RESTRICTED

ORDER OF BATTLE
OF THE
GERMAN ARMY

FEBRUARY 1944

This document must not fall into enemy hands

MILITARY INTELLIGENCE DIVISION
WAR DEPARTMENT
WASHINGTON 25, D. C.

RESTRICTED

The Naval & Military Press Ltd

Published by
The Naval & Military Press Ltd
Unit 10 Ridgewood Industrial Park,
Uckfield, East Sussex,
TN22 5QE England
Tel: +44 (0) 1825 749494
Fax: +44 (0) 1825 765701
www.naval-military-press.com
www.military-genealogy.com
www.militarymaproom.com

In reprinting in facsimile from the original, any imperfections are inevitably reproduced and the quality may fall short of modern type and cartographic standards.

FOREWORD

This revised edition of the *Order of Battle of the German Army* brings up to date the mass of factual data given in the earlier edition concerning the organization, composition, disposition, and commanders of German ground forces. Although it maintains the general arrangement of the previous issue for the benefit of those who have become accustomed to it, this edition embodies a number of improvements designed to make it more accurate, more complete, and easier to use. Notable among these are an entirely new exposition of the replacement-training system, a corrected and much more exhaustive catalog of the types of small units in the German Army, cross references to divisions by page number from section VII to section VI, and complete indexes of German names and of German terms and designations used in the book.

In general, sections I to VI, inclusive, which deal with the organization and administrative structure of the German Army, the types of units, the militarized and auxiliary organizations, and the histories and compositions of divisions and higher headquarters, are written in a manner readily comprehensible to anyone not familiar with the German language and not a specialist in the German order of battle. Wherever German designations are used, the English equivalent is given or the meaning is explained. Section VII, on the other hand, consisting of numerical tables of the composition and affiliations of units, is intended for the order-of-battle specialist, and in it German terms and abbreviations are used freely in order to avoid ambiguity.

This text should be used in conjunction with these publica-

RESTRICTED

tions of the Military Intelligence Division: TM-E 30-451, *Handbook on German Military Forces* (1 Sep 1943); TM 30-255, *Military Dictionary* (*English-German, German-English*) (5 Aug 1941); "German Military Abbreviations," *Special Series*, No. 12 (12 Apr 1943); *German Military Symbols* (Jan 1943). In addition to order-of-battle studies, various handbooks, and miscellaneous publications, the Military Intelligence Division issues the following:

Tactical and Technical Trends (biweekly);
Intelligence Bulletin (monthly);
Military Reports on the United Nations (monthly);
Special Series (approximately once a month).

Requests for additional copies of any MID publication should be made through channels.

All comments on this publication, as well as corrections of factual detail, should be transmitted promptly and may be addressed directly to the **Dissemination Unit, Military Intelligence Division, War Department, Washington 25, D. C.**

RESTRICTED

CONTENTS

	Page
SECTION I. THE GERMAN HIGH COMMAND	1
1. Introduction	1
2. Armed Forces High Command (OKW)	3
3. Army High Command (OKH)	5
a. Field headquarters	5
b. Army Personnel Office (Heerespersonalamt)	7
c. Home Command	7
II. BASIC ADMINISTRATIVE STRUCTURE OF THE ARMY	11
4. Introduction	11
5. Regional Organization	11
a. Corps areas in peacetime	11
b. Wartime function of corps areas	12
c. Control of replacement training	13
d. Control of recruiting	13
6. Conscription System	14
7. Replacement Training System	15
a. Basic principle	15
b. Original operation of the system	16
c. Later modifications	18
d. Recapitulation	24
8. Corps Areas	24
a. General	24
b. List of corps areas	25
9. Army Administration in Occupied Countries	49
a. General	49
b. Occupied countries	50
10. Army Organization in the Communications Zone	60

RESTRICTED

TABLE OF CONTENTS

	Page
III. TYPES OF SMALL UNITS	62
11. Introduction	62
a. General	62
b. Numbering System	63
12. Combat Troops (Fechtende Truppen)	66
a. Infantry (Infanterie)	66
b. Panzer troops (Panzertruppen)	71
c. Artillery (Artillerie)	74
d. Chemical warfare troops (Nebeltruppen)	79
e. Engineers (Pioniere)	81
f. Railway engineers (Eisenbahnpioniere)	86
g. Signal troops (Nachrichtentruppen)	88
h. Propaganda troops (Propagandatruppen)	91
13. Service Troops (Versorgungstruppen)	91
a. Supply troops (Nachschubtruppen)	91
b. Motor maintenance troops (Kraftfahrparktruppen)	94
c. Medical troops (Sanitätstruppen)	96
d. Veterinary troops (Veterinärtruppen)	97
e. Military police (Feldgendarmerie)	98
f. Administrative troops (Verwaltungstruppen)	99
14. Security Troops (Sicherungstruppen)	102
a. Area security units	102
b. Local security units	102
c. Native security units	105
d. Prisoner of war administration units	105
e. Secret field police	105
15. Special Purpose Units	106
a. Intelligence and sabotage units	106
b. Unique units	107
c. Penal units	107
16. Air Force Ground Units	108
a. Antiaircraft units (Flakeinheiten)	108
b. Parachute units (Fallschirmeinheiten)	110
c. Ground combat units	111

RESTRICTED

TABLE OF CONTENTS

	Page
IV. OTHER MILITARIZED AND AUXILIARY ORGANIZATIONS	113
17. Introduction	113
18. SS and Police	113
a. The SS organization	114
b. The Police	116
c. The Waffen-SS	118
19. Semimilitary Services	120
a. Organisation Todt, O.T. (Todt Organization)	120
b. Nationalsozialistisches Kraftfahrerkorps (Nazi Party Motor Transport Corps)	121
c. Reichsarbeitsdienst, R.A.D. (Reich Labor Service)	121
d. Technische Nothilfe, T.N. or Teno (Technical Emergency Corps)	122
20. Party Organizations	122
a. NSDAP (the National-Socialist Party as such)	123
b. Sturmabteilungen, SA (Storm Troops)	123
c. Nationalsozialistisches Fliegerkorps, NSFK (Nazi Party Aviation Corps)	123
d. Hitler-Jugend, HJ (Hitler Youth Organization)	123
V. THE GERMAN FORCES IN ACTION	125
21. Introduction	125
22. Formation of Task Forces	125
VI. DIVISIONS AND HIGHER HEADQUARTERS	129
23. Introduction	129
24. Types of Higher Headquarters	130
a. Army groups	130
b. Armies	130
c. Corps	130
d. Divisions	131

RESTRICTED

TABLE OF CONTENTS

	Page
25. Army Groups (Heeresgruppen)	134
26. Armies (Armeeoberkommandos)	138
27. Panzer Armies (Panzerarmeeoberkommandos)	145
28. Infantry Corps (Armeekorps)	148
29. Panzer Corps (Panzerkorps)	164
30. Mountain Corps (Gebirgskorps)	169
31. Corps Commands and Reserve Corps (Höhere Kommandos z.b.V and Reservekorps)	172
32. Infantry Divisions (Infanteriedivisionen)	176
33. Motorized Divisions (Panzergrenadierdivisionen)	263
34. Light Divisions (Jägerdivisionen)	272
35. Panzer Divisions (Panzerdivisionen)	277
36. Mountain Divisions (Gebirgsdivisionen)	292
37. Sicherungs Divisions (Sicherungsdivisionen)	296
38. Administrative, Reserve, Frontier Guard, and Field Training Divisions	302
39. Divisions and Higher Headquarters of the Waffen-SS	322
40. Air Force Ground Units	333
a. General	333
b. Parachute Divisions (Fallschirmdivisionen)	334
c. Air Force Field Corps (Luftwaffenfeldkorps)	335
d. Air Force Field Divisions (Luftwaffenfelddivisionen)	336
e. Flak Corps (Flakkorps)	344
f. Flak Divisions (Flakdivisionen)	344
VII. TABLES OF IDENTIFIED UNITS	351
41. Introduction	351
42. Armies and Panzer Armies	353

RESTRICTED

TABLE OF CONTENTS

		Page
43.	Corps	354
44.	Infantry and Miscellaneous Divisions	357
45.	Panzer Divisions	367
46.	Mountain Divisions	368
47.	Waffen-SS Units	369
48.	Brigades	371
49.	Infantry Regiments	373
50.	Reconnaissance Units	382
51.	Panzer Units	385
52.	Antitank Units	387
53.	Artillery Units	391
54.	Artillery Observation Units	400
55.	Engineer Units	401
56.	Signal Units	407
57.	Auxiliary Unit Numbers	413
58.	Antiaircraft Units	416

VIII. ROSTERS OF SENIOR OFFICERS _____ 425

 59. Introduction _____ 425
  a. General _____ 425
  b. German surnames _____ 425
  c. German titles _____ 426
  d. German military ranks _____ 426
  e. Categories of officers _____ 427
 60. Army Generals _____ 429
  a. Generalfeldmarschall (Field Marshal) __ 429
  b. Generaloberst (General) _____ 430
  c. General der Infanterie, Kavallerie, etc. (Lieutenant General) _____ 431
  d. Generalleutnant (Major General) _____ 439
  e. Generalmajor (Brigadier General) _____ 464

RESTRICTED

	Page
61. Air Force Generals	**492**
a. Reichsmarschall (Marshal of the Reich)	492
b. Generalfeldmarschall (Field Marshal)	**492**
c. Generaloberst (General)	492
d. General der Flieger, Flakartillerie, etc. (Lieutenant General)	493
e. Generalleutnant (Major General)	495
f. Generalmajor (Brigadier General)	499
62. Senior Officers of the Waffen-SS	506
a. Reichsführer-SS (Field Marshal)	506
b. SS-Oberstgruppenführer und Generaloberst der Waffen-SS (General)	506
c. SS-Obergruppenführer und General der Waffen-SS (Lieutenant General)	507
d. SS-Gruppenführer und Generalleutnant der Waffen-SS (Major General)	509
e. SS-Brigadeführer und Generalmajor der Waffen-SS (Brigadier General)	**511**
f. Lower ranking Waffen-SS officers	513
IX. INDEX OF NAMES	515
X. INDEX OF GERMAN TERMS AND DESIGNATIONS	549

RESTRICTED

Section I. THE GERMAN HIGH COMMAND

1. Introduction.

Under the German military system the basic principle is unity of command. This principle applies not only in the lower echelons but at the top as well. Thus the Army, Navy and Air Force are not regarded as separate services but as branches of a single service, the Armed Forces (*die Wehrmacht*), the head of which has a seat in the Cabinet and represents the joint interests of the Armed Forces with respect to other governmental departments. This joint High Command is responsible for the whole preparation of defense in time of peace and for the general conduct of war; it appoints commanders for the joint task forces in the field and sees to it that the efforts of the three branches of the Armed Forces are thoroughly coordinated.

Under the *Oberkommando der Wehrmacht* (*OKW*), each branch has its own high command: the Army High Command (*Oberkommando des Heeres, OKH*), the Navy High Command (*Oberkommando der Kriegsmarine, OKM*), and the Air Force High Command (*Oberkommando der Luftwaffe, OKL*), usually referred to as the Air Ministry (*Reichsluftfahrtministerium, RLM*). These are responsible for organizing in detail, under the general direction of the *OKW*, the military, naval, and air establishments, respectively, and for carrying out the strategic planning of the *OKW* in their particular spheres.

With this system it is quite usual in a task force for units of one branch of the armed forces to come under the immediate command of another branch, and all personnel may be

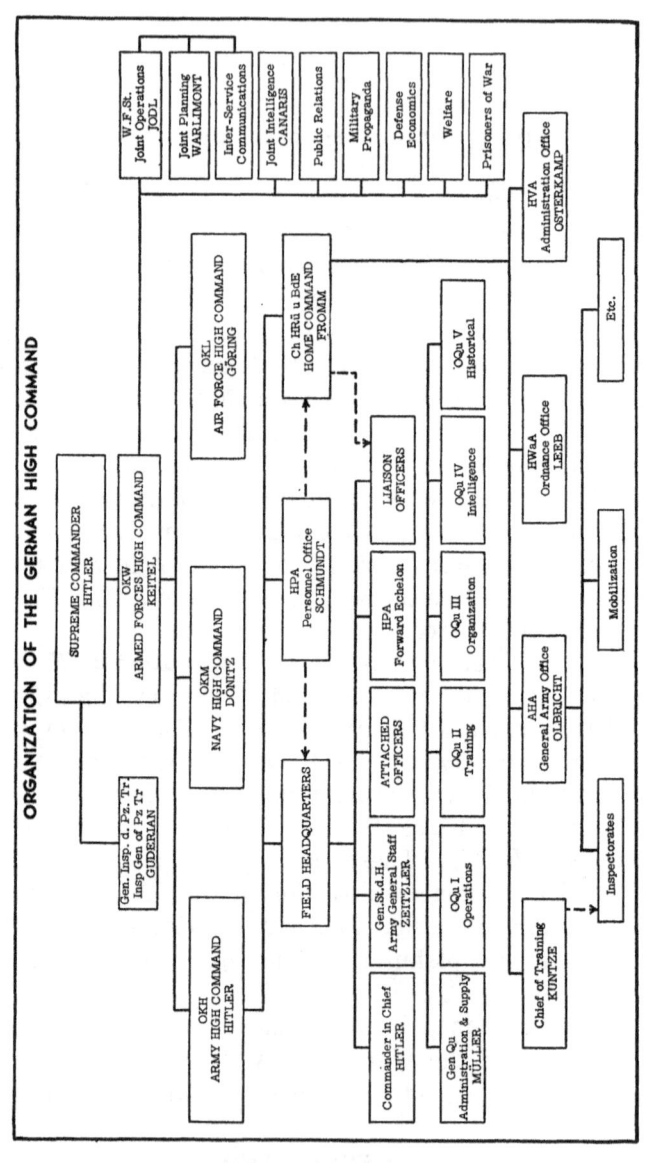

transferred from one branch to another in the same or equivalent rank. In all cases, the *OKW* alone decides what is most expedient in the national interest.

In time of war the *OKW* as well as the High Command of each of the three branches establishes a field headquarters away from Berlin for the conduct of operations. Its location at any given time depends on the theater to which the main attention is being directed; in the case of the Navy it is usually at one of the naval bases, while the headquarters of the Army, the Air Force, and the *OKW* have been in close proximity to each other at some point in the East since the spring of 1941. The Commander in Chief and the bulk of the General Staff of each High Command are stationed at field headquarters, while the non-operational branches back in Berlin continue to handle all basic administrative matters, procurement, mobilization, training, and replacement of personnel and equipment.

2. Armed Forces High Command (*OKW*).

HITLER is the Supreme Commander of the Armed Forces (*Oberster Befehlshaber der Wehrmacht*). His deputy as such is Generalfeldmarschall Wilhelm KEITEL, Chief of the Armed Forces High Command (*Chef des Oberkommandos der Wehrmacht*). KEITEL is responsible for the smooth functioning of the High Command and sees to it that HITLER's orders are carried out, but he has comparatively little to do with major decisions of policy.

Under the *OKW* the functions of a joint general staff are performed by what is known as the Armed Forces Operations Staff (*Wehrmachtführungsstab, W.F.St.*). The chief of this staff, Generaloberst Alfred JODL, is HITLER'S principal adviser on strategy and planning. Under JODL, the *W.F.St.* is divided into sections entrusted with particular functions. The most important of these sections is the Joint Planning

RESTRICTED

Staff, which is responsible for strategic planning and plans for future operations; it is headed by Generalleutnant Walter WARLIMONT, Deputy Chief of the *W.F.St.* Another section of the *W.F.St.* is solely concerned with interservice communications and maintains a special network of land cables and radio channels between the Army, Navy, and Air Force headquarters and the principal subordinate headquarters.

The field headquarters of the *OKW*, which includes the principal sections of the Armed Forces Operations Staff, is known as the *Führerhauptquartier*. During the Polish campaign it was situated between Berlin and the Polish frontier, moving to the Rhineland for the western campaign in 1940 and to East Prussia for the early stages of the attack on the U.S.S.R. It is now (January 1944) probably near Rastenburg in East Prussia.

The various sections of the *OKW* which remain in Berlin are responsible for the following matters:

a. Joint intelligence of a long-range and non-operational nature. This includes both intelligence of the enemy and counterintelligence (security) and is conducted by a section known as *Abwehr*, hitherto under Admiral CANARIS. Tactical intelligence is of course handled by the intelligence staffs of lower echelons in the three branches.

b. Public relations, including the issuance of the daily joint communiques on the course of operations.

c. Military propaganda addressed to the German troops, the enemy troops, the population of occupied territories, and the home front. The *Wehrmachtpropagandaamt* issues all propaganda directives and controls the training and employment of the propaganda companies which are attached to the forces in the field.

d. Defense economics (*Wehrwirtschaft*) including the overall planning of production, the allocation of raw materials, and

RESTRICTED

the exploitation of the economic resources of occupied territories. This work is carried out in conjunction with other branches of the government, such as the Ministry of Economic Affairs, the Ministry of Munitions, the rationing authorities, the Reich control offices for raw materials, the district economic chambers, and the Reich Food Estate.

e. Welfare, including questions of family allowances, pensions, indemnities, and rehabilitation. This is conducted by the *Wehrmachtfürsorge- und -versorgungsamt.*

f. Prisoner of war matters such as the administration of PW camps, the employment of PW labor, and relations with the protecting powers and the International Red Cross. The head of this section is known as *Generalinspekteur des Kriegsgefangenenwesens.* The interrogation of prisoners of war is handled by the lower echelon intelligence officers.

The personnel of the *OKW* is drawn from all three branches, but the Army naturally has the largest representation.

The name of a command, organization, or unit deriving from the *OKW* is often prefixed by *Wehrmacht-* or *Führungs-* in order to distinguish it from a similar command, organization, or unit in one of the three branches.

3. **Army High Command (*OKH*).**

a. Field headquarters.—Since December 1941, when von BRAUCHITSCH was dismissed as Commander in Chief of the Army (*Oberbefehlshaber des Heeres*) and HITLER took direct control of the Army, the field headquarters of the *OKH* has been virtually merged with that of the *OKW*. The functions of the two, however, have remained distinct, and there has been no personal union except at the top. KEITEL acts as HITLER's deputy in the latter's capacity as Commander in Chief of the Army as well as in his capacity as Supreme Commander of the Armed Forces.

RESTRICTED

The field headquarters of the Army includes the following:

(1) The Commander in Chief of the Army, HITLER, with his deputy.

(2) The bulk of the General Staff, under the Chief of Staff, Generaloberst Kurt ZEITZLER. The General Staff is divided into twelve sections, which are placed under the control of the following six senior officers:

(a) *Generalquartiermeister.*—In charge of all matters relating to the supply and administration of the armies in the field. He gives advice to the Commander in Chief and the Chief of Staff on all matters of supply, maintenance, and replacement of equipment, establishment and upkeep of transportation lines, and control of pay, rations, and other administrative services. Since the beginning of the war the *Generalquartiermeister* has been General der Artillerie Eugen MÜLLER.

(b) *Oberquartiermeister I.*—The chief operations officer (roughly equivalent to our G-3). This position is less important than one would suppose, since all important operational matters are handled by the Armed Forces Operations Staff under the *OKW,* to which the task force commanders are directly responsible.

(c) *Oberquartiermeister II.*—In charge of training within the Field Army (as distinct from training in the Replacement Training Army).

(d) *Oberquartiermeister III.*—In charge of organization of the armies in the field, including the setting up of special staffs and definition of their functions.

(e) *Oberquartiermeister IV.*—In charge of operational intelligence.

(f) *Oberquartiermeister V.*—In charge of the historical section.

(3) Attached general officers of the various arms and services. These act as the principal advisers on the employment

RESTRICTED

of troops of their respective arms and have authority down to the lowest echelons on various technical matters relating to these troops. They include the *General der Infanterie* (chief infantry officer), *General der Artillerie* (chief artillery officer), *Chef des Heeresnachrichtenwesens* (chief signal officer), *General der Pioniere* (chief engineer officer), *General der Nachschubtruppen* (chief supply troop officer), *General der Nebeltruppen* (chief chemical warfare officer), *Chef des Transportwesens* (chief transportation officer), and others.

(4) The forward echelon of the Army Personnel Office (see *b*, below).

(5) Liaison officers from the various bureaus in the Home Command (see *c*, below).

b. Army Personnel Office (Heerespersonalamt).—This important bureau is independent of both the General Staff and the Home Command and comes directly under the Commander in Chief. Its chief, Generalleutnant Rudolf SCHMUNDT, is also the Chief Armed Forces Adjutant (*Chefadjutant der Wehrmacht*) to HITLER. The *Personalamt* (abbreviated *PA* or *HPA*) handles officer appointments, promotions, and other matters relating to Army personnel. Much of its work is done in Berlin, but it has a forward echelon at field headquarters, where SCHMUNDT himself is stationed.

c. Home Command.—All Army activities in the Zone of the Interior (*Heimatkriegsgebiet*) are controlled by a senior officer who was appointed for this purpose on mobilization with the title Chief of Army Equipment and Commander of the Replacement Training Army (*Chef der Heeresrüstung und Befehlshaber des Ersatzheeres*). This post has been held by Generaloberst Fritz FROMM since the beginning of the war; his high rank indicates the importance of his position. It is his duty to administer all Army installations within Germany, to control all army units which are permanently or temporarily

RESTRICTED

stationed in the Zone of the Interior, and above all to supply the Field Army with all the equipment and trained personnel that it requires.

(1) *General Army Office* (Allgemeines Heeresamt). This includes separate sections to deal with mobilization, budgetary matters, the issuance of Army regulations, design of uniforms and insignia, and training. The latter function is supervised by the Chief of Training in the Replacement Training Army (*Chef des Ausbildungswesens im Ersatzheer*), General der Pioniere Walter KUNTZE, who is directly responsible to FROMM and operates through the various inspectorates of arms and services (*Inspektion der Infanterie, Inspektion der Artillerie*, etc.) in the General Army Office. The Chief of the General Army Office is General der Infanterie Friedrich OLBRICHT.

(2) *Army Ordnance Office* (Heereswaffenamt). This office is responsible for the design, procurement, and acceptance of weapons and other equipment and for their storage in suitable depots for the use of the Field Army. It is divided into numerous sub-sections for the different categories of equipment (*Waffenrüstungsabteilungen 1-10*) and for their testing (*Waffenprüfungsabteilungen 1-12*). The Ordnance Office is headed by General der Artillerie Emil LEEB.

(3) *Army Administration Office* (Heeresverwaltungsamt). This office includes sections concerned with the affairs of Armed Forces officials (*Wehrmachtbeamte*) and civilian employees of the Armed Forces, pay, rations, barracks and training grounds, and the administration of Army buildings. It is headed by General der Artillerie OSTERKAMP.

The office formerly known as Chief of Mobile Troops (*Chef der Schnellen Truppen*) under FROMM's command has been superseded by the *Generalinspekteur der Panzertruppen* responsible direct to HITLER. This position was created in

RESTRICTED

March 1943 for Generaloberst GUDERIAN, who was placed in complete control of the equipment, organization, and training of tank, motorized, armored infantry, armored reconnaissance, antitank, and heavy assault gun units.

Most of the functions of the Home Command are decentralized as much as possible to the Corps Area Commands (*Wehrkreise*). This applies particularly to the mobilization, training, and replacement of personnel, which are dealt with in section II, below. The bureaus in Berlin confine themselves largely to overall planning, the issuance of directives, and supervision of the operation of the system.

RESTRICTED

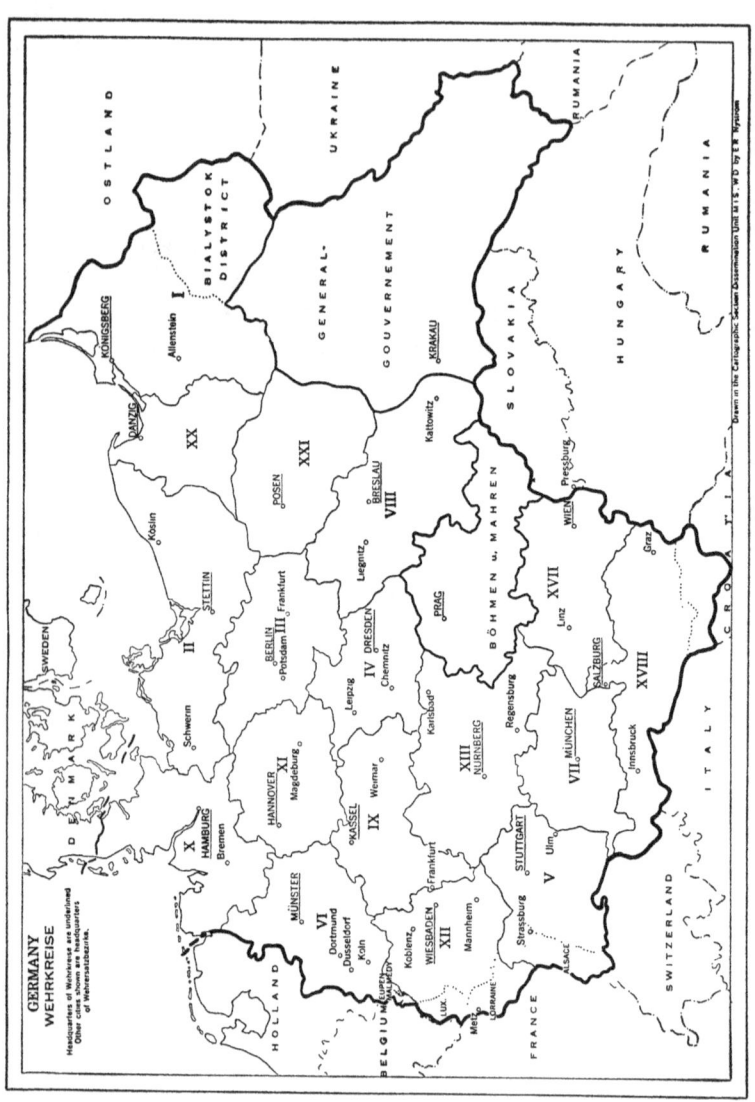

Section II. BASIC ADMINISTRATIVE STRUCTURE OF THE ARMY

4. Introduction.

The German Army in wartime is divided into the Field Army (*Feldheer*) and the Replacement Training Army (*Ersatzheer*). The Field Army is under the direct control of the Commander in Chief and his staff at field headquarters, who are thus enabled to devote themselves primarily to military operations. All other Army matters—the conscription of personnel, training of replacements, procurement of equipment, and administration of permanent military posts and installations within Germany—are entrusted to the Home Command in Berlin, and all units and men regularly stationed in the Zone of the Interior are comprised in the Replacement Training Army. The present section describes this permanent home structure and the manner in which it supplies replacements to the Field Army in time of war.

5. Regional Organization.

a. Corps areas in peacetime.—Germany is divided for administrative purposes into nineteen corps areas (*Wehrkreise*). There were fifteen at the outbreak of the war, and four more have been formed from Polish and Czechoslovak territory. In peacetime the *Wehrkreise* contained the headquarters and components of the active infantry corps and were numbered concurrently with them. Thus the II Infantry Corps, which is now in the field, had its peacetime headquarters in Stettin in *Wehrkreis II*, and its original component divisions and smaller units are permanently affiliated with this *Wehrkreis* and normally receive replacements from it.

Before the war there were also four non-territorial corps— XIV, XV, XVI, and XIX—to control the organization and training of Panzer and motorized units. Each included several divisions, but these were located in different parts of the country, and the corps themselves had no corresponding *Wehrkreise*.

In peacetime, the commander of the infantry corps was also commander of the corps area, but because he was destined to take his corps into the field his chief concern was to develop and maintain the fighting efficiency of the troops under his command. All administrative matters, therefore, were assigned to a second in command or deputy *Wehrkreis* commander—normally a general officer whose health or age rendered him unsuited for active service in the field, while his seniority and experience qualified him for a post of responsibility. (The present average age of these officers is about ten years above that of field corps commanders.)

b. Wartime function of corps areas.—At the beginning of the war the commander of the infantry corps departed with his corps to join the Field Army and the second in command assumed command of the corps area. His staff was composed of reserve officers who had understudied their opposite numbers on the regular corps staff in peacetime. This new *Wehrkreis* command put into effect the mobilization plans worked out in Berlin, and its primary concern since then has been to provide trained manpower to all units of the Field Army mobilized in its area.

These Field Army units include not only the active units of the peacetime army which moved out with the active infantry corps but also all units formed during or after the initial mobilization in the area in question. To illustrate this point,

RESTRICTED

a corps area which contained the peace stations of three divisions under one corps staff might by now have mobilized as many as four corps staffs and anywhere from twelve to twenty divisions for the Field Army.

c. *Control of replacement training.*—The functions of the *Wehrkreis* command in wartime in supplying trained personnel and equipment to the Field Army are controlled by the *OKH* in Berlin through the General Army Office (*AHA*) and the Chief of Training in the Replacement Training Army. The detailed work is decentralized as much as possible, however, and the corps areas are left a large measure of freedom in applying the policies decided in Berlin. Central control is exercised by special staffs to keep close watch over any special program (such as the conversion of infantry to motorized or Panzer divisions), as well as by the inspectors of the different arms, who supervise the training of units of those arms throughout Germany.

d. *Control of recruiting.*—For purposes of the draft of personnel each *Wehrkreis* is subdivided into recruiting areas (*Wehrersatzbezirke*) and recruiting sub-areas (*Wehrbezirke*). Most *Wehrkreise* contain two or three recruiting areas, but *Wehrkreis VI*, comprising the populous Ruhr and Rhineland region, has four, while *Wehrkreise VII, XX,* and *XXI* consist of only one such area each. The number of recruiting sub-areas in each recruiting area varies between three and a dozen according to local needs. Each recruiting area is controlled by an inspector of recruiting area (*Wehrersatzinspekteur*), who is usually a Generalmajor or Generalleutnant similar in his qualifications to the corps area deputy commander. He has the status and disciplinary authority of a division commander. (In some cases he may be a naval or air force officer, since the recruiting system operates jointly for all three branches.) Recruiting sub-areas are normally commanded

RESTRICTED

by colonels selected from the class of officers whose suitability for active service in the field has ceased. They have the status of regimental commanders.

6. Conscription System.

Universal compulsory military service has existed in Germany ever since the Napoleonic wars, with the exception of the period from 1918 to 1935. In March 1935 conscription was reintroduced by law, with the period of active service fixed at one year; this was extended to two years in August 1936. The law provides that all males between the ages of 18 and 45 are subject to military service in peacetime; in wartime these age limits may be extended and in addition all citizens of both sexes are liable to "service for the Fatherland."

Before the outbreak of war military service usually began at the age of 20. The first registration (*Musterung*), however, took place at the age of 18 and was accompanied by a preliminary medical examination and a classification according to degree of physical fitness as well as a provisional assignment to an arm or branch of the service (infantry, artillery, air force, navy, etc.). This procedure was carried out in small local registration areas (*Musterungsbezirke*) with the active collaboration of the district police and other local civil authorities. The recruits then awaited the next stage, their actual drafting (*Aushebung*), which involved a second physical examination, a definite assignment to an arm, and a decision regarding any request for deferment. If found fit (*tauglich*), they were then sent home pending their call to the colors (*Einberufung*) and their induction (*Einstellung*). Between their first registration and their induction the men ordinarily performed their required period of labor service (*Arbeitsdienst*).

All German men over 18 (except those considered totally

unfit) are classified at any given time into the following categories:

aktiv Dienende—on active service.
Reserve I—fully trained, under 35 years of age.
Reserve II—partly trained, under 35.
Ersatzreserve I—untrained, not yet called up, under 35.
Ersatzreserve II—untrained, physically unfit, under 35.
Landwehr I—trained, between 35 and 45.
Landwehr II—untrained, between 35 and 45.
Landsturm I—trained, over 45.
Landsturm II—untrained, over 45.

In wartime the procedure for conscripting personnel for the German military forces is essentially the same as that outlined above for peacetime, except that is has been greatly accelerated and expanded. For example, the *Musterung* and *Aushebung* are now combined into a single operation. The usual age of induction has been lowered to 17, and older classes have also been called up. Members of the *Ersatzreserve II* and *Landwehr II* are subject to call, and occupational and other deferments are strictly limited.

The entire conscription system is organized under the General Army Office (*AHA*), but its operation is highly decentralized through the corps areas, recruiting areas, and sub-areas down to the reporting areas (*Wehrmeldebezirke*) and local registration districts. Navy and Air Force interests are represented by officers specially detailed to the Army recruiting organization for this purpose.

7. Replacement Training System.

a. Basic principle.—Every unit in the Field Army is affiliated for personnel replacement purposes with a specific unit of the Replacement Training Army located in its own original *Wehrkreis* and known as an *Ersatz* unit. The func-

RESTRICTED

tion of the latter is to induct recruits, to provide for their training, and to see that they are held in readiness to be sent off to the field unit in batches or individually as required.

The normal location of the *Ersatz* unit is the home station of the affiliated field unit, to which the soldiers expect ultimately to return for their discharge or for reassignment. For example, a soldier who is wounded and goes to a reserve hospital in the Zone of the Interior will be sent, on leaving the hospital, to his affiliated *Ersatz* unit before being returned to the field.

Whenever feasible trained replacements are sent by an *Ersatz* unit to a field unit with which it is affiliated. If, however, a man is for any reason diverted to a different field unit, or if he is subsequently transferred from one field unit to another, the affiliated *Ersatz* unit of his new field unit must be entered on Page 4 of his paybook under the heading "present competent *Ersatz* unit" (*jetzt zuständiger Ersatztruppenteil*).

In order to understand the intricacies of the present *Ersatz* system it is well to trace the successive stages of its development.

b. Original operation of the system.—Each infantry regiment which took the field at the beginning of the war left behind at its home station a battalion cadre bearing its own number and known as its *Ersatz* battalion. The primary purpose of this battalion was to receive recruits, train them, and dispatch them as replacements to the field regiment. At any given time it included one or more of each of the following types of companies:

(1) Recruit companies, known either as *Rekrutenkompanien* or as *Stammkompanien,* consisting of men undergoing training.

(2) Convalescent companies (*Genesendenkompanien*), con-

sisting of men released from reserve hospitals who were being prepared for return to the field.

(3) Companies known as *Marschkompanien*, which were pools of trained replacements ready to depart for the field unit.

The three *Ersatz* battalions corresponding to the three infantry regiments of a field division were controlled by a regimental staff known as an infantry *Ersatz* regiment and bearing the number of the division. Thus the 2d, 23d, and 44th Infantry Regiments, belonging to the 11th Infantry Division, were represented by the 2d, 23d, and 44th Infantry *Ersatz* Battalions controlled by the 11th Infantry *Ersatz* Regiment at Allenstein in *Wehrkreis I*, the home station of the division.

The *Ersatz* regiment also controlled four specialist *Ersatz* companies which trained the personnel for the infantry howitzer companies, antitank companies, signal sub-units, and engineer platoons of the three field infantry regiments.

The other components of the field division—the artillery regiment, reconnaissance battalion, antitank battalion, engineer battalion, and signal battalion, were similarly affiliated with *Ersatz* units of their respective arms back in the *Wehrkreis* from which they came. All the artillery *Ersatz* battalions in any *Wehrkreis* were controlled by two or more artillery *Ersatz* regiments bearing the numbers of artillery field regiments originally raised in that area. The *Ersatz* battalions for the smaller divisional components likewise bore the numbers of some of the corresponding field units from the *Wehrkreis*, but usually one such *Ersatz* battalion would provide replacements for the corresponding field battalions of several divisions.

All the *Ersatz* units in a *Wehrkreis* were controlled by one or more special divisional staffs known simply as *Div. Nr.* . . . For the purposes of this book these are referred to as mobilization and training divisions up to the latter part

RESTRICTED

of 1942, and subsequently (for reasons which will be shown presently) as mobilization divisions. Their function was to supervise the induction and replacement procedure of the *Ersatz* units under them and particularly to coordinate their training activities. Their numbers were taken from the series 141 to 198.

It should be clearly understood that the *Ersatz* regiments and the mobilization and training divisions were nothing more than administrative and supervisory staffs, while the actual manpower was to be found in the *Ersatz* battalions and companies.

c. Later modifications.—(1) *1940.*—The above system of *numerical* affiliation between *Ersatz* and field units, applying particularly to the infantry units and to a lesser extent to the other arms, was valid in general for the four initial waves of divisions sent to the field by each *Wehrkreis* in the summer and autumn of 1939. These were the "active," or peacetime, divisions, numbered from 1 to 30; those raised from reservists, numbered from 52 to 98; those raised from *Landwehr* personnel, from 205 to 231; and those formed from so-called *Ergänzungs* units (special "supplementary" peacetime units for short training of men in the intermediate classes 1901 to 1913), from 251 to 269. In the list of corps areas in paragraph 8*b* below it will be noted that in most cases the infantry replacement regiments shown are identical in their numbering to the original divisions of these four blocks which were formed in the *Wehrkreis*.

The component units of divisions formed subsequently to the initial mobilization period, on the other hand, were usually not given new *Ersatz* units of their own but were assigned an affiliation with existing *Ersatz* units of their respective arms. Thus each infantry *Ersatz* battalion eventually had to feed replacements to several field regiments, only one of which bore its own number. Similarly, when the infantry in the Panzer divisions was increased from one regiment to two in

RESTRICTED

1940, the second regiment was usually affiliated to the existing *Ersatz* battalion of the original regiment. Some *Ersatz* units were converted outright into field units and organized under the previous mobilization and training division staffs (Nos. 161, 162, 163, etc., for example) as regular field divisions; on the other hand some field units were later dissolved. These changes tended to upset the principle of numerical affiliation, although it will still be found to hold with a majority of the original divisions.

(2) *1941*.—It was the practice from the very beginning to collect groups of trained replacements of the various arms in the *Wehrkreis* and organize them into special personnel transfer battalions known as *Marschbataillone* for the purpose of conducting them to the combat zone. Originally each such transfer unit was normally destined for a particular division and often carried the number of that division preceded by the Roman numeral of the *Wehrkreis* and followed by a serial number. For example I/11/3 would be the third *Marschbataillon* raised in *Wehrkreis I* to replace personnel in the 11th Division. Such battalions were usually attached to the rear echelon of the division in the field, and from there the personnel was filtered into the various divisional components as needed. In many cases these units acquired a more permanent status as replacement pools for the divisions in the field and were renamed field replacement battalions (*Feldersatzbataillone*).

After the start of the Russian campaign it was found expedient, in view of the long distances involved, to draw on these field replacement pools in some cases without regard to their *Wehrkreis* of origin or the division for which they were originally intended. Thus a division which had suffered particularly heavy losses might receive a large proportion of the personnel which had been trained and dispatched to the field

RESTRICTED

for a different division in an adjacent and less active sector. In other cases all the divisions under a given corps or in a particular area would share a single field replacement battalion. In the African theater, for a time at least, there was one field replacement battalion for all the divisions of the Africa Corps, although they came from different *Wehrkreise*. In the middle of 1941, moreover, all units in Africa were assigned affiliations with *Ersatz* units in *Wehrkreise III* and *XII* regardless of the location of their previous *Ersatz* units; this was done in order to concentrate the specialized training which the men required for operations in the desert.

All such measures resulted in a further breaking down of the system of numerical affiliation and in some cases even a departure from the rule that the great majority of men in a given unit should come from the same *Wehrkreis*. It must be borne in mind, however, that all these as well as all subsequent modifications in the detailed operation of the *Ersatz* system have never violated its basic principle: namely, that every field unit must at all times be affiliated with a specified *Ersatz* unit to which all men returning to the Zone of the Interior are automatically sent.

(3) *1942*.—Conditions in the rear areas in Russia made it desirable to organize some of the field replacement units there on a divisional basis, equip them with proper weapons, and employ them for local mopping-up activities and counter-partisan warfare. This practice had the advantage that it gave the men practical experience of combat in the Russian terrain before they were assigned to regular line units. At the same time it meant a further departure from the numerical affiliation system. The new units were at first known as field replacement divisions (*Feldersatzdivisionen*) and later in the year became field training divisions (*Feldausbildungsdivisionen*), of which five (in the series between 381 and 391)

RESTRICTED

have been identified. There is of course a constant turnover of personnel in these units as well as considerable fluctuation in their numerical strength, since it is still the practice to transfer men from them, often in groups as large as a battalion or even a regiment, to fill the gaps in regular field divisions which happen to be in their sector. The field training divisions were subsequently separated from the replacement training command and are now under the Field Army.

The most far-reaching change in the *Ersatz* system took place on or about 1 October 1942, when all *Ersatz* units were divided into two parts, one to handle induction and replacement and the other to handle training. The induction and replacement unit retained the designation *Ersatz* unit but was thenceforth concerned only with receiving recruits from the conscription offices, issuing them their personal equipment and their paybooks, and sending them on as speedily as possible to its sister training unit; with receiving convalescents and sending them back to a field unit; and with processing men from its affiliated field units who for any reason were to be discharged. The newly created training unit (*Ausbildungseinheit*) bore the same number as the *Ersatz* unit and was to receive the men from the *Ersatz* unit, give them their training, and then dispatch them to an affiliated field unit. Infantry training battalions were organized under infantry training regiments numbered in the same manner as the corresponding infantry *Ersatz* regiments, and the same principle applied to the artillery units.

The purpose of this measure was apparently to facilitate a shift of most training activities to the occupied countries, particularly in the west, without seriously affecting the efficiency of the induction and replacement procedure back in the *Wehrkreise*. Under the previous arrangement *Ersatz* units had sometimes been moved out of their *Wehrkreise* for some

RESTRICTED

special reason; early in 1940, for example, those along the western border were temporarily shifted to eastern Germany to release barrack space and other facilities for the initial assembly preparatory to the attack on France and the Low Countries. Some *Ersatz* units were even moved into occupied territory, notably into Denmark, Alsace, and Lorraine. In all such cases it was necessary to establish special collecting points for recruits in the *Wehrkreise* concerned and to send them long distances to the units into which they were to be inducted. By contrast, under the new system established late in 1942, all training units were free to move to whatever areas were thought most suitable while the functions of the *Ersatz* units were carried on in the normal way at their proper home stations.

A special advantage of the new system is a saving of manpower. By taking over considerable areas in occupied territory the training units released offensive combat divisions from occupational duties, and a number of them have moved to coastal sectors in the west where they are apparently intended to absorb the first shock of any invasion.

For these occupational and defensive purposes as well as to conduct combined training exercises, the training units in occupied territory were organized into a new type of training division known as a reserve division (Reservedivision). This was in each case formed by conversion of the staff of one of the former mobilization and training divisions (*Div.Nr.*) in the *Wehrkreise*. If there were then not enough *Div.Nr.* left in a *Wehrkreis* to supervise the induction and replacement activities of the *Ersatz* units, a new one was created, sometimes taking a number 300 higher than that of the departed reserve division. In *Wehrkreis XVII*, for example, one of the two original mobilization and training divisions, Div. Nr.

RESTRICTED

187, was transferred to the Balkans as the 187th Reserve Division, and to take its place a new Div. Nr. 487 (now properly translated mobilization division) was created. Other new mobilization divisions have been obtained by conversion of special divisional administrative staffs (z.b.V. divisions). At the time of writing this text there are some 24 reserve divisions and 20 *Div.Nr.*, against a total of 33 *Div.Nr.* in September 1942.

Since the summer of 1943 four or five new reserve divisions have been formed from Panzer and motorized training units, which until then had all been stationed in the Zone of the Interior. There are indications that several more of these *Reserve-Panzer-Divisionen* are in process of formation.

Training units which go abroad and come under reserve divisions are called reserve units (*Reserveeinheiten*). They retain their original numbering system, so that the number of a Reserve infantry regiment is the same as that of a division from its *Wehrkreis* and the numbers of its battalions are the same as those of the regiments of that division.

In addition to the reserve divisions a number of reserve corps have been formed in occupied territory. It is believed that these supervise the administration of the reserve divisions in something like the same manner in which the *Wehrkreis* headquarters control the *Div. Nr.* and *Ersatz* units in their areas.

Not all training units, however, have left their home stations in Germany. Those which have remained are usually in close proximity to their corresponding *Ersatz* units and may even occupy the same barracks, but they are still distinct from them in function and in nomenclature. For almost every important type of unit new combined regimental and battalion staffs have been formed under the title of "replacement and training" units (*Ersatz- und Ausbildungseinheiten*). These are probably set up to avoid a duplication of administrative personnel in cases where the training and *Ersatz* units are close enough to each other to be administered jointly.

d. Recapitulation.—The essence of the German *Ersatz* system is the affiliation of every field unit with a specific *Ersatz* unit in its own *Wehrkreis*, to which its personnel will return in case of convalescence or discharge. Originally this *Ersatz* unit had the same number as the field unit, but this rule no longer applies generally.

A German recruit today is inducted into an *Ersatz* unit in the vicinity of his place of residence and is then sent almost at once to the training unit of the same number. This is likely to be part of a reserve division in occupied territory. After a period of training and occupational duties he will normally be sent, probably in a *Marschbataillon* with a large group of his fellows, to a field unit which is affiliated with his own original *Ersatz* unit, although he may go to almost any other field unit if circumstances so require.

A convalescent is sent back by the hospital to the affiliated *Ersatz* unit of his last field unit. There he is placed in a convalescent company to be restored to combat fitness. He is then dispatched to the field, preferably to his own former unit and otherwise probably to another unit affiliated with the *Ersatz* unit.

8. Corps Areas.

a. General.—The following section outlines the essential facts concerning the corps areas (*Wehrkreise*): territory comprised, name of commander, units mobilized, recruiting area headquarters and recruiting sub-areas, and training and replacement structure.

RESTRICTED

ORDER OF BATTLE OF THE GERMAN ARMY

American terms are employed for convenience. Geographical names are given in their German form as they will most commonly be encountered in German documents. Places in occupied territories are given in both their German and non-German forms.

The reserve or training regiments and the locations of the reserve or training divisions are omitted in this section. They will be found under the divisional histories in section VI.

b. List of corps areas.

Wehrkreis I (Hq: Königsberg)

Ostpreussen: Extended in March 1939 to include the Memel area, in autumn 1939 the Zichenau (*Ciechanów*) and Sudauen (*Suwałki*) areas, and in 1942 the Bialystok district.

Commander: Gen.d.Art. Albert WODRIG (61)

C of S:

Corps mobilized: I and XXVI Inf

Divisions mobilized:

   Infantry: 1, 11, 21, 61, 161, 206, 217, 228 (since disbanded), 291, 311 (since disbanded), 340, 383, 714 (now 114th L)

   Light: 114 (former 714th Inf)

   Panzer: 24 (former 1st Cav)

Recruiting area Hq: Königsberg (Pr.): Genlt. Alexander RÜHLE v. LILIENSTERN (63)

   Recruiting sub-areas: Königsberg (Pr.) I-II, Tilsit, Gumbinnen, Treuburg, Bartenstein (Ostpr.), Braunsberg (Ostpr.)

Recruiting area Hq: Allenstein:

   Recruiting sub-areas: Allenstein, Lötzen, Zichenau (*Ciechanów*)

Mobilization divisions:

   No. 401: Königsberg

   No. 461: Bialystok

RESTRICTED

*Replacement regiments:
   Infantry:
      1: Königsberg
      11: Allenstein
      21: Mohrungen
      61: Königsberg
      206: Gumbinnen
      217: Allenstein
      228: Lötzen
   Artillery:
      1: Insterburg
      11: Allenstein
Reserve divisions: 141
                   151
Training areas:
   Arys:
   Mielau (*Mlawa*):
   Stablack: Genmaj. DECKMANN (52)
Division staffs:
   421 z.b.V.: Zichenau (*Ciechanów*)

---

*From mid-1940 to mid-1941 most of the replacement training units from this Wehrkreis were stationed in the Protectorate.
For *training* regiments, see Reserve divisions 141 and 151 in section VI, below.

Wehrkreis II (Hq: Stettin)

Pommern, Mecklenburg, and a small section of the northern part of Brandenburg.
Commander: Gen.d.Inf. Werner KIENITZ (59)
C of S:
Corps mobilized: II Inf, LXV (Corps Comd), LVII Pz, and XXXVI Mtn
Divisions mobilized:
   Infantry: 12, 32, 75, 122, 162, 207 (now 207th Sich), 242, 258, 272 (since disbanded), 274, 292, 302, 328, 347, 702
   Motorized: 2 (now 12th Pz)

RESTRICTED

ORDER OF BATTLE OF THE GERMAN ARMY

Panzer: 12 (former 2d Mtz)
Sicherungs: 207 (former 207th Inf)
Recruiting area Hq: Stettin: Genmaj. Carl v. AMMON (61)
  Recruiting sub-areas: Stettin I-II, Swinemünde, Stargard i. Pom.,
    Greifswald, Stralsund
Recruiting area Hq: Köslin: Genlt. Karl MOYSES (60)
  Recruiting sub-areas: Köslin, Stolp, Kolberg, Neustettin, Deutsch-
    Krone, Woldenberg Nm.
Recruiting area Hq: Schwerin (Meckl.)
  Recruiting sub-areas: Schwerin (Meckl.), Rostock, Parchim, Neu-
    strelitz
Mobilization divisions:
  No. 152:   (transferred to Wkr.XX)
  No. 192: Rostock
Replacement regiments:
  Infantry:
    12: Schwerin (Meckl.)
    32: Kolberg
    75: Neustrelitz
    207: Deutsch-Krone
    258: Rostock
  Motorized (Pz. Gren.):
    2: Stettin
  Artillery:
    2 (Mtz): Stettin
    12: Schwerin (Meckl.)
    32: Kolberg
Reserve divisions:
Training areas:
  Altwarp:
  Gross-Born: Genlt. Wilhelm THOFERN (59)
  Hammerstein:
  Wüstrow:
Division staffs:
  402 z.b.V.: Stettin

RESTRICTED

Wehrkreis III (Hq: Berlin)

Brandenburg.
Commander:
C of S: Genmaj. Heinrich ROTH
Corps mobilized: XXVIII, XXXIV, and LII Inf, III Pz and Africa Pz
Divisions mobilized:
    Infantry: 3 (now 3d Mtz), 23, 50 ?, 68, 76, 93, 123, 163, 208, 218, 257, 273 (since disbanded), 293, 333, 719
    Motorized: 3 (former 3d Inf), 90 (former 90th Lt.Africa Div)
    Light: 3 (now 8th Pz), 5 (reorganized into 21st Pz early 1941), 90 (now 90th Mtz)
    Panzer: 3, 8 (former 3d L), 21 (reorganized from former 5th L early 1941), 26, Grossdeutschland
    Sicherungs: 203 ?, 403 (since disbanded)
Recruiting area Hq: Berlin*: Genlt. Ferdinand BOCK v. WÜLFINGEN (61)
    Recruiting sub-areas: Berlin I-X
Recruiting area Hq: Frankfurt (Oder): Genlt. SATOW (56)
    Recruiting sub-areas: Frankfurt (Oder), Küstrin, Landsberg (Warthe), Crossen (Oder), Lübben (Spreewald), Cottbus
Recruiting area Hq: Potsdam: Genlt. Friedrich Frhr. v. WILMOWSKY (63)
    Recruiting sub-areas: Potsdam I-II, Neuruppin, Eberswalde, Bernau b.Berlin, Perleberg
Mobilization divisions:
    No. 433: Berlin
†Replacement regiments:
    Infantry:
        23: Potsdam
        50 ?: Küstrin ?
        68: Guben
        76: Brandenburg
        208: Cottbus

---

*Wehrersatzinspektion Berlin I has recently been identified, commanded by Genlt. Karl Frhr. v. THÜNGEN. This may indicate the presence of more than one recruiting area headquarters in Berlin.

†For *training* regiments, see Reserve divisions 143, 153, and 233 in section VI, below.

RESTRICTED

218: Spandau
257: Landsberg (Warthe)
Motorized:
   3: Frankfurt (Oder)
Motorized (Pz.Gren.):
   83: Eberswalde
   Grossdeutschland: Cottbus
Artillery:
   3 (Mtz): Frankfurt (Oder)
   23: Potsdam
   168: Frankfurt (Oder)
Reserve divisions: 143
                  153
                  233 (Pz)
Training areas:
   Döberitz: Genmaj. Eckhard v. GEYSO (52)
   Jüterbog: Obst. v. MALLINCKRODT (52)
   Tiborlager über Schwiebus:
   Wandern: Genmaj. OELSNER (55)
   Zossen:
Division staffs:
   Kdtr. Gross-Berlin

Wehrkreis IV (Hq: Dresden)

Sachsen and the eastern part of Thüringen: Extended in 1938 to include part of Czechoslovakia.
Commander: Gen.d.Inf. Viktor v. SCHWEDLER (59)
C of S:
Corps mobilized: IV, XXIX, and XLIV Inf
Divisions mobilized:
   Infantry: 4 (now 14th Pz), 14 (now 14th Mtz), 24, 56, 87, 94, 134, 164 (now 164th Mtz), 209 (since disbanded), 223, 255, 256, 294, 304, 336, 370, 384, 704 (now 104th L)
   Motorized: 14 (former 14th Inf), 164 (former 164th Inf)

RESTRICTED

ORDER OF BATTLE OF THE GERMAN ARMY

Light: 104 (former 704th Inf)
Panzer: 14 (former 4th Inf), 18
Recruiting area Hq: Dresden: Genlt. Robert PRAETORIUS (62)
  Recruiting sub-areas: Dresden I-III, Pirna, Bautzen, Zittau, Kamenz, Meissen, Grossenhain, Leitmeritz (*Litoměřice*), Böhmisch-Leipa, Reichenberg (*Liberec*)
Recruiting area Hq: Leipzig:
  Recruiting sub-areas: Leipzig I-III, Naumburg a. d. Saale, Halle a. d. Saale, Altenburg, Eisleben, Bitterfeld, Wittenberg, Grimma, Döbeln
Recruiting area Hq: Chemnitz: Genlt. Fritz HENGEN (57)
  Recruiting sub-areas: Chemnitz I-II, Freiberg, Annaberg, Zwickau, Auerbach, Plauen, Glauchau, Teplitz-Schönau (*Teplice-Sanow*)
Mobilization divisions:
  No. 464: Leipzig
*Replacement regiments:
  Infantry:
    24: Chemnitz
    56: Dresden
    87 ? :
    223: Bautzen
    255: Löbau
    256: Meissen
    294 ? :
  Motorized:
    14: Leipzig
  Motorized (Pz. Gren.):
    4: Dresden
  Artillery:
    4 (Mtz): Dresden
    24 (Mtz): Chemnitz
Reserve divisions: 154
                   174
Training areas:
  Königsbrück:
  Zeithain: Obst. MITSCHERLING

---

*Some of the replacement training units from this Wehrkreis were transferred to the Protectorate in 1941.
For *training* regiments, see Reserve divisions 154 and 174 in section VI, below.

RESTRICTED

Division staffs:
404 z.b.V.: Dresden

Wehrkreis V (Hq: Stuttgart)

Württemberg, Hohenzollern, and southern Baden: Extended after the French campaign to include Alsace.

Commander: Gen.d.Pz.Tr. Rudolf VEIEL (61)
C of S: Genmaj. Otto HERFURTH?
Corps mobilized: V, XXV, and L Inf
Divisions mobilized:
  Infantry: 5 (now 5th L), 25 (now 25th Mtz), 35, 78, 125, 198, 205, 215, 260, 271 (since disbanded), 305, 323, 330, 335, 715
  Motorized: 25 (former 25th Inf)
  Light: 5 (former 5th Inf), 101
  Panzer: 10, 23
Recruiting area Hq: Stuttgart: Genlt. Otto TSCHERNING (63)
  Recruiting sub-areas: Stuttgart I-II, Schwäb.Gmünd, Schwäb. Hall, Heilbronn, Esslingen (Neckar), Ludwigsburg, Horb (Neckar), Calw, Karlsruhe, Pforzheim, Rastatt, Offenburg
Recruiting area Hq: Ulm:
  Recruiting sub-areas: Ulm, Tübingen, Ehingen, Ravensburg, Sigmaringen, Rottweil, Donaueschingen, Konstanz, Freiburg (Breisgau), Lörrach
Recruiting area Hq: Strassburg (*Strasbourg*): Genlt. Ernst VOLK (60)
  Recruiting sub-areas: Strassburg (*Strasbourg*), Mülhausen i. Elsass (*Mulhouse*), Thann i. Elsass, Kolmar (*Colmar*), Schlettstadt (*Sélestat*), Zabern (*Saverne*), Hagenau (*Haguenau*)
Mobilization divisions:
  No. 465: Stuttgart (transferred to Epinal)

RESTRICTED

*Replacement regiments:
  Infantry:
    5: Konstanz
    35: Ulm ?
    78: Tübingen
    205: Ulm
    215: Heilbronn
    260: Tübingen ?
  Motorized:
    25: Stuttgart
  Motorized (Pz.Gren.):
    90 ? : Stuttgart ?
  Artillery:
    5: Ulm
    25 (Mtz): Ludwigsburg
    35: Karlsruhe
Reserve divisions: 155 (Pz)
                   165
Training areas:
  Heuberg/Baden: Genmaj. Franz SEUFFERT (52)
  Münsingen:
Division staffs:
  405 z.b.V.: Stuttgart

---

*From late 1939 to mid-1940 most of the replacement training units from this Wehrkreis were stationed in the Protectorate.
For *training* regiments, see Reserve divisions 155 and 165 in section VI, below.

Wehrkreis VI (Hq: Münster)

Westfalen, Lippe, and the northern part of Rheinprovinz: Extended after the French campaign to include the Eupen-Malmédy district of Belgium.
Commander: Gen.d.Inf. Gerhard GLOKKE (60)
C of S:
Corps mobilized: VI and XXIII Inf, XXXIII (Corps Comd), LVI Pz

RESTRICTED

ORDER OF BATTLE OF THE GERMAN ARMY

Divisions mobilized:
  Infantry: 6, 16 (now 16th Pz and 16th Mtz), 26, 69, 86, 106, 126, 196, 199, 211, 227, 253, 254, 264, 306, 326, 329, 371, 385, 716.
  Motorized: 16 (formed from elements of 16th Inf)
  Light: 1 (now 6th Pz)
  Panzer: 6 (former 1st L), 16 (formed from elements of 16th Inf), 25
Recruiting area Hq: Münster i.W.: Genlt. v.dem KNESEBECK (67)
  Recruiting sub-areas: Münster i.W., Coesfeld, Paderborn, Bielefeld, Herford, Minden, Detmold, Lingen, Osnabrück, Recklinghausen, Gelsenkirchen
Recruiting area Hq: Dortmund:
  Recruiting sub-areas: Dortmund I-II, Arnsberg, Soest, Iserlohn, Bochum, Herne, Hagen (Westf.)
Recruiting area Hq: Düsseldorf:
  Recruiting sub-areas: Düsseldorf, Neuss, Krefeld, München-Gladbach, Wuppertal, Mettmann, Solingen, Essen I-II, Duisburg, Moers, Oberhausen, Wesel
Recruiting area Hq: Köln: Genlt. Kurt Frhr. ROEDER v. DIERSBURG (58)
  Recruiting sub-areas: Köln I-III, Bonn, Siegburg, Aachen, Jülich, Düren, Monschau
Mobilization divisions:
  No. 176: Bielefeld
  No. 526: Wuppertal
*Replacement regiments:
  Infantry:
    6: Osnabrück
    26: Düsseldorf
    69: Soest
    86: Herford?
    211: Köln
    227: Düsseldorf
    253: Aachen
    254: Lingen

---

*From late 1939 to late 1940, most of the replacement training units from this Wehrkreis were stationed in Wehrkreis XX.
For *training* regiments, see Reserve divisions 156 and 166 in section VI, below.

RESTRICTED

Motorized:
   16: Rheine
Motorized (Pz.Gren.):
   57: Wuppertal
Artillery:
   6: Münster
   26: Köln
   211?:
Reserve divisions: 156
                     166
Training areas:
   Deilinghofen:
   Elsenborn:
   Meppen:
   Senne: Obst. PAHL
   Wahn: Obst. BENCZEK
Division staffs:
   406 z.b.V.: Münster

Wehrkreis VII (Hq: München)

Oberbayern, the southern part of Niederbayern, and Schwaben.
Commander: Gen.d.Inf. Kurt KRIEBEL (56)
C of S: Genlt. Johann KASPAR (70)
Corps mobilized: VII and XXVII Inf
Divisions mobilized:
   Infantry: 7, 27 (now 17th Pz), 57, 88, 167, 212, 268, 277 (since disbanded), 337, 376, 387, 707
   Light: 97
   Panzer: 17 (former 27th Inf)
   Mountain: 1, 4
Recruiting area Hq: München: Genlt. Oskar van GINKEL (62)
   Recruiting sub-areas: München I-IV, Rosenheim, Traunstein, Weilheim, Augsburg, Kempten (Allgäu), Landshut, Pfarrkirchen, Ingolstadt

RESTRICTED

ORDER OF BATTLE OF THE GERMAN ARMY 35

Mobilization Divisions:
  No. 467: München
*Replacement regiments:
  Infantry:
    7: München
    157: München
    212: Ingolstadt
    268: München
  Motorized (Pz.Gren.):
    27: Augsburg
  Mountain:
    1: Füssen
  Artillery:
    7: München
    27 (Mtz): Augsburg
    79 (Mtn): Garmisch
Reserve divisions: 147
                  157
Training areas:
  Hohenfels (under jurisdiction of Wkr. VII but located in Wkr. XIII):
  Mittenwald (for mountain troops):
Division staffs:
  407 z.b.V.: München

*For *training* regiments, see Reserve divisions 147 and 157 in section VI, below.

Wehrkreis VIII (Hq: Breslau)

Niederschlesien and Oberschlesien: Extended in 1938 to include part of Czechoslovakia and in 1939 Ost-Oberschlesien and the Teschen (*Cieszyn*) area.
Commander: Gen.d.Kav. Rudolf KOCH-ERPACH (58)
C of S:
Corps mobilized: VIII, XXXV, and XXXVIII ? Inf. XLI Pz

RESTRICTED

Divisions mobilized:
  Infantry: 8 (now 8th L), 18 (now 18th Mtz), 28 (now 28th L), 62, 81, 102, 168, 213 (now 213th Sich), 221 (now 221st Sich), 239 (since disbanded), 252, 298 (now possibly disbanded), 320, 332, 708
  Motorized: 18 (former 18th Inf)
  Light: 8 (former 8th Inf), 28 (former 28th Inf)
  Panzer: 5, 11
  Sicherungs: 213 (former 213th Inf), 221 (former 221st Inf)
  Recruiting area Hq: Breslau: Genlt. Athos v. SCHAUROTH (58)
    Recruiting sub-areas: Breslau I-III, Oels, Brieg, Glatz, Waldenburg (Schles.), Schweidnitz, Mährisch-Schönberg (*Sumperk*), Zwittau, Troppau (*Opava*), Jägerndorf (*Krnov*), Wohlau
  Recruiting area Hq: Liegnitz: Genlt. Konrad SORSCHE (61)
    Recruiting sub-areas: Liegnitz, Glogau, Sagan, Görlitz, Bunzlau, Hirschberg i. Rsgb., Trautenau (*Trutov*)
  Recruiting area Hq: Kattowitz (*Katowice*): Genlt. Georg CARP (57)
    Recruiting sub-areas: Kattowitz (*Katowice*), Königshütte O.S. (*Krolewska Huta*), Loben, Rybnik, Teschen (*Cieszyn*), Bielitz (Beskiden) (*Bielsko*), Oppeln, Neisse, Neustadt O.S., Cosel, Gleiwitz
Mobilization divisions:
  No. 178: Liegnitz
*Replacement regiments:
  Infantry:
    8: Troppau ?
    28: Mährisch-Schönberg ?
    62: Görlitz ?
    213: Mährisch-Schönberg
    221: Breslau
    239: Gleiwitz
    252: Neisse
  Motorized:
    18: Liegnitz ?
  Motorized (Pz. Gren.):
    85: Gleiwitz

---

*For *training* regiments, see Reserve divisions 148 and 158 in section VI, below.

RESTRICTED

Artillery:
  8: Troppau
  18 ? (Mtz): Liegnitz
  44 ? :
  116 (Mtz): Breslau ?
Reserve divisions: 148
                   158
Training areas:
  Hohenelbe:
  Lamsdorf:
  Neuhammer:
Division staffs:
  408 z.b.V.: Breslau
  432 z.b.V.: Kattowitz (*Katowice*)

Wehrkreis IX (Hq: Kassel)

The western part of Thüringen, part of Hessen, and part of Hessen-Nassau.
Commander: Gen.d.Inf. SCHELLERT (57)
C of S: Genmaj. von NIDA
Corps mobilized: IX Inf and XXXIX Pz
Divisions mobilized:
  Infantry: 9, 15, 29 (now 29th Mtz), 52, 82, 95, 129, 169, 214, 251, 299, 319, 339, 356, 377, 389, 709
  Motorized: 29 (former 29th Inf)
  Light: 2 (now 7th Pz)
  Panzer: 1, 7 (former 2d L), 20, 27 (since disbanded)
  Sicherungs: 201
Recruiting area Hq: Kassel: Genlt. PINCKVOSS (58)
  Recruiting sub-areas: Kassel I-II, Korbach, Marburg a.d.Lahn, Hersfeld, Siegen, Wetzlar, Fulda, Giessen
Recruiting area Hq: Frankfurt (Main): Genlt. DETMERING (57)
  Recruiting sub-areas: Frankfurt (Main) I-II, Offenbach a.M., Aschaffenburg, Friedberg, Hanau

RESTRICTED

Recruiting area Hq: Weimar:
  Recruiting sub-areas: Weimar, Sangerhausen, Gera, Rudolstadt, Mühlhausen i. Th., Erfurt, Eisenach, Gotha, Meiningen
Mobilization divisions:
  No. 409: Kassel
*Replacement regiments:
  Infantry:
    9: Siegen ?
    15: Fulda
    52: Kassel
    214: Aschaffenburg
    251: Hanau
  Motorized:
    29: Erfurt
  Motorized (Pz.Gren.):
    81: Meiningen
  Artillery:
    9:
    15 ? : Kassel
    29 (Mtz): Erfurt
Reserve divisions: 159
                   179 (Pz)
                   189
Training areas:
  Ohrdruf:
  Schwarzenborn:
  Wildflecken: Genmaj. Walter HOSSFELD (52)
Division staffs:

*For *training* regiments, see Reserve divisions 159, 179, and 189 in section VI, below.

Wehrkreis X (Hq: Hamburg)

Schleswig-Holstein, Oldenburg, Hamburg, Bremen, Lübeck, and the northern part of Hannover.

RESTRICTED

ORDER OF BATTLE OF THE GERMAN ARMY

Commander: Gen.d.Inf. Walter RASCHICK (62)
C of S:
Corps mobilized: X Inf, XXXI (Corps Comd) ?, XL and XLVI Pz
Divisions mobilized:
    Infantry: 22 (now 22d Mtz), 30, 58, 83, 110, 121, 170, 225, 269, 270, 290, 416 ?, 710
    Motorized: 20, 22 (former 22d Inf)
Recruiting area Hq: Schleswig-Holstein (Hq at Hamburg):
    Recruiting sub-areas: Neumünster, Rendsburg, Schleswig, Kiel, Eutin, Lübeck, Hamburg I-VI
Recruiting area Hq: Bremen:
    Recruiting sub-areas: Bremen I-II, Stade, Wesermünde, Oldenburg i.O. I-II, Aurich (Ostfriesland), Nienburg a.d. Weser, Lüneburg
Mobilization divisions:
    No. 180: Verden
    No. 190: Neumünster
*Replacement regiments:
    Infantry:
        30: Ratzeburg
        58: Lüneburg ?
        225: Itzehoe
        269: Delmenhorst
    Motorized:
        20: Hamburg
        22: Oldenburg
    Artillery:
        20 (Mtz): Hamburg
        22: Bremen
        30: Lübeck
Reserve divisions: 160
Training areas:
    Munster (i. d. Lüneburger Heide): Obst. BECKER
    Putlos:
Division staffs:
    410 z.b.V.: Hamburg

---

*For *training* regiments, see Reserve division 160 in section VI, below.

RESTRICTED

Wehrkreis XI (Hq: Hannover)

The southern part of Hannover; Braunschweig, Anhalt, and Provinz Sachsen.
Commander:
C of S:
Corps mobilized: XI, XXX, and XLIII Inf, XIV Pz, LI Mtn
Divisions mobilized:
    Infantry: 19 (now 19th Pz), 31, 71, 96, 111, 131, 181, 216, 265, 267, 295, 321, 711
    Motorized: 13 (now 13th Pz)
    Panzer: 13 (former 13th Mtz), 19 (former 19th Inf)
Recruiting area Hq: Hannover:
    Recruiting sub-areas: Hannover I-II, Braunschweig, Goslar, Hildesheim, Hameln, Göttingen, Celle
Recruiting area Hq: Magdeburg:
    Recruiting sub-areas: Magdeburg I-II, Stendal, Burg bei Magdeburg, Halberstadt, Dessau, Bernburg
Mobilization divisions:
*Replacement regiments:
    Infantry:
        31: Braunschweig
        71: Hannover
        216: Hameln
        267: Quedlinburg
    Motorized (Pz. Gren.):
        13: Magdeburg
    Artillery:
        13 (Mtz): Magdeburg
        19 (Mtz): Hannover
        31: Braunschweig
Reserve divisions: 171
                    191
Training areas:
    Altengrabow:
    Bergen-Fallingbostel:
Divisional staffs:
    411 z.b.V.: Hannover

---

*For *training* regiments, see Reserve divisions 171 and 191 in section VI, below.

RESTRICTED

Wehrkreis XII (Hq: Wiesbaden)

The southern part of Rheinprovinz, part of Hessen-Nassau, part of Hessen, and Saar-Pfalz: Extended after the French campaign to include Lorraine and the Grand Duchy of Luxembourg.

Commander: Gen.d.Inf. Walther SCHROTH (62)
C of S:
Corps mobilized: XII and LIII Inf, XXIV Pz
Divisions mobilized:
    Infantry: 33 (now 15th Mtz), 34, 36 (now 36th Mtz), 65, 72, 79, 112, 132, 197, 246, 263, 282, 342, 712
    Motorized: 15 (former 15th Pz), 36 (former 36th Inf)
    Panzer: 15 (now 15th Mtz), 22 (since disbanded)
    Sicherungs: 444
Recruiting area Hq: Koblenz: Genlt. Ludwig v. BERG (62)
    Recruiting sub-areas: Koblenz, Trier I-II, Neuwied, Kreuznach, Wiesbaden, Limburg a.d. Lahn, Mainz, Worms, Darmstadt, Luxemburg
Recruiting area Hq: Mannheim:
    Recruiting sub-areas: Mannheim I-II, Saarlautern, Saarbrücken, St. Wendel, Zweibrücken, Kaiserslautern, Neustadt a. d. Weinstrasse, Ludwigshafen a. Rhein, Heidelberg
Recruiting area Hq: Metz:
    Recruiting sub-areas: Metz, Diedenhofen (*Thionville*), St. Avold, Saargemünd (*Sarreguemines*)
Mobilization divisions:
    No. 172: Mainz
    No. 462:   (transferred to Nancy)
*Replacement regiments:
    Infantry:
        34: Heidelberg
        79: Koblenz
      112: Darmstadt
      246: Trier
      263: Idar-Oberstein
      342: Kaiserslautern
      572:

---

*From late 1939 to late 1940 most of the replacement training units from this Wehrkreis were stationed in Wehrkreis XXI.
For *training* regiments, see Reserve division 182 in section VI, below.

RESTRICTED

Motorized:
    36: Wiesbaden
Motorized (Pz. Gren.):
    104: Landau
Artillery:
    33 (Mtz): Darmstadt
    34: Koblenz
    263 ?:
Reserve divisions: 182
Training areas:
    Baumholder:
    Bitsch (*Bitche*):
Division staffs:
    412 z.b.V.: Wiesbaden

Wehrkreis XIII (Hq: Nürnberg)

Unterfranken, Oberfranken, Mittelfranken, Oberpfalz, and the northern part of Niederbayern: Extended in 1938 to include part of Czechoslovakia.

Commander: Gen.d.Inf. Mauriz WIKTORIN (61)
C of S: Genmaj. Paul VOIT (68)
Corps mobilized: XIII Inf, XLV (Corps Comd) (believed disbanded)
Divisions mobilized:
    Infantry: 10 (now 10th Mtz), 17, 46, 73, 98, 113, 183, 231 (since disbanded), 296, 334, 343, 713
    Motorized: 10 (former 10th Inf)
    Light: 99 (now 7th Mtn)
    Panzer: 4
    Mountain: 7 (former 99th L)
Recruiting area Hq: Nürnberg:
    Recruiting sub-areas: Nürnberg I-II, Fürth, Bamberg, Bad Kissingen, Würzburg, Ansbach, Coburg, Bayreuth, Bad Mergentheim, Tauberbischofsheim
Recruiting area Hq: Regensburg: Genlt. Bruno Edler v. KIESLING auf KIESLINGSTEIN (65)

RESTRICTED

ORDER OF BATTLE OF THE GERMAN ARMY 43

Recruiting sub-areas: Regensburg, Passau, Straubing, Weiden, Amberg

Recruiting area Hq: Eger (*Cheb*):
 Recruiting sub-areas: Eger (*Cheb*), Kaaden (*Kadan*), Karlsbad (*Karlovy Vary*), Mies (*Mže*), Marktredwitz

Mobilization divisions:
 No. 193: (transferred to Bohemia)
 No. 473: Regensburg

*Replacement regiments:
 Infantry:
  17: Nürnberg
  46: Bayreuth
  73: Nürnberg
  231: Coburg
  296: Regensburg ?
 Motorized:
  10: Regensburg
 Motorized (Pz.Gren.):
  84: Würzburg ?
 Artillery:
  10 (Mtz): Regensburg
  17: Nürnberg

Reserve divisions: 173

Training areas:
 Grafenwöhr: Genlt. Hans HEBERLEIN (56) ?
 Hammelburg: Obstlt. WITTE

Division staffs:
 413 z.b.V.: Nürnberg

---

*For *training* regiments, see Reserve division 173 in section VI, below.

RESTRICTED

Wehrkreis XVII (Hq: Wien)

Oberdonau and Niederdonau (formerly Ober- and Nieder-Österreich, Wien, and part of Burgenland): Extended in 1938 to include part of Czechoslovakia.

Commander: Gen.d.Inf. Albrecht SCHUBERT (58)

C of S:

Corps mobilized: XVII and LXXXII (former XXXVII Corps Comd) Inf, XL Pz

Divisions mobilized:
    Infantry: 44, 45, 137, 262, 297, 327, 331, 369 (Croatian), 373 (Croatian), 392 (Croatian), 717 (now 117th L)
    Light: 4 (now 9th Pz), 100, 117 (former 717th Inf)
    Panzer: 2, 9 (former 4th L)

Recruiting area Hq: Wien: Genlt. SCHWARZNECKER (60)
    Recruiting sub-areas: Wien I-IV, Melk, Zwettl, St. Pölten, Krems an der Donau, Znaim (*Znojmo*), Wiener-Neustadt, Baden b. Wien, Nikolsburg (*Mikulov*)

Recruiting area Hq: Linz: Genlt. Ludwig RIEBESAM (56)
    Recruiting sub-areas: Linz, Steyr, Wels, Ried im Innkreis, Krummau (*Krumlov Český*)

Mobilization divisions:
    No. 177: Wien
    No. 487: Linz

*Replacement regiments:
    Infantry:
        44: Wien
        45: Krummau
        130: Linz
        131: Wien
        134 ?:
        262: Eggenburg
        462: Wien
    Motorized (Pz.Gren.):
        82: Wien

---

*Since 1941 some of the replacement training units from this Wehrkreis have been stationed in Moravia.

For *training* regiments, see Reserve division 187 in section VI, below.

RESTRICTED

ORDER OF BATTLE OF THE GERMAN ARMY 45

Artillery:
  96: Wien
  98 ?: Linz
  262 ?:
Reserve divisions: 187
Training areas:
  Bruck (Leitha):
  Döllersheim: Genmaj. Konrad OFFENBÄCHER (54)
  Kleinkarpathen (located in Slovakia)
Division staffs:
  417 z.b.V.: Wien

Wehrkreis XVIII (Hq: Salzburg)

Tirol, Vorarlberg, Salzburg, Steiermark, and Kärnten: Extended in 1941 to include Oberkrain and Untersteiermark (districts in northern Yugoslavia).
Commander: Gen.d.Inf. Friedrich MATERNA (59)
C or S:
Corps mobilized: XVIII and XIX (former Norway) Mtn
Divisions mobilized:
  Infantry: 718 (now 118th L)
  Light: 118 (former 718 Inf)
  Mountain: 2, 3, 5, 6, 8
Recruiting area Hq: Graz: Genlt. Emil GUNZELMANN (57)
  Recruiting sub-areas: Graz, Spittal a.d.Drau, Klagenfurt, Judenburg, Leoben, Leibnitz, Fürstenfeld, Marburg a.d.Drau (*Maribor*), Cilli (*Celje*), Krainburg (*Kranj*)
Recruiting area Hq: Innsbruck: Genlt. Wilhelm Frhr.v. WALDENFELS (60)
  Recruiting sub-areas: Innsbruck, Bregenz, Salzburg
Mobilization divisions:
*Replacement regiments:
  Mountain:
    136: Landeck
    137: Salzburg
    138: Leoben
    139: Villach

---
*For *training* regiments, see Reserve division 188 in section VI, below.

RESTRICTED

Artillery:
    111 (Mtn): Hall
    112 (Mtn): Kufstein
Reserve divisions: 188
Training areas:
    Seethaler Alpe:
    Wattener Lizum:
Division staffs:
    537 Grenzwach: Innsbruck
    538 Grenzwach: Klagenfurt

Wehrkreis XX (Hq: Danzig)

Formed after the Polish campaign, comprising Freistaat Danzig, the Polish Corridor, and the part of Westpreussen which between the wars was attached to Ostpreussen.

Commander: Gen.d.Inf. Bodewin KEITEL (55)
C of S:
Corps maintained: XX Inf and XLVII Pz
Divisions maintained:
    Infantry: 60 (now 60th Mtz)
    Motorized: 60 (former 60th Inf), renamed "Pz.Gr.Div. Feldherrnhalle"
Recruiting area Hq: Danzig: Genlt. KURZ
    Recruiting sub-areas: Danzig, Neustadt (Westpr.) (*Wejherowo*), Pr.Stargard (*Starogard*), Marienwerder, Graudenz (*Grudziądz*), Bromberg (*Bydgoszcz*), Thorn (*Toruń*)
Mobilization divisions:
    No. 152: Graudenz (transferred from Wkr. II)
Replacement regiments:
    Motorized:
        60: Danzig

RESTRICTED

Training areas:
  Grossendorf (*Wielkawieś*):
  Thorn (*Toruń*): Genmaj. MELCHERT
Division staffs:
  428 z.b.V.: Graudenz (*Grudziądz*)

Wehrkreis XXI (Hq. Posen *(Poznań)*)

Formed after the Polish campaign, comprising the Wartheland (western Poland).
Commander: Gen.d.Art. Walter PETZEL (61)
C of S:
Corps maintained: XLVIII Pz
Divisions maintained:
Recruiting area Hq: Posen (*Poznań*):
  Recruiting sub-areas: Posen (*Poznań*), Lissa (Wartheland) (*Leszno*), Hohensalza (*Inowracław*), Leslau (*Włocławek*), Kalisch (*Kalisz*), Litzmannstadt (*Łódź*)
Mobilization divisions:
*Replacement regiments:
Training areas:
  Sieradz (*Sjerads*):
  Warthelager:
Division staffs:
  429 z.b.V.: Posen (*Poznań*)
  430 z.b.V.: Gnesen (*Gniezno*)
  431 z.b.V.: Litzmannstadt (*Łódź*)

*Training units were transferred to this area in 1942 from Wehrkreise II and III.

RESTRICTED

Wehrkreis Böhmen und Mähren (Hq: Prag *(Praha)*)

Formed late in 1942. Comprises the whole of the Protectorate.
Commander: Gen.d.Pz.Tr. Ferdinand SCHAAL (55)
C of S:
Corps mobilized: XLIX Mtn
Divisions mobilized:
Recruiting area Hq: Prag (*Praha*): Genlt. von PRONDZYNSKI (63)
    Recruiting sub-areas: Prag (*Praha*), Budweis (*České Budějovice*)
    (now taken over by Prag), Brünn (*Brno*), Olmütz (*Olomouc*)
    (now taken over by Brünn)
Mobilization divisions:
    No. 193: Prag (*Praha*) (**transferred** from Wkr.XIII)
Replacement regiments:
Training areas:
    Kammwald (*Hřebeny*), formerly Brdy-Wald: Genmaj. THAMS (59)
    Milowitz über Lissa a.d. Elbe (*Milovice*):
    Wischau (*Vyškov*):
Division staffs:
    539 Grenzwach: Prag (*Praha*): Genlt. Dr. Richard SPEICH (60)
    540 Grenzwach: Brünn (*Brno*): Genlt. Karl TARBUK v. SEN-SENHORST

Wehrkreis Generalgouvernement (Hq: Krakau *(Kraków)*)

Formed late in 1942. Comprises those parts of Poland not incorporated in Wehrkreise I, VIII, XX, and XXI or in the Reichskommissariate Ostland and Ukraine.
Commander: Gen.d.Inf. Siegfried HAENICKE (66)
C of S: Genmaj. Kurt HASELOFF (49)
Corps maintained:
Divisions maintained:
Recruiting area Hq: Krakau (*Kraków*):
    Recruiting sub-areas: Krakau (*Kraków*), Warschau (*Warszawa*), Lemberg (*Lwów*)

RESTRICTED

Training areas:
Süd (South — Hq. Dęba): Genmaj. Fritz SALITTER
Mitte (Center — Hq. Radom): Genmaj. von KUTZLEBEN
Galizien (Malopolska Wsch. — Hq. Janów near Lemberg (Lwów)):
Genmaj. Helmvt BESCH
Biedruska:
Jablonna—Legionowo near Warschau (Warszawa):
Pustkow near Krakau (Kraków):

9. Army Administration in Occupied Countries.

a. General.—In the following pages the German occupied and satellite countries are set out in the order in which they were occupied by or became associated with Germany. Details are given regarding the military administration of, or German military relations with, each country. It should be understood that this administrative structure is distinct from the operational control of any German combat units stationed in the territory in question.

The administrative relations of the German Army with the different countries under German control vary widely according to German strategic needs as well as political, economic, and psychological considerations. Several areas, for example, are extensively used for training and may be thought of as a projection of the German territorial organization at home (*Wehrkreise*). The nomenclature of the German commands and the entire administrative organization are in each case adapted to the special requirements and objectives.

The lower administrative headquarters and local military administration in several of the occupied areas are organized as follows:

RESTRICTED

(1) *Oberfeldkommandantur* (administrative area headquarters). Headquarters of this type in the theater of operations come under the commander of Army or Army Group Rear Area. In occupied territory outside the theater of operations they come under the military commander in charge of the military administration of the country.

(2) *Subordinate administrative headquarters.*—These include:

(a) *Feldkommandantur* (administrative sub-area headquarters).—Normally commanded by a colonel or a *Generalmajor*.

(b) *Ortskommandantur* (town headquarters).— Major's command in a small town.

(c) *Kreiskommandantur* (district headquarters).—Major's command in a rural district.

(d) *Stadtkommandantur* (city headquarters).—Found in some cities; status varies with the size and importance of the city.

b. Occupied countries.—(1) *Austria.*—Occupied in March 1938 and absorbed into the Reich as *Wehrkreise XVII* and *XVIII*.

(2) *Czechoslovakia.*—First partitioned in September 1938, when the Sudetenland was detached and incorporated into *Wehrkreise IV, VIII, XIII, and XVII*. The remaining territory (except the parts which went to Hungary and Poland) was occupied in March 1939, and was divided into the *Protektorat Böhmen und Mähren* (Protectorate of Bohemia and Moravia) and the protected state of Slovakia.

(a) *Protektorat* (Hq: Prag).—This area became a corps area under the name *Wehrkreis Böhmen und Mähren*, late in 1942. The office of *Wehrmachtbevollmächtigter* (Armed Forces Plenipotentiary) is combined with that of *Wehrkreis* commander under the title of *Wehrmachtbevollmächtigter*

RESTRICTED

ORDER OF BATTLE OF THE GERMAN ARMY

beim Reichsprotektor und Befehlshaber im Wehrkreis Böhmen und Mähren (Armed Forces Plenipotentiary attached to the Reich Protector and Commander in the Corps Area Bohemia and Moravia). For the military administrative structure see *Wehrkreis Böhmen und Mähren* under paragraph 8 *b* above.

(*b*) *Slovakia* (Hq: Pressburg (*Bratislava*)).—This province is nominally an independent country with its own army and its own defense ministry (Minister of Defense and C in C: General CATLOS). It is, however, under complete German domination and the Germans not only have a military mission there but garrison and train their own troops in the territory.

German General with Slovak Defense Ministry and Head of Military Mission (*Deutscher General beim Slowakischen Verteidigungsministerium und Chef der Deutschen Heeresmission*): Genlt. SCHLIEPER (53)
C of S:
Commandant of the Protected Area (Kommandant der Schutzzone):
Training Area: *Kleinkarpathen* (Hq: Malacky): Obstlt. v. GROELING

(3) *Memel District.*—Occupied in March 1939 and incorporated into *Wehrkreis I*.

(4) *Poland.*—The western half was occupied by the Germans after the campaign of September 1939. Parts of this area were incorporated into the Reich in *Wehrkreise I, VIII*, and the newly formed *Wehrkreise XX* and *XXI*. The remainder of German-occupied Poland was established as the Government General (*Generalgouvernement*) under a civilian Governor General. The eastern part of Poland was conquered from the Russians in June 1941 and was eventually divided among *Wehrkreis I* (Bialystok district), *Reichskommissariate Ostland* and *Ukraine,* and the Government General (Galicia). The Government General became a *Wehrkreis* late in 1942; it has, however, retained some of the administrative structure of an occupied country.

RESTRICTED

Administrative Headquarters:
Oberfeldkommandanturen:
225 Warsaw: Genlt. v. KLEIST (57)
365 Lemberg (*Lwów*): Genlt. BEUTTEL (57)
372 Lublin: Genlt. Wilhelm v. ALTROCK (55)?
393 Piaseczno
Krakau: Genlt. Kurt OPPENLÄNDER?
Feldkommandanturen:
768 Mińsk-Mazowiecki
Ortskommandanturen:
II/354 Krakau area?
I/411 Mińsk-Mazowiecki?
I/604 Kielce

(5) *Danzig Free State.*—Occupied in September 1939 and incorporated subsequently into the newly formed *Wehrkreis XX*.

(6) *Denmark.*—Occupied almost without resistance in April 1940 and subsequently allowed a degree of autonomy in internal affairs. The country has been extensively used by the Germans for training purposes.

German Troops in Denmark (Hq: Copenhagen)

Commander of German Troops (*Befehlshaber der deutschen Truppen*): Gen.d.Inf. v.HANNEKEN (54) (XXXI Corps Command)
C of S:
Area Hq: Copenhagen
    Sub-areas: Jutland, Zealand.
Training area: Oxböl.

(7) *Norway.*—Occupied after a brief campaign in April 1940 and subsequently governed by the QUISLING regime under a German civilian commissar (TERBOVEN).

German Forces in Norway (Hq: Oslo)

Armed Forces Commander (*Wehrmachtbefehlshaber**): Genobst. Nikolaus v. FALKENHORST (59)
C of S: Genlt. Rudolf BAMLER (48)

*Also commanding the Twenty-first Army (Army of Norway).

RESTRICTED

ORDER OF BATTLE OF THE GERMAN ARMY

Areas:
North (Hq: Rundhaug): Gen.d.Art. Willi MOSER (56) (LXXI Corps Command)
  Sub-areas: Skoganvarre, Saetermoen
Center (Hq: Trondhjem): Gen.d.Kav. Erwin ENGELBRECHT (53) (XXXIII Corps Command)
  Sub-area: Mo, Steinkjaer, Dombaas
South (Hq: Oslo):
  Sub-area: Bergen, Arendal

The administrative areas are corps commands, each having two or three sub-areas which are divisional commands. These in turn are subdivided into three sectors, each under the control of an infantry regiment. The commanders of areas and sub-areas are described as *Territorial-Befehlshaber* and the commanders of sectors as *Territorial-Abschnittsbefehlshaber*.

(8) *Holland*.—Occupied in May 1940 and subsequently governed by a German civilian commissar (SEYSS-INQUART), with the help of the existing Dutch administrative agencies.

German Forces in Holland (Hq: Hilversum)

Armed Forces Commander (*Wehrmachtbefehlshaber*): Gen.d.Flieger Friedrich CHRISTIANSEN (65)
Commander of Army Troops in the Netherlands (*Befehlshaber der Truppen des Heeres in den Niederlanden*): Gen.d.Inf. Hans REINHARD (56) (LXXXVIII Army Corps)
C of S:
Administrative Headquarters:
  Feldkommandanturen:
    674 Breda
    724 Utrecht
  Ortskommandanturen:
    Rotterdam
    The Hague

(9) *Luxemburg*.—Occupied in May 1940 and incorporated into *Wehrkreis XII*.

(10) *Belgium*.—Occupied in May 1940, subsequently gov-

RESTRICTED

erned by a German military commander with the help of the existing Belgian administrative agencies. For military administration purposes it is combined with coastal northern France above the river Somme into the unified command *Belgien-Nordfrankreich*.

German Forces in *Belgien-Nordfrankreich* (Hq: Brussels)

Military Commander (*Militärbefehlshaber*): Gen.d.Inf. Alexander v. FALKENHAUSEN (66)
C of S: Obstlt. v. HARBOU
Administrative Headquarters:

Oberfeldkommandanturen:
520 Mons
570 Ghent
589 Liége
670 Lille
672 Brussels: Genlt. Günther Freiherr v. HAMMERSTEIN-EQUORD (67)
Feldkommandanturen:
178 Bruges
503 Courtrai
520 Antwerp: Genmaj. Otto SCHMIDT
569 Lille
598 Arlon
611 Ghent
681 Hasselt
682 Namur
683 Liége
718 Douai
Kreiskommandanturen:
510 Bruges
598 Wervicq
616 Charleroi

636 Lille
636 Neufchateau?
652 Courtrai?
I/685 Tongres
687 Huy?
694 Malines?
703 Valenciennes?
708 Alost?
714 Dunkirk?
718 Douai
772 Saint-Omer
913 Louvain
Ortskommandanturen:
II/630 Ghent
I/644 Verviers
I/699 Tirlemont
I/702 Antwerp
759 Berck
853 Roulers
914 Lille
I/940 Liége
942 Namur
Brussels

(11) *France.*—Partially occupied after the capitulation of June 1940; allowed a degree of autonomy in matters of local

RESTRICTED

government throughout the occupied area, with the exception of Alsace and Lorraine, which have since been incorporated into *Wehrkreise V* and *XII*. Divided for purposes of military administration into the areas "France" and "Northern France" (included in Belgium). The remainder of metropolitan France was occupied in November 1942; it has retained its autonomy in civil affairs under the government at Vichy, but for the purposes of military administration the Commander of the Army Group Rear Area South France has the same status and powers as the commanders of the Military Districts of "Occupied" **France.**

German Forces in France (Hq: Paris)

Military Commander (*Militärbefehlshaber*): Gen.d.Inf. Otto v. STÜLP-NAGEL (65)
C of S:
Military Districts (*Militärverwaltungsbezirke*):
   Northern France (Hq: Paris)
     Commander:
     C of S:
   Northwestern France (Hq: Angers)
     Commander: Genlt. Kurt FELDT (55)?
     C of S:
   Northeastern France (Hq: Dijon)
     Commander: Genlt. Heinrich Ritter v. FÜCHTBAUER (64)
     C of S:
   Southwestern France (Hq: Bordeaux)
     Commander:
     C of S:
   Southern France (*Kommandeur des Heeresgebiets Südfrankreich*)
     Commander: Genlt. Heinrich NIEHOFF (61)
     C of S:
   Greater Paris (*Kommandantur Gross-Paris*)
     Commander: Genlt. Wilhelm Freiherr v. BOINEBURG-LENGSFELD (55)
     C of S:

RESTRICTED

Administrative Headquarters:
Oberfeldkommandanturen:
592 Laon
Feldkommandanturen:
515 Channel Islands
517 Rouen
529 Bordeaux: Genmaj. Hans KNOERZER (56)
531 Châlons-sur-Marne
541 Biarritz:Genmaj. BOIE?
545 Genmaj. Artur BISLE (56)
549 Rennes: Genmaj. JACOBI
560 Besançon
563 Saint-Dizier
580 Amiens
588 Le Mans
590 Bar-le-Duc
591 Nancy: Genmaj. Franz Karl v. BOCK (68)
595 Angers: Genmaj. Jürgen BAARTH (53)?
602 Laon
605 La Roche-sur-Yon: Genmaj. v. KURNATOWSKI (64)?
622 Dijon
638 Beauvais
651 Niort
677 **Poitiers**
680 Melun
684 Charleville
722 Saint-Lô
723 Caen
734 Paris Area?
746 Montdidier
750 Vannes: Genmaj. Ritter v. REISS?
751 Chartres
752 Quimper?
758 Marseille
788 Tours
801 Evreux
Kreiskommandanturen:
554 Belfort
563 Dijon
583 Cherbourg?
593 Nancy
612 Sedan
623 Brest
626 Abbeville
637 Le Havre
672 Verdun
704 Marseille
713 Boulogne?
735 Lorient
781 Fontainebleau
800 Amiens
892 Longwy

(12) *Italy*.—Entered the war in June 1940, after which German infiltration continued with growing intensity. After Marshal Badoglio's government made a separate peace with the Allies in September 1943, a puppet Republican Fascist Government was set up in German-occupied Italy, under the nominal leadership of Mussolini. The form of German military administration in this area (much of which is in the communications zone for the Italian front) is not yet clear.

RESTRICTED

ORDER OF BATTLE OF THE GERMAN ARMY 57

(13) *Rumania.*—Under German domination since November 1940.
Head of Military Mission: Gen.d.Kav. Erik HANSEN (55)
C of S:

(14) *Hungary.*—Allied with Germany since the summer of 1940. Since the autumn of that year German domination has increased. The Hungarians have retained, however, a much greater degree of independence than the Rumanians.
Head of Military Mission:
C of S:

(15) *Bulgaria.*—Passively associated with Germany since March 1941; at war with the United States and Great Britain but not with Russia.
Head of Military Mission:
C of S:

(16) *Southeast* (Südost).—A composite occupied territory, formed by Yugoslavia (less those parts annexed to Germany, ceded to Italy, Hungary or Bulgaria, or incorporated into the theoretically independent state of Croatia), Greece and the Greek Islands.

(a) *Yugoslavia.*—Occupied in April 1941. Portions of the country annexed by Germany, Italy, Hungary, and Bulgaria, the rest under German occupation. Part of Slovenia was incorporated into *Wehrkreis XVIII.*

(i) Serbia (Hq: Belgrade)
Military Commander (*Kommandierender General und Befehlshaber in Serbien*): Gen.d.Inf. Hans Gustav FELBER (56)
C of S: Obst. BODE
Administrative Headquarters:
Feldkommandanturen:
809 Nisch

(ii) Croatia (Hq: Agram (*Zagreb*)).—Formed into a theoretically independent kingdom under the Duke of Spoleto, who was deposed shortly after Italy made a separate peace.

RESTRICTED

German General Plenipotentiary in Croatia (*Bevollmächtigter Deutscher General in Kroatien*) : Genlt. Dr. Edmund v. GLAISE-HORSTENAU (62)

C of S: Obst. KAULBACH

Administrative Headquarters:
Feldkommandanturen:
735 Agram (*Zagreb*): Genmaj. Walter KOSSACK (61)

(*b*) *Greece.*—Occupied after the campaign of May 1941. Portions ceded to Bulgaria; the rest divided into German and Italian spheres of influence. Since the Italian Armistice, the whole country has been administered by the Germans with the help of a puppet Greek regime.

(i) Salonika-Aegean (Northern Greece and the Aegean Islands) (Hq: Salonika).

Commander (*Befehlshaber Saloniki-Ägäis*): Genlt. Kurt PFLUG-RADT (53)

C of S:

(ii) Southern Greece (Hq: Athens).

Commander (*Befehlshaber Südgriechenland*): Gen.d.Flieger Wilhelm SPEIDEL

C of S:

(iii) Fortress of Crete (Hq: Heraklion).

Commander (*Kommandant der Festung Kreta*): Genlt. (Luftwaffe) Bruno BRÄUER (51)

C of S: Obst. Hans EHLERT

Administrative Headquarters:
Feldkommandanturen:
599 Belgrade: Genmaj. Adalbert LONTSCHAR
606 Crete?
808 Salonika
810 (Greece)
Ortskommandanturen:
I/856 Langadas (Greece)
I/825 Athens
I/866 Demotika (Greece)
II/941 Crete?
II/981 Crete?

RESTRICTED

(17) *Finland*.—Allied to Germany since June 1941. A German Army Headquarters controls German forces in northern Finland; any German units that may be stationed in southern Finland come under the Finnish High Command, to which a German Military Mission is accredited.

Head of Military Mission: Gen.d.Inf. Waldemar ERFURTH (65)
C of S: Obstlt. HÖLTER

(18) *Union of Soviet Socialist Republics*.—Attacked in June 1941. The Baltic States and White Russia (collectively termed the *Ostland*) and the western Ukraine were subsequently placed under the German Ministry for the Occupied Eastern Area (ROSENBERG). The occupied regions farther east were under German military administration. The province of Galicia was incorporated into the Government General and the Bialystok district into *Wehrkreis I*.

(a) *Ostland* (Hq: Riga). Governed by a German Reich Commissar (LOHSE).

 Armed Forces Commander (*Wehrmachtbefehlshaber*): Gen.d.Kav. Walter BRAEMER (61)
 C of S:
 Districts (*Generalbezirke*), governed by German Commissars with the aid of native so-called autonomous administrations:
  Estonia (*Estland*) (Hq: Reval (*Talinn*))
   Commander: Gen.d.Inf. Cuno Hans v. BOTH (60)
   C of S:
  Latvia (*Lettland*) (Hq: Riga)
   Commander: Genlt.Dipl.Ing. Friedrich-Wilhelm JOHN
   C of S:
  Lithuania (*Litauen*) (Hq: Kovno, Kauen, (*Kaunas*))
   Commander: Genmaj. Emil JUST (54)
   C of S:
  White Russia (*Weiss-Ruthenien*) (Hq: Minsk)
   Commander:
   C of S:

RESTRICTED

Administrative Headquarters:
Oberfeldkommandanturen:
392 Minsk?
Feldkommandanturen:
768 Minsk
Ortskommandanturen:
I/257 Minsk

(*b*) **Ukraine** (Hq: formerly Rowno (*Równe*)): Includes southwestern Russia (except Transnistria and the Odessa area, which were ceded to Rumania), the Crimea, and the Brest-Litowsk-Rowno-Luck area of Poland. The recent Russian advances in this area make it unnecessary to give details of this occupied territory, which was administered in a manner similar to the *Ostland*, with an Armed Forces Commander (*Wehrmachtbefehlshaber*) and divided into six districts (*Generalbezirke*).

10. Army Organization in the Communications Zone.

In the communications zone of the theater of operations each army group has a Commander of Army Group Rear Area (*Befehlshaber des rückwärtigen Heeresgebiets*), and each army has a Commandant of Army Rear Area (*Kommandant des rückwärtigen Armeegebiets*). Their main task is to provide for the administration and particularly for the security of the communications zone so that the army group or army commander can concentrate exclusively on combat operations.

The Commander of Army Group Rear Area has charge of Sicherungs (security) units—specially organized divisions and regiments formed to undertake mopping-up operations in the rear of the combat zone. He is also in charge of such administrative headquarters as may be set up within the area assigned to him and of all guard units and supply organizations of the GHQ pool stationed within the area.

His functions, therefore, correspond very closely to those of the military commanders of occupied countries, and on the close of active operations he may in fact remain as military commander over the country or portion of a country which he has hitherto commanded as a rear area.

The functions of the Commandant of an Army Rear Area are less extensive, and his status compares more closely with that of the area commander within an occupied country.

RESTRICTED

Section III. TYPES OF SMALL UNITS

11. Introduction.

a. General.—This section consists of a list of all the principal types of units in the German ground forces of the status of regiments and below, with particulars of their German designations, their numbering, and the method of their allotment and employment. They are arranged according to the arms and services (*Waffengattungen*) and subdivided into organic units (integral parts of divisions or higher units) and GHQ units (*Heerestruppen*) (units held in the GHQ pool and allotted temporarily to army groups, armies, corps, and divisions, for specific operations). GHQ units also include static units controlled by administrative headquarters in Germany and occupied countries.

Each German *Waffengattung* has a distinguishing color which appears on the piping of the shoulder straps. In the course of the war, however, a number of types of units have been reclassified under different arms and have retained their original color, so that today the color does not always coincide with the arm. For example, the cavalry as a separate arm has been abolished and its units absorbed by the infantry, but all cavalry units have retained golden yellow as their distinguishing color.

Air Force ground units are listed separately. They include antiaircraft units, parachute units, and Air Force field units (ground combat troops).

All units of the Field Army are comprised in the following three categories:
Combat Troops (*Fechtende Truppen*)
Service Troops (*Versorgungstruppen*)
Security Troops (*Sicherungstruppen*)
In addition units may be found organized for specific missions. Those identified are listed in this section under special purpose units (*Sondereinheiten*). The combat and service troops are divided into the various arms (*Waffengattungen*), whereas the security troops consist principally of infantry.

It should be noted that with the exception of the various types of infantry regiments all units listed as organic may also be found as GHQ troops. They are not included here under the latter heading. Each arm includes demonstration units (*Lehreinheiten*) and equipment parks (e.g., *Infanteriepark, Artilleriepark*), which are listed at the end of their respective paragraphs. All parks are serviced by companies (e.g., *Infanterieparkkompanie, Pionierparkkompanie*) the personnel of which are believed to belong to the supply troops; these are not included in this section.

The supporting units of the mountain and Panzer divisions are usually found prefixed by *Gebirgs-* and *Panzer-*, respectively. They are usually not listed separately in this section since their nomenclature is automatic.

b. Numbering system.—(1) *Purpose.*—The overall system for the numbering of German small units was originally designed to provide various blocks of numbers for all categories of units in the German Army, so arranged that the number of any unit would indicate, within certain limits of security, the status of the unit, i.e., whether it was divisional, corps, army, or independent, and in some cases, its affiliation.

This overall system was based on three main categories or groups, each of which contained numerous series of units. For convenience these are referred to here as categories A, B, and C.

RESTRICTED

Category A was designed for all organic divisional units as well as those GHQ units which were intended to be attached to divisions, corps, and armies, with the important exception of infantry, artillery, Panzer, and chemical warfare units.

Category B was designed for infantry, artillery, Panzer, and chemical warfare units.

Category C was designed for those GHQ units which were to be directly or indirectly under the control of the O.K.H. in Berlin and not under the Field Army or its subordinate armies, corps, and divisions.

(2) *Category A.*—Units in this category received numbers from 1 to 700. This series was subdivided into three distinct blocks as follows:

(*a*) 1-400 for organic divisional units. The number given such a unit was in most cases either the number of the division itself, 100 greater than the number of the division, or the same as the auxiliary unit number of the division.

(*b*) 401-500 for organic corps units. The last two digits correspond to the number of the corps; thus Feldgendarmerietrupp 442 belonged organically to the XLII Corps and Brückenkolonne 404 to the IV Corps.

(*c*) 501-600 for organic army units. Here there was apparently no relationship between the number of the unit and the number of the army headquarters to which it belonged.

(*d*) 601-700 for attached army units. Here also the number of the unit did not correspond to that of the army to which it was attached.

(2) *Category B.*—The numbers of infantry, artillery, Panzer, and chemical warfare units were taken from various blocks between 1 and 1000. Organic and GHQ units are mixed throughout the numerical series. In the case of the artillery regiments in divisions, there is usually a close relationship between the regimental and divisional numbers, and there is

RESTRICTED

ORDER OF BATTLE OF THE GERMAN ARMY

usually a pattern for the assignment of infantry regiments to the divisions of any given wave. The numbers for chemical warfare units do not go above 150.

(3) *Category C.*—Each type of unit in this category was numbered in a separate series from 1 up. Units in the zone of the interior often took their numbers from the *Wehrkreis;* other types may have been numbered on a pattern based on the *Wehrkreis* of origin. With many types of units in Category C only very low numbers will be found, and this often serves to distinguish them from the same types belonging to Category A. For example, units of the Secret Field Police which operate in Germany and in occupied countries are numbered below 200, while those belonging or attached to armies in the field have numbers above 500.

(4) *Variations and exceptions.*—While the system outlined above is still in general operation and can usually be relied on for identifications and affiliations, a number of minor variations have occurred in the course of the war due to various circumstances.

(*a*) *Use of the 700, 800, and 900 series.*—When the fifteen divisions of the 15th wave, formed in the spring of 1941, were assigned numbers in the 700 series (702, 704, and 707-719), their minor components were all given the divisional number instead of a number from the series 1-400. (When four of the divisions were subsequently converted into light divisions in the 100 series their minor components likewise changed their numbers.) Since then the remaining numbers in the 700 series (720-800) as well as the 800 and 900 series have been drawn upon to a limited extent for the numbering of attached army units instead of the 600 series.

(*b*) *Change in status of units.*—When a unit hitherto attached to an army changes its status to that of an organic army unit, it does not necessarily change its number. Propa-

RESTRICTED

ganda companies, for example, which were numbered in the 600 series because they were intended to be attached to armies, have actually been incorporated as organic army troops but have retained their original numbers instead of adopting new ones in the 500 series. The opposite policy has apparently been followed with the *Arkos*. These were originally numbered between 1 and 150 in an independent artillery series (Category B), but some have been found renumbered in the 400 series, indicating that they are now intended to be organic to corps (Category A).

(*c*) *Change in the employment of units.*—When units belonging to Category C which are employed in the zone of the interior under *Wehrkreis* control or in occupied countries under the occupational authorities (*Oberfeldkommandanturen*, etc.) are transferred to the theater of operations and attached to an army or subordinate field command, they may retain their previous numbering. For example, many *Landesschützen* battalions, formerly employed in Germany and consisting of low-grade personnel, have moved into the rear areas of the Russian front and have since operated under a *Korück* or directly under an army headquarters; in some cases they have been renamed as *Sicherungs, Wach,* or *Baupionier* battalions, but without changing their numbers. Hence today there are some *Baupionier* units numbered above 500 (originally intended as army troops) and some below 500 (converted from *Landesschützen* units).

(*d*) *Possible future changes.*—As has been shown, the system here outlined is not a rigid one, and any form of violation of it may take place in the course of the extensive changes in the affiliations of German units which may be expected in the future.

12. Combat Troops *(Fechtende Truppen).*

a. Infantry (Infanterie).—Under an order issued in April

RESTRICTED

1943 this arm does not include the infantry units in Panzer and motorized divisions, which are now classified as Panzer troops. Under the same order, however, it does include reconnaissance and other former cavalry units.

The distinguishing color of the infantry is white, except for light and mountain infantry and former cavalry units.

(1) *Organic units.*—(*a*) Grenadierregiment (*regular infantry regiment*).—Usually three, sometimes two, to an infantry division.

(*b*) Füsilierregiment.—A special honorary name for certain infantry regiments which carry on the traditions of *Füsilierregimenter* of the old Imperial Army. No different in organization from *Grenadierregimenter*. Nos. 22, 26, 27, 34, 39, 68, 230, and 334 have been identified.

(*c*) Jägerregiment (*light infantry regiment*).—Infantry regiment in a light division. Usually two to a division.

(Distinguishing color: light green.)

(*d*) Gebirgsjägerregiment (*mountain infantry regiment*). —Organized especially for mountain warfare by making the three battalions self-sufficient. The normal infantry howitzer company (*Infanteriegeschützkompanie*) is lacking, but pack howitzers (75 mm) are organic in each battalion.

(Distinguishing color: light green.)

(*e*) Aufklärungsabteilung (*reconnaissance battalion.*)— Two types exist:

(i) Found in regular infantry divisions. Consists of three troops: one mounted, one cyclist, and one heavy weapons.

(ii) Found in light and mountain divisions. Formerly known as *Radfahrabteilung* (cyclist battalion). Consists of one or two cyclist troops, one motorcycle company and one heavy weapons troop.

Any of the above companies except the heavy weapons com-

RESTRICTED

pany may be replaced by a company of troops riding in armored carriers (*Schützenpanzerwagenkompanie*).
(Distinguishing color: golden yellow.)

(*f*) Schnelle Abteilung (*mobile battalion*).—Combined reconnaissance and antitank battalion. Consists of horse and cyclist units, which belong to the infantry, and antitank units, which belong to the Panzer troops. *Schnelle Abteilungen* 602, 608, and 621, as well as those of the *Schnelle Brigaden* 20 and 30 (see section VII, paragraph 50) are classified as infantry throughout.

(*g*) Divisionsbataillon (*divisional battalion*).—Believed to be similar in composition and purpose to the *Jägerbataillon*, described under (2) (*j*), below.

(*h*) Feldersatzbataillon (*field replacement battalion*).—A field reserve for divisional units. Consists of three to five companies containing replacement elements for the various arms. May be organic to a division, but its personnel may also go to several divisions in a given area.

(*i*) Maschinengewehrkompanie (*machine-gun company*).—Found in all infantry battalions. Has heavy machine guns and heavy mortars.

(*j*) Infanteriegeschützkompanie (*infantry howitzer company*).—Found in infantry regiments, normally as the 13th company (except in mountain divisions).

(*k*) Infanteriepanzerjägerkompanie (*antitank company*).—Found in all types of infantry regiments, normally as the 14th company (16th in the mountain division).

(*l*) Schwere Kompanie (*heavy weapons company*).—Found in light and mountain infantry battalions.

(*m*) Reiterschwadron (*mounted troop*).—Found in reconnaissance battalions of infantry, light, and mountain divisions.
(Distinguishing color: golden yellow.)

(*n*) Aufklärungsschwadron (*cyclist troop*). — Formerly

RESTRICTED

Radfahrschwadron; found in reconnaissance battalions of infantry, light, and mountain divisions.
(Distinguishing color: golden yellow.)

(*o*) Schwere Schwadron (*heavy weapons troop*).—Found in reconnaissance battalions of infantry, light, and mountain divisions.
(Distinguishing color: golden yellow.)

(*p*) Kradschützenkompanie (*motorcycle company*).—Found in reconnaissance battalions of light and mountain divisions.
(Distinguishing color: grass green.)

(2) *GHQ units.*—(*a*) Festungsregiment (*fortress regiment*).—Regimental staffs controlling fortress battalions. Several identified in the 900 series.

(*b*) Festungsbataillon (*fortress battalion*).—Static infantry battalion specifically trained for the defense of fixed fortifications. Consists largely of *Landesschützen* personnel.

(*c*) Sturmregiment (*assault regiment*).—A special regiment with heavy firepower. The name *Sturmregiment* is also used as an honorary title for outstanding regiments (such as those of the 78th Infantry Division).

(*d*) Sturmbataillon (*assault battalion*).—A special battalion with heavy firepower. The name *Sturmbataillon* is also used as an honorary title for outstanding battalions. Nos. 186, 262, 293, 393, 395, and 826 have been identified.

(*e*) Reiterregiment (*mounted regiment*).—None of the original cavalry regiments have been recently identified. A new table of organization for cavalry regiments exists, however, and new units may be formed.

(*f*) Schweres Granatwerferbataillon (*heavy mortar battalion*).—Consists of three companies. Each company has twelve heavy mortars (120 mm).

(*g*) Fliegerabwehrbataillon (Fla-Bataillon) (*antiaircraft machine-gun battalion*).—Has light antiaircraft guns (20 &

RESTRICTED

37 mm) in addition to machine guns. Used for both antitank and antiaircraft defense. Two types exist:

(i) Consists of three companies, which may be found operating independently although the battalion is the tactical unit. Identified in the 600 series and 501.

(ii) Battalion staff controlling five or six companies. These companies were used independently as tactical units and carried the numbers of their battalion (e.g., *6. Kp./Fla Btl. 66*), which ran from 22 to 66. Since none have been identified recently, it is possible that this type of unit has been abolished.

Fla units belong to the infantry, although German orders have at times referred to them as a separate arm. They wear white infantry piping with the addition of the Gothic letters "Fl" on the shoulder straps.

(*h*) Grenadierbataillon (*infantry battalion*).—Independent battalion. Often found composed of foreign legion personnel.

(*i*) Grenadierbataillon z.b.V. (*special duty infantry battalion*).—An independent infantry battalion for special employment (*zu besonderer Verwendung*). Identified in the 100, 500, and 800 series.

(*j*) Jägerbataillon (*raiding battalion*).—Formed during the winter of 1941-1942 as *Jagdkommandos* (raiding detachments) for special raiding or mopping-up purposes in Russia. Later renamed *Jägerbataillone*. About twenty have been identified in the 1-100, 100, and 200 series.

(*k*) Skibataillon (*ski infantry battalion*).—This is the *Jägerbataillon* reorganized for winter service. Some of its machine guns are fixed on boat sleds (*Akjas*). Identified in Russia, northern Italy, Finland, and Norway.

(*l*) Maschinengewehrbataillon (mot.) (*motorized machine gun battalion*).—Independent machine gun battalions. Identified in the 1-100 series.

RESTRICTED

(*m*) Panzerzerstörer Kompanie (*antitank rifle company*). —Equipped with 36 antitank rifles (*Panzerbüchsen*).

(*n*) Infanteriepark (*infantry equipment park*).—One to an army; numbered in the 500 series. Probably now combined with the *Artilleriepark* into *Heeresgerätpark* (see sub-paragraph *f*, below. (The officers wear the color of their arm, but enlisted men wear light blue, in each case with the Arabic number of the park.)

(*o*) Infanterie-Lehr-Regiment (*infantry demonstration regiment*).—Normally stationed at the Infantry School at Döberitz (Wkr. III) to demonstrate tactics and perform experiments with new infantry weapons. It is possible that such regiments may be found, in whole or in part, on active service in the field. Nos. 900 and 901 have been identified.

(*p*) Aufklärungs- und Kavallerie-Lehr-Abteilung (*reconnaissance and cavalry demonstration battalion*).—Normally stationed at the reconnaissance and cavalry school at Hannover (Wkr. XI).

b. *Panzer troops* (Panzertruppen).—The arm *Panzertruppen*, created in April 1943, includes all elements of the former *Schnelle Truppen* (mobile troops) with the exception of their horse and cyclist units, which were transferred to the infantry but retain the original color of the cavalry.

The distinguishing color of the Panzer troops is pink. Antitank units wear in addition a Gothic "P" on the shoulder straps. Armored and motorized infantry regiments have retained their original colors.

(1) *Organic units.*—(*a*) Panzerregiment (*tank regiment*). —One to a Panzer division; consists of two or three tank battalions or two tank battalions and one assault gun battalion (*Sturmgeschützabteilung*).

(*b*) Panzerabteilung (*tank battalion*).—Two or three to a Panzer regiment; one to a motorized division.

RESTRICTED

(c) Panzergrenadierregiment (*armored infantry regiment.*)—Two to a Panzer division. Normally composed of only two battalions and an added support echelon of four to six 150 mm infantry howitzers.
(Distinguishing color: grass green.)
(d) Grenadierregiment (mot.) (*motorized infantry regiment*).—Normally two to a motorized (*Panzergrenadier*) division. Similar in organization and armament to regular infantry, but transported in organic motor vehicles.
(Distinguishing color: white.)
(e) Panzeraufklärungsabteilung (*Panzer reconnaissance battalion*).—Formerly *Kradschützenbataillon* found in Panzer and motorized divisions. Consists of various combinations of scout car, armored car, motorcycle, and armored troop carrier companies, plus a heavy weapons company.
(Distinguishing color: pink. Previous colors copper brown and grass green may still be encountered.)
(f) Panzeraufklärungskompanie (Krad) (*motorcycle company*).—Found in all Panzer reconnaissance battalions.
(g) Panzeraufklärungskompanie (Volkswagen) (*scout car company*).—May be found in all Panzer reconnaissance battalions.
(h) Panzerspähkompanie (*armored car company*).—May be found in all Panzer reconnaissance battalions.
(i) Schützenpanzerwagenkompanie (*armored troop carrier company*).—May be found in motorized infantry and armored infantry regiments as well as in Panzer reconnaissance battalions, replacing any company except the heavy weapons company.
(j) Schwere Kompanie (*heavy weapons company*).—Found in the armored infantry regiment, mobile battalion, and Panzer reconnaissance battalion. Table of organization varies.
(k) Panzerjägerabteilung (*antitank battalion*).—Organic

RESTRICTED

in all types of divisions. Composed of three motorized companies usually equipped with 50 mm antitank guns.

(*l*) Feldersatzbataillon (*field replacement battalion*).—A field reserve for divisional units. Consists of three to five companies containing various replacement elements. May be organic to a division, but its personnel may also go to several divisions in a given area.

(*m*) Infanteriegeschützkompanie (*infantry howitzer company*).—Found in the motorized infantry regiment (Grenadierregiment (mot.)) as the 13th company.

(*n*) Schwere Infanteriegeschützkompanie (*heavy infantry howitzer company*).—Usually organic in the armored infantry regiment. Has four to six heavy infantry howitzers (often self-propelled). Identified in the 700 series.

(*o*) Divisionsbegleitkompanie (*divisional headquarters comany*).—Collective name of various machine gun, heavy weapons, and antiaircraft platoons composing the headquarters detachment of a Panzer division. Possibly also in infantry divisions.

(*p*) Fliegerabwehrkompanie (Fla-Kompanie) (*antiaircraft machine-gun company*).—Has light antiaircraft guns (20 & 37 mm) in addition to machine guns. Used for both antitank and antiaircraft defense. Found organically in the Panzer regiment, sometimes also in the armored infantry regiment. May also be found replacing the third company of an antitank battalion (*Panzerjägerabteilung*).

(See Fliegerabwehrbataillon, *Infantry*, sub-paragraph a (2) (*g*), above.)

(2) *GHQ units.*—(*a*) Schwere Panzerjägerabteilung (*heavy antitank battalion*).—Equipped with either 75 mm antitank guns (on self-propelled mount) or 88 mm antitank guns (tractor-drawn or on self-propelled mount). Identified in the 500 series.

RESTRICTED

(b) Panzerabteilung (Flammenwerfer) (*tank flamethrower battalion*).—Independent flamethrower tank battalions (series 100) normally found employed under Panzer corps in the spearhead of the attack.

(c) Panzerinstandsetzungsabteilung (*tank repair battalion*).—Formerly belonged to motor maintenance troops (*Kraftfahrparktruppen*), but now incorporated into the Panzer arm.

(d) Eisenbahnpanzerzug (*armored train*).—Twenty identified in the 1-100 series.

(Distinguishing color: pink, with a Gothic "E" on the shoulder straps.)

(e) Panzer-Lehr-Regiment (*tank demonstration regiment*).—Stationed at the tank school at Bergen (Wkr. XI); consists of I and II (tank) and III (antitank) battalions. Like other demonstration units, it is potentially available for service in the field.

c. *Artillery* (Artillerie).—In the Germany Army much of the field artillery and all the Army coast artillery and railway artillery belongs to the GHQ pool. Navy coast artillery is normally under the Army area command in which it is located. Units are allotted from this pool to army groups or armies according to the estimated needs. They may then be suballotted to corps or divisions, in which case they are usually placed under the control of special artillery commanders and staffs, also provided from the GHQ pool. With the exception of artillery commanders and staffs and artillery observation units, all types of artillery carry numbers allotted from a single series.

The distinguishing color of the artillery is bright red. Some specialized units are distinguished, in addition, by Gothic letters on the shoulder straps.

(1) *Organic divisional artillery.*—The division artillery

RESTRICTED

ORDER OF BATTLE OF THE GERMAN ARMY

regiment (*Artillerieregiment*) varies in composition according to the type and manner of employment of the division. It is frequently reinforced by GHQ artillery, army antiaircraft artillery (*Heeresflakartillerie*), and projector units (*Werfereinheiten*).

(a) *In Panzer divisions.*—One regiment consisting of four battalions (I and II equipped with 105 mm gun-howitzers, III with 150 mm howitzers, and IV with 88 mm and 20 mm self-propelled antiaircraft guns). In addition, the artillery regiment in Panzer and motorized divisions has an observation battery (*Panzerbeobachtungsbatterie*) organically assigned to it.

(b) *In motorized divisions.*—Identical with the organization in Panzer divisions.

(c) *In light divisions.*—One regiment consisting of three battalions (I and II equipped with 105 mm gun-howitzers and III with 150 mm howitzers). Its degree of motorization depends on the manner of its employment. An antiaircraft battalion similar to that in the Panzer division may also be found.

(d) *In mountain divisions.*—One regiment consisting of four battalions (I, II, and III equipped with 75 mm mountain pack howitzers and IV with 105 mm mountain howitzers).

(e) *In infantry divisions.*—One regiment consisting of four battalions (I, II, and III equipped with 105 mm gun-howitzers; the organization of IV may vary, but it is normally equipped with two batteries of 150 mm howitzers and one battery of 105 mm guns).

(f) *In infantry divisions in defensive sectors.*—Artillery may be modified to suit local conditions. For example, part of the division's regiment may be transferred for service in the field; or one or more units of coast defense or railway artillery from GHQ pool may be attached to the division. In

RESTRICTED

such cases the units concerned retain their original numbers but do not display divisional emblems.

(2) *Artillery commanders.*—When the division artillery regiment is not reinforced from the GHQ pool, its commander is known as *Artillerieführer* (*Arfü*) and he is the division artillery commander. When GHQ artillery units are attached to the division the *Arfü* is usually subordinated to a special artillery commander known as *Artilleriekommandeur* (*Arko*) whose small special staff is supplemented in action by the organic staff of the organic artillery regiment. An *Arko* may also be assigned to command an allotment of artillery to a corps. In this case a GHQ artillery regimental staff and an artillery observation unit are normally included in the allotment. The following echelons in the chain of artillery command exist:

(*a*) *At GHQ.*—The GHQ artillery general (*OKH/Gen. d. Art.*) is the principal adviser on artillery employment; units from the GHQ pool are probably allotted to army groups and armies on his recommendation.

(*b*) *At army group and army headquarters.*—An artillery general known as *Höherer Artilleriekommandeur* (*Höh. Arko*) with a special staff advises the commander on artillery matters and recommends the sub-allotment of GHQ artillery to lower units.

(*c*) *At corps.*—Artillery may be commanded by an *Arko*; but a corps not in action may have only a junior artillery staff officer known as *Stabsoffizier der Artillerie* (*Stoart*).

(*d*) *At division.*—Artillery may be commanded by an *Arko* or *Arfü* (see above).

The *Höh. Arkos* are numbered in the 300 series; the *Arkos* are numbered in the 1-100 and the 100 series. There is no apparent connection between any of these numbers and that of the unit with which the commander concerned is operating.

RESTRICTED

(3) *GHQ artillery.*—(*a*) Artillerieregimenter (*artillery regimental staffs*).—Staffs on the peacetime division medium regiments (Nos. 37-72, 97, 99, and 115) and special staffs formed on or after mobilization (numbered above 500). The latter are chiefly independent staffs with no battalions carrying the same number. All GHQ artillery regimental staffs except coast defense staffs are fully motorized.

(*b*) Artillerieabteilungen (*artillery battalion staffs*).—Independent staffs controlling independent GHQ medium, heavy, and super-heavy batteries (motorized or railway) or coast defense batteries.

(*c*) Artillerieabteilungen und Batterien (*artillery battalions and batteries*).—Light, medium, heavy, and super-heavy units which may be horse-drawn, motorized, tractor-drawn, self-propelled, railway, or fixed. Numbers allotted to them are not necessarily connected with their particular type. Motorized medium battalions formerly belonging to peacetime medium regiments consist of three batteries of four guns each, but many of the battalions formed on or after mobilization may have three-gun batteries, and heavy or super-heavy batteries may have only two guns, or sometimes only one.

(*d*) Beobachtungsabteilung (*artillery observation battalion*).—Normally allotted to corps, but often attached to divisional artillery regiments. Identified in the 1-100 and 500 series.

(*e*) Sturmgeschützabteilung (*assault gun battalion*).—Consists of three six-gun batteries equipped with 75 mm guns on self-propelled mounts. Known for a short period as *Sturmartillerieabteilung*. Numbered in the main artillery series. Identified between 177 and 667.

(*f*) Sturmgeschützbatterie (*assault gun battery*).—Similar to batteries in the *Sturmgeschützabteilung*. Identified in the 600 series.

RESTRICTED

(g) Heeresflakartillerieabteilung (mot.) (*motorized Army antiaircraft artillery battalion*).—Consists of three 88 mm gun batteries and two 20 mm gun batteries. Numbered in the same series as Air Force antiaircraft units. Identified in the 200 and 300 series.

(h) Heeresküstenartillerieabteilung (*Army coast artillery battalion*).—Composition varies. Independent battalions and batteries have been identified in the regular artillery series.

(i) Eisenbahnartillerieabteilung (*railway artillery battalion*).—Composition not clear. Five battalions have been identified in the regular artillery series.

(j) Marineartillerieabteilung (*Naval coast artillery battalion*).—Composition varies. Belongs to the German Navy (*Kriegsmarine*) but may come under the Army area command in which it is located. Numbered concurrently with Army artillery units.

(k) Vermessungs- und Kartenabteilung (*survey and mapping battalion*).—In GHQ pool, but may be allocated to army groups or armies. Identified in the 500 and 600 series.

(l) Armee- or Korpskartenstelle (*army or corps map reproduction center*).—Previously known as *Armee-* or *Korpskartenlager*. Identified in the 400 and 500 series.

(m) Astronomischer Messzug (*astronomical survey platoon*).—Identified in the 700 series.

(n) Ballonbatterie (*observation balloon battery*).—Identified in the 100 series.

(o) Velozitätsmesszug (*velocity measurement platoon*).—Identified in the 500 series.

(p) Wetterpeilzug (*meteorological platoon*).—Identified in the 500 series.

(q) Artilleriepark (*artillery equipment park*).—Normally one to an army. Identified in the 500 series. Probably now combined with the *Infanteriepark* into *Heeresgerätpark* (see

RESTRICTED

sub-paragraph *f*, below). (The officers wear the color of their arm, but enlisted men wear light blue, in each case with the Arabic number of the park.)

(*r*) Artillerie- Lehr- Regiment (*artillery demonstration regiment*).—Three regiments stationed at the Artillery School at Jüterbog (Wkr. III). No. 1 is horse-drawn, No. 2 is motorized (including an assault gun battery), No. 3 consists of artillery observation, survey and mapping, range-finding, and balloon battalions. Portions of one or more of these regiments may be found in the field.

(*s*) Lehr- und Ersatzabteilung für Eisenbahnartillerie (mot.) (*Motorized demonstration and replacement battalion for railway artillery*).—Location unknown.

(*t*) Heeresflakartillerie-Lehr-Abteilung (*Army antiaircraft artillery demonstration battalion*).—Stationed at the Army antiaircraft artillery school in Wkr. II; available for service in the field.

d. *Chemical warfare troops* (Nebeltruppen).—Most chemical warfare units belong to the GHQ pool. Except for decontamination units, all units are equipped to launch chemical, smoke, and high-explosive projectiles. While they were originally used only for smoke projection, they have recently been employed more and more as artillery for the launching of high-explosive projectiles. The German Army may include such projector units (*Werfereinheiten*) organically in divisional artillery regiments. The 150 mm or 210 mm projectors would be the probable weapons to replace some of the 105 mm gun-howitzers.

Every German Army unit down to company strength has a small group of its own men trained in defensive chemical warfare. In a company these normally consist of one noncommissioned officer and three enlisted men, called the gas detection detachment (*Gasspürtrupp*).

RESTRICTED

The distinguishing color of chemical warfare troops is wine red.

(1) *Organic units.*—There are no organic units in this arm.

(2) *GHQ units.*—(a) Werferregiment z.b.V. (*regimental staff for special employment*).—May also be known as *Regimentsstab der Nebeltruppen*. Regimental staff controlling projector battalions in action. Nos. 3 and 4 have been identified.

(b) Werferregiment (*projector regiment*). — Formerly called *Nebelwerferregiment*. Consists of three battalions equipped with 105 mm mortars. The number of mortars in a regiment is approximately 72. Identified in the 1-100 series.

(c) Schweres Werferregiment (*heavy projector regiment*). —Consists of three or four battalions, probably equipped with 150 mm (six-barreled) and 210 mm (five-barreled) mortars (*Werfer "41"* or *"Do- Gerät"*). The number of mortars in the regiment varies from 54 to 72. Nos. 1, 2, 56, and 71 have been identified.

(d) Werferabteilung (*projector battalion*). — Formerly known as *Nebelwerferabteilung;* independent battalion, controlled in action by a special regimental staff. Identified in the series 1-13.

(e) Schwere Werferbatterie (*heavy projector battery*).— Independent battery equipped with 150 mm (six-barreled) and 210 mm (five-barreled) mortars. Identified in the 100 and 200 series.

(f) Gebirgswerferabteilung (*mountain projector battalion*). —A unit of this type is known to exist, but no identification has been made.

(g) Entgiftungsabteilung (*decontamination battalion*).— —Organized and equipped for decontamination work. Identified in the 100 series.

(h) Strassenentgiftungsabteilung (*road decontamination battalion*).—Organized and equipped for road decontamination work. No. 132 identified.

RESTRICTED

ORDER OF BATTLE OF THE GERMAN ARMY   81

(*i*) Gasmaskentrupp (*gas mask supply detachment*).—For the supply and fitting of gas masks. No. 38 identified.

(*j*) Gasschutzgerätpark (*gas defense equipment park*).— Normally one to an army. Numbered in the 500 series. Also 463 for Army of Norway. (Officers wear the color of their arm, but enlisted men wear light blue, in each case with the Arabic number of the park).

(*k*) Werfer-Lehr-Regiment (*chemical warfare demonstration regiment*).—Stationed at the Army Chemical Warfare School at Celle (Wkr. XI), but may be found serving at the front.

(*l*) Gebirgswerfer-Lehr-Batterie (*mountain projector demonstration battery*).—No. 8 located at Villach (Wkr. XVIII).

e. Engineers (Pioniere).—This arm includes the regular combat engineers as well as fortress engineers (*Festungspioniere*). Under a recent order it now also includes the construction engineers (*Baupioniere*), which were hitherto a separate arm known as construction troops (*Bautruppen*). On the other hand, it is probable that the engineer arm does not include the railway engineers (*Eisenbahnpioniere*), and these are therefore here treated separately. (See sub-paragraph *f*, below.)

It should be noted that the personnel of engineer platoons in organic divisional units (other than the organic engineer battalion) belong to the arm of the unit which they are serving and not to the engineer arm, although they are trained to perform minor engineer tasks.

The distinguishing color of the engineers is black. Fortress and construction engineers are further distinguished by Gothic letters on their shoulder straps.

(1) *Organic units.*—(*a*) Pionierbataillon (*engineer battalion*).—One to a division. Table of organization varies according to type of division. Carries division auxiliary number.

RESTRICTED

(b) Pionierkompanie (mot.) (*motorized heavy engineer company*).—One or two to an engineer batallion.

(c) Pionierkompanie (tmot.) (*partly motorized engineer company*).—One or two to an engineer battalion.

(d) Brückenkolonne (Brüko) (*bridge column*).—One or two to an engineer battalion. Different types are distinguished by Arabic letters. In addition, there are two series of independent bridge columns in the GHQ pool. One carries numbers in the 400-450 series and consists of units of two columns (e.g. 1/403, 2/403) which operate independently. The other, numbered in the 600, 800, and 900 series, consists of single columns. All are fully motorized.

(2) *GHQ units.*—(a) *Combat engineers* (Pioniere).—(i) *Pionierregiment* (engineer regiment).—Nos. 59 and 414 have been identified.

(ii) *Pionierregiment z.b.V.* (engineer regiment for special employment) or *Pionierregimentsstab* (engineer regimental staff).—Staff controlling independent engineer battalions bridge columns, and sometimes construction units of the GHQ pool. Identified in the 500 and 600 series.

(iii) *Pionierbataillon z.b.V.* (engineer battalion for special employment).—Staff controlling independent engineer units. Nos. 300 and 750 have been identified.

(iv) *Minensuchbataillon z.b.V.* (mine detection battalion for special employment).—One identified.

(v) *Minensuchkompanie* (mine detection company).—Independent company. No. 3 identified.

(vi) *Pionierlandungsbataillon* (engineer assault landing battalion).—Equipped with assault boats using outboard motors. Used in assault landing operations.

(vii) *Pionierlandungskompanie* (engineer assault landing company).—Equipped with assault boats using outboard motors. Used in assault landing operations.

RESTRICTED

(viii) *Feldwasserstrassenräumabteilung* (waterway clearing battalion).—Engaged in clearing and maintaining waterways which are essential for military transport.

(ix) *Sturmbootkompanie* (assault boat company) and *Sturmbootkommando* (assault boat detachment).—No companies have been identified as yet, but they are known to exist. Detachment Nos. 904 and 905 have been identified.

(x) *Sprengkommando* (demolition detachment).—Responsible for the demolition of military and industrial establishments preceding a retreat.

(xi) *Technisches Bataillon* (technical battalion).—Intended for such specialized functions as the production and treatment of mineral oil and coal mining. They are supplied with personnel by the Technical Replacement Training Battalion at Pirna (Wkr. IV). Identified in the 1-100 series. Technical troops are believed to belong to the engineers, although German orders have at times been ambiguous as to their classification.

(xii) *Pionierpark* (engineer equipment park).—One to an army; numbered in the 500 and 600 series. (Officers wear the color of their arm, but enlisted men wear light blue, in each case with the Arabic number of the park.)

(xiii) *Pionier-Lehr-Bataillon* (engineer demonstration battalion).—Nos. 1 and 2 are stationed at the Engineer School at Dessau-Rösslau (Wkr. XI). There is also a *Pionier-Lehr-Bataillon z.b.V.* at Offenbach am Main (Wkr. IX), which specializes in mining and similar activities. These units may also be found serving in the field.

(xiv) *Pionier-Lehr-Bataillon für schweren Brückenbau* (heavy bridge building engineer demonstration battalion).— Located at Speyer am Rhein (Wkr. XII).

(b) *Fortress engineers* (Festungspioniere). — Peacetime units wear the Gothic letters "Fp", while units formed on or

RESTRICTED

after mobilization wear the Gothic letter "F" on the shoulder straps.

(i) *Festungspionierregiment* (fortress engineer regiment).—Nos. 14, 21, and 29 have been identified.

(ii) *Festungspionierstab* (fortress engineer staff).—Regimental staff in the field, normally controlling two sector groups *Festungspionierabschnittsgruppen*). Numbered in the 1-50 series.

(iii) *Festungspionierabschnittsgruppe* (fortress engineer sector group).—Battalion staff in charge of engineer units in a fortified sector. Carries the number of the controlling staff (*Festungspionierstab*), preceded by the number I or II.

(iv) *Festungspionierpark* (fortress engineer equipment park).—Normally one to an army. Numbered in the 500 series. (Officers wear the color of their arm, but enlisted men wear light blue, in each case with the Arabic number of the park.)

(v) *Heimatfestungspionierpark* (home fortress engineer equipment park).—Three have been identified, one at Pardubitz (Prot.), one at Modlin (Wkr. I), and one at Rehagen-Klausdorf (Wkr. III).

(c) *Construction engineers* (Baupioniere).—Hitherto a separate arm of inferior status known as *Bautruppen;* reclassified as engineers under an order issued in October 1943. Most of the units were then renamed as indicated below. (Personnel wear black as their distinguishing color. Previous color light brown may still be encountered.)

(i) *Pionierregimentsstab z.b.V.* (hitherto called *Kommandeur der Bautruppen*) (construction engineer command staff for special employment).—Equivalent in status to a regimental commander. It should be noted that construction engineers are often employed under combat, fortress, or railway engineer staffs, and often operate in conjunction with units

RESTRICTED

of the Reich Labor Service (*Reichsarbeitsdienst*) and of the Air Force construction troops. Identified in the 1-100 and 100 series.

(ii) *Baupionierregiment* (construction engineer regiment). —Probably a railway construction regiment. Number 992 has been identified.

(iii) *Baupionierbataillon, Pionierbrückenbataillon, Festungspionierbataillon* (hitherto known as *Baubataillon, Brückenbaubataillon* and *Festungsbaubataillon*), *Eisenbahnbaubataillon* and *Marinebaubataillon* (construction battalion, bridge construction battalion, fortress construction battalion, railway construction battalion, and naval construction battalion).— Older personnel engaged in general construction work in rear areas, specializing in such tasks as are designated by their title. A number of *Baubataillone* were converted in 1941-1942 into guard and cyclist guard battalions (*Wachbataillon B* and *Radfahrwachbataillon B;* see paragraph 14 e, below). These units may, however, be used for construction work if necessary. All types of construction battalions have been identified in the 1-500 series.

(iv) *Radfahrbaupionierbataillon* (*leicht und schwer*), *Pionierbrückenbataillon* (hitherto known as *Radfahrstrassenbaubataillon* (*leicht und schwer*) and *Brückenbaubataillon*), and *Eisenbahnbaubataillon* (cyclist construction battalion (light and heavy), bridge construction battalion, and railway construction battalion).—These construction battalions, numbered in the 500 and 600 series, differ from the preceding units in that they are composed of technically better trained personnel.

(v) *Schneeräumregiment* (snow removal regiment).—Construction troops specializing in snow removal. Identified in the 500 series.

(vi) *Schneeräumabteilung* (snow removal battalion). — Construction troops specializing in snow removal. Nos. 602, 603, 604, and 605 have been identified.

RESTRICTED

(vii) *Landesbaupionierbataillon* (hitherto known as *Landesbaubataillon*) (regional construction battalion).—Engaged in general construction work. Nos. 1-11 have been identified.

(viii) *Kriegsgefangenenbau- und Arbeitsbataillon* (prisoner of war construction and labor battalion).—Engaged in rear areas as well as in theater of operations. German cadre personnel act as guards. Numbered from 1-125.

(ix) *Kriegsgefangenarbeitskommando* (prisoner of war labor detachment).—May be engaged in rear areas, as well as in the theatre of operations. German cadre personnel act as guards. Numbered between 200 and 5200.

f. Railway engineers (Eisenbahnpioniere).—These units are believed to constitute a separate arm, although they wear the same color as the regular engineers and German documents are confusing as to their proper classification. It is believed that they also include the railway operating units (*Feldeisenbahnbetriebstruppen*).

The distinguishing color of the railway engineers is black with the Gothic letter "E" on the shoulder straps.

(1) *Organic units.*—There are no organic units in this arm.

(2) *GHQ units.*—(*a*) Eisenbahnpionierregiment (*railway engineer regiment*).—Consists of two battalions of four companies each. Nos. 1-8 have been identified.

(*b*) Eisenbahnpionierbataillon (*railway engineer battalion*).—No. 3 identified.

(*c*) Eisenbahnpionierstab z.b.V. (*railway engineer staff for special employment*).

(*d*) Eisenbahnpionierbaukompanien (*railway construction companies*).—Specialist companies engaged in various types of railway construction work. Their function is usually defined by their title. The following types have been identified in the 100 series:

(i) *Eisenbahnfernsprechkompanie* (railway telephone company).

RESTRICTED

ORDER OF BATTLE OF THE GERMAN ARMY

(ii) *Eisenbahnfunkkompanie* (railway radio company).

(iii) *Eisenbahnpfeilerbaukompanie* (railway pier building company).

(iv) *Eisenbahnwasserstationskompanie* (railway waterpoint company).

(v) *Seilbahnkommandotrupp* (cableway detachment).

(vi) *Eisenbahnunterwasserschneidetrupp* (underwater welding section).

(vii) *Eisenbahnstellwerkskompanie* (railway signal box company).

It should be noted that the above are specialist units, in contrast to the railway construction units of the construction engineers.

(e) Feldeisenbahnbetriebstruppen (*railway operating units*)—Formerly Feldeisenbahneinheiten.—Troops engaged in the maintenance and operation of railways in rear areas. Often work in conjunction with railway engineer construction companies (see above). The following types have been identified in the 1-500 series:

(i) *Feldeisenbahnkommando* (field railway command).

(ii) *Feldeisenbahnbetriebsabteilung* (field railway operating unit).

(iii) *Feldeisenbahnmaschinenabteilung* (field railway machinery battalion).

(iv) *Feldeisenbahnwerkstattabteilung* (field railway workshop battalion).

(v) *Eisenbahnbetriebskompanie* (railway operating company).

(vi) *Feldbahnabteilung* (field railway battalion).

(vii) *Feldbahnkompanie* (field railway company).

(viii) *Feldeisenbahnnachschublager* (field railway supply depot).

(f) Eisenbahnpionierpark (*railway equipment park*).—

RESTRICTED

Nos. 402 and 403 have been identified. (Officers wear the color of their arm, but enlisted men wear light blue, in each case with the Arabic number of the park.)

(g) Heimateisenbahnpionierpark (*home railway equipment park*).—One stationed at the Railway Engineer School at Rehagen-Klausdorf (Wkr. III) and one at Fürstenwalde/Spree (Wkr. III).

g. *Signal troops* (Nachrichtentruppen).

It should be noted that the personnel of signal platoons in organic divisional units other than the organic signal battalion belong to the arm of the units in which they serve, although they are trained to perform minor signal tasks. The propaganda troops, which formerly belonged to the signal troops, are now a separate arm. (See sub-paragraph *h*, below.)

The distinguishing color of the signal troops is lemon yellow.

(1) *Organic units*.—(a) Heeres- or Armeenachrichtenregiment (*army group or army signal regiment*).—One to an army group or army. Identified in the 1-100 and 500 series.

(b) Korpsnachrichtenabteilung (*corps signal battalion*).—One to an army. Identified in the 1-100 and 400 series.

(c) Nachrichtenabteilung (*signal battalion*).—One to a division. Table of organization varies according to type of division.

(d) Nachrichtenkompanie (*signal company*).—May be found in place of a signal battalion in some of the recently formed divisions. Also identified in the GHQ pool in the 1-100, 300, 500, and 700 series.

(e) Fernsprechkompanie (*telephone company*).—One to a signal battalion.

(f) Funkkompanie (*radio company*).—One to a signal battalion.

(g) Divisionsfernsprechkompanie (*divisional telephone*

RESTRICTED

company).—Directly under division headquarters in some divisions.

(*h*) Divisionsfunkkompanie (*Divisional radio company*).—Same as (*g*), above.

(2) *GHQ units.*—(*a*) Feldnachrichtenkommandantur (*field signal command*).—Static signal headquarters for a sector of occupied territory or in rear areas of the zone of operations. Identified in the 1-100 series.

(*b*) Festungsnachrichtenkommandantur (*fortress signal command*).—Carries the same number as the fortress engineer staff (*Festungspionierstab*, see sub-paragraph *e*, above) to which it is attached.

(*c*) Wehrmachtnachrichtenkommandantur (*Armed Forces signal command*).—Nos. 306 and 313 have been identified.

(*d*) Führungsnachrichtenregiment (*Armed Forces signal regiment*).—Under direct control of the Armed Forces high command. Provides and maintains signal communications between Hitler's headquarters and army group and army headquarters, as well as among the three branches of the Armed Forces. Nos. 40, 601, 602, and 603 have been identified.

(*e*) Heeresnachrichtenregiment (*army group signal regiment*).—One to an army group. Identified in the 500 and 600 series.

(*f*) Nachrichtenregimentsstab z.b.V. (*signal regimental staff for special employment*).—Regimental staff controlling independent battalions and other units. Nos 597 and 604 have been identified.

(*g*) Eisenbahnnachrichtenregiment (*railway signal regiment*).—No. 517 has been identified.

(*h*) Eisenbahnnachrichtenabteilung (*railway signal battalion*).

(*i*) Nachrichtenabteilungsstab z.b.V. (*signal battalion staff*

RESTRICTED

for special employment) and Nachrichtenführer z.b.V. (*signal commander for special employment*).—Battalion staffs controlling independent signal companies in the field. Identified in the 600 and 700 series.

(*j*) Feldkabelbauabteilung (*field wire laying battalion*).

(*k*) Nachrichtenhelferinnenabteilung (*women's auxiliary signal battalion*).—Engaged in auxiliary signal work such as radio, telephone, and telegraph operation. When used in the field, the letter "E" (*Einsatz*) follows the name of the unit. No. 52 has been identified.

(*l*) *Independent signal companies.*—Specialist companies engaged in various types of signal work. Their function is usually defined by their title. The following types have been identified in the 600 series:

(i) *Fernsprechbaukompanie* (telephone construction company).

(ii) *Fernsprechbetriebskompanie* (telephone operating company).

(iii) *Fernschreibkompanie* (telegraph company).

(iv) *Funküberwachungskompanie* (radio supervision company).

(v) *Horchkompanie* (interception company).—Identical with (vii) and (viii) below.

(vi) *Nachrichtenauswertekompanie* (signal evaluation company).—For evaluating radio intercepts.

(vii) *Nachrichtenfernaufklärungskompanie* (long - range signal reconnaissance company).—Radio interception company.

(viii) *Nachrichtennahaufklärungskompanie* (short - range signal reconnaissance company).—Radio interception company.

(*m*) Nachrichtenpark (*signal equipment park*).—One to an army. Numbered in the 500 series. (Officers wear the

RESTRICTED

color of their arm, but enlisted men wear light blue, in each case with the Arabic number of the park.)

(n) Nachrichten-Lehr-Regiment (*signal demonstration regiment*).—Stationed at the Army Signal School at Halle (Wkr. IV).

h. *Propaganda troops* (Propagandatruppen).—Under an order issued in January 1943, propaganda troops, formerly belonging to the signal troops, were made into a separate arm. They consist mainly of news reporters, photographers, film cameramen, and radio commentators. Their main function is front line reporting, but they also conduct propaganda addressed to the enemy as well as to German troops. Replacements are provided from the Propaganda Replacement Training Battalion, Berlin (Wkr. III).

The distinguishing color of the Propaganda troops is light grey.

(1) *Organic units.*—There are no organic units in this arm.

(2) *GHQ units.*—(a) Propagandaabteilung (*propaganda battalion*).—Several have been identified, normally named after an occupied country or area in which they function (e.g., Frankreich, Südost, Ostland, Ukraine, etc.)

(b) Propagandakompanie (*propaganda company*).—About twenty have been identified in the 500, 600, and 900 series. One normally attached to each army, from which small teams are sub allotted to corps and divisions.

13. Service Troops (*Versorgungstruppen*).

a. *Supply troops* (Nachschubtruppen).—The supply and motor maintenance units of the German Army, originally combined under transport troops (*Fahrtruppen*), were later divided into two separate arms. The motor maintainance units were grouped under the motor maintainance troops (*Kraftfahrparktruppen*) see sub-paragraph b, below), while

RESTRICTED

the transport and supply units were classified as supply troops (*Nachschubtruppen*).

Railway operating units (*Feldeisenbahnbetriebstruppen*) are believed to belong to the railway engineers, although they work in conjunction with the supply troops (see paragraph 12 *f.*).

The distinguishing color of the supply troops is light blue.

(1) *Organic units.*—Every unit in the German Army has its own supply echelon, the composition of which varies according to the type and size of the unit. It is to be noted that battalions normally get most of their supplies at division and are therefore not dependent upon regiment.

(*a*) Kommandeur der Divisionsnachschubtruppen (Kodina) (*commander of the division rear services*).—Formerly known as *Divisionsnachschubführer* (*Dinafü*); commands the divisional service troops. Normally carries the divisional auxiliary number.

(*b*) Kraftfahrabteilung (*motor transport battalion*).—One to a division; carries the division auxiliary number.

(*c*) Leichte Kolonne (*light column*).—One to a regiment. Consists of 39 wagons carrying all types of supplies except rations; serves as a supply reserve for the subordinate battalions.

(*d*) Trosse (*trains*).—Battalion and company supply units. Consist of combat train (*Gefechtstross*), ration train (*Verpflegungstross*) (two per battalion), and baggage train (*Gepäcktross*). The company baggage train and one battalion ration train are usually motorized.

(2) *GHQ units.*—(*a*) Kraftwagentransportregiment (*motor transport regiment*).—Used primarily for moving non-motorized units, but may also be used for the transportation of supplies. About twenty have been identified in the 300, 500, 600, 900 series.

RESTRICTED

(b) Kraftwagentransportabteilung (*motor transport battalion*).—Independent battalions similar in function to the above units. About twenty have been identified in the 500, 600, 700, and 900 series.

(c) Nachschubkolonnenabteilung (*supply column battalion*).—Horse-drawn or motorized; allotted to armies according to estimated needs. Identified in the 500, 600, 700, and 900 series; also 463 for Army of Norway. (Their component columns are distinguished by an Arabic number preceding that of the battalion.)

(d) Nachschubkolonnenabteilung z.b.V. (*supply column battalion for special employment*).

(e) Nachschubbataillon (*supply battalion*).—Independent battalion. Two types exist: 1-100 and 100 series (non-motorized); 500 and 600 series (fully motorized).

(f) Nachschubstab z.b.V. (*supply staff for special employment*).—Independent staff, probably of battalion status. Its function is often defined by its title, such as *Verladestab* (loading staff), *Entladestab* (unloading staff) and *Umschlagstab* (reloading staff). Identified in the 100, 300, 400, 600, and 900 series.

(g) Gebirgsträgerbataillon (*mountain supply bearer battalion*).—Used for the movement of supplies and ammunition in mountainous terrain where ordinary supply columns cannot be employed. No. 56 has been identified.

(h) *Independent supply companies and columns.*—Specialist companies performing various supply duties. Their function is usually defined by their title. The following types have been identified in the 500, 600, 700, and 900 series.

(i) *Nachschubkompanie z.b.V.* (supply column for special employment).

(ii) *Munitionsverwaltungskompanie* (ammunition administration company).

RESTRICTED

(iii) *Betriebsstoffverwaltungskompanie* (fuel and lubricant administration company).

(iv) *Destillationskompanie* (water distilling company).

(v) *Kraftwagentransportkolonne* (motor transport column).

(vi) *Grosse Kraftwagenkolonne* (large motor transport column)—Capacity 60 tons.

(vii) *Kleine Kraftwagenkolonne* (small motor transport column).—Capacity 30 tons.

(viii) *Kombinierte Kolonne* (combined column).—Probably consists of both horse-drawn and motor transportation.

(ix) *Fahrkolonne* (horse-drawn column).

(x) *Tragtierkolonne* (pack train).

(xi) *Grosse Betriebsstoffkolonne* (large fuel and lubricant column).—50 cubic meters (5,500 gallons).

(xii) *Kleine Betriebsstoffkolonne* (small fuel and lubricant column).—Capacity 25 cubic meters (11,000 gallons).

(xiii) *Kesselwagenkolonne für Betriebsstoff* (tank truck column for fuel and lubricants).

(xiv) *Filterkolonne* (water filter column).

(xv) *Wasserkolonne* (water supply column).

b. *Motor maintenance troops* (Kraftfahrparktruppen).— The supply and motor maintenance units of the German Army, originally combined under transport troops (*Fahrtruppen*), were divided into two separate arms in October 1942. The transport and supply units are now classified as supply troops (*Nachschubtruppen*) (see sub-paragraph *a*, above), while the motor maintenance units are grouped under the motor maintenance troops (*Kraftfahrparktruppen*).

The distinguishing color of the motor maintenance troops is pink with the letter "J" on the shoulder straps.

(1) *Organic units.*—There are no organic units in this arm. Workshops attached to troop units do not belong to the *Kraft-*

ORDER OF BATTLE OF THE GERMAN ARMY 95

fahrparktruppen but to the arm of the units to which they are attached. These are usually designated *Werkstattkompanie* (workshop company) or *Kraftwagenwerkstatt* (mobile repair shop).

(2) *GHQ units.* — (*a*) Kommandeur der Kraftfahrparktruppe (*motor maintenance command staff*).

(*b*) Heeres- or Armeekraftfahrbezirk (*motor maintenance area command*).—Controls motor maintenance and repair work in a specified area. No. 123 has been identified.

(*c*) Heimatkraftfahrbezirk (*home motor maintenance area command*).—Controls motor maintenance and repair work in a specified area within the zone of the interior. Identified carrying Roman numbers in the 1-100 series or names of cities in which they are located.

(*d*) Kraftfahrzeuginstandsetzungsregiment (*motor maintenance and repair regiment*).—Controls various maintenance and repair units. Possibly constitutes the mobile equivalent to a *Kraftfahrbezirk*. No. 548 has been identified.

(*e*) Kraftfahrzeuginstandsetzungsabteilung (*motor maintenance and repair battalion*).—Identified in the 500 series.

(*f*) Kraftfahrzeuginstandsetzungskompanie (*motor maintenance and repair company*).—Independent company. Identified in the 100 series.

(*g*) Kraftfahrzeugabschleppzug (*motor transport recovery platoon*).—Identified in the 700 series.

(*h*) Reifeninstandsetzungsstaffel (*tire repair detachment*).

(*i*) Zentralersatzteillager (*central spare parts depot*).— Identified in the 1-100, 200, and 300 series.

(*j*) Heeres- or Armeekraftfahrpark (*GHQ or army motor transport park*).—Motor transport park in occupied territory and with field armies. Handles maintenance and repair jobs for both industry and the Armed Forces. Western territory, where most of the divisions returning from the Russian front

RESTRICTED

are reformed and refitted, is divided into recommissioning areas (*Auffrischungsräume*); several motor maintenance parks handle the motor repair work of all the units within their area. They are also responsible for the upkeep of lines of transportation within their area. Identified in the 500, 600, 700, 800, and 900 series; also 463 with Army of Norway.

(*k*) Heimatkraftfahrpark (*home motor transport park*).— Handles the more complicated and difficult repair jobs which cannot be easily done in the occupied areas. Eleven have been identified, carrying Roman numbers in the 1-100 series or names of cities in which they are located. (The abbreviation *H.K.P.* is used for both *Heimat-* and *Heereskraftfahrpark*.)

(*l*) Kraftfahrpark Eisenbahn (*motor transport park on rails*).

c. *Medical troops* (Sanitätstruppen).—The distinguishing color for medical troops is dark blue.

(1) *Organic units.*—(*a*) *Sanitätskompanie* (*medical company*).—Normally two to a division, carrying the division auxiliary number.

(*b*) Feldlazarett (*field hospital*). — Usually motorized. Normally one to a division in all except Panzer divisions. Carries the auxiliary number preceded by 1, 2, 3, or 4.

(*c*) Krankenkraftwagenzug (*motorized ambulance platoon*). —Normally three to a medical battalion. Identified in the GHQ pool in the 500, 600, and 700 series.

(2) *GHQ units.*—(*a*) Sanitätsabteilung (*medical battalion*).—Identified in the GHQ pool in the 500, 600, and 700 series. (Numbers usually end in 2.)

(*b*) Krankentransportabteilung (*ambulance transport battalion*).—One attached to a medical battalion or station hospital. Provides for the transportation of wounded to rear areas. Identified in the 500, 600, and 700 series.

RESTRICTED

(c) Kriegslazarettabteilung (*station hospital battalion*).— Staff controlling a group of hospitals. A hospital subordinate to such a staff is shown with an Arabic numeral before the number of the staff (e.g. 4/520). An "R" after a number indicates that the hospital was previously a *Reservekriegslazarettabteilung* (auxiliary station hospital battalion). These have been abolished.

(d) Kriegslazarett (*station hospital, communications zone*).—Independent hospital in the army rear area. Numbered in the 900 series.

(e) Leichtkrankenkriegslazarett (*station hospital for minor cases*).—Not separate hospitals but detachments of hospital staffs. Located in army rear area.

(f) Entseuchungszug (*disinfecting train*).

(g) Lazarettzug (*hospital train*).—Identified in the 500, 600, and 700 series.

(h) Leichtkrankenzug (*hospital train for minor cases*).

(i) Truppenentgiftungskompanie (*personnel decontamination company*).—These are medical units not to be confused with chemical warfare decontamination units. Nos. 607, 617, 620, 622, and 624 have been identified.

(j) Truppenverbandplatz (*first aid station*).—Established by medical battalion. Identified in the 500 series.

(k) Sanitätspark (*medical equipment park*).—Identified in the 500 and 600 series. (Both officers and enlisted personnel wear dark blue with the Arabic number of the park.)

d. Veterinary troops (Veterinärtruppen).— The distinguishing color of veterinary troops is carmine.

(1) *Organic units.*—(a) Veterinärkompanie (*veterinary company*).—Normally one to an infantry, light, and mountain division. Has collecting, hospital, and fodder platoon.

(2) *GHQ units.* — (a) Heeres- or Armeepferdelazarett (*army group or army veterinary hospital*).—Identified in the 500 and 600 series.

RESTRICTED

(b) Heimatpferdelazarett (*home veterinary hospital*).—Located in the zone of the interior. Those located in Germany carry their *Wehrkreis* number; those treating horses with epidemic diseases carry the *Wehrkreis* number plus 100.

(c) Pferdetransportkolonne (mot.) (*motorized horse transport column*).—Identified in the 500 and 600 series.

(d) Heeres- or Armeepferdepark (*army group or army horse park*).—Provides replacements for horse casualties. Normally one to an army. Identified in the 500 and 600 series.

(e) Veterinärpark (*veterinary equipment park*).—Identified in the 500 and 600 series. (Both officers and enlisted personnel wear carmine with the Arabic number of the park.)

e. *Military police* (*Feldgendarmerie*).—Military police duties are divided between the *Feldgendarmerie* (military police), whose main task is the maintenance of traffic discipline, and *Wachtruppen* (guard troops), who are primarily concerned with the guarding of parks, dumps, etc., in the field. The latter also take charge of prisoners of war and escort them to the rear areas. The arm to which the *Wachtruppen* belong has not been definitely established, and they are therefore listed here. Patrol duties and the maintenance of military discipline are carried out both by army patrols (*Heeresstreifen*, see sub-paragraph f) and by military policemen (*Feldgendarme*).

The distinguishing color of the *Feldgendarmerie* is orange. They carry no number, but on the left upper arm they wear the Nazi eagle and swastika surrounded by an oak wreath and on the lower arm a brown band with the word "Feldgendarmerie" inscribed in silver.

(1) *Organic units.*—(a) Feldgendarmerietrupp (*military police detachment*).—One to a division. Carries the divisional auxiliary number. Those in the GHQ pool which are allocated to the military administration of an occupied country are

RESTRICTED

believed to carry the number of the headquarters to which they are attached.

(2) *GHQ units.*—(a) **Wach**regiment (*guard regiment*).— Staff controlling guard units in a large city. Four have been identified: Wachregiment Clüwer (named after its commander) and Wachregiment Paris 1, 2, and 3.

(b) Wachbataillon (*guard battalion*).—Independent guard battalions assigned to army groups or armies. Identified in the 500, 600, and 700 series. There is also a Wachbataillon Grossdeutschland stationed at Berlin.

(c) Heimatwachbataillon (*home guard battalion*).—In the zone of the interior. Includes bridge guard battalions (*Brückenwachbataillone*) and cyclist guard battalions (*Radfahrwachbataillone*). Identified in the 1-100, 100, 300, and 600 series.

(d) Feldgendarmerieabteilung (*military police battalion*). —One allotted to each army. Identified in the 500 and 600 series.

(e) Feldgendarmeriekompanie (*military police company*). —Independent company.

(f) Verkehrsregelungsbataillon (*traffic control battalion*). —A battalion or a company may be allotted for as long as necessary to an army on the move. Seven units of this type have been identified in the series 751-760.

f. Administrative troops (Verwaltungstruppen).—There is no distinguishing color for administrative units. Civilian specialists (*Beamte*), in various administrative positions, wear uniforms with dark green piping. Officers wear the color of their original arm; piping of enlisted personnel varies.

Personnel of area security and prisoner of war administration units may belong to the administrative arm; they are classified as security troops and are described in paragraph 14 *a* and *b*, below.

(1) *Organic units.*—(a) Bäckereikompanie (*bakery company*).—One to each division.

RESTRICTED

(*b*) Schlächtereizug (*slaughter platoon*). — One to each division.

(*c*) Verpflegungsamt (*ration supply office*). — Supervises the requisitioning and supply of rations for troop units. Erects *Verpflegungsausgabestellen* (ration supply distributing points) which are refilled daily by the bakery and slaughter units and from which troop units obtain their rations.

(*d*) Gerätsammelstelle (*equipment salvage depot*).—Found in division. Collects salvagable equipment and forwards it to field workshops (see *Feldwerkstattkompanie,* below).

(*e*) Feldpostamt (*field post office*).—One to each army. In addition to its proper number, each field post office (including those in higher echelons) uses a code number (*Kenn-Nummer*) selected at random in the 1-1000 series. Thus K 943 might be the code number for the 571st Army Field Post Office; hence it is necessary to exercise particular care in studying identifications of field post offices. Each field post office has branches concerned with the collection and delivery of mail (*Armeebriefstellen*). Both *Feldpostämter* and **Armeebriefstellen** are numbered in the 500 series.

(2) *GHQ units.*—(a) *Administration of supplies.*—(i) *Grossbäckereikompanie* (large bakery company.)—Normally allotted to army. Identified in the 500 and 600 series.

(ii) *Schlächtereiabteilung* (slaughter battalion).—Normally allotted to army group. Identified in the 500 and 600 series.

(iii) *Schlächtereikompanie* (slaughter company). — Allotted to army. Identified in the 500 and 600 series.

(iv) *Heereskühldienststelle* (army group refrigeration unit).

(v) *Heeresunterkunftsverwaltung* (army group billetting staff).

(vi) *Heeresbaudienststelle* (army group construction unit).

(vii) *Heeres-* or *Armeebekleidungsamt* (army group or army clothing office).

RESTRICTED

(b) *Administration of ordnance stores.*—Ordnance troops (*Feldzeugtruppen*) may belong to the administrative troops, although German orders have at times referred to them as a separate arm. (Officers wear the color of their original arm but enlisted personnel wear light blue, in each case with the Latin letters "FZ" on their shoulder straps.)

(i) *Heereszeugamt* (army group ordnance office).

(ii) *Oberfeldzeugstab* (higher ordnance staff).—Of regimental status.

(iii) *Feldzeugstab* (ordnance staff).—Of battalion status.

(iv) *Feldzeugbataillon* (ordnance battalion).—Identified in the 1-100 series.

(v) *Feldzeugkraftwagenkolonne* (ordnance motor transport column).

(vi) *Feldwerkstattkompanie* (field workshop company).—Attached in full or in part to an *Armeegerätpark* (see below). Repairs salvageable equipment forwarded from equipment salvage depots (*Gerätsammelstellen*).

(vii) *Heeres-* or *Armeegerätpark* (army group or army equipment park).—Maintains and repairs various types of equipment except motor transport, medical, and veterinary. Has also assumed control of infantry and artillery parks.

(viii) *Heeres-* or *Armeefeldzeugpark* (army group or army ordnance park).—Maintains and repairs ordnance equipment.

(c) *Transport and welfare administration.*—These units do not properly belong to the administrative troops, and are normally referred to as "Other troops and establishments" (*Sonstige Truppen und Dienststellen*). Personnel wear the color of their particular arm.

(i) *Bahnhofskommandantur I & II* (railway station headquarters I & II).—Formerly called *Transportdienststelle*. *I* is a station headquarters at an important station; *II* is at a smaller station and was until recently referred to as *Bahnhofsoffizier*.

RESTRICTED

(ii) *Frontleitstelle* (front directing office).—Handles the movement of troops to and from the front lines.

(iii) *Kommandeur des Streifendienstes* (Army patrol service command staff).—Supervises army patrols (*Heeresstreifen*) in a *Wehrkreis* or in an army rear area. These patrols are not formed by the military police, but from picked officers and noncommissioned officers of the army. Their authority exceeds that of ordinary military police (see sub-paragraph *e*, above).

(iv) *Streifenabteilung* (Army patrol battalion).—See (iii), above.

(v) *Streifenkompanie* (Army patrol company).—See (iii), above.

(vi) *Heeresbetreuungsabteilung* (Army welfare battalion).—Nos. 1 to 6 have been identified.

(vii) *Heeresbetreuungskompanie* (*E*) (Army delousing company).—Formerly called *Entlausungskompanie*.

(viii) *Betreuungshelferinnenabteilung* (women's auxiliary welfare battalion).—Performs various special service functions.

(ix) *Eisenbahnküchenwagenabteilung* (railway kitchen car battalion).—Nos. 1, 2, and 3 have been identified.

(x) *Eisenbahnverpflegungszug* (railway ration supply train).

(xi) *Zugwachabteilung* (train guard battalion).

14. Security Troops (*Sicherungstruppen*)

a. Area security units.—The various types of administrative headquarters in certain occupied countries (*Feldkommandantur, Kreiskommandantur, Ortskommandantur,* and *Stadtkommandantur* are described in section II, paragraph 9 *a.*

b. Local security units.—(1) Sicherungsregiment (*security regiment*).—A special mopping-up regiment for the line of

RESTRICTED

communications, usually attached to commanders of army group or army rear area. May be either independent security regiments or regimental staffs controlling several converted *Landesschützen* battalions (see below). Numbered in a separate series, they have special units such as cyclist companies or motor transport echelons. (The personnel is distinguished by the Latin letter "S" with an Arabic number on the shoulder straps.)

(2) Landesschützen-Einheiten (*local defense units*).—These units are normally composed of older personnel (*Landesschützen*) and may be found in Germany itself as well as in all German-held territory.

(a) *Employment and organization.*—Within Germany local defense units are employed for guard duties at prisoner of war camps and at vulnerable points, such as railway bridges and airfields. In occupied countries they provide the main support for the military administration. In rear areas they may be used to guard dumps, parks, etc. They are also employed in the maintenance of river security and for the protection of railway communications in occupied territory. The tactical unit is normally the battalion, controlled by a regimental staff. All *Landesschützen* battalions can be converted at any time to perform any of the functions mentioned. When given additional transportation and equipment, they can also be used as *Sicherungsbataillone* (see below). A battalion comprises from two to six companies. Some are designated *z.b.V.* (for special employment) and have special tables of organization.

(b) *Types of units.*—The following types have been identified:

(i) *Landesschützenregiment* (*Landesschützen* regimental staff).

(ii) *Landesschützenbataillon* (*Landesschützen* battalion).

RESTRICTED

(iii) *Stromsicherungsregiment* (river security regimental staff).

(iv) *Stromsicherungsbataillon* (river security battalion). —Normally located at important river crossings.

(v) *Transportbegleitregiment* (railway escort regimental staff).

(vi) *Transportbegleitbataillon* (railway escort battalion). Provides protection for railway trains against guerilla forces.

(vii) *Sicherungsbataillon* (security battalion).—Normally a mobile *Landesschützen* battalion used for mopping-up purposes (see *Sicherungsregiment* above).

For *Wachregiment, Wachbataillon,* and *Radfahrwachbataillon,* see sub-paragraph 13 *e*; for *Zugwachabteilung,* see sub-paragraph 13 *f* (2) (*c*).

(*c*) *Numbering system.* — (i) *Regiments.* — Regimental numbers normally include that of the *Wehrkreis* from which they originate. In the case of two-digit numbers the first, and in the case of three-digit numbers the first two digits give the *Wehrkreis* of origin (e.g., *Landesschützen* Regiment 115 comes from Wehrkreis XI).

(ii) *Battalions.*—Battalions carry numbers from 201 to 999, according to the series allotted to their *Wehrkreis* as follows:

Wkr.	Series	Wkr.	Series
I	201-250	IX	601-650
II	251-300	X	651-700
III	301-350	XI	701-750
IV	351-400	XII	751-800
V	401-450	XIII	801-850
VI	451-500	XVII	851-900
VII	501-550	XVIII	901-950
VIII	551-600	Various	951-999

(iii) *Air Force* Landesschützen *units.*—The Air Force also has *Landesschützen* units. These may be distinguished from the Army *Landesschützen* since they carry double numbers,

RESTRICTED

Roman for the air district (*Luftgau*) of origin and Arabic for the particular unit.

c. *Native security units* (Landeseigene Sicherungsverbände).—Units maintaining order and security within a specified area. Formed by the native population in the occupied portions of Russia.

d. *Prisoner of war administration units.*—(1) *In the theater of operations.*—The following units handle prisoners of war from the time of their capture to the time of their delivery to the zone of the interior:

(a) Heeres- or Armeegefangenensammelstellen (*army group or army prisoner of war enclosures*).

(b) Kommandeur der Kriegsgefangenen (*prisoner of war command staff*).

(c) Kriegsgefangenenbezirkskommandant (*district commander of prisoners of war*).

(d) Kriegsgefangenenfrontstammlager (Frontstalag) (*forward area prisoner of war camp*).—Twenty-five identified.

(e) Kriegsgefangenendurchgangslager (Dulag) (*prisoner of war transit camp*).—Twenty identified.

(2) *In the zone of the interior.*—Prisoner of war camps located in a *Wehrkreis* normally carry the Roman numeral of the *Wehrkreis* followed by a letter of the alphabet (*e.g. Stalag XXI A*). Others are numbered serially.

(a) Kriegsgefangenenoffizierslager (Oflag) (*camp for officer prisoners of war*).—Numbered by *Wehrkreise* and in the 1-100 series.

(b) Kriegsgefangenenstammlager (Stalag) (*camp for enlisted prisoners of war*).—Numbered by *Wehrkreise* and in the 300 series.

e. *Secret field police* (Geheime Feldpolizei).—Designed to combat any subversive activities within the armed forces. Groups (*Gruppen*) are assigned to Army or Air Force organi-

RESTRICTED

zations and work in close cooperation with the *SS–Sicherheitsdienst* and the *Geheime Staatspolizei (Gestapo)* (see section IV, paragraph 18, below). Normally one *Gruppe* to an army and one or more attached to the military administration of each occupied country. There is no indication that they are associated with the military police (*Feldgendarmerie*). (Personnel wear Army uniforms with light blue facings and the letters "G.F.P." in white on the shoulder straps. Officers wear the letters in yellow on their epaulettes. Sometimes the personnel wear civilian clothing or even the uniform of another arm.) Identified in the 1–100, 100, 500, 600, and 700 series.

15. Special Purpose Units (*Sondereinheiten*)

a. Intelligence and sabotage units.—(1) *Lehr-Regiment Brandenburg z.b.V. 800* (demonstration regiment Brandenburg 800 for special employment).—This unit was formed on the outbreak of the war as *Bau-Lehr-Bataillon 800;* it was later expanded to a regiment and has recently been upgraded to divisional status. Its home station is at Brandenburg (Wkr. III), where its recruits are trained, but detachments from it may be encountered wherever German forces are operating. Its primary function is sabotage (by companies, platoons, and individuals). Its personnel includes Germans who have lived abroad and speak foreign languages fluently, as well as foreigners of many nationalities. Different companies of the regiment specialize in preparation for operations in specific countries. Its members often operate in civilian clothes, in some cases dropping by parachute into enemy-occupied territory. The unit is under the direct control of the Intelligence Branch of the High Command (*OKW/Abwehr*—see section I, paragraph 2, above).

(2) *Brandenburg-Regimenter* (Brandenburg regiments).—

RESTRICTED

Believed to be field units set up by the above *Lehr-Regiment Brandenburg z.b.V. 800.* Several have been identified.

(3) *Sonderstab "F"* (special staff "F").—Believed to have some connection with the Brandenburg organization.

(4) *Sonderverband 287* (special unit 287).—Believed to have some connection with the Brandenburg organization.

b. Unique units.—(1) *Führerbegleitbataillon* (Hitler's escort battalion).—A special unit formed to protect Hitler's headquarters in the field. Its personnel is provided in rotation by the Grossdeutschland Division. (See section VI, paragraph 34, below.) It is fully motorized and contains elements of all the principal combat arms. It is sometimes referred to as the "vest-pocket corps" (*Westentaschenkorps*).

(2) *Führergrenadierbataillon* (Führer's infantry battalion).—Personnel belongs to the Grossdeutschland Division. Probably a new name for the *Führerbegleitbataillon.*

(3) *Versuchsbataillon* (experimental battalion).—A unit in an experimental stage, normally renamed before joining the Field Army.

c. Penal units.—(1) *Feld-Sonderbataillon* (special field battalion).—Soldiers who, because of serious and repeated misconduct, have been declared "wehrunwürdig" (undeserving the honor of being a soldier) are placed in this unit for a period of six months, where they perform dangerous tasks (such as clearing mine fields), normally without the benefit of weapons.

(2) *Sonderbataillon* or *Bewährungsbataillon* (special or rehabilitation battalion).—Similar to *Feld-Sonderbataillon* (see above), but believed intended for the rehabilitation rather than the punishment of offenders who are not considered entirely incorrigible.

(3) *Feldstrafgefangenenabteilung* (field penal battalion).—For convicts serving terms of more than three months. (Convicts serving less than three months serve in *Straf-*

RESTRICTED

vollzugszüge formed by division and higher echelons.) Service is similar to that in the *Feld-Sonderbataillon*.

16. Air Force Ground Units.

a. Antiaircraft units (Flakeinheiten).—The great bulk of antiaircraft units found cooperating with the Army ground forces belongs to the Air Force and is known as *Flak*, in contrast to Army antiaircraft artillery (*Heeresflak*) (see paragraph 12 *c.*) and antiaircraft machine gun battalions (*Fla-Bataillone*) (see paragraph 12 *a.*). It should always be remembered that all *Flak* weapons can be used for both antiaircraft and antitank purposes; *Flak* units are therefore commonly used against ground targets such as tanks, pillboxes, and personnel.

(1) *Organic units.*—(*a*) Flakregiment (*antiaircraft artillery regiment*).—One in the Hermann Göring Division. Has 20 and 88 mm antiaircraft guns.

(*b*) Flakabteilung (*antiaircraft artillery battalion*).—One to an Air Force field division (see section VI, paragraph 40 *d*, below). May have 20, 37, and 88 mm guns.

(2) *GHQ units.*—It is believed that all *Flak* units found cooperating with Army ground units are attached to the GHQ pool, from which they are sub-allotted to lower units.

(*a*) Schwere Flakabteilung (*heavy antiaircraft artillery battalion*).—Normally consists of three to four heavy batteries.

(*b*) Gemischte Flakabteilung (*mixed antiaircraft artillery battalion*).—Normally consists of three heavy and two light batteries.

(*c*) Leichte Flakabteilung (*light antiaircraft artillery battalion*).—Normally consists of four light batteries.

(*d*) Reserve-Flakabteilung (*reserve antiaircraft artillery battalion*).—"Reserve" may be prefixed to the name of any of the above units and denotes a difference in its strength and equipment (usually the lack of organic transportation) from the regular table of organization.

(e) Scheinwerferabteilung (*searchlight battalion*).—Consists of three batteries; each battery usually has nine 150 cm searchlights (some of which may be replaced by 250 cm searchlights).

(f) Schwere Flakbatterie (*heavy antiaircraft artillery battery*).—Normally has six heavy antiaircraft guns (usually 88 mm, sometimes 150 mm), and two or three light antiaircraft guns.

(g) Leichte Flakbatterie (*light antiaircraft artillery battery*).—Normally has twelve light antiaircraft guns (usually 20 mm, sometimes 37 mm) and three *Flakvierlinge* (four-barreled light antiaircraft guns).

(3) *Cooperation with ground forces.*—Air Force antiaircraft units operating with Army ground forces are subordinated operationally to the army units to which they are attached, but administratively (for replacements, etc.) to a parent Air Force ground unit.

The tactical unit is the battalion and not the regiment. In action, battalions, whether regimental or independent, rarely operate under a regimental staff carrying the same number. All antiaircraft artillery found cooperating with Army ground forces is fully motorized. It is equipped for cross-country operation when used with the spearhead of an attack.

(4) *Allotment of units.*—Allotment of units varies according to the estimated needs, but an army corps normally has a *Flak* battalion attached to it during operations, and a Panzer division may have a light or a mixed battalion attached to it. An infantry division is not likely to be allotted more than an antiaircraft artillery battery.

RESTRICTED

(5) Numbering system.—All units of this type are numbered in the series 1 - 1000. The following are the principal groups:

1 - 69 *Flak* regiments consisting of: Headquarters and four to six battalions if in static defense, or headquarters and four battalions if in the field.

71 - 99 light *Flak* battalions consisting of: Headquarters and three to four light batteries.

100 - 999 *Flak* units formed on or after mobilization. In general the numbering of *Flak* regiments and *Flak* battalions is believed to be systematic. Germany is divided into *"Luftgaue"* (abbr. *LG*), or Air Service Commands under a system which is somewhat similar to the *Wehrkreis* system, although *Wehrkreis* and *Luftgau* do not always coincide. At the time the German Air Force was founded each *LG* was allotted a key number. This accounts for the fact that *LG II* which was formed after the Polish campaign does not fall into the regular series. The key numbers are the following:

LG	I—1	LG	VII—5
LG	II—(not included)	LG	XI—6
LG	III—2	LG	VIII—7
LG	IV—3	LG	XVII—8
LG	VI—4	LG	XII/XIII—9

In numbering *Flak* regiments, the key number was used as the last digit. Thus *LG VI* (key number 4) had, among others, *Flak* regiments 4, 14, and 24. As for *Flak* battalions, the key number was used as the middle digit; i.e., *LG VI* (key number 4) had, among others, *Flak* battalions 140, 149, and 240.

This procedure was generally adopted for all *LG's*. However, due to later developments, the system was somewhat altered to provide for numbers stemming from newly acquired territories, as well as for other reasons.

RESTRICTED

b. *Parachute units* (Fallschirmeinheiten).—The following are the principal types of parachute units:

(1) *Fallschirmjägerregiment* (parachute regiment).—Nos. 1, 3, and 4 have been identified as belonging to the 1st Parachute Division and Nos. 2, 6, and 7 to the 2d Parachute Division.

(2) *Fallschirmartillerieregiment* (parachute artillery regiment).—Nos. 1 and 2 have been identified.

(3) *Fallschirmpanzerjägerabteilung* (parachute antitank battalion).

(4) *Fallschirmmaschinengewehrbataillon* (parachute machine gun battalion).—Nos. 1 and 2 have been identified.

(5) *Fallschirmnachrichtenabteilung* (parachute signal battalion).—Nos. 1 and 2 have been identified.

(6) *Fallschirmfliegerabwehrbataillon* (parachute antiaircraft machine gun battalion).

(7) *Fallschirmpionierbataillon* (parachute engineer battalion).—Nos. 1 and 2 have been identified.

(8) *Fallschirmsanitätskompanie* (parachute medical company).

(9) *Sturmregiment* (glider-borne assault regiment).—No. 1 has been identified.

c. *Ground combat units.*—The following are the types of units found in the Air Force field divisions (*Luftwaffenfelddivisionen*). Their organization and purpose is similar to that of the corresponding Army units described in the previous paragraphs of this section. Other units with special designations are found in the Hermann Göring Division (see section VI, paragraph 35, below).

(1) *Luftjägerregiment* (light infantry regiment).
(2) *Artillerieregiment* (artillery regiment).
(3) *Flakabteilung* (antiaircraft artillery battalion).

RESTRICTED

(4) *Aufklärungsabteilung* (reconnaissance battalion).
(5) *Panzerjägerabteilung* (antitank battalion).
(6) *Schnelle Abteilung* (mobile battalion).
(7) *Pionierbataillon* (engineer battalion).
(8) *Nachrichtenabteilung* (signal battalion).
(9) *Nachschub* (division rear services).

Section IV. OTHER MILITARIZED AND AUXILIARY ORGANIZATIONS.

17. Introduction.

The German ground forces whose organization and composition have been outlined in sections I to III, inclusive, of this text are supplemented to an increasing extent by combat forces and service organizations which are not part of the German Army proper, but are directly or indirectly affiliated to the National-Socialist Party. No picture of the German field forces would be complete without a consideration of these independent formations and their important roles. They may be subordinated to regular army commands or may function autonomously. In any event, they cooperate, mostly in close harmony, with the *Wehrmacht* and relieve the field forces of the regular German Army of many responsibilities and tasks. On the other hand, they absorb a considerable portion of its potential manpower.

18. SS and Police.

The most important combat force affiliated to the Nazi Party is the *Waffen-SS*. A branch of the *Schutzstaffeln,* or Party Elite Corps, it is sometimes designated the "fourth arm" of the *Wehrmacht,* along with the German Army, Navy, and Air Force. Since the SS and the German Police are closely integrated and the officers of one are often officers in the other, they are treated together in this section. Heinrich HIMMLER is Commander in Chief of both and since 1936 has borne the official title of *Reichsführer-SS und Chef der Deutschen Polizei.* (It should be noted that the Germans always print and write the abbreviation SS as a runic symbol: ᛋᛋ.)

a. The SS *Organization.*—Originally formed in the 1920's to furnish protective squads for political meetings and bodyguards for the leaders of the Party, the *SS* has been vastly expanded. Its formations employed for internal security duties in Germany and German-occupied territories include cadres for at least 124 regular *Standarten,* or "Regiments," which in 1941 numbered up to 2,500 men each. To these must be added cadres for about 20 mounted *Standarten,* engineer, motorized, signal, light artillery, mountain, and medical units. The *Waffen-SS,* which is the combat field force of this organization, has expanded from three to at least eighteen divisions since 1939, one new division having been identified for every 35 days of 1943.

HITLER is the supreme commander of all *SS* formations, to whom unswerving loyalty is sworn. The words "Germany" or "Fatherland" do not appear in the oath of the *SS*. Under HITLER, Heinrich HIMMLER, now also Reich Minister of the Interior, General Plenipotentiary for Administration, and Commissar of Internal Defense, is the executive chief of the *SS*. The *SS* High Command is maintained in Berlin and Munich, while the *Reichsführer-SS* has also established a field headquarters. The *Reichsführung-SS,* as this high command is called, is organized on the scale of a complete cabinet with ministries and departments. One of these departments is comparable to the organization of the three regular branches of the *Wehrmacht.* It handles the recruiting, training, equipment, administration, and assignment of all *SS* forces in the field and at home.

The *SS* includes the following main branches:

(1) *Allgemeine SS* ("General" *SS*).—Originally consisting of part-time volunteers (with a permanent administrative staff), these formations are mainly cadres employed for internal security duties and in occupied countries. They also form a reserve from which personnel for the other branches is

RESTRICTED

drawn. The men are subject to strict discipline and are increasingly subjected to military training.

(2) *Waffen-SS* ("Armed" *SS*).—Takes active part in military campaigns (see *c*, below).

(3) *SS-Totenkopfverbände* (*SS-TV;* SS Death's Head Formations).—Guard units for concentration camps and uniformed force of the Gestapo. Some of these units have been expanded and incorporated into the *Waffen-SS* as the *SS-Totenkopf-Division* and elements of the *SS* Cavalry Division.

(4) *SS-Sicherheitsdienst* (*SD;* SS Security Service).—A political intelligence service against internal and foreign enemies of the regime, working in close collaboration and often in personal union with the *Sicherheitspolizei* and the *Geheime Staatspolizei*. (See *b*, below.)

The SS, in Greater Germany and some occupied countries, is regionally organized into twenty-one *SS-Oberabschnitte* (Corps Areas), of which fourteen almost coincide with the seventeen *Wehrkreise* of the *Wehrmacht*. (One *SS-Oberabschnitt* comprises Norway, one the Netherlands, and one the Baltic countries. All others are situated within the boundaries of "Greater Germany" as of 1940). Each *SS-Oberabschnitt* is normally subdivided into either two or three *SS-Abschnitte* (Districts), of which there are forty-five altogether. *SS-Oberabschnitte* carry such regional name designations as "West" or "Rhein", and *SS-Abschnitte* consecutive Roman numerals from I to XLV. The *SS-Oberabschnitte* comprising occupied countries are not subdivided. (*SS-Abschnitt XXXIX* appears to be independent. It comprises the "Protectorate of Bohemia and Moravia", with headquarters at Prague.)

Each *SS-Oberabschnitt* is commanded by a senior *SS* officer, who is also HIMMLER's representative at the headquarters of the *Wehrkreis* which regionally corresponds most closely

RESTRICTED

to it. As commander of the *SS-Oberabschnitt* he is referred to as *Führer;* in his capacity at *Wehrkreis* headquarters he is described as *Höherer SS und Polizeiführer* (Superior SS and Police Commander) in the *Wehrkreis* concerned. As *H SS Pf* he is directly or indirectly commander of all *SS* and Police Forces in his region, including those of the *Waffen-SS* and its replacement training system.

Each *SS-Abschnitt* is commanded by a *Führer* who is described as *SS und Polizeiführer* (SS and Police Commander). Within his sub-region he holds a position not unlike that of the Superior *SS* and Police Commander in the *SS-Oberabschnitt.*

In occupied territory (so far as it is not considered a theater of operations) all *SS* forces as well as fully militarized and regular police are commanded by a *Höherer SS und Polizeiführer* cooperating with the authorities of the military administration but closely controlled by the *SS* High Command in Berlin. Sub-regions within occupied countries may be assigned, if necessary, to an *SS und Polizeiführer,* corresponding to the commander of an *Abschnitt* in Germany. In Norway, the Netherlands, and the Baltic countries local *SS* forces are nominally headed by natives of these countries but are subordinated to the German *SS.*

b. The Police.—The German police, like those of most European countries, are formally placed under the Ministry of the Interior. Until August 1943, HIMMLER, in his capacity as chief of the police, was nominally subordinated to Reich Minister Wilhelm FRICK, although he was responsible only to HITLER in his capacity as Commander in Chief of the *SS.* At that time he was appointed Minister of the Interior and thus gained even formal independence.

All German police forces at present are under the strictest *SS* control. Their local commanders, officer corps, and a considerable number of their personnel are members of the

RESTRICTED

ORDER OF BATTLE OF THE GERMAN ARMY

SS. For the last seven years all police personnel have been drawn exclusively from the *SS*.

The German police force is divided into the following two main branches:

(1) *Ordnungspolizei* (*Orpo*).—The uniformed or regular police, including the municipal *Schutzpolizei* (*Schupo*), the rural *Gendarmerie*, the river police (*Flusspolizei*), the building inspection police (*Baupolizei*), the fire-fighting police (*Feuerschutzpolizei*), and the air raid protection services (*Sicherheits- und Hilfsdienste—S. H. D.*). The Chief of the *Ordnungspolizei* is General der Polizei SS-Obergruppenführer Alfred WÜNNENBERG.

(2) *Sicherheitspolizei* (*Sipo*).—The security police, comprising primarily the criminal investigation police (*Kriminalpolizei*) and the state police (*Staatspolizei*). Partly administered by the latter is the secret state police (*Geheime Staatspolizei* or *Gestapo*), which has as its special task the prevention and liquidation of all activity hostile to the regime. In this it is closely associated with the *Sicherheitsdienst* of the *SS*, and its personnel is believed to be drawn wholly from the *SS*. Until his death in 1942 Reinhard HEYDRICH was *Chef der Sicherheitspolizei und des SS-Sicherheitsdienstes;* his successor, the present chief, is General der Polizei SS-Obergruppenführer Dr. Ernst KALTENBRUNNER. The *Sicherheitspolizei* also works in close touch with and frequently furnishes personnel to the Secret Field Police (see paragraph 14*e*), which is largely recruited from the Gestapo.

Police headquarters is in Berlin. Within each *Wehrkreis* there is a unified chain of command subordinate to the *Höherer SS und Polizeiführer* (see *a*, above), but various police forces and authorities are organized independently, thus serving as controlling agencies for one another. Variety also exists in the local structure, which shows traces of the

RESTRICTED

old federal system. Below the *Höherer SS und Polizeiführer*, command is exercised by *Inspekteure* (inspectors), *Kommandeure* (commanders), and *Befehlshaber* (commanding officers); these posts may be held independently or concurrently, and the titles are qualified by *d.O.* or *d. Sipo u.d.S.D.*, according to the branch of the service.

Regular German police units are used in varying degrees in the occupied countries, depending on the extent to which the local national police are thought strong and reliable enough to maintain law and order and to cooperate with the German military and civil authorities.

Militarized units of the regular police force are formed into police battalions, either fully or partially motorized, for use outside Germany. A battalion consists of about 550 men organized into a headquarters and four companies and equipped with rifles, machine guns, antitank guns, and armored cars. The personnel is drawn from the *Ordnungspolizei*. These battalions are normally used for internal security or mopping up duties behind the front, but they may on occasion be employed in the line under regular Army command. They are numbered in the series 1-325; about a hundred have been identified. Their uniform is field grey like that of the Army, but they are distinguished by dark green collar and cuffs, white metal buttons, and the police version of the national emblem (eagle and swastika enclosed in and resting on a wreath of oak leaves) worn on the left sleeve and on the cap or steel helmet. Police battalions may be controlled within an occupied country by a regimental staff.

The above-mentioned police units in the field and immediately behind the front are not components of the *Waffen-SS*. Exceptions are an *SS-Polizei-Division* and various independently operating *SS-Polizei* regiments and battalions.

c. The Waffen-SS.—Ever since 1933 a portion of the *SS* has

RESTRICTED

been armed and trained along military lines and served on a full-time basis, living in special barracks. These troops were known as the *SS-Verfügungstruppe*, the name indicating that they were held at the disposition of HITLER for any purpose whatever. They included the *Leibstandarte-SS "Adolf Hitler,"* which was HITLER's own bodyguard regiment, and several other regiments. Shortly before the present war they were reorganized as purely military units to take part in the Polish campaign, and subsequently divisions were formed and given the title *Waffen-SS*.

The *Waffen-SS* at present consists of at least eighteen divisions and a number of independent smaller units. About half of these are Panzer divisions and most of the others are motorized. Four *SS-Panzer-Korps* and one *SS* Mountain Corps have been identified, while the existence of the First *SS* Panzer Army appears to be likely. At least half of the identified eighteen *SS* divisions are now engaged in combat, some of them proving themselves to be among Germany's best.

HITLER is the supreme commander of the *Waffen-SS*. For military operations, however, its divisions are placed under command of the *OKH* and individual units are assigned to army groups and armies as needed, although an effort is made to give them independent tasks wherever possible. On the other hand, regular Army units may be subordinated to larger *Waffen-SS* formations, especially when the latter are given a specific mission.

The uniform of the *Waffen-SS* is grey-green as in the Army, but the national emblem is worn on the upper left sleeve instead of on the right breast. The cap insignia is a skull and cross-bones, and the ᛋᛋ sign is worn on the right-hand side of the steel helmet. The collar patches of the *Waffen-SS* are black, and rank designations similar to those of the *Allgemeine SS* are worn on the left collar patch, in addition to

RESTRICTED

shoulder insignia like those of the Army. On the right patch the runic *SS* symbol in white distinguishes *Waffen-SS* personnel. Death's Head formations wear the skull and crossbones, and the Prinz Eugen Division a distinctive rhombic symbol on the left collar patch.

19. Semimilitary Services.

The following are the principal semimilitary organizations which perform service duties behind the lines. They are thoroughly disciplined and are usually equipped at least with small arms.

    a. Organisation Todt, O.T. (*Todt Organization*).—This was first formed by the late Dr. TODT in 1938 to build the western defenses known in Germany as the Westwall. It is now widely employed to assist army engineer units in road building, road repairs, bridge construction, etc., in the wake of advancing troops and for longer-term work in occupied territory such as improving communications, preparing sites for airfields, building fortifications, and clearing harbors of wreckage. It is organized into battalions with a nucleus of specialist German personnel and a large amount of hired or impressed foreign labor. Its motor transport is provided mainly by the *NSKK* (see below) but in part by local contractors.

    The *Organisation Todt* is now headed by Prof. Albert SPEER, who succeeded Dr. TODT after the latter's death early in 1942 and incorporated into the *O.T.* his own similar organization known as the *Baustab Speer*. The uniform of the *O.T.*, ordinarily worn only by its German personnel, is a khaki blouse, open at the neck, and khaki breeches. On the left sleeve is a red armband with a black swastika set in a white circle, and immediately above the left cuff is a narrow armband with the inscription "*Org. Todt*" in white Gothic letters on a black background. Foreign workers employed by the

RESTRICTED

organization wear civilian work-clothes and an armband displaying the Arabic number of the battalion.

b. **Nationalsozialistisches Kraftfahrkorps, NSKK** (*Nazi Party Motor Transport Corps*).—The principal functions of this organization are to provide motor transport units to supplement the transport services of the armed forces and the *O.T.* and to assist police in traffic control duties on the line of communications. These are organized under four brigades bearing the titles *Heer, Luftwaffe, Speer,* and *Todt*. Within Germany and in the annexed territories, the *NSKK* also trains men in its motor schools and training units for service with the Army's mobile troops. Its basic unit is the *Motorstandarte* (literally a regiment but in reality a battalion), which carries a number in the series 1-400. The Corps is headed by Korpsführer Erwin KRAUS.

The regular uniform of the *NSKK* is a brown shirt and black breeches; however, impressed non-German *NSKK* men may appear in almost any uniform. The national emblem is mounted on a wheel enclosing a swastika and is worn on the cap or black crash helmet. White Arabic numerals preceded by the letter M or the *NSKK* emblem are worn on the right-hand collar patch. The numeral designates the number of the battalion. Rank insignia are worn on the left collar patch. The nomenclature of the *NSKK* differs but slightly from that of the *Waffen-SS*. The color of the edging of the epaulets varies: Walloon members wear yellow, Frenchmen blue, and Flemings and Dutchmen red. In addition, distinctive escutcheons are worn on the upper sleeve by the various nationalities serving in the *NSKK*. Equipment consists of light weapons only.

c. **Reichsarbeitsdienst, R.A.D.** (*Reich Labor Service*).— All German men who are physically fit are in peacetime required to perform six months' labor service in the *R.A.D.* before beginning their military service. In some cases members sign up for longer periods, but the term of service for conscripts today is usually only three or four months. They are organized into companies under a cadre of permanent officers and NCOs and are available for service in the communications zone and in occupied countries, often in conjunction with the work of the *O.T.* or the Army engineers. Their leader is Reichsarbeitsführer Konstantin HIERL. The uniform is a brownish-grey blouse with dark collar and trousers. The *R.A.D.* emblem (a spade-head containing the Arabic number of the company) is worn on the left sleeve, and under it a red armband with a black swastika set in a white circle.

d. Technische Nothilfe, T.N. *or* Teno (*Technical Emergency Corps*).—This is an auxiliary police organization actually used in the combat zone or in occupied territory for such tasks as the restoration of public utilities, the demolition of damaged buildings, the removal of unexploded bombs, and the reconstruction, maintenance, and guarding of installations of all kinds. In Germany it plays an important part in passive air defense.

The *Teno* is officially subordinated to the Regular Police and is commanded by SS-Gruppenführer Generalleutnant der Polizei SCHMELCHER under the control of WÜNNENBERG and HIMMLER. The uniform for service in the field is field grey with a narrow armband immediately above the left cuff with the words *"Technische Nothilfe"* in white. Above this is a yellow armband with *"Deutsche Wehrmacht"* in black. The national emblem is worn on the upper left sleeve, superimposed on a black triangle. The *Teno* emblem, a cog-wheel, is worn on the collar patches.

20. Party Organizations.

Certain uniformed organizations of the Party, in addition to those described above, may also be considered as potential auxiliary units to the military forces and are likely to be

RESTRICTED

encountered performing important functions in the occupied countries. The following are the principal organizations of this type:

    a. NSDAP (*the National-Socialist Party as such*).—It is organized regionally down to the smallest local units, and its officials, known as *politische Leiter*, keep close control of the activities of all German civilians at home and abroad.

    b. Sturmabteilungen, SA (*Storm Troops*).—These are organized on a pattern similar to that of the SS and are now used for a great variety of purposes on the home front, including the pre-military training of men over 18 who for some reason have not yet been called to the colors. The great majority of SA men, and particularly of SA officers, are now serving in the Army as regular soldiers. The 60th Motorized Division is officially stated to consist of volunteers from the SA and has been given the honorary designation of *Panzer-Grenadier-Division "Feldherrnhalle"*.

    The present chief of the SA is Stabschef Wilhelm SCHEPMANN.

    c. Nationalsozialistisches Fliegerkorps, NSFK (*Nazi Party Aviation Corps*).—This organization performs an important function in training personnel for the Air Force and particularly in developing the use of gliders. Until recently it was headed by General der Flieger Friedrich CHRISTIANSEN; its present chief, with the title *Korpsführer*, is Generaloberst Alfred KELLER.

    d. Hitler-Jugend, HJ (*Hitler Youth Organization*).—All German youths up to their 17th birthday belong to this organization, which is in charge of their thorough pre-military training and indoctrination. This has recently been greatly expanded in the so-called military fitness camps (*Wehrertüchtigungslager*). The HJ is headed by Reichsjugendführer Arthur AXMANN.

RESTRICTED

METHOD OF FORMING A GERMAN TASK FORCE

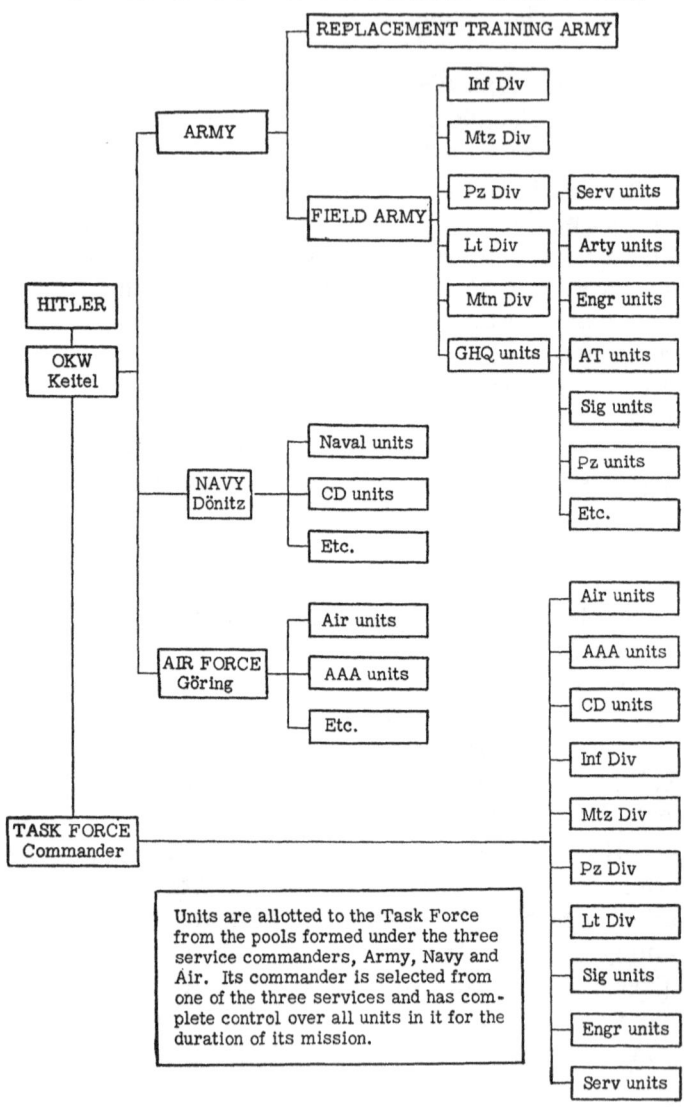

Units are allotted to the Task Force from the pools formed under the three service commanders, Army, Navy and Air. Its commander is selected from one of the three services and has complete control over all units in it for the duration of its mission.

RESTRICTED

Section V. THE GERMAN FORCES IN ACTION

21. Introduction.

Sections I to IV, inclusive, have described in some detail the structure of the German Army and the basic organization of its various elements. It is the purpose of the present section V to explain briefly how these elements are combined, under the exigencies of war, to form effective combat teams. The accompanying chart should be consulted in conjunction with this text.

Like the Army, the German Navy and Air Force are composed of many different types of units for the various purposes which these branches of the service must fulfill. The Navy includes battalions of coast artillery, naval antiaircraft artillery, naval aviation units, and the various types of combat ship formations. The German Air Force has, in addition to the regular aviation units, its different types of antiaircraft units, aircraft warning service organizations, communications, engineer, balloon barrage, and administrative units.

22. Formation of Task Forces.

All types of units in the German Army, Navy, and Air Force may be considered as groups or pools. Unit organizations are withdrawn from these pools to form task forces, which then function as teams for a specific mission. In any given situation the following factors will be considered in selecting units to form a German task force:

(1) Mission.
(2) Judgment of the commander.
(3) Availability of units.

The commander will be selected from one of the three services, normally from the one which predominates in the task force or whose interests are paramount. He will of course be of a rank commensurate with the size of the force and the importance of its mission.

Since missions and circumstances vary almost without limit, it is obvious that every German task force engaged in combat is likely to be composed differently from any other. German organizations above the division should be regarded merely as basic command frameworks, with a minimum of organically assigned combat and administrative units; task forces are formed around these frameworks. Thus the only sure method of determining the composition of the larger German formations at any particular time is by aggressive reconnaissance.

An effort is always made to retain a maximum number of combat units in the various types of GHQ pools. Consequently, when a large German unit, such as a corps or a division, is engaged in combat it will almost always be reinforced by units from the GHQ pools. When the amount of reinforcement is large, additional commanders and staffs will also be attached. The great influence which GHQ reinforcements can have on the combat power of a standard organization, such as a division, should not be overlooked.

The German system as thus outlined is both rigid and flexible. It is rigid in the sense that all the units in any single pool are as nearly alike as possible; it is flexible because the principle of combining units from the various pools is utilized to obtain any sort of combat organization which may be required for a given purpose.

Every German task force assigned to a mission is tactically and administratively an independent and self-contained organization. Coordination with other units is arranged in advance. The force is never required to depend on other units to carry out its mission.

RESTRICTED

It is hardly necessary to point out that the German system of organization for combat is economical and still effective. It enables the commanders to concentrate combat power at the most vulnerable points without changing basic dispositions. The method is also deceptive to the enemy in that it is difficult to estimate German strength in any particular situation.

The German administrative organization for supply and evacuation is arranged in a manner similar to that of the combat organization and is employed in conformance with the principle that the administrative plan must support the tactical or strategical plan. Like the tactical organization the German administrative organization will be different in almost every situation.

One of the outstanding characteristics of the German military system is unity of command. All units engaged on a single mission are under one commander, who is charged by one authority with responsibility for the success of the mission. As a corollary, two or more German commands are never assigned the same mission simultaneously. Units from the Air Force, the Navy, and the Army all serve together under a commander chosen from any of the three branches. In basic training, likewise, great emphasis is placed on cooperation among the services and among different branches of the same service. Although members of the Air Force, Navy, and Army wear different uniforms and have somewhat diverging interests, rivalry or competitive spirit among them is practically nonexistent.

To sum up, it should always be borne in mind in confronting any situation involving German forces that the predominating note in all German military thought is the combination of all arms and services necessary for any specific mission into a task force (or mission force) under a single **commander.**

RESTRICTED

SECTION VI. DIVISIONS AND HIGHER HEADQUARTERS

23. Introduction.

This section consists of a catalogue of large German units, from army groups down to divisions, with the names of their commanders, particulars of their composition, and brief notes on their origin and the campaigns in which they have taken part. Divisional components are included whose numbers can be surmised with virtual certainty, even though they may not yet have been actually identified. No attempt is made to give exact or last-minute locations, and it should be remembered that these as well as the commanders change at frequent intervals. The ages shown in parentheses after the names of commanders are usually those reached in 1944.

All *SS* units are listed separately in paragraph 39. Ground units belonging to the Air Force, including parachute divisions, Air Force field corps and divisions, and antiaircraft corps and divisions, are listed separately in paragraph 40 at the end of this section.

Under the German system the higher command is extremely fluid, and units from the division upwards may be transferred from one larger formation to another without warning, in accordance with the needs of the immediate situation. Thus there is no permanent allocation of divisions to corps, corps to armies, or armies to army groups and there is no standard equation such as 2 divisions—1 corps or 2 corps—1 army.

The following outline shows the chain of command and the various types of armies, corps, and divisions.

24. Types of Higher Headquarters.

a. Army groups (Heeresgruppenkommandos).—These are the highest command frameworks below the Army High Command itself and are formed for particular campaigns to control two or more armies in a single theater of operations or in an important and more or less self-contained sector of such a theater. Each army group has a special signal regiment (*Heeresnachrichtenregiment*) at its disposal and includes numerous staffs and special units to deal with the many administrative and operational matters within its territory, including the rear area. Since the beginning of the Russian campaign the total number of army groups has been between four and eight.

b. Armies (Armeeoberkommandos).—These are more permanent command frameworks than army groups and are not formed only for a specific campaign, although several have been disbanded since the war began. They consist of headquarters to which one or more corps are allotted in a particular sector with a particular objective, whether offensive or defensive. Each one has a signal regiment (Armeenachrichtenregiment) and certain administrative units permanently assigned to it. They are of two main types: ordinary armies, of which about fifteen now exist, and Panzer armies, of which there are four. The latter do not necessarily have only Panzer corps under them, but usually the Panzer element predominates. There is also one mountain army.

c. Corps.—These are permanent staffs to which groups of divisions as well as GHQ artillery and other units are temporarily allotted for specific missions. Each one has a signal battalion and various services permanently assigned to it. The following types exist, all numbered in the same series from I to XC:

(1) Infantry corps (*Armeekorps*) to control a group of divisions in which infantry divisions predominate.

RESTRICTED

(2) Panzer corps (*Panzerkorps*) to control a group of divisions in which Panzer divisions usually predominate.

(3) Mountain corps (*Gebirgskorps*) to control a group of divisions in mountainous or other difficult terrain.

(4) Corps command (*Höheres Kommando z.b.V.*) to control an area in occupied territory in which certain defensive units are located.

(5) Reserve corps (*Reservekorps*) to control a group of reserve divisions in occupied territory. A new variety is the reserve Panzer corps.

A corps of any type may be converted into another type and retain its number. Corps are sometimes expanded into armies.

d. *Divisions.*—These are the basic large units of the German Army having permanently assigned components. They include the following main types, all numbered in the same series from 1 to 719 except the Panzer and mountain divisions:

(1) Infantry division (*Infanteriedivision*).—Normally consists of three infantry regiments, an artillery regiment, a reconnaissance battalion, an antitank battalion, an engineer battalion, a signal battalion, and services. May be of either offensive or defensive character. Some formed since the beginning of 1941 have only two infantry regiments, and there is a tendency to replace the reconnaissance and antitank elements by a single mobile battalion.

(2) Motorized division (*Panzergrenadierdivision*).—All elements are carried in organic motor transport. Similar in composition to the infantry division but with only two infantry regiments and with the addition (since 1942) of a tank battalion.

(3) Light division (*Jägerdivision*).—Similar in organization and mode of employment to the mountain division, except Nos. 5, 8, and 28, which are believed to be more akin to motorized divisions.

RESTRICTED

(4) Panzer division (*Panzerdivision*).—Includes a tank regiment, two motorized infantry regiments, and supporting arms. Some of the infantry is carried in armored vehicles. Numbered in a separate series from 1 to 26.

(5) Mountain division (*Gebirgsdivision*).—Has two mountain infantry regiments which are distinguished from ordinary infantry not only in the special training of the personnel but in the fact that each battalion is tactically and administratively self-sufficient. Normally uses pack transport. Numbered in a separate series from 1 to 8.

(6) Sicherungs ("security") division (*Sicherungsdivision*).—Designed for mopping up duties in the rear areas and along the lines of communication in Russia. May consist of two reinforced regiments or of a number of independent Sicherungs battalions.

(7) Coast defense division (*Küstenverteidigungsdivision*).—Consists of a divisional staff controlling fortress battalions and coast artillery units in a coastal sector.

(8) Assault division (*Sturmdivision*).—Probably intended as an honorary title for divisions with a reduced amount of infantry and a concentration of heavy firepower and automatic weapons. Only two identified.

(9) Frontier guard division (*Grenzwachdivision*).—A divisional staff controlling certain frontier guard units.

(10) Special administrative division (*Divisionskommando z.b.V.*)—A divisional staff controlling *Landesschützen* battalions as well as Army GHQ troops temporarily stationed in a corps area in Germany.

(11) Mobilization division (*Div. Nr.*   ).—A divisional staff within a corps area in Germany to supervise the induction and replacement functions of *Ersatz* units. (See section II, paragraph 7.)

(12) Reserve division (*Reservedivision*).—Controls reserve units sent out to occupied territory from their corps area to

RESTRICTED

receive training and perform occupational and defensive duties. (See section II, paragraph 7.)

(13) Field training division (*Feldausbildungsdivision*).—Controls field training regiments in Russia. (See section II, paragraph 7.)

Types of divisions and higher headquarters of the *Waffen-SS* and of the Air Force ground troops are described in paragraphs 39 and 40, respectively, at the end of this section.

25. Army Groups *(Heeresgruppen)*.

Army Group North

Commander: Genfldm. Georg v. KÜCHLER (63)
C of S: Genlt. Eberhardt KINZEL (47)

Formed at the time of the initial attack on Russia in 1941 to control the armies advancing into the Baltic states. Subsequently in charge of operations in the Leningrad and Lake Ilmen sectors.

Army Group Center

Commander: Genfldm. Günther v. KLUGE (62)
C of S:

Formed at the time of the initial attack on Russia in 1941 to control the armies advancing toward the Moscow region. Subsequently in charge of operations in the entire central sector.

Army Group South

Commander: Genfldm. Fritz Erich v. LEWINSKI gen. v. MANSTEIN (57)
C of S: Genlt. Theodor BUSSE (48)

First formed at the time of the initial attack on Russia in 1941 to control the armies advancing toward Kiev and Rostov.

RESTRICTED

ORDER OF BATTLE OF THE GERMAN ARMY 135

Split at the start of the German offensive in June 1942 into Army Group A for the Caucasus sector and Army Group B for the Stalingrad drive. Reconstituted as Army Group South in the spring of 1943 to control the subsequent defensive and counteroffensive operations on the southern part of the Russian front.

Army Group A

Commander: Genfldm. Ewald v. KLEIST (63)
C of S:

Formed at the start of the German offensive in June 1942 to control the armies advancing into the North Caucasus. Withdrew to the Crimea during the Russian winter offensive and later probably to the lower Dnieper area. May have been reabsorbed into Army Group South, or may still exist to control the units operating in the Crimea and the Dnieper estuary region.

Army Group B

Commander:
C of S:

First formed at the start of the German offensive in June 1942 to control the armies advancing into the region between Stalingrad and Kursk. Replaced by Army Group South in the

RESTRICTED

spring of 1943 after the retreat beyond Rostov. The designation Army Group B may now possibly be used for a headquarters to control operations as well as occupational forces in Italy.

Army Group West

Commander: Genfldm. Gerd v. RUNDSTEDT (69)
C of S: Genlt. BLUMENTRITT (51)

Sometimes referred to as Army Group D. Formed after the French campaign to control the armies which have since been stationed in western Europe.

Army Group E

Commander: Genobst. (Luftwaffe) Alexander LÖHR (59)
C of S:

Formed in 1942-43 in the Balkans by expansion of the Twelfth Army. Now controls German and possibly some Bulgarian units in the Aegean area. May be subordinate to Army Group F.

RESTRICTED

Army Group F

Commander: Genfldm. Maximilian Frhr. v. WEICHS (63)
C of S: Genlt. Hermann FOERTSCH (49)

Formed in the summer of 1943 to control German operational and occupational forces in the Balkans.

26. Armies *(Armeeoberkommandos)*.

First Army

Commander: Genobst. Johannes BLASKOWITZ (61)
C of S: Genlt. Anton Frhr. v. MAUCHENHEIM gen. BECHTOLSHEIM (50)

Formed on mobilization. Took part in the French campaign and has since remained in France. In southwestern France.

Second Army

Commander: Gen.d.Pz.Tr. Josef HARPE (54)
C of S: Genlt. Gustav HARTENECK

Formed on mobilization. Took part in the Polish, French, and Balkan campaigns. In Russia since 1941; now on the central sector.

Third Army

Formed on mobilization. Took part in the Polish campaign under von KÜCHLER. Disbanded late in 1939.

RESTRICTED

ORDER OF BATTLE OF THE GERMAN ARMY 139

Fourth Army

Commander: Genobst. Gotthard HEINRICI (57)
C of S:
Formed on mobilization. Took part in the Polish and western campaigns. In Russia on the central sector since June 1941.

Fifth Army

Formed on mobilization for service in the west during the Polish campaign. Disbanded late in 1939.

Sixth Army

Commander: Genobst. Karl HOLLIDT (53)
C of S:
Formed early in 1940. Took part in the western campaign under von REICHENAU. In Russia on the southern sector from June 1941 and engaged at Kiev, Kharkov, and Stalingrad. Encircled and destroyed at Stalingrad under PAULUS in January 1943. Reformed in southern Russia in the spring of 1943.

RESTRICTED

Seventh Army

Commander: Genobst. Friedrich DOLLMANN (62)
C of S: Genlt. Friedrich SIXT (47)

Formed on mobilization. Took part in the western campaign and has subsequently remained in western France.

Eighth Army

Commander: Gen. d. Inf. Otto WÖHLER (50)
C of S:

Formed on mobilization. Took part in the Polish campaign under BLASKOWITZ. Subsequently disbanded. Reformed in July 1943 and since then on the southern sector in Russia.

Ninth Army

Commander: Genobst. Walter MODEL (53)
C of S: Genlt. KREBS

Formed in the spring of 1940. Took part in the Western campaign. In Russia on the central sector since June 1941.

RESTRICTED

Tenth Army

Commander: Genobst. Heinrich v. VIETINGHOFF gen. SCHEEL (57)
C of S:

Formed on mobilization. Took part in the Polish campaign under von REICHENAU. Subsequently disbanded. Reformed in August 1943 and now operating in southern Italy.

Eleventh Army

Probably formed late in 1940. In Russia on the southern sector from June 1941 under von MANSTEIN. Carried out the successful assault on Sevastopol. Subsequently moved to the northern sector and was there disbanded.

Twelfth Army

Probably formed in the spring of 1940. Took part in the Western and Balkan campaigns and subsequently remained in the Balkans. Expanded into Army Group E in the winter of 1942-43.

Fourteenth Army

Commander:
C of S:

Formed on mobilization. Took part in the Polish campaign under LIST. Disbanded late in 1939. Reformed in the autumn of 1943.

Fifteenth Army

Commander: Genobst. Hans v. SALMUTH (56)
C of S:

Probably formed late in 1940. Since then in northwestern France and Belgium.

Sixteenth Army

Commander: Genfldm. Ernst BUSCH (59)
C of S: Genlt. Hans BOECKH-BEHRENS (48)

Formed in the spring of 1940. Took part in the western campaign. In Russia on the northern sector since June 1941.

Seventeenth Army

Commander: Genobst. Erwin JAENECKE (52)
C of S:

Probably formed late in 1940. In Russia on the southern sector since June 1941.

RESTRICTED

ORDER OF BATTLE OF THE GERMAN ARMY 143

Eighteenth Army

Commander: Genobst. Georg LINDEMANN (60)
C of S: Genmaj. SPETH

Formed in the spring of 1940. Took part in the western campaign. In Russia on the northern sector since June 1941.

Nineteenth Army

Commander: Gen. d. Inf. Georg v. SODENSTERN (55)
C of S: Genmaj. Walter BOTSCH

Formed in the spring of 1943 in southern France, where it has remained.

Twentieth Army

Commander: Genobst. Eduard DIETL (54)
C of S: Genlt. Friedrich SCHULZ (47)

Referred to as a mountain army. Known until the summer of 1942 as the Army of Lapland. Formed in the winter of 1941-42 in northern Finland to control operations on the Murmansk front, where it has since remained.

RESTRICTED

Twenty-first Army

Commander: Genobst. Nikolaus v. FALKENHORST (59)
C of S: Genlt. Rudolf BAMLER (48)

Also known as the Army of Norway. Formed on mobilization as the XXI Infantry Corps, taking part as such in the Polish campaign. As Gruppe XXI organized the conquest of Norway. Expanded to an army in the summer of 1941, absorbing the LXIII Corps Command, and continued to control occupational forces in Norway. Also responsible for German operations in Finland until the formation of the Army of Lapland (Twentieth Army).

27. Panzer Armies (*Panzerarmeeoberkommandos*).

First Panzer Army

Commander: Gen. d. Pz. Tr. Hans HUBE (54)
C of S:

Formed on or shortly before mobilization as the XXII Infantry Corps, taking part as such in the Polish campaign. Fought in the west as Gruppe Kleist and in the Balkans as Panzergruppe 1. Toward the end of 1941 became the First Panzer Army on the southern sector in Russia, where it has remained.

Second Panzer Army

Commander: Gen. d. Inf. Dr. Lothar RENDULIĆ (57)
C of S:

Formed in May 1939 as the XIX Motorized Corps in the peacetime standing army. As such took part in the Polish campaign. Fought in the west as Gruppe Guderian and in the early stages of the campaign in Russia as Panzergruppe 2. Became the Second Panzer Army at the close of 1941 and continued to operate on the central sector in Russia until the latter part of 1943, when it was transferred to the Balkans.

Third Panzer Army

Commander: Genobst. Georg-Hans REINHARDT (57)
C of S:

Part of the peacetime standing army as the XV Motorized

RESTRICTED

Corps. Fought as such in the Polish campaign, as Gruppe Hoth in the west, and as Panzergruppe 3 in the early stages of the Russian campaign. Became the Third Panzer Army at the close of 1941 and has since operated on the central sector.

Fourth Panzer Army

Commander: Genobst. Hermann HOTH (60)
C of S: Genlt. RÖTTIGER

Part of the peacetime standing army as the XVI Motorized Corps. Fought as such in Poland and the west and as Panzergruppe 4 in the early stages of the Russian campaign. Became the Fourth Panzer Army at the close of 1941. Moved from the central to the southern sector in the early summer of 1942 and heavily engaged at Stalingrad. Still on the southern sector.

Fifth Panzer Army

Formed late in 1942 by expansion of the XC Panzer Corps to control operations in northern Tunisia. Destroyed there in May 1943.

RESTRICTED

Panzer Army of Africa

Formed in June 1941 as Panzergruppe Afrika to control the Africa Panzer Corps and Italian units. Became a Panzer Army at the close of 1941. Entered Tunisia in the winter of 1942-43 and was destroyed there the following May.

28. Infantry Corps *(Armeekorps)*.

I Infantry Corps

Commander:
C of S:
Home station: Königsberg (Wkr. I)

Part of the peacetime standing army.

Campaigns: Polish, Western, Russian. On the northern sector.

II Infantry Corps

Commander: Gen. d. Inf. Paul LAUX (57)
C of S: Obst. SCHMIDT-RICHBERG
Home station: Stettin (Wkr. II)

Part of the peacetime standing army.

Campaigns: Polish, Western, Russian. On the northern sector.

III Corps—See III Pz Corps

IV Infantry Corps

Commander:
C of S:
Home station: Dresden (Wkr. IV)

RESTRICTED

ORDER OF BATTLE OF THE GERMAN ARMY 149

Part of the peacetime standing army.
Campaigns: Polish, Western, Russian; destroyed at Stalingrad. Reformed summer 1943; since then in Russia in the southern sector.

V Infantry Corps

Commander:
C of S:
Home station: Stuttgart (Wkr. V)

Part of the peacetime standing army.
Campaigns: Western, Russian. On the southern sector.

VI Infantry Corps

Commander:
C of S:
Home station: Münster (Wkr. VI)

Part of the peacetime standing army.
Campaigns: Western, Russian. On the central sector.

VII Infantry Corps

Commander: Gen. d. Art. Ernst-Eberhard HELL (57)
C of S:
Home station: München (Wkr. VII)

RESTRICTED

Part of the peacetime standing army.
Campaigns: Polish, Western, Russian. On the southern sector.

VIII Infantry Corps

Commander: Gen. d. Pz. Tr. Erhard RAUS (55)?
C of S:
Home station: Breslau (Wkr. VIII)

Part of the peacetime standing army.
Campaigns: Polish, Western, Russian; destroyed at Stalingrad. Probably reformed in Russia and now on the southern sector.

IX Infantry Corps

Commander: Gen. d. Inf. Hans SCHMIDT (66)
C of S:
Home station: Kassel (Wkr. IX)

Part of the peacetime standing army.
Campaigns: Western, Russian. On the central sector.

RESTRICTED

X Infantry Corps

Commander: Gen. d. Art. Christian HANSEN (59)
C of S:
Home station: Hamburg (Wkr. X)
Part of the peacetime standing army.
Campaigns: Polish, Western, Russian. On the northern sector.

XI Infantry Corps

Commander:
C of S:
Home station: Hannover (Wkr. XI)
Part of the peacetime standing army.
Campaigns: Polish, Western, Russian; destroyed at Stalingrad. Reformed summer 1943; since then in Russia on the southern sector.

XII Infantry Corps—See XII Pz. Corps

XIII Infantry Corps

Commander: Gen. d. Inf. Erich JASCHKE (54)
C of S:
Home station: Nürnberg (Wkr. XIII)
Part of the peacetime standing army.
Campaigns: Polish, Western, Russian. On the southern sector.

XIV Corps—See XIV Panzer Corps

XV Corps—See Third Panzer Army

XVI Corps—See Fourth Panzer Army

XVII Infantry Corps

Commander: Gen. d. Art. Erich BRANDENBERGER (52)
C of S:
Home station: Wien (Wkr. XVII)

Part of the peacetime standing army since April 1938.
Campaigns: Polish, Western, Russian. On the southern sector.

XVIII Corps—See XVIII Mountain Corps

XIX Corps—See Second Panzer Army

XX Infantry Corps

Commander: Gen. d. Art. Rudolf Frhr. v. ROMAN (51)
C of S:
Home station: Danzig (Wkr. XX)

Formed shortly before mobilization.
Campaigns: Polish, Russian. On the central sector.

RESTRICTED

XXI Infantry Corps—See Army of Norway

XXII Infantry Corps—See First Panzer Army

XXIII Infantry Corps

Commander: Gen. d. Inf. Karl HILPERT (56)
C of S:
Home station: Bonn (Wkr. VI)

Part of the peacetime standing army (as "Grenzkommando Eifel").
Campaigns: Western, Russian. On the central sector.

XXIV Infantry Corps—See XXIV Panzer Corps

XXV Infantry Corps

Commander: Gen. d. Inf. Wilhelm FAHRMBACHER (56)?
C of S:
Home station: Baden-Baden (Wkr. V)

Part of the peacetime standing army ("Grenzkommando Oberrhein").
Campaign: Western. In western France.

XXVI Infantry Corps

Commander:
C of S:
Home station: (Wkr. I)

RESTRICTED

Formed on mobilization.
Campaigns: Polish, Western, Russian. On the northern sector.

XXVII Infantry Corps

Commander:
C of S:
Home station: (Wkr. VII)

Formed on mobilization.
Campaigns: Western, Russian. On the central sector.

XXVIII Infantry Corps

Commander: Gen. d. Art. Herbert LOCH (58)
C of S:
Home station: (Wkr. III)

Formed in early summer 1940.
Campaign: Russian. On the northern sector.

XXIX Infantry Corps

Commander: Gen. d. Art. Hans v. OBSTFELDER (58)
C of S:
Home station: (Wkr. IV)

Formed in early summer 1940.
Campaign: Russian. On the southern sector.

RESTRICTED

XXX Infantry Corps

Commander: Gen. d. Art. Maximilian FRETTER-PICO (53)
C of S:
Home station: (Wkr. XI)

Formed on mobilization. Campaigns: Polish, Western, Balkan, Russian. On the southern sector.

XXXI-XXXIII Corps—See XXXI-XXXIII Corps Commands

XXXIV Infantry Corps

Commander:
C of S:
Home station: (Wkr. III)

Probably formed shortly after mobilization as a corps command.

In Poland from late in 1939 until June 1941; thereafter operating as an infantry corps in Russia, on the central sector. Unlocated since September 1943.

XXXV Infantry Corps

Commander: Gen. d. Art. Rudolf KAEMPFE (61)
C of S:
Home station: (Wkr. VIII)

Probably formed shortly after mobilization as a corps command.

RESTRICTED

In Poland late in 1939 until June 1941; thereafter operating as an infantry corps in Russia; designation changed in May 1942. On the central sector.

XXXVI and XXXVII Corps—
See XXXVI and XXXVII Corps Command

XXXVIII Infantry Corps

Commander: Gen. d. Inf. Kurt HERZOG (56)
C of S:
Home station: (Wkr. VIII?)

Formed on mobilization.

Campaigns: Polish, Western, Russian. On the northern sector.

XXXIX-XLI Corps—See XXXIX-XLI Panzer Corps

XLII Infantry Corps

Commander:
C of S:
Home station: (Wkr. III)

Formed on mobilization.

Campaigns: Polish, Western, Russian. On the southern sector.

RESTRICTED

XLIII Infantry Corps

Commander: Gen. d. Inf. Karl von OVEN (56)
C of S: Obst. Otto SCHULZ
Home station: Hannover (Wkr. XI)

Formed in early summer 1940.
Campaigns: Western, Russian. On the northern sector.

XLIV Infantry Corps

Commander: Gen. d. Art. Maximilian ANGELIS (55)
C of S:
Home station: Dresden (Wkr. IV)

Formed in early summer 1940.
Campaigns: Western, Russian. On the southern sector.

XLV Corps—See XLV Corps Command

XLVI-XLVIII Corps—See XLVI-XLVIII Panzer Corps

XLIX Corps—See XLIX Mountain Corps

L Infantry Corps

Commander: Gen. d. Inf. Philipp KLEFFEL (57)
C of S:
Home station: (Wkr. X)

Formed late in 1940.
Campaigns: Balkan, Russian. On the northern sector.

RESTRICTED

LI Infantry Corps—See LI Mountain Corps

LII Infantry Corps

Commander:
C of S:
Home station: (Wkr. III)

Formed late in 1940.
Campaign: Russian. On the southern sector.

LIII Infantry Corps

Commander: Gen. d. Inf. Erich CLÖSSNER (58)
C of S:
Home station: (Wkr. XII)

Formed late in 1940.
Campaign: Russian. On the central sector.

LIV Infantry Corps

Commander: Gen. d. Inf. Gustav HÖHNE (51)
C of S:
Home station:

Formed as a corps command in 1940 and became an active corps in the spring of 1941.
Campaign: Russian. On the northern sector.

RESTRICTED

LV Infantry Corps

Commander: Gen. d. Inf. Paul VÖLCKERS (53)?
C of S:
Home station:
Probably formed in the spring of 1941.
Campaign: Russian. On the central sector.

LVI-LVII Corps—See LVI-LVII Panzer Corps

LVIII Infantry Corps—Not yet reported

LIX Infantry Corps

Commander: Gen. d. Inf. Kurt v. d. CHEVALLERIE (53)
C of S:
Home station:
Probably formed in the spring of 1941.
Campaign: Russian. On the southern sector.

LX-LXVII Corps—See LX-LXVII Corps Commands

LXVIII Infantry Corps

Commander:
C of S: Genmaj: Heinz von GYLDENFELDT
Home station:
Probably formed in the summer of 1943. In Greece.

RESTRICTED

LXIX-LXXI Corps—See LXIX-LXXI Corps Command

LXXII-LXXV Corps—Not yet reported

LXXVI Corps—See LXXVI Panzer Corps

LXXVII-LXXIX Corps—Not yet reported

LXXX Infantry Corps

Commander:
C of S:
Home station:

Probably formed in early summer 1942, in France, where it has remained.

LXXXI Infantry Corps

Commander: Gen. d. Pz. Tr. Adolf KUNTZEN (55)
C of S:
Home station:

Formed as the XXXII Corps Command and became an active corps in the summer of 1942, in northwestern France, where it has remained.

LXXXII Infantry Corps

Commander: Gen. d. Art. SINNHUBER (57)
C of S: Obst. von DITFURTH ?
Home station: (Wkr. XVII)

RESTRICTED

Formed as the XXXVII Corps Command and became an active corps in summer 1942, in northwestern France, where it has remained.

LXXXIII Infantry Corps

Commander:
C of S:
Home station:

Formed in early summer 1942 in France, and subsequently moved into former unoccupied France. Possibly dissolved.

LXXXIV Infantry Corps

Commander: Gen. d. Art. BEHLENDORFF (55)
C of S:
Home station:

Formed as the LX Corps Command and became an active Corps in summer 1942, in northwestern France, where it has remained.

RESTRICTED

LXXXV Corps—Not yet reported

LXXXVI Infantry Corps

Commander: Gen. d. Inf. Bruno BIELER (56)
C of S:
Home station:

Formed probably late in 1942 in southwestern France, where it has remained.

LXXXVII Infantry Corps

Commander:
C of S:
Home station:

Formed probably late in 1942 in France; moved into northern Italy in latter part of 1943.

LXXXVIII Infantry Corps

Commander: Gen. d. Inf. Hans REINHARD (56)
C of S:
Home station:

Formed in early summer 1942 and subsequently in Holland.

RESTRICTED

LXXXIX Infantry Corps

Commander: Gen. d. Pz. Tr. Dr. Alfred Ritter von HUBICKI (57)
C of S:
Home station:
Formed as "Schelde" Corps in summer 1942, in Belgium, where it has remained. Renamed LXXXIX Corps in December 1942 or January 1943.

XC Corps—See XC Panzer Corps

29. Panzer Corps (Panzerkorps).

III Panzer Corps

Commander: Gen. d. Pz. Tr. Hermann BREITH (52)
C of S:
Home station: Berlin (Wkr. III)

Part of the peacetime standing army as III Inf Corps.

Campaigns: Polish and Western (as III Inf Corps), Russian. On the southern sector.

XII Panzer Corps

Commander:
C of S:
Home station: Wiesbaden (Wkr. XII)

Part of peacetime standing army as XII Infantry Corps. Converted to XII Panzer Corps in 1943.

XIV Panzer Corps

Commander:
C of S:
Home station: Magdeburg (Wkr. XI)

Part of the peacetime standing army. Destroyed in Stalingrad. Reformed in the summer of 1943.

Campaigns: Polish and Western (as XIV Mtz Corps). Balkan, Russian, Sicilian, Italian.

RESTRICTED

XXIV Panzer Corps

Commander: Gen. d. Pz. Tr. Walter NEHRING (52)
C of S:
Home station: Kaiserslautern (Wkr. XII)

Part of the peacetime standing army (as "Grenzkommando Saarpfalz").
Campaigns: Polish and Western (as XXIV Inf. Corps), Russian. On the southern sector.

XXXIX Panzer Corps

Commander: Gen. d. Art. Robert MARTINEK (60)
C of S:
Home station: (Wkr. IX)

Formed late in 1939.
Campaigns: Western, Russian. On the central sector.

XL Panzer Corps

Commander: Gen. d. Art. Sigfrid HENRICI (56)
C of S: Obst. HESSE
Home station: (Wkr. X)

Formed late in 1939.
Campaigns: Western, Balkan, Russian. On southern sector.

RESTRICTED

XLI Panzer Corps

Commander:
C of S:
Home station:

Formed late in 1939.
Campaigns: Western, Balkan, Russian. On the central sector.

XLVI Panzer Corps

Commander: Genlt. Friedrich HOSSBACH (50)
C of S:
Home station: (Wkr. X)

Formed in early summer 1940.
Campaigns: Balkan, Russian. On the central sector.

XLVII Panzer Corps

Commander:
C of S:
Home station: Danzig (Wkr. XX)

Formed in early summer 1940.
Campaign: Russian. On the southern sector.

RESTRICTED

XLVIII Panzer Corps

Commander: Gen. d. Pz. Tr. Otto v. KNOBELSDORFF (58)
C of S:
Home station: Posen (Wkr. XXI)

Formed in early summer 1940.
Campaign: Russian. On the southern sector.

LVI Panzer Corps

Commander:
C of S:
Home station: (Wkr. VI)

Formed late in 1940.
Campaign: Russian. On the central sector.

LVII Panzer Corps

Commander: Gen. d. Pz. Tr. Friedrich KIRCHNER (59)
C of S:
Home station: (Wkr. II)

Formed late in 1940.
Campaign: Russian. On the southern sector.

RESTRICTED

LXXVI Panzer Corps

Commander: Gen. d. Pz. Tr. Traugott HERR (54)
C of S:
Home station:
Formed in the summer of 1943 in Italy.
Campaign: Italian.

XC Panzer Corps

Formed in the summer of 1942 for operations in Tunisia, but soon expanded into the Fifth Panzer Army, subsequently disbanded.

Africa Panzer Corps (Pz.K.Afrika)

Formed as the German Africa Corps in the spring of 1941. Campaigns: Libya and Egypt. Destroyed in Tunisia.

RESTRICTED

ORDER OF BATTLE OF THE GERMAN ARMY 169

30. Mountain Corps *(Gebirgskorps)*.

XV Mountain Corps

Commander: Gen. d. Inf. Rudolf LÜTERS (61)
C of S:
Home station:
Formed in the summer of 1943. In Croatia.

XVIII Mountain Corps

Commander: Gen. d. Inf. Franz BÖHME (59)
C of S:
Home station: Salzburg (Wkr. XVIII)
Part of the peacetime standing army since April 1938. Campaigns. Polish, Western, Balkan. Now in Finland.

XIX Mountain Corps

Commander: Genlt. Ritter von HENGL
C of S:
Home station: (Wkr. XVIII)
Formed in the summer of 1940 in northern Norway as Norway Mountain Corps. Renamed XIX Mountain Corps in the summer of 1942.
Campaigns: Murmansk front.

RESTRICTED

XXI Mountain Corps

Commander: Gen. d. Art. Paul BADER (59)
C of S:
Home station:

Formed late in the summer of 1943. In Albania and Montenegro.

XXII Mountain Corps

Commander: Gen. d. Geb. Tr. Hubert LANZ (48)
C of S:
Home station:

Formed late in the summer of 1943 in Greece.

XXXVI Mountain Corps

Commander: Gen. d. Inf. Karl WEISENBERGER (54)
C of S: Obstlt. HOLTER
Home station: (Wkr. II)

Formerly XXXVI Corps Command, probably formed shortly after mobilization. In Norway from summer 1940 until June 1941. Moved to northern Finland as an infantry corps and subsequently converted to a mountain corps.

RESTRICTED

XLIX Mountain Corps

Commander: Gen. d. Geb. Tr. Rudolf KONRAD (53)
C of S:
Home station: Prag (Wkr. Böhmen u Mähren)

Formed in early summer 1940.
Campaigns: Balkan, Russian. On the southern sector.

LI Mountain Corps

Commander: Gen. d. Geb. Tr. Valentin FEURSTEIN (59)
C of S:
Home station: (Wkr. XI)

Formerly LI Infantry Corps. Destroyed at Stalingrad. Reformed as the LI Mountain Corps in the summer of 1943.

Norway Mountain Corps

Formed in the summer of 1940 in northern Norway. Renamed XIX Mountain Corps in the winter of 1942-43.

RESTRICTED

31. Corps Commands and Reserve Corps *(Höhere Kommandos z.b.V.* and *Reservekorps).*

XXXI Corps Command

Commander: Gen. d. Inf. von HANNEKEN (54)
C of S:
Home station: (Wkr. X?)

Probably formed shortly after mobilization.
Since April 1940 at Copenhagen, Denmark.

XXXII Corps Command—See LXXXI Infantry Corps

XXXIII Corps Command

Commander: d. Kav. Erwin ENGELBRECHT (53)
C of S:
Home station: (Wkr. VI)

Probably formed shortly after mobilization.
Since summer 1940 in central Norway.

XXXIV Corps Command—See XXXIV Infantry Corps
XXXV Corps Command—See XXXV Infantry Corps
XXXVI Corps Command—See XXXVI Mountain Corps
XXXVII Corps Command—See LXXXII Infantry Corps

XLV Corps Command

Probably formed early in 1940. Subsequently in France. Believed disbanded in 1943.

RESTRICTED

ORDER OF BATTLE OF THE GERMAN ARMY 173

LX Corps Command—See LXXXIV Infantry Corps

LXI Reserve Corps

Commander: Gen. d. Art. Edgar THEISEN (55)
C of S:
Home station:

Formed in September of 1942, in Poland, where it has remained.

LXII Reserve Corps

Commander: Gen. d. Inf. Ferdinand NEULING (59)
C of S:
Home station:

Formed in September of 1942, in Poland, where it has remained.

LXIII Corps Command—See Twenty-first Army (Army of Norway)

LXIV Reserve Corps

Commander: Gen. d. Inf. Wilhelm WETZEL (56)
C of S:
Home station:

Formed as LXIV Corps Command. Converted into the LXIV Reserve Corps in the autumn of 1942, in France, now in eastern France.

RESTRICTED

LXV Corps Command

Commander:
C of S:
Home station: (Wkr. II)

Probably formed early in 1941. Continued existence uncertain.
At Belgrade, Serbia, from May 1941.

LXVI Reserve Corps

Commander: Gen. d. Inf. Baptist KNIESS (59)
C of S:
Home station:

Formed in the autumn of 1942, in France, now in southeastern France.

LXVII Reserve Corps

Commander:
C of S:
Home station:

Formed as LXVII Corps Command. Converted to LXVII Reserve Corps in the autumn of 1942 in France, now in southern France.

RESTRICTED

LXIX Reserve Corps

Commander: Genlt. Erich DENECKE (52)
C of S:
Home station:
Formed probably late in 1942, in Croatia, where it has remained.

LXX Corps Command

Commander: Gen. d. Art. Hermann TITTEL (55)
C of S:
Home station: (Wkr. VI?)
Formed in southern Norway in autumn 1941.
In southern Norway.

LXXI Corps Command

Commander: Gen. d. Art. Willi MOSER (57)
C of S:
Home station:
Formed in northern Norway in the spring of 1942.
In northern Norway.

32. Infantry Divisions *(Infanteriedivisionen)*.

1st Infantry Division

Commander: Genlt. Martin GRASE (53)
Composition: 1st Gren Regt, 22d Füsilier Regt, 43d Gren Regt, 1st Arty Regt, 1st Rcn Bn, 1st AT Bn, 1st Engr Bn, 1st Sig Bn
Auxiliary unit number: 1
Home station: Insterburg (Wkr. I)

Active division. Took part in the Polish and French campaign. Engaged on the northern sector of the Russian front since June 1941. Heavily engaged south of Lake Ladoga in the summer of 1943.

2d Infantry Division—See 12th Pz Div

3d Infantry Division—See 3d Mtz Div

4th Infantry Division—See 14th Pz Div

5th Infantry Division—See 5th L Div

6th Infantry Division

Commander: Genlt. Horst GROSSMANN (53)
Composition: 18th Gren Regt, 37th Gren Regt, 58th Gren Regt, 6th Arty Regt, 6th Rcn Bn, 6th AT Bn, 6th Engr Bn, 6th Sig Bn
Auxiliary unit number: 6
Home station: Bielefeld (Wkr. VI)

Active division. Fought throughout the French campaign. Engaged on the central sector of the Russian front since the

RESTRICTED

ORDER OF BATTLE OF THE GERMAN ARMY 177

beginning of the campaign. Took part in the Kursk offensive in the summer of 1943 and recently in the defense of the middle Dnieper.

7th Infantry Division

Commander: Genlt. Fritz v. RAPPARD
Composition: 19th Gren Regt, 61st Gren Regt, 62d Gren Regt, 7th Arty Regt, 7th Rcn Bn, 7th AT Bn, 7th Engr Bn, 7th Sig Bn
Auxiliary unit number: 7
Home station: München (Wkr. VII)

Active division. Took part in the Polish and Belgian campaign. Continuously engaged on the central sector of the Russian front since the beginning of the campaign. (The 638th Infantry Regiment, composed of French volunteers, is believed to have operated under its command). Took part in the Kursk offensive in the summer of 1943 and recently in the defense of the middle Dnieper.

8th Infantry Division—See 8th L Div

9th Infantry Division

Commander: Genlt. Siegmund Frhr. v. SCHLEINITZ (54)
Composition: 36th Gren Regt, 57th Gren Regt, 116th Gren Regt, 9th Arty Regt, 9th Rcn Bn, 9th AT Bn, 9th Engr Bn, 9th Sig Bn
Auxiliary unit number: 9
Home station: Giessen (Wkr. IX)

Active division. Fought in France. Engaged on the southern sector on the Russian front since the beginning of the

RESTRICTED

campaign. In the Caucasus in the summer of 1942; later withdrew to the Kuban, where it remained until evacuated to the lower Dnieper area in the autumn of 1943.

10th Infantry Division—See 10th Mtz Div

11th Infantry Division

Commander: Genlt. Karl BURDACH (50)
Composition: 2d Gren Regt, 23d Gren Regt, 44th Gren Regt, 11th Arty Regt, 11th Rcn Bn, 11th AT Bn, 11th Engr Bn, 11th Sig Bn
Auxiliary unit number: 11
Home station: Allenstein (Wkr. I)

Active division. Fought in Poland. Not identified during the French campaign. Engaged on the northern sector of the Russian front from the beginning of the campaign. Heavily engaged south of Lake Ladoga in the summer of 1943.

12th Infantry Division

Commander: Genlt. Kurt-Jürgen Frhr. v. LÜTZOW (52)
Composition: 27th Füsilier Regt, 48th Gren Regt, 89th Gren Regt, 12th Arty Regt, 12th Rcn Bn, 12th AT Bn, 12th Engr Bn, 12th Sig Bn
Auxiliary unit number: 12
Home station: Schwerin (Wkr. II)

Active division. Fought in Poland and France. On the northern sector of the Russian front.

RESTRICTED

13th Infantry Division—See 13th Pz Div

14th Infantry Division—See 14th Mtz Div

15th Infantry Division

Commander: Genlt. Erich BUSCHENHAGEN (52)
Composition: 81st Gren Regt, 88th Gren Regt, 106th Gren Regt, 15th Arty Regt, 15th Rcn Bn, 15th AT Bn, 15th Engr Bn, 15th Sig Bn
Auxiliary unit number: 15
Home station: Kassel (Wkr. IX)

Active division. Not active in the French campaign. Engaged on the central sector of the Russian front until April 1942, when it was transferred to France. Returned to the southern sector of the Russian front in March 1943. Suffered heavy losses in the Dnepropetrovsk area in the summer of 1943.

16th Infantry Division—See 16th Pz Div and 16th Mtz Div

17th Infantry Division

Commander:
Composition: 21st Gren Regt, 55th Gren Regt, 95th Gren Regt, 17th Arty Regt, 17th Rcn Bn, 17th AT Bn, 17th Engr Bn, 17th Sig Bn
Auxiliary unit number: 17
Home station: Nürnberg (Wkr. XIII)

Active division. Distinguished in Poland and France. Engaged on the central sector of the Russian front from the beginning of the campaign. Transferred to France in the summer of 1942 and returned to the southern sector in Russia in February 1943. Suffered severe losses during the encirclement of Taganrog in the summer of 1943. Later took part in the defense of the lower Dnieper.

RESTRICTED

18th Infantry Division—See 18th Mtz Div

19th Infantry Division—See 19th Pz Div

20th Infantry Division—See 20th Mtz Div

21st Infantry Division

Commander: Genlt. PRIESS
Composition: 3d Gren Regt, 24th Gren Regt, 45th Gren Regt, 21st Arty Regt, 21st Rcn Bn, 21st AT Bn, 21st Engr Bn, 21st Sig Bn
Auxiliary unit number: 21
Home station: Mohrungen (Wkr. I)

Active division. Fought in Poland and France.

Engaged on the northern sector of the Russian front since the beginning of the campaign.

22d Infantry Division—See 22d Mtz Div

23d Infantry Division

Commander:
Composition: 68th Füsilier Regt, 9th(?) Gren Regt, 67th(?) Gren Regt, 23d Arty Regt, 23d(?) Rcn Bn, 23d AT Bn, 23d Engr Bn, 23d(?) Sig Bn
Auxiliary unit number: 23
Home station: Potsdam (Wkr. III)

Active division. Operated in Poland and in France. Engaged continuously and apparently with heavy losses on the central sector of the Russian front in the first few months. Transferred to France in the spring of 1942, where the bulk of its personnel was used in the formation of the 26th Pz Div. A new 23d Infantry Division was formed in Wkr. III and went to the northern sector of the Russian front in the winter of 1942-1943. Transferred to the central sector of the Russian front in the autumn of 1943.

RESTRICTED

24th Infantry Division

Commander: Genlt. Hans v. TETTAU (56)
Composition: 31st Gren Regt, 32d Gren Regt, 102d Gren Regt, 24th Arty Regt, 24th Rcn Bn, 24th AT Bn, 24th Engr Bn, 24th Sig Bn
Auxiliary unit number: 24
Home station: Chemnitz (Wkr. IV)

Active division. Took part in the Polish and French campaigns. Engaged on the southern sector of the Russian front and in the Crimea from the beginning of the campaign. Transferred to the northern sector in the winter of 1942-1943, where it has remained.

25th Infantry Division—See 25th Mtz Div

26th Infantry Division

Commander: Genlt. Friedrich HOCHBAUM (50)
Composition: 39th Füsilier Regt, 77th Gren Regt, 78th Gren Regt, 26th Arty Regt, 26th Rcn Bn, 26th AT Bn, 26th Engr Bn, 26th Sig Bn
Auxiliary unit number: 26
Home station: Köln (Wkr. VI)

Active division. Took part in the French campaign. Continuously engaged on the central sector of the Russian front since the beginning of the campaign. Took part in the Kursk offensive in the summer of 1943 with heavy losses.

27th Infantry Division—See 17th Pz Div

28th Infantry Division—See 28th L Div

RESTRICTED

29th Infantry Division—See 29th Mtz Div

30th Infantry Division

Commander: Genlt. Emil von WICKEDE (51)
Composition: 6th Gren Regt, 26th Gren Regt, 46th Gren Regt, 30th Arty Regt, 30th Rcn Bn, 30th AT Bn, 30th Engr Bn, 30th Sig Bn
Auxiliary unit number: 30
Home station: Lübeck (Wkr. X)

Active division. Fought in Poland and Belgium. Engaged on the northern sector of the Russian front since the beginning of the campaign. Referred to as the Briesen Division, after its late commander.

31st Infantry Division

Commander:
Composition: 12th Gren Regt, 17th Gren Regt, 82d Gren Regt, 31st Arty Regt, 31st Rcn Bn, 31st AT Bn, 31st Engr Bn, 31st Sig Bn
Auxiliary unit number: 31
Home station: Braunschweig (Wkr. XI)

Active division. Took part in the Polish and French campaigns. Continuously engaged on the central sector of the Russian front since the beginning of the campaign. Engaged in the Kursk offensive in the summer of 1943 and later in the defense of the middle Dnieper.

RESTRICTED

32d Infantry Division

Commander: Genlt. Wilhelm WEGENER (49)
Composition: 4th Gren Regt, 94th Gren Regt, 96th Gren Regt, 32d Arty Regt, 32d Rcn Bn, 32d AT Bn, 2d Engr Bn, 32d Sig Bn
Auxiliary unit number: 32
Home station: Köslin (Wkr. II)

Active division. Operated in Poland and France. On the northern sector of the Russian front since the beginning of the campaign.

33d Infantry Division—See 15th Mtz Div

34th Infantry Division

Commander:
Composition: 80th Gren Regt, 107th Gren Regt, 253d Gren Regt, 34th Arty Regt, 34th Rcn Bn, 34th AT Bn, 34th Engr Bn, 34th Sig Bn
Auxiliary unit number: 34
Home station: Heidelberg (Wkr. XII)

Active division. Took part in the French campaign. Continuously engaged on the central sector of the Russian front from the beginning of the campaign. Transferred in August 1943 to the southern sector, where it fought hard in the Kharkov area.

35th Infantry Division

Commander: Genlt. Ludwig MERKER (50)
Composition: 34th Füsilier Regt, 109th Gren Regt, 111th Gren Regt, 35th Arty Regt, 35th Rcn Bn, 35th AT Bn, 35th Engr Bn, 35th Sig Bn
Auxiliary unit number: 35
Home station: Karlsruhe (Wkr. V)

RESTRICTED

Active division. Fought in Belgium. Continuously engaged on the central sector of the Russian front, where it suffered considerable losses in the summer of 1943.

36th Infantry Division—See 36th Mtz Div

38th Infantry Division

Commander: Genlt. EBERHARDT (51)
Composition: 108th Gren Regt, 112th Gren Regt, 138th Arty Regt, 138th Mobile Bn, 138th Engr Bn, 138th Sig Bn
Auxiliary unit number: 138
Home station:

Formed in Brittany in the summer of 1942. First identified on the southern sector of the Russian front in April 1943, where it was last reported. Appears to include many Poles and other non-Germans. Contains only two infantry regiments.

39th Infantry Division

Commander:
Composition: 113th Gren Regt, 114th Gren Regt, 139th Arty Regt, 139th Mobile Bn, 139th Engr Bn, 139th Sig Bn
Auxiliary unit number: 139
Home station:

Formed in the summer of 1942 and identified in Holland in the Flushing area. Transferred to the southern sector of the Russian front in March 1943, where it has since been heavily engaged. Contains many Poles and other non-Germans. Contains only two infantry regiments.

RESTRICTED

44th Infantry Division

Commander: Genlt. Dr. Franz BEYER (54)
Composition: 131st Gren Regt, 132d Gren Regt, 134th Gren Regt, 96th Arty Regt, 44th Rcn Bn, 46th AT Bn, 80th Engr Bn, 64th Sig Bn
Auxiliary unit number: 44
Home station: Wien (Wkr. XVII)

Active division, formed in 1938. Operated in Poland and in France. Engaged on the southern sector of the Russian front from the beginning of the campaign. Virtually destroyed at Stalingrad. Reformed in France in April 1943. Was honored in June 1943 with the traditional Viennese title of "Reichsgrenadierdivision Hoch- und Deutschmeister." Transferred to northern Italy in August 1943, then to Slovenia in October, and subsequently to the southern Italian front in December 1943.

45th Infantry Division

Commander: Genmaj. Hans Frhr. v. FALKENSTEIN (51)
Composition: 130th Gren Regt, 133d Gren Regt, 135th Gren Regt, 98th Arty Regt, 45th Rcn Bn, 45th AT Bn, 81st Engr Bn, 65th Sig Bn
Auxiliary unit number: 45
Home station: Linz (Wkr. XVII)

Active division, formed in 1938. Operated in Poland and in France. Continuously engaged on the central sector of the Russian front. Possibly transferred to the southern sector but returned to the central sector in the spring of 1943 and appears to have taken part in the Kursk offensive in the summer of that year. Engaged in the defense of the Sozh River in the autumn.

RESTRICTED

46th Infantry Division

Commander: Genmaj. Kurt RÖPKE (58)
Composition: 42d Gren Regt, 72d Gren Regt, 97th Gren Regt, 114th Arty Regt, 46th Rcn Bn, 52d AT Bn, 88th Engr Bn, 76th Sig Bn
Auxiliary unit number: 46
Home station: Karlsbad (Wkr. XIII)

Active division, formed at the close of 1938. Saw little fighting before the Russian campaign. Engaged on the southern sector, especially in the Crimea and in the Caucasus. Later fought on the Donets front and took a prominent part in the Belgorod offensive in the summer of 1943. Heavily engaged at Dnepropetrovsk in the autumn of 1943.

50th Infantry Division

Commander:
Composition: 121st Gren Regt, 122d Gren Regt, 123d Gren Regt, 150th Arty Regt, 150th Rcn Bn, 150th AT Bn, 150th Engr Bn, 150th Sig Bn
Auxiliary unit number: 150
Home station: (Wkr. III?)

Active division as "Grenzkommando Küstrin" (Küstrin Frontier Command). Took part in the Polish and French campaigns. Continuously engaged on the southern sector of the Russian front, especially in the Crimea and in the Caucasus. Withdrew to the Kuban in the winter of 1942-1943 and was evacuated to the lower Dnieper area in the autumn of 1943.

RESTRICTED

52d Infantry Division

Commander:
Composition: 163d Gren Regt, 181st Gren Regt, 205th Gren Regt, 152d
Arty Regt, 152d Rcn Bn, 152d AT Bn, 152d Engr Bn,
152d Sig Bn
Auxiliary unit number: 152
Home station: Kassel (Wkr. IX)

Formed in the summer of 1939 from reservists. Operated partly in France and partly in Norway in 1940. Engaged in the central sector of the Russian front from the beginning. Was in the Smolensk area in the autumn of 1943.

56th Infantry Division

Commander: Genlt. Otto LÜDECKE (50)
Composition: 171st Gren Regt, 192d Gren Regt, 234th Gren Regt, 156th
Arty Regt, 156th Rcn Bn, 156th AT Bn, 156th Engr Bn,
156th Sig Bn
Auxiliary unit number: 156
Home station: Dresden (Wkr. IV)

Formed on mobilization from reservists. Personnel Saxon. Took part in the Polish campaign. Fought against the British in Belgium. Identified on the central sector of the Russian front in November 1941, where it has since remained. Took part in the Kursk offensive in summer 1943 and appears to have suffered very heavy casualties.

RESTRICTED

57th Infantry Division

Commander:
Composition: 179th Gren Regt, 199th Gren Regt, 217th Gren Regt, 157th Arty Regt, 157th Rcn Bn, 157th AT Bn, 157th Engr Bn, 157th Sig Bn
Auxiliary unit number: 157
Home station: Bad Reichenhall (Wkr. VII)

Formed in the summer of 1939 from reservists. Operated in Poland and in France. Continuously engaged in Russia on the southern sector from the outset and has suffered appreciable losses.

58th Infantry Division

Commander:
Composition: 154th Gren Regt, 209th Gren Regt, 220th Gren Regt, 158th Arty Regt, 158th Rcn Bn, 158th AT Bn, 158th Engr Bn, 158th Sig Bn
Auxiliary unit number: 158
Home station: Rendsburg ? (Wkr. X)

Formed in the summer of 1939 from reservists. On the Saar front in April 1940. Identified on the northern sector of the Russian front in December 1941, but did not see much action. Transferred to the central sector in the autumn of 1943.

60th Infantry Division—See 60th Mtz Div

RESTRICTED

61st Infantry Division

Commander: Genlt. Günther KRAPPE (51)
Composition: 151st Gren Regt, 162d Gren Regt, 176th Gren Regt, 161st Arty Regt, 161st Rcn Bn, 161st AT Bn, 161st Engr Bn, 161st Sig Bn
Auxiliary unit number: 161
Home station: Königsberg (Wkr. I)

Formed in the summer of 1939 from reservists. Fought in Belgium. Identified on the northern sector of the Russian front but has not seen much action.

62d Infantry Division

Commander:
Composition: 164th Gren Regt, 183d Gren Regt, 190th Gren Regt, 162d Arty Regt, 162d Rcn Bn, 162d AT Bn, 162d Engr Bn, 162d Sig Bn
Auxiliary unit number: 162
Home station: Glatz (Wkr. VIII)

Formed in the summer of 1939 from reservists. Fought in Poland and Flanders. Identified on the southern Russian front and suffered heavy casualties on the withdrawal from Stalingrad. Has since been constantly engaged on the southern sector.

65th Infantry Division

Commander: Genlt. Dr. phil. Georg PFEIFFER (54)
Composition: 145th Gren Regt, 146th Gren Regt, 165th Arty Regt, 165th Mobile Bn, 165th Engr Bn, 165th Sig Bn
Auxiliary unit number: 165
Home station: (Wkr. XII)

Formed in the summer of 1942. First identified in the Flushing area in Holland late in 1942. Remained there until

RESTRICTED

August 1943, when it was transferred to northern Italy. In October 1943 it was moved to southern Italy and was identified in the front lines in November 1943. Contains only two infantry regiments.

68th Infantry Division

Commander: Obst. Paul SCHEUERPFLUG (48)
Composition: 169th Gren Regt, 188th Gren Regt, 196th Gren Regt, 168th Arty Regt, 168th Rcn Bn, 168th AT Bn, 168th Engr Bn, 168th Sig Bn
Auxiliary unit number: 168
Home station: Guben (Wkr. III)

Formed in the summer of 1939 from reservists. Took part in the operations in France. Engaged on the southern sector of the Russian front from the outset. Suffered heavy losses in the autumn of 1943 during the retreat from Kiev.

69th Infantry Division

Commander: Genlt. Bruno ORTNER
Composition: 159th Gren Regt, 193d Gren Regt, 236th Gren Regt, 169th Arty Regt, 169th Mobile Bn, 169th Engr Bn, 169th Sig Bn
Auxiliary unit number: 169
Home station: Soest (Wkr. VI)

Formed in the summer of 1939 from reservists. Fought in Norway where it remained on occupational and defense duties until early in 1943, when it was transferred to the central sector of the Russian front. Sent to the northern sector of the Russian front in the spring of 1943. It does not appear to have seen much fighting. Gren. Regt. 193 was known to have

RESTRICTED

ORDER OF BATTLE OF THE GERMAN ARMY 191

been detached for employment in northern Finland while the division was in Norway.

71st Infantry Division

Commander: Genmaj. RAAPKE (46)
Composition: 191st Gren Regt, 194th Gren Regt, 211th Gren. Regt, 171st Arty Regt, 171st Rcn Bn, 171st AT Bn, 171st Engr Bn, 171st Sig Bn
Auxiliary unit number: 171
Home station: Hildesheim (Wkr. XI)

Formed in the summer of 1939 from reservists. Took part in the French campaign. Fought in Russia on the southern sector for the first four months of the campaign, then returned to France, and left again for the eastern front in April 1942. Virtually destroyed at Stalingrad. Reformed in Denmark in April 1943 and transferred to the Istria-Slovenia area in August 1943.

72d Infantry Division

Commander: Obst. Dr. HOHN
Composition: 105th Gren Regt, 124th Gren Regt, 266th Gren Regt, 172d Arty Regt, 172d Rcn Bn, 172d AT Bn, 172d Engr Bn, 172d Sig Bn
Auxiliary unit number: 172
Home station: Trier (Wkr. XII)

Formed in the summer of 1939 in Wkr. IX and XII, incorporating two active infantry regiments and one reserve. Originally known as "Grenzkommando Trier" (Trier Frontier Command). Took part in the French and Balkan campaigns. Continuously engaged on the southern sector of the Russian

RESTRICTED

front and in the Crimea until the autumn of 1942 when it was transferred to the central sector. Took part in the Kursk offensive in the summer of 1943 and was later transferred to the southern sector, where it has seen action in the Dnieper bend.

73d Infantry Division

Commander: Genlt. Rudolf v. BÜNAU (54)
Composition: 170th Gren Regt, 186th Gren Regt, 213th Gren Regt, 173d Arty Regt, 173d Rcn Bn, 173d AT Bn, 173d Engr Bn, 173d Sig Bn
Auxiliary unit number: 173
Home station: Würzburg (Wkr. XIII)

Formed in the summer of 1939 from reservists. Took part in the Polish, French, and Balkan campaigns. Continuously engaged in Russia on the southern sector, especially in the Crimea and in the Caucasus. Withdrew to the Kuban in the winter of 1942-1943 and was evacuated to the lower Dnieper area in the autumn of 1943.

75th Infantry Division

Commander: Genlt. Erich DIESTEL
Composition: 172d Gren Regt, 202d Gren Regt, 222d Gren Regt, 175th Arty Regt, 175th Rcn Bn, 175th AT Bn, 175th Engr Bn, 175th Sig Bn
Auxiliary unit number: 175
Home station: Neustrelitz (Wkr. II)

Formed in the summer of 1939 from reservists. Took part

RESTRICTED

in the French campaign. Continuously engaged on the southern sector of the Russian front. Sustained heavy losses in the retreat from Kiev in the autumn of 1943.

76th Infantry Division

Commander: Genmaj. Erich ABRAHAM (49)
Composition: 178th Gren Regt, 203d Gren Regt, 230th Füsilier Regt, 176th Arty Regt, 176th Rcn Bn, 176th AT Bn, 176th Engr Bn, 176th Sig Bn
Auxiliary unit number: 176
Home station: Berlin (Wkr. III)

Formed in the summer of 1939 from reservists. Took part in the French campaign. Engaged on the southern sector of the Russian front from the outset. Virtually destroyed at Stalingrad. Reformed in Brittany in the spring of 1943 and was sent to northern Italy in the following summer. In the autumn of 1943 it was transferred to the southern sector of the Russian front and has seen action in the Dnieper bend.

78th Infantry Division

Commander:
Composition: 14th Gren Regt, 195th Gren Regt, 215th Gren Regt, 178th Arty Regt, 178th Mobile Bn, 178th Engr Bn, 178th Sig Bn
Auxiliary unit number: 178
Home station: Ulm (Wkr. V)

Formed in the summer of 1939 from reservists. Took part in the French campaign. Continuously engaged from the outset on the central sector of the Russian front. Took part in

RESTRICTED

the Kursk offensive in the summer of 1943; subsequently identified west of Smolensk. It is usually referred to as an assault (*Sturm*) division.

79th Infantry Division

Commander: Genlt. SCHERBENING (53)
Composition: 208th Gren Regt, 212th Gren Regt, 226th Gren Regt, 179th Arty Regt, 179th Rcn Bn, 179th AT Bn, 179th Engr Bn, 179th Sig Bn
Auxiliary unit number: 179
Home station: Koblenz (Wkr. XII)

Formed in the summer of 1939 from reservists. Took part in the French campaign. Identified on the southern sector of the Russian front. Virtually destroyed at Stalingrad. Reformed on the southern sector of the Russian front in the spring of 1943 and was identified in action in the Kuban in the early summer. In the autumn of 1943 it was transferred to the lower Dnieper area.

81st Infantry Division

Commander:
Composition: 161st Gren Regt, 174th Gren Regt, 189th Gren Regt, 181st Arty Regt, 181st Rcn Bn, 181st AT Bn, 181st Engr Bn, 181st Sig Bn
Auxiliary unit number: 181
Home station: (Wkr. VIII)

Formed in the summer of 1939 from reservists. Took part in the French campaign. Apparently arrived on the northern sector of the Russian front from France in January 1942. Transferred to the central sector in the late autumn of 1943.

RESTRICTED

ORDER OF BATTLE OF THE GERMAN ARMY

82d Infantry Division

Commander:
Composition: 158th Gren Regt, 166th Gren Regt, 168th Gren Regt, 182d Arty Regt, 182d Mobile Bn, 182d Engr Bn, 182d Sig Bn
Auxiliary unit number: 182
Home station: Frankfurt/Main(?) (Wkr. IX)

Formed in the summer of 1939 from reservists. Not identified during the French campaign. In Holland late in 1941 but left for Russia in May 1942, where it has since operated on the southern sector. Apparently transferred to the central sector in the summer of 1943, where it took part in the Kursk offensive, and returned to the southern sector in the autumn. Suffered severe losses in the retreat from Kiev in November 1943.

83d Infantry Division

Commander: Genlt. Theodor SCHERER (55)
Composition: 251st Gren Regt, 257th Gren Regt, 277th Gren Regt, 183d Arty Regt, 183d Mobile Bn, 183d Engr Bn, 183d Sig Bn
Auxiliary unit number: 183
Home station: Hamburg (Wkr. X)

Formed in the summer of 1939 from reservists. Took part in the Polish and French campaigns. Left France for Russia early in 1942. Has been operating near the boundary between the northern and central sectors and is now located in the northern sector.

RESTRICTED

86th Infantry Division

Commander: Genlt. Helmuth WEIDLING (52)
Composition: 167th Gren Regt, 184th Gren Regt, 216th Gren Regt, 186th Arty Regt, 186th Rcn Bn, 186th AT Bn, 186th Engr Bn, 186th Sig Bn
Auxiliary unit number: 186
Home station: (Wkr. VI)

Formed in the summer of 1939. Took part in the French campaign. Continuously engaged on the central sector of the Russian front from the outset. Took part in the Kursk offensive in the summer of 1943.

87th Infantry Division

Commander:
Composition: 173d Gren Regt, 185th Gren Regt, 187th Gren Regt, 187th Arty Regt, 187th Mobile Bn, 187th Engr Bn, 187th Sig Bn
Auxiliary unit number: 187
Home station: (Wkr. IV)

Formed in Wehrkreis IV and Wehrkreis IX from reservists in the summer of 1939. First in action during the French campaign. Continuously engaged on the central sector of the Russian front from the outset. Saw action in the Nevel area in the late autumn of 1943.

RESTRICTED

ORDER OF BATTLE OF THE GERMAN ARMY 197

88th Infantry Division

Commander: Genlt. Friedrich GOLLWITZER (55)
Composition: 245th Gren Regt, 246th Gren Regt, 248th Gren Regt, 188th Arty Regt, 188th Mobile Bn, 188th Engr Bn, 188th Sig Bn
Auxiliary unit number: 188
Home station: (Wkr. VII)

Formed in the summer of 1939 from reservists. Took part in the French campaign. Left France for Russia early in 1942 and has fought on the southern sector. Apparently suffered heavy losses in the retreat from Kiev in the autumn of 1943.

93d Infantry Division

Commander: Genlt. Otto TIEMANN (56)
Composition: 270th Gren Regt, 272d Gren Regt, 193d Arty Regt, 193d Rcn Bn, 193d AT Bn, 193d Engr Bn, 193d Sig Bn
Auxiliary unit number: 193
Home station: Berlin (Wkr. III)

Formed in September 1939 from reservists. On the Saar front for several months. On the northern sector of the Russian front from the outset. In the summer of 1943 it was transferred to Poland, where Infantry Regiment 271 (Feldherrnhalle) was withdrawn and became part of the new 60th Motorized Division then reforming in France. The division later returned to the northern sector of the Russian front.

94th Infantry Division

Commander: Genlt. STEINMETZ
Composition: 267th Gren Regt, 274th Gren Regt, 276th Gren Regt, 194th Arty Regt, 194th Mobile Bn, 194th Engr Bn, 194th Sig Bn
Auxiliary unit number: 194
Home station: (Wkr. IV)

Formed in September 1939 from reservists. Took part in

RESTRICTED

the French campaign. Engaged on the southern sector of the Russian front. Virtually destroyed at Stalingrad. Believed to have reformed in Brittany, where it was identified in July 1943. Transferred to northern Italy in August 1943 and reported in action in southern Italy in October 1943.

95th Infantry Division

Commander:
Composition: 278th Gren Regt, 279th Gren Regt, 280th Gren Regt, 195th Arty Regt, 195th Rcn Bn, 195th AT Bn, 195th Engr Bn, Sig Bn
Auxiliary unit number: 195
Home station: (Wkr. IX)

Formed in September 1939 from reservists. Identified on the Saar front. Continuously engaged on the southern sector of the Russian front; transferred to the central sector late in 1942. Suffered heavy losses at Bryansk in the late summer of 1943 and is still engaged on the central sector.

96th Infantry Division

Commander:
Composition: 283d Gren Regt, 284th Gren Regt, 287th Gren Regt, 196th Arty Regt, 196th Mobile Bn, 196th Engr Bn, 196th Sig Bn
Auxiliary unit number: 196
Home station: (Wkr. XI)

Formed in September 1939 mainly from reservists. Took part in the French campaign. Engaged on the northern sector of the Russian front.

RESTRICTED

ORDER OF BATTLE OF THE GERMAN ARMY

98th Infantry Division

Commander: Genlt. Martin GAREIS (53)
Composition: 282d Gren Regt, 289th Gren Regt, 290th Gren Regt, 198th Arty Regt, 198th Mobile Bn, 198th Engr Bn, 198th Sig Bn
Auxiliary unit number: 198
Home station: (Wkr. XIII)

Formed in September 1939 mainly from reservists. Took part in the French campaign. Identified on the central sector of the Russian front in November 1941. Transferred to the Kuban in the summer of 1943 and later took part in the defense of the Crimea.

102d Infantry Division

Commander: Obst. von BERCKEN
Composition: 84th Gren Regt, 232d Gren Regt, 233d Gren Regt, 104th Arty Regt, 102d Rcn Bn, 102d AT Bn, 102d Engr Bn, 102d Sig Bn
Auxiliary unit number: 102
Home station: (Wkr. VIII)

Formed in December 1940. First identified in action on the central sector of the Russian front in August 1941. Constantly engaged until February 1942, when it may have been withdrawn to Germany to rest. Returned to the central sector in mid-April 1942. Took part in the Kursk offensive in the summer of 1943. Still engaged on the central sector.

RESTRICTED

106th Infantry Division

Commander: Genlt. Werner FORST (52)
Composition: 239th Gren Regt, 240th Gren Regt, 241st Gren Regt, 107th Arty Regt, 106th Rcn Bn, 106th AT Bn, 106th Engr Bn, 106th Sig Bn
Auxiliary unit number: 106
Home station: (Wkr. VI)

Formed in December 1940. First identified in action on the central Russian front in August 1941. Fought in that sector throughout the winter, sustaining heavy casualties, particularly in the latter half of January 1942. Subsequently returned to France for rest and refit. Transferred back to Russia in the spring of 1943 where it was heavily engaged at the Dnieper bend in the autumn.

110th Infantry Division

Commander: Genlt. SEYFFARDT (50)
Composition: 252d Gren Regt, 254th Gren Regt, 255th Gren Regt, 120th Arty Regt, 110th Rcn Bn, 110th AT Bn, 110th Engr Bn, 110th Sig Bn
Auxiliary unit number: 110
Home station: Oldenburg (Wkr. X)

Formed in December 1940. First identified in action on the Russian front in August 1941, where it has been heavily engaged in the central sector. Sustained heavy losses at Bryansk in the summer of 1943.

RESTRICTED

111th Infantry Division

Commander: Genlt. Hermann RECKNAGEL (52)
Composition: 50th Gren Regt, 70th Gren Regt, 117th Gren Regt, 117th? Arty Regt, 117th? Rcn Bn, 111th AT Bn, 111th Engr Bn, 111th Sig Bn
Auxiliary unit number: 111
Home station: (Wkr. XI)

Formed in December 1940. Has been in action in Russia on the southern sector, where it took part in the fighting for Mozdok. Withdrew to the Kuban in the winter of 1942-1943 and was transferred to the Mius front in the following summer, sustaining heavy losses at Taganrog. Later took part in the defense of the lower Dnieper.

112th Infantry Division

Commander:
Composition: 110th Gren Regt, 256th Gren Regt, 258th Gren Regt, 86th Arty Regt, 120th Rcn Bn, 112th AT Bn, 112th Engr Bn, 112th Sig Bn
Auxiliary unit number: 112
Home station: Darmstadt (Wkr. XII)

Formed in December 1940. Engaged on the Russian front, central sector, since August 1941. Took part in the Kursk offensive in the summer of 1943, sustaining heavy losses. Later transferred to the southern sector.

RESTRICTED

113th Infantry Division

Commander:
Composition: 260th Gren Regt, 261st Gren Regt, 268th Gren Regt, 87th Arty Regt, 113th Rcn Bn, 113th AT Bn, 113th Engr Bn, 113th Sig Bn
Auxiliary unit number: 113
Home station: (Wkr. XIII)

Formed in December 1940. In the Balkans on occupational duties during November and December 1941. Later transferred to the southern sector of the Russian front, where it was virtually destroyed at Stalingrad. It was reformed in Brittany in the spring of 1943 and returned to the central sector in Russia in the summer of 1943.

121st Infantry Division

Commander:
Composition: 405th Gren Regt 407th Gren Regt, 408th Gren Regt, 121st Arty Regt, 121st Rcn Bn, 121st AT Bn, 121st Engr Bn, 121st Sig Bn
Auxiliary unit number: 121
Home station: (Wkr. X)

Formed in October 1940. In action on the northern Russian front from the outset. Appears to include many non-Germans.

122d Infantry Division

Commander: Genlt. Kurt CHILL (49)
Composition: 409th Gren Regt, 411th Gren Regt, 414th(?) Gren Regt, 122d Arty Regt, 122d Rcn Bn, 122d AT Bn, 122d Engr Bn, 122d Sig Bn
Auxiliary unit number: 122
Home station: (Wkr. II)

Formed in October 1940. In action on the northern Russian

RESTRICTED

front from the outset. Transferred to the central sector in the autumn of 1943. In action at Nevel in the late autumn of 1943.

123d Infantry Division

Commander: Genlt. Erwin RAUCH (55)
Composition: 415th Gren Regt, 416th Gren Regt, 418th Gren Regt, 123d Arty Regt, 123d Rcn Bn, 123d AT Bn, 123d Engr Bn, 123d Sig Bn
Auxiliary unit number: 123
Home station: (Wkr. III)

Formed in October 1940. In action on the northern sector of the Russian front, where it appears to have been heavily engaged. Transferred to the southern sector in the autumn of 1943, where it was heavily engaged in the Zaporozhe area.

125th Infantry Division

Commander:
Composition: 419th Gren Regt, 420th Gren Regt, 421st Gren Regt, 125th Arty Regt, 125th Rcn Bn, 125th AT Bn, 125th Engr Bn, 125th Sig Bn
Auxiliary unit number: 125
Home station: (Wkr. V)

Formed in October 1940. Continuously engaged on the southern sector of the Russian front, especially in the Crimea and in the Caucasus. Withdrew to the Kuban in the winter of 1942-1943. Evacuated to the Dnieper bend area in the autumn of 1943.

RESTRICTED

126th Infantry Division

Commander: Genlt. Arthur HOPPE (49)
Composition: 422d Gren Regt, 424th Gren Regt, 426th Gren Regt, 126th Arty Regt, 126th Rcn Bn, 126th AT Bn, 126th Engr Bn, 126th Sig Bn
Auxiliary unit number: 126
Home station: (Wkr. VI)

Formed in October 1940. In action on the northern sector of the Russian front from the outset, where it appears to have been fairly continuously engaged.

129th Infantry Division

Commander: Genlt. Albert PRAUN (50)
Composition: 427th Gren Regt, 428th Gren Regt, 430th Gren Regt, 129th Arty Regt, 129th Rcn Bn, 129th AT Bn, 129th Engr Bn, 129th Sig Bn
Auxiliary unit number: 129
Home station: Fulda (Wkr. IX)

Formed in October 1940. Continuously engaged on the central sector of the Russian front from the outset. Heavily engaged at Nevel in the late autumn of 1943.

131st Infantry Division

Commander: Genlt. Heinrich MEYER-BUERDORF (56)
Composition: 431st Gren Regt, 432d Gren Regt, 434th Gren Regt, 131st Arty Regt, 131st Rcn Bn, 131st AT Bn, 131st Engr Bn, 131st Sig Bn
Auxiliary unit number: 131
Home station: (Wkr. XI)

RESTRICTED

ORDER OF BATTLE OF THE GERMAN ARMY

Formed in October 1940. Appeared on the central sector of the Russian front in August 1941 and took part in the Moscow offensive in November 1941. Transferred to the southern sector in the late summer of 1943 and subsequently back to the central sector.

132d Infantry Division

Commander:
Composition: 436th Gren Regt, 437th Gren Regt, 438th Gren Regt, 132d Arty Regt, 132d Mobile Bn, 132d Engr Bn, 132d Sig Bn
Auxiliary unit number: 132
Home station: (Wkr. XII)

Formed in Wehrkreis VII in October 1940. Subsequently transferred to Wehrkreis XII. Engaged on the southern sector of the Russian front and in the Crimea from July 1941, where it sustained heavy losses. Transferred in the autumn of 1942 to the northern sector, where it has remained.

134th Infantry Division

Commander: Genlt. Dipl. Ing. Hans SCHLEMMER (51)
Composition: 439th Gren Regt, 445th Gren Regt, 446th Gren Regt, 134th Arty Regt, 134th Rcn Bn, 134th AT Bn, 134th Engr Bn, 134th Sig Bn
Auxiliary unit number: 134
Home station: (Wkr. IV)

Formed in Wehrkreis XIII in October 1940. Subsequently transferred to Wehrkreis IV. Continuously and heavily en-

RESTRICTED

gaged on the central sector of the Russian front from the outset. Heavily engaged at Bryansk in the summer of 1943 and later in the defense of Gomel.

137th Infantry Division

Commander:
Composition: 447th Gren Regt, 448th Gren Regt, 449th Gren Regt, 137th Arty Regt, 137th Rcn Bn, 137th AT Bn, 137th Engr Bn, 137th Sig Bn
Auxiliary unit number: 137
Home station: (Wkr. XVII)

Formed in October 1940. Identified on the central sector of the Russian front in August 1941, where it appears to have been fairly heavily engaged. Took part in the Kursk offensive in the summer of 1943.

161st Infantry Division

Commander: Genlt. Heinrich RECKE (54)
Composition: 336th Gren Regt, 364th Gren Regt, 371st Gren Regt, 241st Arty Regt, 241st Mobile Bn, 241st Engr Bn, 241st Sig Bn
Auxiliary unit number: 241
Home station: (Wkr. I)

Formed in January 1940 from Ersatz units. Continuously engaged on the central sector of the Russian front, where it suffered heavy losses. May have been withdrawn from Russia for rest and refit during the winter of 1942-1943. Again identified on the southern sector of the Russian front in the spring of 1943; in the autumn it was heavily engaged at Dnepropetrovsk.

RESTRICTED

162d Infantry Division

Commander: Genmaj. Prof. Dr. Oskar Ritter v. NIEDERMAYER (59)
Composition: 303d Gren Regt, 314th Gren Regt, 329th? Gren Regt, 236th Arty Regt, Rcn Bn, 236th AT Bn, 236th Engr Bn, 236th Sig Bn
Auxiliary unit number: 236
Home station: Rostock (Wkr. II)

Formed in January 1940 from Ersatz units. Continuously engaged on the central sector of the Russian front from the outset until the late summer 1942, when it was transferred to the southern sector. Transferred to Slovenia in the summer of 1943, where it has remained. Known to contain a number of Turanian battalions.

163d Infantry Division

Commander: Genmaj. Karl RÜBEL (49)
Composition: 307th Gren Regt, 310th Gren Regt, 324th Gren Regt, 234th Arty Regt, 234th Mobile Bn, 234th Engr Bn, 234th Sig Bn
Auxiliary unit number: 234
Home station: Berlin (Wkr. III)

Formed in January 1940 from Ersatz units. Fought in the Gudbransdal during the Norwegian campaign. Transferred to Finland at the beginning of the Russian campaign, where it took an active part in the fighting in 1942. Has remained in Finland ever since.

RESTRICTED

164th Infantry Division—See 164th Mtz Div

167th Infantry Division

Commander: Genlt. Wolf TRIERENBERG (53)
Composition: 315th Gren Regt, 331st Gren Regt, 339th Gren Regt, 238th Arty Regt, 238th Rcn Bn, 238th AT Bn, 238th Engr Bn, Sig Bn
Auxiliary unit number: 238
Home station: (Wkr. VII)

Formed in January 1940 from Ersatz units. First in action during the French campaign. Continuously engaged on the central sector of the Russian front from the outset. Transferred to Holland in the summer of 1942. Returned to the southern sector of the Russian front early in 1943. Took part in the Belgorod offensive in the summer of 1943, sustaining heavy losses.

168th Infantry Division

Commander:
Composition: 417th Gren Regt, 429th Gren Regt, 442d Gren Regt, 248th Arty Regt, 248th Rcn Bn, 248th AT Bn, 248th Engr Bn, 248th Sig Bn
Auxiliary unit number: 248
Home station: (Wkr. VIII)

Formed in January 1940 from Ersatz units. Identified on the southern sector of the Russian front in July 1941, where it has been continuously engaged. Took part in the Belgorod offensive in the summer of 1943, where it suffered heavy losses. Subsequently in action west of Kiev.

RESTRICTED

ORDER OF BATTLE OF THE GERMAN ARMY 209

169th Infantry Division

Commander: Genmaj. RADZIEJ
Composition: 378th Gren Regt, 379th Gren Regt, 392d Gren Regt, 230th
 Arty Regt, Rcn Bn, 230th AT Bn, 230th Engr Bn,
 230th Sig Bn
Auxiliary unit number: 230
Home station: (Wkr. IX)

Formed in January 1940 from Ersatz units. First in action during the French campaign. Apparently arrived in Finland from Norway during the early stages of the Russian campaign and was in action on the Kandalaksha front in 1942. Has remained in Finland ever since.

170th Infantry Division

Commander: Genlt. Erwin SANDER (52)
Composition: 391st Gren Regt, 399th Gren Regt, 401st Gren Regt, 240th
 Arty Regt, 240th Rcn Bn, 240th AT Bn, 240th Engr Bn,
 240th Sig Bn
Auxiliary unit number: 240
Home station: Bremen (Wkr. X)

Formed in January 1940 from Ersatz units. Fairly continuously engaged on the southern sector of the Russian front and in the Crimea from the outset. Transferred to the northern sector in the late summer of 1942, where it has since remained.

RESTRICTED

181st Infantry Division

Commander: Genlt. BAYER (57)
Composition: 334th Füsilier Regt, 349th Gren Regt, 359th Gren Regt, 222d Arty Regt, 222d Rcn Bn, 222d AT Bn, 222d Engr Bn, 222d Sig Bn
Auxiliary unit number: 222
Home station: (Wkr. XI)

Formed in January 1940 from Ersatz units. Employed in Norway (Dombaas area) from April 1940 until October 1943, when elements of it were reported on the Russian front, while the main body of the division appears to have been transferred to Yugoslavia.

183d Infantry Division

Commander: Genlt. DETTLING (53)
Composition: 330th Gren Regt, 343d Gren Regt, 351st Gren Regt, 219th Arty Regt, 219th Rcn Bn, 219th AT Bn, 219th Engr Bn, 219th Sig Bn
Auxiliary unit number: 219
Home station: (Wkr. XIII)

Formed in January 1940 from Ersatz units. Identified on the central sector of the Russian front late in 1941, where it was fairly constantly in action. Transferred to the southern sector in the autumn of 1943 and suffered heavy losses in the fighting in the Kiev area.

RESTRICTED

196th Infantry Division

Commander: Genlt. Dr. Friedrich FRANEK (53)
Composition: 340th Gren Regt, 345th Gren Regt, 362d Gren Regt, 233d Arty Regt, 233d Rcn Bn, 233d AT Bn, 233d Engr Bn, 233d Sig Bn
Auxiliary unit number: 233
Home station: Bielefeld ? (Wkr. VI)

Formed early in 1940 from Ersatz units. Participated in the Norwegian campaign and has remained as a garrison division in central Norway.

197th Infantry Division

Commander: Genlt. Ehrenfried BOEGE (50)
Composition: 321st Gren Regt, 332d Gren Regt, 347th Gren Regt, 229th Arty Regt, 229th Rcn Bn, 229th AT Bn, 229th Engr Bn, 229th Sig Bn
Auxiliary unit number: 229
Home station: Speyer (Wkr. XII)

Formed early in 1940 from Ersatz units. Identified on the central sector of the Russian front in August 1941, where it has since remained. West of Smolensk in the autumn of 1943.

198th Infantry Division

Commander:
Composition: 305th Gren Regt, 308th Gren Regt, 326th Gren Regt, 235th Arty Regt, 235th Rcn Bn, 235th AT Bn, 235th Engr Bn, 235th Sig Bn
Auxiliary unit number: 235
Home station: (Wkr. V)

Formed early in 1940 from Ersatz units. Has been in Russia continuously from the outset. Took part in operations in the Crimea and in the Caucasus. Still in action in the southern sector.

RESTRICTED

199th Infantry Division

Commander:
Composition: 341st Gren Regt, 357th Gren Regt, 410th Gren Regt, 199th Arty Regt, 199th Mobile Bn, 199th Engr Bn, 199th Sig Bn
Auxiliary unit number: 199
Home station: Düsseldorf (Wkr. VI)

Formed late in 1939. In southern Norway from the end of 1940 until the middle of May 1941, when it was moved to northern Norway. In the Narvik area since December 1941.

205th Infantry Division

Commander:
Composition: 335th Gren Regt, 353d Gren Regt, 358th Gren Regt, 205th Arty Regt, 205th Mobile Bn, 205th Engr Bn, 205th Sig Bn
Auxiliary unit number: 205
Home station: (Wkr. V)

Formed in the summer of 1939 with a high proportion of Landwehr personnel (later largely replaced by younger men). Identified in France in August 1941 and transferred to the central sector in Russia early in 1942. Moved to the northern sector in the autumn of 1943.

206th Infantry Division

Commander: Genlt. Alfons HITTER
Composition: 301st Gren Regt, 312th Gren Regt, 413th Gren Regt, 206th Arty Regt, 206th Mobile Bn, 206th Engr Bn, 206th Sig Bn
Auxiliary unit number: 206
Home station: Gumbinnen (Wkr. I)

RESTRICTED

ORDER OF BATTLE OF THE GERMAN ARMY 213

Formed in the summer of 1939 with a high proportion of Landwehr personnel (later largely replaced by younger men). Engaged on the central sector of the Russian front from the outset and in the Smolensk sector in the autumn of 1943.

207th Infantry Division—See 207th Sicherungs Division

208th Infantry Division

Commander: Genmaj. Karl Wilhelm von SCHLIEBEN (50)
Composition: 309th Gren Regt, 337th Gren Regt, 338th Gren Regt, 208th Arty Regt, 208th Mobile Bn, 208th Engr Bn, 208th Sig Bn
Auxiliary unit number: 208
Home station: Cottbus (Wkr. III)

Formed in the summer of 1939 with a high proportion of Landwehr personnel (later largely replaced by younger men). Identified in France in April 1941. Engaged on the central sector of the Russian front since January 1942. Took part in the Kursk offensive in the summer of 1943 and sustained very heavy losses. Transferred to the southern sector in the following autumn.

209th Infantry Division

Landwehr division formed in the summer of 1939. Disbanded after the French campaign in the summer of 1940.

RESTRICTED

210th Infantry Division

Commander: Genlt. Karl WINTERGERST (52)
Composition:
Auxiliary unit number:
Home station:

Identified in northern Finland late in 1942. Probably a coast defense division consisting of a divisional staff controlling fortress battalions and coastal batteries.

211th Infantry Division

Commander:
Composition: 306th Gren Regt, 317th Gren Regt, 365th Gren Regt, 211th Arty Regt, 211th Rcn Bn, 211th AT Bn, 211th Engr Bn, 211th Sig Bn
Auxiliary unit number: 211
Home station: Köln (Wkr. VI)

Formed in the summer of 1939 with a high proportion of Landwehr personnel (later largely replaced by younger men). In southwestern France during most of 1941. Transferred to Russia at the beginning of 1942, where it has been continuously engaged on the central sector. Took part in the Kursk offensive in the summer of 1943, where it sustained very heavy losses. Subsequently heavily engaged at Nevel.

RESTRICTED

212th Infantry Division

Commander:
Composition: 316th Gren Regt, 320th Gren Regt, 423d Gren Regt, 212th Arty Regt, 212th Mobile Bn, 212th Engr Bn, 212th Sig Bn
Auxiliary unit number: 212
Home station: München (Wkr. VII)

Formed in the summer of 1939 with a high proportion of Landwehr personnel (later largely replaced by younger men). On the Saar front for a time, later in France. Left France for Russia late in 1941, where it was identified on the central sector and subsequently on the northern sector.

213th Infantry Division—See 213th Sicherungs Division

214th Infantry Division

Commander: Genlt. Max HORN (56)
Composition: 355th Gren Regt, 367th Gren Regt, 214th Arty Regt, 214th Mobile Bn, 214th Engr Bn, 214th Sig Bn
Auxiliary unit number: 214
Homestation: Hanau (Wkr. IX)

Formed in the summer of 1939 with a high proportion of Landwehr personnel (later largely replaced by younger men). On the Saar front until December 1939. In southern Norway from May 1940. Since December 1941, the 388th Regiment has been detached for service in northern Finland.

215th Infantry Division

Commander: Genlt. FRANKEWITZ
Composition: 380th Gren Regt, 390th Gren Regt, 435th Gren Regt, 215th Arty Regt, 215th Rcn Bn, 215th AT Bn, 215th Engr Bn, 215th Sig Bn
Auxiliary unit numbers: 215
Home station: Heilbronn (Wkr. V)

Formed in the summer of 1939 with a high proportion of Landwehr personnel (later largely replaced by younger men).

RESTRICTED

On the Saar front in May 1940. In central France during the summer of 1941, but left for Russia late in that year. Identified in the northern sector.

216th Infantry Division

Commander: Genlt. GIMMLER (54)
Composition: 348th Gren Regt, 396th Gren Regt, 398th Gren Regt, 216th Arty Regt, 216th Rcn Bn, 216th AT Bn, 216th Engr Bn, 216th Sig Bn
Auxiliary unit number: 216
Home station: Hameln (?) (Wkr. XI)

Formed in the summer of 1939 with a high proportion of Landwehr personnel (later largely replaced by younger men). Fought in Holland and Belgium. Apparently arrived on the central sector of the Russian front from France early in January 1942. Took part in the Kursk offensive in the summer of 1943.

217th Infantry Division

Commander: Genlt. POPPE (51)
Composition: 311th Gren Regt, 346th Gren Regt, 389th Gren Regt, 217th Arty Regt, 217th Rcn Bn, 217th AT Bn, 217th Engr Bn, 217th Sig Bn
Auxiliary unit number: 217
Home station: Allenstein (Wkr. I)

Formed in the summer of 1939 with a high proportion of Landwehr personnel (later largely replaced by younger men). Fought in Poland and Flanders. Identified on the northern

RESTRICTED

sector of the Russian front in July 1941, where it was subsequently employed on coastal defense duties. Transferred to the southern sector in the autumn of 1943, where it fought in the Kiev area and suffered heavy losses.

218th Infantry Division

Commander:
Composition: 323d Gren Regt, 386th Gren Regt, 397th Gren Regt, 218th Arty Regt, 218th Mobile Bn, 218th Engr Bn, 218th Sig Bn
Auxiliary unit number: 218
Home station: Spandau (Wkr. III)

Formed in the summer of 1939 with a high proportion of Landwehr personnel (later largely replaced by younger men). Heavily engaged in Poland and France. In Denmark from May 1941 until January 1942, when it left for the eastern front. Has since fought on the northern sector.

221st Infantry Division—See 221st Sicherungs Division

223d Infantry Division

Commander:
Composition: 344th Gren Regt, 385th Gren Regt, 425th Gren Regt, 223d Arty Regt, 223d Mobile Bn, 233d Engr Bn, 233d Sig Bn
Auxiliary unit number: 223
Home station: Dresden (Wkr. IV)

Formed in the summer of 1939 with a high proportion of Landwehr personnel (later largely replaced by younger men). Identified in southwestern France in May 1941, where it remained until transferred to Russia at the end of the year.

RESTRICTED

Subsequently fought on the northern sector. Transferred to the southern sector in the summer of 1943, where it has been heavily engaged.

225th Infantry Division

Commander:
Composition: 333d Gren Regt, 376th Gren Regt, 377th Gren Regt, 225th Arty Regt, 225th Mobile Bn, 225th Engr Bn, 225th Sig Bn
Auxiliary unit number: 225
Home station: Hamburg (Wkr. X)

Formed in the summer of 1939 with a high proportion of Landwehr personnel (later largely replaced by younger men). Arrived on the northern sector of the Russian front from France in January 1942, and has since remained there.

227th Infantry Division

Commander:
Composition: 328th Gren Regt, 366th Gren Regt, 412th Gren Regt, 227th Arty Regt, 227th Rcn Bn, 227th AT Bn, 227th Engr Bn, 227th Sig Bn
Auxiliary unit number: 227
Home station: Düsseldorf (Wkr. VI)

Formed in the summer of 1939 with a high proportion of Landwehr personnel (later largely replaced by younger men). Took part in operations in Belgium. In northeastern France in the latter part of 1941. Transferred to the northern sector of the Russian front in April 1942, where it has since remained.

RESTRICTED

228th Infantry Division

Landwehr division formed in the summer of 1939. Fought in northern Poland and in Holland and Belgium. Disbanded in the late summer of 1940.

230th Infantry Division

Commander: Genmaj. MENKEL
Composition:
Auxiliary unit number:
Home station:

Formed in the summer of 1942 as a coast defense division in northern Norway consisting of a divisional staff controlling fortress battalions and coastal batteries.

231st Infantry Division

Landwehr division formed in the summer of 1939. No evidence of any active operation. Disbanded in the late summer of 1940.

239th Infantry Division

Formed in the summer of 1939. In the Protectorate during the winter of 1940-1941. Engaged in the southern sector at the beginning of the Russian campaign. Disbanded late in 1941.

RESTRICTED

240th Infantry Division

Commander:
Composition:
Auxiliary unit number:
Home station:

Formed in the summer of 1942 as a coast defense division consisting of a divisional staff controlling fortress battalions and coastal batteries. Location uncertain.

242d Infantry Division

Commander:
Composition: 916th(?) Gren Regt, 917th Gren Regt, Gren Regt, 242d Arty Regt
Auxiliary unit number: 242
Home station: (Wkr. II)

Formed in Belgium in the summer of 1943. Subsequently transferred to southeastern France.

246th Infantry Division

Commander:
Composition: 352d Gren Regt, 404th Gren Regt, 689th Gren Regt, 246th Arty Regt, 246th Mobile Bn, 246th Engr Bn, 246th Sig Bn
Auxiliary unit number: 246
Home station: Trier (Wkr. XII)

Formed in the latter part of 1939. On the Saar front for a time. In southwestern France from August 1941 until January 1942, when it left for Russia. Has since operated on the central sector. Exchanged Gren Regt 313 for Gren Regt 689 of the 337th Inf Div prior to its transfer to Russia.

RESTRICTED

ORDER OF BATTLE OF THE GERMAN ARMY

250th Infantry Division (Blue Division)

Commander: General de Division Emilio ESTEBAN-INFANTES (52)
Composition: 262d Gren Regt, 263d Gren Regt, 269th Gren Regt, 250th Arty Regt,
Auxiliary unit number: 250
Home station:

Formed at Grafenwöhr (Wkr. XIII) in August 1941 from Spanish volunteers. Originally destined for the southern sector of the Russian front, but was sent to the northern sector, where it was heavily engaged. Probably disbanded in the autumn of 1943.

251st Infantry Division

Commander: Genmaj. Maximilian FELZMANN (50)
Composition: 451st Gren Regt, 459th Gren Regt, 471st Gren Regt, 251st Arty Regt, 251st Rcn Bn, 251st AT Bn, 251st Engr Bn, 251st Sig Bn
Auxiliary unit number: 251
Home station: Frankfurt/Main(?) (Wkr. IX)

Formed in the summer of 1939 from men already serving in Ergänzungs units. First identified on the central sector of the Russian front in July 1941, where it has been fairly continuously engaged. Took part in the Kursk offensive in the summer of 1943 and has since been engaged in defensive fighting. Identified in the middle Dnieper area in the autumn.

RESTRICTED

252d Infantry Division

Commander:
Composition: 452d Gren Regt, 461st Gren Regt, 472d Gren Regt, 252d Arty Regt, 252d Rcn Bn, 252d AT Bn, 252d Engr Bn, 252d Sig Bn
Auxiliary unit number: 252
Home station: Neisse (Wkr. VIII)

Formed in the summer of 1939 from men already serving in Ergänzungs units. Took part in the attack on the Maginot line. Continuously and heavily engaged on the central sector of the Russian front from the outset.

253d Infantry Division

Commander: Genlt. Fritz BECKER (52)
Composition: 453d Gren Regt, 464th Gren Regt, 473d Gren Regt, 253d Arty Regt, 253d Mobile Bn, 253d Engr Bn, 253d Sig Bn
Auxiliary unit number: 253
Home station: Aachen (Wkr. VI)

Formed in the summer of 1939 from men already serving in Ergänzungs units. Took part in the French campaign. First identified on the northern sector of the Russian front in July 1941. Subsequently transferred to the central sector.

254th Infantry Division

Commander:
Composition: 454th Gren Regt, 474th Gren Regt, 484th Gren Regt, 254th Arty Regt, 254th Rcn Bn, 254th AT Bn, 254th Engr Bn, 254th Sig Bn
Auxiliary unit number: 254
Home station: Dortmund (Wkr. VI)

Formed in the summer of 1939 from men already serving in

RESTRICTED

Ergänzungs units. Took part in operations in Holland, Belgium, and Northern France. Identified on the northern sector of the Russian front in July, where it has remained.

255th Infantry Division

Commander:
Composition: 455th Gren Regt, 465th Gren Regt, 475th Gren Regt, 255th Arty Regt, 255th Rcn Bn, 255th AT Bn, 255th Engr Bn, 255th Sig Bn
Auxiliary unit number: 255
Home Station: Löbau (Wkr. IV)

Formed in the summer of 1939 from men already serving in Ergänzungs units. Took part in the French campaign. Identified on the central sector of the Russian front in August 1941. Transferred to the southern sector in the spring of 1943, where it has been fairly continuously engaged.

256th Infantry Division

Commander: Genlt. Paul DANHAUSER (51)
Composition: 456th Gren Regt, 476th Gren Regt, 481st Gren Regt, 256th Arty Regt, 256th Mobile Bn, 256th Engr Bn, 256th(?) Sig Bn
Auxiliary unit number: 256
Home station: Meissen(?) (Wkr. IV)

Formed in Wehrkreise IV and XIII in the summer of 1939 from men already serving in Ergänzungs units. Fought in Holland and Belgium. Continuously engaged on the central sector of the Russian front from the outset. In action northwest of Smolensk in the autumn of 1943, where it suffered heavy losses.

RESTRICTED

257th Infantry Division

Commander: Genlt. PÜCHLER
Composition: 457th Gren Regt, 466th Gren Regt, 477th Gren Regt, 257th Arty Regt, 257th Rcn Bn, 257th AT Bn, 257th Engr Bn, 257th Sig Bn
Auxiliary unit number: 257
Home station: Frankfurt/Oder (Wkr. III)

Formed in the summer of 1939 from men already serving in Ergänzungs units. On the Saar front for a time. Identified on the southern sector of the Russian front in July 1941, where it was continuously and heavily engaged. Transferred to France in the autumn of 1942 for rest and refit and returned to the southern sector of the Russian front in April 1943. Heavily engaged at Dnepropetrovsk and in the Dnieper bend in the autumn of 1943.

258th Infantry Division

Commander: Genlt. Hans-Kurt HÖCKER (50)
Composition: 458th Gren Regt, 478th Gren Regt, 479th Gren Regt, 258th Arty Regt, 258th Rcn Bn, 258th AT Bn, 258th Engr Bn, 258th Sig Bn
Auxiliary unit number: 258
Home station: Rostock (Wkr. II)

Formed in Wehrkreise II and III in the summer of 1939 from men already serving in Ergänzungs units. Took part in the attack on the Maginot line. Continuously engaged on the central sector of the Russian front from the outset. Transferred to the southern sector in the late summer of 1943.

RESTRICTED

ORDER OF BATTLE OF THE GERMAN ARMY 225

260th Infantry Division

Commander: Obst. Alexander CONRADY (41)
Composition: 460th Gren Regt, 470th Gren Regt, 480th Gren Regt, 260th Arty Regt, 260th Rcn Bn, 260th AT Bn, 260th Engr Bn, 260th Sig Bn
Auxiliary unit number: 260
Home station: Karlsruhe (Wkr. V)

Formed in the summer of 1939 from men already serving in Ergänzungs units. No evidence of active operations prior to the Russian campaign. Continuously and heavily engaged on the central sector of the Russian front until transferred to France in the summer of 1942. Returned to the central sector in the following winter, where it was heavily engaged during the summer of 1943. In action in the area west of Gomel in the autumn of 1943.

262d Infantry Division

Commander:
Composition: 462d Gren Regt, 482d Gren Regt, 486th Gren Regt, 262d Arty Regt, 262d Rcn Bn, 262d AT Bn, 262d Engr Bn, 262d Sig Bn
Auxiliary unit number: 262
Home station: Wien (Wkr. XVII)

Formed in the summer of 1939 from men already serving in Ergänzungs units. On the Saar front for several months. Identified on the central sector of the Russian front in September 1941, where it remained. Took part in the Kursk offensive in the summer of 1943 and sustained very heavy losses in the operations which followed. Considered disbanded late in the autumn of 1943.

RESTRICTED

263d Infantry Division

Commander:
Composition: 463d Gren Regt, 483d Gren Regt, 485th Gren Regt, 263d
Arty Regt, 263d Rcn Bn, 263d AT Bn, 263d Engr Bn,
263d Sig Bn
Auxiliary unit number: 263
Home station: Idar-Oberstein (Wkr. XII)

Formed in the summer of 1939 from men already serving in Ergänzungs units. Took part in the French campaign. Identified on the central sector of the Russian front in July 1941. Transferred to the northern sector in the autumn of 1943.

264th Infantry Division

Commander: Genmaj. Wilhelm METGER ?
Composition: 891st Gren Regt, 892d Gren Regt, 893d Gren Regt, 264th
Arty Regt, Rcn Bn, 264th AT Bn, 264th Engr Bn, Sig Bn
Auxiliary unit number: 264(?)
Home station: (Wkr. VI)

Formed in the summer of 1943 in Belgium and transferred to Croatia in October 1943. Subsequently in Dalmatia.

265th Infantry Division

Commander: Genlt. Wilhelm RUSSWURM (56)
Composition: 894th Gren Regt, 895th Gren Regt, 896th Gren Regt,
Arty Regt, Rcn Bn, AT Bn, Engr Bn, Sig Bn
Auxiliary unit number:
Home station: (Wkr. XI)

Formed early in 1943. Identified in Brittany in September 1943.

RESTRICTED

267th Infantry Division

Commander:
Composition: 467th Gren Regt, 487th Gren Regt, 497th Gren Regt, 267th Arty Regt, 267th Rcn Bn, 267th AT Bn, 267th Engr Bn, 267th Sig Bn
Auxiliary unit number: 267
Home station: Hannover(?) (Wkr. XI)

Formed in the summer of 1939 from men already serving in Ergänzungs units. Identified on the central sector of the Russian front in July 1941, where it has been fairly continuously engaged.

268th Infantry Division

Commander: Genlt. Heinz GREINER (49)
Composition: 468th Gren Regt, 488th Gren Regt, 499th Gren Regt, 268th Arty Regt, 268th Mobile Bn, 268th Engr Bn, 268th Sig Bn
Auxiliary unit number: 268
Home station: München (Wkr. VII)

Formed in Wehrkreise VII and XVII in the summer of 1939 from men already serving in Ergänzungs units. On the Saar front for several months. Continuously engaged on the central sector of the Russian front from the outset. Suffered heavy losses in the summer of 1943.

RESTRICTED

269th Infantry Division

Commander: Genlt. Kurt BADINSKI (49)
Composition: 469th Gren Regt, 489th Gren Regt, 490th Gren Regt, 269th Arty Regt, 269th Mobile Bn, 269th Engr Bn, 269th Sig Bn
Auxiliary unit number: 269
Home station: Delmenhorst (Wkr. X)

Formed in the summer of 1939 from men already serving in Ergänzungs units. Fought in northern France. Transferred to Denmark in the late summer of 1940, where it remained until May 1941. Engaged on the northern sector of the Russian front until the winter of 1942-1943, when it was transferred to the Bergen area in Norway.

270th Infantry Division

Commander: Genlt. Ralf SODAN (64)
Composition:
Auxiliary unit number:
Home station: (Wkr. X)

Probably formed in the summer of 1942 as a coast defense division in central Norway. Consists of a divisional staff with fortress battalions and coastal batteries under its control.

271st Infantry Division

Formed in Wehrkreis V and disbanded in the summer of 1940.

RESTRICTED

272d Infantry Division

Formed and disbanded in the summer of 1940.

273d Infantry Division

Formed in Wehrkreis III and disbanded in the summer of 1940.

274th Infantry Division

Commander:
Composition:
Auxiliary unit number:
Home station: (Wkr. II)

Formed in the summer of 1943 and transferred to the Drammen area in Norway in the early autumn of 1943. May include the 862d and 865th Gren Regts from the 347th and 348th Infantry Divisions, respectively.

276th Infantry Division

Formed and disbanded in the summer of 1940.

277th Infantry Division

Formed and disbanded in the summer of 1940.

RESTRICTED

280th Infantry Division

Commander: Genlt. v. BEEREN (53)
Composition:
Auxiliary unit number:
Home station:

Probably formed in the summer of 1942 as a coast defense division in southern Norway. Consists of a divisional staff with fortress battalions and coastal batteries under its control.

282d Infantry Division

Commander: Genmaj. KOHLER
Composition: 848th Gren Regt, 849th Gren Regt, 850th Gren Regt, 282d Arty Regt
Auxiliary unit number: 282
Home station: (Wkr. XII)

Formed in France in the winter of 1942-1943. Identified on the southern sector of the Russian front in April 1943, where it has been continuously engaged.

290th Infantry Division

Commander: Genlt. HEINRICHS (52)
Composition: 501st Gren Regt, 502d Gren Regt, 503d Gren Regt, 290th Arty Regt, 290th Mobile Bn, 290th Engr Bn, Sig Bn
Auxiliary unit number: 290
Home station: (Wkr. X)

Formed in March/April 1940 from newly trained personnel. First in action in June 1940 during the French campaign.

RESTRICTED

Continuously engaged on the northern sector of the Russian front since July 1941. Transferred to the central sector and heavily engaged at Nevel in late autumn 1943.

291st Infantry Division

Commander: Genlt. Werner GOERITZ (52)
Composition: 504th Gren Regt, 505th Gren Regt, 506th Gren Regt, 291st Arty Regt, 291st Mobile Bn, 291st Engr Bn, 291st Sig Bn
Auxiliary unit number: 291
Home station: Insterburg (Wkr. I)

Formed in March/April 1940 from newly trained personnel. First in action during the French campaign. Identified on the northern sector of the Russian front in July 1941. Transferred to the southern sector in the late summer of 1943, where it has been heavily engaged.

292d Infantry Division

Commander: Genmaj. JOHN
Composition: 507th Gren Regt, 508th Gen Regt, 509th Gren Regt, 292d Arty Regt, Rcn Bn, 292d AT Bn, 292d Engr Bn, 292d Sig Bn
Auxiliary unit number: 292
Home station: (Wkr. II)

Formed in March/April 1940 from newly trained personnel. Took part in the French campaign. Identified on the central sector of the Russian front in August 1941, where it was last

RESTRICTED

reported. Took part in the Kursk offensive in the summer of 1943 and saw action on the Sozh River in the following autumn.

293d Infantry Division

Commander: Genmaj. Karl ARNDT
Composition: 510th Gren Regt, 511th Gren Regt, 512th Gren Regt, 293d Arty Regt, 293d Rcn Bn, 293d AT Bn, 293d Engr Bn, 293d Sig Bn
Auxiliary unit number: 293
Home station: (Wkr. III)

Formed in March/April 1940 from newly trained personnel. Took part in the French campaign. Identified on the central sector of the Russian front in July 1941. Took part in the Kursk offensive in the summer of 1943, suffering very heavy losses. Transferred to the southern sector in the following autumn.

294th Infantry Division

Commander: Genlt. Johannes BLOCK (50)
Composition: 513th Gren Regt, 514th Gren Regt, 515th Gren Regt, 294th Arty Regt, 294th Rcn Bn, 294th AT Bn, 294th Engr Bn, 294th Sig Bn
Auxiliary unit number: 294
Home station: (Wkr. IV)

Formed in March/April 1940 from newly trained personnel. First identified in action during the Balkan campaign. Has fought on the southern sector of the Russian front since

RESTRICTED

September 1941. Suffered heavy losses on the withdrawal from Stalingrad, and later during the encirclement of Taganrog.

295th Infantry Division

Commander:
Composition: 516th Gren Regt, 517th Gren Regt, 518th Gren Regt, 295th Arty Regt, Rcn Bn, 295th AT Bn, 295th Engr Bn, 295th Sig Bn
Auxiliary unit number: 295
Home station: (Wkr. XI)

Formed in March/April 1940 from newly trained personnel. Continuously engaged on the southern sector of the Russian front from July 1941. Virtually destroyed at Stalingrad. Subsequently reformed and identified in the Trondelaeg area of Norway late in 1943.

296th Infantry Division

Commander: Genlt. Artur KULLMER (48)
Composition: 519th Gren Regt, 520th Gren Regt, 521st Gren Regt, 296th Arty Regt, 296th Rcn Bn, 296th AT Bn, 296th Engr Bn, 296th Sig Bn
Auxiliary unit number: 296
Home station: Nürnberg(?) (Wkr. XIII)

Formed in March/April 1940 from newly trained personnel. Has operated on the central sector of the Russian front. Actively engaged in the Gomel area late in the summer of 1943.

RESTRICTED

297th Infantry Division

Commander:
Composition: 522d Gren Regt, 523d Gren Regt, 524th Gren Regt, 297th Arty Regt, 297th Rcn Bn, 297th AT Bn, 297th Engr Bn, 297th Sig Bn
Auxiliary unit number: 297
Home station: Wien (Wkr. XVII)

Formed in March/April 1940 from newly trained personnel. Operated on the southern sector of the Russian front from July 1941. Virtually destroyed at Stalingrad. Reformed in the summer of 1943 in the Belgrade area. Transferred to Albania in September 1943.

298th Infantry Division

Commander: Genlt. SZELINSKI (53)
Composition: 525th Gren Regt, 526th Gren Regt, 527th Gren Regt, 298th Arty Regt, 298th Rcn Bn, 298th AT Bn, 298th Engr Bn, 298th Sig Bn
Auxiliary unit number: 298
Home station: (Wkr. VIII)

Formed in March/April 1940 from newly trained personnel. Operated on the southern sector of the Russian front from July 1941. Now considered disbanded.

299th Infantry Division

Commander: Genlt. Graf v. ORIOLA
Composition: 528th Gren Regt, 529th Gren Regt, 530th Gren Regt, 299th Arty Regt, 299th Rcn Bn, 299th AT Bn, 299th Engr Bn, Sig Bn
Auxiliary unit number: 299
Home station: Weimar (Wkr. IX)

RESTRICTED

Formed in March/April 1940 from newly trained personnel. First in action during the French campaign in June 1940. Continuously engaged on the southern sector of the Russian front and later on the central sector. In action west of Gomel in the late autumn of 1943.

302d Infantry Division

Commander:
Composition: 570th Gren Regt, 571st Gren Regt, 572d Gren Regt, 302d Arty Regt, 302d Mobile Bn, 302d Engr Bn, 302d Sig Bn
Auxiliary unit number: 302
Home station: Schwerin (Wkr. II)

Formed late in 1940, but not reliably identified until early in 1942 in northern France. Transferred to the southern sector of the Russian front early in 1943.

304th Infantry Division

Commander: Genlt. Heinrich KRAMPF (56)
Composition: 573d Gren Regt, 574th Gren Regt, 575th Gren Regt, 304th Arty Regt, Rcn Bn, 304th AT Bn, 304th Engr Bn, 304th Sig Bn
Auxiliary unit number: 304
Home station: (Wkr. IV)

Formed late in 1940. From April 1942 in Belgium. Transferred to the southern sector of the Russian front early in 1943, where it has been constantly engaged, suffering heavy losses at Taganrog.

RESTRICTED

305th Infantry Division

Commander: Genmaj. Bruno HAUCK
Composition: 576th Gren Regt, 577th Gren Regt, 578th Gren Regt, 305th Arty Regt, 305th Rcn Bn, AT Bn, 305th Engr Bn, 305th Sig Bn
Auxiliary unit number: 305
Home station: Konstanz (Wkr. V)

Formed late in 1940. In western France from the end of 1941 until the beginning of May 1942, when it left for the southern sector of the Russian front. Virtually destroyed at Stalingrad. Reformed in France in May 1943. Transferred to Italy in August 1943, where it has since been in action. Known as the "Bodensee Division."

306th Infantry Division

Commander:
Composition: 579th Gren Regt, 580th Gren Regt, 581st Gren Regt, 306th Arty Regt, 306th Mobile Bn, 306th Engr Bn, 306th Sig Bn
Auxiliary unit number: 306
Home station: (Wkr. VI)

Formed late in 1940. In Belgium from late in 1941. Transferred to the southern sector of the Russian front in December 1942, where it has been constantly engaged, sustaining heavy losses at Taganrog.

307th Infantry Division

Probably formed and disbanded in 1940.

RESTRICTED

310th Infantry Division

Probably formed and disbanded in 1940.

311th Infantry Division

Commander:
Composition:
Auxiliary unit number:
Home station: (Wkr. I)

Classification uncertain. Stationed in Poland during 1940. No recent evidence for location and continued existence. Believed disbanded.

317th Infantry Division

Probably formed and disbanded in 1940.

319th Infantry Division

Commander: Genlt. Erich MÜLLER (55)
Composition: 582d Gren Regt, 583d Gren Regt, 584th Gren Regt, 319th Arty Regt, 319th Mobile Bn, 319th Engr Bn, Sig Bn
Auxiliary unit number: 319
Home station: (Wkr. IX)

Formed late in 1940. In Brittany since August 1941, where it holds a coastal sector including the Channel Islands.

RESTRICTED

320th Infantry Division

Commander: Genlt. Georg POSTEL (48)
Composition: 585th Gren Regt, 586th Gren Regt, 587th Gren Regt, 320th Arty Regt, Rcn Bn, 320th AT Bn, 320th Engr Bn, 320th Sig Bn
Auxiliary unit number: 320
Home station: (Wkr. VIII)

Formed late in 1940. Moved early in January 1942 from Belgium to Brittany. Transferred to northeastern France in April 1942 and to the southern sector of the Russian front early in 1943, where it has been continuously and heavily engaged. Took part in the summer offensive at Belgorod.

321st Infantry Division

Commander:
Composition: 588th Gren Regt, 589th Gren Regt, 590th Gren Regt, 321st Arty Regt, Rcn Bn, AT Bn, 321st Engr Bn, 321st Sig Bn
Auxiliary unit number: 321
Home station: (Wkr. XI)

Formed late in 1940. In northeastern France from the end of 1941 until it was transferred to the central sector of the Russian front early in 1943, where it has been heavily engaged.

323d Infantry Division

Commander: Genlt. Johann BERGEN (53)
Composition: 591st Gren Regt, 592d Gren Regt, 593d Gren Regt, 323d Arty Regt, 323d Mobile Bn, 323d Engr Bn, 323d Sig Bn
Auxiliary unit number: 323
Home station: (Wkr. V)

RESTRICTED

Formed late in 1940. In northwestern France from the end of 1941 until early in May 1942, when it left for the southern sector of the Russian front. It fought in the retreat from Kiev in the autumn of 1943, sustaining heavy losses.

326th Infantry Division

Commander: Genlt. Viktor v. DRABICH-WAECHTER (53)
Composition: 751st Gren Regt, 752d Gren Regt, 753d Gren Regt, 326th Arty Regt, Rcn Bn, 326th AT Bn, 326th Engr Bn, 326th Sig Bn
Auxiliary unit number: 326
Home station: (Wkr. VI)

Probably formed late in 1942. In former unoccupied France, where it holds a Mediterranean coastal sector. It is a static (*bodenständig*) division.

327th Infantry Division

Commander:
Composition: 595th Gren Regt, 596th Gren Regt, 597th Gren Regt, 327th Arty Regt, Rcn Bn, 327th AT Bn, 327th Engr Bn, 327th Sig Bn
Auxiliary unit number: 327
Home station: (Wkr. XVII)

Formed late in 1940. In eastern France in the latter half of 1941 and southwestern France from January 1942. Took part in the occupation of former unoccupied France and trans-

RESTRICTED

ferred to the southern sector of the Russian front early in 1943. Suffered heavy losses in the retreat from Kiev in the autumn of 1943. Considered absorbed into the 377th Infantry Division.

328th Infantry Division

Commander: Genlt. Joachim v. TRESCKOW (50)
Composition: 547th Gren Regt, 548th Gren Regt, 549th Gren Regt, 328th Arty Regt, 328th Rcn Bn, AT Bn, 328th Engr Bn, 328th Sig Co
Auxiliary unit number: 328
Home station: (Wkr. II)

Formed late in 1941. First identified in March 1942 in the central sector of the Russian front. Transferred to former unoccupied France in November 1942 and back to the southern sector of the Russian front in the summer of 1943, where it has since remained.

329th Infantry Division

Commander:
Composition: 551st Gren Regt, 552d Gren Regt, 553d Gren Regt, 329th Arty Regt, 329th Mobile Bn, 329th Engr Bn, 329th Sig Bn
Auxiliary unit number: 329
Home station: (Wkr. VI)

Formed late in 1941. First identified in May 1942 on the northern sector of the Russian front, where it has since remained.

RESTRICTED

ORDER OF BATTLE OF THE GERMAN ARMY 241

330th Infantry Division

Commander:
Composition: 554th Gren Regt, 555th Gren Regt, 556th Gren Regt, 330th Arty Regt, 330th Rcn Bn, AT Bn, 330th(?) Engr Bn, 330th Sig Bn
Auxiliary unit number: 330
Home station: (Wkr. V)

Formed late in 1941. First identified in February 1942. Has subsequently been in action on the central sector of the Russian front.

331st Infantry Division

Commander: Genmaj. Karl RHEIN (50)
Composition: 557th Gren Regt, 558th Gren Regt, 559th Gren Regt, 331st Arty Regt, 331st(?) Rcn Bn, 331st AT Bn, 331st Engr Bn, 331st Sig Bn
Auxiliary unit number: 331
Home station: (Wkr. XVII)

Formed late in 1941. First identified in February 1942. Has operated on the central sector of the Russian front. Transferred to the northern sector in the autumn of 1943.

332d Infantry Division

Commander:
Composition: 676th Gren Regt, 677th Gren Regt, 678th Gren Regt, 332d Arty Regt, Rcn Bn, 332d AT Bn, 332d Engr Bn, 332d Sig Co
Auxiliary unit number: 332
Home station: (Wkr. VIII)

RESTRICTED

Formed in January 1941. In Normandy from August 1941 to the spring of 1943, when it was transferred to the southern sector of the Russian front. In action in the Belgorod area in the summer of 1943.

333d Infantry Division

Commander:
Composition: 679th Gren Regt, 680th Gren Regt, 681st Gren Regt, 333d Arty Regt, 333d Mobile Bn, 333d Engr Bn, 333d Sig Co
Auxiliary unit number: 333
Home station: (Wkr. III)

Formed in January 1941. Moved in May 1941 from Wkr. III to southwestern France. Transferred to Brittany in March 1942 and to the southern sector of the Russian front early in 1943. Appears to have included many Poles. Believed disbanded in the late autumn of 1943.

334th Infantry Division

Commander:
Composition: 754th Gren Regt, 755th Gren Regt, 756th Gren Regt, 334th Arty Regt, 334th Mobile Bn, 334th Engr Bn, 334th Sig Bn
Auxiliary unit number: 334
Home station: (Wkr. XIII)

Formed in the autumn of 1942. Sent to Tunisia in December 1942, where it was destroyed in May 1943. Reformed in south-

RESTRICTED

ORDER OF BATTLE OF THE GERMAN ARMY 243

western France in July and August 1943. Transferred to northern Italy in November 1943 and to the southern Italian front in December 1943, where it has since been in action.

335th Infantry Division

Commander: Genlt. CASPER (51)
Composition: 682d Gren Regt, 683d Gren Regt, 684th Gren Regt, 335th Arty Regt, Rcn Bn, 335th AT Bn, 335th Engr Bn, 335th Sig Co
Auxiliary unit number: 335
Home station: (Wkr. V)

Formed in January 1941. First identified in northern France in October 1941. Moved to Brittany in February 1942. Took part in the occupation of former unoccupied France. Transferred to the southern sector of the Russian front early in 1943, where it has been fairly constantly in action. Appears to include a large proportion of Poles.

336th Infantry Division

Commander: Genlt. Walter LUCHT (62)
Composition: 685th Gren Regt, 686th Gren Regt, 687th Gren Regt, 336th Arty Regt, Rcn Bn, 336th AT Bn, 336th Engr Bn, 336th Sig Bn
Auxiliary unit number: 336
Home station: (Wkr. IV)

Formed in January 1941 with cadres from the 256th Infantry Division and moved to Normandy. Transferred to

RESTRICTED

Brittany at the end of March 1942. Left for the Russian front at the end of May 1942, where it has operated in the southern sector. Sustained heavy losses during the encirclement of Taganrog.

337th Infantry Division

Commander: Genlt. Otto SCHÜNEMANN (53)
Composition: 313th Gren Regt, 688th Gren Regt, 690th Gren Regt, 337th Arty Regt, Rcn Bn, 337th AT Bn, 337th Engr Bn, 337th Sig Co
Auxiliary unit number: 337
Home station: (Wkr. VII)

Formed in January 1941. In central France from August 1941 until late in 1942, when it was transferred to the central sector of the Russian front, where it has remained. Exchanged Gren. Regt. 689 for Gren. Regt. 313 of the 246th Infantry Division prior to its transfer to Russia.

338th Infantry Division

Commander: Genlt. FOLTTMANN (55)
Composition: 757th Gren Regt, 758th Gren Regt, 759th Gren Regt, 338th Arty Regt, Rcn Bn, 338th AT Bn, 338th Engr Bn, 338th Sig Bn
Auxiliary unit number: 338
Home station:

Probably formed in France early in 1943. Subsequently in southern France.

RESTRICTED

339th Infantry Division

Commander:
Composition: 691st Gren Regt, 692d Gren Regt, 693d Gren Regt, 339th Arty Bn, 339th Mobile Bn, 339th Engr Bn, 339th Sig Co
Auxiliary unit number: 339
Home station: Jena (Wkr. IX)

Formed in January 1941. In central France until it left for the Russian front at the end of 1941. Subsequently in action on the central sector. Transferred to the southern sector in the autumn of 1943, where it has remained.

340th Infantry Division

Commander: Genlt. BUTZE (53)
Composition: 694th Gren Regt, 695th Gren Regt, 696th Gren Regt, 340th Arty Regt, Rcn Bn, 340th AT Bn, 340th Engr Bn, 340th Sig Bn
Auxiliary unit number: 340
Home station: Königsberg (Wkr. I)

Formed in January 1941, but first identified in April 1942 in northeastern France. Left in May 1942 for the Russian front, where it has operated on the southern sector. Suffered losses in the retreat from Kiev in the autumn of 1943.

341st Infantry Division

Probably formed and disbanded in 1940.

RESTRICTED

342d Infantry Division

Commander:
Composition: 697th Gren Regt, 698th Gren Regt, 699th Gren Regt, 342d
Arty Regt, 342d Rcn Bn, 342d AT Bn, 342d Engr Bn,
342d Sig Bn
Auxiliary unit number: 342
Home station: Kaiserslautern (Wkr. XII)

Formed in January 1941. Engaged in mopping up operations in Yugoslavia from late 1941 until February 1942, when it was transferred to the central sector of the Russian front, where it has remained.

343d Infantry Division

Commander:
Composition: 851st Gren Regt, 852d Gren Regt, 853d(?) Gren Regt,
Art Regt, Rcn Bn, AT Bn, 343d Engr Bn, Sig Bn
Auxiliary unit number: 343
Home station: (Wkr. XIII)

Formed late in 1942 and identified in Brittany in April 1943, where it has remained. It is a static (*bodenständig*) division.

344th Infantry Division

Commander:
Composition: 854th Gren Regt, 855th Gren Regt, 856th Gren Regt,
344th Arty Regt, Rcn Bn, AT Bn, Engr Bn, Sig Bn
Auxiliary unit number: 344
Home station:

RESTRICTED

ORDER OF BATTLE OF THE GERMAN ARMY 247

Probably formed late in 1942. Identified in France in the Bordeaux area. In the autumn of 1943 it was holding the coastal sector from Arcachon to Hendaye. It is a static (*bodenständig*) division.

346th Infantry Division

Commander:
Composition: 857th Gren Regt, 858th Gren Regt, 859th(?) Gren Regt, Arty Regt, Rcn Bn, AT Bn, Engr Bn, Sig Bn
Auxiliary unit number:
Home station:

Probably formed in the autumn of 1942. Since early in 1943, it has occupied a coastal sector in western France. It is a static (*bodenständig*) division.

347th Infantry Division

Commander:
Composition: 860th Gren Regt, 861st Gren Regt, 862d(?) Gren Regt, Arty Regt, Rcn Bn, AT Bn, Engr Bn, Sig Bn
Auxiliary unit number: 347 (?)
Home station: (Wkr. II)

Probably formed in 1942. In Holland since March 1943. It is a static (*bodenständig*) division. The 862d Gren Regt may belong to the 274th Infantry Division in Norway.

RESTRICTED

348th Infantry Division

Commander:
Composition: 863d Gren Regt, 864th Gren Regt, 865th(?) Gren Regt, Arty Regt, Rcn Bn, AT Bn, Engr Bn, Sig Bn
Auxiliary unit number:
Home station:

Formed late in 1942. Holds the Dieppe sector in France. It is a static (*bodenständig*) division. The 865th Gren Regt may belong to the 274th Infantry Division in Norway.

351st Infantry Division

Probably formed and disbanded in 1940.

355th Infantry Division

Commander:
Composition: 866th Gren Regt, 867th Gren Regt, 868th Gren Regt, Arty Regt, Rcn Bn, AT Bn, Engr Bn, Sig Bn
Auxiliary unit number:
Home station:

Formed in eastern France in the winter of 1942-1943. Identified on the southern sector of the Russian front in August 1943, where it has remained.

356th Infantry Division

Commander: Genlt. FAULENBACH (52)
Composition: 869th Gren Regt, 870th Gren Regt, 871st Gren Regt, 356th Arty Regt, Rcn Bn, AT Bn, Engr Bn, Sig Bn
Auxiliary unit number: 356
Home station: (Wkr. IX)

RESTRICTED

Formed in France in the summer of 1943. Elements are reported to have been in Corsica. The division moved to northern Italy in October 1943.

358th Infantry Division

Home station: (Wkr. III)

Landwehr division formed late in 1939 and disbanded after the French campaign.

365th Infantry Division

Home station: (Wkr. V)

Landwehr division formed late in 1939. Now Oberfeldkommandantur 365 at Lemberg (Lwow), Poland.

369th Infantry Division

Commander: Genmaj. Fritz NEIDHOLDT (54)
Composition: 369th Gren Regt, 370th Gren Regt, 369th Arty Regt, Rcn Bn, AT Bn, Engr Bn, Sig Bn
Auxiliary unit number: 369
Home station: Stockerau (Wkr. XVII)

Croatian division. Formed in the latter part of 1942 by the expansion of the 369th Infantry Regiment, consisting of Croatians, which formerly operated under the 100th Light Division. Now in Croatia. Referred to as the "Teufels (Devil's) Division."

RESTRICTED

370th Infantry Division

Commander:
Composition: 666th Gren Regt, 667th Gren Regt, 668th Gren Regt, 370th Arty Regt, Rcn Bn, 370th AT Bn, 370th Engr Bn, 370th Sig Bn,
Auxiliary unit number: 370
Home station: (Wkr. VIII)

Completed formation in France in May 1942. Transferred to the southern sector of the Russian front, where it operated in the Caucasus in the winter of 1942-1943. Evacuated to the lower Dnieper area in the autumn of 1943.

371st Infantry Division

Commander: Genmaj. Johannes NIEHOFF
Composition: 669th Gren Regt, 670th Gren Regt, 671st Gren Regt, 371st Arty Regt, Rcn Bn, 371st AT Bn, 371st Engr Bn, Sig Bn
Auxiliary unit number: 371
Home station: (Wkr. VI)

Completed formation in France in May 1942. Transferred to the Russian front, where it operated on the southern sector. Virtually destroyed at Stalingrad. Reformed in France in April and May 1943 and transferred to Italy and Slovenia in the following autumn.

372d Infantry Division

Home station: (Wkr. IV)

Landwehr division formed late in 1939. Now Oberfeldkommandantur 372 at Kielce, Poland.

RESTRICTED

ORDER OF BATTLE OF THE GERMAN ARMY

373d Infantry Division

Commander: Genlt. Emil ZELLNER
Composition: 383d Gren Regt, 384th Gren Regt, 373d Arty Regt, Rcn Bn, 373d AT Bn, 373d Engr Bn, Sig Bn
Auxiliary unit number: 373
Home station: (Wkr. XVII)

Formed early in 1943 in Croatia and Bosnia, where it has remained. Consists principally of Croatian personnel.

376th Infantry Division

Commander:
Composition: 765th Gren Regt, 766th Gren Regt, 767th Gren Regt, 376th Arty Regt, Rcn Bn, 376th AT Bn, Engr Bn, Sig Bn
Auxiliary unit number: 376
Home station: (Wkr. VII)

Completed formation in France in May 1942. Transferred to the Russian front, where it operated on the southern sector. Virtually destroyed at Stalingrad. Reformed in Holland during the summer of 1943 and returned to the southern sector of the Russian front in the following autumn. In action in the Dnieper bend.

377th Infantry Division

Commander: Genmaj. Erich BAESSLER (52)
Composition: 768th Gren Regt, 769th Gren Regt, 770th Gren Regt, 377th Arty Regt, 377th Rcn Bn, 377th AT Bn, 377th Engr Bn, 377th Sig Bn
Auxiliary unit number: 377
Home station: (Wkr. IX)

RESTRICTED

Completed formation in France in May 1942. Transferred to the Russian front, where it has operated on the southern sector. May have recently absorbed the remnants of the 327th Infantry division.

379th Infantry Division

Home station: (Wkr. IX)

Formed after mobilization. Now Oberfeldkommandantur 379 at Lublin, Poland.

380th Infantry Division

Probably formed and disbanded in 1940.

383d Infantry Division

Commander:
Composition: 531st Gren Regt, 532d Gren Regt, 533d Gren Regt, 383d Arty Regt, 383d Mobile Bn, 383d Engr Bn, 383d Sig Bn
Auxiliary unit number: 383
Home station: (Wkr. I)

Formed in the winter of 1941-1942. Continuously and heavily engaged on the southern sector of the Russian front since June 1942. In the Orel area in the summer of 1943.

RESTRICTED

384th Infantry Division

Commander:
Composition: 534th Gren Regt, 535th Gren Regt, 536th Gren Regt, 384th Arty Regt, Rcn Bn, 384th AT Bn, Engr Bn, 384th Sig Bn
Auxiliary unit number: 384
Home station: (Wkr. IV)

Formed in the winter of 1941-1942. In action on the southern sector of the Russian front from May 1942. Virtually destroyed at Stalingrad. Partially reformed in southern Russia in 1943 and transferred to France in the spring of that year for completion and training. Returned to the southern sector of the Russian front in the autumn. In action in the Dnieper bend.

385th Infantry Division

Commander:
Composition: 537th Gren Regt, 538th Gren Regt, 539th Gren Regt, 385th Arty Regt, Rcn Bn, 385th AT Bn, 385th Engr Bn, 385th Sig Bn
Auxiliary unit number: 385
Home station:

Formed in the winter of 1941-1942. In action on the central sector of the Russian front from May 1942; later transferred to the southern sector. Now considered disbanded.

RESTRICTED

387th Infantry Division

Commander:
Composition: 541st Gren Regt, 542d Gren Regt, 543d Gren Regt, 387th Arty Regt, Rcn Bn, 387th AT Bn, 387th Engr Bn, 387th Sig Bn
Auxiliary unit number: 387
Home station: (Wkr. VII)

Formed in the winter of 1941-1942. On the southern sector of the Russian front since May 1942, where it has been continuously in action. During the latter part of 1943 it was referred to as the "Rheingold Division."

389th Infantry Division

Commander: Genmaj. Paul Herbert FORSTER (52)
Composition: 544th Gren Regt, 545th Gren Regt, 546th Gren Regt, 389th Arty Regt, Rcn Bn, 389th AT Bn, Engr Bn, Sig Bn
Auxiliary unit number: 389
Home station: (Wkr. IX)

Formed in the winter of 1941-1942. In action on the southern sector of the Russian front from May 1942 until its virtual destruction at Stalingrad. Reformed in Brittany during the summer of 1943 and returned to the southern sector of the Russian front in the following autumn.

392d Infantry Division

Commander:
Composition: Gren Regt, Gren Regt, Arty Regt, Rcn Bn, AT Bn, Engr Bn, Sig Bn
Auxiliary unit number:
Home station: Stockerau (Wkr. XVII)

Probably formed in the autumn of 1943; believed to be Croatian.

RESTRICTED

393d Infantry Division

Formed late in 1939 in Wkr. X. Now Oberfeldkommandantur 393 at Warsaw, Poland.

395th Infantry Division

Formed after mobilization. Disbanded late in 1940. Now Oberfeldkommandantur 395.

399th Infantry Division

Formed after mobilization in Wkr. I. Disbanded late in 1940. Now Oberfeldkommandantur 399, last reported in eastern Poland.

416th Infantry Division

Commander: Genlt. PFLIEGER (54)
Composition: 930th Gren Regt, 931st Gren Regt
Auxiliary unit number: 466 (?)
Home station: (Wkr. X)

Previously 416th Division z.b.V. stationed in the Silkeborg area, Denmark.

RESTRICTED

554th Infantry Division

Formed in Wkr. V early in 1940. Disbanded after the French campaign.

555th Infantry Division

Formed in Wkr. VI in 1940. Disbanded after the French campaign.

556th Infantry Division

Formed in Wkr. XII in 1940 and disbanded after the French campaign.

557th Infantry Division

Formed in Wkr. IV in 1940 and disbanded after the French campaign.

702d Infantry Division

Commander: Genmaj. Otto SCHMIDT (52)
Composition: 722d Gren Regt, 742d Gren Regt, 662d Arty Regt, 702d(?) Engr Bn, 702d Sig Bn
Auxiliary unit number: 702
Home station: (Wkr. II)

Static defensive division. Formed in April 1941 and sent

RESTRICTED

ORDER OF BATTLE OF THE GERMAN ARMY 257

to southern Norway in May 1941. Moved to northern Norway at the end of June 1941, where it has remained.

704th Infantry Division—See 104th L Div

707th Infantry Division

Commander:
Composition: 727th Gren Regt, 747th Gren Regt, 657th Arty Regt, 707th Engr Bn, 707th Sig Bn
Auxiliary unit number: 707
Home station: (Wkr. VII)

Formed in April 1941. Identified on the central sector of the Russian front in October 1941, where it was employed on rear area duties. Believed to have been in action in the Bryansk area in the summer of 1943. Unlike the others in this series, this is regarded as an offensive division.

708th Infantry Division

Commander: Genlt. Hermann WILCK (59)
Composition: 728th Gren Regt, 748th Gren Regt, Arty Regt, 708th Engr Bn, 708th Sig Bn
Auxiliary unit number: 708
Home station: (Wkr. VIII)

Static defensive division. Formed in April 1941. Probably in central France in November 1941; in southwestern France from December 1941. Moved to the central sector of the Russian front in late autumn 1943, where it has operated in the rear area.

RESTRICTED

709th Infantry Division

Commander:
Composition: 729th Gren Regt, 739th Gren Regt, Arty Regt, 709th Engr Bn, 709th Sig Bn
Auxiliary unit number: 709
Home station: (Wkr. IX)

Static defensive division. Formed in April 1941. In Brittany from November 1941 to early 1943, when it moved to the Cherbourg peninsula.

710th Infantry Division

Commander: Genlt. PETSCH (56)
Composition: 730th Gren Regt, 740th Gren Regt, Arty Regt, 710th Engr Bn, 710th Sig Bn
Auxiliary unit number: 710
Home station: (Wkr. X)

Static defensive division. Formed in April 1941. In southern Norway since June 1941.

711th Infantry Division

Commander: Genmaj. DEUTSCH (52)
Composition: 731st Gren Regt, 744th Gren Regt, 651st Arty Regt, 711th Engr Bn, 711th Sig Bn
Auxiliary unit number: 711
Home station: (Wkr. XI)

Static defensive division. Formed in April 1941. In northeastern France from August to December 1941. In Normandy since January 1942.

RESTRICTED

712th Infantry Division

Commander: Genlt. Friedrich-Wilhelm NEUMANN (64)
Composition: 732d Gren Regt, 745th Gren Regt, 652d Arty Regt, 712th Engr Bn, 712th Sig Bn
Auxiliary unit number: 712
Home station: (Wkr. XII)

Static defensive division. Formed in April 1941.. In France early in 1942; subsequently moved to Belgium. Has held a coastal sector in the Bruges area since June 1942.

713th Infantry Division

Commander:
Composition: 733d Gren Regt, 746th Gren Regt, 653d Arty Regt, 713th Engr Bn, 713th Sig Bn
Auxiliary unit number: 713
Home station: (Wkr. XIII)

Static defensive division. Formed in April 1941. One of its regiments, the 746th Gren Regt, has been identified in Crete under "Festungsbrigade Kreta." The continued existence of the division as such is uncertain.

715th Infantry Division

Commander: Genlt. Kurt HOFFMANN (53)
Composition: 725th Gren Regt, 735th Gren Regt, Arty Regt, 715th Engr Bn, Sig Bn
Auxiliary unit number: 715
Home station: (Wkr. V)

RESTRICTED

Static defensive division. Formed in April 1941. In southwestern France from August 1941 to June 1943, when it moved to the Cannes-Nice coastal sector.

716th Infantry Division

Commander:
Composition: 726th Gren Regt, 736th Gren Regt, 656th Arty Regt, 716th Engr Bn, Sig Bn
Auxiliary unit number: 716
Home station (Wkr. VI)

Static defensive division. Formed in April 1941 and identified in Brittany in February 1942. In Normandy since 1942.

717th Infantry Division—See 117th L Div

718th Infantry Division—See 118th L Div

719th Infantry Division

Commander: Genlt. Erich HÖCKER (61)
Composition: 723d Gren Regt, 743d Gren Regt, 663d Arty Regt, 719th Engr Bn, 719th Sig Bn
Auxiliary unit number: 719
Home station: (Wkr. III)

Static defensive division. Formed in April 1941. Has been in Brabant, Holland, since late 1942.

RESTRICTED

999th Africa Division

Commander:
Composition: 961st Gren Regt, 962d Gren Regt, 963d Gren Regt, 999th Arty Regt, 999th Sig Bn
Auxiliary unit number: 999
Home station: Heuberg/Baden (Wkr. V)

"Afrika Brigade 999" was formed in Antwerp in October 1942 and in March 1943 was converted into "Afrika-Division 999." Much of its personnel was taken from criminal elements and political offenders. Two of its regiments were transferred to Tunisia in March 1943, where they were virtually destroyed. Since May 1943 it appears to have ceased to exist as a division and to consist merely of a regimental headquarters for the control of fortress battalions in Greece. Its original supporting arms and services have been incorporated in Assault Division Rhodes.

Assault Division Rhodes

Commander: Genlt. Ulrich (Werner) KLEEMANN (52)
Composition: Miscellaneous units
Auxiliary unit number:
Home station:

The "Sturm-Division Rhodos" was formed in Rhodes in early summer 1943 from the former assault brigade Rhodes. Its infantry components appear to have been formed largely from the 440th Gren Regt of the 164th Light Division and from elements of the 22d Motorized Division. Its supporting arms and services were largely provided by the 999th Division. It has so far been employed only for the garrisoning of the island of Rhodes.

RESTRICTED

1st Cossack Division

Commander: Genmaj. Helmuth v. PANNWITZ (46)
Composition:
Auxiliary unit number:
Home station:

Cavalry division formed in the latter part of 1943 from units of Don, Kuban, and Terek Cossacks which had previously operated as separate squadrons against Russian guerillas. Probably consists of two cavalry brigades including all the principal supporting units. Contains some German officers and NCOs and possibly elements of other nationalities. In action against the partisans in Yugoslavia.

ORDER OF BATTLE OF THE GERMAN ARMY

33. Motorized Divisions *(Panzergrenadierdivisionen)*.

2d Motorized Division—See 12th Pz Div

3d Motorized Division

Commander: Genlt. Fritz Hubert GRÄSER (56)
Composition: 103d Pz Bn, 8th Mtz Inf Regt, 29th Mtz Inf Regt, 3d Mtz Arty Regt, 103d Pz Rcn Bn, 3d AT Bn, 3d Mtz Engr Bn, 3d Mtz Sig Bn
Auxiliary unit number: 3
Home station: Frankfurt/Oder (Wkr. III)

Originally the 3d Infantry Division, an active division. As such took part in the Polish and French campaigns. Motorized in the autumn of 1940. Fought in Russia from the outset, at first on the central and subsequently on the southern sector. Virtually destroyed at Stalingrad. Reformed in southwestern France in the spring of 1943, when it absorbed the bulk of the 386th Motorized Division. Transferred to Italy in June 1943. In action intermittently on the southern Italian front.

10th Motorized Division

Commander: Genlt. August SCHMIDT (51)
Composition: 110th (?) Pz Bn, 20th Mtz Inf Regt, 41st Mtz Inf Regt, 10th Mtz Arty Regt, 110th Pz Rcn Bn, 10th AT Bn, 10th Mtz Engr Bn, 10th Mtz Sig Bn
Auxiliary unit number: 10
Home station: Regensburg (Wkr. XIII)

Originally the 10th Infantry Division, an active division. As such took part in the Polish and French campaigns. Motorized in the autumn of 1940. Fought in the Balkan campaign. Has operated on the central sector of the Russian front from

RESTRICTED

the outset. Took part in the Kursk offensive in the summer of 1943 and was subsequently transferred to the southern sector, where it was heavily engaged west of Kiev.

13th Motorized Division—See 13th Pz Div

14th Motorized Division

Commander: Genmaj. FLÖRKE
Composition: 114th (?) Pz Bn, 11th Mtz Inf Regt, 53d Mtz Inf Regt, 14th Mtz Arty Regt, 114th Pz Rcn Bn, 14th AT Bn, 14th Mtz Engr Bn, 14th Mtz Sig Bn
Auxiliary unit number: 14
Home station: Leipzig (Wkr. IV)

Originally the 14th Infantry Division, an active division. Took part in the campaigns in Poland and France. Motorized in the autumn of 1940. Continuously in action on the central sector of the Russian front since the summer of 1941. Sustained heavy casualties in the autumn of 1943, when it fought in the Smolensk-Vitebsk area.

15th Motorized Division

Commander: Genmaj. Eberhardt RODT (49)
Composition: 115th Pz Bn, 104th Pz Gren Regt, 115th Pz Gren Regt, 129th Pz Gren Regt, 33d Mtz Arty Regt, 115th Pz Rcn Bn, 33d AT Bn, 33d Mtz Engr Bn, 78th Mtz Sig Bn
Auxiliary unit number: 33
Home station: Kaiserslautern (Wkr. XII)

Originally the 33d Infantry Division, an active division.

RESTRICTED

As such fought in the French campaign. Reorganized as the 15th Panzer Division in the autumn of 1940. Transferred to Libya in the spring of 1941. Entered Tunisia early 1943, where it was virtually destroyed in May 1943. In July 1943 "Division Sizilien," formed from miscellaneous units in Sicily was renamed the 15th Panzer Grenadier Division. It incorporated elements of the former 15th Panzer Division and has since been engaged in operations in Sicily and Italy. Its regiments retain the title of "Panzer-Grenadier-Regiment." Panzer-Grenadier-Regiment 115 has been possibly withdrawn to the GHQ pool.

16th Motorized Division

Commander: Genlt. Gerhard Graf v. SCHWERIN (45)
Composition: 116th Pz Bn, 60th Mtz Inf Regt, 156th Mtz Inf Regt, 146th Mtz Arty Regt, 116th Pz Rcn Bn, AT Bn, 146th (?) Mtz Engr Bn, 228th Mtz Sig Bn
Auxiliary unit number: 66
Home station: Rheine (Wkr. VI)

Formed in the late summer of 1940 from elements of the 16th Infantry Division, an active division which took part in the French campaign. Engaged in the Balkan campaign and later in the Ukraine. Has since remained on the southern sector of the Russian front. Took part in the retreat from the Mius in the summer of 1943 and has been engaged in the Zaporozhe area.

RESTRICTED

18th Motorized Division

Commander: Genmaj. Hans-Georg LEYSER
Composition: 118th (?) Pz Bn, 30th Mtz Inf Regt, 51st Mtz Inf Regt, 18th Mtz Arty Regt, 118th Pz Rcn Bn, 18th AT Bn, 18th Mtz Engr Bn, 18th Mtz Sig Bn
Auxiliary unit number: 18
Home station: Liegnitz (Wkr. VIII)

Originally the 18th Infantry Division, an active division. As such fought in Poland and in northern France. Motorized in the autumn of 1940. Fought in Russia from the beginning of the campaign, first on the central and subsequently on the northern sector. Transferred back to the central sector in the autumn of 1943, where it was engaged west of Smolensk.

20th Motorized Division

Commander:
Composition: 120th Pz Bn, 76th Mtz Inf Regt, 90th Mtz Inf Regt, 20th Mtz Arty Regt, 120th Pz Rcn Bn, 20th AT Bn, 20th Mtz Engr Bn, Mtz 20th Sig Bn
Auxiliary unit number: 20
Home station: Hamburg (Wkr. X)

Active division. Fought in Poland and in France. Morale very high. First identified in Russia in the Minsk area and later on the northern sector. Engaged at Velikie Luki (central) sector) in the spring of 1943. Fought on the central sector in the summer of 1943 and was later transferred to the southern sector, where it sustained very heavy losses in the retreat from Kiev in November 1943.

RESTRICTED

ORDER OF BATTLE OF THE GERMAN ARMY 267

22d Motorized Division (Airborne)

Commander: Genlt. Friedrich Wilhelm MÜLLER (47)
Composition: 212th (?) Pz Bn, 16th Mtz Inf Regt, 65th Mtz Inf Regt, 22d Mtz Arty Regt, 122d Pz Rcn Bn, 22d AT Bn, 22d Mtz Engr Bn, 22d Mtz Sig Bn
Auxiliary unit number: 22
Home station: Oldenburg (Wkr. X)

Active division. Employed as an airborne division in Holland. Engaged continuously on the southern sector of the Russian front. Transferred from the Crimea to Salonika and thence to Crete in the late summer of 1942. Sent one regiment (Grenadier Regiment 47) to Tunisia at the end of 1942, where it was destroyed. The remaining two regiments stayed in Crete, where the division was reorganized as a motorized division in the spring of 1943. Has the honorary designation of Luftlande-Division (air landing division).

25th Motorized Division

Commander: Genlt. Anton GRASSER (53)
Composition: 125th (?) Pz Bn, 35th Mtz Inf Regt, 119th Mtz Inf Regt, 25th Mtz Arty Regt, 125th Pz Rcn Bn, 25th AT Bn, 25th Mtz Engr Bn, 25th Mtz Sig Bn
Auxiliary unit number: 25
Home station: Ludwigsburg (Wkr. V)

Originally the 25th Infantry Division, an active division. Took little part in early operations. Motorized in the autumn of 1940. Has fought on the central sector of the Russian front since the beginning of the campaign. Took part in the Kursk offensive in the summer of 1943, where it appears to have sustained heavy losses. Subsequently engaged west of Smolensk.

RESTRICTED

29th Motorized Division

Commander: Genmaj. FRIES (48)
Composition: 129th Pz Bn, 15th Mtz Inf Regt, 71st Mtz Inf Regt, 29th Mtz Arty Regt, 129th Pz Rcn Bn, 29th AT Bn, 29th Mtz Engr Bn, 29th Mtz Sig Bn
Auxiliary unit number: 29
Home station: Erfurt (Wkr. IX)

Active division. Fought in Poland and France. Identified on the central sector of the Russian front in July 1941. Transferred to the southern sector in the summer of 1942 and virtually destroyed at Stalingrad. Reformed in southwestern France in the spring of 1943, where it absorbed the bulk of the 345th Motorized Division. The greater part of the division took part in the Sicilian campaign in July 1943, and it has since been engaged in the operations in southern Italy.

36th Motorized Division

Commander:
Composition: 136th (?) Pz Bn, 87th Mtz Inf Regt, 118th Mtz Inf Regt, 36th Mtz Arty Regt, 136th Pz Rcn Bn, 36th AT Bn, 36th Mtz Engr Bn, 36th Mtz Sig Bn
Auxiliary unit number: 36
Home station: Wiesbaden (Wkr. XII)

Originally the 36th Infantry Division, an active division. Fought in France. Motorized in the autumn of 1940. Entered Russia via the Baltic States and has since operated on the central sector. Suffered heavy losses in the Rzhev area in the summer of 1942 and again in the summer of 1943 when taking part in the Kursk offensive.

RESTRICTED

60th Motorized Division

Commander: Genlt. Otto KOHLERMANN
Composition: 160th Pz Bn, (120th) "Füsilier Regt Feldherrnhalle", (271st) "Grenadier Regt Feldherrnhalle", 160th Mtz Arty Regt, 160th Pz Rcn Bn, 160th AT Bn, 160th Mtz Engr Bn, 160th Mtz Sig Bn
Auxiliary unit number: 160
Home station: Danzig (Wkr. XX)

Originally the 60th Infantry Division, formed at Danzig in August 1939 and embodying the Danzig Heimwehr (SA-Brigade Eberhardt). As such took part in the attack on the Hela Peninsula in September 1939 and in the French campaign. Motorized in the late summer of 1940 and fought in Yugoslavia in April 1941. Subsequently on the southern sector of the Russian front. Virtually destroyed at Stalingrad. Reformed in southern France in the summer of 1943, incorporating the 271st "Feldherrnhalle" Regiment, which previously belonged to the 93d Infantry Division, in place of the 92d Motorized Regiment, later reconstituted in Croatia as an independent unit. The division was given the honorary name of Panzer-Grenadier-Division "Feldherrnhalle" and is said to be principally made up of volunteers from the Nazi storm troops (SA) from all parts of Germany. It remained in France until the late autumn of 1943, when it was transferred to the central sector of the Russian front.

90th Motorized Division

Commander: Genlt. Carl Hans LUNGERSHAUSEN (48)
Composition: 190th Pz Bn, 155th Pz Gren Regt, 200th Pz Gren Regt, 361st Pz Gren Regt, 190th Mtz Arty Regt, 190th Pz Rcn Bn, 190th AT Bn, 190th Mtz Engr Bn, 190th Mtz Sig Bn
Auxiliary unit number: 190
Home station: (Wkr. III)

RESTRICTED

Formed as "Afrika-Division z.b.V." early in 1941. First identified in Africa during the autumn. Renamed "90th Light Division" in November 1941. Reorganized in March 1942 and renamed 90th Light Africa Division in the latter part of 1942. Entered Tunisia early in 1943 and was destroyed there in May 1943. In June 1943 Division Sardinien, formed from miscellaneous units in Sardinia, was renamed the 90th Panzer Grenadier Division. It withdrew to Corsica in the autumn of 1943 and then to northern Italy. Subsequently went into action on the southern Italian front. Its regiments bear the honorary title of Panzer-Grenadier-Regiment.

164th Motorized Division

Commander:
Composition: 164th (?) Pz Bn, 125th Pz Gren Regt, 382d (?) Pz Gren Regt, 433d Pz Gren Regt, 220th Mtz Arty Regt, 164th (?) Pz Rcn Bn, 220th AT Bn, 220th Mtz Engr Bn, 220th Mtz Sig Bn
Auxiliary unit number: 220
Home station: Leipzig (Wkr IV)

Formed in January 1940 as the 164th Infantry Division. In reserve on the western front; first identified in action in Greece. Remained in the Aegean area after the Balkan campaign, based first at Salonika and, from early in 1942, on Crete. Transferred to the Panzer Army of Africa during the summer of 1942 and there classified as a light division. Renamed 164th Light Africa Division toward the end of the year. Entered Tunisia early in 1943, where it was destroyed in May. Reformed in Brittany in the autumn of 1943 as a Panzer Grenadier Division. Its regiments are believed to bear the honorary title of Panzer-Grenadier-Regiment. Panzer-Grenadier-Regiment 382 is now possibly a GHQ unit.

RESTRICTED

345th Motorized Division

Commander:
Composition: 148th Mtz Inf Regt, 152d Mtz Inf Regt
Auxiliary unit number:
Home station:

Formed late in 1942. In southern France until the spring of 1943, when the bulk of its personnel was incorporated into the reforming 29th Motorized Division; in effect, the 148th Motorized Infantry Regiment was converted into the 15th, and the 152d into the 71st. Its continued existence as a division is improbable, although it may reform.

386th Motorized Division

Commander:
Composition: 149th Mtz Inf Regt, 153d Mtz Inf Regt
Auxiliary unit number:
Home station:

Formed in October 1942. First identified in March 1943 in southwestern France, where the bulk of its personnel was shortly thereafter incorporated into the reforming 3d Motorized Division; in effect, the 149th Motorized Infantry Regiment was converted into the 8th, and the 153d into the 29th. Its continued existence as a division is doubtful, although it may be reforming.

RESTRICTED

34. Light divisions (Jägerdivisionen).

5th Light Division

Commander: Genlt. Helmuth THUMM (49)
Composition: 56th Jäger Regt, 75th Jäger Regt, 5th Mtz Arty Regt, 5th Rcn Bn, 5th AT Bn, 5th Mtz Engr Bn, 5th Mtz Sig Bn
Auxiliary unit number: 5
Home station: Konstanz (Wkr. V)

Originally the 5th Infantry Division, an active division. As such took part in the French campaign. Identified in Russia during the summer of 1941. After suffering heavy casualties on the Vyazma sector, it was withdrawn to France during December for rest and conversion to a light division. Returned to the northern sector of the Russian front in February 1942. It has remained on that sector, mostly in the Staraya Russia area, ever since.

8th Light Division

Commander:
Composition: 28th Jäger Regt, 38th Jäger Regt, 8th Mtz Arty Regt, 8th Rcn Bn, 8th AT Bn, 8th Mtz Engr Bn, 8th Mtz Sig Bn
Auxiliary unit number: 8
Home station: Neisse (Wkr. VIII)

Originally the 8th Infantry Division, an active division. As such fought in Poland and France and took part in the Russian campaign from the outset. After suffering heavy casualties, it was withdrawn to France in December 1941 for rest and conversion to a light division. Returned to the northern sector of the Russian front in the early spring of 1942, where it has remained.

RESTRICTED

28th Light Division

Commander:
Composition: 49th Jäger Regt, 83d Jäger Regt, 28th Mtz Arty Regt, 28th Rcn Bn, 28th AT Bn, 28th Mtz Engr Bn, 28th Mtz Sig Bn
Auxiliary unit number: 28
Home station: Breslau (Wkr. VIII)

Originally the 28th Infantry Division, an active division. As such engaged in the Polish and French campaigns. Identified on the central sector of the Russian front during the late summer of 1941. Withdrawn to France in November for rest and conversion to a light division. Returned to Russia at the end of the winter and took part in operations on the Kerch sector during May 1942. Transferred to the northern sector in the late summer of 1942, where it has since remained.

90th Light Africa Division—See 90th Mtz Div

97th Light Division

Commander: Genlt. Ludwig MÜLLER (52)
Composition: 204th Jäger Regt, 207th Jäger Regt, 81st Arty Regt, 97th Rcn Bn, 97th AT Bn, 97th Engr Bn, 97th Sig Bn
Auxiliary unit number: 97
Home station: (Wkr. VII)

Formed in December 1940. First identified in action on the southern sector of the Russian front during the summer of 1941. Took part in the advance into the Caucasus in the summer of 1942 and later retreated to the Kuban. Evacuated to the lower Dnieper area in the autumn of 1943.

RESTRICTED

99th Light Division—See 7th Mtn Div

100th Light Division

Commander: Genmaj. Willibald UTZ
Composition: 54th Jäger Regt, 227th Jäger Regt, 83d Arty Regt, 100th Rcn Bn, 100th AT Bn, 100th Engr Bn, 100th Sig Bn
Auxiliary unit number: 100
Home station: (Wkr. XVII)

Formed in December 1940. First identified in action during the summer of 1941 on the southern sector of the Russian front. The 369th Reinforced Infantry Regiment (Croatian) was attached to it until late in 1942. The division was virtually destroyed at Stalingrad. Reformed in the Belgrade area in May 1943 and transferred to Albania in the summer of that year, where it has remained.

101st Light Division

Commander: Genlt. Emil VOGEL (50)
Composition: 228th Jäger Regt, 229th Jäger Regt, 85th Arty Regt, 101st Rcn Bn, 101st AT Bn, 101st Engr Bn, 101st Sig Bn
Auxiliary unit number: 101
Home station: (Wkr. V)

Formed in December 1940. First identified in action on the southern sector of the Russian front during the summer of 1941. Took part in the advance into the Caucasus in the summer of 1942 and later retreated to the Kuban. Evacuated to the lower Dnieper area in the autumn of 1943.

RESTRICTED

104th Light Division

Commander: Genmaj. Hartwig v. LUDWIGER (49)
Composition: 724th Jäger Regt, 734th Jäger Regt, 654th Arty Regt, 104th (?) Rcn Bn, AT Bn, 104th Engr Bn, 104th Sig Bn
Auxiliary unit number: 104
Home station: (Wkr. IV)

Formed in April 1941 as the 704th Infantry Division. In Yugoslavia between September 1941 and April 1943, where it was converted into a light division and renumbered. In June 1943 it moved to western Greece, where it has since been engaged in occupational duties.

114th Light Division

Commander: Genlt. Karl EGLSEER
Composition: 721st Jäger Regt, 741st Jäger Regt, 661st Arty Regt, Rcn Bn, AT Bn, 114th Engr Bn, 114th Sig Bn
Auxiliary unit number: 114
Home station: (Wkr. I)

Formed in April 1941 as the 714th Infantry Division. Engaged in mopping-up duties in Yugoslavia from November 1941 to April 1943, when it was converted into a light division and renumbered. Still in Yugoslavia.

117th Light Division

Commander: Genmaj. von LE SUIRE (48)
Composition: 737th Jäger Regt, 749th Jäger Regt, 670th Arty Regt, Rcn Bn, AT Bn, 117th Engr Bn, 117th Sig Bn
Auxiliary unit number: 117(?)
Home station: (Wkr. XVII)

RESTRICTED

Formed in April 1941 as the 717th Infantry Division. Engaged in mopping-up operations in Yugoslavia from November 1941 to April 1943, when it was converted into a light division and renumbered. In May 1943 it moved to Greece and has since been engaged in occupational duties in the Peloponnesus.

118th Light Division

Commander: Genmaj. Josef KÜBLER
Composition: 738th Jäger Regt, 750th Jäger Regt, 668th Arty Regt, Rcn Bn, AT Bn, 118th Engr Bn, 118th Sig Bn
Auxiliary unit number: 118
Home station: (Wkr. XVIII)

Formed in April 1941 as the 718th Infantry Division. Stationed in Yugoslavia since the summer of 1941. In April 1943 it was converted into a light division and renumbered.

164th Light Africa Division—See 164th Mtz Div

RESTRICTED

… ORDER OF BATTLE OF THE GERMAN ARMY

35. Panzer Divisions *(Panzerdivisionen)*.

1st Panzer Division

Commander: Genlt. Eugen (Walter) KRÜGER (54)
Composition: 1st Pz Regt, 1st Pz Gren Regt, 113th Pz Gren Regt, 73d Pz Arty Regt, 1st Pz Rcn Bn, 37th AT Bn, 37th Pz Engr Bn, 37th Pz Sig Bn
Auxiliary unit number: 81
Home station: Weimar (Wkr. IX)

Active division. Took part in the Polish and French campaigns. Continuously engaged in Russia, at first on the northern sector and subsequently on the central sector. Transferred to France early in 1943. Sent to the Balkans in the late spring of 1943 and returned to Russia in the late autumn.

2d Panzer Division

Commander: Genlt. Vollrath LÜBBE (50)
Composition: 3d Pz Regt, 2nd Pz Gren Regt, 304th Pz Gren Regt, 74th Pz Arty Regt, 2nd Pz Rcn Bn, 38th AT Bn, 38th Pz Engr Bn, 38th Pz Sig Bn
Auxiliary unit number: 82
Home station: Wien (Wkr. XVII)

Active division. Fought in the Polish, French, and Balkan campaigns. Engaged in Russia on the central sector since September 1941. Took part in the Kursk offensive in the summer of 1943 and was later active in the middle Dnieper area.

RESTRICTED

3d Panzer Division

Commander: Genmaj. Fritz BAYERLEIN (55)
Composition: 6th Pz Regt, 3d Pz Gren Regt, 394th Pz Gren Regt, 75th Pz Arty Regt, 3d Pz Rcn Bn, AT Bn, 39th Pz Engr Bn, 39th Pz Sig Bn
Auxiliary unit number: 83
Home station: Berlin (Wkr. III)

Active division. Fought in Poland and in the campaign in Belgium and France. Continuously engaged in Russia from the outset, first on the central and subsequently on the southern sector. Suffered heavy losses in the Mozdok area at the end of 1942. Heavily engaged in the Kharkov area during the summer of 1943 and subsequently in the Dnieper bend.

4th Panzer Division

Commander: Genlt. Dietrich v. SAUCKEN (52)
Composition: 35th Pz Regt, 12th Pz Gren Regt, 33d Pz Gren Regt, 103d Pz Arty Regt, 4th Pz Rcn Bn, 49th AT Bn, 79th Pz Engr Bn, 79th Pz Sig Bn
Auxiliary unit number: 84
Home station: Würzburg (Wkr. XIII)

Active division. Fought in Poland and in the campaigns in Belgium and France. Continuously engaged on the central sector of the Russian front. Took part in the Kursk offensive in the summer of 1943 and subsequently fought west of the middle Dnieper.

RESTRICTED

5th Panzer Division

Commander: Genmaj. Karl DECKER
Composition: 31st Pz Regt, 13th Pz Gren Regt, 14th Pz Gren Regt, 116th Pz Arty Regt, 5th Pz Rcn Bn, 53d AT Bn, 89th Pz Engr Bn, 85th(?) Pz Sig Bn
Auxiliary unit number: 85
Home station: Oppeln (Wkr. VIII)

Active division, formed late in 1938. Took part in the Polish campaign and was prominent in the French and Balkan campaigns. Continuously engaged on the central sector of the Russian front. Took part in the Kursk offensive in the summer of 1943, where it apparently suffered heavy losses. Subsequently fought west of the middle Dnieper.

6th Panzer Division

Commander:
Composition: 11th Pz Regt, 4th Pz Gren Regt, 114th Pz Gren Regt, 76th Pz Arty Regt, 6th Pz Rcn Bn, 41st AT Bn, 57th Pz Engr Bn, 82d Pz Sig Bn
Auxiliary unit number: 57
Home station: Wuppertal (Wkr. VI)

Active division (formerly 1st Light Division). Fought in Poland and in France. Has been continuously engaged on the Russian front, first on the northern sector and later on the central sector, where it apparently suffered serious losses. Transferred to France for rest and refit in May 1942. In December 1942 it returned to the southern sector of the Russian front and was heavily engaged in the Belgorod offensive in the summer of 1943.

RESTRICTED

7th Panzer Division

Commander: Genmaj. Hasso Eccard v. MANTEUFFEL (47)
Composition: 25th Pz Regt, 6th Pz Gren Regt, 7th Pz Gren Regt, 78th Pz Arty Regt, 7th Pz Rcn Bn, 42d AT Bn, 58th Pz Engr Bn, 83d Pz Sig Bn
Auxiliary unit number: 58
Home station: Gera (Wkr. IX)

Active division (formerly 2d Light Division). Fought in Poland and with outstanding dash in France, where it was commanded by the then Genmaj. ROMMEL. Heavily and continuously engaged on the central sector of the Russian front in 1941-1942. Transferred to France for rest and refit in May 1942. Took part in the occupation of former unoccupied France. Returned to the southern sector of the Russian front in February 1943. Engaged in the Belgorod offensive in the summer of 1943 and apparently suffered heavy losses in the retreat west of Kiev in November 1943.

8th Panzer Division

Commander: Obst.(?) FRÖHLICH
Composition: 10th Pz Regt, 8th Pz Gren Regt, 28th Pz Gren Regt, 80th Pz Arty Regt, 8th Pz Rcn Bn, 43d AT Bn, 59th Pz Engr Bn, 59th Pz Sig Bn
Auxiliary unit number: 59
Home station: Cottbus (Wkr. III)

Active division (formerly 3d Light Division). Fought in Poland, France, and Yugoslavia. Continuously and heavily engaged on the northern sector of the Russian front up to the end of 1941. Identified on the central sector in the autumn of 1942. Transferred to the southern sector after the Orel

RESTRICTED

offensive in the summer of 1943. Apparently suffered heavy casualties in the following autumn during the retreat west of Kiev.

9th Panzer division

Commander: Genlt. Walther SCHELLER (52)
Composition: 33d Pz Regt, 10th Pz Gren Regt, 11th Pz Gren Regt, 102d Pz Arty Regt, 9th Pz Rcn Bn, 50th AT Bn, 86th Pz Engr Bn, 81st Pz Sig Bn
Auxiliary unit number: 60
Home station: Wien (Wkr. XVII)

Active division (formerly 4th Light Division). Took part in the Polish, French, and Balkan campaigns. Continuously engaged in Russia during the advance through the Ukraine and during the offensive on the southern sector in 1942. Later transferred to the central sector, where it took part in the Kursk offensive in the summer of 1943. Returned to the southern sector in the following autumn, where it has been heavily engaged in the Dnieper bend.

10th Panzer Division

Commander:
Composition: 7th Pz Regt, 69th Pz Gren Regt, 86th Pz Gren Regt, 90th Pz Arty Regt, 10th Pz Rcn Bn, 90th AT Bn, 49th Pz Engr Bn, 90th Pz Sig Bn
Auxiliary unit number: 90
Home station: Stuttgart (Wkr. V)

Composite division, made up of active units from various parts of Germany. Fought in Poland and France. Heavily

RESTRICTED

engaged on the central sector of the Russian front up to the end of 1941. Transferred to France for rest and refit in May 1942. Took part in the occupation of former unoccupied France. Transferred to Tunisia late in 1942, where it was destroyed in May 1943. Reconstituted in northwestern France late in 1943.

11th Panzer Division

Commander: Genmaj. Wend v. WIETERSHEIM (44)
Composition: 15th Pz Regt, 110th Pz Gren Regt, 111th Pz Gren Regt, 119th Pz Arty Regt, 11th Pz Rcn Bn, AT Bn, 209th Pz Engr Bn, 341st Pz Sig Bn
Auxiliary unit number: 61
Home station: Görlitz (Wkr. VIII)

Formation completed after the French campaign, during which the 11th Motorized Infantry Brigade fought as an independent command. Took part in the Balkan campaign. Continuously engaged in Russia, first in the advance through the Ukraine and subsequently on the central sector. Transferred to the southern sector in the summer of 1942. Took part in the Belgorod offensive in the summer of 1943 and heavily engaged in the Krivoi Rog area in the autumn of 1943.

12th Panzer Division

Commander:
Composition: 29th Pz Regt, 5th Pz Gren Regt, 25th Pz Gren Regt, 2d Pz Arty Regt, 12th Pz Rcn Bn, 2d AT Bn, 32d Pz Engr Bn, 2d Pz Sig Bn
Auxiliary unit number: 2
Home station: Stettin (Wkr. II)

RESTRICTED

Originally the 2d Motorized Division, an active division. As such saw little fighting in Poland, but was actively engaged in France. Reorganized as the 12th Panzer Division in the autumn of 1940. Continuously engaged on the Russian front, first on the central and later on the northern sector up to the end of 1941, when, after sustaining considerable losses, it was withdrawn to Estonia for rest and refit. Subsequently returned to the northern sector of the Russian front. It was later transferred to the central sector and took part in the Kursk offensive in the summer of 1943. Has since been heavily engaged west of the middle Dnieper.

13th Panzer Division

Commander: Genmaj. HAUSER
Composition: 4th Pz Regt, 66th Pz Gren Regt, 93d Pz Gren Regt, 13th Pz Arty Regt, 13th Pz Rcn Bn, 13th AT Bn, 4th Pz Engr Bn, 13th Pz Sig Bn
Auxiliary unit number: 13
Home station: Magdeburg (Wkr. XI)

Formed in the autumn of 1940 out of the former 13th Motorized Division, an active division, which had fought in Poland and in France. Spent the winter of 1940-41 in Rumania. Continuously engaged on the southern sector of the Russian front, where it took part in the encirclement of Kiev in 1941 and in the advance to Mozdok in 1942. Suffered heavy losses late in 1942. Took part in the retreat from the Caucasus in the following winter and remained in the Kuban area until evacuated to the lower Dnieper in the autumn of 1943. Last reported in the Dnieper bend.

RESTRICTED

14th Panzer Division

Commander:
Composition: 36th Pz Regt, 103d Pz Gren Regt, 108th Pz Gren Regt, 4th Pz Arty Regt, 14th Pz Rcn Bn, 4th AT Bn, 13th Pz Engr Bn, 4th Pz Sig Bn
Auxiliary unit number: 4
Home station: Dresden (Wkr. IV)

Originally the 4th Infantry Division, an active division. As such fought in Poland and in the French campaign. Reorganized as the 14th Panzer Division in the late summer of 1940. Fought in Yugoslavia in the Balkan campaign and was continuously engaged on the southern sector of the Russian front, where it was finally encircled and virtually destroyed at Stalingrad. Reformed in Brittany in the summer of 1943 and transferred to the southern sector of the Russian front in October 1943, where it was last reported in the Dnieper bend.

15th Panzer Division—See 15th Motorized Division

16th Panzer Division

Commander:
Composition: 2d Pz Regt, 64th Pz Gren Regt, 79th Pz Gren Regt, 16th Pz Arty Regt, 16th Pz Rcn Bn, 16th AT Bn, 16th Pz Engr Bn, 16th Pz Sig Bn
Auxiliary unit number: 16
Home station: Münster (Wkr. VI)

Originally the 16th Infantry Division, an active division. As such took part in the French campaign. Reorganized as the 16th Panzer Division in the late summer of 1940. First identified in action during the early weeks of the Russian campaign and then continuously engaged on the southern

RESTRICTED

sector. Virtually destroyed at Stalingrad. Reformed in France in the spring of 1943. Moved to Italy in June 1943 and was in action at Salerno and north of Naples. Transferred to Russia in the winter of 1943-44 for the German counterdrive west of Kiev.

17th Panzer Division

Commander: Genmaj. Karl-Friedrich v. der MEDEN (48)
Composition: 39th Pz Regt, 40th Pz Gren Regt, 63d Pz Gren Regt, 27th Pz Arty Regt, 17th Pz Rcn Bn, 27th AT Bn, 27th Pz Engr Bn, 27th Pz Sig Bn
Auxiliary unit number: 27
Home station: Augsburg (Wkr. VII)

Originally the 27th Infantry Division, an active division. As such fought in Poland and in France. Reorganized as the 17th Panzer Division in the autumn of 1940. First identified on the central sector of the Russian front in late June 1941 and subsequently was continuously in action. Transferred to the southern sector at the time of the Russian offensive in November 1942. Heavily engaged during the defensive operations in the Donets and Dnieper bend areas in the summer and autumn of 1943.

18th Panzer Division

Commander:
Composition: 18th Pz Regt, 52d Pz Gren Regt, 101st Pz Gren Regt, 88th Pz Arty Regt, 18th Pz Rcn Bn, 88th AT Bn, 98th Pz Engr Bn, 88th Pz Sig Bn
Auxiliary unit number: 88
Home station: (Wkr. IV)

RESTRICTED

Formed in the autumn of 1940. First identified in action on the central sector of the Russian front in late June 1941. Operated on the southern sector in the summer of 1942 and subsequently transferred back to the central sector. In action west of Kiev in the autumn of 1943.

19th Panzer Division

Commander: Genlt. Gustav SCHMIDT (50)
Composition: 27th Pz Regt, 73d Pz Gren Regt, 74th Pz Gren Regt, 19th Pz Arty Regt, 19th Pz Rcn Bn, 19th AT Bn, 19th Pz Engr Bn, 19th Pz Sig Bn
Auxiliary unit number: 19
Home station: Hannover (Wkr. XI)

Originally the 19th Infantry Division, an active division. As such fought in Poland and in Belgium. Reorganized as the 19th Panzer Division in the autumn of 1940. Took part in the initial attack on Russia and has since operated on the central sector. Transferred to the southern sector in the spring of 1943 and took part in the Belgorod offensive in the summer, where it apparently suffered heavy casualties.

20th Panzer Division

Commander: Genlt. Heinrich Frhr. v. LÜTTWITZ (48)
Composition: 21st Pz Regt, 59th Pz Gren Regt, 112th Pz Gren Regt, 92d Pz Arty Regt, 20th Pz Rcn Bn, 92d AT Bn, 92d Pz Engr Bn, 92d Pz Sig Bn
Auxiliary unit number: 92
Home station: Gotha (Wkr. IX)

RESTRICTED

Formed in the autumn of 1940, First identified in action on the central sector of the Russian front at the outset of the campaign, where it has been continuously engaged ever since. It took part in the Orel offensive in the summer of 1943.

21st Panzer Division

Commander:
Composition: 5th Pz Regt, 192d(?) Pz Gren Regt, 492d(?) Pz Gren Regt, 155th Pz Arty Regt, 21st Pz Rcn Bn, 39th AT Bn, 200th Pz Engr Bn, 200th Pz Sig Bn
Auxiliary unit number: 200
Home station: Berlin (Wkr. III)

At first known as the 5th Light Division. Formed after the French campaign partly from units of the 3d Panzer Division. Reorganized as a Panzer division in Africa in the summer of 1941. Entered Tunisia early in 1943, where it was destroyed in May. Reformed in Normandy in the summer of 1943.

22d Panzer Division

Commander:
Composition: 204th Pz Regt, 129th Pz Gren Regt, 140th Pz Gren Regt, 140th Pz Arty Regt, 22d Pz Rcn Bn, 140th AT Bn, 140th Pz Engr Bn, 140th Pz Sig Bn
Auxiliary unit number:
Home station: (Wkr. XII)

Formed in France in 1941. Transferred to the southern

RESTRICTED

sector of the Russian front early in 1942 and thrown immediately into action. Subsequently suffered heavy casualties both in the Crimea and at Stalingrad. It is believed to have since been disbanded. (Panzer-Grenadier-Regiment 129 is now under the control of the 15th Mtz Div.)

23d Panzer Division

Commander: Genlt. Nikolaus v. VORMANN (49)
Composition: 201st Pz Regt, 126th Pz Gren Regt, 128th Pz Gren Regt, 128th Pz Arty Regt, 23d Pz Rcn Bn, 128th AT Bn, 128th Pz Engr Bn, 128th Pz Sig Bn
Auxiliary unit number: 128
Home station: (Wkr. V)

Formed in France in 1941. Transferred to Russia in the spring of 1942 and identified in action in the Kharkov area. Later fought at Mozdok; transferred to the Stalingrad area at the time of the Russian breakthrough. Retreated from the Mius front in the summer of 1943 and was subsequently heavily engaged in the Dnieper bend.

24th Panzer Division

Commander: Genmaj. Reichsfrhr. von EDELSHEIM
Composition: 24th Pz Regt, 21st Pz Gren Regt, 26th Füsilier Regt, 89th Pz Arty Regt, 24th Pz Rcn Bn, 40th AT Bn, 40th Pz Engr Bn, 86th Pz Sig Bn
Auxiliary unit number: 40
Home station: (Wkr. I)

Formed in France in February 1942, largely from the for-

RESTRICTED

mer 1st Cavalry Division, which had fought as a brigade in Poland and as a division in France and in the early stages of the Russian campaign. Transferred to the southern sector of the Russian front in the summer of 1942 and virtually destroyed at Stalingrad. Reformed in France, went to northern Italy in the summer of 1943, and returned to the southern sector of the Russian front in the following autumn.

25th Panzer Division

Commander: Genlt. Adolf v. SCHELL (50)
Composition: 9th Pz Regt, 146th Pz Gren Regt, 147th Pz Gren Regt, 91st Pz Arty Regt, 25th Pz Rcn Bn, AT Bn, 75th(?) Pz Engr Bn, 87th (?) Pz Sig Bn
Auxiliary unit number: 87
Home station: (Wkr. VI)

Formed in Norway early in 1942 at a strength below normal. Transferred to northern France in August 1943, where it was brought up to strength. Sent to the southern sector of the Russian front in October 1943, where it was engaged in the area west of Kiev.

26th Panzer Division

Commander: Genlt. Smilo Frhr. v. LÜTTWITZ (49)
Composition: 26th Pz Regt, 9th Pz Gren Regt, 67th Pz Gren Regt, 93d Pz Arty Regt, 26th Pz Rcn Bn, 93d AT Bn, 93d Pz Engr Bn, 93d Pz Sig Bn
Auxiliary unit number: 93
Home station: Potsdam (Wkr. III)

RESTRICTED

Formed in France in the autumn of 1942 from elements of the 23d Infantry Division. Remained in France until July 1943, when it was transferred to Italy, where it has since been engaged in combat.

27th Panzer Division

Commander:
Composition:
Auxiliary unit number:
Home station:

Formed in France during the summer and autumn of 1942. Operated on the southern sector of the Russian front in the winter of 1942–43 and is now believed to have been disbanded.

Panzer Division "Hermann Göring"

Commander: Genlt. (LW) Paul CONRATH (48)
Deputy Commander: Obst. SCHMALZ
Composition: Pz Regt HG, Gren Regt 1 HG, Gren Regt 2 HG, Jäger(?) Regt HG, Arty Regt HG, AA Regt HG, Pz Rcn Bn HG, Pz Engr Bn HG, Pz Sig Bn HG
Auxiliary unit number: All units bear the name "Hermann Göring"
Home station: Berlin (Wkr. III)

The Hermann Göring Brigade was formed in the summer 1942 from the Regiment General Göring and in January 1943 was converted into a Panzer division. The greater part of it was sent to Tunisia, where it was virtually destroyed. In May and June 1943 it was rapidly reformed from elements which had remained in southern France and was sent to

RESTRICTED

Sicily. It was heavily engaged in the Sicilian campaign and withdrew to the Italian mainland in August, where it has since been constantly in action.

Panzer Grenadier Division "Grossdeutschland"

Commander: Genlt. Walter HOERNLEIN (51)
Deputy Commander: Obst. Hyazinth Graf STRACHWITZ (51)
Composition: Pz Regt GD, Gren Regt GD, Füsilier Regt GD, Arty Regt GD, Pz Rcn Bn GD, AT Bn GD, Pz Engr Bn GD, Sig Bn GD
Auxiliary unit number: All units bear the name "Grossdeutschland"
Home station: Berlin (Wkr. III)

Formed in the spring of 1942 as a motorized division by the expansion of the former independent regiment of the same name, which had been operating on the central sector of the Russian front. In peacetime this regiment was stationed in Berlin, its personnel being drawn from all over Germany. In action as a division on the southern sector of the Russian front from June 1942. Transferred to the central sector in September 1942 and back to the southern sector at the time of the Russian offensive in the following winter, where it was fairly heavily and continuously engaged. At the time of the German offensive in the summer of 1943 it was transferred to the Orel area, but was hastily switched back to the southern sector shortly afterwards. Heavily engaged in the withdrawal from Kharkov and the Donetz and subsequently in the Dnieper bend. Although known as Panzer Grenadier Division "Grossdeutschland" it is rated as a full Panzer division as it includes a tank regiment. This division is a corps d'élite and has the honor of providing the guard for the Führer's headquarters.

RESTRICTED

36. Mountain Divisions (*Gebirgsdivisionen*).

1st Mountain Division

Commander: Genmaj. Walter STETTNER Ritter v. GRABENHOFEN (52)
Composition: 98th Mtn Inf Regt, 99th Mtn Inf Regt, 79th Mtn Arty Regt, 54th Rcn Bn, 44th Mtn AT Bn, 54th Mtn Engr Bn, 54th Mtn Sig Bn
Auxiliary unit number: 54
Home station: Garmisch (Wkr. VII)

Active division. Took part in the Polish, French, and Balkan campaigns. In action on the southern sector of the Russian front in July 1941 and in the Caucasus in 1942. Transferred to northern Greece in March 1943 and to the Greco-Albanian frontier in the summer of 1943. Subsequently in western Serbia and Montenegro.

2d Mountain Division

Commander: Obst. DEGEN
Composition: 136th Mtn Inf Regt, 137th Mtn Inf Regt, 111th Mtn Arty Regt, 67th Rcn Bn, 55th Mtn AT Bn, 67th Mtn Engr Bn, 67th Mtn Sig Bn
Auxiliary unit number: 67
Home station: Innsbruck (Wkr. XVIII)

Active division. Took part in the Polish and Norwegian campaigns. Part of the Mountain Corps (later expanded to the Lapland Army) at the opening of the Russian campaign. After suffering casualties in operations on the Murmansk front was withdrawn to northern Norway and held in reserve during the winter of 1941–42. Since then operating in northern Finland.

RESTRICTED

3d Mountain Division

Commander: Genmaj. WITTMANN (49)
Composition: 138th Mtn Inf Regt, 144th Mtn Inf Regt, 112th Mtn Arty Regt, 68th Rcn Bn, 48th Mtn AT Bn, 83d Mtn Engr Bn, 68th Mtn Sig Bn
Auxiliary unit number: 68
Home station: Graz (Wkr. XVIII)

Active division. Took part in the Polish and Norwegian campaigns. Part of the Mountain Corps (later expanded to the Lapland Army) at the opening of the Russian campaign. Reported partly in Norway and partly in Finland during the winter 1941-42. Transferred from Norway to the Baltic states in the autumn of 1942. Moved to the southern sector of the Russian front early in 1943. Took part in the retreat from the Mius in the summer of 1943 and was in action in the Zaporozhe area in the following autumn.

4th Mountain Division

Commander:
Composition: 13th Mtn Inf Regt, 91st Mtn Inf Regt, 94th Mtn Arty Regt, 94th Rcn Bn, 94th Mtn AT Bn, 94th Mtn Engr Bn, 94th Mtn Sig Bn
Auxiliary unit number: 94
Home station: (Wkr. VII)

Formed in the autumn of 1940. First identified during the Balkan campaign. Has operated on the southern sector of the Russian front from the outset. Took part in the advance into the Caucasus in the summer of 1942. Withdrawn to the Kuban in the winter of that year and evacuated to the Crimea in the autumn of 1943.

RESTRICTED

5th Mountain Division

Commander: Genlt. Julius RINGEL (55)
Composition: 85th Mtn Inf Regt, 100th Mtn Inf Regt, 95th Mtn Arty Regt, 95th Rcn Bn, 95th Mtn AT Bn, 95th Mtn Engr Bn, 95th Mtn Sig Bn
Auxiliary unit number: 95
Home station: Salzburg (Wkr. XVIII)

Formed in the autumn of 1940. First identified in Greece, where it was heavily engaged during the Balkan campaign. Subsequently took part in the airborne attack on Crete. Remained in the Aegean area during 1941. Transferred to the Leningrad sector early in 1942 and to Italy late in 1943, where it has fought on the southern front.

6th Mountain Division

Commander: Genlt. Christian PHILIPP
Composition: 141st Mtn Inf Regt, 143d Mtn Inf Regt, 118th Mtn Arty Regt, 112th Rcn Bn, 47th Mtn AT Bn, 91st Mtn Engr Bn, 91st Mtn Sig Bn
Auxiliary unit number: 91
Home station: Klagenfurt(?) (Wkr. XVIII)

Formed in the winter of 1939-40. Took part in the latter stages of the French campaign. In Greece it played a leading part in the advance on Salonika. Elements took part in the attack on Crete. Transferred in the late summer of 1941 from Greece to Finland, where it has since operated as part of the Twentieth (Lapland) Army on the northern Finnish front.

RESTRICTED

7th Mountain Division

Commander: Genlt. August KRAKAU (50)
Composition: 206th Mtn Inf Regt, 218th Mtn Inf Regt, 82d Mtn Arty Regt, 99th Rcn Bn, 99th Mtn AT Bn, 99th Mtn Engr Bn, 99th Mtn Sig Bn
Auxiliary unit number: 99
Home station: (Wkr. XIII)

Formed during the winter of 1941-42, mainly by conversion of the former 99th Light Division (formed in December 1940), which had operated for a time on the southern sector of the Russian front. First fought in Finland in the late spring of 1942 and has since remained there.

8th Mountain Division

Commander:
Composition: 142d(?) Mtn Inf Regt, Mtn Inf Regt, Mtn Arty Regt, Rcn Bn, Mtn AT Bn, Mtn Engr Bn, Mtn Sig Bn
Auxiliary unit number:
Home station: (Wkr. XVIII)

Probably formed late in 1942. Present location believed to be in Germany. Existence very uncertain.

37. Sicherungs Divisions *(Sicherungsdivisionen)*.

201st Sicherungs Division

Commander: Genlt. Alfred JACOBI (58)
Composition: 406th Gren Regt
Auxiliary unit number:
Home station: (Wkr. IX) (?)

Expanded from the 201st Sicherungs Brigade during the summer of 1942. Employed in the rear area of the northern sector of the Russian front on line of communications duty. May have moved to the forward area in the autumn of 1943.

203d Sicherungs Division

Commander:
Composition:
Auxiliary unit number:
Home station: (Wkr. III)

Expanded from the 203d Sicherungs Brigade during the summer of 1942. Employed in the rear area of the central sector of the Russian front on line of communications duty. Identified in the front lines in the autumn of 1943 in the Kiev area.

RESTRICTED

207th Sicherungs Division

Commander: Genmaj. Paul HOFFMANN
Composition: 322d Gren Regt, 374th Gren Regt, 207th Rcn Bn, 207th AT Bn, 207th Engr Bn
Auxiliary unit number: 207
Home station: Stargard (Wkr. II)

Formed in the summer of 1939 as the 207th Infantry Division. Fought in Poland. Converted into a Sicherungs division in the winter of 1940-1941, when it lost one infantry regiment and its artillery. Employed on rear area duties on the northern sector of the Russian front from the outset.

213th Sicherungs Division

Commander:
Composition: 318th Gren Regt, 354th Gren Regt, 213th Arty Regt, 213th Rcn Bn, 213th AT Co, 213th Engr Bn, 213th Sig Bn
Auxiliary unit number: 213
Home station: Glogau (Wkr. VIII)

Formed in the summer of 1939 as the 213th Infantry Division. Converted into a Sicherungs division in the winter of 1940-1941, when it lost one infantry regiment. Employed on rear area duties on the southern sector of the Russian front from the outset. Identified in the front line in the Kiev area in the autumn of 1943, where it appears to have been fairly heavily engaged. At one time Cossack units were apparently subordinated to the division.

RESTRICTED

221st Sicherungs Division

Commander: Genlt. LENDLE (52)
Composition: 350th Gren Regt, 360th Gren Regt, 221st Arty Regt, 221st
　　　　　　Rcn Bn, 221st AT Bn, 221st Engr Bn, 221st Sig Bn
Auxiliary unit number: 221
Home station: Breslau (Wkr. VIII)

Formed in the summer of 1939 as the 221st Infantry Division. Saw active fighting in Poland. Converted into a Sicherungs division in the winter of 1940-1941, when it lost one infantry regiment. Employed on rear area duties, first on the central sector of the Russian front, and subsequently on the southern sector. Identified on the front line in the autumn of 1943 in the Kiev area.

281st Sicherungs Division

Commander: Genmaj. Dipl. Ing. v. STOCKHAUSEN (54)
Composition: 368th(?) Gren Regt, 107th Sicherungs Regt
Auxiliary unit number:
Home station: (Wkr. II)

Probably formed in the summer of 1942. On rear area duties on the northern sector of the Russian front. May have been moved to the forward area in the autumn of 1943.

284th Sicherungs Division

Commander:
Composition:
Auxiliary unit number:
Home station:

Date of formation uncertain. On rear area duties on the northern sector of the Russian front since early in 1943.

RESTRICTED

285th Sicherungs Division

Commander: Genlt. Gustav ADOLPH-AUFFENBERG-KOMAROW
Composition: 113th Sicherungs Regt,
Auxiliary unit number:
Home station:

Date of formation uncertain. On rear area duties on the northern sector of the Russian front since early in 1942.

286th Sicherungs Division

Commander: Genlt. RICHERT (52)
Composition: 31st Sicherungs Regt, 61st Sicherungs Regt, 122d Sicherungs Regt
Auxiliary unit number:
Home station:

Date of formation uncertain. On rear area duties on the central sector of the Russian front since the autumn of 1942.

403d Sicherungs Division

Commander:
Composition:
Auxiliary unit number:
Home station: Berlin (Wkr. III)

Formed in the spring of 1940 as a z.b.V. division staff. Given security functions on the Russian front and employed in the rear area of the central sector from November 1941, later moving to the southern sector. It is believed that per-

RESTRICTED

sonnel from this division was used to reform the 79th and 384th Infantry Divisions early in 1943, and the division as such has probably been disbanded.

442d Sicherungs Division

Commander:
Composition:
Auxiliary unit number:
Home station:

Formed early in 1940. In the rear area of the central sector of the Russian front.

444th Sicherungs Division

Commander: Genlt. AULEB (57)
Composition:
Auxiliary unit number:
Home station: (Wkr. XII)

Formed early in 1940. In the rear area of the southern sector of the Russian front since the autumn of 1941.

RESTRICTED

454th Sicherungs Division

Commander:
Composition: 375th Gren Regt(?)
Auxiliary unit number: 375
Home station:

Date of formation uncertain. In the rear area of the southern sector of the Russian front since the autumn of 1941.

455th Sicherungs Division

Commander:
Composition:
Auxiliary unit number:
Home station:

Date of formation uncertain. Operated in the rear area of the southern sector of the Russian front from the autumn of 1941. Believed disbanded.

RESTRICTED

38. Administrative, Reserve, Frontier Guard, and Field Training Divisions.

The divisions and division staffs listed below are of the following types:

Mobilization divisions (*Div. Nr....*).—Established at the beginning of the war or later and located at their home stations unless otherwise stated. (See section II, paragraph 7 *c*, above.)

Reserve divisions (*Reservedivisionen*).—Established since 1 October 1942 and located in occupied territory. (See section II, paragraph 7 *c*, above.)

Field training divisions (*Feldausbildungsdivisionen*).—Established during 1942 in the rear areas in Russia. Belong to the Field Army although made up of replacements intended for other field divisions. (See section II, paragraph 7 *c*, above.)

Special administrative staffs (*Divisionskommandos z.b.V.*).—Established early in the war to control GHQ units temporarily stationed in their respective *Wehrkreise* and for other special administrative purposes.

Frontier guard divisions (*Grenzwachdivisionen*).—Established in 1939 in certain frontier districts and made up of frontier guard units.

141st Reserve Division

Commander:
Composition: 1st Res Gren Regt (1st, 22d, 43d Res Gren Bns), 11th Res Gren Regt (2d(?), 23d, 44th(?) Res Gren Bns), 61st Res Gren Regt (151st, 162d, 176th(?) Res Gren Bns), 1st(?) Res Arty Bn
Home station: Insterburg (Wkr. I)

Originally a mobilization and training division. Transferred to White Russia as a reserve division early in 1943.

RESTRICTED

ORDER OF BATTLE OF THE GERMAN ARMY

143d Reserve Division

Commander: Genlt. Paul STOEWER (55)
Composition: 68th Res Gren Regt (169th, 188th, 512th(?) Res Gren Bns), 76th Res Gren Regt (178th(?), 203d(?), 230th Res Gren Bns), 218th(?) Res Gren Regt (122d(?), 323d, 397th Res Gren Bns), 257th Res Arty Bn
Home station: Frankfurt/Oder (Wkr. III)

Originally a mobilization and training division. Converted into a reserve division late in 1942, probably in Wkr. XXI. Transferred to northwestern Ukraine early in 1943.

147th Reserve Division

Commander: Genlt. Otto MATTERSTOCK (55)
Composition: 212th(?) Res Gren Regt (316th, 320th, 423d Res Gren Bns), 268th(?) Res Gren Regt (468th, 488th, 499th Res Gren Bns), 268th(?) Res Arty Bn
Home station: Augsburg (Wkr. VII)

Originally a mobilization and training division. Transferred to Russia as a reserve division late in 1943.

148th Reserve Division

Commander: Genlt. Hermann BOETTCHER (58)
Composition: 8th Res Jäg Regt (38th, 54th(?), 84th Res Jäg Bns), 239th Res Gren Regt (7th(?), 28th(?), 372d Res Gren Bns), 252d Res Gren Regt (452d, 461st, 472d(?) Res Gren Bns), 8th Res Arty Regt, (8th(?) Res L Arty Bn, 239th(?) Res L Arty Bn, 252d Res M Arty Bn)
Home station: Neisse (Wkr. VIII)

RESTRICTED

First identified at Metz (Wkr. XII) in 1941 as a mobilization and training division controlling Wkr. VIII replacement training units which had been transferred to Lorraine to make room in Silesia for field units assembling for the initial offensive against Russia. Became a reserve division late in 1942 and took part in the occupation of former unoccupied France. In October 1943 it was transferred to the Italian Riviera.

151st Reserve Division

Commander:
Composition: 21st(?) Res Gren Regt (3d, 24th, 45th Res Gren Bns), 217th Res Gren Regt (311th, 346th, 389th Res Gren Bns), 228th Res Gren Regt (312th(?), 356th, 400th Res Gren Bns), 21st(?) Res Arty Bn
Home station: Allenstein (Wkr. I)

Originally a mobilization and training division. Converted into a reserve division in the southern (Polish) part of the Wehrkreis late in 1942. Believed to have been transferred to Lithuania.

152d Mobilization Division

Commander: Genlt. Arthur BOLTZE (66)
Home station: Stettin (Wkr. II)

Transferred to Wkr. XX early in 1943.

RESTRICTED

153d Reserve Division

Commander: Genlt. René de l'HOMME de COURBIÈRE (57)
Composition: 23d(?) Res Gren Regt (67th(?), 68th(?), 270th(?) Res Gren Bns), 208th Res Gren Regt (309th(?), 337th(?), 338th Res Gren Bns), 257th Res Gren Regt (457th, 466th, 477th Res Gren Bns), 218th(?) Res Arty Bn
Home station: Potsdam (Wkr. III)

Originally a mobilization and training division. Transferred to the Crimea as a reserve division late in 1942.

154th Reserve Division

Commander: Genlt. Dr. Friedrich ALTRICHTER (53)
Composition: 56th Res Gren Regt (171st, 475th, 514th Res Gren Bns), 223d Res Gren Regt (192d, 234th, 465th Res Gren Bns), 255th Res Gren Regt (385th(?), 425th(?), 440th, 455th Res Gren Bns), 24th(?) Res Arty Bn
Home station: Dresden (Wkr. IV)

Originally a mobilization and training division. Transferred to the Government General as a reserve division late in 1942.

155th Reserve Panzer Division

Commander:
Composition: 7th Res Pz Bn, 90th Res Pz Gren Regt (86th, 215th Res Pz Gren Bns), 25th Res Mtz Gren Regt (35th, 119th Res Mtz Gren Bns), 25th Res Mtz Arty Regt (25th(?), 90th(?) Res Mtz Arty Bns)
Home station: Ulm (Wkr. V)

RESTRICTED

Originally a mobilization and training division. Transferred to northwestern France as a reserve Panzer division late in 1943.

156th Reserve Division

Commander:
Composition: 6th Res Gren Regt (18th, 37th, 58th Res Gren Bns), 227th Res Gren Regt (328th, 366th, 412th Res Gren Bns), 254th Res Gren Regt (454th, 474th, 484th Res Gren Bns), 6th(?) Res Arty Regt (6th(?), 169th, 211th(?) Res Arty Bns)
Home station: Köln (Wkr. VI)

Originally a mobilization and training division. Transferred as a reserve division in the autumn of 1942 to Belgium and in the autumn of 1943 to the Boulogne area.

157th Reserve Division

Commander: Genlt. Karl PFLAUM (54)
Composition: 1st Res Mtn Inf Regt (98th, 99th, 100th Res Mtn Inf Bns), 7th Res Gren Regt (19th, 61st, 62d Res Gren Bns), 157th Res Gren Regt (179th, 199th, 217th Res Gren Bns), 7th(?) Res Arty Regt (7th Res Arty Bn, 157th Res Arty Bn, 79th Res Mtn Arty Bn)
Home station: München (Wkr. VII)

Originally a mobilization and training division. Became a reserve division late in 1942 and took part in the occupation of former unoccupied France. Transferred to the Grenoble area after the Italian evacuation of southeastern France.

*** RESTRICTED ***

ORDER OF BATTLE OF THE GERMAN ARMY

158th Reserve Division

Commander: Genlt. Ernst HAECKEL (54)
Composition: 62d Res Gren Regt (164th(?), 183d, 190th Res Gren Bns), 213th Res Gren Rgt (318th, 354th Res Gren Bns), 221st Res Gren Regt (350th, 360th Res Gren Bns), 221st Res Arty Regt (221st Res L Arty Bn, 213th Res L Arty Bn, 213th Res M Arty Bn)
Home station: Liegnitz (Wkr. VIII)

First identified at Strassburg (Wkr. V) in 1941 as a mobilization and training division controlling Wkr. VIII replacement training units which had been transferred to Alsace to make room in Silesia for field units assembling for the initial offensive against Russia. Became a reserve division late in 1942 and took part in the occupation of former unoccupied France. In March 1943 it was transferred to the La Rochelle area.

159th Reserve Division

Commander: Genlt. Hermann MEYER-RABINGEN (55)
Composition: 9th Res Gren Regt (36th, 57th, 116th Res Gren Bns), 214th(?) Res Gren Regt (355th, 367th, 388th Res Gren Bns), 251st Res Gren Regt (451st, 459th, 471st Res Gren Bns), 9th Res Arty Regt (9th Res L Arty Bn, 214th L Arty Bn, 251st Res M Arty Bn)
Home station: Frankfurt/Main (Wkr. IX)

Originally a mobilization and training division. Became a reserve division late in 1942 and took part in the occupation of former unoccupied France.

RESTRICTED

160th Reserve Division

Commander: Genlt. Horst Frhr. v. UCKERMANN (52)
Composition: 30th Res Gren Regt (6th, 26th, 46th Res Gren Bns),
58th Res Gren Regt (209th, 220th, 469th Res Gren Bns),
225th Res Gren Regt (333d, 376th, 377th Res Gren Bns),
58th (?) Res Arty Regt (30th, 58th, 290th Res Arty Bns)
Home station: (Wkr. X)

Identified as a mobilization and training division in 1940 in the Copenhagen area. Transferred to Jutland as a reserve division early in 1943.

165th Reserve Division

Commander: Genlt. Sigmund Frhr. v. SCHACKY auf SCHÖNFELD (58)
Composition: 205th Res Gren Regt (111th(?), 335th, 358th Res Gren Bns), 215th Res Gren Regt (380th, 390th, 435th Res Gren Bns), 260th Res Gren Regt, (460th, 470th, 480th(?) Res Gren Bns), 5th Res Arty Regt (5th, 61st Res Arty Bns)
Home station: Stuttgart (Wkr. V)

Originally a mobilization and training division. Transferred to the Epinal area in the spring of 1942. Became a reserve division in the autumn of 1942.

166th Reserve Division

Commander: Genmaj. Dipl. Ing. Helmut CASTORF (54)
Composition: 26th(?) Res Gren Regt (77th, 78th, 306th(?) Res Gren Bns), 69th Res Gren Regt (159th, 193d, 236th Res Gren Bns), 86th Res Gren Regt (167th, 184th, 216th Res Gren Bns), 26th(?) Res Arty Bn
Home station: Bielefeld (Wkr. VI)

RESTRICTED

ORDER OF BATTLE OF THE GERMAN ARMY

Originally a mobilization and training division. Transferred to Copenhagen, probably as a reserve division, early in 1943.

171st Reserve Division

Commander: Genlt. Friedrich FÜRST (54)
Composition: 71st Res Gren Regt (191st, 194th, 211th Res Gren Bns), 216th Res Gren Regt (348th, 396th, 398th Res Gren Bns), 267th(?) Res Gren Regt (467th, 487th, 497th Res Gren Bns), 171st(?) Res Arty Regt (171st Res L Arty Bn, 216th Res L Arty Bn, 267th Res M Arty Bn)
Home Station: Hannover (Wkr. XI)

Originally a mobilization and training division. Transferred as a reserve division late in 1942 to France and early in 1943 to the Belgian coast.

172d Mobilization Division

Commander:
Home station: Mainz (Wkr. XII)

173d Reserve Division

Commander:
Composition: 17th Res Gren Regt (21st, 55th, 95th Res Gren Bns), 73d Res Gren Regt (42d(?), 170th, 186th Res Gren Bns), 114th(?) Res Arty Bn
Home station: Würzburg (Wkr. XIII)

Originally a mobilization and training division. Transferred as a reserve division to eastern Croatia in September 1943.

RESTRICTED

174th Reserve Division

Commander:
Composition: 24th Res Gren Regt (32d, 456th(?), 476th(?) Res Gren Bns), 87th(?) Res Gren Regt (10th(?), 31st(?), 102d(?), 185th Res Gren Bns), 256th Res Gren Regt (173d(?), 513th(?), 515th(?) Res Gren Bns), 14th Res Arty Bn
Home station: Leipzig (Wkr. IV)

Originally a mobilization and training division. Reorganized as a reserve division in Bohemia late in 1942. Transferred to the Government General early in 1943.

176th Mobilization Division

Commander:
Home station: Bielefeld (Wkr. VI)

177th Mobilization Division

Commander:
Home station: Wien (Wkr. XVII)

178th Mobilization Division

Commander:
Home station: Liegnitz (Wkr. VIII)

RESTRICTED

ORDER OF BATTLE OF THE GERMAN ARMY 311

179th Reserve Panzer Division

Commander:
Composition: 1st(?) Res Pz Bn, 81st Res Pz Gren Regt (1st, 59th Res Pz Gren Bns), 29th Res Mtz Gren Regt (15th, 71st Res Mtz Gren Bns), 29th(?) Res Mtz Arty Regt (29th, 73d Res Mtz Arty Bns)
Home station: Weimar (Wkr. IX)

Originally a mobilization and training division. Transferred to northern France as a reserve Panzer division in the autumn of 1943.

180th Mobilization Division

Commander:
Home station: Verden (Wkr. X)

182d Reserve Division

Commander: Genmaj. Paul LETTOW (53)
Composition: 34th Res Gren Regt (80th, 105th(?), 107th Res Gren Bns), 79th Res Gren Regt (208th, 212th, 226th Res Gren Bns), 112th Res Gren Regt (110th, 256th, 437th(?) Res Gren Bns), 179th(?) Res Arty Regt (34th(?), 70th(?), 179th(?) Res Arty Bns)
Home station: Koblenz (Wkr. XII)

Originally a mobilization and training division. Transferred to the Nancy area early in 1942. Reorganized in the autumn of 1942 as a reserve division.

RESTRICTED

187th Reserve Division

Commander: Genlt. Josef BRAUNER
Composition: 45th Res Gren Regt (II./130, II./133, II./135 Res Gren Bns), 462nd(?) Res Gren Regt (II./462, II./482(?), II./486 Res Gren Bns), 96th Res Arty Bn
Home station: Linz (Wkr. XVII)

Originally a mobilization and training division. Transferred to northern Croatia as a reserve division in the autumn of 1942.

188th Reserve Mountain Division

Commander: Genlt. Wilhelm v. HÖSSLIN (66)
Composition: 136th(?) Res Mtn Inf Regt (I./136, II./136, II./137 Res Mtn Inf Bns), 139th(?) Res Mtn Inf Regt (I./137, I./139, II./139 Res Mtn Inf Bns) 112th(?) Res Mtn Arty Bn
Home station: Salzburg (Wkr. XVIII)

Originally a mobilization and training division. Transferred to the Merano area as a reserve mountain division in the autumn of 1943.

189th Reserve Division

Commander: Genmaj. Bogislav Graf v. SCHWERIN (48)
Composition: 15th(?) Res Gren Regt (81st, 88th, 106th Res Gren Bns), 28th Res Jäg Regt (49th, 83d Res Jäg Bns), 52d Res Gren Regt (163d, 181st, 205th Res Gren Bns), 28th(?) Res Arty Regt (15th(?), 28th 152d(?) Res Arty Bns)
Home station: Kassel (Wkr. IX)

RESTRICTED

Originally a mobilization and training division. Became a reserve division late in 1942 and took part in the occupation of former unoccupied France.

190th Mobilization Division

Commander:
Home station: Neumünster (Wkr. X)

191st Reserve Division

Commander:
Composition: 31st(?) Res Gren Regt (12th, 17th, 82d Res Gren Bns), 267th Res Gren Regt (467th, 487th, 497th Res Gren Bns), 19th Res Arty Regt (19th Res L Arty Bn, 31st Res L Arty Bn, 267th Res M Arty Bn)
Home station: Braunschweig (Wkr. XI)

Originally a mobilization and training division. Transferred to Belgium as a reserve division in the autumn of 1942. Moved in March 1943 to northern France where it has since remained.

192d Mobilization Division

Commander:
Home station: Rostock (Wkr. II)

193d Mobilization Division

Commander:
Home station: Regensburg (Wkr. XIII)
Transferred to Bohemia in the autumn of 1942.

RESTRICTED

233d Reserve Panzer Division

Commander: Genlt. Heinrich WOSCH (54)
Composition: 5th(?) Res Pz Bn, 83d Res Pz Gren Regt (3d, 8th Res Pz Gren Bns), 3d Res Mtz Gren Regt (8th, 29th Res Mtz Gren Bns), 3d(?) Res Mtz Arty Regt (3d, 75th Res Mtz Arty Bns)
Home station: Frankfurt a.d. Oder (Wkr. III)

Originally a mobilization and training division for Panzer and motorized troops in Wehrkreis III. Transferred to Denmark as a reserve Panzer division late in 1943.

381st Field Training Division

Commander: Genmaj. Helmut EISENSTUCK (50)
Composition: 616th Field Tng Regt
Home station:

First identified on the southern sector of the Russian front in January 1943, where it is believed to have remained.

382d Field Training Division

Commander:
Composition: 617th Field Tng Regt, 618th Field Tng Regt, 619th Field Tng Regt
Home station:

First identified in Russia in January 1943; it is believed that it has been operating on the southern sector.

RESTRICTED

388th Field Training Division

Commander: Genlt. Johann PFLUGBEIL (62)
Composition:
Home station:

First identified in Russia in May 1943, where it has been operating on the northern sector.

390th Field Training Division

Commander:
Composition:
Home station:

First identified in Russia in May 1943, where it has possibly been operating on the central sector.

391st Field Training Division

Commander: Genlt. Albrecht Baron DIGEON v. MONTETON (52)
Composition: 718th Field Tng Regt, 719th Field Tng Regt, 720th Field Tng Regt
Home station: Koblenz (Wkr. XII)

First identified in Russia in March 1943, where it has been operating on the central sector.

RESTRICTED

401st Mobilization Division

Commander: Genlt. v. DIRINGSHOFEN
Home station: Königsberg (Wkr. I)
Converted from the 401st Special Administrative Division toward the end of 1943.

402d Special Administrative Division

Commander:
Home station: Stettin (Wkr. II)

404th Special Administrative Division

Commander:
Home station: Dresden (Wkr. IV)

405th Special Administrative Division

Commander:
Home station: Stuttgart (Wkr. V)

406th Special Administrative Division

Commander:
Home station: Münster (Wkr. VI)

407th Special Administrative Division

Commander:
Home station: München (Wkr. VII)

RESTRICTED

408th Special Administrative Division

Commander:
Home station: Breslau (Wkr. VIII)

409th Mobilization Division

Commander: Genmaj. Hans EHRENBERG (55)
Home station: Kassel (Wkr. IX)

Converted from the 409th Special Administrative Division in the spring or summer of 1943.

410th Special Administrative Division

Commander: Genlt. Karl MADERHOLZ (59)?
Home station: Hamburg (Wkr. X)

411th Special Administrative Division

Commander: Genlt. KANNENGIESSER ?
Home station: Hannover (Wkr. XI)

412th Special Administrative Division

Commander: Genlt. Kurt FISCHER (67)
Home station: Wiesbaden (Wkr. XII)

413th Special Administrative Division

Commander:
Home station: Nürnberg (Wkr. XIII)

RESTRICTED

417th Special Administrative Division
Commander:
Home station: Wien (Wkr. XVII)

421st Special Administrative Division
Commander:
Home station: Zichenau (*Ciechanów*) (Wkr. I)

428th Special Administrative Division
Commander:
Home station: Graudenz (*Grudziądz*) (Wkr. XX)

429th Special Administrative Division
Commander: Genlt. SCHARTOW (53)
Home station: Posen (*Poznań*) (Wkr. XXI)

430th Special Administrative Division
Commander:
Home station: Gnesen (*Gniezno*) (Wkr. XXI)

431st Special Administrative Division
Commander:
Home station: Litzmannstadt (*Łodz*) (Wkr. XXI)

RESTRICTED

ORDER OF BATTLE OF THE GERMAN ARMY

432d Special Administrative Division

Commander:
Home station: Kattowitz (*Katowioe*) (Wkr. VIII)

433d Mobilization Division

Commander:
Home station: Berlin (Wkr. III)
Created in 1943.

461st Mobilization Division

Commander: Genlt. Hans Erich NOLTE (62)
Home station: Bialystok (Wkr. I)
Formerly known as Special Purpose Division Bialystok (Division z.b.V.) Converted into a mobilization division in 1943.

462d Mobilization Division

Commander:
Home station: (Wkr. XII)
Created in the winter of 1942-43. In the Nancy area since early in 1943.

464th Mobilization Division

Commander:
Home station: Leipzig (Wkr. IV)
Created early in 1943.

RESTRICTED

465th Mobilization Division

Commander:
Home station: Stuttgart (Wkr. V)

Created in the winter of 1942-43. In the Epinal area since early in 1943.

467th Mobilization Division

Commander: Genlt. Karl GRAF (61) ?
Home station: München (Wkr. VII)

Created in 1943.

473d Mobilization Division

Commander:
Home station: Regensburg (Wkr. XIII)

Created in 1943.

487th Mobilization Division

Commander:
Home station: Linz (Wkr. XVII)

Created in 1943.

526th Mobilization Division

Commander: Genlt. Albin NAKE
Home station: Wuppertal (Wkr. VI)

Formerly a frontier guard division, when it was located in the Namur area in Belgium. Converted to a mobilization division in 1943 and returned to its home station.

RESTRICTED

537th Frontier Guard Division

Commander:
Home station: Innsbruck (Wkr. XVIII)

538th Frontier Guard Division

Commander:
Home station: Klagenfurt (Wkr. XVIII)

539th Frontier Guard Division

Commander: Genlt. Dr. Richard SPEICH (60)
Home station: Prag (Wkr. Böhmen u. Mähren)

540th Frontier Guard Division

Commander: Genlt. Karl TARBUK v. SENSENHORST
Home station: Brünn (Wkr. Böhmen u. Mähren)

RESTRICTED

39. Divisions and Higher Headquarters of the *Waffen-SS*.
Nomenclature of *Waffen-SS* units is somewhat different from that of the Army. In particular, it should be remembered that Panzer Grenadier Division, which in the Army is always a motorized division, may mean either a Panzer division or a motorized division in the *Waffen-SS*. Actually, no clear distinction is made between these two types, and the classification of *SS* divisions must therefore be made on the basis of their composition.

The nomenclature of subordinate units varies widely among the different divisions and is also subject to frequent change.

In the following lists the proper German designations are used wherever known.

a. Armies.

1st SS Panzer Army

Commander:

This headquarters may exist or may be in process of formation.

b. Corps.

I SS Panzer Corps

Commander: SS-Oberstgruppenführer Josef ("Sepp") DIETRICH (52)
C of S:
Home station:

Probably formed in the summer of 1943 to replace the II SS Panzer Corps in control of the Adolf Hitler, Reich, and Totenkopf SS divisions. Probably on the southern sector in Russia.

RESTRICTED

ORDER OF BATTLE OF THE GERMAN ARMY 323

II SS Panzer Corps

Commander: SS-Obergruppenführer Paul HAUSSER (64)
C of S:
Home station: (Wkr. XI)

Formed in France in the summer of 1942 to control the three traditional SS divisions—Adolf Hitler, Reich, and Totenkopf—which were then undergoing conversion to Panzer divisions. Moved to southern Russia after the start of the Russian winter offensive and achieved distinction in the recapture of Kharkov and Belgorod in March 1943. Moved to northern Italy in the summer of 1943, where it has remained.

III SS Panzer Corps

Commander: SS-Obergruppenführer Felix STEINER (48)
C of S:
Home station:

Also known as the SS Germanisches Korps. Formed in the early part of 1943 to control the training and the subsequent operations of the new Scandinavian and Dutch SS divisions. Moved to Croatia in the summer of 1943; present location uncertain.

RESTRICTED

IV SS Panzer Corps

Commander:
C of S:
Home station:

Probably formed in 1943 to control SS divisions in France and Belgium.

V SS Mountain Corps

Commander: SS-Obergruppenführer Artur PHLEPS (63)
C of S:
Home station:

Formed in Yugoslavia in the late summer of 1943. Controls the Prinz Eugen as well as regular Army divisions in Bosnia.

ORDER OF BATTLE OF THE GERMAN ARMY

c. *Divisions.*

SS-Panzer-Grenadier-Division Leibstandarte-SS "Adolf Hitler"

Commander: SS-Oberführer WISCH
Composition Pz Regt, SS-Pz. Gren. Rgt. 1, SS-Pz. Gren. Rgt. 2, SS-Pz. Gren. Rgt., 3 (?), Pz. Arty Regt, Pz Rcn Bn, AT Bn, Pz Engr Bn, Pz Sig Bn
Home station: Berlin-Lichterfelde (Wkr. III)

Formed in the winter of 1940-41 as a motorized division by expansion of the elements of the Leibstandarte (Hitler's bodyguard regiment) which had taken part in the Polish and western campaigns as a motorized regiment. Fought with distinction in the Balkan campaign and was heavily engaged on the southern sector in Russia until the summer of 1942. Transferred to France to be reorganized as a Panzer division and returned to southern Russia for the German counteroffensive toward Kharkov in March 1943. Moved to northern Italy in the summer of 1943 and back to Russia in the autumn. Recently heavily engaged west of Kiev.

SS-Panzer-Grenadier-Division "Das Reich"

Commander: SS-Gruppenführer Walter KRÜGER (54)
Composition: Pz Regt, SS-Pz. Gren. Rgt. Deutschland, SS-Pz. Gren. Rgt. Der Führer, SS-Pz. Gren Rgt. Langemarck, Pz Arty Regt, Pz Rcn Bn, AT Bn, Pz Engr Bn, Pz Sig Bn
Home station: Regt Deutschland: München (Wkr. VII) Regt Der Führer: Wien (Wkr. XVII)

Formed in the winter of 1940-41 as a motorized division from two regiments of the former SS-Verfügungs-Division

RESTRICTED

and a third regiment (Langemarck) composed partly of Germanic volunteers. Fought in the Balkan campaign and heavily engaged on the central sector in Russia from the outset. Transferred to France in the summer of 1942 to be reorganized as a Panzer division and returned to the southern sector in Russia early in 1943 for the German counteroffensive toward Kharkov. Recently heavily engaged west of Kiev.

SS-Panzer-Grenadier-Division "Totenkopf"

Commander: SS-Brigadeführer Hermann PRIESS (43)
Composition: SS-Pz. Rgt. "Totenkopf", SS-Pz. Gren. Rgt. "Theodor Eicke", Pz Gren Regt, Pz Arty Regt, Pz Rcn Bn, AT Bn, Pz Engr Bn, Pz Sig Bn
Home station: Oranienburg (Wkr. III)

Formed in October 1939 as a motorized division, mainly from existing concentration camp guard units. Fought in Flanders and in France. Engaged on the northern sector in Russia from the outset until September 1942, when it was transferred to France for reorganization as a Panzer division. Returned to the southern sector in Russia early in 1943 for the German counteroffensive toward Kharkov. Recently engaged in the Dnieper bend area.

SS-Polizei-Division

Commander:
Composition: SS-Polizei-Gren. Rgt. 1, SS-Polizei-Gren. Rgt. 2, SS-Polizei-Gren. Rgt. 3, SS-Polizei-Art. Rgt., Rcn Bn, AT Bn, Engr Bn, Sig Bn
Home station:

RESTRICTED

Formed in October 1939 from members of police units in all parts of Germany. Fought in the western campaign and constantly engaged on the northern sector in Russia from the outset until the summer of 1943. A large part of the division is now in Greece, but some of it is believed to remain in northern Russia. Regarded as a motorized division.

SS-Panzer-Grenadier-Division "Wiking"

Commander: SS-Gruppenführer Herbert GILLE (47)
Composition Pz Regt (?), SS-Pz. Gren. Rgt. Germania, SS-Pz-Gren-Rgt. Nordland, SS-Pz. Gren. Rgt. Westland, Pz Arty Regt, Pz Rcn Bn, AT Bn, Pz Engr Bn, Pz Sig Bn
Home station: Regt Germania: Hamburg (Wkr. X) Regts Nordland and Westland: Klagenfurt (Wkr. XVIII)

Formed in December 1940 from the Germania regiment of the former SS-Verfügungs-Division and two regiments of Scandinavian, Dutch, Flemish and other Germanic volunteers. Contains many racial Germans from the Balkans. Continuously in action on the southern sector in Russia from the outset. Recently engaged in the Dnieper bend area. Was a motorized division until the end of 1942 but is probably now to be regarded as a Panzer division.

SS-Gebirgsdivision "Nord"

Commander: SS-Gruppenführer Matthias KLEINHEISTERKAMP (51)
Composition: SS-Geb.Jg.Rgt. 6 "Reinhard Heydrich", SS-Geb.Jg.Rgt. 7, SS-Geb.Art.Rgt., Rcn Bn, AT Bn, Engr Bn, Sig Bn
Home station: Trautenau (Wkr. VIII)

RESTRICTED

Formed in the summer of 1941 as a mountain division. Sent to Finland for operations against Russia and has remained there.

SS-Freiwilligen-Gebirgsdivision "Prinz Eugen"

Commander: SS-Brigadeführer Carl Reichsritter v. OBERKAMP (50)
Composition: May include either SS-Geb.Jg.Rgtr. 1 and 2 or SS Regts 10 and 11
Home station:

Formed in the spring of 1942 as a mountain division, consisting principally of racial Germans from Rumania and Yugoslavia. Stationed in northern Serbia until the spring of 1943, since when it has been heavily engaged against Partisans in Bosnia and Dalmatia.

SS-Kavalleriedivision

Commander: SS-Brigadeführer Hermann FEGELEIN (37)
Composition: Two cavalry brigades with SS-Kav.Rgtr. 1, 2, 3, and 4
Home station: Debica (Gen.Gouv.)

Raised to divisional status in the autumn of 1942 from the former SS Cavalry Brigade, which had been in action in Russia since 1941. Continued operations on the southern and central sectors until late in 1943, when it appears to have been withdrawn from the combat zone.

RESTRICTED

ORDER OF BATTLE OF THE GERMAN ARMY 329

SS-Panzer-Grenadier-Division "Hohenstaufen"

Commander: SS-Gruppenführer Willi BITTRICH (50)
Composition:
Home station:

Formed in northeastern France in the winter of 1942-43 as a Panzer division. Moved to Belgium and subsequently to northern France, where it has remained.

SS-Panzer-Grenadier-Division "Frundsberg"

Commander:
Composition: Believed to include SS-Pz.Gren.Rgt. "Hermann Göring"; minor components bear the number 10
Home station:

Formed in southwestern France in the winter of 1942-43. Contains many non-Germans. Moved to southeastern France in the summer of 1943 and to northwestern France in the autumn. Classified as a Panzer division.

SS-Panzer-Division "Hitler-Jugend"

Commander: SS-Oberführer Fritz WITT
Composition:
Home station:

Formed during 1943, largely of recruits from the military fitness camps of the Hitler Youth organization. Stationed in Belgium, where it has thus far served largely as a training division for other SS divisions.

RESTRICTED

SS-Schützendivision "Galizien"

Commander:
Composition:
Home station:

Formed in the spring and summer of 1943 of Ukrainian volunteers in the Polish province of Galicia. Includes some German and Austrian officers and NCOs. No evidence that it has seen action or left Galicia. Classed as an infantry division.

SS-Panzer-Grenadier-Division "Nordland"

Commander: SS-Brigadeführer Fritz SCHOLZ (47)
Composition: Pz Bn, SS-Pz.Gren.Rgt. Norge (?), SS-Pz.Gren.Rgt. Danmark (?), Arty Regt, Pz Rcn Bn, AT Bn, Engr Bn, Sig Bn
Home station:

Formed in Germany as a motorized division in the summer of 1943. Consists partly of Norwegian and Danish volunteers and partly of racial Germans from the Balkans. Stationed in northern Croatia in the autumn of 1943 but may have left for Russia toward the end of the year.

SS-Panzer-Grenadier-Division "Nederland"

Commander:
Composition:
Home station:

RESTRICTED

ORDER OF BATTLE OF THE GERMAN ARMY 331

Formed in Germany as a motorized division in the summer of 1943. Contains Dutch and possibly Flemish volunteers as well as racial Germans from the Balkans. Recently located in Croatia.

SS-Freiwilligen-Division "Lettland"

Commander: SS-Brigadeführer Carl-Friedrich Graf v. PÜCKLER-BURGHAUS
Composition:
Home station: Riga

Formed in the summer of 1943 of Latvians. Considered an infantry division. Has not seen action and is still stationed in Latvia.

Croatian or Bosnian SS Division

Commander: SS-Brigadeführer SAUBERZWEIG
Composition:
Home station:

Proper designation uncertain; referred to as BH division, probably for Bosanska-Hrvatska (Bosnian-Croat). Began forming in the spring of 1943 with Bosnian Moslem and Croat volunteers and probably a cadre from the Prinze Eugen Division. Subsequently stationed in southern France and now believed to be in Germany. Classified as a mountain division.

RESTRICTED

SS-Panzer-Grenadier-Division Reichsführer-SS

Commander:
Composition:
Home station:

First formed as an assault brigade (SS-Sturmbrigade Reichsführer-SS) in the first half of 1943, some of the personnel coming from Himmler's escort battalion. Took part in operations on Corsica in the autumn and was evacuated to the Italian mainland, where it was expanded to a motorized division. Stationed in the Livorno-Rome area until late in 1943 and subsequently located in northeastern Italy.

SS-Panzer-Grenadier-Division "Götz von Berlichingen"

Commander:
Composition:
Home station:

Formed in the latter part of 1943 and stationed in **France**. Believed to be a motorized division but may possibly be Panzer.

RESTRICTED

40. Air Force Ground Units.

a. General.—Since the middle of 1942 the German Air Force, partly because of its relative surplus of manpower as compared with the Army and partly for prestige reasons, has formed several types of divisions for ground combat operations. These include the Hermann Göring Division, which is listed under Panzer divisions (see paragraph 35, above); the parachute divisions, which are a new form of organization of the previously existing parachute units; and the Air Force field divisions.

The Air Force field divisions, originally 22 in number, were formed in the latter part of 1942 from surplus personnel of the antiaircraft artillery, the air signal troops, the ground crews of the flying troops, and administrative units as well as a certain number of recruits and foreigners. They were organized and trained for ground combat at Mielau (*Wkr. I*) and other training grounds and in most cases sent to the Russian front in the winter of 1942-43. Some of them are under the tactical control of Air Force field corps formed for the purpose, but they may also operate under regular Army corps. No further Air Force field divisions appear to have been formed since the initial wave, and at least two have been disbanded. It is possible that others will be disbanded or that the entire force will be reorganized.

The functions of the Flak units which are listed in subparagraphs *e* and *f*, below, are described in section III, paragraph 16 *a*, above.

RESTRICTED

b. *Parachute divisions* (Fallschirmdivisionen).

1st Parachute Division

Commander: Genlt. Richard HEIDRICH (48)
Composition: 1st Para Inf Regt, 3d Para Inf Regt, 4th Para Inf Regt, 1st Para Arty Regt, 1st Para Flak Bn, 1st Para AT Bn, 1st Para Engr Bn, 1st Para Sig Bn
Home station:

Formed in France in the spring of 1943. Considerable elements went into action in Sicily and the division has subsequently been operating in southern Italy.

2d Parachute Division

Commander: Genlt. Hermann Bernhard RAMCKE (56)
Composition: 2d Para Inf Regt, 6th Para Inf Regt, 7th Para Inf Regt, 2d Para Arty Regt, 2d Para Flak Bn, 2d Para AT Bn, 2d Para Engr Bn, 2d Para Sig Bn
Home station:

Formed in France in the summer of 1943. Subsequently in the Rome area; elements took part in operations in the Aegean islands. Transferred to the southern sector in Russia in the late autumn of 1943.

RESTRICTED

ORDER OF BATTLE OF THE GERMAN ARMY

c. *Air Force field corps* (Luftwaffenfeldkorps).

II Air Force Field Corps

Commander:
Home station:
Formed early in 1943. On the northern sector in Russia.

III Air Force Field Corps

Commander: Gen. d. Fl. ODEBRECHT
Home station:
Formed in the winter of 1942-43. On the northern sector in Russia.

IV Air Force Field Corps

Commander:
Home station:
Formed in the winter of 1942-43. On the southern sector in Russia.

RESTRICTED

d. *Air Force field divisions* (Luftwaffenfelddivisionen).

1st Air Force Field Division

Commander:
Composition: 1st Air Force Field Regt, 2d Air Force Field Regt, 1st Air Force Field Arty Regt, 1st Air Force Field Flak Bn, 1st Air Force Field Rcn Co, 1st Air Force Field AT Bn, 1st Air Force Field Engr Bn, 1st Air Force Field Sig Co
Home station:

Formed in the latter part of 1942. On the northern sector in Russia.

2d Air Force Field Division

Commander:
Composition: 3d Air Force Regt, 4th Air Force Field Regt, 2d Air Force Field Arty Regt, 2d Air Force Field Flak Bn, 2d Air Force Field Rcn Co, 2d Air Force Field AT Bn, 2d Air Force Field Engr Bn, 2d Air Force Field Sig Co
Home station:

Formed in the latter part of 1942. On the central sector in Russia.

3d Air Force Field Division

Commander:
Composition: 5th Air Force Field Regt, 6th Air Force Field Regt, 3d Air Force Field Arty Regt, 3d Air Force Field Flak Bn, 3d Air Force Field Rcn Co. 3d Air Force Field AT Bn, 3d Air Force Field Engr Bn, 3d Air Force Field Sig Co
Home station:

Formed in the latter part of 1942. On the central sector in Russia.

RESTRICTED

ORDER OF BATTLE OF THE GERMAN ARMY

4th Air Force Field Division

Commander:
Composition: 7th Air Force Field Regt, 8th Air Force Field Regt, 4th Air Force Field Arty Regt, 4th Air Force Field Flak Bn, 4th Air Force Field Rcn Co, 4th Air Force Field AT Bn, 4th Air Force Field Engr Bn, 4th Air Force Field Sig Co
Home station:
Formed in the latter part of 1942. On the central sector in Russia.

5th Air Force Field Division

Commander:
Composition: 9th Air Force Field Regt, 10th Air Force Field Regt, 5th Air Force Field Arty Regt, 5th Air Force Field Flak Bn, 5th Air Force Field Rcn Co, 5th Air Force Field AT Bn, 5th Air Force Field Engr Bn, 5th Air Force Field Sig Co
Home station:
Formed in the latter part of 1942. On the southern sector in Russia.

6th Air Force Field Division

Commander: Genlt. Rüdiger von HEYKING
Composition: 11th Air Force Field Regt, 12th Air Force Field Regt, 6th Air Force Field Arty Regt, 6th Air Force Field Flak Bn, 6th Air Force Field Rcn Co, 6th Air Force Field AT

RESTRICTED

Bn, 6th Air Force Field Engr Bn, 6th Air Force Field Sig Co

Home station:

Formed in the latter part of 1942. On the central sector in Russia.

7th Air Force Field Division

Formed in the latter part of 1942. Operated on the southern sector in Russia, believed to have been disbanded in the autumn of 1943.

8th Air Force Field Division

Formed in the latter part of 1942. Operated on the southern sector in Russia, believed to have been disbanded in the autumn of 1943.

9th Air Force Field Division

Commander:
Composition: 17th Air Force Field Regt, 18th Air Force Field Regt, 9th Air Force Field Arty Regt, 9th Air Force Field Flak Bn, 9th Air Force Field Rcn Co, 9th Air Force Field AT Bn, 9th Air Force Field Engr Bn, 9th Air Force Field Sig Co

Home station:

Formed in the latter part of 1942. On the northern sector in Russia.

RESTRICTED

10th Air Force Field Division

Commander:
Composition: 19th Air Force Field Regt, 20th Air Force Field Regt, 10th Air Force Field Arty Regt, 10th Air Force Field Flak Bn, 10th Air Force Field Rcn Co, 10th Air Force Field AT Bn, 10th Air Force Field Engr Bn, 10th Air Force Field Sig Co
Home station:

Formed in the latter part of 1942. On the northern sector in Russia.

11th Air Force Field Division

Commander: Genlt. Karl DRUM (50)
Composition: 21st Air Force Field Regt, 22d Air Force Field Regt, 11th Air Force Field Arty Regt, 11th Air Force Field Flak Bn, 11th Air Force Field Rcn Co, 11th Air Force Field AT Bn, 11th Air Force Field Engr Bn, 11th Air Force Field Sig Co
Home station:

Formed in the latter part of 1942. Elements operated in the Aegean islands. Now in Greece.

12th Air Force Field Division

Commander:
Composition: 23d Air Force Field Regt, 24th Air Force Field Regt, 12th Air Force Field Arty Regt, 12th Air Force Field Flak Bn, 12th Air Force Field Rcn Co, 12th Air Force

RESTRICTED

Field AT Bn, 12th Air Force Field Engr Bn, 12th Air Field Sig Co

Home station:

Formed in the latter part of 1942. On the northern sector in Russia.

13th Air Force Field Division

Commander:
Composition: 25th Air Force Field Regt, 26th Air Force Field Regt, 13th Air Force Field Arty Regt, 13th Air Force Field Flak Bn, 13th Air Force Field Rcn Co, 13th Air Force Field AT Bn, 13th Air Force Field Engr Bn, 13th Air Force Field Sig Co

Home station:

Formed in the latter part of 1942. On the northern sector in Russia.

14th Air Force Field Division

Commander: Genmaj. LOHMANN (51)
Composition: 27th Air Force Field Regt, 28th Air Force Field Regt, 14th Air Force Field Arty Regt, 14th Air Force Field Flak Bn, 14th Air Force Field Rcn Co, 14th Air Force Field AT Bn, 14th Air Force Field Engr Bn, 14th Air Force Field Sig Co

Home station:

Formed in the latter part of 1942. Stationed in Norway.

RESTRICTED

15th Air Force Field Division

Commander: Genlt. Willibald SPANG (57)
Composition: 29th Air Force Field Regt, 30th Air Force Field Regt, 15th Air Force Field Arty Regt, 15th Air Force Field Flak Bn, 15th Air Force Field Rcn Co, 15th Air Force Field AT Bn, 15th Air Force Field Engr Bn, 15th Air Force Field Sig Co
Home station:

Formed in the latter part of 1942. On the southern sector in Russia.

16th Air Force Field Division

Commander:
Composition: 31st Air Force Field Regt, 32d Air Force Field Regt, 16th Air Force Field Arty Regt, 16th Air Force Field Flak Bn, 16th Air Force Field Rcn Co, 16th Air Force Field AT Bn, 16th Air Force Field Engr Bn, 16th Air Force Field Sig Co
Home station:

Formed in the latter part of 1942. Stationed in Holland.

17th Air Force Field Division

Commander:
Composition: 33d Air Force Field Regt, 34th Air Force Field Regt, 17th Air Force Field Arty Regt, 17th Air Force Field Flak Bn, 17th Air Force Field Rcn Co, 17th Air Force Field AT Bn, 17th Air Force Field Engr Bn, 17th Air Force Field Sig Co
Home station:

Formed in the latter part of 1942. Stationed in northwestern France.

RESTRICTED

18th Air Force Field Division

Commander:
Composition: 35th Air Force Field Regt, 36th Air Force Field Regt, 18th Air Force Field Arty Regt, 18th Air Force Field Flak Bn, 18th Air Force Field Rcn Co, 18th Air Force Field AT Bn, 18th Air Force Field Engr Bn, 18th Air Force Field Sig Co
Home station:

Formed in the latter part of 1942. Stationed in northwestern France.

19th Air Force Field Division

Commander:
Composition: 37th Air Force Field Regt, 38th Air Force Field Regt, 19th Air Force Field Arty Regt, 19th Air Force Field Flak Bn, 19th Air Force Field Rcn Co, 19th Air Force Field AT Bn, 19th Air Force Field Engr Bn, 19th Air Force Field Sig Co
Home station:

Formed in the latter part of 1942. Located in France in the summer of 1943, subsequently in Holland.

20th Air Force Field Division

Commander:
Composition: 39th Air Force Field Regt, 40th Air Force Field Regt, 20th Air Force Field Arty Regt, 20th Air Force Field Flak Bn, 20th Air Force Field Rcn Co, 20th Air Force Field AT Bn, 20th Air Force Field Engr Bn, 20th Air Force Field Sig Co
Home station:

Formed in the latter part of 1942. Stationed in Denmark.

RESTRICTED

ORDER OF BATTLE OF THE GERMAN ARMY

21st Air Force Field Division

Commander:
Composition: 41st Air Force Field Regt, 42d Air Force Field Regt, 21st Air Force Field Arty Regt, 21st Air Force Field Flak Bn, 21st Air Force Field Rcn Co, 21st Air Force Field AT Bn, 21st Air Force Field Engr Bn, 21st Air Force Field Sig Co

Home station:

Formed in the latter part of 1942. On the northern sector in Russia.

22d Air Force Field Division

Commander:
Composition: 43d Air Force Field Regt, 44th Air Force Field Regt, 22d Air Force Field Arty Regt, 22d Air Force Field Flak Bn, 22d Air Force Field Rcn Co, 22d Air Force Field AT Bn, 22d Air Force Field Engr Bn, 22d Air Force Field Sig Co

Home station:

Formed in the latter part of 1942. On the northern sector in Russia in 1943, in northern Italy in the autumn of 1943, subsequent location uncertain.

RESTRICTED

e. Flak corps (Flakkorps).

I Flak Corps

Commander:

Operated in France in 1940 and in Russia in 1941-43, at first on the central and later on the southern sector.

II Flak Corps

Commander:

Operated in France in 1940 and in Russia in 1941-43, at first on the southern and later on the central sector.

f. Flak divisions (Flakdivisionen).

1st Flak Division

Commander: Genmaj. SCHALLER
Headquarters: Berlin

2d Flak Division (Mtz)

Commander:

Transferred from the Paris area to the northern sector in Russia early in 1942.

3d Flak Division

Commander:
Headquarters: Hamburg

RESTRICTED

4th Flak Division

Commander:
Headquarters: Düsseldorf

5th Flak Division

Commander:
Operated in western Germany late in 1941 (Hq: Frankfurt am Main) and during 1942 (Hq: Darmstadt). Transferred to southeastern Europe late in 1943.

6th Flak Division (Mtz)

Commander:
Operated in western Europe (probably Belgium and Northern France) in 1941 and early 1942. Transferred to the northern sector in Russia later in 1942.

7th Flak Division

Commander: Genlt. Dipl. Ing. Heinrich BURCHARD
Headquarters: Köln

8th Flak Division

Commander: Genlt. WAGNER
Headquarters: Bremen

RESTRICTED

9th Flak Division (Mtz)

Commander: Genmaj. Wolfgang PICKERT (47)

Transferred from the Paris area to the central sector of Russia early in 1942 and to the Crimea in 1943.

10th Flak Division (Mtz)

Commander: Genlt. Johann SEIFERT

Controlled all Flak in Rumania and Bulgaria in 1941; on the southern sector in Russia since early in 1942.

11th Flak Division (Mtz)

Commander: Genlt. Hellmuth RICHTER (52)
Headquarters: Avignon

Operated in northern France (Rennes-Paris area) late in 1941 until autumn 1942 when it was transferred to southern France.

12th Flak Division (Mtz)

Commander: Genlt. Rudolf EIBENSTEIN (50)

Operating on the central sector in Russia since late in 1941.

13th Flak Division

Commander: Genlt. Theodor SPIESS (52)
Headquarters: Caen

RESTRICTED

14th Flak Division

Commander:
Headquarters: Leipzig

15th Flak Division (Mtz)

Commander:

Believed to have been formed in Rumania by expansion of the III Flak Brigade late in 1941; transferred to the southern sector of Russia early in 1942.

16th Flak Division

Commander:
Headquarters: Lille

17th Flak Division (Mtz)

Commander:

Transferred from Germany to the southern sector in Russia early in 1942.

18th Flak Division (Mtz)

Commander: Genmaj. Heinrich XXXVII Prinz von REUSS

Operating on the central sector in Russia since early in 1942.

RESTRICTED

19th Flak Division (Mtz)

Commander:

Operated in North Africa in 1942 and early in 1943. Reformed and operating in Greece since late in 1943.

20th Flak Division (Mtz)

Commander:

Operated in North Africa in 1942 and early in 1943. Believed to have been reformed for operations in southeastern Europe late in 1943.

21st Flak Division

Commander:

Believed to be operating in southwestern Germany.

22d Flak Division

Commander:

Believed to be operating in western Germany.

RESTRICTED

Section VII. TABLES OF IDENTIFIED UNITS

41. Introduction.

Whereas the foregoing pages (section VI) have contained data on all units of the German ground forces from division upward, including those whose existence or composition can only be surmised, the present section records only those units, from armies down to companies, which have actually been identified. These are listed in tabular form with details as to their component elements and the higher units to which they belong, so far as these are known.

It should be noted that in the case of armies and army corps the only component elements given are the special units (such as the Armee-Nachrichten-Regiment and the field police units) which are organically attached to the staffs of these large organizations. The divisions which make up the combat strength of armies and corps are not included, since they are allocated to them only on a temporary basis for a specific operation or series of operations.

Where a blank (....) is left in the tables, it means that the unit may exist but has not been identified. A dash (—) indicates that the unit is believed not to exist. Gaps in the numerical sequence of units are indicated by dotted lines and may be filled in later as information is received regarding such missing units.

Abbreviations used in these tables are not necessarily those most frequently encountered in German documents but are chosen for their brevity. In each case they are explained at the top of the table and will be found in the Index.

RESTRICTED

Under the divisions, the column headed "Aux. No." gives the number which is assigned to the various service units, such as the medical, veterinary, and supply troops. The second column from the right indicates whether the division in question is considered to be offensive, defensive, or administrative, respectively.

The right-hand column in the tables of armies, corps, and divisions refers to the page in section VI on which the history and other pertinent data regarding the unit will be found.

ORDER OF BATTLE OF THE GERMAN ARMY 353

42. Armies and Panzer Armies. — Armeeoberkommando (A.O.K.), Panzerarmeeoberkommando (Pz.A.O.K.)

A.O.K.	Wkr.	A.N.R.	K.A.N.	Korück	F.G.A.	G.F.P.	F.P.A.	P.K.	See page
1	IX		579		591	590	591		*138*
Pz. 1		Pz. 1	Pz. 1				422	691	*145*
2	XIII?	563?		550?					*138*
Pz. 2	XVII	Pz. 2	Pz. 2	532?			419		*145*
[1]3									*139*
Pz. 3	IX	Pz. 3	Pz. 3		551			697?	*145*
4	VI	589		580		721?	580	689?	*139*
Pz. 4	III	Pz. 4	Pz. 4					694	*146*
[1]5									*139*
[2]Pz. 5									*146*
6	IV	549		585?			540?	637	*139*
7	V	531	551		690?			649?	*140*
8									*140*
9		520?					583?	583?	*140*
10		512?			498	741			*141*
[3]11									*141*
[4]12									*141*
14									*141*
15		509				625?		698?	*142*
16	I?	501?				616?			*142*
17		596?					550	666?	*142*
18			516						*143*
19		445?	445?						*143*
[5]20		550		525			537		*143*
[6]21	XXI	463	463			629	463		*144*
[2]Pz. Afrika									*147*

[1] Formed and disbanded in 1939.
[2] Destroyed in Tunisia.
[3] Disbanded late in 1942.
[4] Expanded to Heeresgruppe E.
[5] Formerly A.O.K. Lappland.
[6] Formerly A.O.K. Norwegen.

A.N.R. = Armeenachrichtenregiment.
K.A.N. = Kommandeur der Armeenachschubtruppen.
Korück = Kommandant des rückwärtigen Armeegebietes.
F.G.A. = Feldgendarmerieabteilung.
G.F.P. = Geheime Feldpolizei.
F.P.A. = Feldpostamt.
P.K. = Propagandakompanie.

RESTRICTED

43. Corps. — Armeekorps (A.K.), Panzerkorps (Pz.K.), Gebirgskorps (Geb.K.), Höheres Kommando zu besonderer Verwendung (Höh.Kdo.), Reservekorps (Res.K).

No.	Type	Wkr.	Nachr. Abt.	Services	Home Station	See page
I	A. K	I		41 401	Königsberg	148
II	A. K	II		42 402	Stettin	148
III	Pz. K	III	Pz.	43 403	Berlin	164
IV	A. K	IV		44 404	Dresden	148
V	A. K	V		45 405	Stuttgart	149
VI	A. K	VI		46 406	Münster	149
VII	A. K	VII		47 407	München	149
[1] VIII	A. K	VIII				150
IX	A. K	IX		49 409	Kassel	150
X	A. K	X		50 410	Hamburg	151
XI	A. K	XI		51 411	Hannover	151
XII	Pz. K	XII		52 412	Wiesbaden	164
XIII	A. K	XIII		53 413	Nürnberg	151
XIV	Pz. K	XI	Pz.	60 414	Magdeburg	164
[2] XV						
XV	Geb. K					169
[3] XVI						
XVII	A. K	XVII		66 417	Wien	152
XVIII	Geb. K	XVIII	Geb.	70 418	Salzburg	169
[4] XIX						
[5] XIX	Geb. K	XVIII				169
XX	A. K	XX		420 420	Danzig	152
[6] XXI						
XXI	Geb. K					170
[7] XXII						
XXII	Geb. K					170
XXIII	A. K	VI		423 423?	Bonn	153
XXIV	Pz. K	XII	Pz.	424 424	Kaiserslautern	165
XXV	A. K	V		425 425?	Baden-Baden	153
XXVI	A. K	I		426 426		153
XXVII	A. K	VII		427 427		154
XXVIII	A. K	III		428 428		154
XXIX	A. K	IV		429 429		154
XXX	A. K	XI		430 430		155
XXXI	Höh. Kdo	X?		431 431		172

[1] Destroyed at Stalingrad; now reformed.
[2] Expanded to 3 Panzerarmee.
[3] Expanded to 4 Panzerarmee.
[4] Expanded to 2 Panzerarmee.
[5] Formerly Geb.K. Norwegen.
[6] Expanded to A.O.K. Norwegen.
[7] Expanded to 1 Panzerarmee.

RESTRICTED

ORDER OF BATTLE OF THE GERMAN ARMY 355

No.	Type	Wkr.	Nachr. Abt.	Services	Home Station	See page
[8]XXXII	Höh. Kdo					
XXXIII	Höh. Kdo	VI	433	433		*172*
[9]XXXIV	A. K	III	434	434?		*155*
XXXV	A. K	VIII	435	435		*155*
XXXVI	Geb. K	II	436	436		*170*
[10]XXXVII	Höh. Kdo					
XXXVIII	A. K	VIII?	438?	438?		*156*
XXXIX	Pz. K	IX	Pz. 439	439		*165*
XL	Pz. K	VII	Pz. 440	440		*165*
XLI	Pz. K	VIII	Pz. 441	441?		*166*
XLII	A. K	III	442	442		*156*
XLIII	A. K	XI	443	443	Hannover	*157*
XLIV	A. K	IV	444	444	Dresden	*157*
[11]XLV						*172*
XLVI	Pz. K	X	Pz. 446	446		*166*
XLVII	Pz. K	XX	Pz. 447	447	Danzig	*166*
XLVIII	Pz. K	XXI	Pz. 448	448	Posen	*167*
XLIX	Geb. K	Böhm & Mähr.	Geb.449	449	Prag	*171*
L	A. K	V		450	450	*157*
LI	Geb. K	XI		451	451	*171*
LII	A. K	III		452	452	*158*
LIII	A. K	XII		453	453	*158*
LIV	A. K			454	454	*158*
LV	A. K			455	455	*159*
LVI	Pz. K	VI	Pz. 456	456		*167*
LVII	Pz. K	II	Pz. 457	457		*167*
LIX	A. K			459	459	*159*
[12]LX	A. K					
LXI	Res. K					*173*
LXII	Res. K					*173*
[13]LXIII						
LXIV	Res. K		464?			*173*
LXV	Höh. Kdo	II	465	465?		*174*
LXVI	Res. K					*174*
LXVII	Res. K		467	467?		*174*
LXVIII	A. K		468	468		*159*
LXIX	Res. K			469?		*175*
LXX	Höh. Kdo	VI?				*175*
LXXI	Höh. Kdo					*175*

[8] Reorganized as LXXXI A.K.
[9] Possibly disbanded.
[10] Reorganized as LXXXII A.K.
[11] Believed disbanded.
[12] Reorganized as LXXXIV A.K.
[13] Incorporated into A.O.K. Norwegen.

RESTRICTED

No.	Type	Wkr.	Nachr. Abt.	Services	Home Station	See page
LXXVI	Pz. K					168
LXXX	A. K		480	480		160
LXXXI	A. K		432?			160
LXXXII	A. K	XVII	437?	437?		160
LXXXIII	A. K					161
LXXXIV	A. K		460?	460?		161
LXXXVI	A. K					162
LXXXVII	A. K					162
LXXXVIII	A. K					162
LXXXIX	A. K					163
[14] XC	Pz. K					168
[14] Afrika	Pz. K					168

[14] Destroyed in Tunisia.

44. Infantry and Miscellaneous Divisions.

— Infanteriedivision (Inf.), Panzergrenadierdivision (Pz.Gr.), Jägerdivision (Jäg.) Sicherungsdivision (Sich.), Grenzwachdivision (Grz.W.), Reservedivision (Res.), Feldausbildungsdivision (F. Ausb.), Divisionsnummer (Div.Nr.), Divisionskommando zu besonderer Verwendung (z.b.V.).

Div.	Type	Grenadier-regimenter			Art. Rgt.	Aufkl. Abt.	Pz.Jg. Abt.	Pi. Btl.	Nachr. Abt.	Pz. Abt.	Aux. No.	Wkr.	Class	See Page
1	Inf	¹1	²22	43	1	¹1	1	1	1		1	I	Off	176
3	Pz.Gr.	8	29		3	103	3	3	3	103	3	III	Off	263
5	Jäg.	⁵56	⁵75		5	5	5	5	5		5	V	Off	272
6	Inf	18	37	58	6	6	6	6	6		6	VI	Off	176
7	Inf	19	61	62	7	7	7	7	7		7	VII	Off	177
8	Jäg.	²28	²38		8	8	8	8	8		8	VIII	Off	272
9	Inf	36	57	116	9	9	9	9	9		9	IX	Off	177
10	Pz.Gr.	20	41		10	¹³110	10	10	10	110?	10	XIII	Off	263
11	Inf	2	23	44	11	11	11	11	11		11	I	Off	178
12	Inf	²27	48	89	12	12	12	12	12		12	II	Off	178
14	Pz. Gr.	11	53	106	14	¹³114	14	14	14	114?	14	IV	Off	264
15	Inf	81	88	²129	15	¹³115	15	15	15	115	15	IX	Off	179
15	Pz. Gr.	⁵104	⁵115		33	¹³116	33	33	33	116	33	XII	Off	264
16	Pz. Gr.	60	156	95	146	17		146	228		66	VI	Off	265
17	Inf	21	55		17	¹³117	17	17	17		17	XIII	Off	179
18	Pz. Gr.	30	51		18	¹³118	18	18	18	118?	18	VIII	Off	266
20	Pz. Gr.	76	90		20	¹³120	20	20	20	120	20	X	Off	266
21	Inf	3	24	45	21	21	21	21	21		21	I	Off	180
22	Pz. Gr.	16	65		22	¹³122	22	22	22	212?	22	X	Off	267
23	Inf	⁶68	³¹9	²167	23	23	23	23	23		23	III	Off	180
24	Inf	31	32	102	24	24	24	24	24		24	IV	Off	181
25	Pz. Gr.	35	119		25	¹³125	25	25	25	125?	25	V	Off	267
26	Inf	⁶39	77	78	26	26	26	26	26		26	VI	Off	181

For footnotes see Page 366.

Div.	Type	Grenadier-regimenter			Art. Rgt.	Aufkl. Abt.	Pz.Jg. Abt.	Pi. Btl.	Nachr. Abt.	Pz. Abt.	Aux. No.	Wkr.	Class	See Page
28	Jäg.	49	⁸83		28	28	28	28	28		28	VIII	Off	*273*
29	Pz. Gr.	15	71		29	¹⁸129	29	29	29	129	29	IX	Off	*268*
30	Inf.	6	26	46	30	30	30	30	30		30	X	Off	*182*
31	Inf.	12	17	82	31	31	31	31	31		31	XI	Off	*182*
32	Inf.	4	94	96	32	32	32	2	32		32	II	Off	*182*
34	Inf.	80	107	253	34	34	34	34	34		34	XII	Off	*183*
35	Inf.	⁶34	109	111	35	35	35	35	35		35	V	Off	*183*
36	Pz. Gr.	87	118		36	¹⁸136	36	36	36	136?	36	XII	Off	*268*
38	Inf.	108	112		138			138	138		138		Off	*184*
39	Inf.	113	114	134	139			139	139?		139		Off	*184*
44	Inf.	131	132	135	96	44	46	80	64		44	XVII	Off	*185*
45	Inf.	130	133	97	98	45	45	81	65		45	XVII	Off	*185*
46	Inf.	42	72	123	114	46	52	88	76		46	XIII	Off	*186*
50	Inf.	121	122	205	150	150	150	150	150		150	III?	Off	*186*
52	Inf.	163	181	234	152	152	152	152	152		152	IX	Off	*187*
56	Inf.	171	192	217	156	156	156	156	156		156	IV	Off	*187*
57	Inf.	179	199	220	157	157	157	157	157		157	VII	Off	*188*
58	Inf.	154	209		158	158	158	158	158		158	X	Off	*188*
60	Pz. Gr.	⁶120	271		160	¹⁸160	160	160	160	160	160	XX	Off	*269*
61	Inf.	151	162	176	161	161	161	161	161		161	I	Off	*188*
62	Inf.	164	183	190	162	162	162	162	162		162	VIII	Off	*189*
65	Inf.	145	146	196	165	168		165	165		165	XII	Off	*189*
68	Inf.	169	188	236	168	¹⁹165	168	168	168		168	III	Off	*190*
69	Inf.	159	193	211	169	¹⁹169		169	169		169	VI	Off	*190*
71	Inf.	191	194	266	171	171	171	171	171		171	XI	Off	*191*
72	Inf.	105	124	213	172	172	172	172	172		172	XII	Off	*191*
73	Inf.	170	186	222	173	173	173	173	173		173	XIII	Off	*192*
75	Inf.	172	202	⁶230	175	175	175	175	175		175	II	Off	*192*
76	Inf.	178	203	215	176	176	176	176	176		176	III	Off	*193*
78	Inf.	14	195	226	178	¹⁹178		178	178		178	V	Off	*193*
79	Inf.	208	212	189	179	179	179	179	179		179	XII	Off	*194*
81	Inf.	161	174		181		181	181	181		181	VIII	Off	*194*

ORDER OF BATTLE OF THE GERMAN ARMY

82	Inf	158	166	168	182		182	182	182	IX	Off	*195*
83	Inf	251	257	277	183		183	183	183	X	Off	*195*
86	Inf	167	184	216	186		186	186	186	V	Off	*196*
87	Inf	173	185	187	187		187	187	187	IV	Off	*196*
88	Pz.Gr	245	246	248	188		188	188	188	VII	Off	*196*
90	Inf	⁵155	⁵200	⁵361	190	190	190	190		III	Off	*269*
93	Inf	270	272	276	193		193	193	193	III	Off	*197*
94	Inf	267	274	280	194		194		¹⁸194	IV	Off	*197*
95	Inf	278	279	287	195		195		195	IX	Off	*198*
96	Inf	283	284		196		196	196	¹⁹196	XI	Off	*198*
97	Jäg	⁵204	⁵207		81		97		97	VII	Off	*273*
98	Inf	282	289	290	198		198	¹⁹198		XIII	Off	*199*
100	Jäg	⁵354	⁵227		83		100	100	100	XVII	Off	*274*
101	Jäg	⁵228	⁵229	233	85		101	101	101	V	Off	*274*
102	Inf	84	232		104		102	102	102	VIII	Off	*199*
104	Jäg	⁵724	³734		654		104	104?		IV	Off	*275*
106	Inf	239	240	241	107		106	106	106	IV	Off	*200*
110	Inf	252	254	255	120		110	110	110	VI	Off	*200*
111	Inf	50	70	117	117?		111	111	111	X	Off	*201*
112	Inf	110	256	258	86		112	112	112	XI	Off	*201*
113	Inf	260	261	268	87		113	113	113	XII	Off	*201*
114	Jäg	⁵721	³741		661		114			XIII	Off	*275*
117	Jäg	⁵737	³749		670		117			I	Off	*275*
118	Jäg	⁵738	³750		668		118			XVII	Off	*276*
121	Inf	405	407	408	121		121	121	121	XVIII	Off	*202*
122	Inf	409	411	414?	122		122	122	122	X	Off	*202*
123	Inf	415	416	418	123		123	123	123	II	Off	*203*
125	Inf	419	420	421	125		125	125	125	III	Off	*203*
126	Inf	422	424	426	126		126	126	126	V	Off	*204*
129	Inf	427	428	430	129		129	129	129	VI	Off	*204*
131	Inf	431	432	434	131		131	131	131	IX	Off	*204*
132	Inf	436	437	438	13**2**		132		¹⁹132	XII	Off	*204*
134	Inf	439	445	446	134			134	134	IV	Off	*205*
137	Inf	447	448	449	137			137	137	XVII	Off	*206*
141	Inf	121	¹²¹¹	¹²⁶¹	1⁵1?						Off	*302*
143	Res	¹²⁶⁸?	¹²⁷⁶?	¹²²¹⁸?	¹²⁵⁷?					III	Def	*303*
147	Res	¹²²¹²?	¹²⁶⁸?		¹²²⁶⁸?					VII	Def	*303*

For footnotes see Page 366.

RESTRICTED

Div.	Type	Grenadier-regimenter			Art. Rgt.	Aufkl. Abt.	Pz.Jg. Abt.	Pi. Btl.	Nachr. Abt.	Aux. No.	Wkr.	Class	See Page
148	Res.	¹⁷8?	¹²239?	¹²252?	¹68?						VIII	Def	303
151	Res.	¹²21	¹²217	¹²228	¹²21?						I	Def	304
152	Div. Nr.										II	Adm	304
153	Res.	¹²23?	¹²208?	¹²257?	¹⁵218?						III	Def	305
154	Res.	¹56	¹²223	¹255	¹⁶24?						IV	Def	305
²³155	Res. Pz.	⁴²25?	¹⁹0?		¹²25?						V	Def	305
156	Res.	¹26	¹²227?	¹²254?	¹⁶6?						VI	Def	306
157	Res.	¹41	¹¹7	¹²157	¹⁶7?						VII	Def	306
158	Res.	¹²62?	¹²213?	¹²221?	¹⁶221?						VIII	Def	307
159	Res.	¹⁹	¹²214?	¹²251	¹69?						IX	Def	307
160	Res.	¹²30	¹⁵58	¹²225	¹⁴58?						X	Def	308
161	Inf.	336	364	371	241	¹⁹241		241	241	241	I	Off	306
162	Inf.	303	314	329	236		236	236	236	236	II	Off	307
163	Inf.	307	310	324	234	¹⁹234		234	234	234	III	Off	307
¹⁰164	Pz. Gr.	¹²125	²382	³433	220	¹⁸220	220	220	220	220	IV	Off	270
165	Res.	¹²205	¹²215?	¹²260	¹⁶57?						V	Def	308
166	Res.	¹²26?	¹²69?	¹³86?	¹²26?						VI	Def	308
167	Inf.	315	331	339	238	238	238	238	238	238	VII	Def	208
168	Inf.	417	429	442	248	248	248	248	248	248	VIII	Off	208
169	Inf.	378	379	392	230		230	230	230	230	IX	Off	209
170	Inf.	391	399	401	240	240	240	240	240	240	X	Off	209
171	Res.	¹²71	¹²216?		¹⁶171?						XI	Def	309
172	Div. Nr.										XIII	Adm	309
173	Res.	¹²17	¹²73	¹⁸87?	¹⁵114?						IV	Def	309
174	Res.	¹²24?		¹⁸256?	¹⁵14?						VI	Def	310
176	Div. Nr.										XVII	Adm	310
177	Div. Nr.										VIII	Adm	310
²⁴179	Res. Pz.	⁴²29	¹81		¹⁶29?						IX	Def	311
180	Div. Nr.										X	Adm	311
181	Inf.	⁶334	349	359	222	222	222	222	222	222	XI	Def	210
182	Res.	¹²34	¹²79	¹²112	¹⁶179?						XII	Def	311

ORDER OF BATTLE OF THE GERMAN ARMY

Div	Type						Corps	Status	Area
183	Inf	330	343		351		219	XIII	Off	210
187	Res	[14]345	[14]462				[15]196	XVII	Def	312
188	Res. Geb	[14]136?	[14]139?				[15]112?	XVIII	Def	312
189	Res	[14]15?	[14]28		[15]252		[15]128?	IX	Def	312
190	Div. Nr							X	Adm	313
[26]191	Res	[12]31?	[12]267?				[15]19?	XI	Def	313
192	Div. Nr							XIII	Adm	313
193	Div. Nr							VI	Adm	313
196	Inf	340	345	362		233	233	233	XII	Off	210
197	Inf	321	332	347		229	229	229	V	Off	211
198	Inf	305	308	326		235	235	235	VI	Off	211
199	Inf	341	357	410		199	199	199	IX?	Def	212
201	Sich	406						III	Def	296
203	Sich							V	Def	212
205	Inf	335	353	358		[15]205	205	205	I	Off	212
206	Inf	301	312	413		[15]206	206	206	II	Off	297
207	Sich	322	374			207		207	III	Def	213
208	Inf	309	337	338		[15]208	208	208	VI	Off	214
[26]210	Inf							VII	Def	214
211	Inf	306	317	365		211	211	211	VIII	Off	214
212	Inf	316	320	423		[15]212	212	212	IX	Def	297
213	Sich	318	354			213	[8]213	213	V	Off	215
214	Inf	355	367			[15]214	214	214	XI	Off	216
215	Inf	380	390	435		215	215	215	I	Off	216
216	Inf	348	396	398		216	216	216	III	Def	217
217	Inf	311	346	389		217	217	217	VIII	Off	298
218	Inf	323	386	397		[15]218	218	218	IV	Def	217
221	Sich	350	360			221	221	221	X	Def	218
223	Inf	344	385	425		[15]223	223	223	VI	Def	218
225	Inf	333	376	377		[15]225	225	225		Def	219
227	Inf	328	366	412		227	227	227	III	Off	314
[26]230	Inf								Def	220
[26]233	Res. Pz	[4]3?	[18]83?			[16]3?			II	Def	220
240	Inf	916?	917	689					XII	Off	220
242	Inf	352	404			242		242			
246	Inf					[19]246	246	246			

For footnotes see Page 366.

RESTRICTED

Div.	Type	Grenadier-regimenter			Art. Rgt.	Aufkl. Abt.	Pz.Jg. Abt.	Pi. Btl.	Nachr. Abt.	Aux. No.	Wkr.	Class	See Page
³⁰250	Inf	262	263	269	250					250	IX	Off	*221*
251	Inf	451	459	471	251	251	251	251	251	251	VIII	Off	*221*
252	Inf	³¹452	461	472	252	252	252	252	252	252	VI	Off	*221*
253	Inf	453	464	473	253	¹⁰253		253	253	²53	VI	Off	*222*
254	Inf	454	474	484	254	254	254	254	254	254	IV	Off	*222*
255	Inf	455	465	475	255	255	255	255	255	255	IV	Off	*223*
256	Inf	456	476	481	256	¹⁰256		256	256	256	III	Off	*223*
257	Inf	4-7	466	477	257	257	257	257	257	257	II	Off	*224*
258	Inf	458	478	479	258	258	258	258	258	258	II	Off	*224*
260	Inf	460	470	480	260	260	260	260	260	260	V	Off	*225*
³²262	Inf	462	482	486	262	262	262	262	262	262	XVII	Off	*225*
263	Inf	463	483	485	263	263	263	263	263	263	XII	Off	*226*
264	Inf	891	892	893	264		264	264		264?	VI	Off	*226*
265	Inf	894	895	896							XI	Off	*227*
267	Inf	467	487	³³497	267	267	267	267	267	267	VII	Off	*227*
268	Inf	468	488	499	268	¹⁹268		268	268	268	X	Off	*228*
269	Inf	469	489	490	269	¹⁹269		269	269	269	X	Off	*228*
³⁰270	Inf										II	Def	*229*
274	Inf											Def	*230*
²⁰280	Inf										II	Off	*298*
281	Sich.	¹¹107	368?								XII	Def	*230*
282	Inf	848	849	850	282					282		Def	*299*
284	Sich.											Def	*299*
285	Sich.	¹¹113		¹¹122							X	Off	*230*
286	Sich.	¹¹31	¹¹61	503							I	Off	*231*
290	Inf	501	502	506	290	¹⁰290				290	II	Off	*231*
291	Inf	504	505	509	291	¹⁰291		291	291	291	III	Off	*232*
292	Inf	507	508	512	292		292	292	292	292	III	Off	*232*
293	Inf	510	511	515	293	293	293	293	293	293	IV	Off	*233*
294	Inf	513	514	518	294	294	294	294	294	294	IV	Off	*233*
295	Inf	516	517	518	295		295	295	295	295	XI	Off	*233*
296	Inf	519	520	521	296	296	296	296	296	296	XIII	Off	*233*

RESTRICTED

297	Inf.	522	523	524	297	297	297	297	XVII	Off	234
²298	Inf.	525	526	527	298	298	298	298	VIII	Off	234
299	Inf.	528	529	530	299	299	299		IX	Off	234
302	Inf.	570	571	572	¹³302	302		302	II	Off	235
304	Inf.	573	574	575	304	304		304	IV	Off	235
305	Inf.	576	577	578	305	305		305	V	Off	236
306	Inf.	579	580	581	¹⁹306	306		306	VI	Off	236
319	Inf.	582	583	584	¹⁹319	319			IX	Off	237
320	Inf.	585	586	587		320	320	320	VIII	Off	238
321	Inf.	588	589	590		321	321		XI	Off	238
323	Inf.	591	592	593	¹⁹323	323	323		▼	Off	238
326	Inf.	751	752	753		326	326	326	VI	Def	239
²327	Inf.	595	596	597		327	327	327	XVII	Off	239
328	Inf.	547	548	549	328	328	328		II	Off	240
329	Inf.	551	552	553	¹⁹329	329	329		VI	Off	240
330	Inf.	554	555	556	330	330	330		V	Off	241
331	Inf.	557	558	559	331	331	331	331	XVII	Off	241
332	Inf.	676	677	678	332	332	⁸332	332	VIII	Off	242
³³333	Inf.	679	680	681	¹⁹333	333	⁸333		III	Off	242
334	Inf.	754	755	756	¹⁹334	334	334		XII	Off	243
335	Inf.	682	683	684		335	⁸335	335	V	Off	243
336	Inf.	685	686	687		336	336	336	IV	Off	244
337	Inf.	313	688	690		337	⁸337	337	VII	Off	244
338	Inf.	757	758	759		338	338	338		Def	245
339	Inf.	691	692	693	¹⁹339	⁸339	⁸339		IX	Off	246
340	Inf.	694	695	696		340	340	340	I	Off	246
342	Inf.	697	698	699	342	342	342	342	XII	Off	246
343	Inf.	851	852	853?			343		XIII	Off	246
344	Inf.	854	855	856		344				Def	271
³⁷345	Pz. Gr.	148	152							Def	247
346	Inf.	857	858	859?					II	Def	247
347	Inf.	860	861	862?				347		Def	248
348	Inf.	863	864	865?						Off	248
355	Inf.	866	867	868				356	IX	Def	248
356	Inf.	869	870	871			369	369	XVII	Def	249
²⁵369	Inf.	369	370				370	370	VIII	Off	250
370	Inf.	666	667	668							

For footnotes see Page 866.

RESTRICTED

Div.	Type	Grenadier-regimenter				Art. Rgt.	Aufkl. Abt.	Pz.Jg. Abt.	Pi. Btl.	Nachr. Abt.	Aux. No.	Wkr.	Class	See Page
371	Inf	669	670	671		371		371	371		371	VI	Off	250
²⁵373	Inf	383	384			373	373	373	373		373	XVII	Def	251
⁴⁰376	Inf	765	766	767		376		376	376		376	VII	Off	251
377	Inf	768	769	770		377	377	377	377	377	377	IX	Off	251
381	F. Ausb.		³⁶618	³⁶616									Def	314
382	F. Ausb.	³⁶617	³⁶618	³⁶619									Def	314
383	Inf	531	532	533		383	¹⁹383		383	383	383	I	Off	252
384	Inf	534	535	536		384		384		384	384	IV	Off	253
²⁵385	Inf	537	538	539		385		385	385	385	385		Off	253
²⁶386	Pz. Gr.	149	153											271
387	Inf	541	542	543		387		387	387	387	387	VII	Off	253
388	F. Ausb.												Def	315
389	Inf	544	545	546		389		389			389	IX	Off	254
390	F. Ausb.												Def	315
391	F. Ausb.	³⁶718	³⁶719	³⁶720									Def	315
²⁵392	Inf												Def	254
401	Div. Nr.											XII	Adm	316
402	z. b. V.											XVII	Adm	299
403	Sich.											I	Adm	316
404	z. b. V.											II	Adm	316
405	z. b. V.											III	Adm	316
406	z. b. V.											IV	Adm	316
407	z. b. V.											V	Adm	316
408	z. b. V.											VI	Adm	317
409	Div. Nr.											VII	Adm	317
410	z. b. V.											VIII	Adm	317
411	z. b. V.											IX	Adm	317
412	z. b. V.											X	Adm	317
413	z. b. V.											XI	Adm	317
416	Inf	930	931									XII	Adm	317
417	Inf. z. b. V.											XIII	Def	255
421	z. b. V.										466	X XVII	Adm Adm	318 318

RESTRICTED

ORDER OF BATTLE OF THE GERMAN ARMY

428	z. b. V.						XX	Adm	*318*
429	z. b. V.						XXI	Adm	*318*
430	z. b. V.						XXI	Adm	*318*
431	z. b. V.						XXI	Adm	*318*
432	z. b. V.						VIII	Adm	*319*
433	Div. Nr.						III	Adm	*319*
442	Sich.							Def	*300*
444	Sich.							Def	*300*
454	Sich.			375			XII		*301*
[33]455	Sich.								*301*
461	Div. Nr.						I	Adm	*319*
462	Div. Nr.						XII	Adm	*319*
464	Div. Nr.						IV	Adm	*319*
465	Div. Nr.						V	Adm	*320*
467	Div. Nr.						VII	Adm	*320*
473	Div. Nr.						XIII	Adm	*320*
487	Div. Nr.						XVII	Adm	*320*
526	Div. Nr.						VI	Adm	*320*
537	Grz. W						XVIII	Def	*321*
538	Grz. W						XVIII	Def	*321*
539	Grz. W						[20]	Def	*321*
540	Grz. W						[20]	Def	*321*
702	Inf.	722	742		662		702	II Def	*256*
707	Inf.	727	747	707	657	702	707	VII Off	*257*
708	Inf.	728	748	708		707	708	VIII Def	*257*
709	Inf.	729	739	709		708	709	IX Def	*258*
710	Inf.	730	740	710		709	710	X Def	*258*
711	Inf.	731	744	711	651	710	711	XI Def	*258*
712	Inf.	732	745	712	652	711	712	XII Def	*259*
[3]713	Inf.	733	746	713	653	712	713	XIII Def	*259*
715	Inf.	725	735	715		713	715	V Def	*259*
716	Inf.	726	736	716	656		716	VI Def	*260*
719	Inf.	723	743	719	663	719	719	III Def	*261*
[4]999	Inf.	961	962		999	999	999	Off	*261*
[7]Rhodos Inf			963						

There is also a Cossack Cavalry Division; its units are believed not to be numbered. (See Page 262.)

For footnotes see Page 366.

RESTRICTED

Footnotes to Infantry and Miscellaneous Divisions.

[1] One Grenadier-Regt. believed to have been dropped.
[2] Panzergrenadierregiment, possibly withdrawn to Heerestruppen.
[3] Jägerregiment.
[4] Gebirgsjägerregiment.
[5] Panzergrenadierregiment.
[6] Füsilierregiment.
[7] Sturmdivision ; regiment is called Sturmregiment.
[8] Kompanie.
[9] Abteilung.
[10] Also contains Panzerabteilung 164 (?).
[11] Sicherungsregiment.
[12] Reservegrenadierregiment.
[13] Reservepanzergrenadierregiment.
[14] Reservegebirgsjägerregiment.
[15] Reserveartillerieabteilung.
[16] Reserveartillerieregiment.
[17] Reservejägerregiment.
[18] Panzeraufklärungsabteilung.
[19] Schnelle Abteilung.
[20] Wehrkreis Böhmen und Mähren.
[21] Elements converted into Pz.Gr.Rgt. of same number, but probably exist as infantry units also.
[23] May also control Reservepanzerabteilung 7.
[24] May also control Reservepanzerabteilung 1.
[25] Kroatische Division.
[26] Küstenverteidigungsdivision.
[29] May also control Reservepanzerabteilung 5.
[30] Spanish Blue Division ; probably disbanded in 1943.
[31] Possibly replaced by Grenadierregiment 7.
[32] Possibly disbanded.
[33] Probably disbanded.
[34] Disbanded.
[36] Feldausbildungsregiment.
[37] Division disbanded. Furnished elements for Grenadierregimenter (mot.) 15 and 71 of 29 Pz.Gr.Div. Components may still exist.
[38] Division disbanded. Furnished elements for Grenadierregimenter (mot.) 8 and 29 of 3 Pz.Gr.Div. Components may still exist.
[40] May contain Grenadierregimenter 672 and 673.
[41] Division disbanded ; some units may still exist.
[42] Possibly withdrawn to Heerestruppen.
[43] Reservegrenadierregiment (mot.).
[44] Reservepionierbataillon.

RESTRICTED

45. Panzer Divisions—Panzerdivision (Pz. Div.).

Pz. Div.	Pz. Rgt.	Pz. Gr. Rgt.	Pz. Gr. Rgt.	Pz. Art. Rgt.	Pz. Aufkl. Abt.	Pz. Pi. Btl.	Pz. Nachr. Abt.	Pz Jg. Abt.	Pz. Beob. Bttr.	Aux. No.	Wkr.	See page
1	1	1	113	73	1	37	37	37		81	IX	277
2	3	2	304	74	2	38	38	38	320	82	XVII	277
3	6	3	394	75	3	39	39		327	83	III	278
4	35	12	33	103	4	79	79	49	324	84	XIII	278
5	31	13	14	116	5	89	85?	53		85	VIII	279
6	11	4	114	76	6	57	82	41		57	VI	279
7	25	6	7	78	7	58	83	42	325	58	IX	280
8	10	8	28	80	8	59	59	43		59	III	280
9	33	10	11	102	9	86	81	50		60	XVII	281
10	7	69	86	90	10	49	90	90	322	90	V	281
11	15	110	111	119	11	209	341			61	VIII	282
12	29	5	25	2	12	32	2	2		2	II	282
13	4	66	93	13	13	4	13	13		13	XI	283
14	36	103	108	4	14	13	4	4		4	IV	284
15												
16	2	64	79	16	16	16	16	16		16	VI	284
17	39	40	63	27	17	27	27	27		27	VII	285
18	18	52	101	88	18	98	88	88		88	IV	285
19	27	73	74	19	19	19	19	19		19	XI	286
20	21	59	112	92	20	92	92	92		92	IX	286
21	5	192?	492?	155	21	200	200	39	335	200	III	287
22	204	³129	140	140	22	140	140	140		140	XII	287
23	201	126	128	128	23	128	128	128		128	V	288
24	24	21	426	89	24	40	86	40		40	I	288
25	9	146	147	91	25	75	87			87	VI	289
26	26	9	67	93	26	93	593	93		93	I	289

Also classified as Panzer divisions are Panzer Division Hermann Göring (Airforce) and **Panzergrenadier** Division **Grossdeutschland**. Their component units bear the name of their division instead of numbers. (See Pages 290–291.)
¹ 15 Panzerdivision is now listed under 15 Panzergrenadierdivision. ⁴ Füsilierregiment.
² Division possibly disbanded now. ⁵ Contains elements of Panzerjägerabteilung 525.
³ Now in 15 Panzergrenadierdivision.

RESTRICTED

46. Mountain Divisions—Gebirgsdivision (Geb.Div.).

Geb. Div.	Geb. Jäg. Rgt.	Geb. Jäg. Rgt.	Geb. Art. Rgt.	Aufkl. Abt.	Geb. Pi. Btl.	Geb. Nachr. Abt.	Geb. Pz. Jg. Abt.	Aux. No.	Wkr.	See page
1	98	99	79	54	54	54	44	54	VII	*292*
2	136	137	111	67	67	67	55	67	XVIII	*292*
3	138	144	112	68	83	68	48	68	XVIII	*293*
4	13	91	94	94	94	94	94	94	VII	*293*
5	85	100	95	95	95	95	95	95	XVIII	*294*
6	141	143	118	112	91	91	47	91	XVIII	*294*
7	206	218	82	99	99	99	99	99	XIII	*295*
8?	142?								XVIII	*295*

RESTRICTED

ORDER OF BATTLE OF THE GERMAN ARMY 369

47. Waffen-SS units.

In the following tables the designations of SS units are given in abbreviated form. The proper full designations will be found in section VI, paragraph 39, wherever they are known.

a. Divisions.

Division	Type	Minor Units	Infantry Regiments
Leibstandarte A. H.	Pz.		Pz. Gr. 1, 2, 3(?).
Das Reich	Pz.		Deutschland, Der Führer, Langemarck.
Totenkopf	Pz.		Theodor Eicke, —.
Polizei	Mtz.		Pol. Gr. 1, 2, 3.
Wiking	Pz.		Germania, Nordland, Westland.
Nord	Mtn.		Geb. Jg. 6 (Reinhard Heydrich), Geb. Jg. 7.
Prinz Eugen	Mtn.		Geb. Jg. 1 & 2 or 10 & 11.
Kavallerie	Cav.		Kav. 1, 2, 3, 4.
Hohenstaufen	Pz.		
Frundsberg	Pz.	10	Pz. Gr. Hermann Göring, —.
Hitler Jugend	Pz.		
Galizien	Inf.		
Nordland	Mtz.		Norge (?), Danmark(?).
Nederland	Mtz.		
Lettland	Inf.		
Croatian	Mtn.		
Reichsführer	Mtz.		
Götz von Berlichingen	Mtz.		

b. Brigades.

Brigade	Type	Component Regiments
1	Mtz.	8, 10.
2	Mtz.	4, 5, 14(?).
3 Estonian	Inf.(?)	
Pz. Brigade	Pz.	
Walloon Brigade	Inf.(?)	

RESTRICTED

c. Regiments.

Regiment	Home Station	Allotted to Div.
Pz. Gr. 1	Berlin(?)	Leibstandarte A. H.
Pol. Gr. 1		Polizei
Geb. Jg. 1(?)		Prinz Eugen(?)
Kav. 1		Kavallerie
Pz. Gr. 2	Berlin(?)	Leibstandarte A. H.
Pol. Gr. 2		Polizei
Geb. Jg. 2(?)		Prinz Eugen(?)
Kav. 2		Kavallerie
Pz. Gr. 3(?)	Berlin(?)	Leibstandarte A. H.(?)
Pol. Gr. 3		Polizei
Kav. 3		Kavallerie
Kav. 4		Kavallerie
4 (Mtz) (?)		2d Mtz Brigade(?)
5 (Mtz) (?)		2d Mtz Brigade(?)
Geb. Jg. 6 (Heydrich)	Trautenau	Nord
Geb. Jg. 7	Trautenau	Nord
8 (Mtz)		1st Mtz Brigade
10 (Mtz)		1st Mtz Brigade
Geb. Jg. 10(?)		Prinz Eugen(?)
Geb. Jg. 11(?)		Prinz Eugen(?)
14 (Mtz) (?)		2d Mtz Brigade
Danmark (Pz. Gr.)		Nordland(?)
Der Führer (Pz. Gr.)	Wien	Das Reich
Deutschland (Pz. Gr.)	München	Das Reich
Germania (Pz. Gr.)	Hamburg	Wiking
Herman Göring (Pz. Gr.)		Frundsberg
Langemarck (Pz. Gr.)		Das Reich
Nordland (Pz. Gr.)	Klagenfurt	Wiking
Norge (Pz. Gr.)		Nordland
Reinhard Heydrich (Geb. Jg.)		Nord (see Geb. Jg. 6)
Theodor Eicke (Pz. Gr.)	Oranienburg	Totenkopf
Westland (Pz. Gr.)	Klagenfurt	Wiking

ORDER OF BATTLE OF THE GERMAN ARMY

48. Brigades.

The only brigades and brigade staffs which now exist or have recently existed in the German Army are the following special types:

a. Infantry.

(1) Armored infantry brigade (*Schützenbrigade*, later *Panzergrenadierbrigade*).—Found in all Panzer divisions up to the end of 1942 to control the armored infantry regiments and the motorcycle battalion. Now abolished.

(2) Sicherungs brigade (*Sicherungsbrigade*). — Controls Sicherungs unit guarding the line of communications in Russia. Several were formed from *Ersatz* regiments in the 600 series in 1942; Nos. 201 and 203 were subsequently raised to Sicherungs divisions, while No. 202 is believed still to exist as a brigade.

(3) Fortress brigade (*Festungsbrigade*).—Controls fortress battalions, coast artillery, and other units in a fortified zone. Two, Nos. 1 and 2, were formed on Crete; No. 1 is now called *Festungsbrigade Kreta*, and No. 2 has been withdrawn or dissolved.

(4) Replacement training brigade (*Ersatzbrigade*).—Controls *Ersatz* and training units of all arms for a particular division. Ersatzbrigade Grossdeutschland at Cottbus (Wkr. III) and Ersatzbrigade Felderrnhalle at Danzig (Wkr. XX) are known to exist. The term was also used for a preliminary form of the Sicherungs brigades described under (2) above.

(5) Cavalry brigade (*Kavalleriebrigade*).—Two such brigades controlling two cavalry regiments each probably constitute the 1st Cossack Division. The 1st Cavalry Division also consisted of two cavalry brigades before its conversion into the 24th Panzer Division.

(6) Mobile brigade (*Schnelle Brigade*).—A new type of brigade staff formed in 1943 to control a number of mobile battalions (*Schnelle Abteilungen*) belonging to the GHQ pool. Nos. 20 and 30 have been identified, both under the command of Army Group West.

RESTRICTED

(7) Demonstration Brigade 900 (*Lehrbrigade 900*).—Controls the two infantry demonstration regiments whenever they are required to serve together in the field.

b. Panzer troops.—The two tank regiments of a Panzer division were comprised under a Panzer brigade (*Panzerbrigade*) up to the time when these divisions were reorganized on a one-regiment basis in the summer of 1940. Since then some Panzer brigades have existed to control tank units of the GHQ pool; those known to exist in 1943 were Nos. 18 and 100 (the latter responsible for forming and training new tank units in France).

c. Artillery.—An armored artillery brigade (*gepanzerte Artilleriebrigade*) was known to exist until recently under Army Group West. It bore the number 1 and controlled (and may still control) two armored artillery regiments numbered 1 and 2. Also of brigade status are the staffs of the artillery commander (*Artilleriekommandeur, Arko*), the coast artillery commander (*Küstenartilleriekommandeur*), and the fortress artillery commander (*Festungsartilleriekommandeur*).

d. Engineers.—Certain senior officers and their staffs have brigade status; these include the *Höherer Pionierführer*, until recently known as *Oberbaustab* (higher construction staff) and the *Festungspionierkommandeur* (fortress engineer commander).

e. Signal troops.—Certain senior officers and their staffs have brigade status; these include the *Heeresgruppen-, Armee-,* and *Panzerarmee-Nachtrichtenführer* (Chief Signal Officer of an army group, army, or Panzer army) and the *Kommandeur der Führungsnachrichtentruppen* (commander of inter-service communications).

f. Supply troops.—Special brigade staffs may be found controlling motor transport regiments and battalions of the GHQ pool. An example is *Wirtschaftskraftwagentransportbrigade z.b.V. 1* (Special Duty Brigade No. 1 for Industrial Motor Transport).

RESTRICTED

ORDER OF BATTLE OF THE GERMAN ARMY

49. Infantry Regiments.—Grenadierregiment (Gr. Rgt.), Füsilierregiment (Füs. Rgt.), Panzergrenadierregiment (Pz. Gr. Rgt.), Jägerregiment (Jäg. Rgt.), Gebirgsjägerregiment (Geb. Jäg. Rgt.).

Gr. Rgt.	Wkr.	In Div.	Gr. Rgt.	Wkr.	In Div.
1	I	1 Inf.	Pz. Gr. 33	XIII	4 Pz.
Pz. Gr. 1	IX	1 Pz.	Füs. 34	V	35 Inf.
2	I	11 Inf.	35 mot	V	25 Pz. Gr.
Pz. Gr. 2	XVII	2 Pz.	36	IX	9 Inf.
3	I	21 Inf.	37	VI	6 Inf.
Pz. Gr. 3	III	3 Pz.	Jäg. 38	VIII	8 Jäg.
4	II	32 Inf.	Füs. 39	VI	26 Inf.
Pz. Gr. 4	VI	6 Pz.	Pz. Gr. 40	VII	17 Pz.
Pz. Gr. 5	II	12 Pz.	41 mot	XIII	10 Pz. Gr.
6	X	30 Inf.	42	XIII	46 Inf.
Pz. Gr. 6	IX	7 Pz.	43	I	1 Inf.
7	VIII	252 Inf.?	44	I	11 Inf.
Pz. Gr. 7	IX	7 Pz.	45	I	21 Inf.
8 mot	III	3 Pz. Gr.	46	X	30 Inf.
Pz. Gr. 8	III	8 Pz.	47 mot.⁴	X	
9¹	III	23 Inf. Div.	48	II	12 Inf.
Pz. Gr. 9	III	26 Pz.	Jäg. 49	VIII	28 Jäg.
10?²	IV		50	III	111 Inf.
Pz. Gr. 10	XVII	9 Pz.	51 mot	VIII	18 Pz. Gr.
11 mot	IV	14 Pz. Gr.	Pz. Gr. 52	IV	18 Pz.
Pz. Gr. 11	XVII	9 Pz.	53 mot	IV	14 Pz. Gr.
12	XI	31 Inf.	Jäg. 54	XVII	100 Jäg.
Pz. Gr. 12	XIII	4 Pz.	55	XIII	17 Inf.
Geb. Jg. 13	VII	4 Geb.	Jäg. 56	V	5 Jäg.
Pz. Gr. 13	VIII	5 Pz.	57	IX	9 Inf.
14³	V	78 Inf.	58	VI	6 Inf.
Pz. Gr. 14	VIII	5 Pz.	Pz. Gr. 59	IX	20 Pz.
15 mot	IX	29 Pz. Gr.	60 mot	VI	16 Ps. Gr.
16 mot	X	22 Pz. Gr.	61	VII	7 Inf.
17	XI	31 Inf.	62	VII	7 Inf.
18	VI	6 Inf.	Pz. Gr. 63	VII	17 Pz.
19	VII	7 Inf.	Pz. Gr. 64	VI	16 Pz.
20 mot	XIII	10 Pz. Gr.	65 mot	X	22 Pz. Gr.
21	XIII	17 Inf.	Pz. Gr. 66	XI	13 Pz.
Pz. Gr. 21	I	24 Pz.	67⁵	III	23 Inf.
Füs. 22	I	1 Inf.	Pz. Gr. 67	III	26 Pz.
23	I	11 Inf.	Füs. 68	III	23 Inf.
24	I	21 Inf.	Pz. Gr. 69	V	10 Pz.
Pz. Gr. 25	II	12 Pz.	70	XI	111 Inf.
Füs. 26	X	30 Inf.	71 mot	IX	29 Pz. Gr.
Pz. Gr. 26		24 Pz.	72	XIII	46 Inf.
Füs. 27	II	12 Inf.	Pz. Gr. 73	XI	19 Pz.
Jäg. 28		8 Jäg.	Pz. Gr. 74	XI	19 Pz.
Pz. Gr. 28	III	8 Pz.	Jäg. 75	V	5 Jäg.
29 mot	III	3 Pz. Gr.	76 mot	X	20 Pz. Gr.
30 mot	VIII	18 Pz. Gr.	77	VI	26 Inf.
31	IV	24 Inf.	78	VI	26 Inf.
32	IV	24 Inf.	Pz. Gr. 79	VI	16 Pz.

¹Converted into Pz. Gr. Rgt. 9; may still exist.
²I Bn is Jäg. Btl.
³Sturm. Rgt.
⁴Detached from 22 Pz. Gren. Div.
⁵Converted into Pz. Gr. Rgt. 67; may still exist.

RESTRICTED

374 ORDER OF BATTLE OF THE GERMAN ARMY

Gr. Rgt.		Wkr.	In Div.	Gr. Rgt.		Wkr.	In Div.
	80............	XII	34 Inf.	Pz. Gr.	128............	V	23 Pz. Gr.
	81............	IX	15 Inf.	Pz. Gr.	129............	V	15 Pz. Gr.
	82............	XI	31 Inf.		130............	XVII	45 Inf.
Jäg.	83[6]...........	VIII	28 Jäg.		131............	XVII	44 Inf.
	84............	VIII	102		132............	XVII	44 Inf.
Geb. Jg.	85............	XVIII	5 Geb. Jg.		133............	XVII	45 Inf.
Pz. Gr.	86............	V	10 Pz.		134............	XVII	44 Inf.
	87 mot.......	XII	36 Pz. Gr.		135............	XVII	45 Inf.
	88............	IX	15 Inf.	Geb. Jg.	136............	XVIII	2 Geb.
	89............	II	12 Inf.	Geb. Jg.	137............	XVIII	2 Geb.
	90 mot.......	X	20 Pz. Gr.	Jäg.	138............	XVIII	3 Geb.
Geb. Jg.	91............	VII	4 Geb. Jg.	Geb. Jg.	139............	XVIII	
	92 mot.[7].....	XX		Pz. Gr.	140?..........	V	
Pz. Gr.	93............	XI	13 Pz.	Geb. Jg.	141............	XVIII	6 Geb.
	94............	II	32 Inf.	Geb. Jg.?	142............	XVIII?	8 Geb.?
	95............	XIII	17 Inf.	Geb. Jg.	143............	XVIII	6 Geb.
	96............	II	32 Inf.	Geb. Jg.	144[8]..........	XVIII	3 Geb.
	97............	XIII	46 Inf.		145............	XII	65 Inf.
Geb. Jg.	98............	VII	1 Geb.		146............	XII	65 Inf.
Geb. Jg.	99............	VII	1 Geb.	Pz. Gr.	146............		25 Pz.
Geb. Jg.	100...........	XVIII	5 Geb.	Pz. Gr.	147............		25 Pz.
Pz. Gr.	101...........	IV	18 Pz.		148 mot.[10]..		345 Pz. Gr.
	102...........	IV	24 Inf.		149 mot.[11]..		386 Pz. Gr.
Pz. Gr.	103...........	IV	14 Pz.		151............	I	61 Inf.
Pz. Gr.	104...........	XII	15 Pz. Gr.		152 mot.[12]..		345 Pz. Gr.
	105...........	XII	72 Inf.		153 mot.[13]..	VIII	386 Pz. Gr.
	106...........	IX	15 Inf.		154............	X	58 Inf.
	107...........	XII	34 Inf.	Pz. Gr.	155............	III	90 Pz. Gr.
	108...........		38 Inf.		156 mot.......	VI	16 Pz. Gr.
Pz. Gr.	108...........	IV	14 Pz.		...		
	109...........	V	35 Inf.				
	110...........	XII	112 Inf.		158............	IX	82 Inf.
Pz. Gr.	110...........	VIII	11 Pz.		159............	VI	69 Inf.
	111...........	V	35 Inf.	Pz. Gr.	160[14].........		
Pz. Gr.	111...........	VIII	11 Pz.		161............	VIII	81 Inf.
	112...........		38 Inf.		162............	I	61 Inf.
Pz. Gr.	112...........	IX	20 Pz.		163............	IX	52 Inf.
	113...........		39 Inf.		164............	VIII	62 Inf.
Pz. Gr.	113...........	IX	1 Pz.		165?...........	IX	
	114...........		39 Inf.		166............	IX	82 Inf.
Pz. Gr.	114...........	VI	6 Pz.		167............	VI	86 Inf.
Pz. Gr.	115...........	XII	15 Pz. Gr.		168............	IX	82 Inf.
	116...........	IX	9 Inf.		169............	III	68 Inf.
	117...........	XI	111 Inf.		170............	XIII	73 Inf.
	118 mot......	XII	36 Pz. Gr.		171............	IV	56 Inf.
	119 mot......	V	25 Pz. Gr.		172............	II	75 Inf.
	120 mot.[9]...	XX	60 Pz. Gr.		173............	IV	87 Inf.
	121...........	III	50 Inf.		174............	VIII	81 Inf.
	122...........	III	50 Inf.		...		
	123...........	III	50 Inf.		176............	I	61 Inf.
	124...........	XII	72 Inf.		177............		
Pz. Gr.	125...........	IV	164 Pz. Gr.		178............	III	76 Inf.
Pz. Gr.	126...........	V	23 Pz.				

[6]Possibly also Pz. Gren. Rgt. of same number.
[7]Independent Rgt.
[8]Possibly withdrawn to G.H.Q. Troops.
[9]Called Füsilier-Regiment-Feldherrnhalle.
[10]Converted into Gren. Rgt. (mot) 15.
[11]Converted into Gren. Rgt. (mot) 8.
[12]Converted into Gren. Rgt. (mot.) 71.
[13]Converted into Gren. Rgt. (mot.) 29.
[14]Disbanded in 1943.

RESTRICTED

ORDER OF BATTLE OF THE GERMAN ARMY

	Gr. Rgt.	Wkr.	In Div.	Gr. Rgt.	Wkr.	In Div.
	179............	VII	57 Inf.	Jäg. 227............	XVII	100 Jäg.
	...			Jäg. 228............	V	101 Jäg.
				Jäg. 229............	V	101 Jäg.
	181............	IX	52 Inf.	Füs. 230............	III	76 Inf.
	...			...		
	183............	VIII	62 Inf.	232............	VIII	102 Inf.
	184............	VI	86 Inf.	233............	VIII	102 Inf.
	185............	IV	87 Inf.	234............	IV	56 Inf.
	186............	XIII	73 Inf.	235[18]............	VIII	
	187............	IX	87 Inf.	236............	VI	69 Inf.
	188*............	III	68 Inf.			
	189............	VIII	81 Inf.			
	190............	VIII	62 Inf.	238[18]............	V	
	191............	XI	71 Inf.	239............	VI	106 Inf.
	192............	IV	56 Inf.	240............	VI	106 Inf.
Pz. Gr.	192?............		21 Pz.	241............	VI	106 Inf.
	193............	VI	69 Inf.	242[17]............	XX	
	194............	XI	71 Inf.	243[17]............	XX	
	195[15]............	V	78 Inf.	244[17]............	XX	
	196............	III	68 Inf.	245............	VII	88 Inf.
	197............			246............	VII	88 Inf.
	198............					
	199[16]............	VII	57 Inf.	...		
Pz. Gr.	200............	III	90 Pz. Gr.	248............	VII	88 Inf.
	201[17]............			249?............		
	202............	II	75 Inf.	250............		
	203............	III	76 Inf.	251............	X	83 Inf.
Jäg.	204............	VII	97 Jäg.	252............	X	110 Inf.
	205............	IX	52 Inf.	253............	XII	34 Inf.
Geb. Jg.	206............	XIII	7 Geb.	254............	X	110 Inf.
Jäg.	207............	VII	97 Jäg.	255............	X	110 Inf.
	208............	XII	79 Inf.	256............	XII	112 Inf.
	209............	X	58 Inf.	257............	X	83 Inf.
	210?............			258............	XII	112 Inf.
	211............	XI	71 Inf.	...		
	212............	XII	79 Inf.			
	213............	XIII	73 Inf.	260............	XIII	113 Inf.
	214............			261............	XIII	113 Inf.
	215[15]............	V	78 Inf.	262[19]............		
	216............	VI	86 Inf.	263[19]............		
	217............	VII	57 Inf.	264?............	IV	
Geb. Jg.	218............	XIII	7 Geb.	265[17]............	V	
	...			266............	XII	72 Inf.
				267............	IV	94 Inf.
	220............	X	58 Inf.	268............	XIII	113 Inf.
	...			269[19]............		
				270............	III	93 Inf.
	222............	II	75 Inf.	271 mot.[20].....	III	60 Pz. Gr.
	223?............			272............	III	93 Inf.
	224?............			...		
	...			274............	IV	94 Inf.
	226............	XII	79 Inf.			

[15]Sturm Rgt.
[16]Regiment List.
[17]Disbanded late in 1940s
[18]Possibly disbanded.
[19]Spanish; disbanded autumn 1943.
[20]Called Grenadier Regiment Feldherrnhalle.

RESTRICTED

Gr. R.

	Gr. Rgt.	Wkr.	In Div.		Gr. Rgt.	Wkr.	In Div.
	...				328	VI	227 Inf.
	276	IV	94 Inf.		329	II	162 Inf.
	274	X	83 Inf.		330	XIII	183 Inf.
	278	IX	95 Inf.		331	VII	167 Inf.
	279	IX	95 Inf.		332	XII	197 Inf.
	280	IX	95 Inf.		333	X	225 Inf.
	...			Füs.	334	XI	181 Inf.
					335	V	205 Inf.
	282	XIII	98 Inf.		336	I	161 Inf.
	283	XI	96 Inf.		337	III	208 Inf.
	284	XI	96 Inf.		338	III	208 Inf.
	...				339	VII	167 Inf.
	...				340	VI	196 Inf.
	287²¹	XI	96 Inf.		341	VI	199 Inf.
	288²²				...		
	289	XIII	98 Inf.		343	XIII	183 Inf.
	290	XIII	98 Inf.		344	IV	223 Inf.
	291?				345	VI	196 Inf.
	...				346	I	217 Inf.
	...				347	XII	197 Inf.
	294?				348	XI	216 Inf.
	...				343	XI	181 Inf.
	...				350²⁴	VIII	221 Sich.
	298?				351	XIII	183 Inf.
	...				352	XII	246 Inf.
	...				353	V	205 Inf.
	301	I	206 Inf.		354²⁴	VIII	213 Sich.
	302²³	XIII			355	IX	214 Inf.
	303	II	162 Inf.		...		
Pz. Gr.	304	XVII	2 Pz.				
	305	V	198 Inf.		357	VI	199 Inf.
	306	VI	211 Inf.		358	V	205 Inf.
	307	III	163 Inf.		359	XI	181 Inf.
	308	V	198 Inf.		360²⁴	VIII	221 Sich.
	309	III	208 Inf.	Pz. Gr.	361	III	90 Pz. Gr.
	310	III	163 Inf.		362	VI	196 Inf.
	311	I	217 Inf.		...		
	312	I	206 Inf.				
	313	XII	337 Inf.		364	I	161 Inf.
	314	II	162 Inf.		365	VI	211 Inf.
	315	VII	167 Inf.		366	VI	227 Inf.
	316	VII	212 Inf.		367	IX	214 Inf.
	317	VI	211 Inf.		368²⁴	II	281 Sich.
	318²⁴	VIII	213 Sich.		369	XVII	369 Inf.
	319²⁴	XIII			370	XVII	369 Inf.
	320	VII	212 Inf.		371	I	161 Inf.
	321	XII	197 Inf.		...		
	322²⁴	II	207 Sich.		374²⁴	II	207 Sich.
	323	III	218 Inf.		375²⁴	VIII	454 Sich.
	324	III	163 Inf.		376	X	225 Inf.
	...				377	X	225 Inf.
	326	V	198 Inf.		378	IX	169 Inf.
	...				379	IX	169 Inf.
					380	V	215 Inf.
					...		

[21] Disbanded late in 1940.
[22] "Sonderverband 288"—disbanded 1943.
[23] Disbanded.
[24] Reinforced Rgt.

RESTRICTED

ORDER OF BATTLE OF THE GERMAN ARMY

Gr. Rgt.	Wkr.	In Div.	Gr. Rgt.	Wkr.	In Div.
Pz. Gr. 382[25]	IV	164 Pz. Gr.	431	XI	131 Inf.
383		373 Inf.[26]	432	XI	131 Inf.
384		373 Inf.[26]	Pz. Gr. 433	IV	164 Pz. Gr.
385	IV	223 Inf.	434	XI	131 Inf.
386	III	218 Inf.	435	V	215 Inf.
			436	XII	132 Inf.
			437	XII	132 Inf.
			438	XII	132 Inf.
388[31]	IX	210 Inf.	439	IV	134 Inf.
389	I	217 Inf.	440[28]	IV	
390	V	215 Inf.	441		
391	X	170 Inf.	442	VIII	168 Inf.
392	IX	169 Inf.	443		
			444[29]	VIII	230 Inf.
			445	IV	134 Inf.
Pz. Gr. 394	III	3 Pz.	446	IV	134 Inf.
395?			447	XVII	137 Inf.
396	XI	216 Inf.	448	XVII	137 Inf.
397	III	218 Inf.	449	XVII	137 Inf.
398	XI	216 Inf.	450[30]		
399	X	170 Inf.	451	IX	251 Inf.
			452[30]	VIII	252 Inf.
			453	VI	253 Inf.
401	X	170 Inf.	454	VI	254 Inf.
402?			455	IV	255 Inf.
403[27]			456	IV	256 Inf.
404	XII	246 Inf.	457	III	257 Inf.
405	X	121 Inf.	458	II	258 Inf.
406[32]	VIII	201 Sich.	459	IX	251 Inf.
407	X	121 Inf.	460	V	260 Inf.
408	X	121 Inf.	461	VIII	252 Inf.
409	II	122 Inf.	462	XVII	262 Inf.
410	VI	199 Inf.	463	XII	263 Inf.
411	II	122 Inf.	464	VI	253 Inf.
412	VI	227 Inf.	465	IV	255 Inf.
413	I	206 Inf.	466	III	257 Inf.
414	IV	122 Inf.?	467	XI	267 Inf.
415	III	123 Inf.	468	VII	268 Inf.
416	III	123 Inf.	469	X	269 Inf.
417	VIII	168 Inf.	470	V	260 Inf.
418	III	123 Inf.	471	IX	251 Inf.
419	V	125 Inf.	472	VIII	252 Inf.
420	V	125 Inf.	473	VI	253 Inf.
421	V	125 Inf.	474	VI	254 Inf.
422	VI	126 Inf.	475	IV	255 Inf.
423	VII	212 Inf.	476	IV	256 Inf.
424	VI	126 Inf.	477	III	257 Inf.
425	IV	223 Inf.	478	II	258 Inf.
426	VI	126 Inf.	479	III	258 Inf.
427	IX	129 Inf.	480	V	260 Inf.
428	IX	129 Inf.	481	XIII	256 Inf.
429	VIII	168 Inf.	482	XVII	262 Inf.
430	IX	129 Inf.	483	XII	263 Inf.

[25] Possibly withdrawn to G.H.Q. troops.
[26] Croatian.
[27] Kosakenbataillon.
[28] Gr. Rgt. Rhodos.
[29] Div. probably disbanded late in 1941.
[30] Turkestanisches Inf. Btl.; 452 also a Regt. in 252 Inf. Div.
[31] Geb.-Tg. Rgt. detached from 214 Inf. Div.
[32] Reinforced Rgt.

RESTRICTED

Gr. R.

Gr. Rgt.	Wkr.	In Div.	Gr. Rgt.	Wkr.	In Div.
484	VI	254 Inf.	541	VII	387 Inf.
485	XII	263 Inf.	542	VII	387 Inf.
486	XVII	262 Inf.	543	VII	387 Inf.
487	XI	267 Inf.	544	IX	389 Inf.
488	VII	268 Inf.	545	IX	389 Inf.
489	X	269 Inf.	546	IX	389 Inf.
490	X	269 Inf.	547	II	328 Inf.
...			548	II	328 Inf.
Pz. Gr. 492?		21 Pz.	549	II	328 Inf.
...			550[35]		
497[33]	XI	267 Inf.	551	VI	329 Inf.
...			552	VI	329 Inf.
499	XVIII	268 Inf.	553	VI	329 Inf.
500[34]			554	V	330 Inf.
501	X	290 Inf.	555	V	330 Inf.
502	X	290 Inf.	556	V	330 Inf.
503	X	290 Inf.	557	XVII	331 Inf.
504	I	291 Inf.	558	XVII	331 Inf.
505	I	291 Inf.	559	XVII	331 Inf.
506	I	291 Inf.	...		
507	II	292 Inf.	569		
508	II	292 Inf.	570	II	302 Inf.
509	II	292 Inf.	571	II	302 Inf.
510	III	293 Inf.	572	II	302 Inf.
511	III	293 Inf.	572[35]		
512	III	293 Inf.	573	IV	304 Inf.
513	IV	294 Inf.	574	IV	304 Inf.
514	IV	294 Inf.	575	IV	304 Inf.
515	IV	294 Inf.	576	V	305 Inf.
516	XI	295 Inf.	577	V	305 Inf.
517	XI	295 Inf.	578	V	305 Inf.
518	XI	295 Inf.	579	VI	306 Inf.
519	XIII	296 Inf.	580	VI	306 Inf.
520	XIII	296 Inf.	581	VI	306 Inf.
521	XIII	296 Inf.	582	IX	319 Inf.
522	XVII	297 Inf.	583	IX	319 Inf.
523	XVII	297 Inf.	584	IX	319 Inf.
524	XVII	297 Inf.	585	VIII	320 Inf.
525	VIII	298 Inf.	586	VIII	320 Inf.
526	VIII	298 Inf.	587	VIII	320 Inf.
527	VIII	298 Inf.	588	XI	321 Inf.
528	IX	299 Inf.	589	XI	321 Inf.
529	IX	299 Inf.	590	XI	321 Inf.
530	IX	299 Inf.	591	V	323 Inf.
531	I	383 Inf.	592	V	323 Inf.
532	I	383 Inf.	593	V	323 Inf.
533	I	383 Inf.	594	VIII	
534	IV	384 Inf.	595	XVII	327 Inf.
535	IV	384 Inf.	596	XVII	327 Inf.
536	IV	384 Inf.	597	XVII	327 Inf.
537	VI	385 Inf.	598?		
538	VI	385 Inf.	599?		
539	VI	385 Inf.	...		
540[34]			601[36]	V	
			602[36]		
			603[36]	IV	

[33] Possibly disbanded.
[34] Bewähr. Btl. (Probat.).
[35] Bataillon.
[36] Feldausbildungsregiment.

RESTRICTED

ORDER OF BATTLE OF THE GERMAN ARMY   Gr. R.   379

Gr. Rgt.	Wkr.	In Div.	Gr. Rgt.	Wkr.	In Div.
606[38]	III		...		
607[38]	I?		676	VIII	332 Inf.
608[38]	III		677	VIII	332 Inf.
609[38]	XI		678	VIII	332 Inf.
610[38]			679	III	333 Inf.
611[38]			680	III	333 Inf.
612			681	III	333 Inf.
613[38]	IV		682	V	335 Inf.
614[38]	IV		683	V	335 Inf.
...			684	V	335 Inf.
616[38]	IV	381[39]	685	IV	336 Inf.
617[38]		382[39]	686	IV	336 Inf.
618[38]	III	382[39]	687	IV	336 Inf.
619[38]	XVII	382[39]	688	VII	337 Inf.
...			689	VII	246 Inf.
621[40]	V		690	VII	337 Inf.
622[40]	V		691	IX	339 Inf.
623[40]	V		692	IX	339 Inf.
...			693	IX	339 Inf.
...			694	I	340 Inf.
638[41]			695	I	340 Inf.
...			696	I	340 Inf.
...			697	XII	342 Inf.
641[40]	XVII		698	XII	342 Inf.
642[40]	III		699	XII	342 Inf.
643[40]	III		...		
644[40]	VI				
645[40]	VIII				
646[40]	VIII		718[38]	XII	391[39]
647[40]			719[38]	XII	391[39]
648[40]	III		720[38]	XII	391[39]
649[40]			Jäg. 721	I	114 Jäg.
650[40]			722	II	702 Inf.
651[40]	VIII		723	III	719 Inf.
652[40]	VIII		Jäg. 724	IV	104 Jäg.
653[40]	XVII		725	V	715 Inf.
			726	VI	716 Inf.
655[40]			727	VII	707 Inf.
656[40]	VII		728	VIII	708 Inf.
657[40]			729	IX	709 Inf.
658[40]			730	X	710 Inf.
659	XVII		731	XI	711 Inf.
660[40]	XVII		732	XII	712 Inf.
661[40]	IV		733	XIII	713 Inf.
662[40]	VI		Jäg. 734	IV	104 Jäg.
663[40]			735	V	715 Inf.
664[40]	IX		736	VI	716 Inf.
665[40]	XIII		Jäg. 737	XVII	117 Jäg.
666	VIII	370 Inf.	Jäg. 738	XVIII	118 Jäg.
667	VIII	370 Inf.	739	IX	709 Inf.
668	VIII	370 Inf.	740	X	710 Inf.
669	VI?	371 Inf.	Jäg. 741	I	114 Jäg.
670	VI	371 Inf.	742	II	702 Inf.
671	VI?	371 Inf.	743	III	719 Inf.
672	VII?	376 Inf.?	744	XI	711 Inf.
673	VII	376 Inf.?	745	XII	712 Inf.
...			746	XIII	713 Inf

[38] Feldausbildungsregiment.
[39] Feldausbildungsdivision.
[40] Festungbataillon.
[41] French; existence uncertain.

RESTRICTED

Gr. R.

ORDER OF BATTLE OF THE GERMAN ARMY

Gr. Rgt.		Wkr.	In Div.	Gr. Rgt.		Wkr.	In Div.
	747.........	VII	707 Inf.		845[48].........		
	748.........	VIII	708 Inf.		...		
Jäg.	749.........	XVII	117 Jäg.		...		
Jäg.	750.........	XVIII	118 Jäg.		848.........		282 Inf.
	751.........		326 Inf.		849.........		282 Inf.
	752.........		326 Inf.		850.........		282 Inf.
	753.........		326 Inf.		851.........		343 Inf.
	754.........	XIII	334 Inf.		852.........	IV?	343 Inf.
	755.........	XIII	334 Inf.		853.........		343 Inf.?
	756.........	XIII	334 Inf.		854.........		344 Inf.
	757.........		338 Inf.		855.........		344 Inf.
	758.........		338 Inf.		856.........		344 Inf.
	759.........		338 Inf.		857.........		346 Inf.
	...				858.........		346 Inf.
	...				859.........		346 Inf.?
	762?.........				860.........		347 Inf.
	763?.........				861.........		347 Inf.
	...				862.........		347 Inf.
	765.........		376 Inf.		863.........	XII	348 Inf.
	766.........		376 Inf.		864.........		348 Inf.
	767.........		376 Inf.		865.........		348 Inf.
	768.........	IX	377 Inf.		866.........		355 Inf.
	769.........	IX	377 Inf.		867.........		355 Inf.
	770.........	IX	377 Inf.		868.........		355 Inf.
	...				869.........	IX	356 Inf.
	...				870.........	IX	356 Inf.
	781[42].........				871.........	IX	356 Inf.
	782[42].........				...		
	783[42].........				...		
	784[42].........				878?.........		
	785[42].........				879.........	V	
	...				880.........	VI	
	787[42].........				...		
	...				887.........	XIII	
	795[43].........				888.........		
	796[43].........				...		
	...			Verst.	890 mot......		
					891.........	VI	264 Inf.
	800[44].........				892.........	VI	264 Inf.
	801[44].........				893.........	VI	264 Inf.
	802[44].........				894.........	X	265 Inf.
	...				895.........	X	265 Inf.
	804[45].........				896.........	X	265 Inf.
	805[45].........				...		
	...				900.........	III	
	808[46].........			Pz. Gr.	901.........	III	
	809[46].........				902[49].........		
	...				903[49].........		
	...				904[49].........		
	837[47].........				905[49].........		
	...				906[49].........		
	...						

[42]Turk. Inf. Btl.
[43]Georgisches Inf. Btl.
[44]Nordkaukasisches Inf. Btl.
[45]Aserbeidschanisches Inf. Btl.
[46]Armenisches Inf. Btl.
[47]Kaukasisches Inf. Btl. or Regt.
[48]Deutsch-Arabisches Btl.
[49]Festungsbataillon.

RESTRICTED

ORDER OF BATTLE OF THE GERMAN ARMY

Gr. Rgt.	Wkr.	In Div.	Gr. Rgt.	Wkr.	In Div.
907[53]			...		
908[53]			950		
909[53]			...		
910[53]					
...			961[50]	V	999 Inf.[52]
916	V	242 Inf.?	962[50]	V	999 Inf.[52]
917		242 Inf.	963[53]	V	999 Inf.[52]
...			...		
920			965[51]		
...			966[51]		
			967[51]		
923[53]			...		
924[51]			992		
925[51]			993		
926[53]			...		
...			995		
930	X	416 Inf.	...		
931	X	416 Inf.	999[54]		

[50] Afrika Schützen Rgt. probably disbanded; some units might still exist.
[51] Festungsregimentsstab.
[52] Div. disbanded.
[53] Festungsbataillon.
[54] Has 12 Bns. carrying Roman numerals. Consists chiefly of ex-convicts.

RESTRICTED

Aufkl.

50. Reconnaissance Units.—Aufklärungsabteilung (Aufkl. Abt.; A.A.), Panzeraufklärungsabteilung (Pz. Aufkl. Abt.; Pz. A.A.), Panzerjäger und Aufklärungsabteilung (Pz. J. & A.A.), Schnelle Abteilung (Schn. Abt.; Schn. A.).

Aufkl. Abt.	Wkr.	In Div.	Aufkl. Abt.	Wkr.	In Div.
1............	I	1 Inf.	Pz. 40............	renumbered	14 Pz. A.A.
Pz. 1............	IX	1 Pz.	...		
Pz. 2............	XVII	2 Pz.	...		
Pz. 3............	III	3 Pz.	44............	XVII	44 Inf.
Pz. 4............	XIII	4 Pz.	45............	XVII	45 Inf.
5 mot.......	V	5 Jäg.	46............	XIII	46 Inf.
Pz. 5............	VIII	5 Pz.	...		
6............	VI	6 Inf.	...		
Pz. 6............	VI	6 Pz.	Pz. 53............	renumbered	103 Pz. A.A.
7............	VII	7 Inf.	54............	VII	1 Geb.
Pz. 7............	IX	7 Pz.	...		
8............	VIII	8 Jäg.	...		
Pz. 8............	III	8 Pz.	Pz. 57............	renumbered	6 Pz. A.A.
9............	IX	9 Inf.	...		
Pz. 9............	XVII	9 Pz.	Pz. 59............	renumbered	8 Pz. A.A.
Pz. 10............	V	10 Pz.	...		
11............	I	11 Inf.	...		
Pz. 11............	VIII	11 Pz.	67............	XVIII	2 Geb.
12............	II	12 Inf.	68............	XVIII	3 Geb.
Pz. 12............	II	12 Pz.	...		
Pz. 13............	XI	13 Pz.	...		
Pz. 14............	IV	14 Pz.	72............		
15............	IX	15 Inf.	...		
Pz. 16............	VI	16 Pz.	...		
17............	XIII	17 Inf.	Pz. 88............	renumbered	18 Pz. A.A.
Pz. 17............	VII	17 Pz.	...		
Pz. 18............	IV	18 Pz.	Pz. 90............	renumbered	10 Pz. A.A.
Pz. 19............	XI	19 Pz.	...		
Pz. 20............	IX	20 Pz.	Pz. 92............	renumbered	20 Pz. A.A.
21............	I	21 Inf.	...		
Pz. 21............	III	21 Pz.	94............	VII	4 Geb.
Pz. 22............	V?	22 Pz.[1]	95............	XVIII	5 Geb.
Pz. 23............	V?	23 Pz.	...		
24............	IV	24 Inf.	97............	VII	97 Jäg.
Pz. 24............	I	24 Pz.	...		
Pz. 25............	VI	25 Pz.	99............	XVIII	7 Geb.
26............	VI	26 Inf.	100............	XVII	100 Jäg.
Pz. 26............	III	26 Pz.	101............	V	101 Jäg.
Pz. 27[2].......			102............	VIII	102 Inf.
28............	VIII	28 Jäg.	Pz. 103............	III	3 Pz. Gr.
30............	X	30 Inf.	104............	IV	104 Jäg.
31............	XI	31 Inf.	...		
32............	II	32 Inf.	106............	VI	106 Inf.
Pz. 33............	renumbered	115 Pz. A.A.	...		
34............	XII	34 Inf.	110............	X	110 Inf.
35............	V	35 Inf.	Pz. 110............	XII	10 Pz. Gr.
Pz. 36............	renumbered	136 Pz. A.A.	112............	XVIII	6 Geb.
Pz. 37............	renumbered	7 Pz. A.A.	113............	XIII	113 Inf.

[1] Div. probably disbanded.
[2] Renumbered Pz. A.A. 17.

ORDER OF BATTLE OF THE GERMAN ARMY

Aufkl. 383

Aufkl. Abt.	Wkr.	In Div.	Aufkl. Abt.	Wkr.	In Div.
Pz. 114	IV	14 Pz. Gr.			
Pz. 115	XII	15 Pz. Gr.	Schn. Abt. 178	V	78 Inf.
Pz. 116	VI	16 Pz. Gr.	179	XII	79 Inf.
117	XI	111 Inf.			
Pz. 118	VIII	18 Pz. Gr.			
			Schn. Abt. 182	IX	82 Inf.
120	XII	112 Inf.	Schn. Abt. 183	X	83 Inf. Div.
Pz. 120	X	20 Pz. Gr.			
121	X	121 Inf.			
122	II	122 Inf.	186	VI	86 Inf.
Pz. 122	X	22 Pz. Gr.	Schn. Abt. 187	IV	87 Inf.
123	III	123 Inf.	Schn. Abt. 188	XVII	88 Inf.
125	V	125 Inf.	Pz. Aufkl. 190	III	90 Pz. Gr.
Pz. 125	V	25 Pz. Gr.			
126	VI	126 Inf.			
			193	III	93 Inf.
			194	IV	94 Inf.
(Pz. Jg. &			195	IX	95 Inf.
Aufkl. Abt.) 129	IX	129 Inf.	196	XI	96 Inf.
Pz. 129	IX	29 Pz. Gr.			
			Schn. Abt. 198	XIII	98 Inf.
131	XI	131 Inf.	Schn. Abt. 199	VI	199 Inf.
Schn. Abt. 132	XII	132 Inf.			
134	IV	134 Inf.	Schn. Abt. 205	V	205 Inf.
			Schn. Abt. 206	I	206 Inf.
Pz. 136	XII	36 Pz. Gr.	207	II	207 Sich.
Schn. Abt. 137	XVII	137 Inf.	Schn. Abt. 208	III	208 Inf.
Schn. Abt. 139		39 Inf.			
			211	VI	211 Inf.
			Schn. Abt. 212	VII	212 Inf.
150	III	50 Inf.	213	VIII	213 Sich.
			Schn. Abt. 214	IX	214 Inf.
152	X	52 Inf.	215	V	215 Inf.
			216	XI	216 Inf.
			217	I	217 Inf.
156	IV	56 Inf.	Schn. Abt. 218	III	218 Inf.
157	VII	57 Inf.	219	XIII	183 Inf.
158	X	58 Inf.	220	IV	164 Pz. Gr.
			221	VIII	221 Sich.
Pz. 160	XX	60 Pz. Gr.	222	XI	181 Inf.
161	I	61 Inf.	Schn. Abt. 223	IV	223 Inf.
162	VIII	62 Inf.			
			Schn. Abt. 225	X	225 Inf.
			Schn. Abt. 226		
Schn. Abt. 165	XII	65 Inf.	227	VI	227 Inf.
			229	XII	197 Inf.
168	III	68 Inf.			
Schn. Abt. 169	VI	69 Inf.	Pz. 231	renumbered	Pz. A.A. 11
171	XI	71 Inf.	233	VI	196 Inf.
172	XII	72 Inf.	Schn. Abt. 234	III	163 Inf.
173	XIII	73 Inf.	235	V	198 Inf.
175	II	75 Inf.			
176	III	76 Inf.	238	VII	167 Inf.

RESTRICTED

Aufkl.

ORDER OF BATTLE OF THE GERMAN ARMY

Aufkl. Abt.		Wkr.	In Div.	Aufkl. Abt.		Wkr.	In Div.
	240...	X	170 Inf.		...		
Schn. Abt.	241...	I	161 Inf.	Schn. Abt.	323...	XIII	323 Inf.
	...				...		
Schn. Abt.	246...	XII	246 Inf.		328...	IX	328 Inf.
	...			Schn. Abt.	329...	VI	329 Inf.
	248...	VIII	168 Inf.		330...	III	330 Inf.
	...				331...	XVII	331 Inf.
	251...	IX	251 Inf.	Schn. Abt.	333...	III	333 Inf.
	252...	VIII	252 Inf.	Schn. Abt.	334...	XIII	334 Inf.
Schn. Abt.	253...	VI	253 Inf.		...		
	254...	VI	254 Inf.				
	255...	IV	255 Inf.	Schn. Abt.	339...	IX	339 Inf.
Schn. Abt.	256...	IV	256 Inf.		...		
	257...	III	257 Inf.	Pz.	341...	renumbered	116 Pz. A.A.
	258...	II	258 Inf.		342...	XII	342 Inf.
	...				...		
	260...	V	260 Inf.				
	...				377...	IX	377 Inf.
	262...	XVII	262 Inf.		...		
	263...	XII	263 Inf.				
	...			Schn. Abt.	383...	I	383 Inf.
	267...	XI	267 Inf.		...		
Schn. Abt.	268...	VII	268 Inf.		402...		H. Tru.
Schn. Abt.	269...	X	269 Inf.		403...		H. Tru.
	...				...		
Schn. Abt.	290...	X	290 Inf.		580...	III	90 Le. Afr.[5]
Schn. Abt.	291...	I	291 Inf.		...		
	293...	III	293 Inf.	Schn. Abt.	602...		
	294...	IV	294 Inf.		...		
	296...	XIII	296 Inf.	Schn. Abt.	608...		
	297...	XVII	297 Inf.		...		
	298...	VIII	298 Inf.	Schn. Abt.	621...		
	299...	IX	299 Inf.		...		
	...						
Schn. Abt.	302...	II	302 Inf.		670...		H. Tru.
	...				...		
	305...	V	305 Inf.		776...		
Schn. Abt.	306...	VI	306 Inf.		...		
	...			Schn. Abt.	819...		
Schn. Abt.	319...	IX	319 Inf.	Pz.	999...		St. Div. Rhodos

[5] Now 90 Pz. Gr.; unit now numbered 190.

RESTRICTED

51. Panzer Units.—Panzerregiment (Pz. Rgt.), Panzerabteilung (Pz. Abt.).

*Pz. Rgt.	Wkr.	**Allotted to	*Pz. Rgt.	Wkr.	**Allotted to
1	IX	1 Pz. Div.	69		
2	VI	16 Pz. Div.	...		
3	XVII	2 Pz. Div.	...		
4	XI	13 Pz. Div.	72*		
5	III	21 Pz. Div.	...		
6	III	3 Pz. Div.	...		
7	V	10 Pz. Div.	100*	XII	Flammenwerfer
8[1]	V		101*	IX	Flammenwerfer
9	I	25 Pz. Div.	102*		
10	III	8 Pz. Div.	103*	III	3 Pz. Gr. Div.
11	VI	6 Pz. Div.	...		
12			110?*	XIII	10 Pz. Gr. Div.
...			...		
14	V?		...		
15	VIII	11 Pz. Div.			
16			114?*	IV	14 Pz. Gr. Div.
17	XVII		115*	XII	15 Pz. Gr. Div.
18	IV	18 Pz. Div.	116*	VI	16 Pz. Gr. Div.
...			...		
...			118?*	VIII	18 Pz. Gr. Div.
21	V	20 Pz. Div.			
22			120*	X	20 Pz. Gr. Div.
23	XII		...		
24		24 Pz. Div.			
25	XIII	7 Pz. Div.	125?*	V	25 Pz. Gr. Div.
26	III	26 Pz. Div.	...		
27	VI	19 Pz. Div.			
28*			129*	IX	29 Pz. Gr. Div.
29	II	12 Pz. Div.	...		
...					
31	VIII	5 Pz. Div.	136?*	XII	36 Pz. Gr. Div.
32			...		
33	XVII	9 Pz. Div.	157*		
...					
35	XIII	4 Pz. Div.			
36	XIII	14 Pz. Div.	160*	XX	60 Pz. Gr. Div.
37			...		
...					
39	XVII	17 Pz. Div.	164?*	IV	164 Pz. Gr. Div.
40*	XVII	(z.b.V.)	...		
...					
44			190*	III	90 Pz. Gr. Div.
...			...		
60*			201*	V	23 Pz. Div.
...			202[2]	III	26 Pz. Div.
66*			203*		
...			204[3]	V	22 Pz. Div.
...			...		
			...		

*Except where marked with asterisk (in such cases Pz. Abt.).
**Unallotted units probably belong to the G.H.Q. pool.
[1] Possibly disbanded or renumbered.
[2] Converted into Pz. Rgt. 26.
[3] Division believed disbanded, unit may still exist.

RESTRICTED

Pz. Abt.

ORDER OF BATTLE OF THE GERMAN ARMY

*Pz. Abt.	Wkr.	**Allotted to	Pz. Abt.	Wkr.	**Allotted to
211	VIII	22 Pz. Gr. Div.	386		
212			387		
213			...		
214			...		
215[3]	XII	15 Pz. Gr. Div.	500	VI	
...			501	IX	
217			502		
...			503[4]		
...			504[5]		
223			505		
...			...		
300			567		
301			...		
...			...		
330			700	XII	
...			...		
...			745		
339*			[6]Grossdeutschland		Grossdeutschland
...			[7]Hermann Göring		Hermann Göring
			Krimhilde		
377	IX		[8]Paris		
...			[9]Rhodos		Sturmdiv. Rhodos
...			Also: Panzer-Lehr-Regiment.		

*Except where marked with asterisk (in such cases Pz. Rgt.).
**Unallotted units probably belong to H. Tru.
[3]Renumbered Pz. Abt. 115.
[4]Possibly incorporated in Pz. Rgt. 26.
[5]Incorporated into Pz. Rgt. 115.
[6]Panzer-Regiment Grossdeutschland in Pz. Gr. Div. Grossdeutschland.
[7]Panzer-Regiment Hermann Göring in Pz. Div. Hermann Göring.
[8]Panzer Kp. Paris.
[9]Panzer Abt. Rhodos in Sturm Div. Rhodos.

ORDER OF BATTLE OF THE GERMAN ARMY   Pz. Jg. 387

52. Antitank Units.—Panzerjägerabteilung (Pz. Jäg. Abt.), Schnelle Abteilung (Schn. Abt.).

Pz. Jäg. Abt.	Wkr.	In Div.	Pz. Jäg. Abt.	Wkr.	In Div.
1	I	1 Inf.	Geb. 55	XVIII	2 Geb.
2	II	12 Pz.	56	X	
3	III	3 Pz. Gr.	...		
4	IV	14 Pz.	...		
5	V	5 Jäg.	61	III?	
6	VI	6 Inf.	...		
7	VII	7 Inf.	...		
8	VIII	8 Jäg.	67		
9	IX	9 Inf.	...		
10	XIII	10 Pz. Gr.	...		
11	I	11 Inf.	72	IV	
12	II	12 Inf.	...		
13	XI	13 Pz.	...		
14	IV	14 Pz. Gr.	Schn. Abt. 78		
15	IX	15 Inf.	...		
16	VI	16 Pz.	...		
17	XIII	17 Inf.	88	IV	18 Pz.
18	VIII	18 Pz. Gr.	...		
19	XI	19 Pz.	90	V	10 Pz.
20	X	20 Pz. Gr.	...		
21	I	21 Inf.	92	IX	20 Pz.
22	X	22 Pz. Gr.	93		26 Pz.
23	III	23 Inf.	Geb. 94	VII	4 Geb.
24	IV	24 Inf.	Geb. 95	XVIII	5 Geb.
25	V	25 Pz. Gr.	...		
26	VI	26 Inf.	97	VII	97 Jäg.
27	VII	17 Pz.	...		
28	VIII	28 Jäg.	Geb. 99	XIII	7 Geb.
29	IX	29 Pz. Gr.?	100	XVII	100 Jäg.
30	X	30 Inf.	101	V	101 Jäg.
31	XI	31 Inf.	102	VIII	102 Inf.
32	II	32 Inf.	...		
33	XII	15 Pz. Gr.	...		
34	XII	34 Inf.	106	VI	106 Inf.
35	V	35 Inf.	...		
36	XII	36 Pz. Gr.	...		
37	IX	1 Pz.	110	X	110 Inf.
38	XVII	2 Pz.	111	XI	111 Inf.
39	III	21 Pz.	112	XII	112 Inf.
40	I	24 Pz.	113	XIII	113 Inf.
41	VI	6 Pz.	...		
42	IX	7 Pz.	...		
43	III	8 Pz.	121	X	121 Inf.
Geb. 44	VII	1 Geb.	122	II	122 Inf.
45	XVII	45 Inf.	123	III	123 Inf.
46	XVII	44 Inf.	...		
Geb. 47	XVIII	6 Geb.	125	V	125 Inf.
Geb. 48	XVIII	3 Geb.	126	VI	126 Inf.
49	XIII	4 Pz.	127	III	27 Pz.[1]
50	XVII	9 Pz.	128	V	23 Pz.
...			129[2]	IX	129 Inf.
52	XIII	46 Inf.	131	XI	131 Inf.
53	VIII	5 Pz.	Schn. Abt. 132	·XII	132 Inf.

[1] Division dissolved.
[2] Pz. Jäg. und Aufklärungs Abteilung.

RESTRICTED

Pz. Jg.

ORDER OF BATTLE OF THE GERMAN ARMY

Pz. Jäg. Abt.		Wkr.	In Div.	Pz. Jäg. Abt.		Wkr.	In Div.
	... 134............	IV	134 Inf.		...		
	...			Schn. Abt.	205............	V	205 Inf.
	...				206............	I	206 Inf.
	137............	XVII	137 Inf.		207?............	II	207 Sich.
Schn. Abt.	138............		38 Inf.	Schn. Abt.	208............	III	208 Inf.
Schn. Abt.	139............		39 Inf.		...		
	140............		22 Pz.³		211............	VI	211 Inf.
	...			Schn Abt..	212............	VII	212 Inf.
	150............	III	50 Inf.		213?⁴	VIII	213 Sich.
				Schn. Abt.	214............	IX	214 Inf.
	152............	IX	52 Inf.		215............	V	215 Inf.
	...				216............	XI	216 Inf.
					217............	I	217 Inf.
	156............	IV	56 Inf.	Schn. Abt.	218............	III	218 Inf.
	157............	VII	57 Inf.		219............	XIII	183 Inf.
	158............	X	58 Inf.		220............	IV	164 Pz. Gr.
					221?............	VIII	221 Sich.
	160............	XX	60 Pz. Gr.		222............	XI	181 Inf.
	161............	I	61 Inf.	Schn. Abt.	223............	IV	223 Inf.
	162............	VIII	62 Inf.		...		
	...			Schn. Abt.	225............	X	225 Inf.
	164............			Schn. Abt.	226............		
Schn. Abt.	165............		65 Inf.		227............	VI	227 Inf.
	...				229............	XII	197 Inf.
					230............	IX	169 Inf.
	168............	III	68 Inf.		...		
Schn. Abt.	169............	VI	69 Inf.		233............	VI	196 Inf.
	171............	XI	71 Inf.	Schn. Abt.	234............	III	163 Inf.
	172?............	XII	72 Inf.		235............	V	198 Inf.
	173............	XIII	73 Inf.		236............	II	162 Inf.
	175............	II	75 Inf.		238............	VII	167 Inf.
	176............	III	76 Inf.		239............	VIII	239 Inf.⁵
					240............	X	170 Inf.
Schn. Abt.	178............	V	78 Inf.	Schn. Abt.	241............	I	161 Inf.
	179............	XII	79 Inf.		...		
	181............	VIII	81 Inf.	Schn. Abt.	246............	XII	246 Inf.
Schn. Abt.	182............	IX	82 Inf.		247............		
Schn. Abt.	183............	XI	83 Inf.		248............	VIII	168 Inf.
	...				...		
	186............	VI	86 Inf.		251............	IX	251 Inf.
Schn. Abt.	187............	IV	87 Inf.		252............	VIII	252 Inf.
Schn. Abt.	188............	XVII	88 Inf.	Schn. Abt.	253............	VI	253 Inf.
					254............	VI	254 Inf.
	190............	III	90 Pz. Gr.		255............	IV	255 Inf.
	...			Schn. Abt.	256............	IV	256 Inf.
					257............	III	257 Inf.
	193............	III	93 Inf.		258............	II	258 Inf.
Schn. Abt.	194............	IV	94 Inf.		...		
	195............	IX	95 Inf.		260............	V	260 Inf.
Schn. Abt.	196............	XI	96 Inf.		...		
	...				262............	XVII	262 Inf.
Schn. Abt.	198............	XIII	98		263............	XII	263 Inf.
Schn. Abt.	199............	VI	199 Inf.		264?............	VI	264 Inf.

³Division possibly dissolved; the unit (possibly renumbered) may still exist.
⁴Kompanie.
⁵Division dissolved; the unit (possibly renumbered) may still exist.

RESTRICTED

ORDER OF BATTLE OF THE GERMAN ARMY

Pz. Jg.

Pz. Jäg. Abt.		Wkr.	In Div.	Pz. Jäg. Abt.		Wkr.	In Div.
	...				371......	VI	371 Inf.
	267......	XI	267 Inf.		373......		373 Inf.
Schn. Abt.	268......	VII	268 Inf.		...		
Schn. Abt.	269......	X	269 Inf.		376......	VII	376 Inf.
	...				377......	IX	377 Inf.
Schn. Abt.	290......	X	290 Inf.		...		
Schn. Abt.	291......	I	291 Inf.				
	292......	II	292 Inf.	Schn. Abt.	383......	I	383 Inf.
	293......	III	293 Inf.		384......	IV	384 Inf.
	294......	IV	294 Inf.		385......	VI	385 Inf.
	295......	XI	295 Inf.		...		
	296......	XIII	296 Inf.		387......	VII	387 Inf.
	297......	XVII	297 Inf.		...		
	298......	VIII	298 Inf.		389......	IX	389 Inf.
	299......	IX	299 Inf.		...		
	...				427......		
Schn. Abt.	302......	II	302 Inf·		429......		
	304......	IV	304 Inf.		...		
	306......	VI	306 Inf.		463......	V	(Armee Norwegen)
	...						
Schn. Abt.	319......	IX	319 Inf.	Pz. Jäg. Abt.		Wkr.	Allotted to*
	320......	VIII	320 Inf.				
	...				...		
Schn. Abt.	323......	V	323 Inf.		511......	I	H. Tru.
	...				...		
	326......		326 Inf.				
	327......	XVII	327 Inf·		521......		H. Tru.
Schn. Abt.	329......	VI	329 Inf.		522......		H. Tru.
	...				...		
	331......	XVII	331 Inf.		525......	III	26 Pz. Div.
	332......	VIII	332 Inf·		...		
Schn. Abt.	333......	III	333 Inf.				
Schn. Abt.	334......	XIII	334 Inf.		529......	VI	
	335......	V	335 Inf.		...		
	336......	IV	336 Inf.				
	337......	VII	337 Inf.		539......		
	338......		338 Inf.		...		
Schn. Abt.	339......	IX	339 Inf.		541......		
	340......	I	340 Inf.		...		
	...				543......	III	H. Tru.
	342......	XII	342 Inf.		...		
	...				545......	XII	H. Tru.
	354......				...		
	...				552......		
	360......				...		
	...				559......	III	H. Tru.⁴
	369......	XVII	369 Inf.		560......		H. Tru.
	370......	VIII	370 Inf.		561......	IV	H. Tru.
					...		

*Where no allotment is shown it is probable that Heeres-Truppen should be understood.
⁴S.P. mount.

RESTRICTED

Pz. Jg.

	Pz. Jäg. Abt.	Wkr.	Allotted to*	Pz. Jäg. Abt.	Wkr.	Allotted to*
	563		H. Tru.			
	567			635		Pz. A.O.K. 2
	590		H. Tru.	643[8]	XII	H. Tru.
				645	XII	H. Tru.
Ir Abt.	602			652	XI	H. Tru.
	605[7]	III		654	X?	H. Tru.
	606[7]					
	607[7]	III?				
Schn. Abt.	608			670	VII	H. Tru.
	611	II	H. Tru.	672		H. Tru.
	616	XI	H. Tru.	721		H. Tru.
Schn. Abt.	621			Schn. Abt. 819		
	624[7]			Also: (1) Pz. Jäg. Abt. 900 (Lehr-Brig. 900).		
	625		H. Tru.	(2) Pz. Jäg. Lehr-Abt. (Pz. Lehr-Rgt.).		
				(3) Pz. Jäg. Abt. Grossdeutschland.		
	628[7]			(4) Pz. Jäg. Abt. Hermann Göring.		

*Where no allotment is shown it is probable that Heeres-Truppen should be understood.
[7]Present existence doubtful.
[8]47 mm S.P.

RESTRICTED

Art.

ORDER OF BATTLE OF THE GERMAN ARMY 391

53. Artillery Units.—Artillerieregiment (Art. Rgt.), Artillerieabteilung (Art. Abt.), Batterie (Bttr.), Sturmartillerieabteilung (St. Abt.)*, Sturmbatterie (St. Bttr.)**, Heeresküstenartillerieregiment (H. Küst. Art. Rgt.; H.K.R.), Heeresküstenartillerieabteilung (H. Küst. Art. Abt.; H.K.A.), Heeresküstenbatterie (H. Küst. Bttr.; H.K.B.).

Art. Rgt.		Wkr.	In Div.	Art. Rgt.		Wkr.	In Div.
	1	I	1 Inf. Div.		46^1	XIII	H. Tru.
Pz.	2	II	12 Pz. Div.		47^1	I	H. Tru.
	3 mot........	III	3 Pz. Gr. Div.		48^1	II	H. Tru.
Pz.	4	XI	14 Pz. Div.		49^1	XI	H. Tru.
	5 mot........	V	5 Jäg. Div.		50^1	IV	H. Tru.
	6	VI	6 Inf. Div.		51^1	IX	H. Tru.
	7	VII	7 Inf. Div.		52^1	VI	H. Tru.
	8 mot........	VIII	8 Jäg. Div.		53^1	XIII	H. Tru.
	9	IX	9 Inf. Div.		54^1	VIII	H. Tru.
	10 mot......	XIII	10 Pz. Gr. Div.		55^1	XI	H. Tru.
	11	I	11 Inf. Div.		56^1	X	H. Tru.
	12	II	12 Inf. Div.		57^1	XX	H. Tru.
Pz.	13	XI	13 Pz. Div.		58^1	X	H. Tru.
	14 mot......	IV	14 Pz. Gr. Div.		$59^{1\,3}$	III	H. Tru.
	15	IX	15 Inf. Div.		60^1	IV	H. Tru.
Pz.	16	VI	16 Pz. Div.		$61^{1\,2}$	V	H. Tru.
	17	XIII	17 Inf. Div.		62^1	VI	H. Tru.
	18 mot......	VIII	18 Pz. Gr. Div.		63^1	VII	H. Tru.
Pz.	19	XI	19 Pz. Div.		64^1	VIII	H. Tru.
	20 mot......	X	20 Pz. Gr. Div.		$65^{1\,3}$	IX	H. Tru.
	21	I	21 Inf. Div.		66^1	X	H. Tru
	22 mot......	X	22 Pz. Gr. Div.		67^1	XI	H. Tru.
	23	III	23 Inf. Div.		68^1	II	H. Tru.
	24	IV	24 Inf. Div.		69^1	XII	H. Tru.
	25 mot......	V	25 Pz. Gr. Div.		70^1	XII	H. Tru.
	26	VI	26 Inf. Div.		71^1	V	H. Tru.
Pz.	27	VII	17 Pz. Div.		$72^{1\,2}$	XII	H. Tru.
	28 mot......	VIII	28 Jäg. Div.	Pz.	73	IX	1 Pz. Div.
	29 mot......	IX	29 Pz. Gr. Div.	Pz.	74	XVII	2 Pz. Div.
	30	X	30 Inf. Div.	Pz.	$75^{1\,2}$ ...	III	3 Pz. Div.
	31	XI	31 Inf. Div.	Pz.	76	VI	6 Pz. Div.
	32	II	32 Inf. Div.		77 mot.^{4} ...	V	H. Tru.
Pz.	33^5	XII	15 Pz. Gr. Div.	Pz.	78	IX	7 Pz. Div.
	34	XII	34 Inf. Div.	Geb.	79	I	1 Geb. Div.
	35	V	35 Inf. Div.	Pz.	80	III	8 Pz. Div.
	36 mot......	XII	36 Pz. Gr. Div.		81	VII	97 Jäg. Div.
	37^1	I	H. Tru.	Geb.	82	XIII	7 Geb. Div.
	38^1	II	H. Tru.		83	XVII	100 Jäg. Div.
	$39^{1\,2}$ ...	III	H. Tru.		84 mot.$^{2\,3}$	IV	H. Tru.
	$40^{1\,2}$ ...	IV	H. Tru.		85	V	101 Jäg. Div.
	41^1	V	H. Tru.		86	XII	112 Inf. Div.
	$42^{1\,2}$ ...	VI	H. Tru.		87	XIII	113 Inf. Div.
	43^1	VII	H. Tru.	Pz.	88	IV	18 Pz. Div.
	$44^{1\,2}$ ...	VIII	H. Tru.	Pz.	89	I?	24 Pz. Div.
	45^1	IX	H. Tru.	Pz.	90	V	10 Pz. Div.

[1]Hq. and 2d Bn. are mtz GHQ troops; 1st Bn. is usually horse-drawn and attached to a divisional artillery regiment in place of a 4th Bn.
[2]Destroyed, possibly reformed.
[3]Formerly Art. Rgt. Sizilien.
[4]150-mm How.
[5]240-mm How.
*Now called Sturmgeschützabteilung (Stu. Gesch. Abt.)
**Now called Sturmgeschützbatterie (Stu. Gesch. Bttr.)

RESTRICTED

Art.

ORDER OF BATTLE OF THE GERMAN ARMY

Art. Rgt.		Wkr.	In Div.	Art. Rgt.		Wkr.	In Div.
Pz.	91[7]	VI	25 Pz. Div.		142	XII	(Bttr.)
Pz.	92	IX	20 Pz. Div.		143	VII	(H. K. A.)
Pz.	93	XIII	26 Pz. Div.		144	VI	(H. K. A.)
Geb.	94	VII	4 Geb. Div.		145		(H. K. A.)
Geb.	95	XVIII	5 Geb. Div.		146 mot	VI	16 Pz. Gr. Div.
	96	XVII	44 Inf. Div.		147		(H. K. A.)
	97[6 9]	XVII	H. Tru.		148	VI	(H. K. A.)
	98	XVII	45 Inf. Div.		149[13]		(H. K. A.)
	99[6]	XVII	H. Tru.		150	III	50 Inf. Div.
	100 mot	II	H. Tru.		151	I	(Abt. or Rgt.)
	101 mot	XII	(Schw. Abt.)		152	IX	52 Inf. Div.
Pz.	102	XVII	9 Pz. Div.		153	III	(Abt.)
Pz.	103	XIII	4 Pz. Div.		154 mot.[14]	VIII	(Abt.)
	104	III	102 Inf. Div.	Pz.	155	III	21 Pz. Div.
	105 mot	XII	(Abt.)		156	IV	56 Inf. Div.
	106 mot.[8]	XII	(Abt.)		157	VII	57 Inf. Div.
	107	VI	106 Inf. Div.		158	X	58 Inf. Div.
	108 mot	XII	H. Tru. (Schw.)		160 mot	XX	60 Pz. Gr. Div.
	109 mot	XVII	H. Tru. (Schw.)		161	I	61 Inf. Div.
	110 mot	XVIII	H. Tru.		162	VIII	62 Inf. Div.
Geb.	111	XVIII	2 Geb. Div.				
Geb.	112	XVIII	3 Geb. Div.		165	XII	65 Inf. Div.
Geb.	113	XVIII	H. Tru.		167	VII	(Abt.)
	114	XIII	46 Inf. Div.		168	III	68 Inf. Div.
	115[6 9]	XIII	H. Tru.		169	VI	69 Inf. Div.
Pz.	116	VIII	5 Pz. Div.				
	117	XI	111 Inf. Div.		171	XI	71 Inf. Div.
Geb.	118	XVIII	6 Geb. Div.		172	XII	72 Inf. Div.
Pz.	119	VIII	11 Pz. Div.		173	XIII	73 Inf. Div.
	120	X	110 Inf. Div.		175	II	75 Inf. Div.
	121[10]	X	121 Inf. Div.		176	III	76 Inf. Div.
	122	II	122 Inf. Div.		177		(St. Abt.)
	123	III	123 Inf. Div.		178[15]	V	78 Inf. Div.
Geb.	124		(Abt.)		179	XII	79 Inf. Div.
	125	V	125 Inf. Div.		181	VIII	81 Inf. Div.
	126[10]	VI	126 Inf. Div.	s.	182	IX	82 Inf. Div.
	127 mot.[11]		H. Tru.?		183	X	83 Inf. Div.
Pz.	128	V	23 Pz. Div.		184	IV?	(St. Abt.)
	129	IX	129 Inf. Div.		185		(St. Abt.)
	131	XI	131 Inf. Div.		186	VI	86 Inf. Div.
	132	XII	132 Inf. Div.		187	IV	87 Inf. Div.
	133 mot.[11]		H. Tru.?		188	VII	88 Inf. Div.
	134	IV	134 Inf. Div.		189		(St. Abt.)
	135		(Abt.)		190[16] mot	III	90 Pz. Gr. Div.
	137	XVII	137 Inf. Div.				
	138 mot	IV?	38 Inf. Div.				
	139		39 Inf. Div.				
Pz.	140[12]	V	22 Pz. Div.				

[6] Hq. and 2d Bn. are mtz GHQ troops; 1st Bn. is usually horse-drawn and attached to a divisional artillery regiment in place of a 4th Bn.
[7] Possibly Abt.
[8] Possibly Regiment.
[9] Destroyed, possibly reformed.
[10] Also H. K. Bttr. of same number.
[11] Probably disbanded.
[12] Division believed disbanded; the unit (possibly renumbered) may still exist.
[13] Probably converted to H. Flak Regt. 2.
[14] 150-mm. how.
[15] Sturm Art. Rgt. in St. Div. 78.
[16] First Bn. is St. Abt.

RESTRICTED

Art.

ORDER OF BATTLE OF THE GERMAN ARMY   393

Art. Rgt.	Wkr.	In Div.	Art. Rgt.	Wkr.	In Div.
191.........		(St. Abt.)	...		
192.........		(St. Abt.)	248............	VIII	168 Inf. Div.
193.........	III	93 Inf. Div.	249 mot.		(St. Abt.)
194.........	IV	94 Inf. Div.	250²⁰		
195.........	IX	95 Inf. Div.	251	IX	251 Inf. Div.
196.........	XI	96 Inf. Div.	252............	VIII	252 Inf. Div.
197.........		(St. Abt.)	253............	VI	253 Inf. Div.
198.........	XIII	98 Inf. Div.	254............	VI	254 Inf. Div.
199.........	VI	199 Inf. Div.	255............	IV	255 Inf. Div.
200.........	XIII	(St. Abt.)	256²¹	IV	256 Inf. Div.
201.........	I?	(St. Abt.)	257............	III	257 Inf. Div.
202.........		(St. Abt.)	258............	II	258 Inf. Div.
203.........		(St. Abt.)	...		
204.........		(St. Abt.)	260............	V	260 Inf. Div.
205.........	V	205 Inf. Div.	...		
206.........	I	206 Inf. Div.	262............	XVII	262 Inf. Div.
207.........	II	(H. K. R. Stab.)	263............	XII	263 Inf. Div.
208.........	III	208 Inf. Div.	264............		264 Inf. Div.
209.........	XII?	(St. Abt.)	...		
210.........		210 Inf. Div.	...		
211.........	VI	211 Inf. Div.	267............	XI	267 Inf. Div.
212.........	VII	212 Inf. Div.	268............	VII	268 Inf. Div.
213¹⁷	VIII	213 Sich. Div.	269............	X	269 Inf. Div.
214.........	IX	214 Inf. Div.	...		
215.........	V	215 Inf. Div.	271............		
216	XI	216 Inf. Div.	272		
217.........	I	217 Inf. Div.	273............	III	(Abt.)
218.........	III	218 Inf. Div.	274............		(H. K. Bttr.)
219.........	XIII	183 Inf. Div.	...		
220 mot.....	IV	164 Pz. Gr. Div.			
221¹⁷	VIII	221 Sich. Div.	277............		
222..........	XI	181 Inf. Div.	...		
223..........	IV	223 Inf. Div.	279............		
...			...		
225 mot.....	X	225 Inf. Div.	281............		
226..........		(St. Abt)	282............		282 Inf. Div.
227..........	VI	227 Inf. Div.	283............		(H. K. Abt.)
228¹⁸	I	228 Inf. Div.	284............		(H. K. Abt.)
229..........	XII	197 Inf. Div.	285............		(H. K. Abt.)
230..........	IX	169 Inf. Div.	286............		
231¹⁷	XIII	231 Inf. Div.	287............	VII	(H. K. Abt.)
...			288............	VIII	(H. K. Abt.)
233..........	VI	196 Inf. Div.	289............		(H. K. Abt.)
234..........	III	163 Inf. Div.	290............	X	290 Inf. Div.
235..........	V	198 Inf. Div.	291............	I	291 Inf. Div.
236..........	II	162 Inf. Div.	292............	II	292 Inf. Div.
236..........		(St. Abt.)	293............	III	293 Inf. Div.
237..........			294............	IV	294 Inf. Div.
238..........	VII	167 Inf. Div.	295	XI	295 Inf. Div.
239¹⁸	VIII	239 Inf. Div.	296............	XIII	296 Inf. Div.
240..........	X	170 Inf. Div.	297............	XVII	297 Inf. Div.
241...........	I	161 Inf. Div.	298¹⁸	VIII	(298 Inf. Div.)
242¹⁹		242 Inf. Div.	299............	IX	299 Inf. Div.
243..........		(St. Abt.)	300............		(St. Abt.)
244..........		(St. Abt.)	...		
245..........		(St. Abt.)	302............	II	302 Inf. Div.
246..........	XII	246 Inf. Div.	...		

[17]HQ is H. Tru.; the Bns. are attached to reinforced Inf. Rgts.
[18]Division disbanded, but unit may still exist.
[19]First Bn. is St. Abt.
[20]Spanish, probably disbanded Autumn 1943.
[21]Also H. K. Abt. of same number.

RESTRICTED

Art.

ORDER OF BATTLE OF THE GERMAN ARMY

Art. Rgt.	Wkr.	Allotted to	Art. Rgt.	Wkr.	Allotted to
304	IV	304 Inf. Div.	362	XII	(H. K. Bttr.)
305	V	305 Inf. Div.	363	XIII	(H. K. Bttr.)
306	VI	306 Inf. Div.	364	XIII	(H. K. Bttr.)
...			...		
309	IX	(H. K. Bttr.)	369[25]	XVII	369 Inf. Div.
...			370	VIII	370 Inf. Div.
311			371	VI	371 Inf. Div.
...			...		
313	XIII	(H. K. Bttr.)	373[25]		373 Inf. Div.
315			...		
...			376	VII	376 Inf. Div.
...			377	IX	377 Inf. Div.
318		(H. K. Bttr.)	...		
319	IX	319 Inf. Div.			
320	VIII	320 Inf. Div.	383	I	383 Inf. Div.
321	XI	321 Inf. Div.	384	IV	384 Inf. Div.
...			385[26]	VI	385 Inf. Div.
323	V	323 Inf. Div.	...		
324		(Bttr.)	387	VII	387 Inf. Div.
325		(H. K. Rgt.)	...		
326		326 Inf. Div.	389	IX	389 Inf. Div.
327	XVII	327 Inf. Div.	...		
328	II	328 Inf. Div.	...		
329	VI	329 Inf. Div.			
330	V	330 Inf. Div.	Art. Unit	Wkr.	Remarks
331	XVII	331 Inf. Div.			
332	VIII	332 Inf. Div.	392[27]		Abt.
333	III	333 Inf. Div.	...		
334	XIII	334 Inf. Div.	398[27]		Abt.
335	V	335 Inf. Div.	...		
336	IV	336 Inf. Div.	400	III	St. Abt.
337	VII	337 Inf. Div.	401	VI	H. K. Abt.
338[22]		338 Inf. Div.	...		
339[23]	IX	339 Inf. Div.			
340	I	340 Inf. Div.			
...			405[27]		Abt.
342	XII	342 Inf. Div.	...		
...			408 mot.[28]	VII	Abt.
344		344 Inf. Div.	...		
345 mot.[24]		345 Mot. Div.	411		Abt.?
...			412[27]		
351[24]		(Abt.)	413[27]		Abt.
...			...		
353					
354		(H. K. Bttr.)	s. 422[29] [30]	X	Abt.
355	VI	(H. K. Bttr.)	423		Abt.
356	VI	356 Inf. Div.	...		
357			427 mot.[31]		Abt.
358			428		
...					
361	III	(H. K Bttr.)			

[22]Also H. K. Bttr. of same number.
[23]Abt.
[24]Believed disbanded.
[25]Croatian.
[26]Division believed disbanded but unit may still exist.
[27]Existence doubtful.
[28]Was incorporated in Afrika Art. Rgt. 1.
[29]Was incorporated in Art. Rgt. 90.
[30]150 mm. how.
[31]150 mm. guns.

RESTRICTED

ORDER OF THE BATTLE OF GERMAN ARMY

Art. Unit	Wkr.	Remarks	Art. Unit	Wkr.	Remarks
			486	VI	H. K. Abt. Stab. II/853
s. 430 mot.....		Abt.	487.........		H. K. Abt. Stab.
431[31]		H. K. Bttr.	488...		H. K. Abt. Stab.
432[31]		H. K. Bttr.			
433 mot.[33]		Abt.	490............		H. K. Abt. Stab.
434[31]		H. K. Bttr.	491		H. K. Abt. Stab.
			492...... ...		H. K. Abt. Stab.
436 mot.[31]		Abt.	493........ ..	III	H. K. Abt. Stab.
437	XVII	H. K. Rgt. Stab.	494.......		H. K. Abt. Stab.
438		H. K. Abt. Stab.	495		H. K. Abt. Stab.
439		H. K. Abt. Stab.	s. 496.........		Art. Abt.
			497.........		H. K. Abt. Stab.
441		H. K. Abt.	498...... ..		H. K. Abt.
442		H. K. Abt.	499...... ...		H. K. Abt. Stab.
443[33]		Abt.	500.	XI	H. K. Abt.
			501 mot. .		Rgt. Stab.
445		Abt.	502... . ..		H. K. Bttr.
446 mot.[32]	XI	Abt.	503..		H. K. Bttr.
447.....		H. K. Abt.	504		H. K. Abt.
			505	VI	H. K. Abt. Stab.; III/853
450[35]		Abt.	506..	I	Art. Abt.
451		Abt.	507.........	I	H. K. Bttr.
452		H. K. Abt. Stab.	508 . ..		H. K. Bttr.
			509. ...		H. K. Rgt. Stab.
			510 . .	XIII	H. K. Abt.
456[33]		Abt.	s. 511[34] ..	I	Art. Abt.
457		H. K. Abt.	512[35] .		H. K. Bttr.
458		Bttr.	513		H. K. Bttr.
459		Bttr.	514		H. K. Bttr.
			515 . .		H. K. Bttr.
			516 . .		H. K. Bttr.
462 . ..		H. K. Bttr.			
463 .. .		H. K. Bttr.			
			519[35]		H. K. Bttr.
			520.....		H. K. Abt.
468	III	H. K. Bttr.	521..........		H. K Abt
			522..........		H. K. Abt.
470 . . .		H. K. Bttr.	523[36]	III	H. K. Abt.
471		H. K. Bttr.	524...........		H. K. Bttr.
472		H. K. Bttr.	525		H. K. Bttr.
			526	I	Art. Abt.
474	X	H. K. Abt.	527[34]		H. K. Bttr.
475		H. K. Abt.	528[37] [38] ..	XII	H. K. Abt.
			529[38]	IX	H. K. Abt.
477		Rgt., Believed disbanded.	531..........		H. K. Abt.
478	V	H. K. Abt.	532		
479	VI?	H. K. Abt.	533[37] . . .	XII	H. K. Abt.
480	XIII	Abt., believed disbanded.	534........		H. K. Bttr.
			535		H. K. Abt.
			536mot.[35] ..	I	Art. Abt.
482			537............		H. K. Bttr.
			538 ..		H. K. Bttr.
484............	VI	H. K. Abt.			
485............	VI	H. K. Abt. Stab. I./853	540.		Art. Abt.

[31] 105 mm. guns.
[32] Reorganized under a new number.
[33] Existence doubtful.
[34] Also a Mtz. Regt. Staff of this number.
[35] 150 mm. how.
[36] Formerly III Bn. of Afr. Art. Regt. 1.
[37] 155 mm. guns.
[38] Formerly in Afr. Art. Regt. 2.

RESTRICTED

Art. Unit	Wkr.	Remarks	Art. Unit	Wkr.	Remarks
541......		H. K. Bttr.	...		
...			596......		H. K. Bttr.
543......		H. K. Bttr.	...		
...			600 mot.....		St. Abt. Stab.
547......		H. K. Bttr.	601 mot.[42]	II	Art. Abt.
...			602 mot.[43]	XVIII	Art. Abt.
549......		H. K. Bttr.	603[44]......		H. K. Abt.
550......		H. K. Bttr.	604 mot.[42]	XVII?	Art. Abt.
551......			605 mot.[45]	IV	Art. Abt.
...			606 mot.....		Art. Rgt. Stab.
553......		Art. Abt.	607 mot.[46]	IV	Probably H. K. Abt.
554?......		Art. Rgt.	...		
555......	VI?	Art. Rgt. disbanded	609 mot.....	III	Art. Rgt. Stab.
556......	XII	Art. Rgt. disbanded	610 mot.....		Art. Rgt. Stab.
s.557[39]......	XVIII	Art. Abt.	611 mot.[41]	XIII	Art. Rgt. Stab.
...			612 mot.....		Art. Rgt. Stab.
560......	XVIII	Art. Rgt.	613 mot.....		Art. Rgt. Stab.
561......		H. K. Bttr.	614 mot.....		Art. Rgt. Stab.
562......		H. K. Bttr.	615 mot.....	V?	Art. Abt.
563......		H. K. Abt.	616 mot.[47]	VI	Art. Abt.
...			617 mot.....		Art. Rgt. Stab.
...			618 mot.....		Art. Rgt. Stab.
569[40]......		H. K. Bttr.; 22/853	619 mot.....		Art. Rgt. Stab.
570[40]......		H. K. Bttr.; 26/853	s. 620 mot.[41]		Art. Abt.
571[40]......		H. K. Bttr.; 7/853	621 mot.....	VI?	Art. Abt.
572[40]......		H. K. Bttr.; 4/853	Geb. 622[48]......		Geb. Art. Rgt.
573[40]......		H. K. Bttr.; 10/853	623 mot.....		Art. Rgt. Stab.
574[40]......		H. K. Bttr.; 11/853	624 mot.....	VIII	Art. Abt.
575[40]......		H. K. Bttr.; 17/853	625 mot.....	XI	Art. Abt.
576[40]......		H. K. Bttr.; 19/853	626 mot.....	V	Art. Abt., disbanded
577[40]......		H. K. Bttr.; 18/853	627 mot.....		Art. Rgt. Stab.
578[40]......		H. K. Bttr.; 20/853	628 mot.....	III	Bttr.
579[40]......		H. K. Bttr.; 21/853	629 mot.. ..	IV	Art. Abt.
580......		Art. Abt.	630 mot..	IV	Art. Abt., disbanded
...			631 mot.[46]		Art. Abt.
584......	X	Art. Abt.	633 mot.....	IX	Art. Abt.
585[41]......		H. K. Bttr.	634 mot.[46]	X	Art. Abt.
...			635 mot.[47]		Art. Abt.
...			636 mot.[47]		Art. Abt.
588[41]......		H. K. Bttr.; 3/853	637 mot.[47]		Art. Abt.
589[41]......		H. K. Bttr.	638 mot.....		Art. Abt.
590......		H. K. Bttr.	...		
591[41]......		H. K. Bttr.	640 mot.....		Art. Abt.
592[40]......		H. K. Bttr.	641 mot.[49]		Art. Abt.
593[40]......		H. K. Bttr.	642 mot.[49]		Art. Abt.

[39] Reported with 15 Pz. Gr. Div.
[40] 105 mm. guns.
[41] 150 mm.
[42] Also a Regt. Staff of this number.
[43] 150 mm.
[44] Believed disbanded.
[45] Reorganized under new number.
[46] Probably H.K. Bttr.
[47] 210 mm. hows.
[48] Also Mtz. Regt. Staff.
[49] 210 mm. and 300 mm. hows.

RESTRICTED

ORDER OF BATTLE OF THE GERMAN ARMY

Art. Unit	Wkr.	Remarks	Art. Unit	Wkr.	Remarks
643 mot.....	IX	Art. Abt.	699............		H. K. Abt.
644 mot.....	IX	Art. Abt.	...		
645 mot.....		Art. Abt.	701............		Bttr.
646 mot.....	V	Art. Abt.	702............	IV	Art. Abt. Stab.
647 mot.....	XII	Art. Abt. disbanded	...		
648 mot.....	XII	Art. Abt., disbanded	704............		Art. Rgt. Stab.
649 mot.....	XIII	Art. Abt., disbanded	705............	XII	Art. Abt.
650............		Art. Abt.	706............		H. K. Abt.
651............		In 711 Inf. Div.	707 mot....		Art. Abt.
652............	XII	In 712 Inf. Div.	708............		H. K. Abt.
653............		In 713 Inf. Div.	709 mot....	III	Art. Abt.
654............	IV	In 104 Jäg. Div.	710............		Eisb. Bttr.
655[51]......		Eisb. Bttr.	711............	IV	Art. Abt.
656............	VI	In 716 Inf. Div.	712............		Eisb. Bttr.
657............	VII	In 707 Inf. Div.	713............		Bttr.
658............		Art. Abt.	714............	V	Art. Abt.
...			s. 716.........	IX	Art. Abt.; probably disbanded
661............	I	In 114 Jäg. Div.			
662............	II	In 702 Inf. Div.	717............		Eisb. Bttr.
663............		In 719 Inf. Div.	718............		Eisb. Bttr.
...			...		
665............		St. Bttr.	720 mot.[53]		H. K. Bttr.
666............		Art. Abt.	721............		
667............		St. Bttr.	722............		Bttr.
668............	XVIII	In 118 Jäg. Div.	...		
669............			724............		
670............	XVII	In 117 Jäg. Div.	725............	VIII	Eisb. Abt.
671............		Art. Abt.	726............		Bttr.
672............		Bttr.	727............	V	H. K. Abt.
...			728............		H. K. Abt. Stab.
674 mot.....		Bttr.	729............		Art. Abt.
676 mot.....	IV	Art. Abt. Stab.	s. 730 mot.[54]	VI	Art. Abt.
677 mot.....	IX	Art. Rgt. Stab.	s. 731 mot.[55]	VIII	Art. Abt.
...			732 mot.....	X	Art. Abt.
679 mot.....		Art. Abt. Stab.	733 mot.[56]	XII	Art. Abt.
s. 680 mot...	IX	Art. Abt.	...		
681 mot.....	IX	Art. Abt. Stab.	735 mot.....	XI	Art. Abt.
...			s. 736 mot.[56]	XIII	Art. Abt.
685............		Bttr.	737 mot.[55]	XVII	Art. Abt.
686............		Art. Abt.	738............		H. K. Abt.
687............		Bttr.	739............		H. K. Abt.
688............		Bttr.	740............	VII	Art. Abt.
689............		Bttr.	741[58]......		H. K. Abt.
690[52]......		Eisb. Bttr.	742[58]......		H. K. Bttr.
691............		Eisb. Bttr.	...		
...			745............	VI	Art. Abt.
694............	III		746............	VI	H. K. Abt.
695............		Art. Abt.	...		
696[52]......		Eisb. Bttr.	749............	XI	Art. Abt., disbanded
697............		Eisb. Bttr.	750............	II	H. K. Bttr.
...		H. K. Rgt. Stab.	751............		H. K. Bttr.

[51] 280 mm. hows.
[52] 280 mm. guns.
[53] Also Regt. Staff of same number.
[54] 105 mm. guns.
[55] 150 mm. hows.
[56] 210 mm. hows.
[58] Also St. Bttr. of this number.

RESTRICTED

398 ORDER OF BATTLE OF THE GERMAN ARMY

Art. Unit	Wkr.	Remarks	Art. Unit	Wkr.	Remarks
752	II	H. K. Rgt. Stab.	812		
753	IV	Art. Abt.	813	VI	H. K. Bttr.
754		H. K. Rgt. Stab.	814 mot.[60]	IX	Art. Rgt.
755		H. K. Rgt. Stab.	815 mot.[61]	III	Art. Abt.
756		Art. Abt.	s. 816 mot.	III	Art. Abt.
757 mot.		Art. Abt.	817 mot.	IV	Art. Abt.
758		H. K. Rgt. Stab.	818 mot.[62]	XI	Art. Rgt.
759		Art. Abt.; disbanded			
			820		Art. Abt.
761		Art. Abt.	821		H. K. Abt.?
762		Art. Abt.; disbanded	822		Art. Abt.
			823[59]		H. K. Abt.
s. 764	V	Art. Abt.	824[62]		Art. Abt.
765		Bttr.	825		H. K. Rgt. Stab.
766		Art. Rgt. Stab.	826[63]	VI	H. K. Abt.
767 mot.		Art. Abt.	827[63]	VII	H. K. Abt.
768	VII	Art. Abt.	828		H. K. Abt.
769	VI	H. K. Abt. Stab.	829	VI	H. K. Abt.
770	XI	H. K. Abt.			
			831	VII	H. K. Abt.
772	XII	H. K. Abt.	832	IX	H. K. Abt.
773[59]		H. K. Abt.	833	III	Art. Abt.
774	VII	H. K. Abt.	834	XII	H. K. Abt.
...			835		H. K. Rgt.
			836	VI	H. K. Rgt. Stab.
777[64]	VI	Art. Abt.	837	VII	H. K. Rgt. Stab.
778		H. K. Abt.	838		H. K. Abt.
779 mot.		Bttr.	839		H. K. Rgt. Stab.
780	IV	Eisb. Abt.	840		H. K. Rgt. Stab.
781 mot.		Art. Rgt. Stab.	841 mot.		Art. Rgt. Stab.
782 mot.		Art. Rgt. Stab.	842 mot.	VI	Art. Abt.
783 mot.		Art. Rgt. Stab.	843 mot.	VI	Art. Abt.
784 mot.		Bttr.	844		Art. Abt.
785 mot.		Art. Rgt. Stab.	845 mot.		Art. Abt.
786 mot.		Art. Abt.	846	II	Art. Abt.
787 mot.		Art. Rgt. Stab.	847	V	Art. Abt.
788 mot.		Art. Rgt. Stab.	s. 848 mot.		Art. Abt.
789[59]	IV	H. K. Abt.	849 mot.	XII	Art. Abt.
...			850	XII	Art. Abt.
793		Art. Abt.	851 mot.	XII	Art. Abt.
...			852		Art. Abt.
			853*	III	H. K. Rgt. Stab.
797			854	III	Art. Abt.
			855		Art. Abt.; disbanded
799	X	H. K. Abt.	856	VI	Art. Abt.
800 mot.		Art. Abt.	s. 857	XII	Art. Abt.
801	II	Art. Abt.	s. 858 mot.		Art. Abt.
802		Art. Rgt.	859 mot.		Art. Abt.
803 mot.		Art. Rgt. Stab.	860 mot.	X	Art. Abt.
804	XVIII	Art. Abt.	861	XX	Art. Abt.; disbanded
805	VIII	H. K. Abt.	862		Art. Abt.
...			863	IX	Art. Abt.
s. 808		Art. Abt.	865 mot.	XIII	Art. Abt.
809		Art. Abt.	866 mot.	V	Art. Abt.
810 mot.		Bttr.			

[59] 105 mm. guns.
[60] 240 mm. hows.
[61] 300 mm. hows.
[62] Also H.K. Regt. Staff of this number.
[63] 150 mm. guns.
[64] 210 mm. hows.

*Controls 26 H.K. Bttrn. in Norway in the 500 and 900 series.

RESTRICTED

ORDER OF BATTLE OF THE GERMAN ARMY

Art. Unit	Wkr.	Remarks	Art. Unit	Wkr.	Remarks
869		H. K. Bttr.	946[68]		H. K. Bttr.; 1/853
...			947[68]		H. K. Bttr.; 8/853
			948[68]		H. K. Bttr.; 14/853
877		H. K. Bttr.	949[68]		H. K. Bttr.; 16/853
...			950[69]		H. K. Bttr.; 23/853
			951		H. K. Bttr.
880		H. K. Bttr.	952[69]		H. K. Bttr.
...			953		H. K. Bttr.
			954[69]		H. K. Bttr.
884	XVIII	H. K. Bttr.	...		
...			956[69]		H. K. Bttr.; 9/753
			957[69]		H. K. Bttr.; 12/853
887		H. K. Bttr.	958[69]		H. K. Bttr.; 6/853
888[65]		H. K. Bttr.	959[69]		H. K. Bttr.; 15/853
889[65]		H. K. Bttr.	960[69]		H. K. Bttr.
890		H. K. Bttr.	961[68]		H. K. Bttr.
...			962[68]		H. K. Bttr.
			963[68]		H. K. Bttr.
893			964		H. K. Bttr.
894[66]	XI	H. K. Bttr., 24/853	...		
895[66]		H. K. Bttr.	966		H. K. Bttr.
896		H. K. Bttr.	967		H. K. Bttr.
897		H. K. Bttr.	...		
898		H. K. Bttr.	970[68]		H. K. Bttr.
...					
900	III	Art. Abt.	971[68]		H. K. Bttr.
901	V	H. K. Abt.*	972		H. K. Bttr.
902[67]		Bttr.	973[68]		H. K. Bttr.
903	III	H. K. Abt.*	974[68]		H. K. Bttr.
904		St. Abt.	975[68]		H. K. Bttr.
905		St. Abt.	976[68]		H. K. Bttr.
906	VI	H. K. Abt. probably disbanded	977[68]		H. K. Bttr.
			978[68]		H. K. Bttr.
907		H. K. Bttr.	979[68]		H. K. Bttr.
...			980[68]		H. K. Bttr.
909		St. Bttr.	981[68]		H. K. Bttr.
910	X	H. K. Abt.	982[68]		H. K. Bttr.
911	IV	Art. Abt.	983[68]		H. K. Bttr.
912	V	St. Bttr.	984[69]		H. K. Bttr.
...			985		H. K. Bttr.; 25/853
914		H. K. Abt.			
...			987[68]		H. K. Bttr.
			988		H. K. Bttr.
927		H. K. Bttr.	989		H. K. Bttr.
928	V	H. K. Abt.	990		H. K. Bttr.
929	XII	H. K. Abt.	991		H. K. Bttr.
930		H. K. Bttr.	992		H. K. Bttr.
931		H. K. Bttr.	993		H. K. Bttr.
...			995		H. K. Bttr.
938		H. K. Bttr.	996[70]		H. K. Bttr.; 13/853
...			997[70]		H. K. Bttr.; 2/853
940		H. K. Rgt. Stab.	998[70]		H. K. Bttr.; 6/853
941		H. K. Bttr.	999 mot.		H. K. Bttr.
942		H. K. Bttr.	999		999 Inf. Div. disbanded

[65] 120 mm. guns.
[66] 75 mm. guns.
[67] 175 mm. guns.
[68] 105 mm. guns.
[69] 210 mm. guns.
[70] 155 mm. guns.
*Under Art. Rgt. 22 on Crete.

Also: (1) Artillerie-Lehr-Regiment 1.
(2) Artillerie-Lehr-Regiment (mot) 2.
(3) Artillerie-Lehr-Regiment (mot) 3.
(4) Artillerie-Regiment mot. Grossdeutschland.
(5) Sturmgeschütz Abt. G.D.
(6) Pz. Art. Rgt. Hermann Göring in Hermann Göring Pz. Div.

RESTRICTED

54. Artillery Observation Units.—Beobachtungsabteilungen (Beob. Abt.), Panzerbeobachtungsbatterien (Pz. Beob. Bttr.).

Beob. Abt.	Wkr.	Allotted to	Beob. Abt.	Wkr.	Allotted to
1	I	H. Tru.	...		
2	II	H. Tru.	...		
3	III	H. Tru.	60?		
4	IV	H. Tru.	...		
5	V	H. Tru.	...		
6	VI	H. Tru.	Pz. 92		(Bttr.)
7	VII	H. Tru.	...		
8	VIII	H. Tru.	...		
9	IX	H. Tru.	501		
10	XIII	H. Tru.	...		
11	I	H. Tru.	...		
12	II	H. Tru.	531		H. Tru.
13	XI	H. Tru.	532		H. Tru.
14	IV	H. Tru.	...		
15	IX	H. Tru.	...		
16	VI	H. Tru.	555		H. Tru.
17	XIII	H. Tru.	556		H. Tru.
Geb. 18	VIII	H. Tru.			
19	XI	H. Tru.			
20	X	H. Tru.	Pz. Beob. Bttr.*	Wkr.	Allotted to
21	XX	H. Tru.			
22	X	H. Tru.			
23	III	H. Tru.	320	XVII	2 Pz. Div.
24	IV	H. Tru.	321		
25	V	H. Tru.	322	V	10 Pz. Div.
26	VI	H. Tru.	323		
27	VII	H. Tru.	324	XIII	4 Pz. Div.
28	VIII	H. Tru.	325	IX	7 Pz. Div.
29	IX	H. Tru.	326	III	15 Pz. Gr. Div
30	X	H. Tru.	327	III	3 Pz. Div.
31	XI	H. Tru.	328	VIII	
32	II	H. Tru.	...		
33	XII	H. Tru.			
34	XII	H. Tru.	333		
35	V	H. Tru.	...		
36	XII	H. Tru.	335	IX	20 Pz. Div.
Geb. 38	XVIII	H. Tru.	337		
40		H. Tru.	...		
41		H. Tru.	339		
42			...		
43					
44	XVII		647		

*Some if not all *Panzer Beobachtungsbatterien* have been incorporated into Artillery Regiments of the Panzer Divisions. e. g. *Panzer Beobachtungsbatterie* 326 re-numbered *Panzer Beobachtungsbatterie* 33, now found in Artillery Regiment 33.

RESTRICTED

ORDER OF BATTLE OF THE GERMAN ARMY

55. Engineer Units.—Pionierregiment (Pi. Rgt.), Pionierbattalion (Pi. Btl.), Pionierkompanie (Pi. Kp.), Brückenkolonne (Br. Kol.), Sturmbootkommando (Stu. B. Kdo.).

Pi. Btl.		Wkr.	Allotted to	Pi. Btl.		Wkr.	Allotted to
	1......	I	1 Inf. Div.	Pz.	49......	V	10 Pz. Div.
	2 mot......	II	32 Inf. Div.		50 mot......	X	H. Tru.
	3 mot.[1]......	III	3 Pz. Gr. Div.		51 mot......	XI	H. Tru.
Pz.	4......	XI	13 Pz. Div.		52 mot......	XII	H. Tru.
	5 mot......	V	5 Jäg. Div.		53......		H. Tru.
	6[1]......	VI	6 Inf. Div.	Geb.	54......	VII	1 Geb. Div.
	7......	VII	7 Inf. Div.		..		
	8......	VIII	8 Jäg. Div.		...		
	9......	IX	9 Inf. Div.	Pz.	57......	VI	6 Pz. Div.
	10 mot......	XIII	10 Pz. Gr. Div.	Pz.	58......	IX	7 Pz. Div.
	11......	I	11 Inf. Div.	Pz.	59......	III	8 Pz. Div.
	12......	II	12 Inf. Div.		60 mot......	XI	H. Tru.
Pz.	13......	IV	14 Pz. Div.		61 mot......		XIV Pz. K.
	14 mot.[2]..	IV	14 Pz. Gr. Div.		62 mot.	IV	H. Tru.
	15......	IX	15 Inf. Div.		...		
Pz.	16......	VI	16 Pz. Div.		...		
	17......	XIII	17 Inf. Div.	Geb.	67......	XVIII	2 Geb. Div.
	18 mot......	VIII	18 Pz. Gr. Div.		68......		
Pz.	19......	XI	19 Pz. Div.		...		
	20 mot......	X	20 Pz. Gr.Div.		70 mot. ...	XVII	H. Tru.
	21[3]......	I	21 Inf. Div.		71......	III	
	22 mot......	X	22 Pz. Gr. Div.		...		
	23......	III	23 Inf. Div.		73......	XII	
	24......	IV	24 Inf. Div.		74......	XII	
	25 mot......	V	25 Pz. Gr. Div.	Pz.	75......		25 Pz. Div.
	26[3]......	VI	26 Inf. Div.		...		
Pz.	27......	VII	17 Pz. Div.		...		
	28......	VIII	28 Jäg. Div.	Pz.	79......	XIII	4 Pz. Div.
	29 mot......	IX	29 Pz. Gr. Div.		80......	XVII	44 Inf. Div.
	30......	X	30 Inf. Div.		81......	XVII	45 Inf. Div.
	31[3]......	XI	31 Inf. Div.	Geb.	82......	XVIII	XIX A. O. K.
Pz.	32......	II	12 Pz. Div.	Geb.	83......	XVIII	3 Geb. Div.
Pz.	33......	XII	15 Pz. Gr. Div.	Geb.	84[6]......	XVIII	
	34......	XII	34 Inf. Div.	Geb.	85......	XVIII	H. Tru.
	35......	V	35 Inf. Div.	Pz.	86......	XVII	9 Pz. Div.
	36 mot......	XII	36 Pz. Gr. Div.		87......		
Pz.	37......	IX	1 Pz. Div.		88......	XIII	46 Inf. Div.
Pz.	38......	XVII	2 Pz. Div.	Pz.	89......	VIII	5 Pz. Div.
Pz.	39......	III	3 Pz. Div.		...		
Pz.	40...... .	I	24 Pz. Div.	Geb.	91......	XVIII	6 Geb. Div.
	41 mot......	I	H. Tru.	Pz.	92......	IX	20 Pz. Div.
	42 mot......	II	H. Tru.	Pz.	93......		26 Pz. Div.
	43 mot.[4]..	III	H. Tru.	Geb.	94......	VII	4 Geb. Div.
	44 mot·......	IV	H. Tru.	Geb.	95......	XVIII	5 Geb. Div.
	45 mot.[5]..	V	H. Tru.		...		
	46 mot......	VI	H. Tru.		97......	VII	97 Jäg. Div.
	47 mot......	VII	H. Tru.	Pz.	98......	III	18 Pz. Div.
	48 mot......	VIII	H. Tru.	Geb.	99......	XIII	7 Geb. Div.

[1] Also Eisenbahn Pi. of same number.
[2] Also Festungs Pi. of same number.
[3] Also Techn. Btl. of same number.
[4] Sturmpi. Btl.
[5] Present existence doubtful.
[6] Possibly now disbanded.

Pion.

ORDER OF BATTLE OF THE GERMAN ARMY

Pi. Btl.	Wkr.	Allotted to	Pi. Btl.	Wkr.	Allotted to
100	XVII	100 Jäg. Div.	162	VIII	62 Inf. Div.
101	V	101 Jäg. Div.	...		
102	VIII	102 Inf. Div.	...		
...			165		65 Inf. Div.
104		104 Jäg. Div.	...		
106	VI	106 Inf. Div.	168	III	68 Inf. Div.
...			169	VI	69 Inf. Div.
110	X	110 Inf. Div.	171	XI	71 Inf. Div.
111	XI	111 Inf. Div.	172	XII	72 Inf. Div.
112	XII	112 Inf. Div.	173[10]	XIII	73 Inf. Div.
113	XIII	113 Inf. Div.	...		
114		114 Jäg. Div.	175	II	75 Inf. Div.
...			176	III	76 Inf. Div.
117		117 Jäg. Div.	178	V	78 Inf. Div.
118		118 Jäg. Div.	179	XII	79 Inf. Div.
...			181	VIII	81 Inf. Div.
121	X	121 Inf. Div.	182[10]	IX	82 Inf. Div.
122	II	122 Inf. Div.	183	X	83 Inf. Div.
123	III	123 Inf. Div.	...		
125	V	125 Inf. Div.	186	VI	86 Inf. Div.
126	VI	126 Inf. Div.	187	IV	87 Inf. Div.
Pz. 127		27 Pz. Div.[8]	188	VII	88 Inf. Div.
Pz. 128	V	23 Pz. Div.			
129	IX	129 Inf. Div.	190 mot.	III	90 Pz. Gr. Div.
131	XI	131 Inf. Div.			
132	VII	132 Inf. Div.	193	III	93 Inf. Div.
133[7]			194	IV	94 Inf. Div.
134	IV	134 Inf. Div.	195	IX	95 Inf. Div.
...			196	XI	96 Inf. Div.
			197		
137	XVII	137 Inf. Div.	198	XIII	98 Inf. Div.
138		38 Inf. Div.	199	VI	199 Inf. Div.
139		39 Inf. Div.	Pz. 200	III	21 Pz. Div.
Pz. 140		22 Pz. Div.[9]			
...			204		
144 mot.			205	V	205 Inf. Div.
145	V		206	I	206 Inf. Div.
146 mot.	VI	16 Pz. Gr. Div.?	207	II	207 Sich. Div.
...			208	III	208 Inf. Div.
150	III	50 Inf. Div.	Pz. 209	IV	11 Pz. Div.
...			211	VI	211 Inf. Div.
152	IX	52 Inf. Div.	212	VII	212 Inf. Div.
...			213	VIII	213 Sich. Liv.
			214	IX	214 Inf. Div.
156	IV	56 Inf. Div.	215	V	215 Inf. Div.
157	VII	57 Inf. Div.	216	XI	216 Inf. Div.
158	X	58 Inf. Div.	217	I	217 Inf. Div.
...			218	III	218 Inf. Div.
160 mot.	XX	60 Pz. Gr. Div.	219	XIII	183 Inf. Div.
161	I	61 Inf. Div.	220 mot.	IV	164 Pz. Gr. Div.

[7] Bau Pi.
[8] 27 Pz. Div. disbanded.
[9] Div. possibly disbanded; unit may still exist (possibly renumbered).
[10] Brückenkol.

RESTRICTED

Pion.

ORDER OF BATTLE OF THE GERMAN ARMY 403

Pi. Btl.	Wkr.	Allotted to	Pi. Btl.	Wkr.	Allotted to
221	VIII	221 Sich. Div.	297	XVII	297 Inf. Div.
222	XI	181 Inf. Div.	298	VIII	298 Inf. Div.
223	IV	223 Inf. Div.	299	IX	299 Inf. Div.
...			300[12]		
225	X	225 Inf. Div.	...		
...			302	II	302 Inf. Div.
227	VI	227 Inf. Div.	...		
228	I	228 Inf. Div.[11]	304	IV	304 Inf. Div.
229	XII	197 Inf. Div.	305	V	305 Inf. Div.
230	IX	169 Inf. Div.	306	VI	306 Inf. Div.
231	XIII	231 Inf. Div.[11]	...		
...					
233	VI	196 Inf. Div.	311	I	311 Inf. Div.[11]
234	III	163 Inf. Div.	...		
235	V	198 Inf. Div.	313[13]		
236	II	162 Inf. Div.	...		
...			...		
238	VII	167 Inf. Div.	319	IX	319 Inf. Div.
239	VIII	239 Inf. Div.[11]	320	VIII	320 Inf. Div.
240		170 Inf. Div.	321	XI	321 Inf. Div.
241	I	161 Inf. Div.	...		
...			323	VIII	323 Inf. Div·
246	XII	246 Inf. Div.	...		
...			326		326 Inf. Div.
...			327	XVII	327 Inf. Div.
248	VIII	168 Inf. Div.	328	II	328 Inf. Div.
...			329	VI	329 Inf. Div·
...			330[13]	V	330 Inf. Div.
251	IX	251 Inf. Div.	331	XVII	331 Inf. Div.
252	VIII	252 Inf. Div.	332	VIII	332 Inf. Div.
253	VI	253 Inf. Div.	333	III	333 Inf. Div.
254	VI	254 Inf. Div.	334	XIII	334 Inf. Div.
255	IV	255 Inf. Div.	335	V	335 Inf. Div·
256	IV	256 Inf. Div.	336[14]	IV	336 Inf. Div.
257 mot.	III	257 Inf. Div.	337	VII	337 Inf. Div.
258	II	258 Inf. Div.	338		338 Inf. Div.
...			339	IX	339 Inf. Div.
260	V	260 Inf. Div.	340	I	340 Inf. Div.
...					
262	XVII	262 Inf. Div.	342	XII	342 Inf. Div.
263	XII	263 Inf. Div.	343	XIII	343 Inf. Div.
264		264 Inf. Div.	...		
...			369[15]	XVII	369 Inf. Div.
267	XI	267 Inf. Div.	370	VIII	370 Inf. Div.
268	VII	268 Inf. Div.	371	VI	371 Inf. Div.
269	X	269 Inf. Div.	...		
...			373[15]		373 Inf. Div.
...			...		
290	X	290 Inf. Div.	...		
291	I	291 Inf. Div.	376	VII	376 Inf. Div.
292	II	292 Inf. Div.	377	IX	377 Inf. Div.
293	III	293 Inf. Div.	...		
294	IV	294 Inf. Div.			
295	XI	295 Inf. Div.	383	I	383 Inf. Div.
296	XIII	296 Inf. Div.	...		

[11]Div. now disbanded; unit may still exist (possibly renumbered).
[12]Bataillon.
[13]Marine Festungs Pi. Btl.
[14]Possibly disbanded.
[15]Croatian.

Pi. Unit	Wkr.	Remarks	Pi. Unit	Wkr.	Remarks
385......	VI	In 385 Inf. Div.	...		
387......	VII	In 387 Inf. Div.	...		
...			525......		
400 mot...		Br. Kol.	...		
401 mot...		Br. Kol.	531......		
...			532......		
403 mot...	III	Br. Kol.	533......		Br. Kol.
404 mot...		Br. Kol.	534......		Br. Kol.
405......			...		
...			536......		Park Btl.
407 mot...		Br. Kol.	...		
...			538......		
409 mot...		Br. Kol.	...		
410 mot...					
411 mot...		Br. Kol.	540......		Landungskompanie
412 mot...		Br. Kol.	541 mot...		Regt. Stab.
413 mot..		Br. Kol.	...		
415 mot...		Br. Kol.	545......		
...			...		
422 mot..		Br. Kol.	591 mot...		Regt. Stab.
...			592......		
427 mot...		Br. Kol.	593......		Btl.
...			...		
			601 mot...		Regt. Stab.
430 mot...		Br. Kol.	602 mot...		Br. Kol.
...			603 mot...		Br. Kol
			604 mot...		Regt. Stab.
442 mot...		Br. Kol.	605 mot...		Regt. Stab.
...			606 mot...		Br. Kol.
476......			...		
...			610 mot...		Br. Kol.
501......			612 mot...		Br. Kol.
...			...		
			614 mot...		Regt. Stab.
504 mot...		Regt. Stab.	...		
505......		H. Tru.	616 mot...		Br. Kol.
...			617 mot...		Regt. Stab.
507 mot...		Regt. Stab.	...		
508......		H. Tru.	620 mot...		Regt. Stab.
...			...		
510......			622......		
511 mot.[16]		Regt. Stab.	...		
512 mot...		Regt. Stab.	624 mot...		Br. Kol.
...			...		
515 mot...		Regt. Stab.	626 mot...		Br. Kol.
...			627 mot...	III	Btl.
517 mot...	XII	Regt. Stab.	628 mot.		Regt. Stab.
519 mot...		Regt. Stab.?	630 mot...	X	Btl.
520 mot...		Regt. Stab.	...		
521......	XVII	Park Btl.			

*Also Festungs Pi. Park.

Pion.

ORDER OF BATTLE OF THE GERMAN ARMY 405

Pi. Unit	Wkr.	Remarks	Pi. Unit	Wkr.	Remarks
632 mot...		Btl.	...		
633............			700 mot...		Regt. Stab.
634............			...		
635 mot...		Btl.	704[17]......	IV	104 Jäg. Div.
636 mot...		Br. Kol.	...		
...			707............	VII	707 Inf. Div.
639 mot...		Br. Kol.	708............		708 Inf. Div.
...			709............	IX	709 Inf. Div.
643............			710............	X	710 Inf. Div.
644 mot...		Br. Kol.	711............	XI	711 Inf. Div.
...			712............	XII	712 Inf. Div.
646............		Festungs Btl.	713............	XIII	713 Inf. Div.
...			714[18]......	I	114 Jäg. Div.
649 mot...		Br. Kol.	715............	V	715 Inf. Div.
...			716............	VI	716 Inf. Div.
651 mot...	III	Btl.	...		
652 mot...	VI	Btl.	719............	III	719 Inf. Div.
653 mot...		Btl.	...		
654 mot...	III	Btl.	741 mot...	III	Btl.
655 mot...		Btl.	742 mot...		Btl.
656 mot...	III	Btl.	743 mot...		Btl.
657 mot...	VII	Btl.	744 mot...	XII?	Btl.
658 mot...		Btl.	745 mot...	XVII?	Btl.
659 mot...		Btl.	746 mot...		Btl.
660 mot...		Btl.	747 mot...		Btl.
661 mot...		Br. Kol.	...		
662 mot...	II	Btl.	750 mot...	VI?	Btl.
663 mot...		Br. Kol.	751 mot...	III	Btl.
664............			752 mot...	VI	Btl.
665............		Br. Kol.	753 mot...		Btl.
666 mot...	VI	Btl.	754 mot...	VI	Btl.
667 mot...		Regt. Stab.	...		
668 mot...		Br. Kol.	770............	XVII	Regt. Stab.
...			771............		Btl.
671 mot...	VI	Btl.	...		
672 mot...	IX	Btl.	778[19]......		
673 mot...		Regt. Stab.	780............		Landungskompanie
675 mot...		Btl.	...		
676 mot...	XVII	Btl.	816 mot...		Br. Kol.
677 mot...		Regt. Stab.	817 mot...		Br. Kol.
678 mot...	XVII	Regt. Stab.	...		
680 mot...		Regt. Stab.	843 mot...		Br. Kol.
...			...		
685 mot...		Regt. Stab.	850[20]......		
...			...		
688............					
690 mot...		Regt. Stab.			
691............		Festungs			

[17]Renumbered 104.
[18]Renumbered 114.
[19]Kompanie.
[20]Sturm Pi.

RESTRICTED

Pion.

Pi. Unit	Wkr.	Remarks	Pi. Unit	Wkr.	Remarks
900 mot...	III		...		
...			927............		Btl.
904............			...		
905............			999............		Btl/Sturm.Div.Rhodos
906............		Sturmbootkommando			

Also Pionier Bataillon Grossdeutschland in Pz. Gr. Div. Grossdeutschland.
Also Pionier Bataillon Hermann Göring in Pz. Div. Hermann Göring.

ORDER OF BATTLE OF THE GERMAN ARMY

56. Signal Units.—Nachrichtenregiment (Nachr. Rgt.; N.R.), Nachrichtenabteilung (Nachr. Abt.; N.A.), Nachrichtenkompanie (Nachr. Kp.; N.K.).

Nachr. Abt.		Wkr.	Allotted to	Nachr. Abt.		Wkr.	Allotted to
Pz. N. R.	1	I	1 Inf. Div.		51 mot	XI	XI A. K.
Pz.	1		1 Pz. A. O. K.		52 mot	XII	XII A. K.
Pz. N. R.	2	II	12 Pz. Div.		53 mot	XIII	XIII A. K.
	2	XVII	2 Pz. A. O. K.	Geb.	54	VII	1 Geb.
	3 mot	III	3 Pz. Gr. Div.				
Pz. N. R.	3	IX	3 Pz. A. O. K.		56 mot	IV	H. Tru.
Pz.	4	IV	14 Pz. Div.		57 mot	V	H. Tru.
Pz. N. R.	4	III	4 Pz. A. O. K.				
	5 mot	V	5 Jäg. Div.	Pz.	59	III	8 Pz. Div.
	6	VI	6 Inf. Div.	Pz.	60	XI	XIV Pz. K.
	7	VII	7 Inf. Div.				
	8	VIII	8 Jäg. Div.				
	9	IX	9 Inf. Div.		63 mot		H. Tru.
	10 mot	XIII	10 Pz. Gr. Div.		64	XVII	44 Inf. Div.
N. R.	10	III	Pz. A. O. K. Afrika		65	XVII	45 Inf. Div.
	11	I	11 Inf. Div.		66 mot	XVII	XVII A. K.
	12	II	12 Inf. Div.	Geb.	67	XVIII	2 Geb. Div.
Pz.	13	XI	13 Pz. Div.	Geb.	68	XVIII	3 Geb. Div.
	14 mot	IV	14 Pz. Gr. Div.				
	15	IX	15 Inf. Div.	Geb.	70	XVIII	XVIII Geb. K.
Pz.	16	VI	16 Pz. Div.				
	17	XIII	17 Inf. Div.		72		
	18 mot	VIII	18 Pz. Gr. Div.				
Pz.	19	XI	19 Pz. Div.		74	IV	
	20 mot	X	20 Pz. Gr. Div.				
	21	I	21 Inf. Div.		76	XIII	46 Inf. Div.
	22	X	22 Pz. Gr. Div.		77 mot	VIII	A. K.
	23 mot	III	23 Inf. Div.		78	XII	
	24	IV	24 Inf. Div.	Pz.	79	XIII	4 Pz. Div.
	25 mot	V	25 Pz. Gr. Div.	Pz.	81	XVII	9 Pz. Div.
	26	VI	26 Inf. Div.	Pz.	82	VI	6 Pz. Div.
Pz.	27	VII	17 Pz. Div.	Pz.	83	IX	7 Pz. Div.
	28	VIII	28 Jäg. Div.	Pz.	84		
	29 mot	IX	29 Pz. Gr. Div.	Pz.	85	VIII	5 Pz. Div.
	30	X	30 Inf. Div.	Pz.	86	I	24 Pz. Div.
	31	XI	31 Inf. Div.	Pz.	87		25 Pz. Div. (?)
	32	II	32 Inf. Div.	Pz.	88	IV	18 Pz. Div.
Pz.	33	XII	15 Pz. Gr. Div.				
	34	XII	34 Inf. Div.	Pz.	90		10 Pz. Div.
	35	V	35 Inf. Div.	Geb.	91	XVIII	6 Geb. Div.
	36 mot	XII	36 Pz. Gr. Div.	Pz.	92	IX	20 Pz. Div.
Pz.	37	IX	1 Pz. Div.	Pz.	93		26 Pz. Div.
Pz.	38	XVII	2 Pz. Div.	Geb.	94	VII	4 Geb. Div.
Pz.	39	III	3 Pz. Div.	Geb.	95	XVIII	5 Geb. Div.
N. R.	40 mot		H. Tru.		97	VII	97 Jäg. Div.
	41 mot	I	I A. K.	Geb.	99	XIII	7 Geb. Div.
	42 mot	II	II A. K.		100	XVII	100 Jäg. Div.
Pz.	43	III	III Pz. K.		101	V	101 Jäg. Div.
	44 mot	IV	IV A. K.		102	VIII	102 Inf. Div.
	45 mot	V	V A. K.				
	46 mot	VI	VI A. K.		104	IV	104 Jäg. Div.
	47 mot	VII	VII A. K.				
	48 mot	VIII	VIII A. K.		106	VI	106 Inf. Div.
	49 mot	IX	IX A. K.				
	50 mot	X	X A. K.				

RESTRICTED

Nachr.

ORDER OF BATTLE OF THE GERMAN ARMY

	Nachr. Abt.	Wkr.	Allotted to	Nachr. Abt.	Wkr.	Allotted to
	110	X	110 Inf. Div.			
	111	XI	111 Inf. Div.	181	VIII	81 Inf. Div.
	112	XII	112 Inf. Div.	182	IX	82 Inf. Div.
	113	XIII	113 Inf. Div.	183	X	83 Inf. Div.
	114	IV	114 Jäg. Div.	...		
	117	XVII	117 Jäg. Div.			
	118	XVIII	118 Jäg. Div.	186	VI	86 Inf. Div.
	121	X	121 Inf. Div.	187	IV	87 Inf. Div.
	122	II	122 Inf. Div.	188	VII	88 Inf. Div.
	123	III	123 Inf. Div.			
	...			Pz. 190	III	90 Pz. Gr. Div.
	125		125 Inf. Div.	...		
	126	VI	126 Inf. Div.			
Pz.	127¹		27 Pz. Div.	193	III	93 Inf. Div.
Pz.	128	V	23 Pz. Div.	194	IV	94 Inf. Div.
	129	IX	129 Inf. Div.	...		
	...			196	XI	96 Inf. Div.
	131	XI	131 Inf. Div.			
	132	XII	132 Inf. Div.	198	XIII	98 Inf. Div.
	...			199	VI	199 Inf. Div.
	134	IV	134 Inf. Div.	Pz. 200	III	21 Pz. Div.
	...			...		
	137	XVII	137 Inf. Div.	205	V	205 Inf. Div.
	138	IV?	38 Inf. Div.	206	I	206 Inf. Div.
	139?		39 Inf. Div.	...		
Pz.	140		22 Pz. Div.²	208	III	208 Inf. Div.
	...			209	IV	209 Inf. Div.³
	150		50 Inf. Div.	211	VI	211 Inf. Div.
	...			212	VII	212 Inf. Div.
	152	IX	52 Inf. Div.	213⁴	VIII	213 Sich. Div.
	...			214	IX	214 Inf. Div.
	...			215	V	215 Inf. Div.
	156	IV	56 Inf. Div.	216	IX	216 Inf. Div.
	157	VII	57 Inf. Div.	217	I	217 Inf. Div.
	158	X	58 Inf. Div.	218	III	218 Inf. Div.
	...			219	XIII	183 Inf. Div.
	160 mot	XX	60 Pz. Gr. Div.	220	IV	164 Pz. Gr. Div.
	161	I	61 Inf. Div.	221	VIII	221 Sich. Div.
	162	VIII	62 Inf. Div.	222	XI	181 Inf. Div.
	...			223	IV	223 Inf. Div.
	165	XII	65 Inf. Div.	225	X	225 Inf. Div.
	...			...		
	...			227	VI	227 Inf. Div.
	168	III	68 Inf. Div.	228 mot	VI	16 Pz. Gr. Div.
	169	VI	69 Inf. Div.	229	XII	197 Inf. Div.
	...			230		169 Inf. Div.
	171	XI	71 Inf. Div.	231	XIII	231 Inf. Div.³
	172	XII	72 Inf. Div.	...		
	173	XIII	73 Inf. Div.	233	VI	196 Inf. Div.
	...			234	III	163 Inf. Div.
	175	II	75 Inf. Div.	235	V	198 Inf. Div.
	176	III	76 Inf. Div.	236	II	162 Inf. Div.
	...			...		
	178	V	78 Inf. Div.	239	VIII	239 Inf. Div.³
	179	XII	79 Inf. Div.			

¹Division disbanded.
²Div. possibly disbanded.
³Division disbanded. The unit (possibly renumbered) may still exist.
⁴Kompanie.

RESTRICTED

ORDER OF BATTLE OF THE GERMAN ARMY

Nachr.

	Nachr. Abt.	Wkr.	Allotted to		Nachr. Abt.	Wkr.	Allotted to
	240...	X	170 Inf. Div.		...		
	241...	I	161 Inf. Div.		326...		326 Inf. Div.
	...				327...	XVII	327 Inf. Div.
	246...	XII	246 Inf. Div.		328[6]...	II	328 Inf. Div.
	...				329...		329 Inf. Div.
	248...	VIII	168 Inf. Div.		330...	V	330 Inf. Div.
	...				331...	XVII	331 Inf. Div.
	...				332[6]...	VIII	332 Inf. Div.
	251...	IX	251 Inf. Div.		333[6]...	III	333 Inf. Div.
	252...	VIII	252 Inf. Div.		334...	XIII	334 Inf. Div.
	253...	VI	253 Inf. Div.		335[6]...	V	335 Inf. Div.
	254...	VI	254 Inf. Div.		336...	IV	336 Inf. Div.
	255...	IV	255 Inf. Div.		337[6]...	VII	337 Inf. Div.
	256...	IV	256 Inf. Div.		338...		338 Inf. Div.
	257...	III	257 Inf. Div.		339[6]...	IX	339 Inf. Div.
	258...	II	258 Inf. Div.		340...	I	340 Inf. Div.
				Pz.	341...	VIII	11 Pz. Div.
	260...	V	260 Inf. Div.		342...	XII	342 Inf. Div.
	262...	XVII	262 Inf. Div.		...		
	263...	XII	263 Inf. Div.		369[7]...		
	...				370...	VIII	370 Inf. Div.
	267...	XI	267 Inf. Div.		...		
	268...	VII	268 Inf. Div.		377...	IX	377 Inf. Div.
	269...	X	269 Inf. Div.		...		
	...				380...		
	291...	I	291 Inf. Div.		...		
	292...	II	292 Inf. Div.				
	293...	III	293 Inf. Div.		383...	I	383 Inf. Div.
	294...	IV	294 Inf. Div.		384...	IV	384 Inf. Div.
	295...	XI	295 Inf. Div.		385...	VI	385 Inf. Div.
	296...	XIII	296 Inf. Div.				
	297...	XVII	297 Inf. Div.		387...	VII	387 Inf. Div.
	298...	VIII	298 Inf. Div.				
	299...				400...		
	300...				420 mot...	XX	XX A. K.
	301...						
	302...	II	302 Inf. Div.		423 mot...	VI	XXIII A. K.
Eisb.	303...			Pz.	424 mot...	XII	XXIV Pz. K.
	304...	IV	304 Inf. Div.		425 mot...	V	XXV A. K.
	305...	V	305 Inf. Div.		426 mot...	I	XXVI A. K.
	306...	VI	306 Inf. Div.		427 mot...	VII	XXVII A. K.
	...				428 mot...	III	XXVIII A. K.
	309...				429 mot...	IV	XXIX A. K.
	...				430 mot...	XI	XXX A. K.
	...				431 mot...	X?	XXXI Höh. Kdo.
	312...				432 mot...		LXXXI A. K.?
Eisb.	313 mot...				433 mot...	VI	XXXIII Höh. Kdo.
Eisb.	314...				434[6] mot...	III	XXXIV A. K.
	...				435 mot...	VIII	XXXV A. K.
	...				436 mot...	II	XXXVI Geb. K.
	320...	VIII	320 Inf. Div.		437[6] mot...	XVII	LXXXII A. K.?
	321...	XI	321 Inf. Div.		438 mot...	VIII?	XXXVIII A. K.?
	...			Pz.	439...	IX	XXXIX Pz. K.
	323...	V	323 Inf. Div.	Pz.	440...	XVII	XL Pz. K

[6] Kompanie.
[7] Telephone construction unit.

RESTRICTED

ORDER OF BATTLE OF THE GERMAN ARMY

Nachr. Abt.		Wkr.	Allotted to	Nachr. Abt.		Wkr.	Allotted to
Pz.	441	VIII	XLI Pz. K.	N.R.	520 mot	VI	9 A.O.K.?
	442 mot	III	XLII A. K.	N.R.	521 mot	XVII	12 A.O.K.[11]
	443 mot	XI	XLIII A. K.	N.R.	522 mot		
	444 mot	IV	XLIV A. K.		525		
	445 mot	XIII?	19 A.O.K.?				
	446	X	XLVI Pz. K.		526		
Pz.	447	XX	XLVII Pz. K.		527		
Pz.	448	XXI	XLVIII Pz. K.		...		
	449 mot	Prot.	XLIX Geb. K.				
	450 mot	V	L A. K.		530		
	451 mot	XI	LI Geb. K.		531 mot	XIII	7 A.O.K.?
	452 mot	III	LII A. K.		...		
	453 mot	XII	LIII A. K.				
	454 mot		LIV A. K.		536		
	455 mot	V	LV A. K.	N.R.	537 mot		H. Gru.
Pz.	456	VI	LVI Pz. K.		...		
Pz.	457	II	LVII Pz. K.				
	458				540[11]		
	459 mot		LIX A. K.		...		
	460 mot		LXXXIV A. K.?		542		
	...				543[10]		
	463 mot	II	Armee Norwegen		...		
	464 mot		LXIV Res. K.?	N.R.	549 mot	IV	6 A.O.K.
	465	II	LXV Höh. Kdo.	N.R.	550 mot		20 A.O.K.
	467 mot		LXVII Res. K.		...		
	468		LXVIII A. K.	N.R.	558 mot	V	11 A.O.K.?
	470 mot				...		
	...			N.R.	563 mot	III	2 A. O. K.?
Pz.	475	III	Afrika Pz. K.[11]	N.R.	564 mot		
	...				...		
	480 mot		LXXX A. K.	N.R.	570 mot	VII	H. Gru. B.
	...				...		
				N.R.	589 mot	VI	4 A. O. K.
N.R.	501 mot	I	16 A.O.K.?		...		
	...				592		
N.R.	503 mot		A.O.K.?		...		
N.R.	504		H. Gru.		594		
	...				...		
N.R.	506			N.R.	596 mot	XII	17 A. O. K.?
	...			N.R.	597 mot		H. Tru.
				N.R.	598		H. Tru.
	509 mot		15 A.O.K.		...		
	...						
N.R.	511 mot.[9]		A.O.K.?	N.R.	601 mot		H. Tru.
	512 mot		10 A.O.K.?	N.R.	602 mot		H. Tru.
	513.[10]				603 mot		H. Gru.
N.R.	514 mot		Eisb.	N.R.	604 mot		
	...				605 mot.[10]		
N.R.	517 mot		Eisb.		...		
	...				610 mot.[10]		
	...				...		

[9] Also Nachr. Park of same number
[10] Kompanie.
[11] Now disbanded.

RESTRICTED

ORDER OF BATTLE OF THE GERMAN ARMY

Nachr. Abt.		Wkr.	Allotted to	Nachr. Abt.		Wkr.	Allotted to
	612 mot.[12]		H. Tru.	...			
	613 mot.[12]		H. Tru.	682 mot.[13]			H. Tru.
	614 mot.[12]		H. Tru.	...			
N. R.	616 mot...		H. Tru.	685 mot.[13]		III	H. Tru.
	617 mot.[12]		H. Tru.	...			
N. R.	618 mot..		H. Tru.	693 mot.[13]		IV	H. Tru.
	619...		H. Tru.	694 mot.[13]			H. Tru.
	620 mot.[12]						
	621 mot.[12]	IX	H. Tru.	696 mot.[13]			H. Tru.
	622 mot.[12]		H. Tru.	697 mot.[13]			H. Tru.
	623 mot.[12]		H. Tru.	698 mot.[13]			H. Tru.
	...			699[13]			H. Tru.
	627			...			
N. R.	632			702		II	702 Inf. Div.
	633 mot.[13]	IV	H. Tru.	704[15]		IV	104 Jäg. Div.
	635 mot	III		...			
	...			707		VII	707 Inf. Div.
	638 mot.[13]			708		VIII	708 Inf. Div.
N. R.	639 mot	IX	H. Gru. D?	709		IX	709 Inf. Div.
	...			710		X	710 Inf. Div.
				711		XI	711 Inf. Div.
N. R.	642 mot...		H. Tru.	712		XII	712 Inf. Div.
N. R.	643 mot.[14]		H. Tru.	713		XIII	713 Inf. Div.
N. R.	644 mot.[14]		H. Tru.	714 [6]		I	114 Jäg. Div.
N. R.	645 mot.[14]	V	H. Tru.	...			
	646			717[17]		XVII	117 Jäg. Div.
	647[12]						
N. R.	649 mot		H. Tru.	719		III	719 Inf. Div.
	650	XVIII	XVIII Geb. K.	721[12]		XI	Crete Comd.
N. R.	651 mot.		H. Tru.	722[12]			Crete Comd.
	...			...			
	657[12]		H. Tru.	727[12]			
	...			...			
	660 mot.[13]		H. Tru.	751			
	...			...			
	665			756			
	666[12]		H. Tru.	...			
	668[13]			761			
	670[12]		H. Tru.	762			
	671[12]		H. Tru.	...			
	672[12]			806[12]			
	673		H. Tru.	...			

[12]Kompanie.
[13]Bataillonsstab.
[14]Telephone Operating Regiment.
[15]Renumbered 104.
[16]Renumbered 114.
[17]Renumbered 117.

RESTRICTED

Nachr.

Nachr. Abt.	Wkr.	Allotted to	Nachr. Abt.	Wkr.	Allotted to
...			907[20]		
810[18]			...		
811[18]			912[20]		
...			...		
821 mot.[19]			920[20]		
...			921[20]		
824	IX		922[20]		
825			...		
826			930[20]		
827[19]			...		
...			937[20]		
902[20]			...		
904[20]			999[21]		999 Inf. Div.
906[20]					

[18] Kompanie.
[19] Bataillonsstab.
[20] Telephone Operating Platoon.
[21] Division now disbanded. Unit may exist as H. Tru. or may have been renumbered.

RESTRICTED

ORDER OF BATTLE OF THE GERMAN ARMY   Aux. No. 413

57. Auxiliary Unit Numbers.

Aux. No.	In Div.	Aux. No.	In Div.
1	1 Inf.	67	2 Geb.
2	12 Pz.	68	3 Geb.
3	3 Pz. Gr.	...	
4	14 Pz.		
5	5 Jäg.	81	1 Pz.
6	6 Inf.	82	2 Pz.
7	7 Inf.	83	3 Pz.
8	8 Jäg.	84	4 Pz.
9	9 Inf.	85	5 Pz.
10	10 Pz. Gr.	...	
11	11 Inf.	87?	25 Pz.?
12	12 Inf.	88	18 Pz.
13	13 Pz.	...	
14	14 Pz. Gr.	90	10 Pz.
15	15 Inf.	91	6 Geb.
16	16 Pz.	92	20 Pz.
17	17 Inf.	93	26 Pz.
18	18 Pz. Gr.	94	4 Geb.
19	19 Pz.	95	5 Geb.
20	20 Pz. Gr.	...	
21	21 Inf.	97	97 Jäg.
22	22 Pz. Gr.	...	
23	23 Inf.	99	7 Geb.
24	24 Inf.	100	100 Jäg.
25	25 Pz. Gr.	101	101 Jäg.
26	26 Inf.	102	102 Inf.
27	17 Pz.	...	
28	28 Jäg.	104	104 Jäg.
29	29 Pz. Gr.	...	
30	30 Inf.	106	106 Inf.
31	31 Inf.	...	
32	32 Inf.		
33	15 Pz.	110	110 Inf.
34	34 Inf.	111	111 Inf.
35	35 Inf.	112	112 Inf.
36	36 Pz. Gr.	113	113 Inf.
		114	114 Jäg.
...		...	
40	24 Pz.	117	117 Jäg.
...		118	118 Jäg.
44	44 Inf.	...	
45	45 Inf.	121	121 Inf.
46	46 Inf.	122	122 Inf.
...		123	123 Inf.
54	1 Geb.	...	
...		125	125 Inf.
57	6 Pz.	126	126 Inf.
58	7 Pz.	128	23 Pz.
59	8 Pz.	129	129 Inf.
60	9 Pz.	...	
61	11 Pz.	131	131 Inf.
...		132	132 Inf.
66	16 Pz. Gr.	134	134 Inf.

RESTRICTED

414 ORDER OF BATTLE OF THE GERMAN ARMY

Aux. No.	In Div.	Aux. No.	In Div.
...		206	206 Inf.
...		207	207 Sich.
137	137 Inf.	208	208 Inf.
138	38 Inf.	...	
139	39 Inf.	...	
140	22 Pz.[1]	211	211 Inf.
...		212	212 Inf.
...		213	213 Sich.
150	50 Inf.	214	214 Inf.
...		215	215 Inf.
152	52 Inf.	216	216 Inf.
...		217	217 Inf.
...		218	218 Inf.
156	56 Inf.	219	183 Inf.
157	57 Inf.	220	164 Pz. Gr.
158	58 Inf.	221	221 Sich.
...		222	181 Inf.
160	60 Pz. Gr.	223	223 Inf.
161	61 Inf.	...	
162	62 Inf.	225	225 Inf.
...		...	
...		227	227 Inf.
165	65 Inf.	...	
...		229	197 Inf.
...		230	169 Inf.
168	68 Inf.	...	
169	69 Inf.	233	196 Inf.
171	71 Inf.	234	163 Inf.
172	72 Inf.	235	198 Inf.
173	73 Inf.	236	162 Inf.
...		...	
175	75 Inf.	238	167 Inf.
176	76 Inf.	239	239 Inf.[2]
...		240	170 Inf.
178	78 Inf.	241	161 Inf.
179	79 Inf.	...	
181	81 Inf.	246	246 Inf.
182	82 Inf.	...	
183	83 Inf.	248	168 Inf.
...		...	
186	86 Inf.	251	251 Inf.
187	87 Inf.	252	252 Inf.
188	88 Inf.	253	253 Inf.
...		254	254 Inf.
190	90 Pz. Gr.	255	255 Inf.
...		256	256 Inf.
...		257	257 Inf.
193	93 Inf.	258	258 Inf.
194	94 Inf.	...	
195	95 Inf.	260	260 Inf.
196	96 Inf.	...	
...		262	262 Inf.
198	98 Inf.	263	263 Inf.
199	199 Inf.	264	264 Inf.
200	21 Pz.	...	
...		267	267 Inf.
205	205 Inf.	268	268 Inf.

Div. possibly disbanded.
Div. disbanded.

RESTRICTED

ORDER OF BATTLE OF THE GERMAN ARMY

Aux. No.	In Div.	Aux. No.	In Div.
269	269 Inf.	347	347 Inf.
...		349	
282	282 Inf.	...	
...		356	356 Inf.
290	290 Inf.	...	
291	291 Inf.		
292	292 Inf.	369	369 Inf.[4]
293	293 Inf.	370	370 Inf.
294	294 Inf.	371	371 Inf.
295	295 Inf.	...	
296	296 Inf.	373	373 Inf.[4]
297	297 Inf.	...	
298	298 Inf.	375	454 Sich. Div.
299	299 Inf.	376	376 Inf.
300	S.S. Polizei[3]	377	377 Inf.
...		...	
302	302 Inf.		
...		383	383 Inf.
304	304 Inf.	384	384 Inf.
305	305 Inf.	385	385 Inf.
306	306 Inf.	...	
...		387	387 Inf.
319	319 Inf.	389	389 Inf.
320	320 Inf.	...	
321	321 Inf.		
...		400	Grossdeutschland
323	323 Inf.	...	
...			
		466	416 Inf.?
326	326 Inf.	...	
327	327 Inf.		
328	328 Inf.	702	702 Inf.
329	329 Inf.	...	
330	330 Inf.		
331	331 Inf.	707	707 Inf.
332	332 Inf.	708	708 Inf.
333	333 Inf.	709	709 Inf.
334	334 Inf.	710	710 Inf.
335	335 Inf.	711	711 Inf.
336	336 Inf.	712	712 Inf.
337	337 Inf.	713	713 Inf.
338	338 Inf.	...	
339	339 Inf.	715	715 Inf.
340	340 Inf.	716	716 Inf.
		...	
342	342 Inf.		
343	343 Inf.	719	719 Inf.
344	344 Inf.	...	
...		999	

[3]Services only carry this number.
[4]Croatian.

Flak.

58. Antiaircraft Units.—Flugabwehrregiment, Flakregiment (Flak Rgt.), Flakabteilung (Flak. Abt.), Flakbatterie (Flak Bttr.), Heeres– (H.), Marine– (M.), Scheinwerfer– (Sch.).

Flak Unit	Luftgau*	Remarks**	Flak Unit	Luftgau*	Remarks**
1	VII	Rgt.	36	XI	Rgt.
1		Sch. Rgt.	37	VIII	Rgt.
2	VII	Rgt.	38	XVII	Rgt.
2		Sch. Rgt.	39	VI (?)	Rgt.
2		Ballon Abt.	40		Rgt. Stab
3	I/II	Rgt.	41		Rgt. Stab
4	VI	Rgt.	42	III/IV	Rgt.
4		Sch. Rgt.	43	III/IV	Rgt.
5	VII	Rgt.	44	VI	Rgt. (105-mm)
5		Sch. Rgt.	45	VII	Rgt.
6	XI	Rgt.	46		Rgt.
7	III/IV	Rgt.	47		Rgt.
8	XVII	Rgt.	48	VIII	Rgt. (105-mm)
9	XII/XIII	Rgt.	49	XII/XIII	Rgt. (40-mm)
10	III/IV	Rgt.	50		Rgt.
10		Ballon Abt.	51	III/IV	Rgt.
11	III/IV	Rgt.	52	III/IV	Rgt.
12	III/IV	Rgt. (105-mm)	53	VII	Rgt.
12		Eisb. Rgt.	54	VI	Rgt.
13	XI	Rgt.	55	XII/XIII (?)	Rgt.
14	VI	Rgt.	...		
15	XII/XIII	Rgt.	57		Rgt. Stab
16	XI	Rgt.	58		Rgt. Stab
17	XI	Rgt.	59	XI	Rgt.
18	XVII	Rgt.	60	XI	Rgt.
19	III/IV	Rgt.	61	III/IV	Rgt.
20	VIII	Rgt.	62	XI	Rgt.
20		M. Rgt.	63		Rgt. Stab
21	I/II	Rgt.	64	VI	Rgt.
22	III/IV	Rgt.	65		Rgt. Stab
22		M. Rgt.	66	XII/XIII	Rgt.
23	III/IV	Rgt.	67		Rgt.
24	XI	Rgt.	68	XVII (?)	Rgt.
24		M. Rgt.	69	VI	Rgt.
25	XVII	Rgt.	...		
26	XI	Rgt.	71	I/II	l. Abt.
27	XI	Rgt.	72	VI	l. Abt. (mot.)
28	XII/XIII	Rgt.	72		Eisb. Rgt.
29	XI	Rgt.	73	III/IV	l. Abt. (mot.)
30		Rgt.	74	VI	l. Abt.
30		Eisb. Rgt.	74		Rgt. Stab
31		Rgt.	74		Sch. Rgt. Stab
32	III/IV	Rgt. (105-mm)	75	VI	l. Abt.
33	III/IV	Rgt.	76	XI	l. Abt. (mot.)
34	VI	Rgt.	77	VIII	l. Abt.
35	XI	Rgt.	77		Rgt. Stab

*Luftgau (the airforce district corresponding in function to the Wehrkreis): Luftgau I/II=Wkr. I, XX, and XXI; Luftgau III/IV=Wkr. II, III, and IV; Luftgau VI=Wkr. VI and IX; Luftgau VII=Wkr. V and VII; Luftgau VIII=Wkr. VIII and XXI; Luftgau XI=Wkr. II, X, and XI; Luftgau XII/XIII=Wkr. IX, XII, and XIII; Luftgau XVII=Wkr. XVII and XVIII.

**Light battalions are normally equipped with 37 mm and 20 mm guns; heavy battalions with 88 mm guns, and all other battalions are *mixed*, with 88 mm, 37 mm, and 20 mm guns. Where a unit is known to be equipped with other calibres such as 40 mm or 105 mm, a reference is given in this column.

Also Heeresflak-Lehrabteilung and Flak-Lehrregiment (Abt. I-III).

Flak.

ORDER OF BATTLE OF THE GERMAN ARMY

Flak Unit	Luftgau	Remarks	Flak Unit	Luftgau	Remarks
78	III/IV	l. Abt.	122		Abt.
78		Rgt. Stab	122		Eisb. Rgt.
79		Rgt.	123		Abt.
...			123		Rgt. Stab
81		l. Abt. (mot.)	124		Abt.
82	VI	l. Abt.	125		Abt.
83	III/IV	l. Abt.	125		Rgt. Stab
83		Rgt. Stab	126		Abt.
84	VI	l. Abt.	126		Rgt. Stab
85	VII	l. Abt. (mot.)	126		M. Abt.
85		Rgt. Stab	127		Abt.
86	III/IV	l. Abt.	...		
86		Rgt. Stab	129		Rgt. Stab
87 (?)		l. Abt.	130		Sch. Abt.
88		l. Abt.	131		Abt. (mot.)
89		l. Abt. (mot.)	132		Abt.
89		Rgt. Stab	132		Rgt. Stab
90		l. Abt.	133	III/IV	Abt.
90		Rgt. Stab	133		Rgt. Stab
91	XVII	l. Abt.	134	III/IV	Abt.
91		Rgt. Stab	134		Rgt. Stab
92	XVII	l. Abt.	135		Rgt. Stab (Bttr.)
92		Rgt. Stab	136		Abt.
93	XVII	l. Abt.	136		Rgt. Stab
93		Rgt. Stab	137		Rgt. Stab
94	VI	l. Abt. (mot.)	138		Sch. Abt.
95	XII/XIII	l. Abt.	138		Rgt.
95		Rgt. Stab	...		
96	VI	l. Abt.	140		Sch. Abt.
97	VII	l. Abt.	141		Rgt. (mot.)
98		l. Abt. (mot.)	142		Abt.
98		Rgt. Stab	142		Rgt. Stab
99	XVII	l. Abt. (mot.)	143		s. Abt.
99		Rgt. Stab	144		l. Abt.
100		Rgt. Stab	145		Abt.
101		Rgt.	146		Abt.
102		Rgt. Stab	147		Abt.
102		Ballon Abt.	148		Sch. Abt.
103		Rgt.	149		Rgt. Stab
104		Rgt. Stab	...		
105		Rgt. Stab	151		Abt.
106		Rgt. Stab	151		Rgt. Stab
...			152		Abt.
108		Rgt. Stab	152		Rgt. Stab
109		Rgt. Stab	153		Abt.
109		Sch. Rgt. Stab	153		Rgt. Stab
110		Eisb. Rgt.	154		Abt.
111		s. Abt.	155		Abt.
111		Rgt.	155		Rgt.
112		Abt.	156		Abt.
112		Eisb. Rgt.	157		s. Abt.
113		Rgt.	158		Sch. Abt.
114		Abt. (Bttr.)	159		Eisb. Rgt.
115		Abt.	160		Sch. Abt.
116		s. Abt.	160		Sch. Rgt.
117		s. Abt.	161		Abt. (?)
118		Abt.	161		Sch. Rgt.
118		Rgt. Stab	162		Rgt. Stab
...			163		s. Abt.
120		Sch. Abt.	163		Sch. Abt.
120		Rgt. Stab	164		Abt.
121		Abt.	164		Rgt. Stab
121		Rgt.	164		M. Abt.

RESTRICTED

Flak.

Flak Unit	Luftgau	Remarks	Flak Unit	Luftgau	Remarks
166		s. Abt.	224		Eisb. Abt.
167		s. Abt.	224		M. Abt.
168		Sch. Abt.	225		s. Abt.
169		Abt.	226		Abt.
...			226		M. Abt.
172		Abt.	227		Eisb. Abt.
...			229		Rgt. Stab
...			230	VI	s. Abt.
180		Rgt.	231		Rgt. (mot.)
181		Abt.	231		M. Abt.
181	XVII	Rgt. Stab	232		Abt.
182		s. Abt.	232		M. Abt.
182		Rgt. Stab	233		M. Abt.
183		Abt.	234		Abt.
185		Abt. (75-mm)	234		M. Abt.
186		Abt. (75-mm)	235		Abt.
187	XVII	Abt.	236		Abt.
...			236		M. Abt.
...			237		Abt.
190		Abt.	...		
191		Abt.	239		M. Abt.
192		Abt.	240		M. Abt.
193		Abt.	241		Rgt.
194		Abt.	241		M. Abt.
...			242		Abt.
196		s. Abt.	242		M. Abt.
197		s. Abt.	243		s. Abt.
...			244		s. Abt.
199		Abt.	245		Abt.
200		M. Abt.	246		Abt.
201	XVII	Rgt. Stab	246		M. Abt.
201		Ballon Abt.	...		
202		Abt.			
202		Sch. Rgt.	249		Abt.
202		Ballon Abt.	...		
203		Ballon Abt.	251	VII	Abt.
204		M. Abt.	252		Abt.
204		Ballon Abt.	252		Sch. Abt.
205		Ballon Abt.	252		M. Abt.
206		Abt.	253		Abt.
206		Ballon Abt.	254		Abt.
207		Abt.	254		M. Abt.
208		M. Abt.	255		Abt.
209		Ballon Abt.	256		Abt.
210		Ballon Abt.	257		s. Abt.
211		Abt.	258	XI	Abt.
211		M. Abt.	259		Sch. Abt.
212		s. Abt.	260		Sch. Abt.
212		M. Abt.	261		Abt.
...			261		M. Abt.
214		M. Abt.	262		Abt.
			262		M. Abt.
216		M. Abt.	263		Abt.
...			263		Eisb. Abt.
			264		s. Abt.
219		M. Abt.	264		M. Abt.
220		Sch. Abt.	265		s. Abt.
221		Abt.	266	XI	Abt.
222		Abt.	266		M. Abt.
222		M. Abt.	267		Abt.
223		Abt.	...		
224		Abt.	269		Sch. Abt.

Flak

ORDER OF BATTLE OF THE GERMAN ARMY

Flak Unit	Luftgau	Remarks	Flak Unit	Luftgau	Remarks
271		s. Abt.	316		Abt.
271		H. Abt.			
272		s. Abt.	321		s. Abt.
272		H. Abt.	321		Eisb. Abt.
272		M. Abt.	322		Abt.
273		H. Abt.	323		Abt.
274		H. Abt.			
274		M. Abt.	325		Abt.
275		H. Abt.			
276		H. Abt. (mot.)	327		s. Abt.
277		H. Abt. (mot.)			
278		H. Abt.	329		Sch. Abt.
279		H. Abt. (mot.)	330		Abt.
280		Abt.	331	III/IV	Abt.
280		H. Abt.	332		s. Abt.
281		s. Abt.	333		Abt.
281		H. Abt.	334		s. Abt.
282		Abt.	335		Rgt.
283		Abt.			
283		H. Abt.			
284		H. Abt.	340		Abt.
285		Abt.	340		Sch. Abt.
286		s. Abt.	341		Abt.
287		s. Abt.	342		Abt.
288		s. Abt.	343		s. Abt.
288		H. Abt.	344		Abt.
289		H. Abt.	345		Abt.
290		H. Abt.	346		s. Abt.
291		Abt.	347		Abt.
291		H. Abt.			
292		Rgt. (mot.)			
292		H. Abt.	351		s. Abt.
293		s. Abt.	352		s. Abt.
294		Abt.	353		Abt.
294		M. Abt.	354		Abt.
295		s. Abt.	355		Abt.
296		Abt.	356		s. Abt.
297		Abt.	357		s. Abt. (94-mm)
298		Sch. Abt.			
299		Sch. Abt.			
299		H. Abt.	360		Abt.
300		Sch. Abt.	361		Abt.
301		s. Abt.	362		s. Abt.
302		Abt.	363		s. Abt.
302		H. Abt.	364		Abt.
303		s. Abt.	365		s. Abt.
303		H. Abt.			
304		s. Abt.			
304		H. Abt.	368		Sch. Abt.
305		Abt.	369		Sch. Abt.
306		Abt.	370		Sch. Abt.
			371	VIII	Abt.
308	III/IV	Sch. Abt.	372		s. Abt.
308		Rgt.	373		Eisb. Abt.
309		Sch. Abt.	374		Abt.
310		Sch. Abt.	375		s. Abt.
310		M. Abt.	376		s. Abt.
311		s. Abt.			
312		H. Abt. (mot.)			
313		H. Abt. (mot.)	381		Abt.
			382		Abt.
315		H. Abt.	382		Rgt. Stab

RESTRICTED

Flak.

Flak Unit	Luftgau	Remarks	Flak Unit	Luftgau	Remarks
383	XVII	Abt.	445		Abt.
384		s. Abt.	(446)		(s. Abt.) renumbered II/Rgt. 37
385		s. Abt.			
386		Abt.	447		Abt.
387	XVII	Abt.	448		Sch. Abt.
......			449		Sch. Abt.
			450		Sch. Abt. (?)
391		Abt.	(451)		(s. Abt.) renumbered 945 (l. Abt.)
......					
393		s. Abt.	452		s. Abt.
394	XII	Abt.	453		s. Abt.
395		Abt.	454		Abt.
396		Abt.	455		Abt.
397	XVII	s. Abt.	456		Abt.
......			457		Abt.
			458		Sch. Abt.
401		Abt.	......		
402		Abt.			
403		s. Abt.	461		Abt.
404		Abt.	462		s. Abt.
404		Rgt. Stab	462		Eisb. Abt.
405		Abt.	463		Abt.
406	VI	Abt.	464		Abt.
407		Abt.	465		s. Abt.
408		Sch. Abt.	466		Abt.
409		Sch. Abt.	467		s. Abt.
410		Sch. Abt.			
411		Rgt. (mot.)	469		Sch. Abt.
412		s. Abt.	......		
			471		s. Abt.
414		s. Abt.			
415		l. Abt.	473		Eisb. Abt.
416		Eisb. Abt.	......		
......			475		s. Abt.
			......		
419		Abt. (?)	481		Abt.
......					
421		s. Abt.			
422		Abt.	......		
423		Abt.	487		Abt.
424		Eisb. Abt.	......		
425		s. Abt.			
426		s. Abt.	491		Rgt.
427		s. Abt.			
428		s. Abt.	493		Abt.
			494		Abt.
......			495		Abt.
431		Abt.	496		s. Abt.
431		Rgt.	497		s. Abt.
432		Abt.	......		
433		s. Abt.			
434		Abt.	501		Rgt. (mot.)
435		s. Abt.	502	VII	s. Abt.
436		Abt.	503		s. Abt.
			504		Abt.
438		Sch. Abt.	504		Rgt. Stab
			505		Abt. (Fähren)
440		Sch. Abt.	506		l. Abt.
441		Abt.	507		l. Abt.
441		Rgt.			
442		Abt.	509		Sch. Abt.
443		s. Abt.	......		
444		Abt.	511		Abt.

RESTRICTED

Flak

ORDER OF BATTLE OF THE GERMAN ARMY

Flak Unit	Luftgau	Remarks	Flak Unit	Luftgau	Remarks
511		M. Abt.	...		
512		Abt.	591		Abt.
513		s. Abt.	592		s. Abt.
(514)		(Abt.) renumbered I/Rgt. 8 (mot.)	593		s. Abt.
			594		Abt.
515		s. Abt.	...		
516		Abt.	596		Abt.
517		Abt.	597		Abt.
...			...		
519		Sch. Abt.	...		
520		Sch. Abt.	601	XI	s. Abt. (105-mm)
520		M. Abt.	602		Abt.
521		Abt.	603		s. Abt.
522		s. Abt.	604		Rgt.
522		Rgt. Stab	605		Abt.
523		s. Abt.	606		Abt.
524		Abt.	607		Abt.
(525)		(s. Abt.) renumbered II/Rgt. 52	608		Sch. Abt.
			609		Sch. Abt.
526		Abt.	...		
527		s. Abt.	611	XI	Rgt. (mot.)
528		Abt. (?)	612		Abt
529		Sch. Abt.	613		Abt.
530		M. Abt.	614		Abt.
			615		s. Abt.
532		Abt.	616		s. Abt.
			617		s. Abt.
534		s. Abt.	618	XI	Sch. Abt.
...			...		
			620		Sch. Abt.
...			...		
538		Abt.	622		Abt. (?)
538		Eisb. Abt.	...		
541		Abt.			
542		Abt.	...		
543		Abt.	628		s. Abt.
544		s. Abt.	629		Rgt.
545		s. Abt.	...		
546		s. Abt.			
547		s. Abt.	632		s. Abt.
548		s. Abt.	...		
			634		s. Abt.
550		s. Abt.	...		
...			...		
			638		s. Abt.
563		Abt.	...		
...			...		
			641		s. Abt.
567		Abt.	642		s. Abt.
			643		Abt.
569		Abt.	644		s. Abt.
			645		Abt.
...			646		s. Abt.
573		s. Abt.	...		
574		s. Abt.	648		Sch. Abt.
575		s. Abt.	649		Sch. Abt.
...			650		Abt.
			...		
582		Abt.	652		Rgt. Stab
582		Sch. Abt.	653		Rgt. Stab
...			654		Rgt. Stab
			655		Rgt. Stab
585		Sch. Abt.	656		[Rgt. Stab
...			657		Rgt. Stab

RESTRICTED

Flak

ORDER OF BATTLE OF THE GERMAN ARMY

Flak Unit	Luftgau	Remarks	Flak Unit	Luftgau	Remarks
...			713		l. Abt.
660		s. Abt.	...		
661		s. Abt.	715		l. Abt.
662		s. Abt.	...		
...			717		l. Abt.
665		Abt.	...		
...			720		l. Abt.
667		l. Abt.	720		M. Abt.
668		l. Abt.	(722)		(l. Abt.) disbanded
668		Sch. Abt.	723		l. Abt.
...			724		l. Abt.
670		Abt.	725		l. Abt.
671		Abt.	726		l. Abt.
672		Abt.	727		l. Abt.
673		l. Abt.	...		
674		Abt.	729		l. Abt.
675		Abt.	730		Abt.
676		Abt.	731		l. Abt. (50-mm)
677		s. Abt.	732		l. Abt.
678		Abt.	733		l. Abt. (?)
679		l. Abt.	734		l. Abt.
680		l. Abt.	735		l. Abt.
681		Abt.	736		l. Abt.
682		Abt.	737		l. Abt.
683		Abt.	738		l. Abt.
684		Abt.	739		l. Abt.
685		Abt.	740		l. Abt.
686		Sch. Abt.	741		l. Abt. (mot.)
687		l. Abt.	742		l. Abt.
688		s. Abt.	...		
689		l. Abt.	744		l. Abt.
690		Abt.	745		l. Abt.
691		l. Abt.	746		Abt.
691		Eisb. Abt.	747		l. Abt.
692		Abt.	748		Abt
693		s. Abt.	...		
694		Abt.	750		l. Abt.
695		Abt.	751		l. Abt.
696		M. Abt. (?)	752		l. Abt. (50-mm)
...			753		l. Abt.
701		Rgt.	754		l. Abt.
701		M. Abt.	755		Abt.
702		Abt.	756		l. Abt.
702		M. Abt.	757		Abt.
703		(s. Abt.) renumbered 372 (s. Abt.)	758		l. Abt.
			...		
703		M. Abt.	761		l. Abt. (mot.)
704		Rgt.	762		l. Abt.
704		M. Abt.	763		l. Abt.
705		s. Abt.	764		l. Abt.
705		M. Abt.	765		Abt.
706		s. Abt.			
707		s. Abt.	767		l. Abt.
708		Sch. Abt.	768		l. Abt.
708		M. Abt.	769		l. Abt.
...			...		
710		M. Abt.			
711		Abt.	772		l. Abt.
711		M. Abt.	773		l. Abt.
712		Abt.	774		l. Abt.

RESTRICTED

Flak.

ORDER OF BATTLE OF THE GERMAN ARMY 423

Flak Unit	Luftgau	Remarks	Flak Unit	Luftgau	Remarks
775		l. Abt.			
777		l. Abt.	839		l. Abt.
....			841		l. Abt. (mot. Bttr.)
781		l. Abt.	842		l. Abt.
782		s. Abt.	844		l. Abt.
...			845		l. Abt.
...			846		l. Abt.
785		l. Abt.	847		l. Abt.
...			(848)		(s. Abt.) renumbered 534 (s. Abt.)
793		Abt.	849		l. Abt.
...			850		l. Abt.
...			851		l. Abt. (mot.)
797		Abt.	852		l. Abt.
...			853		l. Abt.
			854		Abt.
801		Abt.			
802		Abt.	856		l. Abt.
802		M. Abt.			
803		M. Abt.	858		Abt.
804		Abt. (94-mm, 40-mm)			
804		M. Abt.	860		l. Abt.
805		s. Abt.	860		l. Eisb. Abt.
805		M. Abt.	861		l. Abt. (mot.)
806		s. Abt.	862		l. Abt.
806		M. Abt.	863		l. Abt.
807		M. Abt.	864		l. Eisb. Abt.
808		Sch. Abt.	865		l. Eisb. Abt.
808		M. Abt.			
809		Sch. Abt.			
809		M. Abt.	871		l. Abt.
810		M. Abt.	872		l. Abt.
811		M. Abt.	873		l. Abt.
812		M. Abt.	874		l. Abt.
813		Abt.	875		l. Abt
813		M. Abt.	876		l. Abt.
815		Abt.	878		Abt
			879		l. Abt.
817		M. Abt.			
			885		l. Abt.
820		M. Abt. (?)			
822		l. Abt.	889		l. Abt.
822		Eisb. Abt.			
823		l. Abt.	891		l. Abt.
824		l. Abt.			
825		l. Eisb. Abt.			
826		l. Abt.	901		Abt.
			902		Abt.
828		l. Abt.	902		s. Eisb. Abt.(105-mm)
829		l. Abt.	903		Abt.
830		l. Abt.	904		Abt.
831		l. Abt.	905		Abt.
832		Abt.			
833		Abt.			
			909		Sch. Abt.
835		l. Abt.			
			911		l. Abt.
837		l. Abt.	911		Rgt. Stab
838		l. Abt.	912		l. Abt.

RESTRICTED

Flak.

Flak Unit	Luftgau	Remarks	Flak Unit	Luftgau	Remarks
913		l. Abt.	...		
914		l. Abt.	956		l. Abt.
...			...		
921		l. Abt.	959		Abt.
922		l. Abt.	...		
923		l. Abt.	...		
...			978		l. Abt.
925		l. Abt.	979		l. Abt.
...			980		l. Abt.
928		Abt.	982		l. Abt.
...			983		l. Abt.
931		l. Abt.	984		l. Abt.
932		l. Abt.	985		l. Abt. (40-mm)
933		l. Abt.	...		
...			988		l. Abt.
941	XVII	l. Abt.	...		
942		l. Abt.	990		l. Abt.
...			991		l. Abt.
...			992		l. Abt.
945		l. Abt.	993		l. Abt.
...			994	XII	l. Abt.
...			995		l. Abt.
951		l. Abt.	996		l. Abt.
952		l. Abt.	997		l. Abt.
953		l. Abt.	998		l. Abt.
954		l. Abt.	999		l. Abt.

RESTRICTED

Section VIII. ROSTERS OF SENIOR OFFICERS.
59. Introduction.

a. General.—This section consists of lists of generals of the German Army and Air Force and of important commanders of the *Waffen-SS*. In each category they are arranged alphabetically by rank, together with pertinent data regarding their age, command, seniority, origin, and arm.

The ages given are usually those reached in 1944, but in some cases they are only approximate.

The command or appointment shown is that which the officer is believed to have at the time of publication, but if it has not been recently confirmed the year of latest confirmation is given.

Seniority is the date of promotion to the present rank.

Provincial origin in Germany is shown only when it is other than Prussian.

b. German surnames.—Since the use of German surnames is sometimes confusing to the uninitiated, the following aids are given for understanding the method of their alphabetical listing:

(1) Hyphenated names: listed under first element. Example: KOCH-ERPACH, Rudolf.

(2) Compound names connected by *und:* listed under first element. Example: ROTHKIRCH und PANTHEN, Friedrich Wilhelm von.

(3) Compound names connected by *von:* usually listed under first element, provided this is a surname and not a title (such as Ritter) or a Christian name. Example: FISCHER von WEIKERSTHAL, Walter.

(4) Compound names connected by *zu* or *auf:* same as in (3) above.

(5) Double names connected by *genannt* (abbreviated *gen.*, meaning "called"): may be listed under either of the two names according to which is more commonly used. Examples: von LEWINSKI gen. von MANSTEIN, Fritz Erich—listed under

M; but von HARTLIEB gen. WALSPORN, Maximilian, listed under H.

Christian names are seldom if ever used in signatures. Officers sign orders with family name and rank only. It is therefore difficult, at times, to discover an officer's Christian name or initials, so that in a few cases in the following lists there is a possibility of confusion between officers having the same surname.

c. *German titles.*—The principal German titles of nobility occurring in the following lists are, in descending sequence:

Graf—count.

Freiherr (abbreviated *Frhr.*)—baron. The title *Baron* also exists.

Ritter—knight.

Edler—noble.

von (abbreviated *v.*)—when used alone denotes the lowest rank of nobility and corresponds to the French *de*. Also used in combination with all the above titles. Variants are: *vom, von der, von dem, von und zu, van.* (All such particles are ignored in the alphabetical arrangement of names.)

Academic degrees, such as Dr., Dr. Ing., Dr. h.c., Dr. habil., Dr. phil., Dipl. Ing., Dipl. Wirtsch., are considered more important in German than in English. They are regularly shown before the name both in official documents and in signatures and are therefore included in the following lists.

d. *German military ranks.*—Literal translations of ranks above that of colonel are deceptive. In the following table the corresponding U. S. rank is given for each German rank. It should be noted, however, that the appointments held by officers of any given rank may vary widely in status, and no appointment carries or presupposes specific rank. For example: an infantry regiment may be commanded by a Generalmajor, an Oberst, an Oberstleutnant, or, on occasions, a Major.

RESTRICTED

German Rank	Corresponding U. S. Rank
Reichsmarschall	None (Marshal of the Reich)
Generalfeldmarschall	None (Field Marshal)
Generaloberst	General
General (der Infanterie, Gebirgstruppen, Kavallerie, Panzertruppe, Nachrichtentruppen; der Flieger, Flakartillerie, Luftnachrichtentruppen, Luftwaffe)	Lieutenant General
Generalleutnant	Major General
Generalmajor	Brigadier General
Oberst	Colonel
Oberstleutnant	Lieutenant Colonel
Major	Major
Hauptmann	Captain
Rittmeister	Captain (Cavalry)
Oberleutnant	Lieutenant
Leutnant	Second Lieutenant

e. Categories of officers.—In addition to the regular line officers of the peacetime Army (*aktive Truppenoffiziere*), who carry titles of rank without qualifications, officers may be found carrying the following qualified titles—

(1) *Offiziere i. G. (im Generalstab).*—General Staff Corps Officers. Trained at the General Staff School (*Kriegsakademie*), and assigned to one of the very limited number of General Staff appointments (*Generalstabsstellen*) by the Army General Staff (*Generalstab des Heeres*), to which they are at all times directly responsible.

(2) *Offiziere (Erg), Offiziere (E), Ergänzungsoffiziere.*—Officers on the supplementary list. Retired officers recalled, mainly for administrative duties, between 1934 and 1939. These officers are now authorized to use their titles of rank without qualification.

(3) *Offiziere d. R. (der Reserve).*—Reserve Officers. Men selected for commissions at the time when they completed their two years'

RESTRICTED

service as conscripts or their twelve years' service as professional soldiers.

(4) *Offiziere d. L. (der Landwehr)*.—Qualification formerly used for reserve officers over 35 years of age.

(5) *Offiziere d. B. (des Beurlaubtenstandes)*.—A collective term for *Reserve* and *Landwehr* officers; now apparently dropped.

(6) *Offiziere z. V. (zur Verfügung)*.—Regular or reserve officers who have been technically retired (*entlassen*) on completion of their term of service, but who may be retained in service or recalled for a new assignment. (In the lists below z. V. status is indicated in the *Seniority* column).

(7) *Offiziere z. D. (zur Dienstleistung)*.—Qualification sometimes used by certain types of recalled *Offiziere z. V.*

(8) *Offiziere (W) (des Waffenwesens)*.—Ordnance officers.

(9) *Offiziere a. D. (ausser Dienst)*.—Retired officers, performing no military service.

60. Army Generals.
a. Generalfeldmarschall *(Field Marshal)*.

Name (age)	Command or Appointment	Seniority	Origin	Arm
BOCK, Fedor v. (64)	Retired (?)	19 Jul 40		Inf
BRAUCHITSCH, Walther v. (63)	Retired (Dec 41)	19 Jul 40		Arty
BUSCH, Ernst (59)	Sixteenth Army	1 Feb 43	Westphalia	Inf
KEITEL, Wilhelm (62)	Chief of O K W	19 Jul 40		Arty
KLEIST, Ewald v. (63)	Army Group A	1 Feb 43		Cav
KLUGE, Günther v. (62)	Army Group Center	19 Jul 40		Arty
KÜCHLER, Georg v. (63)	Army Group North	30 Jun 42		Arty
LEEB, Wilhelm Ritter v. (68)	Retired (Jan 42)	19 Jul 40	Bavaria	Arty
LIST, Wilhelm (64)	Retired	19 Jul 40	Württemberg	Inf
MANSTEIN, Fritz Erich v. LEWINSKI gen.v. (57)	Army Group South	1 Jul 42		Inf
PAULUS, Friedrich (54)	Prisoner of War (Feb 43)	31 Jan 43	Baden	Tks
ROMMEL, Erwin (53)	Insp Gen of Defense	22 Jun 42	Württemberg	Tks
RUNDSTEDT, Gerd v. (69)	Army Group West	19 Jul 40		Inf
WEICHS, Maximilian Frhr. v. (63)	Army Group F	1 Feb 43	Bavaria	Cav
WITZLEBEN, Erwin v. (63)	Retired (1940)	19 Jul 40	Silesia	Inf

RESTRICTED

60. Army Generals.—Continued.
b. Generaloberst (General).

Name (age)	Command or Appointment	Seniority	Origin	Arm
ARNIM, Jürgen v. (55)	Prisoner of War	3 Dec 42	Silesia	Tks
BLASKOWITZ, Johannes (61)	First Army	1 Oct 39	Baden	Inf
DIETL, Eduard (54)	Twentieth Army	5 Jun 42	Bavaria	Mtn
DOLLMANN, Friedrich (62)	Seventh Army	19 Jul 40	Bavaria	Arty
FALKENHORST, Nikolaus v. (59)	Twenty - first Army and CG Norway	19 Jul 40	Silesia	Inf
FROMM, Fritz (56)	Ch. d. H. Rü. u. BdE	19 Jul 40		Arty
GUDERIAN, Heinz (56)	Insp Gen of Panzer Arm	19 Jul 40		Tks
HALDER, Franz (60)	Retired	19 Jul 40	Bavaria	Arty
HEINRICI, Gotthard (57)	Fourth Army	1 Jan 43		Inf
HEITZ, Walter (66)	Prisoner of War (Feb 43)	31 Jan 43		Arty
HOEPNER, Erich (58)	Retired (1942)	19 Jul 40		Cav
HOLLIDT, Karl (53)	Sixth Army	1 Sep 43	Hesse	Inf
HOTH, Hermann (60)	Fourth Panzer Army	1 Jul 42		Tks
JAENECKE, Erwin (52)	Seventeenth Army	30 Jan 44		Pion
JODL, Alfred (54)	Chief of Wehrmachtführungsstab, OKW	30 Jan 44	Bavaria	Arty
LINDEMANN, Georg (60)	Eighteenth Army	1 Jul 42		Cav
MACKENSEN, Eberhard v. (55)		6 Jul 43		Cav
MODEL, Walter (53)	Ninth Army	1 Feb 42		Tks
REINHARDT, Georg-Hans (57)	Third Panzer Army	1 Jan 42	Saxony	Tks
RUOFF, Richard (59)	Retired (?)	1 Apr 42	Württemberg	Inf
SALMUTH, Hans v. (56)	Fifteenth Army	1 Jan 43		Inf
SCHMIDT, Rudolf (58)		1 Mar 42		Tks
STRAUSS, Adolf (65)	Retired (1942)	19 Jul 40		Inf
VIETINGHOFF, gen. SCHEEL, Heinrich v. (57)	Tenth Army	1 Sep 43		Tks
WEISS, Walter (54)		30 Jan 44		Inf
ZEITZLER, Kurt (49)	C of S, German Army	30 Jan 44		Inf

RESTRICTED

ORDER OF BATTLE OF THE GERMAN ARMY 431

60. Army Generals.—Continued.
c. General der Infanterie, Kavallerie, etc. (*Lieutenant General*).

Name (age)	Command or Appointment	Seniority	Origin	Arm
ALLMENDINGER, Karl (53)		1 Apr 43	Württemberg	Inf
ANGELIS, Maximilian (55)	XLIV Infantry Corps	1 Mar 42	Austria	Arty
BADER, Paul (59)	XXI Mountain Corps	1 Jul 41		Arty
BARCKHAUSEN, Franz (62)	Mil Economics and Armaments Staff, France	1 Jul 43		Arty
BEHLENDORFF (55)	LXXXIV Infantry Corps	1 Oct 41		Arty
BIELER, Bruno (56	LXXXVI Infantry Corps	1 Oct 41		Inf
BOCK (62)	Retired (Mar 43)	1 Dec 40		Inf
BÖCKMANN, Herbert v. (57)		1 Apr 42	Baden	Inf
BÖHME, Franz (59)	XVIII Mountain Corps.	1 Aug 40	Austria	Inf
BOETTICHER, Friedrich v. (63)		1 Apr 40	Saxony	Arty
BOTH, Cuno Hans v. (60)	CG Esthonia	1 Jan 40		Inf
BRAEMER, Walter (61)	CG Ostland	1 Sep 42		Cav
BRAND, Fritz (56)		1 Aug 40		Arty
BRANDENBERGER, Erich (52)	XVII Infantry Corps	1 Aug 43	Bavaria	Arty
BRANDT, Georg (68)	Retired (?)	1 Aug 41		Cav
BREITH, Hermann (52)	III Panzer Corps	1 Mar 43		Tks
BRENNECKE, Kurt (53)		1 Feb 42		Inf
CHEVALLERIE, Kurt v. der (53)	LIX Infantry Corps	1 Mar 42		Inf
CLÖSSNER, Erich (58)	LIII Infantry Corps	1 Jan 42	Hesse	Inf
COCHENHAUSEN, Friedrich v. (65)	Retired (1942)	1 Dec 40		Arty
CRAMER, Hans (48)	Prisoner of War (May 43)	1 May 43		Tks
CRUEWELL, Ludwig (52)	Prisoner of War (1942)	1 Dec 41		Tks
DALWIGK zu LICHTENFELS, Franz Frhr. v. (68)	Retired	1 Dec 40		Inf
DEHNER, Ernst (55)		1 Dec 42		Inf

RESTRICTED

60. Army Generals.—Continued.
c. General der Infanterie, Kavallerie, etc. (*Lieutenant General*).—Continued.

Name (age)	Command or Appointment	Seniority	Origin	Arm
DOSTLER, Anton (53)	A Corps on Eastern Front (?)	1 Aug 43	Bavaria	Inf
EBERBACH, Hans (49)		1 Aug 43	Württemberg	Tks
ENGELBRECHT, Erwin (53)	XXXIII Corps Comd	1 Sep 42	Silesia	Cav
ERFURTH, Waldemar (65)	Mil Mission to Finland	1 Apr 40		Inf
FAHRMBACHER, Wilhelm (56)	XXV Infantry Corps (?)	1 Nov 40	Bavaria	Arty
FALKENHAUSEN, Alexander v. (66)	CG Belgium and Northern France		Silesia	Inf
FEHN, Gustav (52)		1 Nov 42		Tks
FELBER, Hans Gustav (56)	CG Serbia	1 Aug 40		Inf
FELLGIEBEL, Erich (57)	Insp Gen of Sig Trs	1 Aug 40		Sig C
FESSMANN, Ernst (63)	Retired (1942)	30 Sep 37	Bavaria	Tks
FEURSTEIN, Valentin (59)	LI Mountain Corps	1 Sep 41	Austria	Mtn
FISCHER v. WEIKERSTHAL, Walter (54)		1 Dec 41	Württemberg	Inf
FÖRSTER, Otto (59)		1 Apr 38		Pion
FÖRSTER, Sigismund v. (57)		1 May 43	Thuringia	Inf
FRETTER-PICO, Maximilian (53)	XXX Infantry Corps	1 Jun 42	Baden	Arty
FRIDERICI, Erich (59)		1 Apr 39	Saxony	Inf
FRIESSNER, Johannes (52)	A Corps on E Front	1 Apr 43	Saxony	Inf
GALLENKAMP, Curt (55)		1 Apr 42		Arty
GEIB, Theodor (59)	Director General of Ordnance, OKH	1 Dec 41	Bavaria	Arty
GERCKE, Rudolf (60)	Director of Army Transport, OKH	1 Apr 42		Inf
GEYER, Hermann (62)	Retired (Jul 42)	1 Aug 36	Württemberg	Inf
GEYR v. SCHWEPPENBURG, Leo Frhr. (58)	Gen.of Panzer Troops West	1 Apr 40	Württemberg	Tks
GIENANTH, Frhr. v. (65)		1 Apr 36		Cav
GLOKKE, Gerhard (60)	Wkr. VI	1 Dec 40		Inf

RESTRICTED

ORDER OF BATTLE OF THE GERMAN ARMY 433

60. Army Generals.—Continued.
c. General der Infanterie, Kavallerie, etc. (*Lieutenant General*).—Continued.

Name (age)	Command or Appointment	Seniority	Origin	Arm
GOLLNICK, Hans (52)		1 Oct 43		Inf
GREIFF, Kurt v. (66)	Retired (?)	27 Aug 39	Württemberg	Inf
GRÜN, Otto (61)	Insp of Arty		Bavaria	Arty
HAENICKE, Siegfried (66)	Wehrkreis Govt Gen			Inf
HALM, Hans (65)	Retired (Jun 42)			Inf
HANNEKEN v. (54)	CG Denmark and XXXI Corps Command	1 Dec 41		Inf
HANSEN, Christian (59)	X Infantry Corps	1 Jun 40		Arty
HANSEN, Erik (55)	Mil Mission to Rumania	1 Aug 40		Cav
HARPE, Josef (54)	Second Army	1 Jun 42		Tks
HARTMANN, Otto (60)	Security Troops on Eastern Front	1 Apr 40	Bavaria	Arty
HELL, Ernst-Eberhard (57)	VII Infantry Corps	1 Mar 42		Arty
HENRICI, Sigfrid (56)	XL Panzer Corps	1 Jan. 43	Hesse	Tks
HERR, Traugott (54)	LXXVI Panzer Corps	1 Sep 43		Tks
HERZOG, Kurt (56)	XXXVIII Infantry Corps	1 Jul 42	Saxony	Arty
HILPERT, Karl (56)	XXIII Infantry Corps	1 Sep 42	Bavaria	Inf
HÖHNE, Gustav (51)	LIV Infantry Corps	1 May 43		Inf
HUBE, Hans (54)	First Panzer Army	1 Oct 42	Anhalt	Tks
HUBICKI, Dr. Alfred Ritter v. (57)	LXXXIX Infantry Corps	1 Oct 42	Austria	Tks
JACOB, Alfred (61)	Insp Gen of Engineers and Fortifications	1 Jun 40	Bavaria	Pion
JASCHKE, Erich (54)	XIII Infantry Corps			Inf
JORDAN, Hans (52)		1 Jan 43	Anhalt	Inf
KAEMPFE, Rudolf (61)	XXXV Infantry Corps	1 Jul 41		Arty
KAUPISCH, Leonard (66)	Retired (Jun 42)			Arty

RESTRICTED

60. Army Generals.—Continued.
c. General der Infanterie, Kavallerie, etc. (*Lieutenant General*).—Continued.

Name (age)	Command or Appointment	Seniority	Origin	Arm
KEINER, Walter (54)		1 Jan. 43		Arty
KEITEL, Bodewin (55)	Wkr. XX	1 Apr 41		Inf
KEMPF, Werner (58)		1 Apr 41		Tks
KIENITZ, Werner (59)	Wkr. II	1 Apr 38		Inf
KIRCHNER, Friedrich (59)	LVII Panzer Corps	1 Feb 42	Saxony	Tks
KLEFFEL, Philipp (57)	L Infantry Corps	1 Mar 42		Inf
KNIESS, Baptist (59)	LXVI Reserve Corps	1 Dec 42	Bavaria	Inf
KNOBELSDORFF, Otto v. (58)	XLVIII Panzer Corps	1 Aug 42		Tks
KOCH-ERPACH, Rudolf (58)	Wkr. VIII	1 Dec 40	Bavaria	Cav
KÖSTRING, Ernst (68)		1 Sep 40		Cav
KONRAD, Rudolf (53)	XLIX Mountain Corps	1 Mar 42	Bavaria	Mtn
KORTZFLEISCH, Joachim v. (54)		1 Aug 40		Inf
KRIEBEL, Kurt (Karl) (56)	Wkr. VII	1 Apr 43	Bavaria	Inf
KRUSE, Hermann		z. V		Arty
KÜBLER, Ludwig (55)	Rear Area, Army Group Center	1 Aug 40	Bavaria	Mtn
KÜHN, Friedrich (55)	Gen of Motorization at OKH	1 Apr 43		Tks
KUNTZE, Walter (61)	Chief of Training in Repl Tng Army	1 Mar 38		Pion
KUNTZEN, Adolf (55)	LXXXI Infantry Corps	1 Apr 41		Tks
LANZ, Hubert (48)	XXII Mountain Corps	28 Jan 43	Württemberg	Mtn
LAUX, Paul (57)	II Infantry Corps	1 Dec 42	Saxony	Inf
LEEB, Emil (64)	Army Ordnance Office	1 Apr 39	Bavaria	Arty
LEMELSEN, Joachim (56)		1 Aug 40		Tks
LEYSER, v. (56)		1 Dec. 42		Inf
LICHEL, Walter (59)		1 Dec 42		Inf

RESTRICTED

60. Army Generals.—Continued.

c. General der Infanterie, Kavallerie, etc. (*Lieutenant General*).—Continued.

Name (age)	Command or Appointment	Seniority	Origin	Arm
LOCH, Herbert (58)	XXVIII Infantry Corps	1 Oct 41	Bavaria	Arty
LÜDKE, Erich (62)	Retired (?)	1 Dec 40		Inf
LÜTERS, Rudolf (61)	XV Mountain Corps	1 Jan 43	Hesse	Inf
LUTZ, Oswald (68)	Retired (1942)	1 Oct 35	Württemberg	Tks
MARCKS, Erich (53)		1 Oct 42		Arty
MARTINEK, Robert (60)	XXXIX Panzer Corps	1 Jan 43	Austria	Arty
MATERNA, Friedrich (59)	Wkr. XVIII	1 Nov 40	Austria	Inf
MATTENKLOTT, Franz (60)	An Infantry Corps on Eastern Front	1 Oct 41	Silesia	Inf
METZ, Hermann (65)	Retired (1942)	1941		Inf
MIETH (56)	An Infantry Corps	1 May 43		Inf
MOSER, Willi (56)	LXXI Corps Command	1 Dec 42		Arty
MÜLLER, Eugen (53)	Generalquartiermeister	1 Jun 42	Bavaria	Arty
MUFF, Wolfgang (64)	Retired (Mar 43)	1 Dec 40	Württemberg	Inf
NAGY, Emmerich (62)		1 Aug 42	Austria	Inf
NEHRING, Walter (52)	XXIV Panzer Corps	1 Jul 42		Tks
NEULING, Ferdinand (59)	LXII Reserve Corps	1 Oct 42	Saxony	Inf
NIEBELSCHÜTZ, Günther v. (62)	Retired (?)	z.V.		Inf
OBSTFELDER, Hans v. (58)	XXIX Infantry Corps	1 Jun 40	Thuringia	Inf
OLBRICHT, Friedrich (56)	General Army Office, OKH (AHA)	1 Jun 40	Saxony	Inf
OSSWALD, Erwin (62)	Retired (Sep 43)	1 Dec 40	Württemberg	Inf
OSTERKAMP (52)	Army Admin Office, OKH (HVA)	1 Jun 43		Arty
OTT, Eugen (54)		1 Oct 41		Inf
OTTENBACHER, Otto (56)		1942		Inf
OTTO, Paul (63)	Retired (May 43)	1 Dec 40		Inf

RESTRICTED

60. Army Generals.—Continued.
c. General der Infanterie, Kavallerie, etc. (*Lieutenant General*).—Continued.

Name (age)	Command or Appointment	Seniotiry	Origin	Arm
OVEN, Karl v. (56)	XLIII Infantry Corps	1 Apr 43		Inf
PETRI, Hans (67)	Retired (May 42)	z.V.		Inf
PETZEL, Walter (61)	Wkr. XXI	1 Oct 39		Arty
PFEFFER, Max (59)	Prisoner of War (Feb 43)	22 Jan 43		Arty
POGRELL, Günther v. (65)	Retired (?)	1 Oct 36		Cav
PRAGER, Karl Ritter v. (66)	Retired (Jun 42)	1 Sep 40	Bavaria	Inf
RABENAU, Dr. phil. h. c. Friedrich v. (60)	Retired (Apr 43)	1 Sep 40		Inf
RASCHICK, Walther (62)	Wkr. X	1 Apr 39		Inf
RAUS, Erhard (55)	VIII Infantry Corps (?)	1 May 43	Austria	Tks
REINECKE, Hermann (56)	General Office, OKW	1 Jun 42		Inf
REINHARD, Hans (56)	LXXXVIII Infantry Corps	1 Nov 40	Saxony	Inf
RENDULIC, Dr. Lothar (57)	Second Panzer Army	1 Dec 42	Austria	Inf
RINTELEN, Enno v. (53)		1 Jul 42		Inf
ROESE, Franz v. (66)	Army Museums	1 Feb 42		Inf
ROETTIG, Otto (54)	Insp Gen for PW Affairs, OKW	1 Aug 43		Inf
ROMAN, Rudolf Frhr. v. (51)	XX Infantry Corps	1 Nov 42	Bavaria	Arty
ROQUES, Franz v. (67)	Rear Area, Army Group South	1 Jul 42		Inf
SACHS (58)		1 Oct 42		Pion
SCHAAL, Ferdinand (55)	Wkr. Böhmen u. Mähren	1 Oct 41	Baden	Tks
SCHALLER-KALIDE, Hubert (62)	Retired (Feb. 43)	1 Dec 40		Inf
SCHELLERT (57)	Wkr. IX	1 Jul 43		Inf
SCHMIDT, Hans (66)	IX Infantry Corps	1 Dec 42	Württemberg	Inf
SCHNECKENBURGER, Wilhelm (53)		1 May 43	Württemberg	Inf
SCHNIEWINDT, Rudolf (65)	Retired (Jun 42)	1 Sep 40		Inf

RESTRICTED

60. Army Generals.—Continued.
c. General der Infanterie, Kavallerie, etc. (*Lieutenant General*).—Continued.

Name (age)	Command or Appointment	Seniority	Origin	Arm
SCHÖRNER, Ferdinand (52)		1 Jun 42	Bavaria	Mtn
SCHROTH, Walther (62)	Wkr. XII	1 Feb 38		Inf
SCHUBERT, Albrecht (58)	Wkr. XVII	1 Jun 40	Silesia	Inf
SCHWANDNER, Maximilian (63)	Retired (?)	1 Dec 40	Bavaria	Inf
SCHWEDLER, Viktor v. (59)	Wkr. IV	1 Feb 38		Inf
SEYDLITZ - KURZBACH, Walter v. (56)	Prisoner of War (Feb 43)	1 Jun 42		Arty
SINNHUBER (57)	LXXXII Infantry Corps	1 Oct 43		Arty
SODENSTERN, Georg v. (55)	Nineteenth Army	1 Aug 40		Inf
SPONHEIMER, Otto (58)		1 Aug 43	Bavaria	Inf
STAPF, Otto (54)	Insp of Mil Economics Staff, East	1 Oct 42	Bavaria	Inf
STEMMERMANN, Wilhelm (54)		1 Dec 42	Baden	Arty
STEPPUHN, Albrecht (67)	Retired (May 43)	27 Aug 39		Inf
STRAUBE, Erich (57)		1 Jun 42	Silesia	Inf
STRECCIUS, Alfred (65)	Retired (Sep 43)	z.V.		Inf
STRECKER (58)	Prisoner of War (Feb 43)	1 Apr 42		Inf
STÜLPNAGEL, Heinrich v. (57)		1 Apr 39		Inf
STÜLPNAGEL, Joachim v.	Retired (?)	z.V.		Inf
STÜLPNAGEL, Otto v. (65)	C G Occupied France	1 Jan 32		Inf
THEISEN, Edgar (55)	LXI Reserve Corps	1 Oct 42		Arty
THOMA, Wilhelm Ritter v. (53)	Prisoner of War (Nov 42)	1 Nov 42	Bavaria	Tks
THOMAS, Georg (54)	Mil Economics & Armaments Office, OKW	1 Aug 40		Inf
TIPPELSKIRCH, Kurt v. (53)		27 Aug 42		Inf
TITTEL, Hermann (55)	LXX Corps Command	1 Sep 43		Arty
TOUSSAINT, Rudolf (53)		1 Sep 43	Bavaria	Inf

RESTRICTED

60. Army Generals.—Continued.
c. General der Infanterie, Kavallerie, etc. (*Lieutenant General*).— Continued.

Name (age)	Command or Appointment	Seniority	Origin	Arm.
ULEX, Wilhelm (64)	Retired (1942)	1 Oct 36		Arty
UNRUH, Walter v. (67)	Chief of Special Duties Staff, OKW, (Total Mobilization)	1 Jul 42		Inf
VAERST, Gustav v. (51)	Prisoner of War (May 43)	1 Mar 43	Hesse	Cav
VEIEL, Rudolf (61)	Wkr. V	1 Apr 42	Württemberg	Tks
VIEBAHN, Max v. (56)	Retired (Sep 42)	1 Mar 41		Inf
VIEROW, Erwin (54)	In France	1 Jan 41		Inf
VÖLCKERS, Paul (53)	LV Corps (?)	1 Sep 43		Inf
VOGL, Oskar (63)	Head of Armistice Commission		Bavaria	Arty
VOLLARD-BOCKELBERG v. (70)	Retired (1942)	1 Oct 33		Arty
WACHENFELD, Edmund (66)	Retired (Mar 43)			Arty
WÄGER, Alfred (61)	Retired (?)	1 Nov 38	Bavaria	Inf
WAGNER, Eduard (50)		1 Aug 43	Bavaria	Arty
WANDEL, Max (54)	Prisoner of War (?)	1 Jan 43	Silesia	Arty
WEISENBERGER, Karl (54)	XXXVI Mountain Corps	1 Apr 41	Bavaria	Inf
WETZEL, Wilhelm (56)	LXIV Reserve Corps	1 Mar 42		Inf
WEYER, Peter (65)	Retired	1 Dec 40		Arty
WIESE, Friedrich (52)		1 Oct 43		Inf
WIETERSHEIM, Gustav v. (60)	Retired (?)	1 Feb 38		Inf
WIKTORIN, Mauriz (61)	Wkr. XIII	1 Nov 40	Austria	Inf
WITTHÖFT (57)	Army Rear Area, Northern Italy	1 Mar 42	Thuringia	Inf
WODRIG, Albert (61)	Wkr. I	1 Oct 39		Arty
WÖHLER, Otto (50)	Eighth Army	1 Jun 43		Inf
WÖLLWARTH, Erich (72)	Retired (Jun 42)	1 Sep 40	Württemberg	Inf
ZANGEN, Gustav v. (52)		1 Jun 43		Inf

RESTRICTED

ORDER OF BATTLE OF THE GERMAN ARMY 439

60. Army Generals.—Continued.
d. Generalleutnant (Major General).

Name (age)	Command or Appointment	Seniority	Origin	Arm
ADAM, Wilhelm (67)	Insp of Transport Troops	z.V		H-DrT
ADOLPH-AUFFENBERG-KOMAROW, Gustav	285th Sicherungs Division	1 Sep 43	Austria	Inf
AGRICOLA, Kurt (54)	An Army Rear Area (1942)	z.V	Saxony	Inf
ALDRIAN, Eduard		1 Jun 43	Austria	Arty
ALTRICHTER, Dr. Friedrich (53)	154th Reserve Division	1 Apr 43		Inf
ALTROCK, Wilhelm v. (55)	O F K Lublin (?)	1 Apr 43	Saxony	Inf
AMANN v. (63)	Retired (Jun 42)			Inf
ANDREAS (59)		1 Apr 41		Inf
ANGERN, Günther (51)		1 Dec 42		Cav
ANSAT, Johann (52)		1 Aug 42		Arty
APELL v. (58)		1 Jun 38		Inf
APELL, Wilhelm v. (51)		1 Apr 43		Inf
AULEB (57)	444th Sicherungs Division	1 Dec 40	Hesse	Inf
BADINSKI, Kurt (49)	269th Infantry Division	1 Mar 43		Inf
BAIER, Albrecht (50)		1 Jan 43		Arty
BALCK, Hermann (51)		1 Jan 43		Cav
BALTZER (57)		1 Oct 39		Inf
BAMLER, Rudolf (48)	C of S Twenty-first Army (Army of Norway)	1 Apr 43		Arty
BASSE, Hans v. (55)		1 Apr 42		Inf
BAYER (57)	181st Infantry Division	1 Oct 40		Inf
BECHTOLSHEIM, Anton Frhr. v. MAUCHENHEIM, gen. (50)	C of S First Army	1 June 43		Arty
BECKER, Fritz (52)	253d Infantry Division	1 Apr 43		Inf
BECKMANN, Alfred (67)		1 Oct 43		Inf

RESTRICTED

60. Army Generals.—Continued.
d. Generalleutnant (Major General).—Continued.

Name (age)	Command or Appointment	Seniority	Origin	Arm
BEEREN, v. (53)	280th Coast Defense Division	1 May 43		Inf
BEHR, v. (54)		1 Nov 42		Inf
BEHSCHNITT, Walter (59)		1 Sep 40	Silesia	Inf
BERG, Ludwig v. (62)	Insp. of Recruiting Area, Koblenz, Wkr. XII	1 Nov 40	Baden	Arty
BERGEN, Johann (53)	323d Infantry Division	1 Oct 43	Bavaria	Inf
BERLIN (54)		1 Mar 42	Baden	Arty
BERNARD, Kurt (57)		1 Oct 39	Silesia	Tks
BERNHARD, Friedrich Gustav (54		1 Aug 42		Sig C
BERTRAM, Georg (59)	Cmdt of Lille	1 Aug 39		Cav
BEUKEMANN, Helmuth (50)	An Infantry Division (?)	1 May 43		Inf
BEUTTEL (57)	O F K 365 (Lemberg)	1 Mar 41		Inf
BEYER, Dr. Franz (54)	44th Infantry Division	1 Jan 43		Inf
BIELFELD (55)	Cmdt of Posen, Wkr. XXI	1 Feb 42		Inf
BIESS, Paul (72)	Retired (Nov. 42)	1 Apr 42		Inf
BLOCK, Johannes (50)	294th Infantry Division	1 Jan 43		Inf
BLÜMM, Oskar (60)		1 Mar 40	Bavaria	Inf
BLUMENTRITT (51)	C of S, Army Group West	1 Dec 42	Thuringia	Inf
BOCK v. WÜLFINGEN, Ferdinand (61)	Insp of Recruiting Area Berlin, Wkr. III	1 Apr 38		Arty
BOECKH-BEHRENS, Hans (48)	C of S, Sixteenth Army	1 Sep 43		Inf
BOEGE, Ehrenfried (50)	197th Infantry Division	1 Jan 43	Silesia	Inf
BOEHM-BEZING, Diether v. (64)	Retired (?)	1 Apr 35		Cav
BOETTCHER, Hermann (58)	148th Reserve Division	1 Nov 39		Inf

RESTRICTED

ORDER OF BATTLE OF THE GERMAN ARMY 441

60. Army Generals.—Continued.
d. Generalleutnant (Major General).—Continued.

Name (age)	Command or Appointment	Seniotiry	Origin	Arm
BÖTTCHER, Karl (54)		1 Mar 42	Silesia	Arty
BOHNSTEDT, Wilhelm (54)		1 Apr 42		Inf
BOINEBURG-LENGSFELD, Wilhelm, Frhr. v. (55)	Cmdt of Gross-Paris	1 Dec 42		Cav
BOLTENSTERN, Walter v. (53)	Cmdt of Weimar, Wkr. IV	1 Aug 42		Inf
BOLTZE, Arthur (66)	Division Nummer 152		Saxony	Arty
BORDIHN (55)		1 Nov 42		Pion
BOROWIETZ, Willibald (51)	Prisoner of War (May 43)	1 May 43		Tks
BOTZHEIM, Erich Frhr. v. (73)	Retired		Bavaria	Arty
BOYSEN, Wolf (60)		1 Sep 42	Silesia	Inf
BRABÄNDER (53)		1 Jan 43		Inf
BRAND, Albrecht (56)	Cmdt Königsberg Fortifications	1 Oct 39	Silesia	Arty
BRAUNER, Josef	187th Reserve Division	1 Mar 41	Austria	Inf
BREITH, Friedrich (52)	Arty School I	1 Apr 43	Bavaria	Arty
BREMER (57)	Retired (?)	1 Oct 38		Arty
BRODOWSKI, Fritz v. (58)		1 Feb 41		Cav
BROICH, Friedrich Frhr. v. (48)	Prisoner of War (May 43)	1 May 43		Tks
BÜCHS (58)	Admin Post in Wkr. VI	1 Oct 39	Württemberg	Inf?
BÜLOWIUS, Karl (53)	Prisoner of War (May 43)	1 Apr 43		Pion
BÜNAU, Rudolf v. (54)	73d Infantry Division	1 Sep 42	Württemberg	Inf
BUHLE (50)	Army General Staff (Org. Abt.)	1 Apr 42	Württemberg	Inf
BURCKHARDT (53)	C Sig O, Wkr. VI (?)	1 Mar 42		Sig C
BURDACH, Karl (50)	11th Infantry Division	1 Nov 42	Saxony	Arty
BUSCHENHAGEN, Erich (52)	15th Infantry Division	1 May 43		Inf

RESTRICTED

60. Army Generals.—Continued.
d. Generalleutnant (Major General).—Continued.

Name (age)	Command or Appointment	Seniority	Origin	Arm
BUSCHMANN (55)		1 Nov 41		Arty
BUSSE, Theodor (48)	C of S, Army Group South	1 Sep 43		Inf
BUTZE (53)	340th Infantry Division	1 Jan. 43		Inf
CANTZLER, Oskar (54)	Chief Engineer, Army Group South	1 Aug 42	Bavaria	Pion
CARP, Georg (57)	Insp of Recruiting Area Kattowitz, Wkr. VIII (1941)	1 Jun 41	Hesse	Arty
CASPER (51)	335th Infantry Division	1 Jul 43		Inf
CHEVALLERIE, Helmuth v. d. (48)		1 May 43		Cav
CHILL, Kurt (49)	122d Infantry Division	1 Jun 43		Inf
CHOLTITZ, Dietrich v. (50)		1 Feb 43		Inf
COURBIÈRE, René de l'HOMME de (57)	153d Reserve Division	1 Jun 40		Inf
CURTZE, Heinrich (68)	Retired (Jun 42)			Arty
DANHAUSER, Paul (51)	256th Infantry Division	1 Mar 43	Bavaria	Inf
DANIELS, Alexander Edler v. (53)	Prisoner of War (Feb 43)	1 Dec 42		Inf
DEBOI, Heinrich (51)	Prisoner of War (Feb 43)	1 Dec 42		Inf
DEHMEL (56)		1 Jun 41	Silesia	Pion
DEMOLL (62)		1 Jun 43		Arty
DENECKE, Erich (52)	LXIX Reserve Corps	1 Dec 39	Saxony	Inf
DENNERLEIN, Max (59)		1 Mar 40	Bavaria	Pion
DETMERING (57)	Insp. of Recruiting Area Frankfurt/Main, Wkr. IX (1939)	1 Jun 41	Bavaria	Inf
DETTLING (53)	183d Infantry Division	1 Jan 43	Württemberg	Inf
DIESTEL, Erich	75th Infantry Division	1 Aug 43		Inf

RESTRICTED

ORDER OF BATTLE OF THE GERMAN ARMY 443

60. Army Generals.—Continued.
d. Generalleutnant (Major General).—Continued.

Name (age)	Command or Appointment	Seniority	Origin	Arm
DIGEON v. MONTETON, Baron Albrecht (52)	391st Field Training Division	1 Jun 43		Cav
DIHM, Friedrich (64)		1 Oct 42	Bavaria	Arty
DIPPOLD, Benignus (55)		1 Oct 41	Bavaria	Inf
DIRINGSHOFEN, v	Division Nummer 401	1 Mar 43		Cav
DITFURTH, v	Retired (Jul 42)			Inf
DITTMAR, Kurt (54)	Public Relations, OKH	1 Apr 42		Pion
DOEHLA, Heinrich (63)	A Brigade		Bavaria	Inf
DRABICH-WAECHTER, Viktor v. (53)	326th Infantry Division	1 Aug 42		Inf
DROGAND (61)	Inspector of Welfare, OKW	1 Jul 41		Inf
DÜMLEIN, Friedrich (65)	Retired (Jun 42)			Inf
DÜVERT, Walther (52)		1 Jan 43	Saxony	Arty
EBERHARDT (51)	38th Infantry Division	1 Feb 41		Cav
EBERLE, René (53)	Chief Engr, S. France	1 Sep 43	Austria	Pion
ECKSTEIN (54)		1 Jun 42		Pion
EDELMANN, Karl (52)	Head of a Section, OKH (AHA/AgE Tr)	1 Oct 43	Saxony	Inf
EGLSEER, Karl	114th Light Division	1 Feb 43	Austria	Mtn
ELFELDT, Otto		1 Jul 43		Arty
ENDRES, Theodor (68)	Retired (?)	3 Sep 31	Bavaria	Arty
ERDMANNSDORFF, Werner v. (53)		1 Jan 43	Saxony	Inf
ESEBECK, Hans-Karl Frhr. v. (52)		1 Dec 42		Cav
FABER du FAUR, Moritz v. (58)	Cmdt of Innsbruck Wkr. XVIII (?)	1 Apr 39	Württemberg	Cav
FAECKENSTEDT, Ernst Felix (48)		1 Sep 43		Cav
FAULENBACH (52)	356th Infantry Division	1 Jan 43		Inf

RESTRICTED

60. Army Generals.—Continued.
d. Generalleutnant (*Major General*).—Continued.

Name (age)	Command or Appointment	Seniority	Origin	Arm
FELDT, Kurt (55)	Mil District, NW France (?)	1 Feb 42	----------	Inf
FETT, Albert (70)	Retired (?)	z.V.	----------	Cav
FICHTNER, Sebastian	----------	1 Aug 43	----------	Tks
FISCHER, Herbert (62)	Supply Officer, Marseilles	1 Jan 36	Württemberg.	Inf
FISCHER, Hermann (50)	----------	1 Apr 43	Thuringia	Inf
FISCHER, Kurt (67)	412th z.b.V. Division	----------	----------	Inf
FOERTSCH, Hermann (49)	C of S, Army Group F	1 Jan 43	----------	Inf
FOLTTMANN (55)	338th Infantry Division	1 Feb 41	Silesia	Inf
FORST, Werner (52)	106th Infantry Division	1 Jan 43	----------	Arty
FORTNER, Johann (60)	----------	1 Nov 42	Bavaria	Inf
FRANEK, Dr. Friedrich (53)	196th Infantry Division	1 Apr 43	Austria	Inf
FRANKE, Hermann (66)	Retired (Jun 42)	----------	----------	Inf
FRANKEWITZ	215th Infantry Division	1 Jul 43	----------	Arty
FREMEREY, Max (54)	Cmdt of Hannover, Wkr. XI	1 Jun 43	----------	Cav
FRIEBE, Helmuth	----------	1 Sep 43	----------	Inf
FRIEDRICH, Rudolf (53)	----------	1 Apr 42	Saxony	Arty
FÜCHTBAUER, Heinrich Ritter v. (64)	Mil District, NE France (?)	z.V.	Bavaria	Inf
FÜRST, Friedrich (54)	171st Reserve Division	1 Oct 42	Bavaria	Inf
FUNCK, Hans Frhr. v. (53)	----------	1 Sep 42	----------	Cav
GABLENZ, Eccard, Frhr. v. (53)	In Dresden	1 Aug 40	----------	Inf
GAREIS, Martin (53)	98th Infantry Division	1 Jan 43	----------	Inf
GAUSE, Alfred (50)	C of S to ROMMEL	1 Apr 43	----------	Pion
GENTHE, Friedrich (71)	A PW Camp	z.V.	Saxony	Cav
GERHARDT, Paul (63)	Retired (?)	1 Feb 41	----------	Inf

RESTRICTED

ORDER OF BATTLE OF THE GERMAN ARMY 445

60. Army Generals.—Continued.
d. Generalleutnant (Major General).—Continued.

Name (age)	Command or Appointment	Seniority	Origin	Arm
GERKE, Ernst (54)		1 Jan 43	Saxony	Sig C
GILBERT, Martin (55)		1 Jan 42	Saxony	Inf
GILSA, Werner Frhr. v. u. zu (55)		1 Oct 42		Inf
GIMBORN, Hermann v. (64)	Retired (?)			Inf
GIMMLER (54)	216th Infantry Division	1 Apr 43		Sig C
GINKEL, Oskar van (62)	Insp. of Recruiting Area München, Wkr. VII		Bavaria	Arty
GLAISE-HORSTENAU, Dr. h. c. Edmund v. (62)	Mil Plenipotentiary in Croatia	1 Aug 42	Austria	
GOERITZ, Werner (52)	291st Infantry Division	1 Jan 43	Baden	Inf
GOESCHEN (55)		1 Aug 43	Bavaria	Cav
GOETTKE (59)		1 Nov 41	Silesia	Arty
GOLLWITZER, Friedrich (55)	88th Infantry Division	1 Oct 41	Bavaria	Inf
GRÄSER, Fritz Hubert (56)	3d Panzer Grenadier Division	1 Mar 43		Inf
GRAF, Karl (61)	Division Nummer 467 (?)	1 Feb 41	Bavaria	Inf
GRAFFEN, Karl v. (51)	An Infantry Division	1 Jan 43		Arty
GRASE, Martin (53)	1st Infantry Division	1 Jan 43		Inf
GRASSER, Anton (53)	25th Panzer Grenadier Division	1 Jan 43		Inf
GREIFFENBERG, Hans v. (51)	Military Attache, Budapest	1 Mar 42		Inf
GREINER, Heinz (49)	268th Infantry Division	1 Jan 43	Bavaria	Inf
GRIMMEISS	Liaison with Air Force	1 Apr 43		Arty
GROPPE, Theodor (61)	Retired (?)	1 Nov 39		Arty
GROSCHUPF (62)		1 Jul 42		Arty
GROSSMANN, Horst (53)	6th Infantry Division	1 Jan 43		Inf
GROTE, Waldemar Frhr. (67)	In OKW (?)	1 Nov 39		Cav

RESTRICTED

60. Army Generals.—Continued.
d. Generalleutnant (Major General).—Continued.

Name (age)	Command or Appointment	Seniority	Origin	Arm
GÜMBEL, Karl (56)		1 Jan 43		Inf
GULLMANN, Otto (54)		1 Jan 43	Bavaria	Arty
GUNZELMANN, Emil (57)	Insp of Recruiting Area Graz, Wkr. XVIII (1939)	1 Oct 41	Bavaria	Inf
HAARDE (55)		1 Oct 41		Tks
HAASE, Conrad (56)		1 Jan 42	Saxony	Inf
HABENICHT (53)		1 Jun 43	Hesse	Inf
HAECKEL, Ernst (54)	158th Reserve Division	1 Oct 42	Bavaria	Inf
HAHM, Walter (50)		1 Jan 43	Silesia	Inf
HAMMER, Ernst (Karl) (60)	A Division	1 Nov 40	Hesse	Inf
HAMMERSTEIN-EQUORD, Günther Frhr. v. (67)	O F K 672 (Brussels)			Inf
HARTENECK, Gustav	C of S, Second Army	1 Apr 43		Cav
HARTLIEB gen. WALSPORN, Maximilian v. (61)		1 Apr 39	Württemberg	Tks
HARTMANN, Walter (53)	An Infantry Division	1 Feb 43	Saxony	Arty
HASE, Paul v. (59)	Cmdt of Berlin, Wkr. III	1 Jun 40		Inf
HASSE, Ulrich (49)		1 Jan 43		Inf
HAUFFE, Arthur (52)		1 Jan 43		Inf
HEBERLEIN, Hans (56)	Training Area Grafenwöhr, Wkr. XIII	1 Jun 41	Bavaria	Inf
HEIM, Ferdinand (49)		1 Nov 42		Arty
HEINEMANN, Erich (63)				Arty
HEINRICHS (52)	290th Infantry Division	1 Feb 43		Inf
HEINZ, v. (57)		3 Dec 42		Inf
HELD, Karl (66)	Retired (?)	z.V.		Inf
HELLMICH, Heinz (52)	Gen of Eastern Troops (Osttruppen)	1 Sep 41		Inf

RESTRICTED

60. Army Generals.—Continued.
d. Generalleutnant (Major General).—Continued.

Name (age)	Command or Appointment	Seniority	Origin	Arm
HEMMERICH, Gerlach (62)	Topographical Section, OKH	1 Dec 41		Inf
HENGEN, Fritz (57)	Insp of Recruiting Area Chemnitz, Wkr. IV (1940)	1 Feb 41	Bavaria	Arty
HENGL, Ritter v	XIX Mountain Corps	1 Jan 43	Bavaria	Mtn
HENRICI, Dr. Waldemar (66)		z.V		
HERRGOTT, Adolf (72)	PW Camps in Wkr. V	z.V		
HERRLEIN, Friedrich (54)	Inf Gen at OKH	1 Sep 42		Inf
HEUNERT (56)	Staff of Twentieth Army	1 Oct 40		Cav
HEUSINGER (49)	In OKH	1 Jan 43		Inf
HINDENBURG u. BENECKENDORF, Oscar v. (61)	PW Camps in Wkr. I	z.V		Cav
HINGHOFER, Dr. Walter		1 Jul 41	Austria	Inf
HITTER, Alfons	206th Infantry Division	1 Mar 43		Arty
HOCHBAUM, Friedrich (50)	26th Infantry Division	1 Jul 43		Inf
HÖBERTH, Eugen v			Austria	Cav
HÖCKER, Erich (61)	719th Infantry Division	1 Jan 43		Inf
HÖCKER, Hans-Kurt (50)	258th Infantry Division	1 Nov 42		Inf
HÖFL, Hugo (66)	Retired (Apr 43)	1 Jul 41	Bavaria	Inf
HOEGNER, Hermann (59)	1st Ordnance Group (1941)	1 Feb 41		H-DrT
HOERNLEIN, Walter (51)	Grossdeutschland Division	1 Jan 43		Inf
HÖSSLIN, Wilhelm v. (66)	188th Reserve Division		Bavaria	Inf
HOFFMANN, Kurt (53)	715th Infantry Division	1 Jul 43		Inf
HOFMANN, Erich		1 Sep 43	Austria	Inf
HOFMANN, Rudolf (48)		1 Apr 43	Bavaria	Inf

RESTRICTED

60. Army Generals.—Continued.
d. Generalleutnant (Major General).—Continued.

Name (age)	Command or Appointment	Seniority	Origin	Arm
HOPFF, Hermann (68)	Retired (?)			Pion
HOPPE, Arthur (49)	126th Infantry Division	1 Jun 43		Inf
HORN, Max (56)	214th Infantry Division	1 Oct 41	Saxony	Inf
HOSSBACH, Friedrich (50)	XLVI Panzer Corps.	1 Mar 43	Hesse	Inf
HÜHNER, Werner (52)	An Infantry Division.	1 Jan 43		Inf
HÜTTMANN (64)	Retired (Jun 42)			Inf
HUFFMANN (53)	An Infantry Division.	1 Aug 43		Arty
JACOBI, Alfred (58)	201st Sicherungs Division	1 Mar 43		Inf
JAGOW, v.	Retired (Jul 42)			Cav
JAHN (52)		1 Nov 40		Arty
JODL, Ferdinand		1 Sep 43		Arty
JOHN, Dipl. Ing. Friedrich-Wilhelm.	CG Latvia	1 May 43		Inf
JUPPE, Hans (52)		1 Aug 42		Sig C
KANNENGIESSER	411th z.b.V. Division (?)			Inf
KARL, Franz (56)		1 Mar 41	Bavaria	Inf
KARST, Friedrich (51)		1 Apr 43		Inf
KASPAR, Johann (70)	C of S, Wkr. VII	1 Aug 42		Cav
KAUFFMANN (53)		1 Apr 41		Inf
KEMPSKI, Hans v. (59)		1 Feb 41		Inf
KERN, Emil (52)	Chief Engineer 4th Army (1941)	1 Oct 41	Austria	Pion
KERSTEN	C Sig O, South France (?)	1 Oct 42	Saxony	Sig C
KESSEL, Hans (53)		1 Nov 42		Inf
KIEFFER, Friedrich Ritter v. (63)	Cmdt of Munich, Wkr. VII	1 Jun 42	Bavaria	Inf
KIESLING auf KIESLINGSTEIN, Bruno Edler v. (65)	Insp of Recruiting Area, Regensburg, Wkr. XIII (1939)	1 Nov 41	Bavaria	Inf

RESTRICTED

ORDER OF BATTLE OF THE GERMAN ARMY 449

60. Army Generals.—Continued.
d. Generalleutnant (Major General).—Continued.

Name (age)	Command or Appointment	Seniority	Origin	Arm
KINZEL, Eberhardt (47)	C of S, Army Group North	1 Sep 43		Inf
KIRCHHEIM, Heinrich (62)		1 Jul 42	Saxony	Inf
KLEEMANN, Ulrich (Werner) (52)	Assault Division Rhodes	1 May 43	Baden	Cav
KLEIST, v. (57)	O F K 225 (Warsaw)	1 Apr 41		Cav
KLINGBEIL, Erich (63)	Insp of Army Constr Units (1941)	z.V		Pion
KLUGE, Wolfgang v. (52)	An Infantry Division	1 Apr 43		Arty
KLUTMANN (64)	Retired (1942)	1 Apr 42		Cav
KNESEBECK, v. dem (67)	Insp of Recruiting Area Münster, Wkr. VI (1940)	1 Feb 41		Inf
KOBUS		1 Jul 42		Inf
KOCH, Hellmuth (63)		1 Nov 42		Inf
KÖCHLING, Friedrich (51)		1 Jan 43		Inf
KOEHLER, Carl-Erich (50)	In OKH	1 Jun 43		Cav
KÖRNER, Willy (67)	Insp of Recruiting Area Mannheim, Wkr. XII	1 Nov 39	Saxony	Inf
KOHL, Otto (56)	Army Transport, France	1 Sep 41		Inf
KOHLERMANN, Otto	60th Panzer Grenadier Division	1 Jul 43		M T
KOREUBER (54)		1 Jan 43		Tks
KRAISS, Dietrich (55)	A Silesian Infantry Division	1 Oct 42	Württemberg	Inf
KRAKAU, August (50)	7th Mountain Division	1 Jun 43	Bavaria	Inf
KRAMPF, Heinrich (56)	304th Infantry Division	1 Dec 41	Bavaria	Inf
KRAPPE, Günther (51)	61st Infantry Division	1 Dec 43 (?)		Cav
KRATZERT, Hans (61)	303d Higher Arty Comd (1941)	1 Jan 38	Saxony	Arty
KRAUSE, Walther (53)	A North German Infantry Division	1 Sep 43	Silesia	Inf

RESTRICTED

60. Army Generals.—Continued.
d. Generalleutnant (Major General).—Continued.

Name (age)	Command or Appointment	Seniotiry	Origin	Arm
KREBS	C of S, Ninth Army	1 Apr 43		Inf
KRENZKI, Kurt v. (57)		z.V.		Inf
KREYSING, Hans (54)		1 Jul 42	Oldenburg	Inf
KRISCHER, Friedrich (53)		1 Dec 41	Austria	Arty
KRÜGER, Eugen (Walter) (54)	1st Panzer Division	1 Oct 42	Saxony	Cav
KUBENA, Johann (62)			Austria	Arty
KUCKEIN	Retired (Jul 42)			Pion
KÜHLENTHAL, Erich (64)	Retired	1 Oct 33		Arty
KÜHLWEIN (51)		1 Jan 43		Inf
KÜHNE, Fritz (61)		1 Apr 36	Silesia	Inf
KULLMER, Artur (48)	296th Infantry Division	1 Sep 43	Hesse	Inf
KUROWSKI, Eberhard v. (48)	An Infantry Division	1 Jun 43		Inf
KURZ	Insp of Recruiting Area Danzig, Wkr. XX (1941)	1 Mar 43		Inf
LAHODE, Kurt (55)		1 Jul 42	Saxony	Inf
LANDGRAF, Franz (56)		1 Sep 42	Bavaria	Tks
LANG, Viktor (52)		1 Jan 43		Inf
LASCH (51)		1 Apr 43		Inf
LECHNER, Adolf (60)	112th Artillery Command (1941)	1 Mar 42	Bavaria	Arty
LEHMANN, Joseph (56)	O F K 398 (?)	1 Jun 41	Bavaria	Inf
LEISTER (56)		1 Jan 41		CWS
LEISTNER, v	Retired (Jun 42)			Inf
LENDLE (52)	221st Sicherungs Division	1 Jun 43	Württemberg	Tks
LENSKI, Arno v. (51)	Prisoner of War (Feb 43)	1 Jan 43		Tks
LEYEN, Ludwig v. der (58)		1 Jun 38		Inf
LEYKAUF, Hans (59)	Insp of Armaments, Wkr. VIII	1 Feb 41	Saxony	Inf

RESTRICTED

ORDER OF BATTLE OF THE GERMAN ARMY 451

60. Army Generals.—Continued.

d. Generalleutnant (Major General).—Continued.

Name (age)	Command or Appointment	Seniority	Origin	Arm
LIEB (54)		1 Jun 43	Württemberg	Inf
LIEBER, Hans (62)	Head of Army Archives, Prague	z.V		Arty
LINDEMANN, Fritz (52)		1 Jan 43		Arty
LINDIG, Max (54)	Head of a Section, OKH(H.Abn.Abt)	1 Dec 42		Arty
LINN, Philip	Insp of Technical Troops	1 Jan 42		Inf
LOEPER, v. (56)		1 Sep 40		Inf
LOHMANN, Hans (62)	Insp of Armaments, Wkr. XII	1 Feb 41		Arty
LUCHT, Walter (62)	336th Infantry Division	1 Nov 42		Arty
LÜBBE, Vollrath (50)	2d Panzer Division	1 Apr 43		Inf
LÜDECKE, Otto (50)	56th Infantry Division	1 Oct 43		Pion
LÜTTWITZ, Heinrich Frhr. v. (48)	20th Panzer Division	1 Jun 43		Tks
LÜTTWITZ, Smilo Frhr. v. (49)	26th Panzer Division	1 Oct 42		Tks
LÜTZOW, Kurt-Jürgen Frhr. v. (52)	12th Infantry Division	1 Jan 43		Inf
LUNGERSHAUSEN, Carl Hans (48)	90th Panzer Grenadier Division	1 Sep 43		Cav
MACHOLZ (54)	An Infantry Division	1 Jun 42		Inf
MADERHOLZ, Karl (59)	410th z.b.V. Division (?)	1 Oct 41	Bavaria	Inf
MAJEWSKI, v. (54)		1 Dec 42		Pion
MANTELL (63)		1 Oct 42		Arty
MATTERSTOCK, Otto (55)	147th Reserve Division	1 Nov 42	Bavaria	Inf
MATZKY, Gerhard (51)		1 Apr 43		Inf
MAYER, Dr. Dr.-Ing., Johannes (49)	An Infantry Division	1 Feb 43		Inf
MEDEM (52)	Chemical Warfare, Army Group Center	1 Sep 43		Pion
MEHNERT, Karl (56)	Cmdt of Dresden, Wkr. IV	1 Nov 41	Saxony	Sig C

RESTRICTED

60. Army Generals.—Continued.
d. Generalleutnant (Major General).—Continued.

Name (age)	Command or Appointment	Seniority	Origin	Arm
MEISE, Dr. Wilhelm (53)		1 Sep 42	Bavaria	Pion
MEISSNER, Robert (56)		1 Oct 42	Austria	Inf
MELZER, Karl		1 Aug 43		Arty
MENGE, v		1 Jan 43		
MERKER, Ludwig (50)	35th Infantry Division	1 Nov 43 (?)		Inf
MEYER-BUERDORF, Heinrich (56)	131st Infantry Division	1 Sep 41		Arty
MEYER-RABINGEN, Hermann (55)	159th Reserve Division	1 Nov 41		Inf
MIKULICZ, Adalbert		1 Mar 43	Austria	Inf
MITTELBERGER, Hilmer Ritter v. (66)	Retired (?)	1 Jan 32	Bavaria	Inf
MITTERMAIER, Wilhelm (54)		1 Dec 42		Inf
MOLO, Louis Ritter v. (63)	Cmdt of Stuttgart, Wkr. V	1 Jul 42	Württemberg	Inf
MOYSES, Karl (60)	Insp of Recruiting Area Köslin, Wkr. II (1939)	1 Feb 41	Austria	Pion
MÜHLMANN, Max (55)		1 Sep 41	Saxony	Arty
MÜLLER, Erich (55)	319th Infantry Division	1 Jun 42		Cav
MÜLLER, Ferdinand (62)	In Munich	z.D.		Pion
MÜLLER, Friedrich Wilhelm (47)	22d Panzer Grenadier Division	1 Apr 43		Inf
MÜLLER, Hermann	Retired (May 42)			
MÜLLER, Ludwig	Retired (Jun 42)			
MÜLLER, Ludwig (52)	97th Light Division	1 Jul 43		Inf
MÜLLER, Vincenz (49)		1 Mar 43	Württemberg	Pion
MÜLLER-GEBHARD, Alfred (55)		1 Jan 42	Saxony	Inf
MUNDT, Dr. habil		1 Sep 40		Inf
NAKE, Albin	Division Nummer 526	1 Jul 43	Austria	Inf
NAUMANN (54)		1 Mar 42		Tks

RESTRICTED

60. Army Generals.—Continued.
d. Generalleutnant (*Major General*).—Continued.

Name (age)	Command or Appointment	Seniority	Origin	Arm
NEUBRONN v. EISENBURG, Alexander Frhr. (67)	Army Repr at Vichy	1 Dec 42		Inf
NEUMANN, Friedrich-Wilhelm (64)	712th Infantry Division	1 Feb 42		Inf
NEUMANN-NEURODE, Karl (64)		z.V	Silesia	Inf
NIEHOFF, Heinrich (61)	Mil Distr, South France	1 Feb 38		Inf
NOELDECHEN, Ferdinand (49)	An Infantry Division	1 May 43		Arty
NOLTE, Hans Erich (62)	Division Nummer 461	1 Oct 42		Cav
OBERHÄUSSER, Eugen (55)	C Sig O, Army Group Center	1 Nov 42	Bavaria	Sig C
OBERNITZ, Justin v. (60)		1 Jun 40		Cav
OCHSNER, Hermann (52)	Insp of C W at OKH	1 Jun 43	Bavaria	CWS
OESTERREICH, v. (63)	Rear Area, P W Camps	1 Jul 43		Inf
ONDARZA, Herbert v. (64)	305th Higher Arty Comd (1942)	1 Nov 42	Mecklenburg	Arty
OPPENLÄNDER, Kurt	O F K, Krakau (?)	1 Aug 43	Württemberg	Inf
ORIOLA, Graf v.	299th Infantry Division	1 Nov 43 (?)		Arty
ORTNER, Bruno	69th Infantry Division	1 Oct 42	Austria	Inf
OSTERROHT (63)	Retired (Jul 42)	1 Feb 41		Inf
PELLENGAHR, Richard (61)		1 Jun 40	Westphalia	Arty
PELTZ, Joachim (60)		1 Apr 41	Saxony	Inf
PERFALL, Gustav Frhr. v. (61)	Retired	1 Aug 39	Bavaria	Cav
PESCHEL		1 Jun 43		Inf
PETSCH (56)	710th Infantry Division	1 Nov 42		Inf
PFEIFFER, Dr. phil Georg (54)	65th Infantry Division	1 Jun 42		Arty
PFLAUM, Karl (54)	157th Reserve Division	1 Oct 43		Inf
PFLIEGER (54)	416th Infantry Division	1 Oct 42		Arty

RESTRICTED

60. Army Generals.—Continued.
d. Generalleutnant (Major General).—Continued.

Name (age)	Command or Appointment	Seniority	Origin	Arm
PFLUGBEIL, Johann (62)	388th Field Training Division (1942)	1 Oct 39	Saxony	Inf
PFLUGRADT, Kurt (54)	Cmdr Saloniki-Ägäis, Greece	1 Apr 42		Inf
PHILIPP, Christian	6th Mountain Division	1 Jan 43		Inf
PHILIPPS, Dipl. Ing		1 Oct 43	Saxony	Tks
PILZ		1 Feb 42		Inf
PINCKVOSS (58)	Insp of Recruiting Area Kassel, Wkr. IX (1939)	1 Feb 41		Inf
PLOTHO, Wolfgang Edler Herr u. Frhr. v. (65)				Inf
POETTER, Adolf (60)				Inf
POPPE (51)	217th Infantry Division	1 Jan 43	Thuringia	Inf
POSTEL, Georg (48)	320th Infantry Division	1 Dec 43(?)		Arty
PRAETORIUS, Robert (62)	Insp of Recruiting Area Dresden, Wkr. IV	1 Feb 38	Silesia	Arty
PRAGER, Karl (56)	An Admin Post in Wkr. IX	1 Feb 42	Bavaria	Arty
PRAUN, Albert (50)	129th Infantry Division	1 Feb 43	Franconia	Sig C
PRIESS	21st Infantry Division	1 Jul 43		Inf
PRONDZYNSKI, v. (63)	Insp of Recruiting Area, Prague	1 Apr 42		Arty
PÜCHLER	257th Infantry Division	1 Apr 43		Inf
PUTTKAMER, Alfred v. (59)	Retired (?)	1 Aug 39		M T
RAITHEL (49)		1 May 43	Bavaria	Arty
RAPPARD, Fritz v	7th Infantry Division	1 May 43		Inf
RATHKE (55)		1 Oct 42		Arty
RAUCH, Erwin (55)	123d Infantry Division	1 Nov 42		Inf

RESTRICTED

ORDER OF BATTLE OF THE GERMAN ARMY 455

60. Army Generals.—Continued.
d. Generalleutnant (Major General).—Continued.

Name (age)	Command or Appointment	Seniotiry	Origin	Arm
RAVENSTEIN, Johann v. (55)	Prisoner of War (1941)	1 Oct 43		Inf
RECKE, Heinrich (54)	161st Infantry Division	1 Jun 42		Inf
RECKNAGEL, Hermann (52)	111th Infantry Division	1 Mar 43	Hesse	Inf
REICHE, v. (59)		1 Apr 38		Cav
REICHERT, Josef (53)		1 Sep 43	Bavaria	Inf
RENZ, Maximilian (60)		31 Oct 38	Bavaria	Cav
REYMANN, Helmuth		1 Apr 43		Inf
RICHERT (52)	286th Sicherungs Division	1 Mar 43		Inf
RICHTER (55)		1 Oct 39	Baden	Inf
RICHTER, Werner (51)		1 Mar 43	Saxony	Inf
RIEBESAM, Ludwig (56)	Insp of Recruiting Area, Linz, Wkr. XVII (1939)	1 Jun 41	Austria	Inf
RINGEL, Julius (55)	5th Mountain Division	1 Dec 42	Austria	Mtn
RISSE, Walter		1 Jun 43		Inf
RODENBURG, Karl (50)	Prisoner of War (Feb 43)	1 Dec 42	Baden	Inf
ROEDER v. DIERSBURG, Kurt Frhr. (58)	Insp of Recruiting Area Köln, Wkr. VI	1 Feb 41	Baden	Arty
RÖHRICHT		1 Apr 43		Inf
RÖTTIGER	C of S, Fourth Panzer Army	1 Sep 43		Tks
ROHDE, Hans (51)	M A, Ankara	1 Jan 43		Inf
ROSENBUSCH (54)	Chief Engr, Army of Norway (1941)	1 Apr 42	Silesia	Pion
ROSSI, Franz	Units in N. Finland	1 Sep 43		Arty
ROSSUM (54)		1 Dec 42		Inf
ROTBERG, Frhr. v. (68)	Retired (Jun 42)	1 Jan 42(?)		Inf
ROTHKIRCH u. PANTHEN, Friedrich Wilhelm v. (60)		1 Aug 40	Hesse	Cav

RESTRICTED

60. Army Generals.—Continued.
d. Generalleutnant (Major General).—Continued.

Name (age)	Command or Appointment	Seniority	Origin	Arm
ROTHKIRCH u. TRACH, Edwin Graf v. (56)		1 Mar 42		Cav
RÜDIGER, Dr. Ing.		1 Jun 43		Arty
RÜHLE v. LILIENSTERN, Alexander (63)	Insp of Recruiting Area Königsberg, Wkr. I (1939)	1 Feb 41		Inf
RUPPRECHT, Wilhelm (54)		1 Nov 42	Bavaria	Inf
RUSSWURM, Josef (56)	Insp of Sig Tr in Repl Tng Army	1 Sep 40	Württemberg	Sig C
RUSSWURM, Wilhelm (56)	265th Infantry Division	1 Sep 40	Württemberg	Sig C
SANDER, Erwin (52)	170th Infantry Division	1 Jan 43		Arty
SANNE (54)	Prisoner of War (Feb 43)	1 Apr 42	Hesse	Inf
SATOW (56)	Insp of Recruiting Area Frankfurt/Oder, Wkr. III (1940)	1 Nov 41	Baden	Cav
SAUCKEN, Dietrich v. (52)	4th Panzer Division	1 Apr 43		Tks
SAUER, Otto Ritter v. (68)	Retired (Aug 42)		Bavaria	Inf
SCHACKY auf SCHÖNFELD, Sigmund Frhr. v. (58)	165th Reserve Division	1 Aug 41	Bavaria	Inf
SCHAEFER, Hans (52)	Cmdt of Kassel, Wkr. IX	1 Jan 43		Inf
SCHAEWEN, Dr. v. (57)		1 Feb 41		Pion
SCHARTOW (53)	429th z.b.V. Division	1 Mar 43		Inf
SCHAUM (53)		1 Oct 43		Pion
SCHAUMBURG, Ernst (64)		1 Feb 38		Inf
SCHAUROTH, Athos v. (58)	Insp of Recruiting Area Breslau, Wkr. VIII (1941)	1 Apr 38		Inf
SCHEDE, Wolfgang (56)		1 Jul 40	Baden	Inf
SCHEELE, Hans Karl v. (52)	An Infantry Corps	1 Jan 43		Inf
SCHELL, Adolf v. (50)	25th Panzer Division	1 Apr 42		M T
SCHELLBACH, Oskar (66)	Retired (May 42)			Arty

RESTRICTED

60. Army Generals.—Continued.
d. Generalleutnant (*Major General*).—Continued.

Name (age)	Command or Appointment	Seniority	Origin	Arm
SCHELLER, Walther (52)	9th Panzer Division	1 Jan 43	Hesse	Inf
SCHERBENING (53)	79th Infantry Division	1 Sep 43		Inf
SCHERER, Theodor (55)	83d Infantry Division	1 Nov 42	Bavaria	Inf
SCHIMPF (55)		1 Dec 40	Württemberg	Pion
SCHINDLER, Maximilian (62)	Insp of Armaments, Govt Gen	1 Feb 34	Bavaria	Inf
SCHIRMER, Georg (54)		1 Jan 43		Inf
SCHLEINITZ, Siegmund Frhr. v. (54)	9th Infantry Division	1 Sep 42		Inf
SCHLEMMER, Ernst (55)	Mountain Troops, Innsbruck (?)	1 Dec 42	Bavaria	Mtn
SCHLEMMER, Dipl. Ing. Hans (51)	134th Infantry Division	1 Jan 43	Bavaria	Arty
SCHLENTHER, Eugen (67)		1 Mar 38		Inf
SCHLIEPER (53)	Mil Mission to Slovakia	1 Nov 41		Arty
SCHLÖMER, Helmuth (51)	Prisoner of War (Feb 43)	1 Dec 42		Inf
SCHMETZER, Rudolf (59)	Insp of Fortifications in the West	1 Feb 41	Bavaria	Pion
SCHMID-DANKWARD, Walter (57)		1 Dec 40	Thuringia	Arty
SCHMIDT, Arthur (49)	Prisoner of War (Russian) (Feb 43)	17 Jan 43		Inf
SCHMIDT, August (51)	10th Panzer Grenadier Division	1 Jan 43		Inf
SCHMIDT, Curt (54)		1 Oct 42		Inf
SCHMIDT, Gustav (50)	19th Panzer Division	1 Jan 43		Inf
SCHMIDT-LOGAN, Wolfgang (60)			Württemberg	Arty
SCHMITT, Artur	Prisoner of War (British)	1 Jan 43		Inf
SCHMUNDT, Rudolf (56)	Chief Adjutant to Hitler; Army Personnel Office	1 Apr 43		Inf
SCHNEIDER, Dipl. Ing. Erich (60)		1 Jul 43	Hesse	Arty

RESTRICTED

60. Army Generals.—Continued.
d. Generalleutnant (Major General).—Continued.

Name (age)	Command or Appointment	Seniority	Origin	Arm
SCHNEIDER, Ernst (61)	Fortress Engr. Wkr. XVII	1 Jul 42		Pion
SCHÖNBERG, Wilhelm (71)	Retired (Jun 42)			Arty
SCHÖNHERR, Otto (54)		1 Sep 43	Austria	Inf
SCHONHÄRL, Hans (66)	Retired (?)	1 Dec 40	Bavaria	Inf
SCHOPPER, Erich (52)	A Silesian Infantry Division	1 Feb 43	Thuringia	Arty
SCHRADER, Rudolf (55)	Chief Sig O, Army Group West	1 Jul 42		Sig C
SCHREIBER (67)			Hesse	Inf
SCHROECK (55)		1 Jun 41		Inf
SCHUBERT, Rudolf (54)	C Sig O, Greece	1 Apr 43		Sig C
SCHÜNEMANN, Otto (61)	Retired (Jun 42)	1 Aug 37	Hesse	Inf
SCHÜNEMANN, Otto (53)	337th Infantry Division	1 May 43		Inf
SCHULZ, Friedrich (47)	C of S, Twentieth Army	1 Jul 43		Inf
SCHWARZNECKER (60)	Insp of Recruiting Area Vienna, Wkr. XVII	1 Mar 38		Inf
SCHWERIN, Gerhard Graf v. (45)	16th Panzer Grenadier Division	1 Jun 43		Inf
SCHWERIN, Otto v. (61)				Cav
SCHWERIN, Richard v. (49)		1 Dec 42		Inf
SCOTTI, v. (55)	A Higher Arty Comd.	1 Feb 41		Arty
SEEGER (54)		1 Sep 43	Württemberg	Inf
SEIFERT, Ernst (60)		1 Aug 38	Saxony	Inf
SELLE, v.	113th Arty Comd	1 Jan 42		Arty
SENGER u. ETTERLIN, Fridolin v. (53)	A Corps (?)	1 May 43	Baden	Cav
SEYFFARDT (50)	110th Infantry Division	1 Jan 43		Inf
SIEBERT, Friedrich (56)		1 Apr 41	Bavaria	Inf
SIELER (49)		1 Jul 43		Inf

RESTRICTED

60. Army Generals.—Continued.
d. Generalleutnant (*Major General*).—Continued.

Name (age)	Command or Appointment	Seniority	Origin	Arm
SINTZENICH, Rudolf (55)		1 Dec 41	Bavaria	Inf
SINZINGER, Adolf		1 Jan 43	Austria	Inf
SIRY, Maximilian (53)		1 Jan 43	Bavaria	Arty
SIXT, Friedrich (47)	C of S, Seventh Army	1 Jun 43	Bavaria	Arty
SIXT v. ARMIN, Hans Heinrich (55)	Prisoner of War (Feb 43)	1 Mar 40		Inf
SODAN, Ralf (64)	270th Coast Defense Division	1 Dec 42		Cav
SOMMERFELD, Hans v. (58)		1 Sep 41		Inf
SORSCHE, Konrad (61)	Insp of Recruiting Area Liegnitz, Wkr. VIII	1 Mar 38	Silesia	Arty
SPANG, Karl (58)		1 Apr 40	Württemberg	Arty
SPECHT, Karl-Wilhelm (51)	Infantry School Döberitz, Wkr. III	1 Aug 43		Inf
SPEEMANN, Kurt (67)	An Army Rear Area	z.V		Arty
SPEICH, Dr. Richard (60)	539th Frontier Guard Division			Pion
SPONECK, Graf v. (48)	Prisoner of War (May 43)	1 May 43		Inf
SPONECK, Hans Graf v. (55)	Retired (May 42)	1 Feb 40		Inf
STAHL, Friedrich (54)		1 Sep 42		Tks
STEINBAUER, Gerhard (55)		1 Oct 42	Bavaria	Arty
STEINMETZ	94th Infantry Division	1 Dec 43 (?)		Arty
STENGEL, Hans (64)		1 Apr 41	Saxony	Cav
STEPHAN, Friedrich (52)		1 Jan 43		Inf
STEPHANUS (63)	Retired (?)	z.V		Inf
STEVER (56)		1 Jun 41		Tks
STIELER v. HEYDEKAMPF (63)	Insp of Armaments, Wkr. III	1 Feb 41		Inf
STIMMEL (58)		1 Jun 41	Baden	Inf
STOEWER, Paul (55)	143rd Reserve Division	1 Feb 42		Inf

RESTRICTED

60. Army Generals.—Continued.
d. Generalleutnant (Major General).—Continued.

Name (age)	Command or Appointment	Seniotiry	Origin	Arm
STREICH, Hans (53)		1 Oct 43		Tks
STUD (55)	Armaments and Procurement Staff, France	1 Feb 40		Arty
STÜMPFL, Heinrich (61)	Cmdt of Vienna, Wkr. XVII	1 Jun 40	Austria	Inf
STUMPFELD, v. (61)		1 Apr 43		Arty
STUMPFF, Horst (57)		1 Feb 41		Tks
SUTTNER (58)		1 Apr 40	Württemberg	Inf
SZELINSKI (53)	298th Infantry Division	1 Jan 43		Inf
TARBUK v. SENSENHORST, Karl	540th Frontier Guard Division		Austria	Inf
TAYSEN, Adalbert v		1 Jul 42		Inf
TESCHNER (71)	Retired (Jul 42)			Inf
TETTAU, Hans v. (56)	24th Infantry Division (1940)	1 Mar 42	Saxony	Inf
THOFERN, Wilhelm (59)	Gross-Born Tng Area, Wkr. II	1 Sep 42		Inf
THOMA, Heinrich (53)		1 Sep 43	Bavaria	Inf
THOMAS, Wilhelm (51)	Ordnance School	1 Jul 43		Inf
THOMASCHKI, Siegfried (50)		1 Jan 43		Arty
THÜNGEN, Karl Frhr. v. (51)	Insp of Recruiting Berlin I, Wkr. III	1 Jan 43	Bavaria	Cav
THUMM, Helmuth (49)	5th Light Division	1 Sep 43		Inf
TIEDEMANN, Karl v. (67)	Retired	1 Nov 39		Inf
TIEMANN, Otto (56)	93d Infantry Division	1 Oct 39		Pion
TRAUT, Hans (49)	An Infantry Division	1 Jan 43	Alsace	Inf
TRESCKOW, Joachim v. (50)	328th Infantry Division	1 Mar 43		Inf
TRIERENBERG, Wolf (53)	167th Infantry Division	1 Nov 42	Bavaria	Inf
TROTHA, v	In France	z.V		Inf

RESTRICTED

60. Army Generals.—Continued.
d. Generalleutnant (*Major General*).—Continued.

Name (age)	Command or Appointment	Seniority	Origin	Arm
TSCHERNING, Otto (63)	Insp of Recruiting Area Stuttgart, Wkr. V (1942)	1 Sep 35	Württemberg	Arty
UCKERMANN, Horst Frhr. v. (52)	160th Reserve Division	1 Sep 43		Inf
USINGER		1 Jul 43		Arty
UTHMANN, Bruno v. (53)	M A, Stockholm	1 Sep 41		Inf
VEITH, Richard (54)	With an Army Group (1942)	1 Aug 42	Bavaria	Inf
VOGEL, Emil (50)	101st Light Division	1 Apr 43	Saxony	Inf
VOLCKAMER v. KIRCHENSITTENBACH, Friedrich	An Infantry Division (?)	1 Sep 43		Inf
VOLK, Erich (Ernst?) (60)	Insp of Recruiting Area Strassburg, Wkr. V	1 Feb 41	Thuringia	Cav
VORMANN, Nikolaus v. (49)	23d Panzer Division	1 Jul 43		Inf
VOSS, Hans v	Retired (Jul 42)			Inf
WACHTER, Friedrich Karl v. (55)	Head of a Section, OKH (Ag P4)	1 Apr 42	Hesse	Inf
WAEGER, Kurt	Armaments Office in Min. for War Pr.	1 Jan 43		Arty
WAGNER, August (60)		1 Aug 40	Bavaria	Tks
WALDENFELS, Wilhelm Frhr. v. (60)	Insp of Recruiting Area Innsbruck, Wkr. XVIII	1 Feb 41	Saxony	Inf
WANGER, Rudolf (55)		1 Feb 42	Bavaria	Inf
WARLIMONT, Walter (50)	Deputy Chief W. F. St.	1 Apr 42		Arty
WEDDERKOPF, Magnus v. (62)	Retired (Jul 42)	1 Feb 41		Inf
WEGENER, Wilhelm (49)	32d Infantry Division	1 Feb 43		Inf
WEIDINGER, Wilhelm (54)	Insp of Army Flak	1 Oct 42		Arty
WEIDLING, Helmuth (52)	86th Infantry Division	1 Jan 43		Arty
WEINGART, Erich (57)		1 Aug 40	Bavaria	H-DrT
WESSELY, Marian	An Admin Post in Wkr. XVII (?)		Austria	Inf

RESTRICTED

60. Army Generals.
d. Generalleutnant (*Major General*).—Continued.

Name (age)	Command or Appointment	Seniority	Origin	Arm
WESTHOVEN, Franz (50)		1 May 43		Cav
WICKEDE, Emil v. (51)	30th Infantry Division	1 Jan 43		Inf
WILCK, Hermann (59)	708th Infantry Division	/42	Thuringia	Inf
WILL, Otto (53)	Insp of Railway Engrs, OKH	1 Dec 42	Bavaria	Pion
WILLICH, Fritz (62)	Retired (?)	z.V.	Württemberg	Inf
WILMOWSKY, Friedrich Frhr. v. (63)	Insp of Recruiting Area Potsdam, Wkr. III	1 Aug 35		Cav
WINDECK (55)		1 Apr 42		Inf
WINTER, Paul (49)		1 Jun 43	Bavaria	Arty
WINTERGERST, Karl (52)	210th Coast Defense Division	1 Apr 43	Bavaria	Arty
WINTZER, Heinz (54)	Chief of Mil Economics and Armaments Staff, Norway	1 Oct 41		Arty
WITTKE, Walter (56)		1 Aug 41		Inf
WOLFF, Ludwig (51)	Chief of Army Educational Dept	1 Dec 42	Saxony	Inf
WOLFF	PW Camps in Ukraine (?)	1 Jan 43		Inf
WOLFSBERGER, Franz		1 Oct 43	Austria	Cav
WOLLMANN (54)		1 Jun 40		Pion
WOSCH, Heinrich (54)	233d Reserve Panzer Division	1 Jan 43		Inf
WOYTASCH, Kurt (63)		1 Aug 41		Inf
WREDE, Theodor Frhr. v. (56)		1 Mar 41		Cav
WUTHMANN, Rolf		1 Mar 43		Arty
ZEHLER, Albert (56)	304th Higher Arty Comd (1942)	1 Dec 41	Bavaria	Arty
ZELLNER, Emil	373d Infantry Division	1 Apr 43	Austria	Inf
ZEPELIN, Ferdinand v (58)	Retired (Jul 42)	1 Jun 41		Inf

RESTRICTED

60. Army Generals.
d. Generalleutnant (*Major General*).—Continued.

Name (age)	Command or Appointment	Seniority	Origin	Arm
ZICKWOLFF, Friedrich (55)		1 Oct 41	Württemberg	Inf
ZIEGLER, Heinz (50)		3 Dec 42		Arty
ZIMMERMANN, Georg (65)	Mil Plenipotentiary in N. Italy	z.V		Inf
ZÜLOW, Alexander v. (54)		1 Oct 41	Silesia	Inf
ZUKERTORT, Johannes (59)	Arty Cmdr, Army Group West	1 Feb 41	Saxony	Arty
ZWENGAUER, Karl (62)	Special duties with Insp of Arty	1 Feb 41	Bavaria	Arty

RESTRICTED

60. Army Generals.—Continued.
e. Generalmajor (*Brigadier General*).

Name (age)	Command or Appointment	Seniority	Origin	Arm
ABRAHAM, Erich (49)	76th Infantry Division	1 Jun 43		Inf
ABT (53)		1 Apr 42		Sig C
ADLHOCH		1 Nov 42		Inf
ADOLPH, Ernst (68)	Retired (May 42)			Inf
ALBERTI, Konrad v.		1 Apr 43		Inf
ALTEN, Viktor v. (57)	Retired (Jul 42)	1 Feb 41		Inf
AMMON, Carl v. (61)	Insp of Recruiting Area Stettin, Wkr. II	1 Apr 40		Cav
ANGER (56)	P W Camps in Wkr. XIII	1 Oct 39		Arty
ARNDT (52)		1 Aug 43		Inf
ARNDT, Karl	293d Infantry Division	1 Apr 43		Inf
ARNIM, Friedemund v. (51)	Cmdt of Amiens	1 Nov 42		Cav
ARNOLD, Karl (54)		1 Jun 41		Inf
ARNOLD, Wilhelm	On staff of an Army	1 Oct 43		Sig C
ASCHEBERG, Percy Baron v. (62)	Retired (Jul 42)	1 Jun 42		Sig C
ASCHENBRANDT, Heinrich (59)	Feldkdtr. Rakvere, Estonia	1 Dec 41	Bavaria	Arty
AUER, Franz (65)			Bavaria	Arty
BAARTH, Jürgen (53)	Feldkdtr. Angers (?)	1 Apr 42		Cav
BACHER, Hermann		1 Dec 42	Austria	Pion
BADE, Hans-Albert		1 Apr 43		
BAESSLER, Erich (52)	377th Infantry Division	1 Jan 42		Inf
BAESSLER, Hans (51)	A Panzer Division	1 Feb 42	Silesia	Tks
BALTZER, Martin (53)		1 Apr 41	Saxony	Sig C
BAMBERG, Dr. (55)	Cmdt of Riga	1 Feb 41	Saxony	Inf
BARENDS (63)	WBK Neustrelitz, Wkr. II (1939)	1 Jun 41		Inf
BARTENWERFER, Gustav (62)	Retired	1 Feb 42		Inf

RESTRICTED

ORDER OF BATTLE OF THE GERMAN ARMY 465

60. Army Generals.—Continued.
e. Generalmajor (Brigadier General).—Continued.

Name (age)	Command or Appointment	Seniority	Origin	Arm
BARTON, Gottfried		1 Feb 41	Austria	Cav
BASSE, Max v. (59)	Army Welfare Office, Wkr. XII	1 Apr 42		Inf
BAUER, Franz				Inf
BAUMGARTNER, Richard (61)	Military Economics Off, Balkans	1 Dec 39	Austria	Pion
BAYERLEIN, Fritz (55)	3d Panzer Division	1 Mar 43	Baden	Tks
BAZING (51)	Chief Engr, Twentieth Army	1 Nov 42		Pion
BECHER (51)	Cmdt of Königsberg, Wkr. I	1 Apr 43		Inf
BECHT, Dipl. Wirtsch. Ernst (49)	Chief of a Section, Mil. Economics and Armaments Office	1 Apr 42		Arty
BECHTOLSHEIM, Gustav Frhr. v. MAUCHENHEIM gen. (55)		1 Aug 41	Bavaria	Inf
BECKE (62)	Insp of Armaments, Wkr. XVIII	1 Dec 42		Inf
BECKER, Franz (52)		1 Aug 42		Inf
BECKER, Karl (49)	An Infantry Division	1 Apr 43		Inf
BEHRENS, Wilhelm (53)		1 Jan 42		Inf
BEININGER		1 Aug 41		
BEISSWÄNGER, Hugo (48)		1 Jun 43		Arty
BEISSWÄNGER, Walter	Head of a Section, OKH (Wa Prüf)	1 Apr 43		Arty
BENICKE, Dr. Fritz		1 Jul 43		Pion
BERG, Kurt v. (58)		1 Mar 38	Baden	Arty
BERKA (63)	WBK Neisse, Wkr. VIII (1939)	1 Apr 42		Inf
BERTHOLD				Inf
BESCH, Helmut	Galizien Training Area (Govt Gen)	1 Nov 42		Inf
BESSEL, v	In Albania	1 Jun 41		Inf
BESSELL, Hans		1 Apr 43		Pion

RESTRICTED

60. Army Generals.—Continued.
e. Generalmajor (*Brigadier General*).—Continued.

Name (age)	Command or Appointment	Seniotiry	Origin	Arm
BIERINGER	Supply Officer in Italy	1 Jul 43		M T
BIERMANN (71)	In OKH (Insp of Fortifications)	1 Apr 41		Pion
BILHARZ, Eugen (56)	2d Ordnance Group (1941)	1 Feb 41	Saxony	Inf
BISLE, Artur (56)	Feldkdtr. 545	1 Apr 43		Inf
BLOCK, Lothar v. (52)	Staff of Wkr. XX	1 Feb 42		Inf
BLÜCHER, Johann Albrecht v. (52)		1 Aug 42		CWS
BOCK, Franz Karl v. (68)	Feldkdtr. Nancy			Inf
BODENHAUSEN, Erpo Frhr. v	A Panzer Division	1 Apr 43		Tks
BOEHRINGER, Gustav (52)		1 Feb 42	Württemberg	Pion
BÖMERS, Hans (50)		1 Apr 42		Arty
BOER, John de (47)		1 Oct 43		Arty
BOESSER (65)		1 Apr 42		Arty
BÖTTGER, Karl (53)		1 Apr 41	Saxony	Inf
BOGEN, v		1 Feb 43		Inf
BOIE, Sigurd	Feldkdtr. Biarritz (?)	1 Dec 42		Inf
BORCHERS (62)		1 Dec 42		Pion
BORK, Max		1 Apr 43		
BOROWSKI (62)		1 Apr 41		Arty
BOTSCH, Walter	C of S, Nineteenth Army	1 Sep 43		Inf
BRAUMÜLLER, Hans (61)	Feldkdtr. 679	1 Jun 41		Arty
BRAUN		1 Aug 42		Sig C
BRAUN, Julius		1 Apr 43	Bavaria	Arty
BRAUSE		1 Aug 42		Arty
BREHMER, Walter	In Paris (?)	1 Mar 43		Cav
BRENKEN (63)	WBK Koblenz, Wkr. XII (1939)	1 Jun 42		Cav
BRIESEN, v	Cmdt of Prague	1 Oct 42		Inf
BRUNS (58)	Harskamp Training Area	1 Apr 42		Pion

RESTRICTED

ORDER OF BATTLE OF THE GERMAN ARMY 467

60. Army Generals.—Continued.

e. Generalmajor (*Brigadier General*).—Continued.

Name (age)	Command or Appointment	Seniority	Origin	Arm
BRUNS, Walter	Cmdt of Ghent	1 Apr 42		Inf
BÜGGENMANN		1 Apr 42		
BÜLOW, Cord v. (52)		1 Feb 42		Cav
BURGDORF, Wilhelm (49)	Deputy Chief of Army Personnel Office	1 Oct 42		
BUSICH, Rudolf	707th Infantry Division	1 May 42	Austria	Pion
BUTTLAR, Edgar v		1 Oct 43		Sig C
CABANIS, Horst (Hans) (59)	Staff of Wkr. III	1 Jan 43		Cav
CASTORF, Dipl. Ing. Helmut (54)	166th Reserve Division	1 Feb 42	Thuringia	Inf
CHALES de BEAULIEU		1 Jun 43		Tks
CLAER, Bernhard v. (56)	Cmdt of Liége	1 Apr 42		Inf
CONRADI, Siegfried (55)		1 Jan 40	Saxony	Arty
CRAMOLINI (63)	WBK Leipzig III, Wkr. IV (1939)	1 Jun 41		Cav
CRATO (62)	WBK Düsseldorf, Wkr. VI (1939)	1 Jun 42		Arty
CUNO, Kurt (48)		1 Jul 43	Saar	Tks
CZETTRITZ u. NEUHAUS, Konrad v.		1 Feb 43		Cav
DAHLMANN (54)		1 Jul 40		Inf
DANNEEL	Feldkdtr. 603 (1942)	1 Feb· 43		Inf
DASER, Wilhelm (60)		1 Jul 42		Inf
DAUBER, Julius	PW Camps, in Wkr. XI (1942)	1 Jul 42		
DECKER, Karl	5th Panzer Division	1 Dec 43(?)		Tks
DECKMANN (52)	Stablack Training Area, Wkr. I	1 Sep 42		Inf
DEDEK, Emil		1 Jul 42	Austria	Pion
DEGENER (51)		1 Nov 42		Cav
DEINDL, Otto (54)		1 Feb 42	Bavaria	Tks
DEININGER (62)	Retired	1 Aug 41		Inf

RESTRICTED

60. Army Generals.—Continued.
e. Generalmajor (*Brigadier General*).—Continued.

Name (age)	Command or Appointment	Seniority	Origin	Arm
DETTEN, Gustav v.	Retired (?)	1 Nov 41		Inf
DEUTSCH (52)	711th Infantry Division	1 Jul 42		Inf
DEWALD, Fritz		1 Oct 43		Inf
DEYHLE, Willy	Staff of Eighteenth Army			
DICKMANN (53)	WBK Dortmund I, Wkr. VI (1939)	1 Jun 42		Inf
DINTER, Georg		1 Feb 43		Pion
DITTMEYER		1 May 43		Tks
DÖHREN, v. (58)		1 Jul 41		Inf
DÖPPING		1 Jul 43		Inf
DOHNASCHLOBITTEN, Heinrich Burggraf u. Graf z. (62)		1 Jun 42		Cav
DONAT, Dipl. Ing. Hans v. (53)		1 Nov 41		Pion
DORMAGEN		1 Apr 43		Inf
DORNBERGER, Dr. Ing. h.c.	Head of a Section, OKH (?)	1 Jun 43		CWS
DREBBER, Moritz v. (52)	Prisoner of War (Feb 43)	1 Jan 43		Inf
DRECKMANN, Dipl. Ing. Paul		1 Oct 43		Inf
DREES (60)	Head of a Dept, Army Ordnance (1940)	1 Jul 41		Arty
DRESCHER		1 Jun 43		Arty
DRESSLER, Rudolf (61)	In Stuttgart	1 Jan 43		Arty
DROBNIG (56)		1 Jul 41		Arty
DYBILASZ, Dipl. Ing		1 Aug 42		Pion
EBELING, Fritz (56)		1 Jun 41		Inf
EBELING, Kurt (52)	Arty School, Thorn	1 Apr 42		Arty
EBERDING		1 Aug 43		Inf
EBERHARDT, Kurt	Retired (?)	z.V.		
ECKARDT, Eduard	Army Welfare Office, Wkr. III (1939)	1 Apr 41		Arty

RESTRICTED

ORDER OF BATTLE OF THE GERMAN ARMY   469

60. Army Generals.—Continued.
e. Generalmajor (Brigadier General).—Continued.

Name (age)	Command or Appointment	Seniority	Origin	Arm
ECKHARDT, Hans-Heinrich (48)		1 Oct 43		Inf
EDELSHEIM, Reichsfreiherr v	24th Panzer Division	1 Jun 43		Cav
EHRENBERG, Hans (55)	Division Nummer 409	1 Aug 40	Saxony	Inf
EHRIG, Richard (61)	Staff of Wkr. IV	1 Jun 41	Saxony	Inf
EISENBACH		1 Oct 43		Inf
EISENHART-ROTHE, Hans-Georg v. (54)		1 Apr 42		Cav
EISENSTUCK, Helmut (50)	381st Field Training Division (1942)	1 Sep 42		Inf
ELSTER, Botho (50)	Cmdt of Marseille	1 Mar 43		Arty
ELVERFELDT, Frhr. v		1 Sep 43		
ENGELHARDT, Alfred (51)		1 Nov 42		Inf
ERDMANN, Kurt	Insp of Armaments, Wkr. VI	1 Jan 43		Arty
ERDMANNSDORFF, Gottfried v. (51)		1 Dec 42		Inf
ERTEL, Theodor (70)		1 Sep 41	Bavaria	Arty
ERXLEBEN	With an O F K, South France	1 Oct 43		Sig C
FABRICE, Eberhard v. (52)	An Admin Post, Mainz	1 Mar 42		Inf
FALKENSTEIN, Erich Frhr. v. (64)	Chief Ordnance O, Wkr. VI (1939)	1 Apr 41		Inf
FALKENSTEIN, Hans Frhr. v. (51)	45th Infantry Division	1 May 43		Inf
FANGOHR, Joachim		1 Feb 43		Inf
FEHN, Franz (61)	Cmdt of Augsburg, Wkr. VII	1 Jun 41	Bavaria	Cav
FELBERT, Paul v		1 Oct 43		Inf
FELZMANN, Maximilian (50)	251st Infantry Division	1 Jun 43		Arty
FIEDLER, Erich (60)		1 Jul 42		Pion
FISCHER, Karl (52)		1 Apr 42		Arty
FISCHER, Theodor		1 Aug 42		Inf

RESTRICTED

60. Army Generals.—Continued.
e. Generalmajor (*Brigadier General*).—Continued.

Name (age)	Command or Appointment	Seniority	Origin	Arm
FITZLAFF		1 Jan 43		Arty
FLÖRKE	14th Panzer Grenadier Division	1 Jun 43		Inf
FONCK, Dr	Retired			
FORSTER, Paul Herbert (52)	389th Infantry Division	1 Jul 42		Arty
FRETTER-PICO, Otto		1 Mar 43		Tks
FREYE (66)		1 Jul 42		Pion
FREYTAG, Walter (52)	Cmdt of Besancon	1 Aug 42		Inf
FRIEDRICHS, Walter (60)		1 Oct 37	Bavaria	Inf
FRIEMEL, Georg (53)	Prisoner of War	1 Feb 41		Inf
FRIES (48)	29th Panzer Grenadier Division	1 Jun 43		Inf
FUCHS, Willy v	A PW Camp	1 Jul 42		Inf
FUCIK, Karl		1 Jul 41	Austria	Inf
GALL (53)	In France	1 Jan 43		Inf
GALLWITZ, Werner v		1 Oct 43		Arty
GAUL, Hans (67)	Retired (?)	z.V	Bavaria	Inf
GEBAUER, Artur	Cmdt of Graz, Wkr. XVIII	1 Jun 42	Austria	Inf
GEMP, Fritz (70)	In OKW	z.V		Inf
GENEE, Paul (64)		1 Feb 42		Inf
GERBER, Alexander		1 Sep 42	Austria	Inf
GERLACH, Erwin	Staff of First Army	1 Jun 43		Arty
GERMAR, v. (66)	WBK Stolp. Wkr. II	1 Mar 41		Inf
GEROCK		1 Mar 43		Arty
GERSDORFF, Gero v. (51)		1 Jan 43		Cav
GESCHWANDTNER (53)		1 Oct 42		Arty
GEYSO, Eckhard v. (52)	Döberitz Training Area, Wkr. III	1 Oct 42		Inf
GIEHRACH (62)	Staff of Wkr. XVII (1939)	1 Aug 41		Arty

RESTRICTED

60. Army Generals.—Continued.
e. Generalmajor (Brigadier General).—Continued.

Name (age)	Command or Appointment	Seniotiry	Origin	Arm
GIHR		1 Oct 43		Inf
GLODKOWSKI, Erich (64)	WBK. Essen, Wkr. VI	1 Apr 41		Inf
GOECKEL, Hans v. (55)		1 Feb 41	Thuringia	Inf
GOELDEL, v. (54)		1 Feb 41		Inf
GOTHSCHE, Reinhold	In OKH	1 Oct 43		
GRACHEGG, Gustav (62)	PW Camps in Wkr. VIII	z.V	Austria	Inf
GRAEVENITZ, Hans v. (51)	Head of a Section, OKW (W. Vers.)	1 Feb 42	Württemberg	Inf
GRASSMANN, Kuno		1 Mar 43		Arty
GRAU, Josef (55)				Inf
GROBHOLZ, Dr (51)		1 Oct 42		Cav
GRODDECK, Karl Albrecht, v. (52)		1 Aug 42		Inf
GROENEVELD (64)	Retired (May 42)	1 Feb 42	Baden	Inf
GROSSE, Dr. Walther		1 Apr 43		Pion
GRÜNER, Erich		1 Sep 43		Inf
GÜNDELL, Walther v. (52)	Camp Cmdt, Army G H Q (1941)	1 Dec 41		Inf
GUHR (71)			Silesia	Inf
GURRAN		1 Oct 43		Inf
GUTKNECHT (56)		1 Jul 42		Inf
GYLDENFELDT, Heinz v	C of S, LXVIII Inf Corps	1 Jul 43		Arty
HAACK		1 Apr 43		Arty
HAGL, August (56)		1 Dec 40	Bavaria	Inf
HAHN, Johannes (54)	Cmdt of Lyons	1 Apr 43		
HAMANN, Adolf		1 Jun 42		Inf
HANSTEIN, Hans v. (58)	In OKH	1 Aug 42		Inf
HARTMANN, Martin (59)	Staff of an Army on Eastern Front	1 Apr 43	Württemberg	Inf
HARTMANN, Wilhelm Dipl. Ing	In Ministry of Munitions	1 Aug 42		Arty

RESTRICTED

60. Army Generals.—Continued.
e. Generalmajor (*Brigadier General*).—Continued.

Name (age)	Command or Appointment	Seniority	Origin	Arm
HASELMAYR				
HASELOFF, Kurt (49)	C of S, Govt Gen	1 Jan 43		Inf
HAUCK, Bruno	305th Infantry Division	1 Jun 43		Arty
HAUENSCHILD, Bruno Ritter v. (50)		1 Apr 42	Bavaria	Tks
HAUGER, Dipl. Wirtsch	Insp. of Armaments, Upper Rhine	1 Aug 42		Inf
HAUSER	13th Panzer Division	1 Dec 43 (?)		Tks
HAUSER, Wolfgang		1 Dec 42		Arty
HAUSSER	Retired			
HAVERKAMP, Wilhelm (53)	Special Duties in Govt Gen	1 Aug 41	Bavaria	Inf
HEDERICH, Hans (65)	Retired	1 Apr 41		Arty
HEDERICH, L		z.V		
HEDERICH, Willy (64)		1 Feb 42		Arty
HEIDRICH, Fritz		1 Aug 43		Arty
HEISTERMANN v. ZIEHLBERG, Gustav		1 Aug 43		Inf
HELLWIG, Georg		1 Jun 42		Pion
HELWIG, Hans		1 Oct 43		Inf
HENKE, Gerhard (66)	A PW Camp	1 Feb 43		Cav
HENRICI, Hans Dipl. Ing. (49)	Head of a Section, Army Ordnance Office	1 Jul 43		Arty
HENRICI, Rudolf (52)		1 Aug 42		Arty
HERFURTH, Otto (51)	C of S, Wkr V (?)	1 Oct 43		Inf
HERNEKAMP, Dipl. Ing. Karl (49)	Insp of Armaments, Prague	1 Jun 42		Arty
HERMANN, Hans	WBK Tilsit, Wkr. I	z.V		
HERRMANN, Paul		1 Oct 42		Pion
HESSELBARTH (52)		1 Apr 43		Inf
HEYDENREICH, Dipl. Ing		1 Apr 43		Arty

RESTRICTED

60. Army Generals.—Continued.
e. Generalmajor (Brigadier General).—Continued.

Name (age)	Command or Appointment	Seniority	Origin	Arm
HEYGENDORFF, Ralph v.		1 Jun 43		Inf
HEYL, Friedrich (63)		1 Oct 41	Bavaria	Arty
HEYNE, Hans Walter (60)		1 Jun 43		Arty
HIEPE, Hellmuth (53)		1 Feb 42		Arty
HILDEBRANDT, Hans Georg		1 Mar 43		Tks
HILDEMANN (52)	On Eastern Front	1 Nov 41		Pion
HILLERT, Dipl. Ing. Walter	Insp of Armaments, Wkr. IX	1 Jan 42		Inf
HINTZE (66)		1 Jul 42		Arty
HITZFELD (46)	A Silesian Division	1 Apr 43		Inf
HOCHBAUM, Hans (66)				Inf
HÖRAUF, Franz Ritter v. (66)	Cmdt of Lodz, Wkr. XXI		Bavaria	Inf
HÖRMANN, Dr. Maximilian (53)	C Sig O, First Army (?)	1 Apr 42	Bavaria	Sig C
HÖSSLIN, Hubert v.		1 Sep 43		
HOFERT, Johannes (59)	WBK Munich I, Wkr. VII (1939)			Arty
HOFFMANN, Dr. Heinrich		1 Dec 42		Arty
HOFFMANN, Max (52)	PW Camps in Wkr. II	1 Jan 42		Sig C
HOFFMANN, Paul	207th Sicherungs Division	1 Jun 42		Arty
HOFFMANN, Paul		1 Jun 41		Inf
HOFMANN, Friedrich	Chief of Section in OKH (1941)	1 Nov 42		Inf
HOFMANN, Helmut Frhr. v. (52)		1 Jun 42		Inf
HOFFMEISTER, Edmund	An E Prussian Infantry Division	1 Sep 43		Inf
HOLZHAUSEN (52)	Chief Ordnance O, Wkr. XVII	1 Sep 42		Arty
HORN, Hans-Joachim v.	MA, Helsinki	1 Apr 43		Cav
HORSTIG gen. d'AUBIGNY v. ENGELBRUNNER, Dr. Ing. Ritter v. (50)		1 Mar 42		Arty

RESTRICTED

60. Army Generals.—Continued.
e. Generalmajor (*Brigadier General*).—Continued.

Name (age)	Command or Appointment	Seniority	Origin	Arm
HOSSFELD, Walter (52)	Wildflecken Training Area, Wkr. IX	1 Aug 42		Inf
HOTZY, Dr. Otto		1 Apr 42	Austria	Inf
HÜBNER, Kurt (53)		1 Apr 42	Bavaria	Cav
HÜHNLEIN, Friedrich (70)			Bavaria	Inf
HÜLSEN, Heinrich-Hermann v. (49)	Prisoner of War (May 43)	1 May 43		
HÜNERMANN, Dipl. Ing. Rudolf (50)	Armaments Control Commission, France	1 Apr 42		Arty
HÜPEDEN, v	Retired			
IHSSEN, Hugo (57)	Chief Ordnance O, Wkr. III (1941)	1 Oct 40		Arty
ILGEN, Max		1 Feb 43		Arty
JACOBI	Feldkdtr. 549, Rennes (1941)	1 Dec 41		Tks
JACOBSEN, Heinrich		1 Feb 43		Inf
JAEHN		1 Jan 43		
JAIS, Max	Cmdt of Klagenfurt, Wkr. XVIII	1 Oct 42	Bavaria	Mtn
JAKOWITZ (54)				Inf
JANSEN (63)	Insp of Armaments, Ostland	1 Nov 41		Arty
JANSSEN, Adolf Wilhelm (67)				Arty
JANUSZ, Johann (62)	A PW Camp	z.V		Arty
JATZOW, Hermann (64)	WBK Schwerin, Wkr. II (1939)	1 Oct 41		Inf
JAUER (48)		1 Apr 43		Arty
JESSER, Kurt (54)		1 Dec 42		Tks
JÖRLING		1 Feb 42		Inf
JOHN	292d Infantry Division			
JOLLASSE, Erwin (52)		1 Oct 43		Inf
JORDAN, Gerhard (49)		1 Apr 42	Hesse	Pion

RESTRICTED

ORDER OF BATTLE OF THE GERMAN ARMY 475

60. Army Generals.—Continued.
e. Generalmajor (Brigadier General).—Continued.

Name (age)	Command or Appointment	Seniority	Origin	Arm
JOST, Walter (48)		1 Apr 43		Inf
JUST, Emil (54)	C G Lithuania	1 Oct 42		Arty
KALDRACK, Otto (64)		z.V. (?)		Inf
KALM, Otto v. (54)		1 Feb 41	Hesse	Arty
KAMPFHENKEL		1 Apr 43		Arty
KANITZ, Hans Graf v. (51)	Chemical Warfare School, Celle, Wkr. XI	1 Dec 42		CWS
KARL		1 Sep 42		Inf
KATTNER, Heinz (48)	Cmdt of Toulon	1 Oct 43		Inf
KEIL, Rudolf	Insp of Transport, East	1 Jul 42		Tks
KEIM (63)			Hesse	Inf
KEIPER		1 Mar 43		Cav
KELTSCH, Eduard		1 Nov 42		Tks
KESSEL, Paul v		1 Nov 42		Tks
KIRCHBACH, Harry v		1 Jul 42		Inf
KIRCHENPAUER v. KIRCHDORFF, Wilhelm	Staff of Wkr. IV	1 Jan 43		Inf
KISTNER		1 Apr 43		Arty
KITTEL, Heinrich (52)		1 Apr 42	Bavaria	Inf
KLEINHANS (70)	Retired (May 42)			
KLEINSCHROTH, Dipl. Ing		1 Oct 43		
KLEIST (58)		27 Aug 39		Arty
KLEMM, Kuno		1 Oct 43		Inf
KLEPP, Dr. Ernst		1 Apr 42	Austria	Inf
KLISZCZ, Ing. Otto	Fortress Engrs, Wkr. IV	1 Sep 41	Austria	Pion
KLÜG		1 Sep 43		Inf
KNOERZER, Hans (56)	Feldkdtr. Bordeaux	1 Jul 42		Inf
KOCH, Dipl. Ing. Walter (53)	Ordnance Office, OKH	1 Apr 42		Arty

RESTRICTED

60. Army Generals.—Continued.
e. Generalmajor (*Brigadier General*).—Continued.

Name (age)	Command or Appointment	Seniotiry	Origin	Arm
KÖNIGSDORFER, Josef (69)				Pion
KOHL, Gustav (56)	Cmdt of Linz, Wkr. XVII (1940)	1 Feb 41	Bavaria	Inf
KOHLER	282d Infantry Division	1 Jun 43		Inf
KOHNKE		1 Dec 42		Arty
KOLL		1 Aug 43		
KOPP, Arthur (58)		1 Feb 43		Arty
KORFES, Dr. Otto (55)	Prisoner of War (Feb 43)	1 Jan 43		Inf
KORTE, Heinz (52)	102d Arty Comd (1941)	1 Apr 42	Hesse	Arty
KORTÜM, Dr	An Arty Comd in France (?)	1 Apr 43		Arty
KOSSACK, Walter (61)	Feldkdtr. Zagreb	1 Jun 42		Arty
KRÄTZER, Franz		1 Jun 42	Austria	lnf
KRAUSE, Fritz (49)	Prisoner of War (May 43)	1 Jul 42		Arty
KRAUSE, Johannes	314th Higher Arty Comd, Salonika	1 Feb 43		Arty
KREBS v. DEWITZ gen. v		1 Aug 41		Inf
KRECH, Franz (54)		1 Apr 42		Inf
KREIPE		1 Sep 43		Inf
KRETSCHMER, Alfred	MA Tokyo	1 Jul 42		Inf
KRIEBEL, Friedrich Ritter v. (63)		1 Feb 41		Inf
KRIEGER, Hans (52)		1 Jun 42		Inf
KROPFF, v. (57)		1 Mar 39		Inf
KROSIGK, Ernst Anton v		1 Sep 43		
KRUMMEL, Adolf		1 Dec 42		Pion
KÜBLER, Josef	118th Light Division	1 Jan 43		Inf
KÜHNE, Gerhard		1 Sep 43		
KÜPPER, Hans (51)		1 Nov 42		Cav
KUMMER, v	Retired (May 42)	1 Sep 41		Inf

RESTRICTED

ORDER OF BATTLE OF THE GERMAN ARMY 477

60. Army Generals.—Continued.
e. Generalmajor (Brigadier General).—Continued.

Name (age)	Command or Appointment	Seniority	Origin	Arm
KUNZE, Friedrich (64)		1 Apr 41		Arty
KURNATOWSKI, v. (64)	Feldkdtr. 605, La Roche/Yon (1942)	1 Feb 42		Inf
KUSSIN, Friedrich	Rly Engr School	1 Apr 43		Pion
KUTZLEBEN, v	Radom Training Area (Govt Gen)			
LASSEN	Retired			
LATTMANN, Martin	Prisoner of War (Feb 43)	1 Jan 43		Arty
LECHNER, Heinrich (71)	Fortress Brigade Crete	1 Jul 41	Austria	Inf
LEDEBUR, Frhr. v. (64)				Inf
LEEB, Leopold		1 Sep 42		Inf
LEHMANN, Hans-Albrecht		1 Sep 43		Sig C
LEMKE, Herbert (55)	Prisoner of War	1 Aug 41		Inf
LEOPRECHTING, Waldemar Frhr. v. (64)		1 Jul 42		Pion
LE SUIRE, v. (48)	117th Light Division	1 May 43	Bavaria	Inf
LETTOW, Paul (53)	182d Reserve Division	1 Apr 42		Inf
LEUZE, Walter (53)		1 Apr 42	Bavaria	Cav
LEYERS, Dr. Ing	Mil Economics and Armaments Staff, Italy	1 Jan 43		Arty
LEYSER, Hans-Georg	18th Panzer Grenadier Division	1 Nov 42		Inf
LEYTHÄUSER, Hermann (59)		1 Apr 40	Bavaria	Cav
LICHT (53)		1 Feb 42		Inf
LIEBENSTEIN, Kurt Frhr. v. (45)	Prisoner of War (May 43)	1 Mar 43		Cav
LIEGMANN, Wilhelm (55)		1 Jun 41	Saxony	Inf
LINDE, v. der (53)		1 Mar 42		Cav
LINDEMANN, Wilhelm (71)	An OFK	z.V		Inf
LINDENAU (63)		1 Aug 41		Inf

RESTRICTED

60. Army Generals.—Continued.
e. Generalmajor (*Brigadier General*).—Continued.

Name (age)	Command or Appointment	Seniority	Origin	Arm
LINDNER, Kurt		1 Apr 43		Inf
LINKENBACH (55)		1 Aug 41		Cav
LINNARZ	Army Personnel Office, OKH (Ag Pl)	1 Jan 43		Sig C
LIPPE, von der	In France	z.V.		Cav
LOCHAU, Axel v. der (61)	Retired (?)	1 Jul 41		Inf
OEHNING, Paul (55)		1 Apr 40		Inf
OEWENICH, v		1 Apr 43		Cav
LONTSCHAR, Adalbert	Feldkdtr. 599 (Belgrade)	1 Jul 41	Austria	Inf
LORENZ, Hans (63)		1 Apr 41		Inf
LUDWIGER, Hartwig v. (49)	104th Light Division	1 May 43	Silesia	Inf
LÜER, Hilmar (60)	WBK Liegnitz, Wkr. VIII (1942)	1 Aug 41		Inf
LÜTKENHAUS	Cmdt of Mannheim, Wkr. XII	1 Mar 43		Inf
LUTZ, Ernst Frhr. v. (60)	WBK Wien I, Wkr. XVII (1939)	1 Jul 42		Inf
LUZ, Hellwig (52)	Liquidation Office for Sixth Army and Army Group Africa	1 Apr 42		Cav
MAERCKER				Inf
MAGNUS	Prisoner of War, (Feb 43)	1 Oct 42		Inf
MAHLMANN, Paul		1 Jan 43		Inf
MAISEL, Ernst (48)		1 Jun 43		Inf
MANN, Edler v. TIECHLER, Ferdinand Ritter v. (52)	Cmdt of Bucharest	1 Apr 42	Bavaria	Inf
MANTEUFFEL, Hasso Eccard v. (47)	7th Panzer Division	1 May 43		Cav
MARCINKIEWICZ, August		1 Dec 41	Austria	Pion
MARKGRAF, Emil		1 Sep 41	Austria	Inf
MARLOW	Chief Ordnance O, Wkr. XXI	1 Oct 43		Pion
MARNITZ, Dipl. Ing. Victor v		1 Sep 43		Pion

RESTRICTED

60. Army Generals.—Continued.
e. Generalmajor (*Brigadier General*).—Continued.

Name (age)	Command or Appointment	Seniority	Origin	Arm
MARSEILLE, Joachim				
MARSEILLE, Siegfried (56)		1 Jul 41		Inf
MAYER, Siegfried v.		1 Apr 43		Inf
MEDEN, Karl-Friedrich, v. d. (48)	17th Panzer Division	1 Oct 43		Cav
MEINHOLD (54)		1 Apr 42		Inf
MEISSNER, Hans (60)		1 Apr 41	Saxony	Sig C
MEISSNER, Dipl. Ing. Felix		1 Oct 43		Sig C
MELCHERT	Thorn Training Area, Wkr. XX	1 Feb 43		Inf
MELTZER, Rudolf (53)		1 Apr 42		Sig C
MELTZER, Karl		1 Oct 43		Arty
MENKEL	230th Coast Defense Division	1 Oct 42		Inf
MENNY, Erwin (51)		1 Nov 42		Tks
MERTENS (70)	Retired (?)	1 Sep 41		Inf
METGER, Wilhelm	264th Infantry Division (?)	1 Jul 43		Arty
METSCHER, Karl		1 Jun 42		Arty
METZ		1 Jan 43		Arty
METZ, Eduard (53)		1 Aug 42	Bavaria	Arty
MEYER, Karl Ludwig		1 Apr 42		Arty
MEYER, Fritz (51)	A Higher Constr Staff	1 Apr 43		Pion
MEYER, Heinrich	Cmdt of Mainz, Wkr. XII (1940)			Tks
MICKL, Hans (Johann) (51)		1 Mar 43	Austria	Inf
MIERZINSKY (64)		1 Feb 42		Arty
MILISCH, Leopold (72)		1 Jul 42		Inf
MORITZ, Georg (52)	Feldkdtr. Pärnu	1 Dec 41		Cav
MOST (59)			Württemberg	Inf
MÜLLER, Angelo (51)		1 Apr 42	Bavaria	Arty
MÜLLER, Dipl. Ing. Gerhard (48)		1 Apr 43	Silesia	Arty

RESTRICTED

60. Army Generals.—Continued.
e. Generalmajor *(Brigadier General)*.—Continued.

Name (age)	Command or Appointment	Seniority	Origin	Arm
MÜLLER, Hans Ludwig		1 Dec 42		Sig C
MÜLLER-DERICHSWEILER		1 Sep 43		Inf
MUHL (52)		1 Oct 42		Arty
MYLO, Walther (64)		1 Jan 42		Inf
NAGEL, Friedrich Wilhelm (55)	Insp of Armaments, Army Group South	1 Apr 42		Inf
NAUMANN, Max	Retired (Jun 42)			
NEIDHOLDT, Fritz (54)	369th Infantry Division	1 Oct 42		Inf
NEINDORFF, v		1 Dec 42		Inf
NEUMAYR, Franz (54)	Cmdt of Sofia	1 Apr 42	Bavaria	Inf
NEWIGER, Albert (55)		1 Jan 43		Cav
NEYMANN		1 Feb 42		Inf
NICKELMANN (51)		1 Feb 43		Inf
NIDA, v	C of S, Wkr. IX	1 Jun 43		
NIEBECKER, Georg (67)		z.V		Pion
NIEDENFÜHR, Günther (55)		z.V		Arty
NIEDERMAYER, Prof. Dr. Oskar Ritter v. (59)	162d Infantry Division	1 Sep 42		Arty
NIEHOFF, Johannes	371st Infantry Division	1 Jun 43		Inf
NIEMANN		1 Oct 43		CWS
NOACK, Rudolf (63)	In Belgium (?)	1 Sep 43		Inf
NOSTITZ-WALLWITZ, Gerhard v. (59)		1 Dec 41		Inf
ÖLLER		1 Oct 43		Inf
OELSNER (55)	Wandern Training Area, Wkr. III (1939)	1 Feb 41		Inf
OFFENBÄCHER, Konrad (54)	Döllersheim Training Area, Wkr. XVII	1 Jun 41	Hesse	Inf
OHNACKER, W. (52)		1 Apr 42		Inf
OLBERG v		1 Feb 42		Inf

RESTRICTED

ORDER OF BATTLE OF THE GERMAN ARMY 481

60. Army Generals.—Continued.

e. Generalmajor (*Brigadier General*).—Continued.

Name (age)	Command or Appointment	Seniotiry	Origin	Arm
OSTER, Hans (56)		1 Dec 42		Inf
OTTO (57)		1 Aug 38	Baden	Pion
PACHMAYR (61)	Army Mechanics School (1941)	1 Sep 41		Arty
PANNWITZ, Helmuth v. (46)	1st Cossack Division	1 Jun 43	Silesia	Cav
PAUER, Ernst		1 Sep 41	Austria	Arty
PAWEL		1 Sep 42		Inf
PECHMANN, Albrecht Frhr. v. (64)	In France (?)	1 Sep 41	Bavaria	Arty
PEMSEL, Max		1 Sep 43		Inf
PETERSEN, Matthias	Cmdt of Kaiserslautern, Wkr. XII	1 Feb 42		Inf
PETERSEN, Wilhelm (52)		1 Apr 42		Pion
PETTER (63)	Retired (May 42)			Inf
PFEIFFER, Helmut (50)		1 Sep 43		Inf
PFÜHLSTEIN, Alexander v. (45)	Brandenburg Division	1 Jul 43		Inf
PHILIPP, Ernst	Arty School Jüterbog, Wkr. III	1 May 42		Arty
PIEKENBROCK, Hans	An Infantry Division	1 Apr 43		Cav
PITREICH, August v	Retired (Jul 42)		Austria	
PLAMBÖCK (64)	Lötzen Fortifications, Wkr. I (1941)	1 Apr 41		Arty
PLAMMER	A PW Camp	z.V.		Inf
PLEHWE, v	Feldkdtr. Saare Maa (Estonia)	1 Oct 43		Cav
PLEWIG, Willy (64)		1 Apr 41		Inf
PLOETZ, Egon (66)	WBK Rostock, Wkr. II	1 Aug 42		Cav
POEL, Gerhard (58)		1 Jul 41		Cav
POHL, v. (70)				Arty
POTEN, Ernst		1 Jul 42		Arty
PRESSENTIN, Richard v. (70)	Landesschützen Regiment z.b.V. 26	1 Jul 42		Arty

RESTRICTED

60. Army Generals.—Continued.
e. Generalmajor (*Brigadier General*).—Continued.

Name (age)	Command or Appointment	Seniority	Origin	Arm
PREUSSER, Arnold (67)		z.V		
PRIEM, v. (61)	Admin Post in Holland (?)	1 Jan 42		Inf
PRINNER		1 Mar 43		Arty
PRITTWITZ u. GAFFRON, Max v. (68)	Cmdt of Lemberg (Lwów)	1 Sep 41	Silesia	Inf
PRÜGEL, Dr. Karl (67)		1 Jan 42	Bavaria	Sig C
PRÜTER		1 Jan 43		Inf
PUTTKAMER, v. (63)				Inf
RAAB, Matthias	125th Arty Comd (1941)	1 Apr 42	Austria	Arty
RAAPKE (46)	71st Infantry Division	1 Jun 43		Arty
RABE v. PAPPENHEIM, Friedrich Karl		1 Aug 43		Cav
RABSILBER, Friedrich (65)		1 Apr 41		Inf
RADZIEJ	169th Infantry Division	1 Sep 43		Inf
RAESFELD, Werner v. (52)	Transport Office, Essen Wkr. VI (1939)	1 Jun 42	Silesia	Inf
RÄSSLER, Rudolf (59)		1 Jun 42	Saxony	Cav
RAITZ v. FRENTZ, Maximilian Frhr. (64)		1 Jun 41		Arty
RANFT, Albert (45)		1 Aug 43		Inf
REIBNITZ, Leo v. (55)	A PW Camp	1 Apr 42		Inf
REICHER, Franz			Austria	Inf
REIN		1 Sep 43		Sig C
REINERSDORFF-PACZYNSKI u. TENCZYN, Dietrich v. (67)	Retired (?)			Inf
REINHARDT, Fritz (54)		1 Apr 41	Saxony	Inf
REISS, Ritter v	Feldkdtr. 750 (?)	z.V		
REMLINGER		1 Dec 42		Cav
REXILIUS		1 Feb 43		Inf
RHEIN, Karl (50)	331st Infantry Division	1 May 43		Inf

RESTRICTED

ORDER OF BATTLE OF THE GERMAN ARMY 483

60. Army Generals.—Continued.
e. Generalmajor (*Brigadier General*).—Continued.

Name (age)	Command or Appointment	Seniority	Origin	Arm
RIBBENTROP, Friedrich (64)	Retired (?)	1 Apr 41	Saxony	Arty
RICHTER, Gerhard		1 Aug 42		Inf
RICHTER, Wilhelm		1 Mar 43		Inf
RIEDEL (52)		1 Aug 42		Arty
RIEGER, Leopold (54)	Chief Ordnance O, Wkr. XIII (1939)	1 Jun 41	Saxony	Arty
RIEMHOFER, Gottfried (51)	Admin Post in Wkr. XIII	1 Oct 42		M T
RINCK von BALDENSTEIN, Werner Frhr. von (65)		1 Mar 43		Inf
RINGE, Hans		1 Mar 43		Cav
RITTER, Rene	Retired	1 Apr 42	Austria	Inf
RITTWEGER, Ernst (58)	Cmdt of Karlsruhe, Wkr. V (1941)	1 Feb 42		Inf
RODEN, Enno v		1 Apr 43		Inf
RODEWALD (58)				H-DrT
RODT, Eberhardt (49)	15th Panzer Grenadier Division	1 Mar 43		Cav
ROEDER, v	Retired			
ROEMER, Martin v	Feldkdtr. 579 (1941)	1 Jan 43		Inf
RÖPKE, Kurt (48)	46th Infantry Division	1 Aug 43		Inf
ROESINGER, Otto (54)		1 Apr 42	Bavaria	Pion
RÖSLER, Eberhard (54)		1 Apr 42	Württemberg	Inf
RONICKE, Martin		1 Mar 43		Inf
RORICH (52)		1 Sep 43		Inf
ROSKE, Dipl. Ing. Fritz	Prisoner of War (Feb 43)	27 Jan 43		
ROST, v	In Vichy	1 Mar 43		Arty
ROTH, Hans (60)	Cmdt of Köln, Wkr. VI	1 Aug 42	Alsace	Inf
ROTH, Heinrich	C of S, Wkr. III	1 Jun 43		Inf
ROTHE, Erich	Higher Constr Staff 10, Minsk (1941)	1 Jul 42		Pion

RESTRICTED

60. Army Generals.—Continued.
e. Generalmajor (Brigadier General).—Continued.

Name (age)	Command or Appointment	Seniority	Origin	Arm
RÜBEL, Karl (49)	163d Infantry Division	1 Mar 43		Inf
RÜDT von COLLENBERG, Frhr. Ludwig (60)		1 Apr 41		Arty
RÜGAMER, Ferdinand	Acceptance Off, Wkr. XVII	1 Jul 41	Austria	Arty
RÜGGENMANN, Alfons (52)	Insp of Armaments, Wkr. I	1 Apr 42		H-DrT
RÜHLE v. LILIENSTERN, Kurt (62)		1 Jul 42		Arty
RUFF (49)		1 Dec 42		Arty
RUNGE, Wilhelm (54)	Insp of Engineer Equipment, Wkr. I (1939)	1 Jun 41		Pion
RUPPERT, Hans-Eberhard (52)		1 Jun 42		H-DrT
RUVILLE, v		1 Jul 42		Inf
SACHSSE	Retired	z.V. (?)		Inf
SAGERER		1 Aug 41	Bavaria	Inf
SALENGRÉ-DRABBE, Hans de (50)		1 May 43		Inf
SALITTER, Fritz (62)	Deba Training Area (Govt Gen)	1 Apr 41		Arty
SATTLER		1 Oct 43		Inf
SAUVANT (53)		1 Mar 42		Inf
SCHACK, Friedrich August		1 Jul 43		Inf
SCHACKE (63)		1 Mar 43		Inf
SCHADE (61)		1 Aug 41		Inf
SCHAEFER, Hans (51)		1 Apr 42	Silesia	Inf
SCHAEFER, Dr. Gotthold		1 Apr 43		
SCHAEFFER (57)		1 Feb 41		Inf
SCHAUWECKER (62)	Retired (?)	z.V.		Sig C
SCHEFOLD (56)			Württemberg	Arty
SCHELLER		1 Jun 42		Arty
SCHELLMANN (66)	Retired(?)	1 Apr 41		Inf

RESTRICTED

ORDER OF BATTLE OF THE GERMAN ARMY 485

60. Army Generals.—Continued.
e. Generalmajor (Brigadier General).

Name (age)	Command or Appointment	Seniority	Origin	Arm
SCHELLWITZ, v		1 Jan 43		Inf
SCHERFF	In OKW (7 Abt.)	1 Sep 43		Inf
SCHICKFUS u. NEUDORFF, Erich v. (64)		1 Feb 32		Inf
SCHILLING, Otto (55)		1 Dec 42		Inf
SCHINDKE, Wilhelm (51)		1 Jan 43		Cav
SCHITTNIG		1 Apr 43		Inf
SCHLIEBEN, Dietrich v		1 Jan 43		Cav
SCHLIEBEN, Karl Wilhelm v. (50)	208th Infantry Division	1 Jun 43		Cav
SCHLUETER, Robert		1 Mar 43		Arty
SCHMETTOW, Graf v. (52)	C G, Channel Islands	1 Apr 42	Silesia	Cav
SCHMIDT, Hans		1 Apr 43		Pion
SCHMIDT, Dipl. Ing. Johannes		1 Oct 43		Inf
SCHMIDT, Otto	Feldkdtr. Antwerp (?)	1 Oct 41		Inf
SCHMIDT, Otto (52)	702d Infantry Division	1 Jan 42		Inf
SCHMIDT, Ulrich		1 Oct 43		Inf
SCHMIDT-KOLBOW (64)				Arty
SCHMIDT v. LUISINGEN	A PW Camp	z.V		Inf
SCHNARRENBERGER, Ernst (51)	Prisoner of War (May 43)	1 Nov 42		Inf
SCHNEIDEMESSER, Gustav v. (52)	Head of a Section OKH (P 4, II Abt)	1 Jun 42		Inf
SCHNEIDER, Friedrich (62)	Retired (Jul 42)	1 Apr 41		Inf
SCHNEIDER, Otto		1 Dec 41		Sig C
SCHOEN	Retired (?)	z.V		Cav
SCHÖNFELDER, Fritz (52)	Chief Engr First Army (?)	1 Apr 41	Saxony	Pion
SCHÖNFELDER, Kurt (72)	Retired (?)			Arty
SCHOLZ, Erich (52)		1 Aug 42		Arty
SCHREIBER, Alfred (52)		1 Jun 42		Inf

RESTRICTED

60. Army Generals.—Continued.
e. Generalmajor (*Brigadier General*).—Continued.

Name (age)	Command or Appointment	Seniotiry	Origin	Arm
SCHRÖDER, Fritz		1 Oct 43		
SCHROETER, v. (53)	Cmdt of Breslau, Wkr. VIII	1 Jan 42		Cav
SCHROETTER, Dipl. Ing. (51)		1 Apr 42		Inf
SCHUBERTH (53)	Toulouse Area	1 Jul 42		M T
SCHUCKMANN, Eberhard v		1 Aug 43		Inf
SCHÜTZ, Max v. (67)	In OKH	1 Jul 42		Inf
SCHULENBURG, Winfred v. d. (62)	Special Duties with PWs			Cav
SCHULER, Rüdiger v. (53)		1 Sep 41		Inf
SCHULZ, Otto				Inf
SCHUNCK, Theodor (55)		1 Jun 41		Arty
SCHUSTER, Friedrich (63)		1 Jan 42	Bavaria	Inf
SCHUSTER-WOLDAN		1 Sep 43		Arty
SCHWALBE, Eugen-Felix (52)		1 Oct 42		Inf
SCHWERIN, Bogislav Graf v. (48)	189th Reserve Division	1 Oct 43		Inf
SCULTETUS, Bruno (62)		1 Dec 41		Inf
SCULTETUS, Herbert (66)		1 Dec 41		Inf
SEEBOHM		1 Apr 43		Inf
SEELIG		1 Oct 43		Pion
SEHMSDORF, Hans (54)	3d Ordnance Group (1941)	1 Feb 41		Inf
SENSFUSS, Franz (Johannes ?) (51)		1 Oct 42		Pion
SERINI		1 Apr 43		Inf
SEUFFERT, Franz (52)	Heuberg Training Area, Wkr. V	1 Dec 40	Bavaria	Inf
SICHART, Werner v. (63)	WBK Kiel, Wkr. X	1 Sep 41	Saxony	Inf
SIECKENIUS (48)		1 Jun 43	Silesia	Tks
SIEGLIN, Kurt (60)	An O F K in the Ukraine		Württemberg	Inf
SIEVERS, Karl		1 Oct 43		Inf

RESTRICTED

60. Army Generals.—Continued.
e. Generalmajor (Brigadier General).—Continued.

Name (age)	Command or Appointment	Seniority	Origin	Arm
SOHN (62)		1 Sep 41		Arty
SOUCHAY, Stephan (52)		1 Aug 42		Inf
SPALCKE, Dr	MA Bucharest	1 Nov 43(?)		Inf
SPEIDEL, Dr. Hans		1 Jan 43		Inf
SPENGLER (53)		1 Mar 43		Inf
SPETH	C of S, Eighteenth Army	1 Jan 43		Arty
STAHR, Wolfgang (53)	II Armorers School (1941)	1 Apr 42	Saxony	Inf
STAMM (66)		1 Jul 42		Inf
STAMMER (53)		1 Nov 42		Inf
STEGMANN (49)		1 Aug 43		Inf
STEIGLEHNER, Wilhelm (62)		1 Aug 42		Arty
STEIN, Johann v. (53)		1 Jul 42		Inf
STEINBACH, Paul (55)	Chief Ordnance O, Govt Gen	1 Oct 41	Bavaria	Arty
STENZEL, Richard		1 Apr 42	Austria	Arty
STETTNER Ritter v. GRABENHOFEN, Walter (52)	1st Mountain Division	1 Mar 43		Mtn
STEUDTNER (66)	Retired (?)	z.V		Arty
STILLFRIED u. RATTONITZ, Waldemar Graf v. (67)	Staff of Repl Training Army			Inf
STOCKHAUSEN, Dipl. Ing. v. (54)	281st Sicherungs Division	1 Apr 42	Hesse	Inf
STOCKHAUSEN, v. (72)		1 Sep 41		Inf
STOLBERG-STOLBERG, Christoph Graf zu		1 Sep 43		Inf
STRACK, Karl (58)		1 Feb 42		Inf
STUBENRAUCH, Wilhelm (59)	Feldkdtr. 686	1 Jun 41	Saxony	Cav
STÜLPNAGEL, Siegfried v. (58)	Cmdt of Stettin, Wkr. II	1 Jun 42		Inf
STUMM, Berthold (52)		1 Jun 40		Inf

RESTRICTED

60. Army Generals.—Continued.
e. Generalmajor (*Brigadier General*).—Continued.

Name (age)	Command or Appointment	Seniority	Origin	Arm
STURM, Hans (60)		1 Feb 43		Arty
STURT, Gerhard		1 Oct 43		Inf
SUSCHNIGG, Gustav		1 Feb 43		Mtn
TAEGLICHSBECK		1 Feb 43		Inf
TARBUK, Johann		1 Aug 41	Austria	Inf
THADDEN, v		1 Apr 43		Inf
THÄTER, Maximilian (65)		1 Dec 41	Bavaria	Inf
THAMS (59)	Kammwald Training Area (Brdy Wald)	1 Mar 41		Inf
THEISS, Rudolf (59)		1 Sep 41	Austria	Tks
THIELE, Fritz	Chief of Sig Comd Sec, OKW	1 Oct 42		Sig C
THIELMANN		1 Apr 43		Pion
THOENISSEN	C of S, Procurement Staff, France	1 Aug 42		Tks
THOHOLTE		16 Feb 43		Arty
THOMAS (56)		1 Nov 40		Pion
THOMAS, Alfred (59)		1 Dec 42		Inf
THOMAS, Kurt	Formation of 999th Division Units (?)	1 Apr 43		Inf
THON, Friedrich (67)	Insp of Sig Troops	z.V		Sig C
TRAUCH, Rudolf (52)	Head of a Section, OKH (In 8) (1940)	1 Oct 41	Bavaria	H-Dr T
TRÖGER, Hans		1 Jan 43		Cav
TSCHAMMER u. OSTEN, Eckart v. (56)		1 Dec 40		Inf
TSCHUDI - JACOBSEN, Heinrich (Rudolf ?) v.		1 Feb 43		Inf
UBL, Bruno		1 Jul 42	Austria	Inf
UNRUH, Walter Willy Hermann v		z.V		
USEDOM, v		1 Jan 43		Cav
UTZ, Willibald	100th Light Division	1 Jul 43		Mtn
VASSOLL (60)		1 Jun 42		Arty

RESTRICTED

ORDER OF BATTLE OF THE GERMAN ARMY   489

60. **Army Generals.**—Continued.

e. Generalmajor (*Brigadier General*).—Continued.

Name (age)	Command or Appointment	Seniority	Origin	Arm
VATERRODT (52)	Cmdt of Strassburg, Wkr. V	1 Mar 41		Inf
VERSOCK, Kurt (49)		1 May 43		Mtn
VIEBAHN, Hans Albert v. (55)		1 Jul 42		Inf
VIERKORN		1 Jun 43		
VIEROW, Dipl. Ing. (51)		1 Oct 42		Pion
VOIGT, Adolf (52)	Cmdt of Graudenz, Wkr. XX	1 Jul 42		Cav
VOIT, Paul (68)	C of S, Wkr. XIII	1 Apr 38	Bavaria	Inf
VOSS, Erich	Cmdr PW Camps in Wkr. IX	1 Jun 42		Sig C
WAGNER, Gustav		1 Oct 43		Inf
WAGNER, Georg (66)	Retired (?)	1 Apr 41		Inf
WAGNER, Paul		1 Jan 43		Inf
WAHLE, Karl (51)	Cmdt of Hamburg, Wkr. X	1 Jul 42		Inf
WALTER, Helmuth (53)		1 Jul 43		Inf
WARNICKE (62)	WBK Danzig, Wkr. XX	1 Aug 41		Cav
WARTENBERG, Bodo v. (51)		1 Jan 43		Inf
WEBER, Friedrich (45)		1 Jan 43		
WEBERN, v. (51)		1 Oct 42		Arty
WECKMANN	Cmdt of Kriegsakademie	1 Apr 42		Inf
WEDEL, Hasso v. (56)	In OKW (?)	1 Sep 43		Inf
WEDEL, Hermann v. (51)	On Eastern Front	1 Jun 43		Tks
WEDELSTÄDT, Friedrich Wilhelm v. (57)				Inf
WEHRIG		1 Oct 43		
WEIDEMANN	In OKW	1 Sep 43		Inf
WEINKNECHT		1 Oct 43		Cav
WEISS, Wilhelm (58)		1 Oct 41	Austria	Inf

RESTRICTED

60. Army Generals.—Continued.
e. Generalmajor (Brigadier General).—Continued.

Name (age)	Command or Appointment	Seniority	Origin	Arm
WENCK, Walter (44)		1 Feb 43		Arty
WENING, Ernst (57)		1 Jun 41	Bavaria	Cav
WENNINGER		1 Oct 43		Inf
WERTHERN, Georg Thilo Frhr. v. (52)		1 Jun 42		Arty
WESTPHAL, Siegfried (42)	C of S to KESSELRING	1 Mar 43		Cav
WESTRAM	Mil Police in Wkr. XII (1941)	z.V. (?)		Arty
WIETERSHEIM, Wend v. (44)	11th Panzer Division	1 Nov 43 (?)	Silesia	Cav
WILKE, Carl		1 Sep 43		Inf
WILKE, Kurt (52)		1 Dec 42		Tks
WINDISCH, Alois	On Eastern Front	1 Sep 43		Inf
WINDISCH, Josef		1 Jul 43		
WINKLER, Hermann (56)	Feldkdtr. Nikolaiev	1 Jul 41	Saxony	Inf
WINKLER, Max		1 Oct 43		
WINTER, August	Staff of Army Group F	1 Aug 43		Sig C
WIRTZ, Richard (52)	An Infantry Division	1 Apr 42		Pion
WISSELINCK, Ernst (52)	War College, Dresden (1939)	1 Mar 43		Inf
WITTMANN (49)	3d Mountain Division	1 Jun 43		Arty
WITZLEBEN, Hermann v. (52)		1 Jun 42		Cav
WÖSSNER		1 Oct 43		Arty
WOLF		1 Aug 43		
WOLPERT, Johann (55)	In Luxemburg	1 Sep 41	Bavaria	Inf
WUERST		1 Jan 43		Pion
WULFFEN, Gustav Adolf v. (66)	Cmdt of Potsdam, Wkr. III	z.V.		Inf
WULZ (51)		1 Nov 42		Arty
WUTHENOW		1 Apr 43		Cav
XYLANDER, Rudolf Ritter u. Edler v. (72)	In OKW	1 Jul 42		Arty

RESTRICTED

60. Army Generals.—Continued.
e. Generalmajor (*Brigadier General*).—Continued.

Name (age)	Command or Appointment	Seniority	Origin	Arm
ZÄPFFEL, Alexander (62)	An Arty Ersatz Regiment	z.V		Arty
ZAHN, Alois (54)		1 Aug 41	Württemberg	Inf
ZANTHIER, v. (53)		1 Oct 41		Cav
ZEDNICEK, Franz		1 Apr 42	Austria	Pion
ZEISS, Walter (52)	Chief Ordnance Off, Wkr. VII	1 Jul 42		Arty
ZEITZ, Erich (Hermann ?)		1 Feb 41	Bavaria	Tks
ZELTMANN, Otto		1 Jan 43		
ZIEGENRÜCKER (59)	WBK Stettin, Wkr. II (1939)	1 Feb 43		Pion
ZIMMER, Richard		1 Jun 43		Pion
ZUCKERTORT, Karl (52)		1 Mar 40	Saxony	Tks
ZUTAVERN (51)		1 Jun 42	Baden	Arty
ZWADE	In OKH	1 Oct 43		Inf

RESTRICTED

61. Air Force Generals.

a. Reichsmarschall (*Marshal of the Reich*).

Name (age)	Command or appointment	Seniority	Origin
GÖRING, Hermann (51)	C-in-C Air Force	19 Jul 40	Bavaria

b. Generalfeldmarschall (*Field Marshal*).

KESSELRING, Albert (59)	C-in-C German Forces in Italy	19 Jul 40	Bavaria
MILCH, Erhard (52)	Inspector General, Air Force	19 Jul 40	
RICHTHOFEN, Dipl. Ing. Wolfram Frhr. v. (49)	Second Air Fleet	16 Feb 43	Silesia
SPERRLE, Hugo (59)	Third Air Fleet	19 Jul 40	Württemberg

c. Generaloberst (*General*).

GREIM, Robert Ritter v. (52)		16 Feb 43	Bavaria
KELLER, Alfred (62)	Head of N S F K	19 Jul 40	
LÖHR, Alexander (59)	Army Group E	9 May 41	Austria
LOERZER, Bruno (53)		16 Feb 43	
RÜDEL, Günther (61)	Dept Chief in R L M (Luftwehr)	17 Nov 42	Lorraine]
STUMPFF, Hans-Jürgen (55)		19 Jul 40	
WEISE, Hubert (58)	C-in-C Center	19 Jul 40	

RESTRICTED

ORDER OF BATTLE OF THE GERMAN ARMY 493

61. Air Force Generals.—Continued.
d. General der Flieger, Flakartillerie, etc. (*Lieutenant General*)

Name (age)	Command or appointment	Seniority		Origin
ANDRAE, Waldemar (54)		1 Jul	41	
BIENECK, Hellmuth (57)	Luftgau II	1 Jul	41	
BODENSCHATZ, Karl (54)	C of S to GÖRING	1 Jul	41	Bavaria
BOGATSCH, Rudolf (53)		1 Jul	41	
CHRISTIANSEN, Friedrich (65)	C G Holland	1 Jan	39	
COELER, Joachim (53)		1 Jan	42	
DANCKELMANN (56)		1 Apr	41	
DESSLOCH, Otto (55)	Fourth Air Fleet	1 Jan	42	Bavaria
DOERSTLING, Egon (55)	Supply Depot, R L M	1 Jun	42	Saxony
DRANSFELD, Eduard (61)		1 Oct	40	
FELMY, Helmuth (59)		1 Feb	38	
FIEBIG, Martin (53)	Luftwaffenkdo. South East	30 Jan	43	
FISCHER, Veit		1 Jun	42	
FÖRSTER, Hellmuth (55)		1 May	41	
FRÖLICH, Stefan (45)	Luftgau XVII	1 Jul	43	Austria
GEISLER, Hans (53)		19 Jul	40	
GOSSRAU, Karl Siegfried (63)	R L M	1 Sep	41	Württemberg
HARMJANZ, Willi (53)	Luftgau Norway	1 Oct	42	
HAUBOLD, Alfred (56)	Luftgau III/IV	1 Oct	41	Saxony
HEILINGBRUNNER, Friedrich (53)	(Flak)	1 Jul	42	Bavaria
HIRSCHHAUER, Friedrich (61)	Pres Luftschutzbund	1 Aug	39	Bavaria
HOFFMANN (53)	A Flak Division	1 Dec	42	
KAMMHUBER, Josef (48)	Fliegerkorps XII	30 Jan	43	Bavaria
KASTNER-KIRDORF, Gustav (63)		1 Jul	41	
KITZINGER, Karl (59)	C G, Ukraine	1 Oct	39	
KLEPKE, Waldemar (62)		1 Jan	39	Silesia
KORTEN, Günther (46)	C of S, Air Force	30 Jan	43	
KÜHL, Leonhard (59)	R L M	1 Apr	39	
MAHNCKE, Alfred (56)	Luftgau South	1 Sep	43	
MARTINI, Hermann (53)	C Sig O, Air Force	20 Sep	41	Saxony
MAYER, Wilhelm (58)	Luftgau South East	1 Feb	41	

RESTRICTED

61. Air Force Generals.—Continued.
d. General der Flieger, Flakartillerie, etc. (*Lieutenant General*).—Continued.

Name (age)	Command or appointment	Seniority	Origin
MOHR, Max	Liaison Off, French Air Force	1 Apr 41	
ODEBRECHT	Air Force Field Corps III	1 Dec 42	
PETERSEN (53)		1 Nov 42	
PFLUGBEIL, Kurt (54)	An Air Fleet	1 Feb 42	Saxony
POHL, Erich Ritte rv	In Italy	1 Mar 42	Bavaria
PUTZIER (53)		1 Jul 42	
QUADE, Erich (61)	Public Relations	1 Sep 40	Hesse
RENZ, v. (58)	(Flak)	31 Jan 43	Baden
RITTER, Hans (51)	Liaison with Navy	1 Apr 42	
RUGGERA, Kamillo	Flak, Luftgau II	1 Dec 40	Austria
SCHLEMM		30 Jan 43	
SCHMIDT, August (55)	Flak, Luftgau VI	1 Jul 41	
SCHMIDT, Hugo		1 Apr 41	
SCHUBERT, Dr. (56)		1 Jul 42	Saxony
SCHULZ (55)	Fifth Air Fleet ?	1 Dec 42	Hesse
SCHWEICKHARD, Karl (62)	Retired (?)	1 Jun 38	Baden
SEIDEL, Hans-Georg v. (53)	Gen Qu, Air Force	1 Jan 42	
SIBURG, Ing. Hans (50)	Luftgau, Holland	1 Apr 42	
SOMME, Walter (57)	Luftgau VIII	1 Jun 42	
SPEIDEL, Wilhelm	C G, South Greece	1 Jan 42	Württemberg
STUDENT, Kurt (54)	Fliegerkorps XI	30 May 40	
VIERLING, Albert (57)	Luftgaustab z.b.V. 4	1 Jun 42	Bavaria
WABER, Bernhard		1 Mar 42	Austria
WEISSMANN, Dr. Eugen (53)	Luftgau West France	1 Jun 42	Württemberg
WENNINGER, Ralph (54)		1 Nov 40	Bavaria
WIMMER, Wilhelm (55)	Luftgau Belgium—N. France	1 Oct 39	Bavaria
WOLFF, Ludwig (58)	Luftgau XI	1 Feb 41	Alsace
ZANDER, Konrad (61)	Fliegerführer Crimea	1 Apr 38	
ZENETTI, Emil (61)	Luftgau VII	1 Feb 41	Austria

RESTRICTED

ORDER OF BATTLE OF THE GERMAN ARMY 495

61. Air Force Generals.—Continued.
e. Generalleutnant (Major General).

Name (age)	Command or appointment	Seniority	Origin
ANGERSTEIN (53)	Fliegerkorps I	1 Apr 43	Alsace
v. ARNAULD de la PERRIERE		1 Jan 41	
AXTHELM, Walter v. (51)	Insp Gen, Flak Arty	1 Oct 42	Bavaria
BARLEN, Karl (53)	Air Defense, Slovakia	1 Apr 41	
BAUR de BETAZ (60)	(Admin)	1 Aug 43	
BECKER, Hermann		1 Nov 42	
BECKER, Dipl. Ing. Wilhelm	Sigs	1 Jul 43	
BEHRENDT, Hans (52)		1 Oct 43	
BOENICKE, Walter		1 Sep 43	Silesia
BRÄUER, Bruno (51)	C G, Crete	1 Oct 42	
BRUCH, Hermann (62)		1 Nov 40	
BRUNNER, Josef		1 Oct 43	Austria
BÜLOW, Hilmer Frhr. v. (60)	Military Science Dept, R L M	1 Apr 41	
BÜLOWIUS, Alfred (51)	Fliegerkorps II	1 Mar 43	
BUFFA, Ernst (52)	A Flak Division	1 Feb 43	
BURCHARD, Dipl. Ing. Heinrich	7th Flak Division	1 Aug 42	
CABANIS, Ernst (53)	R L M	1 May 43	
CARLSEN	Air Supply Group XI	1 Oct 40	
CONRAD, Dipl. Ing. Gerhard	Staff of Fliegerkorps XI	1 Apr 43	Anhalt
CONRATH, Paul (48)	Hermann Göring Division	1 Sep 43	
CRANZ (55)	Training Cmd, Prague	1 Nov 40	
CZECH	Naval Air Service	1 Apr 43	
DEINHARDT		1 Jan 42	
DÖRFFLER (54)	Field Equipment Group	1 Apr 43	
DÖRING, Kurt Bertrau v. (55)	1st Jagddivision	1 Nov 41	
DRUM, Karl (50)	11th Air Force Field Division	1 Jan 43	Baden
EGAN-KRIEGER, Jeno v. (59)		1 Dec 42	
EIBENSTEIN, Rudolf (50)	12th Flak Division	1 Aug 43	
FAHNERT, Friedrich (65)	Head of Amtsgruppe W N V (OKW)	1 Apr 40	Saxony
FEYERABEND, Walter (53)	(Flak)	1 Apr 41	

RESTRICTED

61. Air Force Generals.—Continued.
e. Generalleutnant (Major General).—Continued.

Name (age)	Command or appointment	Seniority	Origin
FINK, Dipl. Ing	Insp. d. Kampfflieger	1 Oct 42	Württemberg
FRANSSEN	Insp Armaments, Belgium	1 Aug 42	
FRANTZ, Gotthard	Prisoner of War	1 Apr 43	
FRANTZ, Walter	C Sig O, C-in-C Center	1 Jun 43	
FRIEDENSBURG, Walter		1 Dec 41	
GAUTIER, Theophil	Insp of Armaments, Wkr. XVII	1 Apr 42	
GERSTENBERG, Alfred (51)	Head of Air Force in Rumania	1 Sep 43	
GROSCH, Walter (53)	Chief Q M, Fifth Air Fleet	1 Jun 43	
HAEHNELT, Wilhelm (69)	R L M	1 Dec 40	
HANESSE (63)	Head of Air Force Liaison Staff, Paris	1 Apr 42	Hesse
HEIDRICH, Richard (48)	1st Parachute Division	1 Jul 43	
HERMANN	Cmdt of Pilsen	1 Nov 40	
HEYKING, Rüdiger v	6th Air Force Field Division	1 Jul 43	
HILGERS, Dipl. Ing. (52)		1 Apr 43	Hesse
HOFMANN, Hans	C of S, Fourth Air Fleet	1 Jun 43	
KARLEWSKI			
KEIPER	Head of Air Mission to Slovakia	1 Jan 43	
KESSLER (53)	Fliegerführer Atlantic	1 Apr 41	
KETTEMBEIL, Karl (54)	Air Attache Ankara	1 Jun 43	
KETTNER (51)		1 Oct 43	
KIEFFER, Maximillian (53)		1 Jun 42	Bavaria
KNAUSS, Dr. (52)	Luftgauakademie Gatow	1 Aug 42	Württemberg
KOLB, Alexander (55)	Flak Air Defense Command Stettin	1 Nov 40	
KRAHMER, Eckart (52)	Air Attache Madrid	1 Oct 43	
KROCKER, Viktor (55)		1 Dec 41	
KRUEGER, Ernst		1 Jun 43	
KÜHNE, Otto	C Sig O, Fifth Air Fleet	1 Jun 42	
LACKNER, Walther (53)	10th Fliegerdivision	1 Dec 42	

RESTRICTED

61. Air Force Generals.—Continued.
e. Generalleutnant (Major General).—Continued.

Name (age)	Command or appointment	Seniority	Origin
LANGEMEYER, Otto (59)	Q M Staff of Fourth Air Fleet	1 Apr 42	
LAULE (53)		1 Sep 43	Baden
LECH		1 Nov 40	
LENTZSCH, Johannes (60)	(Flak)	1 Mar 38	
LINDNER	Aviation Ordnance	1 Aug 41	
LORENZ, Walter	Supplies, Norway	1 Feb 43	
MACKENZEN v. ASTFELD, Hans-Georg (58)		1 Apr 41	
MÄLZER, Dipl. Ing. Kurt	Cmdt of Rome	1 Oct 43	Saxony
MANN, Hermann Edler v. TIECHLER, Ritter v. (55)	A Luftgaustab	1 Nov 40	Bavaria
MEISTER	Operational Staff	1 Mar 43	
MENSCHING (56)		1 Apr 43	
MERTITSCH (51)		1 Oct 42	
MOLL (57)	With Fourth Air Fleet (Seaplane expert)	1 Apr 42	
MOOYER	Technical Training Dept, R L M	1 Apr 41	
MÜLLER, Ernst	Air Supply Group XI	1 Jan 42	
MUSSHOFF (58)		1 Nov 40	
NIEHOFF, Heinrich (62)	Transferred to Army	1 Feb 38	
NUBER		1 Sep 43	
OSTERKAMP, Theodor (52)		1 Aug 42	
PISTORIUS	11th Fliegerregiment	1 Jul 43	
RAMCKE, Hermann Bernhard (56)	2d Parachute Division	21 Dec 42	
RANTZAU, Heino v		1 Jun 43	Bavaria
REIMANN, Richard (52)	A Flak Division	1 Mar 43	
RICHTER, Hellmuth (52)	11th Flak Division	1 Aug 41	
RÖMER, Erwin v. (56)		1 Apr 41	Saxony
ROQUES, Karl v.	Retired	1 Oct 38	
RUDLOFF, Werner v.	Personnel Dept, R L M	1 Aug 43	
RÜDT v. COLLENBERG, Kurt Frhr. (62)	Insp of Armaments, Paris and N W France	1 Jul 42	

RESTRICTED

61. Air Force Generals.—Continued.
e. Generalleutnant (Major General).—Continued.

Name (age)	Command or appointment	Seniority	Origin
SATTLER, Ottfried (57)		1 Jan 40	
SCHEURLEN		1 Nov 42	
SCHIMPF, Dipl. Ing. Richard	C of S Luftgau VIII	1 Aug 43	
SCHLEICH, Ritter v. (56)		1 Sep 43	Bavaria
SCHMIDT, Kurt (56)		1 Jan 40	Saxony
SCHUBERT		1 Nov 42	
SCHULTHEISS, Pavel (51)		1 Jan 43	Württemberg
SCHULTZE, Rudolf		1 Sep 43	
SCHWABEDISSEN, Walter		1 Mar 42	
SCHWUB, Albert (57)		1 Oct 40	Bavaria
SEIFERT, Johann	10th Flak Division	1 Jun 42	Austria
SOMMER, Johannes (57)		1 Mar 40	Württemberg
SPANG, Willibald (57)	15th Air Force Field Division	1 Jan 42	Württemberg
SPIESS, Theodor (52)	13th Flak Division	1 Aug 41	
SPRUNER v. MERTZ, Hermann (60)	Staff of Luftgau VII	1 Apr 43	Bavaria
STEUDEMANN, Kurt (54)	Flak, R L M	1 Jan 41	Saxony
STUBENRAUCH, Wilhelm v. (54)	(Flak)	1 Jun 42	
STURM, Alfred (56)		1 Aug 43	
SUREN, Walter (56)		1 Apr 41	
TIPPELSKIRCH, v.		1 Apr 43	
TRIENDL, Theodor (55)	In Schwerin	1 Apr 43	Bavaria
WAGNER	8th Flak Division	1 Nov 42	
WALZ, Franz Josef (59)		1 Apr 41	Bavaria
WEESE		1 Apr 43	
WEIGAND, Dipl. Volksw. Wolfgang (59)	Inspector of Armaments Army Group Center (1942)	1 Nov 40	
WITTING (53)		1 Feb 41	
WÜHLISCH, Heinz-Helmut v. (52)		1 Apr 42	
ZIEGLER, Dr. Günther		1 Feb 43	
ZOCH, Phillip (52)		1 Apr 42	

RESTRICTED

ORDER OF BATTLE OF THE GERMAN ARMY 499

61. Air Force Generals.—Continued.
f. Generalmajor (Brigadier General).

Name (age)	Command or appointment	Seniority	Origin
ADAMETZ		1 Feb 41	
ANTON	(Flak)	1 Feb 43	
ARNIM, Hans v.		1 Nov 42	
ASCHENBRENNER, Heinrich	Staff of C-in-C South	1 Aug 42	
BAIER, Eberhard		1 Apr 42	
BANSE		1 Apr 42	
BARENTHIN	Staff of Fliegerkorps XI (?)	1 Sep 43	
BASSENGE, Dipl. Ing. Gerhard	Prisoner of War	1 May 43?	
BERTHOLD	(Admin)	1 Jul 41	
BERTRAM (53)	(Flak)	1 Jun 39	
BIEDERMANN, Wolf Frhr. v. (51)	An Air Force Field Division	1 Apr 41	Saxony
BIWER (50)		1 Sept 41	
BOENIGK, Oskar Frhr. v. (51)		1 Feb 41	
BOETTGE	Air Recruit Depot 31	1 Oct 41	
BONATZ, Ernst (51)	Head of a Section, R L M	1 Aug 41	
BRAKERT		1 Apr 43	
BRANDT		1 Jan 43	
BUCHHOLZ	Air Transport, Mediterranean	1 Dec 41	Braunschweig
CARGANICO (57)		1 Dec 41	
CHAULIN-EGERSBERG, v.	(Flak)	1 Dec 41	Hesse
CRIEGERN, v.		1 Apr 43	
DAHLMANN, Dr. Hermann	R L M	1 Dec 41	Hesse
DEICHMANN, Paul	C of S, Second Air Fleet	1 Sep 42	
DEWALL, Job v. (64)		1 Nov 40	
DOMMENGET		1 Aug 43	
DRECHSEL, Ernst		1 Feb 42	Bavaria
ERDMANN, Dipl. Ing. Wolfgang	General Staff (Organization Section)	1 Mar 43	
ERDMANN		1 Apr 43	
EXSZ (50)	Armistice Commission, Aix-en-Provence	1 Apr 42	

RESTRICTED

61. Air Force Generals.—Continued.
f. Generalmajor (*Brigadier General*).—Continued.

Name (age)	Command or appointment	Seniority	Origin
FALKENHAYN, Erich v. (54)	(Admin)	1 Nov 41	
FALKOWSKI, v.		1 Nov 41	
FINK, Johannes		1 Jun 43	
FREYBERG-EISENBERG-ALL-MENDINGEN, Egloff Frhr. v. (51)	(Flak) In Avignon	1 Apr 39	
FROMMHERZ		1 Apr 43	
FUCHS		1 Sept 43	
FÜTTERER, Cuno Heribert	Air Attache, Budapest	1 Nov 41	
FUNCKE, Heinz	Flying Training Regiment	1 Oct 41	
GALLAND, Adolf (32)	Insp of Fighters	19 Nov 42	
GANDERT, Hans Eberhardt (52)	R L M	1 Dec 39	
GNAMM, Dr.	A Luftgau in Balkans	1 Jun 43	
GOLTZ	Sea Rescue Service	1 Apr 41	
GOSEWISCH		1 Oct 43	
GRONAU, Wolfgang v. (51)	Air Attache, Tokyo		
HACHENBERG, v. (56)	(Admin)	1 Nov 40	
HAENSCHKE (50)		1 Feb 42	
HAMEL	Air Works Inspectorate R L M	1 Apr 43	
HANTELMANN (52)	An Aerodrome Regional Comd in France	1 Feb 42	
HARLINGHAUSEN, Martin (42)	Insp Gen of Torpedoes		
HARTING		1 Nov 40	
HARTOG (53)	Hq Staff of Luftgau Belgium-North France	1 Apr 41	Baden
HASSE (66)	(Admin)	1 Nov 41	
HEIDENREICH		1 Oct 43	
HEMPEL, Fritz (55)		1 Feb 43	
HERHOTH v. ROHDEN		1 Oct 43	
HERWARTH v. BITTENFELD, Eberhard (56)	An Airfield Regional Comd	1 Apr 40	
HESSE, Max		1 Apr 41	

RESTRICTED

ORDER OF BATTLE OF THE GERMAN ARMY 501

61. Air Force Generals.—Continued.
f. Generalmajor (Brigadier General).—Continued.

Name (age)	Command or appointment	Seniority	Origin
HEYDE, v. der		1 Oct 42	
HEYDENREICH, Leopold	R L M	1 Apr 42	
HINKELBEIN (66)	(Admin)	1 Sep 41	Württemberg
HINTZ	Flak Arty School, Rerik	1 Apr 43	
HIPPEL, Walter v	A Flak Division	1 Apr 43	
HOEFERT, Johannes (61)		1 Apr 41	Saxony
HOHNE, Otto			
HOLLE, Alexander (46)		1 Feb 43	
HOMBURG, Erich (68)	General Staff, Air Force	1 Nov 40	
HORNUNG, Ferdinand (53)		1 Sep 42	
HÜCKEL (52)		1 Sep 41	
HUTH, Joachim		1 Apr 43	
JAKOBY	Sigs	1 Feb 43	
JENNY		1 Sep 43	
JUNCK, Werner	3d Jagddivision	1 Apr 43	
KAHL, Siegfried	Luftgau Kdo VIII	1 Aug 43	
KATHMANN, Dipl. Ing		1 Apr 42	
KLEIN, Dipl. Ing		1 Feb 41	
KLEIN, Hans (53)	A Fighter Command	27 Aug 39	
KLEINRATH, Kurt	Chief of a Dept, R L M	1 Mar 39	
KÖCHY, Karl (49)	Prisoner of War	1 Nov 41	
KOLLER, Karl (46)	C of S, Third Air Fleet	1 Mar 43	
KORTE, Hans		1 Jul 43	
KRAPP	(Admin)	1 Apr 41	
KRAUSS, Dipl. Ing		1 Aug 43	
KREIPE	R L M	1 Mar 43	
KRESSMANN, Erich	(Flak)	1 Feb 42	Baden
KRIEGBAUM (52)	A Cadet School	1 Dec 39	
KRÜGER, Otto (51)		1 May 41	
KRUEGER		1 Nov 41	

RESTRICTED

61. Air Force Generals.—Continued.
f. Generalmajor (*Brigadier General*).—Continued.

Name (age)	Command or appointment	Seniority	Origin
KRUG, Michael		1 Jan 43	
KUDERNA		1 Sep 43	
KUEN		1 Apr 42	
KUTZLEBEN, v. (58)	Possibly transferred to Army.	1 Jan 38	
LICHTENBERGER, Hermann	(Flak)	1 Feb 43	
LÖDERER		1 Sep 43	
LOHMANN (51)	14th Air Force Field Division.	1 Feb 42	
LONGIN, Anton		1 Aug 43	
LORENZ, Heinrich (52)		1 Feb 43	
LUCZNY, Alfons (50)	(Flak)	1 Feb 42	Silesia
MAASS	Staff of Luftgau VII	1 Aug 41	
MAIER, Nikolaus		1 Oct 43	
MASSOW, Albrecht v. (58)	Air Supply Group, Luftgau VIII	1 Jan 41	
MASSOW, v		1 Apr 43	
MEINDL, Eugen (52)	Fliegerkorps XIII	1 Jan 41	
MENSCH (57)	Staff of Fifth Air Fleet	1 Nov 40	
MENTZEL	Recon School, Braunschweig.	1 Jun 41	
MENZEL, Georg-Adolf (57)	Air Defense Command 7	1 Oct 39	Saxony
METZNER		1 Apr 42	
MORZIK		1 Oct 43	
MÜLLER, Gottlob	In Italy	1 Nov 41	Bavaria
MUGGENTHALER, Hermann (52)	(Admin)	1 Jul 41	Bavaria
MUHR, Eduard		1 Jul 43	
NEUFFER	Prisoner of War	1 Dec 41	Bavaria
NIELSEN	C of S, Fifth Air Fleet	1 Mar 43	
NITZSCHE, Martin	3d L G N Regiment	1 Jan 41	
NORDT		1 Apr 41	
NOWACK, Franz	R L M	1 Sep 41	

RESTRICTED

ORDER OF BATTLE OF THE GERMAN ARMY 503

61. Air Force Generals.—Continued.
f. Generalmajor (Brigadier General).—Continued.

Name (age)	Command or appointment	Seniority	Origin
OLBRICH		1 Apr 42	
ORTNER-WEIGAND, Bruno		1 Sep 41	Austria
OVERDYCK	Sigs	1 Aug 43	
PAWELKE		1 Oct 43	
PELTZ, Dietrich	Fliegerkorps IX (?)	1 Dec 43	Saxony
PETRAUSCHKE		1 Jul 43	
PFEIFFER	Insp of Clothing and Rations	1 Jul 42	
PICKERT, Wolfgang (47)	9th Flak Division	1 Oct 42	
PLOCH, Dipl. Ing. August (49)		1 Aug 40	
PLOCHER, Hermann	C of S of an Air Fleet	1 Mar 43	
POETSCH (52)		1 Aug 41	
PRELLBERG	7th Flak Brigade	1 Aug 42	
PREU	Luftgaustab South East	1 Feb 43	
PRINZ		1 Sep 43	
PUESCHEL, Konrad (62)	(Admin)	1 Aug 43	
PULTAR, Josef	43d Fliegerausb. Regiment	1 Jul 40	Austria
PUNZERT, Josef	23d Fliegerregiment	1 Mar 43	
RAITHEL, Dipl. Ing. Hans (47)		1 Apr 42	Bavaria
RAUCH, Hans		1 Jun 42	
REINSHAGEN	Flying School, Hildesheim	1 Jul 43	
REUSS, Heinrich XXXVII Prinz v.	18th Flak Division	1 Feb 43	
RIBENSTEIN		1 Aug 41	
RIECKHOFF, Herbert	C of S, First Air Fleet	1 Mar 43	
RIEKE, Georg	R L M	1 Sep 41	
RIESCH, Dipl. Ing	Aerodrome Regional Command, Werl	1 Nov 41	Bavaria
RIVA, Erich		1 Sep 42	
RÖMER		1 Oct 43	
ROESCH (57)	Insp of Armaments, Wkr. VII	1 Dec 41	Württemberg
ROTH, Ernst-August (46)	Fliegerführer Lofoten	1 Aug 42	

RESTRICTED

61. Air Force Generals.—Continued.
f. Generalmajor (*Brigadier General*).—Continued.

Name (age)	Command or appointment	Seniority	Origin
RÜTER, Wolfgang (52)		1 Dec 39	
SATTLER, Alfred (49)	Sig C	1 Dec 41	Baden
SCHALLER	1st Flak Division	1 Oct 43	
SCHAUER, Ludwig (56)		1 Apr 39	Bavaria
SCHILFFARTH, Ludwig (51)		1 Feb 42	Bavaria
SCHMID, Josef		1 Mar 43	
SCHÖBEL, Otto		1 Oct 41	Austria
SCHÖRGI, Hugo		1 Nov 42	Austria
SCHROEDER, Severin		1 Apr 41	
SCHROTH		1 Aug 41	
SCHÜTZE (63)		1 Nov 41	
SCHÜTZEK		1 Oct 43	
SCHÜLTZE-RHONHOF (54)	C Sig O, Lutfgau XVII	1 Apr 41	
SEIBT	On KESSELRING'S Staff	1 Apr 43	
SEIDEMANN, Hans (42)		1 Aug 42	
SELDNER, Eduard (54)		19 Jul 40	Baden
SEYWALD, Heinz	Bomber School, Thorn	1 Nov 41	Bavaria
SIESS, Gustav (49)		1 Nov 40	Austria
SOELDNER (54)		1 Apr 42	Bavaria
SONNENBURG (53)		1 Jun 41	
SPERLING (51)		1 Apr 41	
STAHEL, Reiner (52)	Special Staff, in Italy	21 Jan 43	
STARKE, Friedrich		1 Jun 41	
STEIN	Insp of Motor Transport	1 Nov 40	
STEINKOPF		1 Nov 40	
STEPHAN		1 Oct 43	
STUTZER (56)	Judge Advocate General's Dept	1 Dec 40	
TESCHNER		1 Nov 40	
THYM, Heinrich		1 Nov 40	Austria

RESTRICTED

61. Air Force Generals.—Continued.
f. Generalmajor (Brigadier General).—Continued.

Name (age)	Command or appointment	Seniority	Origin
TIPPELSKIRCH, v		1 Nov 40	
TSCHOELTSCH, Ehrenfried (51)		1 Nov 41	Saxony
UNGER (53)		1 Jun 41	
VEITH (54)	(Flak)	1 Feb 43	
VODEPP		1 Feb 43	
VOELK		1 Oct 43	
VOIGT-RUSCHEWEYH		1 Oct 43	
VOLKMANN, Dietrich	Staff of C-in-C Air Force	1 Jul 43	
VORWALD, Dipl. Ing. Wolfgang	RLM	1 Mar 43	
WADEHN		1 Sep 43	
WALLAND, Eugen		1 Nov 41	Austria
WALLNER, Otto (62)		1 Nov 41	Bavaria
WANGENHEIM, Edgar Frhr. v. (54)		1 Nov 40	
v. WEECH	Sigs, Luftgau Norway	1 Aug 43	
WEESE		1 Nov 40	
WEIL		1 Oct 43	
WEINER		1 Oct 43	
WICHARD	Staff Airfield Regional Comd Warsaw	1 Jan 43	
WIELAND		1 Oct 43	
WILCK	Insp of Armaments, Ukraine	1 Nov 40	
WILKE, Gustav (46)	R L M	1 Apr 43	
WITZENDORFF, Gotthard v. (52)		1 Feb 43	
ZECH	R L M	1 Apr 42	
ZIERVOGEL, Dr		1 Jan 43	

RESTRICTED

62. Senior Officers of the Waffen-SS.*
a. Reichsführer-SS (*Field Marshal*).

Name (age)	Command or appointment
HIMMLER, Heinrich (44)	Chief of the Waffen-SS.

b. SS-Oberstgruppenführer und Generaloberst der Waffen-SS (*General*).

Name (age)	Command or appointment
DIETRICH, Josef ("Sepp") (52)	Traditional Commander of Leibstandarte "Adolf Hitler" and organizer of Waffen-SS; now Commander I SS Panzer Corps

---

* This list also includes certain officers in the General SS and Police whose activities are closely associated with the Waffen-SS.

RESTRICTED

62. Senior Officers of the Waffen-SS.*—Continued.
c. SS-Obergruppenführer und General der Waffen-SS (Lieutenant General).

Name (age)	Command or appointment
BACH-ZELEWSKI, Erich v. dem (45)	H. SS Pf. Central Sector, Russia
BERGER, Gottlob (58)	Chief of Directorate for Germanic Formations in the Central SS Department
BERKELMANN, Theo (50)	H. SS Pf. Lothringen-Saarpfalz; (part of Wkr. XII)
EBERSTEIN, Friedrich, Karl Frhr. v. (50)	H. SS Pf. Süd (Wkr. VII)
HAUSSER, Paul (64)	Cmdr. II SS Panzer Corps
HILDEBRANDT, Richard (47)	H. SS Pf. Weichsel (Wkr. XX)
HOFMANN, Otto (48)	H. SS Pf. Südwest (Wkr. V)
JECKELN, Friedrich (49)	H. SS Pf. Ostland
JÜTTNER, Hans (50)	Chief of Operational Headquarters of the Waffen-SS
KNAPP	In SS Operational Headquarters
KOPPE, Wilhelm (48)	H. SS Pf. Govt Gen
MAZUW, Emil (43)	H. SS Pf. Ostsee (Wkr. II)
PFEFFER-WILDENBRUCH, Karl v. (55)	Former Cmdr SS Polizei Division
PHLEPS, Artur (63)	Cmdr V SS Mountain Corps
POHL, Oswald (52)	Chief of the SS Dept of Administration
PRÜTZMANN, Hans-Adolf (42)	Inspector General of the General and Waffen-SS; Chief Liaison Officer SS-Wehrmacht
QUERNER Rudolf (50)	H. SS Pf. Donau (Wkr. XVII)

RESTRICTED

62. Senior Officers of the Waffen–SS.*—Continued.

c. SS–Obergruppenführer und General der Waffen–SS (*Lieutenant General*).—Continued.

Name (age)	Command or appointment
RAUTER, Hans (49)	H. SS Pf. Netherlands
REDIESS, Wilhelm (43)	H. SS Pf. Norway
REEDER, Eggert	Chief of Civil Administration Belgium and Northern France
SACHS, Ernst (63)	Chief of Communications in the SS High Command
SCHMAUSER, Ernst Heinrich (54)	H. SS Pf. Südost (Wkr. VIII)
STEINER, Felix (48)	Cmdr III SS Panzer Corps
WALDECK - PYRMONT, Josias Erbprinz zu (48)	H. SS Pf. Fulda-Werra (Wkr. IX)
WOLFF, Karl (44)	Chief of the Personal Staff of the Reichsführer; H. SS Pf. Italy
WOYRSCH, Udo v. (49)	H. SS Pf. Elbe (Wkr. IV)
WÜNNENBERG, Alfred (52)	Chief of the Regular Police; former Cmdr SS Polizei Div

RESTRICTED

62. Senior Officers of the Waffen-SS.*—Continued.

d. SS-Gruppenführer und Generalleutnant der Waffen-SS (*Major General*).

Name (age)	Command or appointment
ALVENSLEBEN, Ludolf v. (43)	SS Pf. Taurien (Black Sea)
BANGERSKI, Rudolf	Inspector General of the Latvian SS Volunteer Legion
BASSEWITZ-BEHR, Georg Graf v. (44)	H. SS Pf. Nordsee (Wkr. X)
BITTRICH, Willi (50)	Cmdr SS Division "Hohenstaufen"
BREITHAUPT, Franz (63)	Chief of SS Legal Department
DEMELHUBER, Karl (48)	Cmdr of Waffen-SS in the Netherlands
FRANK, August (45)	In SS Administration, Munich
GEBHARDT, Prof Dr. Karl (46)	Chief of the SS Medical Corps
GENZKEN, Dr. med. Karl (59)	Chief of SS Medical Hq Berlin
GILLE, Herbert (47)	Cmdr SS Division "Wiking"
GLÜCKS, Richard (55)	Inspector General of all Death's Head Formations
GRAWITZ, Dr. Ernst Robert (45)	Medical Inspector of the Waffen-SS
GUTENBERGER, Karl (39)	H. SS Pf. West (Wkr. VI)
HANSEN	Inspector of SS Artillery
HERFF, Maximilian v	Chief of SS Personnel Office
HÖFLE, Hermann	H. SS Pf. Mitte (Wkr. XI)
HOFMANN, H	
JÜRS, Heinrich (46)	Chief of Replacement Training of the Waffen-SS
JUNGCLAUS, Richard (39)	Cmdr of Waffen-SS in Belgium
KAMMERHOFER, Konstantin	Controls SS activities in Croatia

RESTRICTED

62. Senior Officers of the Waffen–SS.*—Continued.

d. SS–Gruppenführer und Generalleutnant der Waffen–SS (*Major General*).—Continued.

Name (age)	Command or appointment
KATZMANN, Friedrich (Fritz) (38)	SS Pf. Galicia
KEPPLER, Georg (50)	Cmdr of the Waffen-SS in Bohemia and Moravia
KLEINHEISTERKAMP, Matthias (51)	Cmdr SS Mountain Div "Nord"
KORSEMANN	H. SS Pf. White Ruthenia
KRÜGER, Walter (54)	Cmdr SS Division "Das Reich"
MARTIN, Dr. Benno (51)	H. SS Pf. Main (Wkr. XIII)
MEYSSNER, August (57)	H. SS Pf. Serbia
OBERG, Karl Albrecht (47)	H. SS Pf. France
PANCKE, Günter (44)	Controls SS Activities in Denmark
RÖSENER, Erwin (42)	H. SS Pf. Alpenland (Wkr. XVIII)
SCHMELCHER, Willi (49)	Chief of the TN (Technical Emergency Service)
SCHROEDER, Walther (41)	SS Pf. Latvia
SPORRENBERG	H. SS Pf. Nordost (Wkr. I)
STROOP	Former H. SS Pf. Greece
WAPPENHANS, Waldemar (50)	SS Pf. Brest-Litowsk
WOLF, Richard	C of S of SS Signal Corps
ZENNER, Karl (45)	SS Pf Minsk(?)

RESTRICTED

ORDER OF BATTLE OF THE GERMAN ARMY 511

62. Senior Officers of the Waffen–SS.*—Continued.
   e. SS–Brigadeführer und Generalmajor der Waffen–SS (*Brigadier General*).

Name (age)	Command or appointment
BEHR, Max v. (65)	Cmdr SS Guard Regiment "Wien"
BLUMENREUTER, Karl (62)	In SS Medical Dept
BÖTTCHER, Dr. Viktor	SS Pf. District Radom, Govt Gen
FEGELEIN, Hermann (37)	Cmdr SS Cavalry Division
GOEDICKE	SS Garrison Cmdr Vienna
HALTERMANN, Hans Dietrich	Formerly SS Pf. Kiev
HARM, Hermann (49)	SS Pf. Kovno
HARTENSTEIN	Cmdr 1st SS Infantry Brigade (1942)
HELLWIG, Otto (45)	SS Pf. Bialystok
KLINGEMANN, Gottfried (59)	Cmdr SS Junker School Bad Tölz
KRYSSING, Christian Peter (53)	Founder of the Free Corps Denmark
OBERKAMP, Carl Reichsritter v. (50)	Cmdr SS Mountain Division "Prinz Eugen"
PRIESS, Hermann (43)	Cmdr SS Division "Totenkopf"
PÜCKLER - BURGHAUS, Carl - Friedrich Graf v.	Cmdr SS Division "Lettland"
SAUBERZWEIG	Cmdr SS Croatian Mountain Division
SCHMEDES, Dr. Rothard (Fritz?)	Cmdr of an SS Police Artillery Regiment
SCHOLZ, Fritz (47)	Cmdr SS Division "Nordland"
SCHWEDLER, Hans (65)	
SIMON, Max (44)	Former Cmdr SS Division "Totenkopf"
THIELE	Chief of Communications in the SS High Command

RESTRICTED

62. Senior Officers of the Waffen–SS.*—Continued.

e. SS–Brigadeführer und Generalmajor der Waffen–SS (*Brigadier General*).—Continued.

Name (age)	Command or appointment
TREUENFELD, Karl v.	Cmdr of Waffen-SS in the Ukraine
VAHL, Herbert Ernst (48)	Former Cmdr SS Division "Das Reich"
VOGLER, Anton	SS Garrison Cmdr Munich
VOSS, Bernhard	Cmdr SS Training Area Debica (Poland)
WEBER, Christian (61)	Inspector of the SS Cavalry Schools
WEISS	SS Pf. Nikolaev
WERLIN, Jacob	Inspector General for Motorization
WYSOCKI	SS Pf. Lithuania

RESTRICTED

ORDER OF BATTLE OF THE GERMAN ARMY 513

62. Senior Officers of the Waffen-SS.*—Continued.
f. Lower Ranking Waffen-SS Officers.
(1) *SS-Oberführer.*

Name (age)	Command or appointment
ALTVATER-MACKENSEN	Cmdr of an SS Junker School
JENA, von	Cmdr SS Death's Head Regt "Oranienburg"
KARASCH	Deputy Cmdr of Waffen-SS in Bohemia and Moravia
SOODLA	Cmdr Estonian SS Brigade
WAGNER, Jürgen (43)	Cmdr SS Pz Gr Regt "Germania" in SS Division "Wiking"
WISCH	Cmdr SS Division Leibstandarte "Adolf Hitler"
WITT, Fritz	Cmdr SS Division "Hitler Jugend"

(2) *SS-Standartenführer.*

Name (age)	Command or appointment
BECKER, Helmuth (42)	Cmdr SS Pz Gr Regt "Theodor Eicke" in SS Division "Totenkopf"
HARMEL, Heinz (38)	Cmdr SS Pz Gr Regt "Deutschland" in SS Division "Das Reich"
LOMBARD, Gustav	Cmdr an SS Cavalry Regt in SS Cavalry Division
MEYER, Kurt	In SS Division Leibstandarte "Adolf Hitler"
SCHULDT, Hinrich	Cmdr an SS Brigade

RESTRICTED

62. SENIOR OFFICERS OF THE WAFFEN—SS.*—Cont'd
(3) *SS–Obersturmbannführer.*

Name (age)	Command or appointment
BAUM, Otto (33)	Cmdr an SS Pz Gren Regt in SS Division "Totenkopf"
KRAAS, Hugo	Cmdr SS Pz Gr Regt 2 in SS Division Leibstandarte "Adolf Hitler"
KUMM, Otto (35)	Former Cmdr SS Pz Gr Regt "Der Führer" in SS Division "Das Reich"
PETERSEN, Heinrich	Cmdr SS Mtn Inf Regt 1 in SS Division "Prinz Eugen"
REITZENSTEIN, Albin (33)	Cmdr Tank Regt in SS Division "Das Reich"
STADLER, Sylvester (34)	Cmdr SS Regt "Der Führer" in SS Division "Das Reich"
ZEHENDER, August (41)	Cmdr an SS Cavalry Regiment

RESTRICTED

Section IX. INDEX OF NAMES

ABRAHAM, Erich, 193, 464
ABT, 464
ADAM, Wilhelm, 439
ADAMETZ, 499
ADLHOCH, 464
ADOLPH-AUFFENBERG-KOMAROW, Gustav, 299, 439
ADOLPH, Ernst, 464
AGRICOLA, Kurt, 439
ALBERTI, Konrad v., 464
ALDRIAN, Eduard, 439
ALLMENDINGER, Karl, 431
ALTEN, Viktor v., 464
ALTRICHTER, Dr. Friedrich, 305, 439
ALTROCK, Wilhelm v., 52, 439
ALTVATER-MACKENSEN, 513
ALVENSLEBEN, Ludolf v., 509
AMANN, v., 439
AMMON, Carl v., 27, 464
ANDRAE, Waldemar, 493
ANDREAS, 439
ANGELIS, Maximilian, 157, 431
ANGER, 464
ANGERN, Günther, 439
ANGERSTEIN, 495
ANSAT, Johann, 439
ANTON, 499
APELL, v., 439
APELL, Wilhelm, v., 439
ARNAULD de la PERRIERE, v. 495

ARNDT, 464
ARNDT, Karl, 232, 464
ARNIM, Friedemund v., 464
ARNIM, Hans v., 499
ARNIM, Jürgen v., 430
ARNOLD, Karl, 464
ARNOLD, Wilhelm, 464
ASCHEBERG, Percy Baron v., 464
ASCHENBRANDT, Heinrich, 464
ASCHENBRENNER, Heinrich, 499
AUER, Franz, 464
AULEB, 300, 439
AXMANN, Arthur, 123
AXTHELM, Walter v., 495
BAARTH, Jürgen, 56, 464
BACH-ZELEWSKI, Erich v. dem, 507
BACHER, Hermann, 464
BADE, Hans-Albert, 464
BADER, Paul, 170, 431
BADINSKI, Kurt, 228, 439
BAESSLER, Erich, 251, 464
BAESSLER, Hans, 464
BAIER, Albrecht, 439
BAIER, Eberhard, 499
BALCK, Hermann, 439
BALTZER, 439
BALTZER, Martin, 464
BAMBERG, Dr., 464
BAMLER, Rudolf, 52, 144, 439
BANGERSKI, Rudolf, 509

515

BANSE, 499
BARCKHAUSEN, Franz, 431
BARENDS, 464
BARENTHIN, 499
BARLEN, Karl, 495
BARTENWERFER, Gustav, 464
BARTON, Gottfried, 465
BASSE, Hans v., 439
BASSE, Max v., 465
BASSENGE, Dipl. Ing. Gerhard, 499
BASSEWITZ-BEHR, Georg Graf v., 509
BAUER, Franz, 465
BAUM, Otto, 514
BAUMGARTNER, Richard, 465
BAUR de BETAZ, 495
BAYER, 210, 439
BAYERLEIN, Fritz, 278, 465
BAZING, 465
BECHER, 465
BECHT, Dipl. Wirtsch. Ernst, 465
BECHTOLSHEIM, Anton Frhr. v. MAUCHENHEIM gen., 138, 439
BECHTOLSHEIM, Gustav Frhr. v. MAUCHENHEIM gen., 465
BECKE, 465
BECKER, 39
BECKER, Franz, 465
BECKER, Fritz, 222, 439
BECKER, Hermann, 495
BECKER, Helmuth, 513
BECKER, Karl, 465
BECKER, Dipl. Ing. Wilhelm, 495

BECKMANN, Alfred, 439
BEEREN, v., 230, 440
BEHLENDORFF, 161, 431
BEHR, v., 440
BEHR, Max v., 511
BEHRENDT, Hans, 495
BEHRENS, Wilhelm, 465
BEHSCHNITT, Walter, 440
BEININGER, 465
BEISSWÄNGER, Hugo, 465
BEISSWÄNGER, Walter, 465
BENCZEK, 34
BENICKE, Dr. Fritz, 465
BERCKEN, v., 199
BERG, Kurt v., 465
BERG, Ludwig v., 41, 440
BERGEN, Johann, 238, 440
BERGER, Gottlob, 507
BERKA, 465
BERKELMANN, Theo. 507
BERLIN, 440
BERNARD, Kurt, 440
BERNHARD, Friedrich Gustav, 440
BERTHOLD (Genmaj.-Heer), 465
BERTHOLD (Genmaj.-Lw.), 499
BERTRAM, 499
BERTRAM, Georg, 440
BESCH, Helmut, 49, 465
BESSEL, v., 465
BESSELL, Hans, 465
BEUKEMANN, Helmuth, 440
BEUTTEL, 52, 440
BEYER, Dr. Franz, 185, 440

RESTRICTED

INDEX OF NAMES 517

BIEDERMANN, Wolf Frhr. v., 499
BIELER, Bruno, 162, 431
BIELFELD, 440
BIENECK, Hellmuth, 493
BIERINGER, 466
BIERMANN, 466
BIESS, Paul, 440
BILHARZ, Eugen, 466
BISLE, Artur, 56, 466
BITTRICH, Willi, 329, 509
BIWER, 499
BLASKOWITZ, Johannes, 138, 430
BLOCK, Johannes, 232, 440
BLOCK, Lothar v., 466
BLÜCHER, Johann-Albrecht v., 466
BLÜMM, Oskar, 440
BLUMENREUTER, Karl, 511
BLUMENTRITT, 136, 440
BOCK, 431
BOCK, Fedor v., 429
BOCK, Franz Karl v., 56, 466
BOCK v. WÜLFINGEN, Ferdinand, 28, 440
BODE, 57
BODENHAUSEN, Erpo Frhr. v., 466
BODENSCHATZ, Karl, 493
BOECKH-BEHRENS, Hans, 142, 440
BÖCKMANN, Herbert v., 431
BOEGE, Ehrenfried, 211, 440
BOEHM-BEZING, Diether v., 440

BÖHME, Franz, 169, 431
BOEHRINGER, Gustav, 466
BÖMERS, Hans, 466
BOENICKE, Walter, 495
BOENIGK, Oskar Frhr. v., 499
BOER, John de, 466
BOESSER, 466
BOETTCHER, Hermann, 303, 440
BÖTTCHER, Karl, 441
BÖTTCHER, Dr. Viktor, 511
BOETTGE, 499
BÖTTGER, Karl, 466
BOETTICHER, Friedrich v., 431
BOGATSCH, Rudolf, 493
BOGEN, v., 466
BOHNSTEDT, Wilhelm, 441
BOIE, Sigurd, 56, 466
BOINEBURG-LENGSFELD, Wilhelm Frhr. v., 55, 441
BOLTENSTERN, Walter v., 441
BOLTZE, Arthur, 304, 441
BONATZ, Ernst, 499
BORCHERS, 466
BORDIHN, 441
BORK, Max, 466
BOROWIETZ, Willibald, 441
BOROWSKI, 466
BOTH, Cuno Hans v., 59, 431
BOTSCH, Walter, 143, 466
BOTZHEIM, Erich Frhr. v., 441
BOYSEN, Wolf, 441
BRABÄNDER, 441
BRAEMER, Walter, 59, 431
BRÄUER, Bruno, 58, 495

RESTRICTED

BRAKERT, 499
BRAND, Albrecht, 441
BRAND, Fritz, 431
BRANDENBERGER, Erich, 152, 431
BRANDT, 499
BRANDT, Georg, 431
BRAUCHITSCH, Walther v., 5, 429
BRAUMÜLLER, Hans, 466
BRAUN, 466
BRAUN, Julius, 466
BRAUNER, Josef, 312, 441
BRAUSE, 466
BREHMER, Walter, 466
BREITH, Friedrich, 441
BREITH, Hermann, 164, 431
BREITHAUPT, Franz, 509
BREMER, 441
BRENKEN, 466
BRENNECKE, Kurt, 431
BRIESEN, v., 466
BRODOWSKI, Fritz, v., 441
BROICH, Friedrich Frhr. v., 441
BRUCH, Hermann, 495
BRUNNER, Josef, 495
BRUNS, 466
BRUNS, Walter, 467
BUCHHOLZ, 499
BÜCHS, 441
BÜGGENMANN, 467
BÜLOW, Cord v., 467
BÜLOW, Hilmer Frhr. v., 495
BÜLOWIUS, Alfred, 495

BÜLOWIUS, Karl, 441
BÜNAU, Rudolf v., 192, 441
BURCKHARDT, 441
BURDACH, Karl, 178, 441
BURGDORF, Wilhelm, 467
BUSCH, Ernst, 142, 429
BUSCHENHAGEN, Erich, 179, 442
BUSCHMANN, 442
BUSICH, Rudolf, 257, 467
BUSSE, Theodor, 134, 442
BUTTLAR, Edgar v., 467
BUTZE, 245, 442
CABANIS, Ernst, 495
CABANIS, Horst (Hans), 467
CANARIS, 4
CANTZLER, Oskar, 442
CARGANICO, 499
CARLSEN, 495
CARP, Georg, 36, 442
CASPER, 243, 442
CASTORF, Dipl. Ing. Helmut, 308, 467
CHALES de BEAULIEU, 467
CHAULIN-EGERSBERG, v., 499
CHEVALLERIE, Helmuth v. der, 442
CHEVALLERIE, Kurt v. der, 159, 431
CHILL, Kurt, 202, 442
CHOLTITZ, Dietrich v., 442
CHRISTIANSEN, Friedrich, 53, 123, 493
CLAER, Bernhard v., 467

RESTRICTED

INDEX OF NAMES 519

CLÖSSNER, Erich, 158, 431
COCHENHAUSEN, Friedrich v., 431
COELER, Joachim, 493
CONRAD, Dipl. Ing. Gerhard, 495
CONRADI, Siegfried, 467
CONRADY, Alexander, 225
CONRATH, Paul, 290, 495
COURBIÈRE, René de L'HOMME de, 305, 442
CRAMER, Hans, 431
CRAMOLINI, 467
CRANZ, 495
CRATO, 467
CRIEGERN, v., 499
CRUEWELL, Ludwig, 431
CUNO, Kurt, 467
CURTZE, Heinrich, 442
CZECH, 495
CZETTRITZ u. NEUHAUS, Konrad v., 467
DAHLMANN, 467
DAHLMANN, Dr. Hermann, 499
DALWIGK zu LICHTENFELS, Franz Frhr. v., 431
DANCKELMANN, 493
DANHAUSER, Paul, 223, 442
DANIELS, Alexander Edler v., 442
DANNEEL, 467
DASER, Wilhelm, 467
DAUBER, Julius, 467
DEBOI, Heinrich, 442
DECKER, Karl, 279, 467

DECKMANN, 26, 467
DEDEK, Emil, 467
DEGEN, 292
DEGENER, 467
DEHMEL, 442
DEHNER, Ernst, 431
DEICHMANN, Paul, 499
DEINDL, Otto, 467
DEINHARDT, 495
DEININGER, 467
DEMELHUBER, Karl, 509
DEMOLL, 442
DENECKE, Erich, 175, 442
DENNERLEIN, Max, 442
DESSLOCH, Otto, 493
DETMERING, 37, 442
DETTEN, Gustav v., 468
DETTLING, 210, 442
DEUTSCH, 258, 468
DEWALD, Fritz, 468
DEWALL, Job v., 499
DEYHLE, Willi, 468
DICKMANN, 468
DIESTEL, Erich, 192, 443
DIETL, Eduard, 143, 430
DIETRICH, Josef ("Sepp"), 322, 506
DIGEON, v. MONTETON, Baron Albrecht, 315, 443
DIHM, Friedrich, 443
DINTER, Georg, 468
DIPPOLD, Benignus, 443
DIRINGSHOFEN, v., 316, 443

RESTRICTED

DITFURTH, v., (Genlt.), 443
DITFURTH, v., (Obst.), 160
DITTMAR, Kurt, 443
DITTMEYER, 468
DOEHLA, Heinrich, 443
DÖHREN, v., 468
DÖPPING, 468
DÖRFFLER, 495
DÖRING, Kurt Bertrau v., 495
DOERSTLING, Egon, 493
DOHNASCHLOBITTEN, Heinrich Burggraf u. Graf zu, 468
DOLLMANN, Friedrich, 140, 430
DOMMENGET, 499
DONAT, Dipl. Ing.Hans v., 468
DORMAGEN, 468
DORNBERGER, Dr. Ing. h.c., 468
DOSTLER, Anton, 432
DRABICH-WAECHTER, Viktor v., 239, 443
DRANSFELD, Eduard, 493
DREBBER, Moritz v., 468
DRECHSEL, Ernst, 499
DRECKMANN, Dipl. Ing. Paul, 468
DREES, 468
DRESCHER, 468
DRESSLER, Rudolf, 468
DROBNIG, 468
DROGAND, 443
DRUM, Karl, 339, 495
DÜMLEIN, Friedrich, 443
DÜVERT, Walther, 443

DYBILASZ, Dipl. Ing., 468
EBELING, Fritz, 468
EBELING, Kurt, 468
EBERBACH, Hans, 432
EBERDING, 468
EBERHARDT, 184, 443
EBERHARDT, Kurt, 468
EBERLE, René, 443
EBERSTEIN, Friedrich Karl Frhr. v., 507
ECKARDT, Eduard, 468
ECKHARDT, Hans-Heinrich, 469
ECKSTEIN, 443
EDELMANN, Karl, 443
EDELSHEIM, Reichsfrhr. v., 288, 469
EGAN-KRIEGER, Jeno v., 495
EGLSEER, Karl, 275, 443
EHLERT, Hans, 58
EHRENBERG, Hans, 317, 469
EHRIG, Richard, 469
EIBENSTEIN, Rudolf, 346, 495
EISENBACH, 469
EISENHART-ROTHE, Hans Georg v., 469
EISENSTUCK, Helmut, 314, 469
ELFELDT, Otto, 443
ELSTER, Botho, 469
ELVERFELDT, Frhr. v., 469
ENDRES, Theodor, 443
ENGELBRECHT, Erwin, 53, 172, 432
ENGELHARDT, Alfred, 469
ERDMANN, 499

RESTRICTED

INDEX OF NAMES

ERDMANN, Kurt, 469
ERDMANN, Dipl. Ing. Wolfgang, 499
ERDMANNSDORFF, Werner v., 443
ERDMANNSDORFF, Gottfried v., 469
ERFURTH, Waldemar, 59, 432
ERTEL, Theodor, 469
ERXLEBEN, 469
ESEBECK, Hans-Karl Frhr. v., 443
ESTEBAN-INFANTES, Emilio, 221
EXSZ, 499
FABER du FAUR, Moritz v., 443
FABRICE, Eberhard v., 469
FAECKENSTEDT, Ernst Felix, 443
FAHNERT, Friedrich, 495
FAHRMBACHER, Wilhelm, 153, 432
FALKENHAUSEN, Alexander v., 54, 432
FALKENHAYN, Erich v., 499
FALKENHORST, Nikolaus v., 52, 144, 430
FALKENSTEIN, Erich Frhr. v., 469
FALKENSTEIN, Hans Frhr. v., 185, 469
FALKOWSKI, v., 499
FANGOHR, Joachim, 469
FAULENBACH, 248, 443
FEGELEIN, Hermann, 328, 511

FEHN, Franz, 469
FEHN, Gustav, 432
FELBER, Hans Gustav, 57, 432
FELBERT, Paul v., 469
FELDT, Kurt, 55, 444
FELLGIEBEL, Erich, 432
FELMY, Helmuth, 493
FELZMANN, Maximilian, 221, 469
FESSMANN, Ernst, 432
FETT, Albert, 444
FEURSTEIN, Valentin, 171, 432
FEYERABEND, Walter, 496
FICHTNER, Sebastian, 444
FIEBIG, Martin, 493
FIEDLER, Erich, 469
FINK, Dipl. Ing., 496
FINK, Johannes, 500
FISCHER, Herbert, 444
FISCHER, Hermann, 444
FISCHER, Karl, 469
FISCHER, Kurt, 317, 444
FISCHER, Theodor, 469
FISCHER, Veit, 493
FISCHER v. WEIKERSTHAL, Walter, 432
FITZLAFF, 470
FLÖRKE, 264, 470
FÖRSTER, Hellmuth, 493
FÖRSTER, Otto, 432
FÖRSTER, Sigismund v., 432
FOERTSCH, Hermann, 137, 444
FOLTTMANN, 244, 444
FONCK, Dr., 470

RESTRICTED

FORST, Werner, 200, 444
FORSTER, Paul Herbert, 254, 470
FORTNER, Johann, 444
FRANEK, Dr. Friedrich, 210, 444
FRANK, August, 509
FRANKE, Hermann, 444
FRANKEWITZ, 215, 444
FRANSSEN, 496
FRANTZ, Gotthard, 496
FRANTZ, Walter, 496
FREMEREY, Max, 444
FRETTER-PICO, Maximilian, 155, 432
FRETTER-PICO, Otto, 470
FREYBERG-EISENBERG-ALLMENDINGEN, Egloff Frhr. v., 500
FREYE, 470
FREYTAG, Walter, 470
FRICK, Wilhelm, 116
FRIDERICI, Erich, 432
FRIEBE, Helmuth, 444
FRIEDENSBURG, Walter, 496
FRIEDRICH, Rudolf, 444
FRIEDRICHS, Walter, 470
FRIEMEL, Georg, 470
FRIES, 268, 470
FRIESSNER, Johannes, 432
FRÖHLICH, 280
FRÖLICH, Stefan, 493
FROMM, Fritz, 7, 8, 430
FROMMHERZ, 500
FUCHS, 500
FUCHS, Willy v., 470

FUCIK, Karl, 470
FÜCHTBAUER, Heinrich Ritter v., 55, 444
FÜRST, Friedrich, 309, 444
FÜTTERER, Cuno Heribert, 500
FUNCK, Hans Frhr. v., 444
FUNCKE, Heinz, 500
GABLENZ, Eccard Frhr. v., 444
GALL, 470
GALLAND, Adolf, 500
GALLENKAMP, Curt, 432
GALLWITZ, Werner v., 470
GANDERT, Hans Eberhardt, 500
GAREIS, Martin, 199, 444
GAUL, Hans, 470
GAUSE, Alfred, 444
GAUTIER, Theophil, 496
GEBAUER, Artur, 470
GEBHARDT, Prof. Dr. Karl, 509
GEIB, Theodor, 432
GEISLER, Hans, 493
GEMP, Fritz, 470
GENEE, Paul, 470
GENTHE, Friedrich, 444
GENZKEN, Dr. med. Karl, 509
GERBER, Alexander, 470
GERCKE, Rudolf, 432
GERHARDT, Paul, 444
GERKE, Ernst, 445
GERLACH, Erwin, 470
GERMAR, v., 470
GEROCK, 470
GERSDORFF, Gero v., 470
GERSTENBERG, Alfred, 496

RESTRICTED

INDEX OF NAMES 523

GESCHWANDTNER, 470
GEYER, Hermann, 432
GEYR v. SCHWEPPENBURG, Leo Frhr., 432
GEYSO, Eckhard v., 29, 470
GIEHRACH, 470
GIENANTH, Frhr. v., 433
GIHR, 471
GILBERT, Martin, 445
GILLE, Herbert, 327, 509
GILSA, Werner Frhr. v. u. z., 445
GIMBORN, Hermann v., 445
GIMMLER, 216, 445
GINKEL, Oskar van, 34, 445
GLAISE-HORSTENAU, Dr. h. c. Edmund v., 58, 445
GLODKOWSKI, Erich, 471
GLOKKE, Gerhard, 32, 433
GLÜCKS, Richard, 509
GNAMM, Dr., 500
GOECKEL, Hans v., 471
GOEDICKE, 511
GOELDEL, v., 471
GÖRING, Hermann, 492
GOERITZ, Werner, 231, 445
GOESCHEN, 445
GOETTKE, 445
GOLLWITZER, Friedrich, 196, 445
GOLLNICK, Hans, 433
GOLTZ, 500
GOSEWISCH, 500
GOSSRAU, Karl Siegfried, 493
GOTHSCHE, Reinhold, 471
GRACHEGG, Gustav, 471

GRÄSER, Fritz Hubert, 263, 445
GRAEVENITZ, Hans v., 471
GRAF, Karl, 320, 445
GRAFFEN, Karl v., 445
GRASE, Martin, 176, 445
GRASSER, Anton, 267, 445
GRASSMANN, Kuno, 471
GRAU, Josef, 471
GRAWITZ, Dr. Ernst Robert, 509
GREIFF, Kurt v., 433
GREIFFENBERG, Hans v., 445
GREIM, Robert Ritter v., 492
GREINER, Heinz, 227, 445
GRIMMEISS, 445
GROBHOLZ, Dr., 471
GRODDECK, Karl Albrecht v., 471
GROELING, v., 51
GROENEVELD, 471
GRONAU, Wolfgang v., 500
GROPPE, Theodor, 445
GROSCH, Walter, 496
GROSCHUPF, 445
GROSSE, Dr. Walther, 471
GROSSMANN, Horst, 176, 445
GROTE, Waldemar Frhr., 445
GRÜN, Otto, 433
GRÜNER, Erich, 471
GUDERIAN, Heinz, 9, 430
GÜMBEL, Karl, 446
GÜNDELL, Walther v., 471
GUHR, 471
GULLMANN, Otto, 446
GUNZELMANN, Emil, 45, 446

RESTRICTED

INDEX OF NAMES

GURRAN, 471
GUTENBERGER, Karl, 509
GUTKNECHT, 471
GYLDENFELDT, Heinz v., 159, 471
HAACK, 471
HAARDE, 446
HAASE, Conrad, 446
HABENICHT, 446
HACHENBERG, v., 500
HAECKEL, Ernst, 307, 446
HAEHNELT, Wilhelm, 496
HAENICKE, Siegfried, 48, 433
HAENSCHKE, 500
HAGL, August, 471
HAHM, Walter, 446
HAHN, Johannes, 471
HALDER, Franz, 430
HALM, Hans, 433
HALTERMANN, Hans Dietrich, 511
HAMANN, Adolf, 471
HAMEL, 500
HAMMER, Ernst, 446
HAMMERSTEIN-EQUORD, Günther Frhr. v., 54, 446
HANESSE, 496
HANNEKEN, v., 52, 172, 433
HANSEN, 509
HANSEN, Christian, 151, 433
HANSEN, Erik, 57, 433
HANSTEIN, Hans v., 471
HANTELMANN, 500
HARBOU, v., 54

HARLINGHAUSEN, Martin, 500
HARM, Hermann, 511
HARMEL, Heinz, 513
HARMJANZ, Willi, 493
HARPE, Josef, 138, 433
HARTENECK, Gustav, 138, 446
HARTENSTEIN, 511
HARTING, 500
HARTLIEB gen. WALSPORN, Maximilian v., 446
HARTMANN, Martin, 471
HARTMANN, Otto, 433
HARTMANN, Walter, 446
HARTMANN, Wilhelm Dipl. Ing., 471
HARTOG, 500
HASE, Paul v., 446
HASELMAYR, 472
HASELOFF, Kurt, 48, 472
HASSE, 500
HASSE, Ulrich, 446
HAUBOLD, Alfred, 493
HAUCK, Bruno, 236, 472
HAUENSCHILD, Bruno Ritter v., 472
HAUFFE, Arthur, 446
HAUGER, Dipl. Wirtsch., 472
HAUSER, 283, 472
HAUSER, Wolfgang, 472
HAUSSER, 472
HAUSSER, Paul, 323, 507
HAVERKAMP, Wilhelm, 472
HEBERLEIN, Hans, 43, 446
HEDERICH, L., 472

RESTRICTED

HEDERICH, Hans, 472
HEDERICH, Willy, 472
HEIDENREICH, 500
HEIDRICH, Fritz, 472
HEIDRICH, Richard, 334, 496
HEILINGBRUNNER, Friedrich, 493
HEIM, Ferdinand, 446
HEINEMANN, Erich, 446
HEINRICHS, 230, 446
HEINRICI, Gotthard, 139, 430
HEINZ, v., 446
HEISTERMANN v. ZIELBERG, Gustav, 472
HEITZ, Walter, 430
HELD, Karl, 446
HELL, Ernst-Eberhard, 149, 433
HELLMICH, Heinz, 446
HELLWIG, Georg, 472
HELLWIG, Otto, 511
HELWIG, Hans, 472
HEMMERICH, Gerlach, 447
HEMPEL, Fritz, 500
HENGEN, Fritz, 30, 447
HENGL, Ritter v., 169, 447
HENKE, Gerhard, 472
HENRICI, Dipl. Ing. Hans, 472
HENRICI, Rudolf, 472
HENRICI, Sigfrid, 165, 433
HENRICI, Dr. Waldemar, 447
HERFF, Maximilian v., 509
HERFURTH, Otto, 31, 472
HERHOTH v. ROHDEN, 500
HERMANN, 496

HERMANN, Hans, 472
HERNEKAMP, Dipl. Ing. Karl, 472
HERR, Traugott, 168, 433
HERRGOTT, Adolf, 447
HERRLEIN, Friedrich, 447
HERRMANN, Paul, 472
HERWARTH v. BITTENFELD, Eberhard, 500
HERZOG, Kurt, 156, 433
HESSE, 165
HESSE, Max, 500
HESSELBARTH, 472
HEUNERT, 447
HEUSINGER, 447
HEYDE, v. der, 501
HEYDENREICH, Dipl. Ing., 472
HEYDENREICH, Leopold, 501
HEYGENDORFF, Ralph v., 473
HEYKING, Rüdiger v., 337, 496
HEYL, Friedrich, 473
HEYNE, Hans Walter, 473
HIEPE, Hellmuth, 473
HIERL, Konstantin, 122
HILDEBRANDT, Hans Georg, 473
HILDEBRANDT, Richard, 507
HILDEMANN, 473
HILGERS, Dipl. Ing., 496
HILLERT, Dipl. Ing. Walter, 473
HILPERT, Karl, 153, 433
HIMMLER, Heinrich, 113, 114, 115, 116, 122, 506

RESTRICTED

INDEX OF NAMES

HINDENBURG u. BENECKEN-
DORFF, Oskar v., 447
HINGHOFER, Dr. Walter, 447
HINKELBEIN, 501
HINTZ, 501
HINTZE, 473
HIPPEL, Walter v., 501
HIRSCHHAUER, Friedrich, 493
HITLER, Adolf, 3, 5, 6, 7, 8, 114, 119
HITTER, Alfons, 212, 447
HITZFELD, 473
HOCHBAUM, Friedrich, 181, 447
HOCHBAUM, Hans, 473
HÖBERTH, Eugen v., 447
HÖCKER, Erich, 260, 447
HÖCKER, Hans-Kurt, 224, 447
HOEFERT, Johannes, 501
HÖFL, Hugo, 447
HOEGNER, Hermann, 447
HÖFLE, Hermann, 509
HÖHNE, Gustav, 158, 433
HOEPNER, Erich, 430
HÖRAUF, Franz Ritter v., 473
HÖRMANN, Dr. Maximilian, 473
HOERNLEIN, Walter, 291, 447
HÖSSLIN, Hubert v., 473
HÖSSLIN, Wilhelm, v., 312, 447
HOFERT, Johannes, 473
HOFFMANN, Dr. Heinrich, 473
HOFFMANN, Kurt, 259, 447
HOFFMANN, Max, 473
HOFFMANN, Paul, 297, 473
HOFFMANN, Paul, 473

HOFFMANN, Rudolf, 493
HOFFMEISTER, Edmund, 473
HOFMANN, Erich, 447
HOFMANN, Friedrich, 473
HOFMANN, H., 509
HOFMANN, Hans, 496
HOFMANN, Helmut Frhr. v., 473
HOFMANN, Otto, 507
HOFMANN, Rudolf, 447
HOHN, Dr., 191
HOHNE, Otto, 501
HOLLIDT, Karl, 139, 430
HOLLE, Alexander, 501
HOLTER, 59, 170
HOLZHAUSEN, 473
HOMBURG, Erich, 501
HOPFF, Hermann, 448
HOPPE, Arthur, 204, 448
HORN, Hans-Joachim v., 473
HORN, Max, 215, 448
HORNUNG, Ferdinand, 501
HORSTIG gen. d'AUBIGNY v.
ENGELBRUNNER, Dr. Ing.
Ritter v., 473
HOSSBACH, Friedrich, 166, 448
HOSSFELD, Walter, 38, 474
HOTH, Hermann, 146, 430
HOTZY, Dr. Otto, 474
HUBE, Hans, 145, 433
HUBICKI, Dr. Alfred Ritter v., 163, 433
HÜBNER, Kurt, 474
HÜCKEL, 501
HÜHNER, Werner, 448

RESTRICTED

INDEX OF NAMES

HÜHNLEIN, Friedrich, 474
HÜLSEN, Heinrich-Hermann v., 474
HÜNERMANN, Dipl. Ing. Rudolf, 474
HÜPEDEN, v., 474
HÜTTMANN, 448
HUFFMANN, 448
HUTH, Joachim, 501
IHSSEN, Hugo, 474
ILGEN, Max, 474
JACOB, Alfred, 433
JACOBI, 56, 474
JACOBI, Alfred, 296, 448
JACOBSEN, Heinrich, 474
JAEHN, 474
JAENECKE, Erwin, 142, 430
JAGOW, v., 448
JAHN, 448
JAIS, Max, 474
JAKOBY, 501
JAKOWITZ, 474
JANSEN, 474
JANSSEN, Adolf Wilhelm, 474
JANUSZ, Johann, 474
JASCHKE, Erich, 151, 433
JATZOW, Hermann, 474
JAUER, 474
JECKELN, Friedrich, 507
JENA, v., 513
JENNY, 501
JESSER, Kurt, 474
JODL, Alfred, 3, 430
JODL, Ferdinand, 448

JÖRLING, 474
JOHN, 231, 474
JOHN, Dipl. Ing. Friedrich Wilhelm, 59, 448
JOLLASSE, Erwin, 474
JORDAN, Gerhard, 474
JORDAN, Hans, 433
JOST, Walter, 475
JUNCK, Werner, 501
JUNGCLAUS, Richard, 509
JUPPE, Hans, 448
JÜRS, Heinrich, 509
JÜTTNER, Hans, 507
JUST, Emil, 59, 475
KAEMPFE, Rudolf, 155, 434
KAHL, Siegfried, 501
KALDRACK, Otto, 475
KALM, Otto v., 475
KALTENBRUNNER, Dr. Ernst, 117
KAMMERHOFER, Konstantin, 509
KAMMHUBER, Josef, 493
KAMPFHENKEL, 475
KANITZ, Hans Graf v., 475
KANNENGIESSER, 317, 448
KARASCH, 513
KARL, 475
KARL, Franz, 448
KARLEWSKI, 496
KARST, Friedrich, 448
KASPAR, Johann, 34, 448
KASTNER-KIRDORF, Gustav, 493

RESTRICTED

INDEX OF NAMES

KATHMANN, Dipl. Ing., 501
KATTNER, Heinz, 475
KATZMANN, Friedrich (Fritz), 510
KAUFFMANN, 448
KAULBACH, 58
KAUPISCH, Leonard, 434
KEIL, Rudolf, 475
KEIM, 475
KEINER, Walter, 434
KEIPER (Genmaj.—Heer), 475
KEIPER (Genmaj.—Luftwaffe), 496
KEITEL, Bodewin, 46, 434
KEITEL, Wilhelm, 3, 5, 429
KELLER, Alfred, 123, 492
KELTSCH, Eduard, 475
KEMPF, Werner, 434
KEMPSKI, Hans v., 448
KEPPLER, Georg, 510
KERN, Emil, 448
KERSTEN, 448
KESSEL, Hans, 448
KESSEL, Paul v., 475
KESSELRING, Albert, 492
KESSLER, 496
KETTEMBEIL, Karl, 496
KETTNER, 496
KIEFFER, Friedrich Ritter v., 448
KIEFFER, Maximilian, 496
KIENITZ, Werner, 26, 434
KIESLING auf KIESLING-STEIN, Bruno Edler v., 42, 448
KINZEL, Eberhardt, 134, 449

KIRCHBACH, Harry v., 475
KIRCHENPAUER v. KIRCH-DORFF, Wilhelm, 475
KIRCHHEIM, Heinrich, 449
KIRCHNER, Friedrich, 167, 434
KISTNER, 475
KITTEL, Heinrich, 475
KITZINGER, Karl, 493
KLEEMANN, Ulrich (Werner), 261, 449
KLEFFEL, Philipp, 157, 434
KLEIN, Dipl. Ing., 501
KLEIN, Hans, 501
KLEINHANS, 475
KLEINHEISTERKAMP, Matthias, 327, 510
KLEINRATH, Kurt, 501
KLEINSCHROTH, Dipl. Ing., 475
KLEIST, 475
KLEIST, v., 52, 449
KLEIST, Ewald v., 135, 429
KLEMM, Kuno, 475
KLEPKE, Waldemar, 493
KLEPP, Dr. Ernst, 475
KLINGBEIL, Erich, 449
KLINGEMANN, Gottfried, 511
KLISZCZ, Ing. Otto, 475
KLÜG, 475
KLUGE, Günther v., 134, 429
KLUGE, Wolfgang v., 449
KLUTMANN, 449
KNAPP, 507
KNAUSS, Dr., 496
KNESEBECK, v. dem, 33, 449

RESTRICTED

INDEX OF NAMES

KNIESS, Baptist, 174, 434
KNOBELSDORFF, Otto v., 167, 434
KNOERZER, Hans, 56, 475
KOBUS, 449
KOCH-ERPACH, Rudolf, 35, 434
KOCH, Hellmuth, 449
KOCH, Dipl. Ing. Walter, 475
KÖCHLING, Friedrich, 449
KÖCHY, Karl, 501
KOEHLER, Carl-Erich, 449
KÖNIGSDORFER, Josef, 476
KÖRNER, Willy, 449
KÖSTRING, Ernst, 434
KOHL, Gustav, 476
KOHL, Otto, 449
KOHLER, 230, 476
KOHLERMANN, Otto, 269, 449
KOHNKE, 476
KOLB, Alexander, 496
KOLL, 476
KOLLER, Karl, 501
KONRAD, Rudolf, 171, 434
KOPP, Arthur, 476
KOPPE, Wilhelm, 507
KOREUBER, 449
KORFES, Dr. Otto, 476
KORSEMANN, 510
KORTE, Hans, 501
KORTE, Heinz, 476
KORTEN, Günther, 493
KORTÜM, Dr., 476
KORTZFLEISCH, Joachim v., 434
KOSSACK, Walter, 58, 476

KRAAS, Hugo, 514
KRÄTZER, Franz, 476
KRAHMER, Eckart, 496
KRAISS, Dietrich, 449
KRAKAU, August, 295, 449
KRAMPF, Heinrich, 235, 449
KRAPP, 501
KRAPPE, Günther, 188, 449
KRATZERT, Hans, 449
KRAUS, Erwin, 121
KRAUSE, Fritz, 476
KRAUSE, Johannes, 476
KRAUSE, Walther, 449
KRAUSS, Dipl. Ing., 501
KREBS, 140, 450
KREBS v. DEWITZ, gen. v., 476
KRECH, Franz, 476
KREIPE (Genmaj.-Heer), 476
KREIPE (Genmaj.-Luftwaffe), 501
KRENZKI, Kurt v., 450
KRESSMANN, Erich, 501
KRETSCHMER, Alfred, 476
KREYSING, Hans, 450
KRIEBEL, Kurt (Karl), 34, 434
KRIEBEL, Friedrich Ritter v., 476
KRIEGBAUM, 501
KRIEGER, Hans, 476
KRISCHER, Friedrich, 450
KROCKER, Viktor, 496
KROPFF, v., 476
KROSIGK, Ernst Anton v., 476
KRUEGER, 501
KRUEGER, Ernst, 496

RESTRICTED

KRÜGER, Eugen (Walter), 277, 450
KRÜGER, Otto, 501
KRÜGER, Walter, 325, 510
KRUG, Michael, 502
KRUMMEL, Adolf, 476
KRUSE, Hermann, 434
KRYSSING, Christian Peter, 511
KUBENA, Johann, 450
KUCKEIN, 450
KUDERNA, 502
KÜBLER, Josef, 276, 476
KÜBLER, Ludwig, 434
KÜCHLER, Georg v., 134, 139, 429
KUEN, 502
KÜHL, Leonhard, 493
KÜHLENTHAL, Erich, 450
KÜHLWEIN, 450
KÜHN, Friedrich, 434
KÜHNE, Fritz, 450
KÜHNE, Gerhard, 476
KÜHNE, Otto, 497
KÜPPER, Hans, 476
KULLMER, Artur, 233, 450
KUMM, Otto, 514
KUMMER, v., 476
KUNTZE, Walter, 8, 434
KUNTZEN, Adolf, 160, 434
KUNZE, Friedrich, 477
KURNATOWSKI, v., 56, 477
KUROWSKI, Eberhard v., 450
KURZ, 46, 450
KUSSIN, Friedrich, 477
KUTZLEBEN, v., 49, 477, 502

LACKNER, Walther, 497
LAHODE, Kurt, 450
LANDGRAF, Franz, 450
LANG, Viktor, 450
LANGEMEYER, Otto, 497
LANZ, Hubert, 170, 434
LASCH, 450
LASSEN, 477
LATTMANN, Martin, 477
LAULE, 497
LAUX, Paul, 148, 434
LECH, 497
LECHNER, Adolf, 450
LECHNER, Heinrich, 477
LEDEBUR, Frhr. v., 477
LEEB, Emil, 8, 434
LEEB, Leopold, 477
LEEB, Wilhelm Ritter v., 429
LEHMANN, Hans-Albrecht, 477
LEHMANN, Joseph, 450
LEISTER, 450
LEISTNER, v., 450
LEMELSEN, Joachim, 434
LEMKE, Herbert, 477
LENDLE, 298, 450
LENSKI, Arno v., 450
LENTZSCH, Johannes, 497
LEOPRECHTING, Waldemar Frhr. v., 477
LE SUIRE, v., 275, 477
LETTOW, Paul, 311, 477
LEUZE, Walter, 477
LEYEN, Ludwig v. der, 450
LEYERS, Dr. Ing., 477

RESTRICTED

INDEX OF NAMES 531

LEYKAUF, Hans, 450
LEYSER, v., 435
LEYSER, Hans-Georg, 266, 477
LEYTHÄUSER, Hermann, 477
LICHEL, Walter, 435
LICHT, 477
LICHTENBERGER, Hermann, 502
LIEB, 451
LIEBENSTEIN, Kurt Frhr. v., 477
LIEBER, Hans, 451
LIEGMANN, Wilhelm, 477
LINDE, v. der, 477
LINDEMANN, Fritz, 451
LINDEMANN, Georg, 143, 430
LINDEMANN, Wilhelm, 477
LINDENAU, 477
LINDIG, Max, 451
LINDNER, 497
LINDNER, Kurt, 478
LINKENBACH, 478
LINN, Philip, 451
LINNARZ, 478
LIPPE, v. der, 478
LIST, Wilhelm, 429
LOCH, Herbert, 154, 435
LOCHAU, Axel v. der, 478
LÖDERER, 502
LOEHNING, Paul, 478
LÖHR, Alexander, 136, 492
LOEPER, v., 451
LOERZER, Bruno, 492
LOEWENICH, v., 478

LOHMANN, 340, 502
LOHMANN, Hans, 451
LOHSE, 59
LOMBARD, Gustav, 513
LONGIN, Anton, 502
LONTSCHAR, Adalbert, 58, 478
LORENZ, Hans, 478
LORENZ, Heinrich, 502
LORENZ, Walter, 497
LUCHT, Walter, 243, 451
LUCZNY, Alfons, 502
LUDWIGER, Hartwig v., 275, 478
LÜBBE, Vollrath, 277, 451
LÜDECKE, Otto, 187, 451
LÜDKE, Erich, 435
LÜER, Hilmar, 478
LÜTERS, Rudolf, 169, 435
LÜTKENHAUS, 478
LÜTTWITZ, Heinrich Frhr. v., 286, 451
LÜTTWITZ, Smilo Frhr. v., 289, 451
LÜTZOW, Kurt-Jürgen Frhr. v., 178, 451
LUNGERSHAUSEN, Carl Hans, 269, 451
LUTZ, Ernst Frhr. v., 478
LUTZ, Oswald, 435
LUZ, Hellwig, 478
MAASS, 502
MACHOLZ, 451
MACKENSEN, Eberhard v., 430
MACKENZEN v. ASTFELD, Hans-Georg, 497

RESTRICTED

MADERHOLZ, Karl, 317, 451
MÄLZER, Dipl. Ing. Kurt, 497
MAERCKER, 478
MAGNUS, 478
MAHLMANN, 478
MAHNKE, Alfred, 493
MAIER, Nikolaus, 502
MAISEL, Ernst, 478
MAJEWSKI, v., 451
MALLINCKRODT, v., 29
MANN, Edler v. TIECHLER, Ferdinand Ritter v., 478
MANN, Edler v. TIECHLER, Hermann Ritter v., 497
MANSTEIN, Fritz Erich v. LEWINSKI gen v., 134, 141, 429
MANTELL, 451
MANTEUFFEL, Hasso Eccard v., 280, 478
MARCINKIEWICZ, August, 478
MARCKS, Erich, 435
MARKGRAF, Emil, 478
MARLOW, 478
MARNITZ, Dipl. Ing. Victor v., 478
MARSEILLE, Joachim, 479
MARSEILLE, Siegfried, 479
MARTIN, Dr. Benno, 510
MARTINEK, Robert, 165, 435
MARTINI, Hermann, 493
MASSOW, Albrecht v., 502
MASSOW, v., 502
MATERNA, Friedrich, 45, 435
MATTENKLOTT, Franz, 435

MATTERSTOCK, Otto, 303, 451
MATZKY, Gerhard, 451
MAYER, Dr. Ing. Johannes, 451
MAYER, Siegfried v., 479
MAYER, Wilhelm, 494
MAZUW, Emil, 507
MEDEM, 451
MEDEN, Karl-Friedrich v. der, 285, 479
MEHNERT, Karl, 451
MEINDL, Eugen, 502
MEINHOLD, 479
MEISE, Dr. Wilhelm, 452
MEISSNER, Dipl. Ing. Felix, 479
MEISSNER, Hans, 479
MEISSNER, Robert, 452
MEISTER, 497
MELCHERT, Rudolf, 47, 479
MELTZER, Karl, 479
MELTZER, Rudolf, 479
MELZER, Karl, 452
MENGE, v., 452
MENKEL, 219, 479
MENNY, Erwin, 479
MENSCH, 502
MENSCHING, 497
MENTZEL, 502
MENZEL, Georg-Adolf, 502
MERKER, Ludwig, 183, 452
MERTENS, 479
MERTITSCH, 497
METGER, Wilhelm, 226, 479
METSCHER, Karl, 479
METZ, 479

RESTRICTED

INDEX OF NAMES

METZ, Eduard, 479
METZ, Hermann, 435
METZNER, 502
MEYER, Fritz, 479
MEYER, Heinrich, 479
MEYER, Karl Ludwig, 479
MEYER, Kurt, 513
MEYER-BUERDORF, Heinrich, 204, 452
MEYER-RABINGEN, Hermann, 307, 452
MEYSSNER, August, 510
MICKL, Hans (Johann), 479
MIERZINSKY, 479
MIETH, 435
MIKULICZ, Adalbert, 452
MILCH, Erhard, 492
MILISCH, Leopold, 479
MITSCHERLING, 30
MITTELBERGER, Hilmar Ritter v., 452
MITTERMAIER, Wilhelm, 452
MODEL, Walter, 140, 430
MOHR, Max, 494
MOLL, 497
MOLO, Louis Ritter v., 452
MOOYER, 497
MORITZ, Georg, 479
MORZIK, 502
MOSER, Willi, 53, 175, 435
MOST, 479
MOYSES, Karl, 27, 452
MÜHLMANN, Max, 452
MÜLLER, Angelo, 479

MÜLLER, Erich, 237, 452
MÜLLER, Ernst, 497
MÜLLER, Eugen, 6, 435
MÜLLER, Ferdinand, 452
MÜLLER, Friedrich Wilhelm, 267, 452
MÜLLER, Dipl. Ing. Gerhard, 479
MÜLLER, Gottlob, 502
MÜLLER, Hans Ludwig, 480
MÜLLER, Hermann, 452
MÜLLER, Ludwig, 273, 452
MÜLLER, Ludwig, 452
MÜLLER, Vincenz, 452
MÜLLER-DERICHSWEILER, 480
MÜLLER-GEBHARD, Alfred, 452
MUFF, Wolfgang, 435
MUGGENTHALER, Hermann, 502
MUHL, 480
MUHR, Eduard, 502
MUNDT, Dr. habil., 452
MUSSHOFF, 497
MYLO, Walther, 480
NAGEL, Friedrich Wilhelm, 480
NAGY, Emmerich, 435
NAKE, Albin, 320, 452
NAUMANN, 452
NAUMANN, Max, 480
NEHRING, Walter, 165, 435
NEIDHOLDT, Fritz, 249, 480
NEINDORFF, v., 480
NEUBRONN v. EISENBURG, Alexander Frhr., 453

RESTRICTED

INDEX OF NAMES

NEUFFER, 502
NEULING, Ferdinand, 173, 435
NEUMANN, Friedrich Wilhelm, 259, 453
NEUMANN-NEURODE, Karl Ulrich, 453
NEUMAYR, Franz, 480
NEWIGER, Albert, 480
NEYMANN, 480
NIEBELSCHÜTZ, Günther v., 435
NICKELMANN, 480
NIDA, v., 37, 480
NIEBECKER, Georg, 480
NIEDENFÜHR, Günther, 480
NIEDERMAYER, Prof. Dr. Oskar Ritter v., 207, 480
NIEHOFF, Heinrich, 55, 453, 497
NIEHOFF, Johannes, 250, 480
NIELSEN, 502
NIEMANN, 480
NITZSCHE, Martin, 502
NOACK, Rudolf, 480
NOELDECHEN, Ferdinand, 453
NOLTE, Hans Erich, 319, 453
NORDT, 502
NOSTITZ-WALLWITZ, Gerhard v., 480
NOWACK, Franz, 502
NUBER, 497
OBERG, Karl Albrecht, 510
OBERNHÄUSSER, Eugen, 453
OBERKAMP, Carl Reichsritter v., 328, 511
OBERNITZ, Justin v., 453
OBSTFELDER, Hans v., 154, 435
OCHSNER, Hermann, 453
ODEBRECHT, 335, 494
ÖLLER, 480
OELSNER, 29, 480
OESTERREICH, v., 453
OFFENBÄCHER, Konrad, 45, 480
OHNACKER, 480
OLBERG, v., 480
OLBRICH, 503
OLBRICHT, Friedrich, 8, 435
ONDARZA, Herbert v., 453
OPPENLÄNDER, Kurt, 52, 453
ORIOLA, Graf v., 234, 453
ORTNER, Bruno, 190, 453
ORTNER-WEIGAND, Bruno, 503
OSSWALD, Erwin, 435
OSTER, Hans, 481
OSTERKAMP, 8, 435
OSTERKAMP, Theodor, 497
OSTERROTH, 453
OTT, Eugen, 435
OTTENBACHER, Otto, 436
OTTO, 481
OTTO, Paul, 436
OVEN, Karl v., 157, 436
OVERDYK, 503
PACHMAYR, 481
PAHL, 34
PANCKE, Günter, 510
PANNWITZ, Helmuth v., 262, 481
PAUER, Ernst, 481

RESTRICTED

INDEX OF NAMES 535

PAULUS, Friedrich, 429
PAWEL, 481
PAWELKE, 503
PECHMANN, Albrecht Frhr. v., 481
PELLENGAHR, Richard, 453
PELTZ, Dietrich, 503
PELTZ, Joachim, 453
PEMSEL, Max, 481
PERFALL, Gustav Frhr. v., 453
PESCHEL, 453
PETERSEN, 494
PETERSEN, Heinrich, 514
PETERSEN, Matthias, 481
PETERSEN, Wilhelm, 481
PETRAUSCHKE, 503
PETRI, Hans, 436
PETSCH, 258, 453
PETTER, 481
PETZEL, Walter, 47, 436
PFEFFER, Max, 436
PFEFFER-WILDENBRUCH, Karl v., 507
PFEIFFER, 503
PFEIFFER, Dr. phil. Georg, 189, 453
PFEIFFER, Helmut, 481
PFLAUM, Karl, 306, 453
PFLIEGER, 255, 453
PFLUGBEIL, Johann, 315, 454
PFLUGBEIL, Kurt, 494
PFLUGRADT, Kurt, 58, 454
PFÜHLSTEIN, Alexander v., 481
PHILIPP, Christian, 294, 454

PHILIPP, Ernst, 481
PHILIPPS, Dipl. Ing., 454
PHLEPS, Artur, 324, 507
PICKERT, Wolfgang, 346, 503
PIEKENBROCK, Hans, 481
PILZ, 454
PINCKVOSS, 37, 454
PISTORIUS, 497
PITREICH, August v., 481
PLAMBÖCK, 481
PLAMMER, 481
PLEHWE, v., 481
PLEWIG, Willy, 481
PLOCH, Dipl. Ing. August, 503
PLOCHER, Hermann, 503
PLOETZ, Egon v., 481
PLOTHO, Wolfgang Edler Herr u. Frhr. v., 454
POEL, Gerhard, 481
POETSCH, 503
POETTER, Adolf, 454
POGRELL, Günther v., 436
POHL, v., 481
POHL, Erich Ritter v., 494
POHL, Oswald, 507
POPPE, 216, 454
POSTEL, Georg, 238, 454
POTEN, Ernst, 481
PRAETORIUS, Robert, 30, 454
PRAGER, Karl, 454
PRAGER, Karl Ritter v., 436
PRAUN, Albert, 204, 454
PRELLBERG, 503
PRESSENTIN, Richard v., 481

RESTRICTED

PREU, 503
PREUSSER, Arnold, 482
PRIEM, v., 482
PRIESS (Genlt.), 180, 454
PRIESS, Hermann, 326, 511
PRINNER, 482
PRINZ, 503
PRITTWITZ u. GAFFRON, Max v., 482
PRONDZYNSKI, v., 48, 454
PRÜGEL, Dr. Karl, 482
PRÜTER, 482
PRÜTZMANN, Hans-Adolf, 507
PÜCHLER, 224, 454
PÜCKLER-BURGHAUS, Carl-Friedrich v., 331, 511
PUESCHEL, Konrad, 503
PULTAR, Josef, 503
PUNZERT, Josef, 503
PUTTKAMER, v. (Genmaj.), 482
PUTTKAMER, Alfred v., 454
PUTZIER, 494
QUADE, Erich, 494
QUERNER, Rudolf, 507
RAAB, Matthias, 482
RAAPKE, 191, 482
RABE v. PAPPENHEIM, Friedrich Karl, 482
RABENAU, Dr. phil. h.c. Friedrich v., **436**
RABSILBER, Friedrich, 482
RADZIEJ, 209, 482
RAESFELD, Werner v., 482
RÄSSLER, Rudolf, 482

RAITHEL, 454
RAITHEL, Dipl. Ing. Hans, 503
RAITZ v. FRENTZ, Maximilian Frhr., 482
RAMCKE, Hermann Bernhard, 334, 497
RANFT, Albert, 482
RANTZAU, Heino v., 497
RAPPARD, Fritz Georg v., 177, 454
RASCHICK, Walter, 39, 436
RATHKE, 454
RAUCH, Erwin, 203, 454
RAUCH, Hans, 503
RAUS, Erhard, 150, 436
RAUTER, Hans, 508
RAVENSTEIN, Johann v., 455
RECKE, Heinrich, 206, 455
RECKNAGEL, Hermann, 201, 455
REDIESS, Wilhelm, 508
REEDER, Eggert, 508
REIBNITZ, Leo v., 482
REICHE, v., 455
REICHER, Franz, 482
REICHERT, Josef, 455
REIMANN, Richard, 497
REIN,' 482
REINECKE, Hermann, 436
REINERSDORFF-PACZYNSKI u. TENCZYN, Dietrich v., 482
REINHARD, Hans, 53, 162, 436
REINHARDT, Fritz, 482
REINHARDT, Georg-Hans, 145, 430

INDEX OF NAMES

REINSHAGEN, 503
REISS, Ritter v., 56, 482
REITZENSTEIN, Albin, 514
REMLINGER, 482
RENDULIĆ, Dr., Lothar, 145, 436
RENZ, v., 494
RENZ, Maximilian, 455
REUSS, Heinrich XXXVII Prinz v., 347, 503
REXILIUS, 482
REYMANN, Helmuth, 455
RHEIN, Karl, 241, 482
RIBBENTROP, Friedrich, 483
RIBENSTEIN, 503
RICHERT, 299, 455
RICHTER, 455
RICHTER, Gerhard, 483
RICHTER, Hellmuth, 346, 497
RICHTER, Werner, 455
RICHTER, Wilhelm, 483
RICHTHOFEN, Dipl. Ing. Wolfram Frhr. v., 492
RIEBESAM, Ludwig, 44, 455
RIECKHOFF, Herbert, 503
RIEDEL, 483
RIEGER, Leopold, 483
RIEKE, Georg, 503
RIEMHOFER, Gottfried, 483
RIESCH, Dipl. Ing., 503
RINCK v. BALDENSTEIN, Werner Frhr., 483
RINGE, Hans, 483
RINGEL, Julius, 294, 455
RINTELEN, Enno v., 436
RISSE, Walter, 455
RITTER, Hans, 494
RITTER, René, 483
RITTWEGER, Ernst, 483
RIVA, Erich, 503
RODEN, Enno v., 483
RODENBURG, Karl, 455
RODEWALD, 483
RODT, Eberhardt, 264, 483
ROEDER, v., 483
ROEDER v. DIERSBURG, Kurt Frhr., 33, 455
ROEMER, Martin v., 483
RÖHRICHT, 455
RÖMER, 503
RÖMER, Erwin v., 497
RÖPKE, Kurt, 186, 483
ROESCH, 503
ROESE, Franz v., 436
RÖSENER, Erwin, 510
ROESINGER, Otto, 483
RÖSLER, Eberhard, 483
ROETTIG, Otto, 436
RÖTTIGER, 146, 455
ROHDE, Hans, 455
ROMAN, Rudolf Frhr. v., 152, 436
ROMMEL, Erwin, 280, 429
RONICKE, Martin, 483
ROQUES, Franz v., 436
ROQUES, Karl v., 497
RORICH, 483
ROSENBERG, 59
ROSENBUSCH, 455
ROSKE, Dipl. Ing. Fritz, 483

RESTRICTED

ROSSI, Franz, 455
ROSSUM, 455
ROST, v., 483
ROTBERG, Frhr. v., 455
ROTH, Ernst-August, 503
ROTH, Hans, 483
ROTH, Heinrich, 28, 483
ROTHE, Erich, 483
ROTHKIRCH u. PANTHEN, Friedrich Wilhelm v., 455
ROTHKIRCH u. TRACH, Edwin Graf v., 456
RUDLOFF, Werner v., 497
RÜBEL, Karl, 207, 484
RÜDEL, Günther, 492
RÜDIGER, Dr. Ing., 456
RÜDT v. COLLENBERG, Frhr. Ludwig, 484
RÜDT v. COLLENBERG, Frhr. Kurt, 497
RÜGAMER, Ferdinand, 484
RÜGGENMANN, Alfons, 484
RÜHLE v. LILIENSTERN, Alexander, 25, 456
RÜHLE v. LILIENSTERN, Kurt, 484
RUFF, 484
RUGGERA, Kamillo, 494
RUNDSTEDT, Gerd v., 136, 429
RUNGE, Wilhelm, 484
RUOFF, Richard, 430
RUPPERT, Hans-Eberhard, 484
RUPPRECHT, Wilhelm, 456
RUSSWURM, Josef, 456

RUSSWURM, Wilhelm, 226, 456
RÜTER, Wolfgang, 504
RUVILLE, v., 484
SACHS, 436
SACHS, Ernst, 508
SACHSSE, 484
SAGERER, 484
SALENGRÉ-DRABBE, Hans de —, 484
SALITTER, Fritz, 49, 484
SALMUTH, Hans v., 142, 430
SANDER, Erwin, 209, 456
SANNE, 456
SATOW, 28, 456
SATTLER, 484
SATTLER, Alfred, 504
SATTLER, Ottfried, 498
SAUBERZWEIG, 331, 511
SAUCKEN, Dietrich v., 278, 456
SAUER, Otto Ritter v., 456
SAUVANT, 484
SCHAAL, Ferdinand, 48, 436
SCHACK, Friedrich August, 484
SCHACKE, 484
SCHACKY auf SCHÖNFELD, Sigmund Frhr. v., 308, 456
SCHADE, 484
SCHAEFER, Dr. Gotthold, 484
SCHAEFER, Hans (Genlt.), 456
SCHAEFER, Hans (Genmaj.), 484
SCHAEFFER, 484
SCHAEWEN, Dr. v., 456
SCHALLER, 344, 504
SCHALLER-KALIDE, Hubert, 436

RESTRICTED

SCHARTOW, 318, 456
SCHAUER, Ludwig, 504
SCHAUM, 456
SCHAUMBURG, Ernst, 456
SCHAUROTH, Athos v., 36, 456
SCHAUWECKER, 484
SCHEDE, Wolfgang, 456
SCHEELE, Hans Karl v., 456
SCHEFOLD, 484
SCHELL, Adolf v., 289, 456
SCHELLBACH, Oskar, 456
SCHELLER, 484
SCHELLER, Walther, 281, 457
SCHELLERT, 37, 436
SCHELLMANN, 484
SCHELLWITZ, v., 485
SCHEPMANN, Wilhelm, 123
SCHERBENING, 194, 457
SCHERER, Theodor, 195, 457
SCHERFF, Walter, 485
SCHEUERPFLUG, Paul, 190
SCHEURLEN, 498
SCHICKFUS u. NEUDORFF, Erich v., 485
SCHILFFARTH, Ludwig, 504
SCHILLING, Otto, 485
SCHIMPF, 457
SCHIMPF, Dipl. Ing. Richard, 498
SCHINDKE, Wilhelm, 485
SCHINDLER, Maximilian, 457
SCHIRMER, Georg, 457
SCHITTNIG, 485
SCHLEICH, Ritter v., 498

SCHLEINITZ, Siegmund Frhr. v., 177, 457
SCHLEMM, 494
SCHLEMMER, Ernst, 457
SCHLEMMER, Dipl. Ing. Hans, 205, 457
SCHLENTHER, Eugen, 457
SCHLIEBEN, Dietrich v., 485
SCHLIEBEN, Karl Wilhelm v., 213, 485
SCHLIEPER, 51, 457
SCHLÖMER, Helmut, 457
SCHLUETER, Robert, 485
SCHMALZ, 290
SCHMAUSER, Ernst Heinrich, 508
SCHMEDES, Dr. Rothard (Fritz?), 511
SCHMELCHER, Willi, 122, 510
SCHMETTOW, Graf v., 485
SCHMETZER, Rudolf, 457
SCHMID, Josef, 504
SCHMID-DANKWARD, Walter, 457
SCHMIDT, Arthur, 457
SCHMIDT, August (Genlt.-Heer), 263, 457
SCHMIDT, August (Gen.d.Fl.-Lw.), 494
SCHMIDT, Curt, 457
SCHMIDT, Gustav, 286, 457
SCHMIDT, Hans (Gen.d.Inf.), 150, 436
SCHMIDT, Hans (Genmaj.), 485
SCHMIDT, Hugo, 494

RESTRICTED

SCHMIDT, Dipl. Ing. Johannes, 485
SCHMIDT, Kurt, 498
SCHMIDT, Otto (Genmaj.), 54, 485
SCHMIDT, Otto (Genmaj.), 256, 485
SCHMIDT, Rudolf, 430
SCHMIDT, Ulrich, 485
SCHMIDT-KOLBOW, 485
SCHMIDT-LOGAN, Wolfgang, 457
SCHMIDT v. LUISINGEN, 485
SCHMIDT-RICHBERG, 148
SCHMITT, Artur, 457
SCHMUNDT, Rudolf, 7, 457
SCHNARRENBERGER, Ernst, 485
SCHNECKENBURGER, Wilhelm, 437
SCHNEIDEMESSER, Gustav v., 485
SCHNEIDER, Dipl. Ing. Erich, 457
SCHNEIDER, Ernst, 458
SCHNEIDER, Friedrich, 485
SCHNEIDER, Otto, 485
SCHNIEWINDT, Rudolf, 437
SCHÖBEL, Otto, 504
SCHOEN, 485
SCHÖNBERG, Wilhelm, 458
SCHÖNFELDER, Fritz, 485
SCHÖNFELDER, Kurt, 485
SCHÖNHERR, Otto, 458
SCHÖRNER, Ferdinand, 437
SCHÖRGI, Hugo, 504

SCHOLZ, Erich, 485
SCHOLZ, Fritz, 330, 511
SCHONHÄRL, Hans, 458
SCHOPPER, Erich, 458
SCHRADER, Rudolf, 458
SCHREIBER, 458
SCHREIBER, Alfred, 485
SCHROECK, 458
SCHRÖDER, Fritz, 486
SCHROEDER, Severin, 504
SCHROEDER, Walther, 510
SCHROETER, v., 486
SCHROETTER, Dipl. Ing., 486
SCHROTH, 504
SCHROTH, Walther, 41, 437
SCHUBERT (Gen.Lw.), 498
SCHUBERT, Dr., 494
SCHUBERT, Albrecht, 44, 437
SCHUBERT, Rudolf, 458
SCHUBERTH, 486
SCHUCKMANN, Eberhard v., 486
SCHULTZE-RHONHOF, 504
SCHULDT, Heinrich, 513
SCHULENBURG, Winfred v.d., 486
SCHULER, Rüdiger v., 486
SCHULTHEISS, Pavel, 498
SCHULTZE, Rudolf, 498
SCHULZ, 494
SCHULZ, Friedrich, 143, 458
SCHULZ, Otto (Genmaj.), 486
SCHULZ, Otto (Obst.), 157
SCHÜNEMANN, Otto, 244, 458

RESTRICTED

INDEX OF NAMES

SCHÜNEMANN, Otto, 458
SCHÜTZ, Max v., 486
SCHÜTZE, 504
SCHÜTZEK, 504
SCHUNCK, Theodor, 486
SCHUSTER, Friedrich, 486
SCHUSTER-WOLDAN, 486
SCHWABEDISSEN, Walter, 498
SCHWALBE, Eugen-Felix, 486
SCHWANDNER, Maximilian, 437
SCHWARZNECKER, 44, 458
SCHWEDLER, Hans, 511
SCHWEDLER, Viktor v., 29, 437
SCHWEICKHARD, Karl, 494
SCHWERIN, Bogislav Graf v., 312, 486
SCHWERIN, Gerhard Graf v., 265, 458
SCHWERIN, Otto v., 458
SCHWERIN, Richard v., 458
SCHWUB, Albert, 498
SCOTTI, v., 458
SCULTETUS, Bruno, 486
SCULTETUS, Herbert, 486
SEEBOHM, 486
SEEGER, 458
SEELIG, 486
SEHMSDORF, Hans, 486
SEIBT, 504
SEIDEL, Hans-Georg v., 494
SEIDEMANN, Hans, 504
SEIFERT, Ernst, 458
SEIFERT, Johann, 346, 498
SELDNER, Eduard, 504
SELLE, v., 458
SENGER u. ETTERLIN, Fridolin v., 458
SENSFUSS, Franz (Johannes?), 486
SERINI, 486
SEUFFERT, Franz, 32, 486
SEYDLITZ-KURZBACH, Walter v., 437
SEYFFARDT, 200, 458
SEYSS-INQUART, 53
SEYWALD, Heinz, 504
SIBURG, Ing. Hans, 494
SICHART, Werner v., 486
SIEBERT, Friedrich, 458
SIECKENIUS, 486
SIEGLIN, Kurt, 486
SIELER, 458
SIESS, Gustav, 504
SIEVERS, Karl, 486
SIMON, Max, 511
SINNHUBER, 160, 437
SINTZENICH, Rudolf, 459
SINZINGER, Adolf, 459
SIRY, Maximilian, 459
SIXT v. ARMIN, Hans Heinrich, 459
SIXT, Friedrich, 140, 459
SODAN, Ralf, 228, 459
SODENSTERN, Georg v., 143, 437
SOELDNER, 504
SOHN, 487
SOMME, Walter, 494
SOMMER, Johannes, 498

RESTRICTED

INDEX OF NAMES

SOMMERFELD, Hans v., 459
SONNENBURG, 504
SOODLA, 513
SORSCHE, Konrad, 36, 459
SOUCHAY, Stephan, 487
SPALCKE, Dr., 487
SPANG, Karl, 459
SPANG, Willibald, 341, 498
SPECHT, Karl (Wilhelm), 459
SPEEMANN, Kurt, 459
SPEER, Prof. Albert, 120
SPEICH, Dr. Richard, 48, 321, 459
SPEIDEL, Dr. Hans, 487
SPEIDEL, Wilhelm, 58, 494
SPENGLER, 487
SPERLING, 504
SPERRLE, Hugo, 492
SPETH, 143, 487
SPIESS, Theodor, 346, 498
SPONECK, Graf v., 459
SPONECK, Hans Graf v., 459
SPONHEIMER, Otto, 437
SPORRENBERG, 510
SPRUNER v. MERTZ, Hermann, 498
STADLER, Sylvester, 514
STAHEL, Reiner, 504
STAHL, Friedrich, 459
STAHR, Wolfgang, 487
STAMM, 487
STAMMER, 487
STAPF, Otto, 437
STARKE, Friedrich, 504

STEGMANN, 487
STEIGLEHNER, Wilhelm, 487
STEIN, 504
STEIN, Johann v., 487
STEINBACH, Paul, 487
STEINBAUER, Gerhard, 459
STEINER, Felix, 323, 508
STEINKOPF, 504
STEINMETZ, 197, 459
STEMMERMANN, Wilhelm, 437
STENGEL, Hans, 459
STENZEL, Richard, 487
STEPHAN, 504
STEPHAN, Friedrich, 459
STEPHANUS, 459
STEPPUHN, Albrecht, 437
STETTNER Ritter v. GRABENHOFEN, Walter, 292, 487
STEUDEMANN, Kurt, 498
STEUDTNER, 487
STEVER, 459
STIELER v. HEYDEKAMPF, 459
STILLFRIED u. RATTONITZ, Waldemar Graf v., 487
STIMMEL, 459
STOCKHAUSEN, Dipl. Ing. v., 298, 487
STOCKHAUSEN, v., 487
STOEWER, Paul, 303, 459
STOLBERG-STOLBERG, Christoph Graf zu, 487
STRACHWITZ, Hyazinth Graf, 291

RESTRICTED

STRACK, Karl, 487
STRAUBE, Erich, 437
STRAUSS, Adolf, 430
STRECCIUS, Alfred, 437
STRECKER, 437
STREICH, Hans, 460
STROOP, 510
STUBENRAUCH, Wilhelm, 487
STUBENRAUCH, Wilhelm v., 498
STUD, 460
STUDENT, Kurt, 494
STÜLPNAGEL, Heinrich v., 437
STÜLPNAGEL, Joachim v., 437
STÜLPNAGEL, Otto v., 55, 437
STÜLPNAGEL, Siegfried v., 437
STÜMPFL, Heinrich, 460
STUMM, Berthold, 487
STUMPFELD, v., 460
STUMPFF, Hans-Jürgen, 492
STUMPFF, Horst, 460
STURM, Alfred, 498
STURM, Hans, 487
STURT, Gerhard, 488
STUTZER, 504
SUREN, Walter, 498
SUSCHNIGG, Gustav, 488
SUTTNER, 460
SZELINSKI, 234, 460
TAEGLICHSBECK, 488
TARBUK, Johann, 488
TARBUK v. SENSENHORST, Karl, 48, 321, 460
TAYSEN, Adalbert v., 460

TERBOVEN, 52
TESCHNER (Genmaj.), 504
TESCHNER (Genlt.), 460
TETTAU, Hans v., 181, 460
THADDEN, v., 488
THÄTER, Maximilian, 488
THAMS, 48, 488
THEISEN, Edgar, 173, 437
THEISS, Rudolf, 488
THIELE, 511
THIELE, Fritz, 488
THIELMANN, 488
THOENISSEN, 488
THOFERN, Wilhelm, 27, 460
THOHOLTE, 488
THOMA, Heinrich, 460
THOMA, Wilhelm Ritter v., 437
THOMAS, 488
THOMAS, Alfred, 488
THOMAS, Georg, 437
THOMAS, Kurt, 488
THOMAS, Wilhelm, 460
THOMASCHKI, Siegfried, 460
THON, Friedrich, 488
THÜNGEN, Karl Frhr. v., 28, 460
THUMM, Helmuth, 272, 460
THYM, Heinrich, 504
TIEDEMANN, Karl v., 460
TIEMANN, Otto, 197, 460
TIPPELSKIRCH, v. (Genlt.), 498
TIPPELSKIRCH, v. (Genmaj.), 505
TIPPELSKIRCH, Kurt v., 437

RESTRICTED

INDEX OF NAMES

TITTEL, Hermann, 175, 438
TOUSSAINT, Rudolf, 438
TRAUCH, Rudolf, 488
TRAUT, Hans, 460
TRESCKOW, Joachim v., 240, 460
TREUENFELD, Karl v., 512
TRIENDL, Theodor, 498
TRIERENBERG, Wolf, 208, 460
TRÖGER, Hans, 488
TROTHA, v., 460
TSCHAMMER u. OSTEN, Eckart v., 488
TSCHERNING, Otto, 31, 461
TSCHOELTSCH, Ehrenfried, 505
TSCHUDI-JACOBSEN, Heinrich (Rudolf ?), 488
UBL, Bruno, 488
UCKERMANN, Horst Frhr. v., 308, 461
ULEX, Wilhelm, 438
UNGER, 505
UNRUH, Walter v., 438
UNRUH, Walter Willy Hermann v. (Genmaj.), 488
USEDOM, v., 488
USINGER, 460
UTHMANN, Bruno v., 460
UTZ, Willibald, 274, 488
VAERST, Gustav v., 438
VAHL, Herbert Ernst, 512
VASSOLL, 488
VATERRODT, 489
VEIEL, Rudolf, 31, 438
VEITH, 505

VEITH, Richard, 460
VERSOCK, Kurt, 489
VIEBAHN, Hans Albert v., 489
VIEBAHN, Max v., 438
VIERKORN, 489
VIERLING, Albert, 494
VIEROW, Dipl. Ing., 489
VIEROW, Erwin, 438
VIETINGHOFF gen. SCHEEL, Heinrich v., 141, 430
VODEPP, 505
VÖLCKERS, Paul, 159, 438
VOELK, 505
VOGEL, Emil, 274, 460
VOGL, Oskar, 438
VOGLER, Anton, 512
VOIGT, Adolf, 489
VOIGT-RUSCHEWEYH, 505
VOIT, Paul, 42, 489
VOLCKAMER v. KIRCHENSITTENBACH, Friedrich, 461
VOLK, Erich (Ernst ?), 31, 461
VOLKMANN, Dietrich, 505
VOLLARD-BOCKELBERG, v., 438
VORMANN, Nikolaus v., 288, 461
VORWALD, Dipl. Ing. Wolfgang, 505
VOSS, Bernhard, 512
VOSS, Erich, 489
VOSS, Hans v., 461
WABER, Bernhard, 494
WACHENFELD, Edmund, 438
WACHTER, Friedrich Karl v., 461

RESTRICTED

INDEX OF NAMES

WADEHN, 505
WÄGER, Alfred, 438
WAEGER, Kurt, 461
WAGNER, 345, 498
WAGNER, August, 461
WAGNER, Eduard (Gen. d. Art.), 438
WAGNER, Georg, 489
WAGNER, Gustav, 489
WAGNER, Jürgen, 513
WAGNER, Paul, 489
WAHLE, Karl, 489
WALDECK-PYRMONT, Josias Erbprinz zu, 508
WALDENFELS, Wilhelm Frhr. v., 45, 461
WALLAND, Eugen, 505
WALLNER, Otto, 505
WALTER, Helmuth, 489
WALZ, 498
WANDEL, Max, 438
WANGENHEIM, Edgar Frhr. v., 505
WANGER, Rudolf, 461
WAPPENHANS, Waldemar, 510
WARLIMONT, Walter, 4, 461
WARNICKE, 489
WARTENBERG, Bodo v., 489
WEBER, Christian, 512
WEBER, Friedrich, 489
WEBERN, v., 489
WECKMANN, 489
WEDDERKOPF, Magnus v., 461
WEDEL, Hasso v., 489

WEDEL, Hermann v., 489
WEDELSTÄDT, Friedrich Wilhelm v., 489
WEECH, v., 505
WEESE (Genlt.), 498
WEESE (Genmaj.), 505
WEGENER, Wilhelm, 182, 461
WEHRIG, 489
WEICHS, Maximilian Frhr. v., 137, 429
WEIDEMANN, 489
WEIDINGER, Wilhelm, 461
WEIDLING, Helmuth, 196, 461
WEIGAND, Dipl. Volksw. Wolfgang, 498
WEIL, 505
WEINER, 505
WEINGART, Erich, 461
WEINKNECHT, 489
WEISE, Hubert, 492
WEISENBERGER, Karl, 170, 438
WEISS, 512
WEISS, Walter, 430
WEISS, Wilhelm, 489
WEISSMANN, Dr. Eugen, 494
WENCK, Walter, 490
WENING, Ernst, 490
WENNINGER, 490
WENNINGER, Ralph, 494
WERLIN, Jacob, 512
WERTHERN, Georg Thilo Frhr. v., 490
WESSELY, Marian, 461
WESTHOVEN, Franz, 462

RESTRICTED

INDEX OF NAMES

WESTPHAL, Siegfried, 490
WESTRAM, 490
WETZEL, Wilhelm, 173, 438
WEYER, Peter, 438
WICHARD, 505
WICKEDE, Emil v., 182, 462
WIELAND, 505
WIESE, Friedrich, 438
WIETERSHEIM, Gustav v., 438
WIETERSHEIM, Wend v., 282, 490
WIKTORIN, Mauriz, 42, 438
WILCK, 505
WILCK, Hermann, 257, 462
WILKE, Carl, 490
WILKE, Gustav, 505
WILKE, Kurt, 490
WILL, Otto, 462
WILLICH, Fritz, 462
WILMOWSKY, Friedrich Frhr. v., 28, 462
WIMMER, Wilhelm, 494
WINDECK, 462
WINDISCH, Alois, 490
WINDISCH, Josef, 490
WINKLER, Hermann, 490
WINKLER, Max, 490
WINTER, August, 490
WINTER, Paul, 462
WINTERGERST, Karl, 214, 462
WINTZER, Heinz, 462
WIRTZ, Richard, 490
WISCH, 325, 513
WISSELINCK, Ernst, 490

WITT, Fritz, 325, 513
WITTE, 43
WITTHÖFT, 438
WITTING, 498
WITTKE, Walter, 462
WITTMANN, 293, 490
WITZENDORFF, Gotthard v., 505
WITZLEBEN, Erwin v., 429
WITZLEBEN, Hermann v., 490
WODRIG, Albert, 25, 438
WÖHLER, Otto, 140, 438
WÖLLWARTH, Erich, 438
WÖSSNER, 490
WOLF, 490
WOLF, Richard, 510
WOLFF, 462
WOLFF, Karl, 508
WOLFF, Ludwig (Gen.), 494
WOLFF, Ludwig (Genlt.), 462
WOLFSBERGER, Franz, 462
WOLLMANN, 462
WOLPERT, Johann, 490
WOSCH, Heinrich, 314, 462
WOYRSCH, Udo v., 508
WOYTASCH, Kurt, 462
WREDE, Theodor Frhr. v., 462
WÜHLISCH, Heinz-Helmut v., 498
WÜNNENBERG, Alfred, 117, 122, 508
WUERST, 490
WULFFEN, Gustav Adolf v., 490
WULZ, 490
WUTHENOW, 490

RESTRICTED

INDEX OF NAMES

WUTHMANN, Rolf, 462
WYSOCKI, 512
XYLANDER, Rudolf Ritter u. Edler v., 490
ZÄPFFEL, Alexander, 491
ZAHN, Alois, 491
ZANDER, Konrad, 494
ZANGEN, Gustav v., 438
ZANTHIER, v., 491
ZECH, 505
ZEDNICEK, Franz, 491
ZEHENDER, August, 514
ZEHLER, Albert, 462
ZEISS, Walter, 491
ZEITZ, Erich (Hermann?), 491
ZEITZLER, Kurt, 6, 430
ZELLNER, Emil, 251, 462
ZELTMANN, Otto, 491
ZENETTI, Emil, 494
ZENNER, Karl, 510
ZEPELIN, Ferdinand v., 462
ZICKWOLFF, Friedrich, 463
ZIEGENRÜCKER, 491
ZIEGLER, Dr. Günther, 498
ZIEGLER, Heinz, 463
ZIERVOGEL, Dr., 505
ZIMMER, Richard, 491
ZIMMERMANN, Georg, 463
ZOCH, Philipp, 498
ZUCKERTORT, Karl, 491
ZÜLOW, Alexander v., 463
ZUKERTORT, Johannes, 463
ZUTAVERN, 491
ZWADE, 491
ZWENGAUER, Karl, 463

RESTRICTED

Section X. INDEX OF GERMAN TERMS AND DESIGNATIONS

The following list is an index of all German military terms, unit designations, and abbreviations used in this book. Reference is made in each case to the page or pages on which the term is explained or the units of the type in question are listed.

A. (=Artillerie), 74
A.A. (= Aufklärungsabteilung), 67, 382
Abschnitt, 115
Abwehr, 4, 106
a.D. (=ausser Dienst), 428
Adolf Hitler (div), 325
Afrika-Brigade, 261
Afrika-Division, 261
Afrika-Division z.b.V., 270
AHA (= Allgemeines Heeresamt), 8, 13, 15
A.K. (= Armeekorps), 130, 148, 354
Akjas, 70
aktiv Dienende, 15
aktive Truppenoffiziere, 427
Allgemeines Heeresamt, 8, 13, 15
Allgemeine SS, 114
A.N.R. (= Armeenachrichtenregiment), 88, 130, 353
A.O.K. (= Armeeoberkommando), 130, 138, 353
Arbeitsdienst, 14, 121

Arfü (= Artillerieführer), 76
Arko (= Artilleriekommandeur), 66, 76, 372
Armeebekleidungsamt, 100
Armeebriefstelle, 100
Armeefeldzeugpark, 101
Armeegefangenensammelstelle, 105
Armeegerätpark, 101
Armeekartenlager, 78
Armeekartenstelle, 78
Armeekorps, 130, 148, 354
Armeekraftfahrbezirk, 95
Armeekraftfahrpark, 95
Armeenachrichtenführer, 372
Armeenachrichtenregiment, 88, 130, 353
Armee Norwegen, 144, 353
Armeeoberkommando, 130, 138, 353
Armeepferdelazarett, 97
Armeepferdepark, 98
Art. (= Artillerie), 74
Art.Abt. (=Artillerieabteilung), 77, 391
Artillerie, 74

RESTRICTED 549

INDEX OF GERMAN TERMS AND DESIGNATIONS

Artillerieabteilung, 77, 391
Artilleriebrigade, 372
Artillerieführer, 76
Artilleriekommandeur, 66, 76, 372
Artillerie-Lehr-Regiment, 79
Artilleriepark, 63, 71, 78
Artillerieregiment, 75, 77, 391
Art.Rgt. (= Artillerieregiment), 75, 77, 391
Astronomischer Messzug, 78
Auffrischungsraum, 96
Aufkl.Abt. (=Aufklärungsabteilung), 67, 382
Aufklärungsabteilung, 67, 382
Aufklärungsschwadron, 68
Aufklärungs- und Kavallerie-Lehr-Abteilung, 71
Ausbildungseinheit, 21
Aushebung, 14, 15
ausser Dienst, 428
B. (= Beurlaubtenstand), 428
Bäckereikompanie, 99
Bahnhofskommandantur, 101
Bahnhofsoffizier, 101
Ballonbatterie, 78
Batterie, 77, 392
Baubataillon, 85
Bau-Lehr-Bataillon, 106
Bau.Pi. (=Baupioniere), 66, 81, 84
Baupioniere, 66, 81, 84
Baupionierbataillon, 85
Baupionierregiment, 85
Baupolizei, 117
Baustab Speer, 120

Bautruppen, 81, 84
Beamte, 99
Befehlshaber des rückwärtigen Heeresgebietes, 60
Bekleidungsamt, 100
Beob.Abt. (=Beobachtungsabteilung), 77, 400
Beobachtungsabteilung, 77, 400
Berlichingen (div), 332
Betreuungshelferinnenabteilung, 102
Betriebsstoffkolonne, 94
Betriebsstoffverwaltungskompanie, 94
Beurlaubtenstand, 428
Bewährungsbataillon, 107
BH (=Bosanska-Hrvatska), 331
Bialystok (div), 319
Bodensee (div), 236
bodenständig, 239
Böhmen und Mähren, 48, 50
Brandenburg (regt), 106
Briesen (div), 182
Br.Kol. (=Brückenkolonne), 82, 401
Brückenbaubataillon, 85, 401
Brückenkolonne, 82, 401
Brückenwachbataillon, 99
Brüko (=Brückenkolonne), 82, 401
Bttr. (=Batterie), 77, 392
Ch H Rüst u. BdE (=Chef der Heeresrüstung und Befehlshaber des Ersatzheeres), 7, 8
Chefadjutant der Wehrmacht, 7

RESTRICTED

INDEX OF GERMAN TERMS AND DESIGNATIONS 551

Chef der Heeresrüstung und Befehlshaber des Ersatzheeres, 7, 8
Chef der Schnellen Truppen, 8
Chef der Sicherheitspolizei, 117
Chef des Ausbildungswesens im Ersatzheer, 8
Chef des Heeresnachrichtenwesens, 7
Chef des Oberkommandos der Wehrmacht 3
Chef des Transportwesens, 7
D. (=Dienst), 428
D. (=Dienstleistung), 428
Danmark (regt), 330
Das Reich (div), 325
d.B. (=des Beurlaubtenstandes), 428
Der Führer (regt), 325
der Sicherheitspolizei und des Sicherheitsdienstes, 117
Destillationskompanie, 94
Deutschland (regt), 325
Dienst, 428
Dienstleistung, 428
Dinafü (=Divisionsnachschubführer), 92
Divisionsbataillon, 68
Divisionsbegleitkompanie, 73
Divisionsfernsprechkompanie, 88
Divisionsfunkkompanie, 89
Divisionskommando z.b.V., 23, 132, 302, 357
Divisionskommando zu besonderer Verwendung, 23, 132, 302, 357

Divisionsnachschubführer, 92
Division Nummer ..., 17, 22, 132, 302, 357
Div.Kdo.z.b.V. (=Divisionskommando zu besonderer Verwendung), 23, 132, 302, 357
Div.Nr. (Division Nummer ___), 17, 22, 132, 302, 357
Division Sizilien, 265
Division zu besonderer Verwendung, 23
Division z.b.V. Bialystok, 319
d.L. (=der Landwehr), 428
d.O. (=der Ordnungspolizei), 118
Do-Gerät, 80
d.R. (=der Reserve), 427
d.Sipo u.d.S.D. (=der Sicherheitspolizei und des Sicherheitsdienstes), 118
Dulag (=Kriegsgefangenendurchgangslager), 105
E (=Einsatz), 90
E (=Ergänzungs-), 18, 221, 427
Eberhardt (brigade), 269
Eicke (regt), 326
Eifel (frontier command), 153
Einberufung, 14
Einstellung, 14
Eisenbahnartillerieabteilung, 78
Eisenbahnbaubataillon, 85
Eisenbahnbetriebskompanie, 87
Eisenbahnfernsprechkompanie, 86
Eisenbahnfunkkompanie, 87
Eisenbahnküchenwagenabteilung, 102

RESTRICTED

INDEX OF GERMAN TERMS AND DESIGNATIONS

Eisenbahnnachrichtenabteiling, 89
Eisenbahnnachrichtenregiment, 89
Eisenbahnpanzerzug, 74
Eisenbahnpfeilerbaukompanie, 87
Eisenbahnpioniere, 81, 86
Eisenbahnpionierbataillon, 86
Eisenbahnpionierbaukompanie, 86
Eisenbahnpionierpark, 87
Eisenbahnpionierregiment, 86
Eisenbahnpionierstab z.b.V., 86
Eisenbahnstellwerkskompanie, 87
Eisenbahnunterwasserschneidetrupp, 87
Eisenbahnverpflegungszug, 102
Eisenbahnwasserstationskompanie, 87
Entgiftungsabteilung, 80
Entgiftungskompanie, 97
Entladestab, 93
entlassen, 428
Entlausungskompanie, 102
Entseuchungszug, 97
Erg. (=Ergänzungs-), 18, 221, 427
Ergänzungs- (units), 18, 221
Ergänzungsoffiziere, 427
Ers. (=Ersatz), 15, 17, 18
Ersatz, 15, 17, 18
Ersatzbrigade, 371
Ersatzheer, 11
Ersatzreserve, 15
Ersatz- und Ausbildungseinheiten, 24
Eugen (div), 328
Fahrkolonne, 94

Fahrtruppen, 91, 94
Fallschirmartillerieregiment, 111
Fallschirmdivision, 334
Fallschirmeinheiten, 110
Fallschirmfliegerabwehrbataillon, 111
Fallschirmjägerregiment, 110
Fallschirmmaschinengewehrbataillon, 111
Fallschirmnachrichtenabteilung, 111
Fallschirmpanzerjägerabteilung, 111
Fallschirmpionierbataillon, 111
Fallschirmsanitätskompanie, 111
F.Ausb. (=Feldausbildungsdivision), 20, 133, 302, 357
Fechtende Truppen, 63, 66
Feldausbildungsdivision, 20, 133, 302, 357
Feldausbildungsregiment, 366
Feldbahnabteilung, 87
Feldbahnkompanie, 87
Feldeisenbahnbetriebsabteilung, 87
Feldeisenbahnbetriebstruppen, 86, 87, 92
Feldeisenbahneinheiten, 87
Feldeisenbahnkommando, 87
Feldeisenbahnmaschinenabteilung, 87
Feldeisenbahnnachschublager, 87
Feldeisenbahnwerkstattabteilung, 87
Feldersatzbataillon, 19, 68, 73
Feldersatzdivision, 20

RESTRICTED

INDEX OF GERMAN TERMS AND DESIGNATIONS 553

Feldgendarme, 98
Feldgendarmerie, 98, 106
Feldgendarmerieabteilung, 99, 353
Feldgendarmeriekompanie, 99
Feldgendarmerietrupp, 98
Feldheer, 11
Feldherrnhalle, 123, 197, 269, 371
Feldkabelbauabteilung, 90
Feldkommandantur, 50, 102
Feldlazarett, 96
Feldnachrichtenkommandantur, 89
Feldpolizei, 105, 353
Feldpostamt, 100, 353
Feld-Sonderbataillon, 107
Feldstrafgefangenenabteilung, 107
Feldwasserstrassenräumabteilung, 83
Feldwerkstattkompanie, 100, 101
Feldzeugbataillon, 101
Feldzeugkraftwagenkolonne, 101
Feldzeugpark, 101
Feldzeugstab, 101
Feldzeugtruppen, 101
Fernschreibkompanie, 90
Fernsprechbaukompanie, 90
Fernsprechbetriebskompanie, 90
Fernsprechkompanie, 88
Festungs-, 69, 372
Festungsartilleriekommandeur, 372
Festungsbataillon, 69
Festungsbaubataillon, 85
Festungsbrigade, 371
Festungsbrigade Kreta, 259, 371

Festungsnachrichtenkommandantur, 89
Festungspioniere, 81, 83
Festungspionierabschnittsgruppe, 84
Festungspionierbataillon, 85
Festungspionierkommandeur, 372
Festungspionierpark, 84
Festungspionierregiment, 84
Festungspionierstab, 84
Festungsregiment, 69
Feuerschutzpolizei, 117
F.G.A. (=Feldgendarmerieabteilung), 99, 353
Filterkolonne, 94
Fla-bataillon, 69, 70, 108
Flak, 108
Flakabteilung, 108, 111, 416
Flakbatterie, 109, 416
Flakdivision, 344
Flakeinheiten, 108
Flakkorps, 344
Flak-Lehr-Regiment, 416
Fla-Kompanie, 70, 73
Flakregiment, 108, 416
Flakvierling, 109
Flammenwerfer, 74
Fliegerabwehr, 69
Fliegerabwehrbataillon, 69, 73
Fliegerabwehrkompanie, 70, 73
Flugabwehrregiment, 416
Flusspolizei, 117
F.P.A. (=Feldpostamt), 100, 353
Freiwilligendivision Lettland, 331

RESTRICTED

INDEX OF GERMAN TERMS AND DESIGNATIONS

Freiwilligen-Gebirgsdivision Prinz Eugen, 328
Frontleitstelle, 102
Frontstalag (=Kriegsgefangenenfrontstammlager), 105
Frundsberg (div), 329
Führer, 116
Führer (regt), 325
Führerbegleitbataillon, 107
Führergrenadierbataillon, 107
Führerhaptquartier, 4
Führungs-, 5
Führungsnachrichtenregiment, 89
Füsilierregiment, 67, 373
Funkkompanie, 88
Funküberwachungskompanie, 90
G. (=Generalstab), 427
Galizien (div), 330
Gasmaskentrupp, 81
Gasschutzgerätpark, 81
Gasspürtrupp, 79
G.D. (=Grossdeutschland), 107, 291, 371
Geb. (=Gebirgs-), 63
Geb.Div. (=Gebirgsdivision), 132, 292, 368
Gebirgs-, 63
Gebirgsdivision, 132, 292, 368
Gebirgsjägerregiment, 67, 373
Gebirgskorps, 131, 169, 354
Gebirgsträgerbataillon, 93
Gebirgswerferabteilung, 80
Gebirgswerfer-Lehr-Batterie, 81

Geb.Jäg.Rgt. (=Gebirgsjägerregiment), 67, 373
Geb.Jg. (=Gebirgsjäger-), 67
Geb.K. (=Gebirgskorps), 132, 354
Gefangenensammelstelle, 105
Gefechtstross, 92
Geheime Feldpolizei, 105, 353
Geheime Staatspolizei, 106, 115, 117
gemischte Flakabteilung, 108
genannt, 425
Gendarmerie, 117
General, 427
Gen.d.Art. (=General der Artillerie), 7, 431
Gen.d.Fl. (=General der Flieger), 493
Gen.d.Flakart. (=General der Flakartillerie), 493
Gen.d.Inf. (=General der Infanterie), 431
Gen.d.Kav. (=General der Kavallerie), 431
Gen.d.Pion. (=General der Pioniere), 431
Gen.d.Pz.Tr. (=General der Panzertruppen), 431
Generalbezirk, 59, 60
General der Artillerie, 7, 431
General der Flakartillerie, 493
General der Flieger, 493
General der Gebirgstruppen, 431
General der Infanterie, 7, 431
General der Kavallerie, 431
General der Luftwaffe, 493

RESTRICTED

INDEX OF GERMAN TERMS AND DESIGNATIONS 555

General der Luftnachrichtentruppen, 493
General der Nachrichtentruppen, 431
General der Nachschubtruppen, 7
General der Nebeltruppen, 7
General der Panzertruppe, 431
General der Pioniere, 7, 431
Generalfeldmarschall, 427, 429
Generalfeldmarschall (air), 492
Generalgouvernement, 48, 51
Generalinspekteur der Panzertruppen, 8
Generalinspekteur des Kriegsgefangenenwesens, 5
Generalleutnant, 427, 439
Generalleutnant (air), 495
Generalmajor, 427, 464
Generalmajor (air), 499
Generaloberst, 427, 430
Generaloberst (air), 492
Generalquartiermeister, 6
Generalstab, 427
Generalstab des Heeres, 427
Generalstabsstelle, 427
Genesendenkompanie, 16
Genfldm. (=Generalfeldmarschall), 427, 429, 492
Genlt. (=Generalleutnant), 427, 439, 495
Genmaj. (=Generalmajor), 427, 464, 499
Genobst. (=Generaloberst), 427, 430, 492

Gen St d H (=Generalstab des Heeres), 427
Gepäcktross, 92
gepanzert, 48
Gerätpark, 101
Gerätsammelstelle, 100, 101
Germania (regt), 327
Germanisches Korps, 323
Gestapo (=Geheime Staatspolizei), 106, 115, 117
G.F.P. (=Geheime Feldpolizei), 105, 353
Göring (div), 290, 333
Götz von Berlichingen (div), 332
Granatwerferbataillon, 69
Grenadierbataillon, 70
Grenadierbataillon z.b.V., 70
Grenadierregiment, 67, 373
Grenadierregiment (mot.) 72, 73
Gren.Rgt. (=Grenadierregiment), 67, 373
Gren.Rgt.(mot.) (=Grenadierregiment (motorisiert)), 72, 73
Grenzkommando Eifel, 153
Grenzkommando Küstrin, 186
Grenzkommando Oberrhein, 153
Grenzkommando Saarpfalz, 165
Grenzkommando Trier, 192
Grenzwachdivision, 132, 302, 357
Grossbäckerei, 100
Grossdeutschland (div), 107, 291, 371
grosse Betriebsstoffkolonne, 94
grosse Kraftwagenkolonne, 94

RESTRICTED

INDEX OF GERMAN TERMS AND DESIGNATIONS

Gr.Rgt. (=Grenadierregiment), 67, 373
Gruppen, 105
Grz.W. (=Grenzwach-), 132
H.Abt. (=Heeresflakartillerieabteilung), 78
Hauptmann, 427
Heeresbaudienststelle, 100
Heeresbekleidungsamt, 100
Heeresbetreuungsabteilung, 102
Heeresbetreuungskompanie (E), 102
Heeresfeldzeugpark, 101
Heeresflak, 75, 108, 416
Heeresflakartillerieabteilung, 78
Heeresflakartillerie-Lehr-Abteilung, 79
Heeresgefangenensammelstelle, 105
Heeresgerätpark, 71, 78, 101
Heeresgruppe, 130, 134
Heeresgruppenkommando, 130
Heeresgruppenachrichtenführer, 372
Heereskraftfahrbezirk, 95
Heereskraftfahrpark, 95
Heereskühldienststelle, 100
Heeresküstenartillerieabteilung, 78, 391
Heeresküstenartillerieregiment, 391
Heeresküstenbatterie, 391
Heeresnachtrichtenregiment, 88, 89, 130
Heerespersonalamt, 7
Heerespferdelazarett, 97
Heerespferdepark, 98
Heeresstreifen, 98, 102
Heerestruppen, 62
Heeresunterkunftsverwaltung, 100
Heeresverwaltungsamt, 8
Heereswaffenamt, 8
Heereszeugamt, 101
Heimateisenbahnpionierpark, 88
Heimatfestungspionierpark, 84
Heimatkraftfahrbezirk, 95
Heimatkraftfahrpark, 96
Heimatkriegsgebiet, 7
Heimatpferdelazarett, 98
Heimatwachbataillon, 99
Heimwehr, 269
Hermann Göring (div), 108, 290, 333
Hermann Göring (regt), 329
Heydrich (regt), 327
H.G. (=Hermann Göring), 108, 290, 329, 333
H.Gru. (=Heeresgruppe), 130, 134
Hitler-Jugend, 123
Hitler-Jugend (div), 329
H.J. (=Hitler-Jugend), 123, 329
H.K.A. (=Heeresküstenartillerieabteilung), 78, 391
H.K.B. (=Heimatkraftfahrbezirk), 95
H.K.P. (=Heereskraftfahrpark), 95
H.K.P. (=Heimatkraftfahrpark), 96

RESTRICTED

INDEX OF GERMAN TERMS AND DESIGNATIONS 557

H.Küst.Art.Abt. (=Heeresküstenartillerieabteilung), 78, 391
Hoch- und Deutschmeister (div), 185
Hohenstaufen (div), 329
Horchkompanie, 90
Höh.Arko. (=Höherer Artilleriekommandeur), 76
Höherer Artilleriekommandeur, 76
Höherer Pionierführer, 372
Höherer SS und Polizeiführer, 116
Höheres Kommando z.b.V., 131, 172, 354
Höheres Kommando zu besonderer Verwendung, 131, 172, 354
Höh.Kdo. (=Höheres Kommando zu besonderer Verwendung), 131, 172, 354
HPA (=Heerespersonalamt), 7
H SS Pf (=Höherer SS und Polizeiführer), 116
H.Tru. (=Heerestruppen), 62
i.G. (=im Generalstab), 427
Inf. (=Infanterie), 66
Infanterie, 66
Inf.Div. (=Infanteriedivision), 131, 176, 357
Infanteriedivision, 131, 176, 357
Infanteriegeschützkompanie, 67, 68, 73
Infanterie-Lehr-Regiment, 71
Infanteriepanzerjägerkompanie, 68
Infanteriepark, 63, 71, 78
Infanterieparkkompanie, 63
Inspektion der Artillerie, 8

Inspektion der Infanterie, 8
Jäg.Btl. (=Jägerbataillon), 68, 70
Jäg.Div. (=Jägerdivision), 131, 272, 357
Jägerbataillon, 68, 70
Jägerdivision, 131, 272, 357
Jägerregiment, 67, 373
Jäg.Rgt. (=Jägerregiment), 67, 373
Jagdkommando, 70
J.D. (=Infanteriedivision), 131, 176, 357
jetzt zuständiger Ersatztruppenteil, 16
Kartenlager, 78
Kartenstelle, 78
Kavalleriebrigade, 371
Kavalleriedivision, 328
Kenn-Nummer, 100
Kesselwagenkolonne für Betriebsstoff, 94
kleine Betriebsstoffkolonne, 94
kleine Kraftwagenkolonne, 94
Kodina (=Kommandeur der Divisionsnachschubtruppen), 92
Kombinierte Kolonne, 94
Kommandant des rückwärtigen Armeegebietes, 60, 66, 353
Kommandantur, 50
Kommandeur der Armeenachschubtruppen, 353
Kommandeur der Bautruppen, 84
Kommandeur der Divisionsnachschubtruppen, 92

RESTRICTED

Kommandeur der Führungsnachrichtentruppen, 372
Kommandeur der Kraftfahrparktruppe, 95
Kommandeur der Kriegsgefangenen, 105
Kommandeur des Streifendienstes, 102
Korpsführer, 121, 123
Korpskartenlager, 78
Korpskartenstelle, 78
Korpsnachrichtenabteilung, 88
Korück (=Kommandeur des rückwärtigen Armeegebietes), 60, 66, 353
Kradschützenbataillon, 72
Kradschützenkompanie, 69
Kraftfahrabteilung, 92
Kraftfahrbezirk, 95
Kraftfahrpark, 95
Kraftfahrpark Eisenbahn, 96
Kraftfahrparktruppen, 74, 91, 94
Kraftfahrzeugabschleppzug, 95
Kraftfahrzeuginstandsetzungsabteilung, 95
Kraftfahrzeuginstandsetzungskompanie, 95
Kraftfahrzeuginstandsetzungsregiment, 95
Kraftwagentransportabteilung, 93
Kraftwagentransportkolonne, 94
Kraftwagentransportregiment, 92
Kraftwagenwerkstatt, 95
Krankenkraftwagenzug, 96

Krankentransportabteilung, 96
Kreiskommandantur, 50, 102
Kriegsakademie, 427
Kriegsgefangenenarbeitskommando, 86
Kriegsgefangenenbau- und Arbeitsbataillon, 86
Kriegsgefangenenbezirkskommandant, 105
Kriegsgefangenendurchgangslager, 105
Kriegsgefangenenfrontstammlager, 105
Kriegsgefangenenmannschaftslager, 105
Kriegsgefangenenoffizierslager, 105
Kriegsgefangenenstammlager, 105
Kriegslazarett, 97
Kriegslazarettabteilung, 97
Kriegsmarine, 78
Kriminalpolizei, 117
Küstenartilleriekommandeur, 372
Küstenverteidigungsdivision, 132, 366
Küstrin (frontier command), 186
L. (=Landwehr), 15, 18, 428
Landesbaupionierbataillon, 86
Landesbaubataillon, 86
Landeseigene Sicherungsverbände, 105
Landesschützen, 66, 103, 104
Landesschützenbataillon, 66, 103
Landesschützeneinheiten, 103
Landesschützenregiment, 103

RESTRICTED

INDEX OF GERMAN TERMS AND DESIGNATIONS 559

Landsturm, 15
Landungskompanie, 82
Landwehr, 15, 18, 212, 428
Langemarck (regt), 326
Lazarettzug, 97
Lehrbrigade, 372
Lehreinheit, 63
Lehrregiment Brandenburg z.b.v., 106
Lehr- und Ersatzabteilung für Eisenbahnartillerie (mot), 79
Leibstandarte (div), 119, 325
Leibstandarte SS "Adolf Hitler", 119, 325
leichte Flakabteilung, 108
leichte Flakbatterie, 109
leichte Kolonne, 92
Leichtkrankenkriegslazarett, 97
Leichtkrankenzug, 97
Lettland (div), 331
Leutnant, 427
LG (=Luftgau), 105, 110, 416
Luftgau, 105, 110, 416
Luftjägerregiment, 111
Luftlande-Division, 267
Luftwaffenfelddivision, 111, 336
Luftwaffenfeldeinheiten, 111
Luftwaffenfeldkorps, 335
M. (=Marine), 416
Major, 427
Marine, 416
Marineartillerieabteilung, 78
Marinebaubataillon, 85
Marineflak, 416

Marschbataillon, 19, 24
Marschkompanie, 17
Maschinengewehrbataillon, 70
Maschinengewehrkompanie, 68
Militärbefehlshaber, 54, 55
Militärverwaltungsbezirk, 55
Minensuchbataillon z.b.V., 82
Minensuchkompanie, 82
Motorstandarte, 121
Munitionsverwaltungskompanie, 93
Musterung, 14, 15
Musterungsbezirk, 14
N.A. (=Nachrichtenabteilung), 88, 407
Nachr.Abt. (=Nachrichtenabteilung), 88
Nachrichtenabteilung, 88, 407
Nachrichtenabteilungsstab z.b.V., 89
Nachrichtenauswertekompanie, 90
Nachrichtenfernaufklärungskompanie, 90
Nachrichtenführer, 372
Nachrichtenführer z.b.V., 90
Nachrichtenhelferinnenabteilung, 90
Nachrichtenkompanie, 88, 407
Nachrichten-Lehr-Regiment, 91
Nachtrichtennahaufklärungskompanie, 90
Nachrichtenpark, 90
Nachrichtenregiment, 407
Nachrichtenregimentsstab z.b.V., 89

RESTRICTED

Nachrichtentruppen, 88
Nachr.Kp. (=Nachrichtenkompanie), 88, 407
Nachr.Rgt. (=Nachrichtenregiment), 88, 407
Nachschubbataillon, 93
Nachschubkolonnenabteilung, 93
Nachschubkolonnenabteilung z.b.V., 93
Nachschubkompanie z.b.V., 93
Nachschubstab z.b.V., 93
Nachschubtruppen, 91, 94
Nationalsozialistische Deutsche Arbeiterpartei, 123
Nationalsozialistisches Fliegerkorps, 123
Nationalsozialistisches Kraftfahrkorps, 121
Nebeltruppen, 79
Nebelwerferabteilung, 80
Nebelwerferregiment, 80
Nederland (div), 330
N.K. (=Nachrichtenkompanie), 88, 407
Nord (div), 327
Nordland (div), 327, 330
Nordland (regt), 327
Norge (regt), 330
N.R. (=Nachrichtenregiment), 88, 407
N.S.D.A.P. (=Nationalsozialistische Deutsche Arbeiterpartei), 123
N.S.F.K. (=Nationalsozialistisches Fliegerkorps), 123

N.S.K.K. (=Nationalsozialistisches Kraftfahrkorps), 121
Oberabschnitt, 115
Oberbaustab, 372
Oberbefehlshaber des Heeres, 5
Oberfeldkommandantur, 50
Oberfeldzeugstab, 101
Oberkommando der Kriegsmarine, 1
Oberkommando der Luftwaffe, 1
Oberkommando der Wehrmacht, 1, 3
Oberkommando des Heeres, 1, 5, 64
Oberleutnant, 427
Oberquartiermeister, 6
Oberrhein (frontier command), 153
Oberst, 427
Oberster Befehlshaber der Wehrmacht, 3
Oberstleutnant, 427
Offiziere a.D., d.B., d.L., d.R., (E), Erg., i.G., (W), z.D., z.V., 427
Oflag (=Kriegsgefangenenoffizierslager), 105
OKH (=Oberkommando des Heeres), 1, 5, 64
OKL (=Oberkommando der Luftwaffe), 1
OKM (=Oberkommando der Kriegsmarine), 1
OKW (=Oberkommando der Wehrmacht), 1, 3
Ordnungspolizei, 117
Organisation Todt, 120
Org.Todt (=Organisation Todt), 120

RESTRICTED

INDEX OF GERMAN TERMS AND DESIGNATIONS 561

Orpo (=Ordnungspolizei), 117
Ortskommandantur, 50, 102
OT (=Organisation Todt), 120
PA (=Personalamt), 7
Panzer-, 63
Panzerabteilung, 71, 385
Panzerabteilung (Flammenwerfer), 74
Panzerarmeeoberkommando, 145, 352
Panzerarmeenachrichtenführer, 372
Panzeraufklärungsabteilung, 72, 382
Panzeraufklärungskompanie (Krad), 72
Panzeraufklärungskompanie (Volkswagen), 72
Panzerbeobachtungsbatterie, 75, 400
Panzerbrigade, 372
Panzerbüchse, 71
Panzerdivision, 132, 277, 367
Panzergrenadierbrigade, 371
Panzergrenadierdivision, 131, 263, 357
Panzergrenadierregiment, 71, 373
Panzergruppe, 145
Panzerinstandsetzungsabteilung, 74
Panzerjägerabteilung, 72, 73, 387
Panzerjäger- und Aufklärungsabteilung, 382
Panzerkorps, 119, 131, 164, 354
Panzer-Lehr-Regiment, 74

Panzerregiment, 71, 385
Panzerspähkompanie, 72
Panzertruppen, 71
Panzerzerstörerkompanie, 71
Parkkompanie, 63
Personalamt, 7
Pferdelazarett, 97
Pferdepark, 98
Pferdetransportkolonne, 98
PGR (=Panzergrenadierregiment), 71, 373
Pi.Btl. (=Pionierbataillon), 81, 401
Pi.Kp. (=Pionierkompanie), 82
Pioniere, 81, 82
Pionierbataillon, 81, 401
Pionierbataillon z.b.V., 82
Pionierbrückenbataillon, 85
Pionierkompanie, 82
Pionierkompanie (mot.), 82, 401
Pionierkompanie (tmot.), 82
Pionierlandungsbataillon, 82
Pionierlandungskompanie, 82
Pionier-Lehr-Bataillon, 83
Pionier-Lehr-Bataillon für schweren Brückenbau, 83
Pionier-Lehr-Bataillon z.b.V., 83
Pionierpark, 63, 83
Pionierparkkompanie, 63
Pionierregimentsstab, 82, 401
Pionierregimentsstab, z.b.V., 84
Pionierregiment z.b.V., 82
P.K. (=Propagandakompanie), 91, 353

RESTRICTED

INDEX OF GERMAN TERMS AND DESIGNATIONS

politischer Leiter, 123
Polizei, 116
Polizei (regt), 118
Polizei-Division, 118, 326
Prinz Eugen (div), 328
Propagandaabteilung, 91
Propagandakompanie, 91, 353
Propagandatruppen, 91
Pz. (=Panzer-), 63
Pz.A.A. (=Panzeraufklärungsabteilung), 72, 382
Pz.Abt. (=Panzerabteilung), 71, 74, 385
Pz.A.O.K. (=Panzerarmeeoberkommando), 145, 352
Pz.Aufkl.Abt. (=Panzeraufklärungsabteilung), 72, 382
Pz.Beob.Bttr. (=Panzerbeobachtungsbatterie), 75, 400
Pz.Div. (=Panzerdivision), 132, 277, 367
Pz.Gr.Div. (=Panzergrenadierdivision), 131, 263, 357
Pz.Gren.Div. (=Panzergrenadierdivision), 131, 263, 357
Pz.Gr.Rgt. (=Panzergrenadierregiment), 71, 373
Pz.J. & A.A. (=Panzerjäger- und Aufklärungsabteilung), 382
Pz.Jäg.Abt. (=Panzerjägerabteilung), 72, 73, 387
Pz.Jg.Abt. (=Panzerjägerabteilung), 72, 73, 387
Pz.K. (=Panzerkorps), 119, 131, 164, 354

Pz.Rgt. (=Panzerregiment), 71, 385
R. (=Reserve), 427
R.A.D. (=Reichsarbeitsdienst), 121
Radfahrabteilung, 67
Radfahrbaupionierbataillon, 85
Radfahrschwadron, 69
Radfahrstrassenbaubataillon, 85
Radfahrwachbataillon, 99, 104
Radfahrwachbataillon B., 85
Regimentsstab der Nebeltruppen, 80
Reich (div), 325
Reichsarbeitsdienst, 121
Reichsarbeitsführer, 122
Reichsführer-SS 114, 506
Reichsführer-SS (div), 332
Reichsführer-SS und Chef der Deutschen Polizei, 113
Reichsführung-SS, 114
Reichsgrenadierdivision Hoch- und Deutschmeister, 185
Reichsjugendführer, 123
Reichskommissariat, 48, 51
Reichsluftfahrtministerium, 1
Reichsmarschall, 427, 492
Reifeninstandsetzungsstaffel, 95
Reinhard Heydrich (regt), 327
Reiterregiment, 69
Reiterschwadron, 68
Rekrutenkompanie, 16
Res. (=Reserve-), 15, 427
Reserve, 15, 427
Reserveartillerieabteilung, 366

RESTRICTED

INDEX OF GERMAN TERMS AND DESIGNATIONS 563

Reserveartillerieregiment, 366
Reservedivision, 22, 132, 302, 357
Reserveeinheit, 23
Reserve-Flakabteilung, 108
Reservegebirgsjägerregiment, 366
Reservegrenadierregiment, 366
Reservejägerregiment, 366
Reservekorps, 131, 172, 354
Reserve-Kriegslazarettabteilung, 97
Reservepanzerabteilung, 366
Reservepanzerdivision, 23
Reservepanzergrenadierregiment, 366
Reservepionierbataillon, 366
Res.K. (=Reservekorps), 131, 172, 354
Rheingold (div), 254
Rhodos (div), 261
Rittmeister, 427
RLM (=Reichsluftfahrtministerium), 1
SA (=Storm Troops), 123
Saarpfalz (frontier command), 165
SA-Brigade Eberhardt, 269
Sanitätsabteilung, 96
Sanitätskompanie, 96
Sanitätspark, 97
Sanitätstruppen, 96
Sch. (=Scheinwerfer), 109, 416
Sch.Abt. (=Scheinwerfer Abteilung), 109, 416
Scheinwerfer, 109, 416
Scheinwerferabteilung, 109, 416

Schelde (corps), 163
Schlächtereiabteilung, 100
Schlächtereikompanie, 100
Schlächtereizug, 100
Schn.A. (=Schnelle Abteilung), 68, 382, 387
Schn.Abt. (=Schnelle Abteilung), 68, 382, 387
Schneeräumabteilung, 85
Schneeräumregiment, 85
Schnelle Abteilung, 68, 382, 387
Schnelle Brigade, 371
Schnelle Truppen, 71
Schupo (=Schutzpolizei), 117
Schützenbrigade, 371
Schützendivision, 330
Schützenpanzerwagenkompanie, 68, 72
Schutzpolizei, 117
Schutzstaffel, 113
schwere Flakabteilung, 108
schwere Flakbatterie, 109
schwere Infanteriegeschützkompanie, 73
Schwere Kompanie, 68, 72
schwere Panzerjägerabteilung, 73
Schwere Schwadron, 69
schweres Werferregiment, 80
schweres Granatwerferbataillon, 69
schwere Werferbatterie, 80
SD (=Sicherheitsdienst), 117
Seilbahnkommandotrupp, 87

RESTRICTED

INDEX OF GERMAN TERMS AND DESIGNATIONS

S.H.D. (=Sicherheits- und Hilfsdienste), 117
Sich. (=Sicherungs-), 66
Sich.Div. (=Sicherungsdivision), 132, 296, 357
Sicherheitsdienst, 117
Sicherheitspolizei, 115, 117
Sicherheits- und Hilfsdienste, 117
Sicherungs-, 66
Sicherungs- (units), 102
Sicherungsbataillon, 103, 104
Sicherungsbrigade, 371
Sicherungsdivision, 132, 296, 357
Sicherungsregiment, 102
Sicherungstruppen, 63, 102
Sipo (=Sicherheitspolizei), 115, 117
Sizilien (div), 265
Skibataillon, 70
Sonderbataillon, 107
Sondereinheit, 63, 106
Sonderstab "F", 107
Sonderverband, 107
Sonstige Truppen und Dienststellen, 101
Speer (Baustab), 120
Sprengkommando, 83
SS, 113
SS-Abschnitt, 115
SS-Brigade, 369
SS-Brigadeführer und Generalmajor der Waffen-SS, 511
SS-Division, 325, 369

SS-Gruppenführer und Generalleutnant der Waffen-SS, 509
SS-Oberabschnitt, 115
SS-Oberführer, 513
SS-Obergruppenführer und General der Waffen-SS, 507
SS-Oberstgruppenführer und Generaloberst der Waffen-SS, 506
SS-Obersturmbannführer, 514
SS-Panzer-Korps, 119, 322
SS-Polizei (div), 326
SS-Regiment, 370
SS-Sicherheitsdienst, 106, 115
SS-Standartenführer, 513
SS-TV (=SS-Totenkopfverbände), 115
SS-Totenkopfverbände, 115
SS- und Polizeiführer, 116
SS-Verfügungstruppe, 119
Staatspolizei, 117
Stabschef, 123
Stabsoffizier der Artillerie, 76
St.Abt. (=Sturmartillerieabteilung), 77, 391
St.Abt. (=Sturmgeschützabteilung), 71, 77, 391
Stadtkommandantur, 50, 102
Stalag (=Kriegsgefangenenstammlager), 105
Stammkompanie, 16
Standarte, 114
St.Bttr. (=Sturmbatterie), 77

RESTRICTED

INDEX OF GERMAN TERMS AND DESIGNATIONS 565

Stoart (=Stabsoffizier der Artillerie), 76
Strafvollzugszug, 107
Strassenentgiftungsabteilung, 80
Streifenabteilung, 102
Streifenkompanie, 102
Stromsicherungsbataillon, 104
Stromsicherungsregiment, 104
Stu.B.Kdo. (=Sturmbootkommando), 83, 401
Stu.Gesch.Abt. (=Sturmgeschützabteilung), 71, 77, 391
Stu.Gesch.Bttr. (=Sturmgeschützbatterie), 77, 391
Sturm-, 194
Sturmabteilung, 123
Sturmartillerieabteilung, 77, 391
Sturmbataillon, 69
Sturmbatterie, 391
Sturmbootkommando, 83, 401
Sturmbootkompanie, 83
Sturmbrigade Reichsführer-SS, 332
Sturm (div), 132, 194
Sturmdivision Rhodos, 261
Sturmgeschützabteilung, 71, 77, 391
Sturmgeschützbatterie, 77
Sturmregiment, 69, 111
Sturm Rgt. (=Sturmregiment), 69, 111
tauglich, 14
Techn.Btl. (=Technisches Bataillon), 83
Technische Nothilfe, 122

Technisches Bataillon, 83
Teno (=Technische Nothilfe), 122
Territorial-Abschnittsbefehlshaber, 53
Territorial-Befehlshaber, 53
Teufels-Division, 249
Theodor Eicke (regt), 326
T.N. (=Technische Nothilfe), 122
Todt, 120, 121
Totenkopf (div), 115, 326
Totenkopf (regt), 326
Tragtierkolonne, 94
Transportbegleitbataillon, 104
Transportbegleitregiment, 104
Transportdienststelle, 101
Trier (frontier command), 192
Trosse, 92
Truppenentgiftungskompanie, 97
Truppenverbandplatz, 97
Umschlagstab, 93
V. (=Verfügung), 428
Velozitätsmesszug, 78
Verfügung, 428
Verfügungstruppe, 119
Verkehrsregelungsbataillon, 99
Verladestab, 93
Vermessungs- und Kartenabteilung, 78
Verpflegungsamt, 100
Verpflegungsausgabestelle, 100
Verpflegungstross, 92
Versorgungstruppen, 63, 91
Versuchsbataillon, 107
Verwaltungstruppen, 99

RESTRICTED

Veterinärkompanie, 97
Veterinärpark, 98
Veterinärtruppen, 97
W (=des Waffenwesens), 428
Wach-, 66
Wachbataillon, 99, 104
Wachbataillon B, 85
Wachregiment, 99, 104
Wachtruppen, 98
Waffengattung, 62, 63
Waffenprüfungsabteilung, 8
Waffenrüstungsabteilung, 8
Waffen-SS, 113, 118
Waffen-SS (units), 322, 369
Waffenwesen, 428
WaPrüf (Waffenprüfungsabteilung), 8
Wasserkolonne, 94
Wehrbezirk, 13
Wehrersatzbezirk, 13
Wehrersatzinspekteur, 13
Wehrersatzinspektion, 28
Wehrertüchtigungslager, 123
Wehrkreis, 9, 11, 25
Wehrmacht, 1
Wehrmacht-, 5
Wehrmachtbeamte, 8
Wehrmachtbefehlshaber, 52, 53
Wehrmachtbevollmächtigter, 50
Wehrmachtführungsstab, 3, 4

Wehrmachtfürsorge- und -versorgungsamt, 5
Wehrmachtnachrichtenkommandantur, 89
Wehrmachtpropagandaamt, 4
Wehrmeldebezirk, 15
wehrunwürdig, 107
Wehrwirtschaft, 4
Werfer, 80
Werferabteilung, 80
Werfereinheiten, 75, 79
Werfer-Lehr-Regiment, 81
Werferregiment, 80
Werferregiment z.b.V., 80
Werkstattkompanie, 95
Westentaschenkorps, 107
Westland (regt), 327
Wetterpeilzug, 78
W.F.St. (=Wehrmachtführungsstab), 3, 4
Wiking (div), 327
Wirtschaftskraftwagentransportbrigade z.b.V., 372
Wkr. (=Wehrkreis), 9, 11, 25
z.b.V. (=zu besonderer Verwendung), 70, 103, 132
z.D. (=zur Dienstleistung), 428
Zentralersatzteillager, 95
zu besonderer Verwendung, 70, 103, 132
Zugwachabteilung, 102, 104
z.V. (=zur Verfügung), 428

RESTRICTED

www.ingramcontent.com/pod-product-compliance
Lightning Source LLC
Chambersburg PA
CBHW031128160426
43193CB00008B/69